DANIEL L. MIGLIORE is the
Arthur M. Adams Professor of
Systematic Theology at Princeton
Theological Seminary. He has also
written *The Power of God* and *Called
to Freedom: Liberation Theology and the
Future of Christian Doctrine.*

FAITH SEEKING UNDERSTANDING

Faith Seeking Understanding

An Introduction to Christian Theology

Daniel L. Migliore

William B. Eerdmans Publishing Company
Grand Rapids, Michigan

Copyright © 1991 by Wm. B. Eerdmans Publishing Co.
255 Jefferson Ave. S.E., Grand Rapids, Mich. 49503
All rights reserved
Printed in the United States of America

Library of Congress Cataloging-in-Publication Data

Migliore, Daniel L., 1935-
   Faith seeking understanding: an introduction to Christian
theology / Daniel L. Migliore
        p.   cm.
   Includes bibliographical references.
   ISBN 0-8028-0601-5 (pbk.)
   ISBN 0-8028-3695-X (hbk.)
   1. Theology, Doctrinal — Introductions.   I. Title.
BT65.M54   1991
230 — dc20   91-13551
                                                        CIP

Contents

Acknowledgments

MANY STUDENTS, COLLEAGUES, AND FRIENDS HAVE ASSISTED ME IN the writing of this book. I especially wish to thank those who read the manuscript in whole or in part and offered helpful comments: Cornelius Plantinga, Jr. (Professor of Systematic Theology, Calvin Theological Seminary), and several colleagues at Princeton Theological Seminary: George S. Hendry (Charles Hodge Professor Emeritus of Systematic Theology), Hugh T. Kerr (Benjamin B. Warfield Professor Emeritus of Systematic Theology), Nancy Duff (Assistant Professor of Ethics), and Kathleen D. Billman and Leanne Van Dyk (Ph.D. candidates).

I am also indebted to George Stroup (Professor of Systematic Theology, Columbia Theological Seminary), Michael Welker (Professor of Systematic Theology, University of Münster), and Sang Hyun Lee, Mark Kline Taylor, and David E. Willis-Watkins (Professors of Systematic Theology, Princeton Theological Seminary), with each of whom at various times I have team taught the basic course in theology at Princeton. Just how much their ideas have enriched my own would be embarrassing to relate in detail. For the flaws of the book I alone am responsible.

I am grateful to President Thomas Gillespie and the Trustees of Princeton Theological Seminary for a sabbatical leave in 1990-1991 that enabled me to complete the writing of this book. Joe Herman, a faculty assistant with extraordinary talents, helped with the typing and other details.

My gratitude to my wife Margaret for her love and support as well as for her wise editorial advice is far greater than I can say.

Finally, I want to express my thanks to the many first-year M.Div. students in TH01 who patiently listened to earlier versions of some of these chapters. Their questions, suggestions, and encouragement have been a continuous source of strength and joy to me. To all these students this book is gratefully dedicated.

Preface

THE PAST FEW DECADES HAVE BEEN A TIME OF REMARKABLE FERMENT
in Christian theology. Many new emphases, proposals, and movements
have appeared — black theology, feminist theology, Latin American liberation theology, process theology, narrative theology, metaphorical theology, to mention only the more prominent. It has been a time of
unprecedented ecumenical dialogue, of intense reflection on theological
method, of dramatic paradigm shifts, of insistence on the importance of
praxis, and of many experiments in conversation between theology and
other areas of inquiry. Some observers of this ferment have suggested that
theology is in utter disarray; I do not share that pessimistic judgment.

Still, the present situation is not without its dangers, especially for
the beginning student in theology. The exciting diversity of new theological proposals and programs can easily lead to confusion or thoughtless
eclecticism. These dangers are heightened if certain perennial tasks of
theology are neglected. One writer warns, for example, of the "abdication
of responsibility" for constructive or systematic theological work in our
time, due in part to a preoccupation with methodological issues. "There
is a growing danger," he says, "that the work of theology is being replaced
by the work of preparing to do theology."[1]

My purpose in writing this book is to offer an introduction to
Christian theology that is both critically respectful of the classical theological tradition and critically open to the new voices and emphases of
recent theology. I hope that the influence of the liberation theologies of

---

1. Theodore W. Jennings, Jr., *The Vocation of the Theologian* (Philadelphia: Fortress,
1985), pp. 2-3.

our time — especially feminist, black, and Latin American — will be evident throughout the book. I am fairly certain that my Reformed theological heritage and orientation will not go unnoticed. I will consider my work successful if it helps to strengthen younger theologians in the conviction that a mutually critical and a mutually enriching interaction between liberation theologies and classical theological traditions is both possible and worth the effort.

Everyone who does theology today must be self-critically aware of his or her own social location and ecclesial context. While I am Protestant, North American, white, and male, my background and experience do not conform to the stereotypical WASP profile. My formative experience of Christian community was in a small Presbyterian congregation in Pittsburgh, Pennsylvania, of which my father was pastor. Almost all of the members of the church were struggling Italian immigrants and their families. Years before my encounter with the Civil Rights movement in the 1960s and with various liberation theologies in the 1970s, I learned some important lessons about the inseparability of faith and practice in that small congregation. Communication of the gospel in that context was always more than a theoretical affair, and concern for those at the margins of society was always a priority of Christian ministry.

While I do not pretend that my presentation of Christian doctrine will be adequate for all times and places, I hope that I have expressed a measure of the fullness of the faith of the worldwide Christian community. I further hope that readers will find that I have tried to listen to a large chorus of old and new voices and that I welcome the help and correction that comes from continuing dialogue with Christians whose experience and context are quite different from my own. I am grateful for the assistance I have received in this learning process from many students and colleagues, male and female, black and white, North and South American, European, African, and Asian.

The immediate context of my own theological work is a seminary of a "mainline" Protestant church in North America. While I am aware of the hazards of any attempt to write an outline of Christian doctrine at the present time, I am equally aware of the likely consequences of failing to make such an effort. In the context of North American schools of theology with which I am familiar, the absence of the risk of systematic reinterpretation of Christian doctrine results in the victory of unexamined orthodoxy or the triumph of nontheological professionalism.

Several convictions about the nature of theology inform this introduction. One is that Christian theology, or any other theology for that matter, arises out of, and remains importantly linked to, a *particular community of faith*. Whether theology is pursued in a seminary or in a university setting is not what is at issue here. The point is that theological inquiry does not arise in a vacuum. It is not built on amorphous religious experiences or on the pious imaginations of isolated individuals. On the contrary, the work of theology is inseparably bound to an identifiable faith community that worships God, attends to Scripture and its accounts of God's work and will, and engages in manifold ministries of education, reconciliation, and liberation. In short, theological inquiry requires continuing participation in the common life of a community of faith, prayer, and service. Apart from such participation, theology would soon become an empty exercise.

As I hope this book makes clear, I am also convinced that theology must be *critical reflection* on the community's faith and practice. Theology is not simply reiteration of what has been or is currently believed and practiced by a community of faith. It is a quest for truth, and that presupposes that the proclamation and practice of the community of faith are always in need of examination and reform. When this responsibility for critical reflection is neglected or relegated to a merely ornamental role, the faith of the community is invariably threatened by shallowness, arrogance, and ossification. The surge of fundamentalism in Christianity and Islam in recent years may yet persuade even the cultured despisers of religion that, for good or ill, religious commitment continues to exercise immense influence on human life. In our religiously pluralistic world the importance of *internal* critical reflection on the doctrines and practices of faith communities should not be overlooked.

Most decisively, critical reflection on the faith of the Christian community involves the deployment of a comprehensive theological vision, an interpretation of the *central Christian message* in interaction with the culture, experience, and need of a particular time and place. As we become increasingly aware today of our need for a thoroughgoing critique of domination in all spheres of life, systematic theology has the task of a consistent rethinking of God's power and presence in trinitarian terms, in which God is seen not as an all-controlling heavenly monarch but as the triune God who lives and acts in mutual self-giving and community-forming love. As the philosophy of individualism shows itself to be not only intellectually bankrupt but a contributor to ways of life that exploit the poor and ravage the environment, theology today is challenged to rethink the meaning of salvation along relational and communitarian lines, defining it not as a rescue of individual souls from the world but as the creation of a new and deeper freedom in community with God and solidarity with others. As mere theory and empty rhetoric come under fire because of their impotence in the face of the urgent crises of our time — racial injustice, political oppression, ecological deterioration, exploitation of women, the threat of nuclear holocaust — theology must understand itself not as abstract speculation but as concrete reflection that arises out of and is directed to the praxis of Christian faith, hope, and love. Thus a revised trinitarian theology, a corresponding relational understanding of creation, redemption, and consummation, and an orientation of theology to praxis are the major components of the theological vision that informs the following outline of Christian doctrine.

Finally, a word about the organization of the material. The order follows the classical loci of theology for the most part and is by intention trinitarian in both structure and content. The primary position given to the doctrine of the Trinity reflects my conviction concerning the central importance of this doctrine not only for classical Christian theology but for contemporary liberation faith and theology as well. After a lengthy period of Christological concentration in theology, we must reclaim for our time the fullness of trinitarian faith.[2]

The sole novelty in the presentation of topics is the inclusion of three imaginary dialogues of representative theologians and theological positions of the twentieth century. The dialogue form is, I think, not only pedagogically appealing, but often captures the vitality of theological inquiry and the open-endedness of theological discussions much better than more conventional expositions.

---

2. The constitution of the World Council of Churches states, "The World Council of Churches is a fellowship of churches which confess the Lord Jesus Christ as God and Savior according to the scriptures and therefore seek to fulfill together their common calling to the glory of the one God, Father, Son, and Holy Spirit."

Sources Frequently Cited

Karl Barth, *Church Dogmatics,* 13 vols. (Edinburgh: T. & T. Clark, 1936-1969).

John Calvin, *Institutes of the Christian Religion,* 2 vols., ed. John T. McNeill (Philadelphia: Westminster Press, 1960).

Paul Tillich, *Systematic Theology,* 3 vols. (Chicago: University of Chicago Press, 1951-1963).

1

The Task of Theology

CHRISTIAN THEOLOGY HAS MANY TASKS. THIS IS EVIDENT BOTH FROM a reading of the history of theology and from the wide variety of current understandings of its nature and task. Some theologians today contend that the task of Christian theology is to provide a clear and comprehensive description of the Christian faith. Other theologians emphasize the importance of translating Christian faith into terms that are intelligible to the wider culture. For others theology is defined broadly as thinking about important issues from the perspective of Christian faith. And still others insist that theology is reflection on the praxis of Christian faith within an oppressed community.[1]

Underlying each of these understandings of the task of theology is the assumption that faith and inquiry are inseparable. Theology arises from the freedom and responsibility of the Christian community to inquire about its faith in God. In this chapter I propose to describe the work of theology as a continuing search for the fullness of the truth of God made known in Jesus Christ. Defining the theological task in this way emphasizes that theology is not mere repetition of traditional doctrines but a persistent search for the truth to which they point and which they only partially and brokenly express. As continuing inquiry, the spirit of theology is interrogative rather than doctrinaire; it presupposes a readiness to question and to be questioned. Like the search of a woman

---

1. See *The Vocation of the Theologian,* ed. Theodore W. Jennings, Jr. (Philadelphia: Fortress Press, 1985).

for her lost coin (Luke 15:8), the work of theology is strenuous but may bring great joy.

Theology as Faith Raising Questions

ACCORDING to a classical definition, theology is *fides quaerens intellectum,* "faith seeking understanding" (Anselm). It is faith venturing to inquire, daring to raise questions. If Christian faith is basically trust in and obedience to the freely gracious God made known in Jesus Christ, theology is faith asking questions and struggling to find at least provisional answers to these questions. Christian faith is no sedative for world-weary souls, no satchelful of ready answers to the deepest questions of life. Instead, Christian faith invariably prompts questions, sets an inquiry in motion, fights the inclination to accept things as they are, continually calls in question unexamined assumptions about God, ourselves, and our world. Consequently, faith has nothing in common with indifference to the search for truth, or fear of it, or the arrogant claim to possess it fully. True faith must be distinguished from fideism. Fideism says we reach a point where we must stop our inquiry and simply believe; faith keeps on seeking and asking.

Theology grows out of this dynamism of Christian faith that incites reflection, inquiry, and pursuit of the truth not yet possessed, or only partially possessed. There are at least two fundamental roots of this quest of faith for understanding that we call theology. The first has to do with the unique *object* of Christian faith. Faith is faith in God, and God is and remains a mystery beyond human comprehension. Precisely as the "object" of faith, God does not cease to be "subject." Faith is a relation to the living God and not to a dead, manipulable idol. In Jesus Christ the living, inexhaustibly rich God has been revealed as sovereign love. To know God in this revelation is to acknowledge the infinite and incomprehensible depth of the mystery called God. Christians are confronted by mystery in all the central affirmations of their faith: the mystery of the holy love of God manifest in the creation of the world, the mystery of the forgiveness of sins in Jesus Christ, and the mystery of the renewal and promised transformation of broken human lives and of the entire world by the power of the Holy Spirit. To the eyes of faith, the world is encompassed by the mystery of God.

As Gabriel Marcel has explained, a mystery is very different from a problem. While a problem can be solved, a mystery is inexhaustible. A problem can be held at arm's length; a mystery encompasses us and will not let us keep a safe distance.[2] Christian faith prompts inquiry not least because it points to the shocking mystery that in the humble service and terrible passion of Jesus, God is at work for our salvation. So while Christians affirm that God has decisively spoken (Heb. 1:1-2), there is much that they do not understand. Perhaps there will come a time when no questions need be asked (John 16:23), but here and now faith sees only dimly, not face to face (1 Cor. 13:12), and the questions of faith abound.

The second root of the quest of faith for understanding is the *situation* of faith. Believers do not live in a vacuum. Like all people, they live in particular historical situations that have their own distinctive problems and possibilities. The changing, ambiguous, and often precarious world poses ever new questions for faith, and many answers that sufficed yesterday are no longer compelling today.

Questions arise at the edges of what we can know and what we can do as human beings. They thrust themselves on us with special force in times and situations of crisis such as sickness, suffering, guilt, injustice, personal or social upheaval, and death. Believers are not immune to the questions that arise in these situations. Indeed, they may be more perplexed than others because they have to relate their faith to what is happening in their lives and in the world. Precisely as believers, they experience the frequent and disturbing incongruity between faith and lived reality. They believe in a sovereign and good God, but they live in a world where evil often seems triumphant. They believe in a living Lord, but more often than not they experience the absence rather than the presence of God. They believe in the transforming power of the Spirit of God, but they know all too well the impotence of the church and of themselves. They know that they should obey God's will, but they find that it is often difficult to know what God's will is in regard to particular issues. And even when they know God's will, they frequently resist doing it. Christian faith asks questions, seeks understanding, both because God is always greater than our ideas of God, and because the public world that faith inhabits confronts it with challenges and contradictions that cannot be ignored. Edward Schillebeeckx puts the point succinctly: Christian faith "causes us to think."[3]

---

2. Marcel, *The Mystery of Being* (Chicago: Henry Regnery, 1960), 1: 260-61.
3. Schillebeeckx, preface to *Interim Report on the Books Jesus and Christ* (New York: Crossroad, 1981).

In emphasizing the point that far from producing a closed or complacent attitude, faith causes wonder, inquiry, and questioning, we underscore the humanity of the life of faith and of the discipline of theology. Human beings are open when they ask questions, when they keep seeking, when they are, as Augustine says, "ravished with love for the truth." To be human is to ask all sorts of questions: Who are we? What is of highest value? Is there a God? What can we hope for? Can we rid ourselves of our flaws and improve our world? What should we do? When persons enter on the pilgrimage of faith, they do not suddenly stop being human; they do not stop asking questions. Becoming a Christian does not put an end to the human impulse to question and to seek for deeper understanding. On the contrary, being a pilgrim of faith intensifies and transforms many old questions and generates new and urgent questions: What is God like? How does Jesus Christ redefine true humanity? Is God present in the world today? What does it mean to be responsible disciples of the crucified and risen Lord? Those who have experienced something of the grace of God in Jesus Christ find themselves wanting to enter more fully into that mystery and to understand the world and every aspect of their lives in its light.

According to the philosopher Descartes, the only reliable starting point in the pursuit of truth is self-consciousness. *Cogito ergo sum,* "I think, therefore I am." The logic of Christian faith differs radically from this Cartesian logic in at least two respects. First, the starting point of inquiry for the Christian is not self-consciousness but awareness of the reality of God, who is creator and redeemer of all things. Not "I think, therefore I am," but "God is, therefore we are." As the Psalmist writes, "O Lord, our Sovereign, how majestic is your name in all the earth. . . . When I look at your heavens, the work of your fingers, the moon and the stars that you have established; what are human beings that you are mindful of them, mortals that you care for them" (Ps. 8:1, 3-4).

Second, for Christian faith and theology inquiry is elicited by faith in God rather than being an attempt to arrive at certainty apart from God. Not "I seek certainty by doubting everything but my own existence," but "Because God has shown mercy to us, therefore we inquire." If we believe in God, we must expect that our old ways of thinking and living will be continually shaken to the foundations. If we believe in God, we will have to become seekers, pilgrims, pioneers with no permanent residence. We will no longer be satisfied with the unexamined beliefs and practices of our everyday personal and social world. If we believe in God, we will necessarily question the gods of power, wealth, nationality, and race that clamor for our allegiance. Christian faith is thinking faith.[4]

As long as Christians remain pilgrims of faith, they will continue to raise questions — hard questions — for which they will not always find answers. Rather than having all the answers, believers often find that they have a new set of questions. This is surely the experience of the women and men in the Bible. The Bible is no easy answer book, although it is sometimes read that way. If we are ready to listen, the Bible has the power to shake us violently with its terrible questions: "Adam, where are you?" (Gen. 3:9). "Cain, where is your brother Abel?" (Gen. 4:9). To judge the cause of the poor and needy — "Is not this to know me? says the Lord" (Jer. 22:16). "Who do you say that I am?" (Mark 8:29). "My God, my God, why have you forsaken me?" (Mark 15:34). When faith no longer frees people to ask the hard questions, it becomes inhuman and dangerous. Unquestioning faith soon slips into ideology, superstition, fanaticism, self-indulgence, and idolatry. Faith seeks understanding passionately and relentlessly, or it languishes and eventually dies. If faith raises ever new questions, then the theological task of the Christian community is to pursue these questions, to keep them alive, to prevent them from being forgotten or suppressed. Human life ceases to be human not when we do not have all the answers but when we no longer have the courage to ask the really important questions. By insisting that these questions be raised, theology serves not only the community of faith but also the wider purpose of God "to make and to keep human life human in the world."[5]

Theology is strenuous inquiry, a process of seeking, contending, wrestling, like Jacob with the angel until dawn, wanting to be blessed and limping away from the struggle (Gen. 32:24ff.)

The Questionableness of Theology

If Christian faith causes us to think, this is not to say that being Christian is exhausted in thinking, even in thinking about the doctrines of the

---

4. See Douglas John Hall, *Thinking the Faith: Christian Theology in a North American Context* (Minneapolis: Augsburg, 1989).

5. Paul Lehmann, *Ethics in a Christian Context* (New York: Harper & Row, 1963), p. 112.

church. Christian faith causes us to do more than think. Faith sings, confesses, rejoices, suffers, and acts. When faith and theology are exhausted in thinking, they become utterly questionable. This is because the understanding that is sought by faith is not speculative knowledge but the wisdom that illumines life and practice. As John Calvin explains, genuine knowledge of God is inseparable from worship and service.[6] Faith seeks the truth of God that wants not only to be known by the mind but also to be enjoyed and practiced by the whole person. Theology as thoughtful faith comes from and returns to the service of God and the neighbor.

No doubt there is such a thing as too much theology — or, more precisely, there is such a thing as unfruitful, abstract theology that gets lost in a labyrinth of academic trivialities. When this happens, theology comes under judgment. In a paraphrase of the prophet Amos, Karl Barth humorously expresses the likely judgment of God on theology that has become pointless and endless talk: "I hate, I despise your lectures and seminars, your sermons, addresses and Bible studies. . . . When you display your hermeneutic, dogmatic, ethical and pastoral bits of wisdom before one another and before me, I have no pleasure in them. . . . Take away from me your . . . thick books and . . . your dissertations . . . your theological magazines, monthlies and quarterlies."[7]

Simple Christian piety has always objected to speculative and useless theology that frivolously asks how many angels can dance on the head of a pin or presumptuously deals with the mystery of God as with a problem in algebra. It is entirely understandable why some Christians find such theological activity completely questionable. In their frustration, they say: "Away with theology and all its clever distinctions and wearisome debates. What we need is not more theology but simple faith, not more elegant arguments but transformed hearts, unadorned commitment to Christ, unqualified acceptance of what the Bible teaches, and uncompromising trust in the Holy Spirit."

But while this criticism of theology in the name of simple piety is important and stands as a constant warning against detached, insensitive, and overly intellectualized theology, it cannot itself go unchallenged

---

6. Calvin, *Institutes of the Christian Religion,* 1.2.1. Note also that for Calvin the gospel is not "a doctrine of the tongue but of life" (3.6.4).

7. Barth, *Evangelical Theology* (Garden City, N.Y.: Doubleday-Anchor, 1964), p. 120.

without serious injury to the life of individual Christians and the well-being of the Christian community. Christian faith is indeed simple, but it is not simplistic. Loyalty to and heartfelt trust in Christ are indeed basic and necessary, but Christians are enjoined to bring their whole life and their every thought into captivity to Christ (2 Cor. 10:5), and this is always an arduous process. While the church is indeed to stand under the authority of the biblical witness, it must avoid bibliolatry. While Christians are certainly to rely on the power of the Holy Spirit, they are also commanded to test the spirits to see whether they are from God (1 John 4:1). The grace of God is indeed a mystery in which men and women are invited to participate rather than an intellectual puzzle that they are to solve. But to speak of God as a mystery is one thing; to revel in mystagogy and obscurantism is quite another. "Theology," Karl Barth writes, "means taking rational trouble over the mystery. . . . If we are unwilling to take the trouble, neither shall we know what we mean when we say that we are dealing with the mystery of God."[8] An appeal to the Bible or the Holy Spirit should not be considered an alternative to serious reflection. Christian faith must not be reduced to a euphoric feeling or to a homiletical cliché. Christ is indeed the answer, but what was the question? And who is Christ? Christian faith is no authoritarian, uncritical, unreflective set of answers to the human predicament. Genuine faith does not suppress any questions; it may give people a lot more questions than they had before. Thus the anxiety of simple piety is misplaced. The sort of thinking that Christian faith sets in motion does not replace trust in God but acts as a critical ingredient that helps to distinguish faith from mere illusion or pious evasion.

The attack on theology as a questionable pursuit, however, comes from another quarter as well. It is launched by the representatives of practical faith who find theology, at least as it is often done, useless and even pernicious. The charge is that theology is a mere intellectual game that causes paralysis rather than leading to action. So these critics of theology say: "Let us Christians have done with all this theorizing and get on with doing something for Christ's sake. Did not the Apostle Paul say that the kingdom of God is not talk but power (1 Cor. 4:20)? Surely faith is more than thinking correctly (a notion that might be called the heresy of orthodoxy). Faith is a matter of transformation — personal, social, and world transformation. It is being willing to put your life on

---

8. Barth, *Church Dogmatics*, I/1 (2d ed., 1975): 423.

the line for the sake of Christ and his gospel." Here again, there is some truth in this line of criticism. Questionable indeed is the theology whose theory is no longer linked to transforming praxis. But the criticism is one-sided. If theory without praxis is empty, praxis without theory is blind. How are Christians to know whether this or that action is "for the sake of Christ and the coming kingdom of God" if they impatiently shrug off the questions: Who is Christ? and What is his kingdom? Mindless leaps into action are no more Christian than thinking for thinking's sake. God's call to faithfulness can sometimes be a summons to be still and wait. There is a creative waiting as well as a creative acting. Christian faith causes us to think, to raise questions, to be suspicious of the bandwagons, the movements that are intolerant of questions, the generals on the right or the left who demand unquestioning allegiance and simply bark: Forward, march!

But the critics of theology may go further and charge that it is not only speculative and impractical but that it often assumes a quite sinister and despicable form. It often serves to give religious justification to the rule of the powerful and to conditions of injustice; doctrines are often invoked in defense of the way things are. According to Karl Marx, the criticism of religion and theology is the beginning of all criticism. This suspicion of the mystifying function of much religion and theology is by no means original to Marxism. We find it at work in the judgments of the Old Testament prophets and in the teaching of Jesus; they knew very well the extent to which religion and its official custodians can stand in opposition to God's intentions for human life. Theology indeed becomes questionable when it ceases to ask itself what powers it is in fact serving and whose interests it may be promoting. It is clear that much Christian theology has not yet learned to take these questions with the seriousness that they deserve.

Theology, I have been contending, is the continuous process of inquiry that is prompted both by the surprising grace of God and by the distance between God's coming kingdom on the one hand and our experience of the brokenness of life on the other. If the task of theology is properly understood, it will not be seen as an activity that can be abandoned to a cadre of professional theologians in the church. It is an activity in which all members of the community of faith participate in appropriate ways. In the life of faith "no one is excused the task of asking questions or the more difficult one of providing and assessing answers."9

9. Barth, *Church Dogmatics*, III/4: 498.

If theology has been put to uses that make it questionable and even contemptible, all members of the community of faith must ask themselves to what extent they have contributed to this misuse by their own surrender of theological responsibility. To be sure, faith and theology are not identical. An advanced degree in theology is no more a guarantee of a living faith than a life of faith is deficient because of the absence of a theological degree. Still, faith and theological inquiry are closely related. If faith is the direct response to the hearing of God's word of grace and judgment, theology is second-order reflection on the church's language and practice of faith. And this second-order reflection happens at many levels and in many different life contexts.

The Questions of Theology

UP to this point, I have been speaking of Christian theology in an undifferentiated way. There are, however, several branches of theology, and it is important to see how they relate to each other.[10] *Biblical theology* studies in detail the canonical writings of the Old and New Testaments that are acknowledged by the church as the primary witnesses to the work and word of God. *Historical theology* traces the many ways in which Christian faith and life have come to expression in different times and places. *Philosophical theology* employs the resources of philosophical inquiry to examine the meaning and truth of Christian faith in the light of reason and experience. *Practical theology* is concerned with the specific tasks of ministry such as preaching, educating, pastoral counseling, caring for the poor, and visiting the sick, the dying, and the bereaved.

In this book we take up that aspect of the larger theological task of the community of faith that is called *systematic theology* (also called doctrinal or constructive theology). Informed by the other theological disciplines, its particular task is to venture a faithful, coherent, timely, and responsible articulation of Christian faith. This is both a critical and an imaginative activity. It involves continuous reinterpretation of the

---

10. On the need for rethinking the nature and organization of theological studies, see Edward Farley, *Theologia: The Fragmentation and Unity of Theological Education* (Philadelphia: Fortress Press, 1983); and Charles M. Wood, *Vision and Discernment: An Orientation in Theological Study* (Atlanta: Scholars Press, 1985).

doctrines and practices of the church in the light of what the church itself avows to be of central importance — namely, the gospel of Jesus Christ that liberates and renews life. All Christians, and especially those who exercise leadership in the Christian community as pastors and teachers, participate in the task of systematic theology insofar as they are constrained to ask at least four basic questions that bear upon every phase of Christian life and ministry.

1. *Are the proclamation and practice of the church true to the revelation of God in Jesus Christ as attested in Scripture?* All of the questions of theology are finally aspects of this question. What is the Christian gospel, the "good news" of God made known in Christ, and how is it to be distinguished from its many misrepresentations and distortions? On this question hangs the very identity of the Christian community and the faithfulness of its proclamation and life.

The Apostle Paul pursues this critical inquiry of theology when he argues in Galatians and Romans that trust in the grace and forgiveness of God is radically different from a religion based on achievements and merits. Paul is blunt and uncompromising. There is for him only one true gospel (Gal. 1:6ff.). False gospels are to be exposed and rejected. In later centuries, Irenaeus argued against the Gnostics, Athanasius against Arianism, Augustine against Pelagianism, Luther against a late medieval system of salvation by works, Barth against a liberal Christianity that had become the domesticated religion of bourgeois culture. From time to time, a creed or confession has been hammered out — the creeds of Nicea and Chalcedon, the Augsburg Confession, the Barmen Declaration, to name a few — marking a time and place where the church has been compelled to state its faith, in the midst of controversy, as unambiguously as possible, lest the gospel be obscured, or even lost.

In our own time, there are all sorts of facsimiles of the gospel being proclaimed, all the way from the seductive cults of self-fulfillment to the ugly arrogance of apartheid Christianity. Is what is purported to be Christian proclamation an appropriate representation of the gospel? No responsible member of the Christian community — certainly no leader of the community — can avoid asking this question. If the gospel is never simply identical with everything that is called Christian or that wraps itself in religious garb, and if it resists identification with many things that we have gotten used to in our personal and social life, then the community of faith cannot cease to ask itself whether it has rightly heard and properly understood what Scripture attests as the "gospel of God"

(Rom. 1:1). Theology as a formal discipline exists to keep that question alive, to ask it over and over again.

2. *Do the proclamation and practice of the community of faith give adequate expression to the whole truth of the revelation of God in Jesus Christ?* This second question of systematic theology tests the wholeness and coherence of the affirmations of the Christian community.

Many people are suspicious of anything called systematic theology, and with good reason. When theology undertakes to derive the whole of Christian doctrine from a single principle or group of principles, or when it expresses a rationalistic attitude that tries to master the revelation of God instead of faithfully following its lead, then it becomes a "system" antithetical to faith. Nevertheless, the effort of theology to be "systematic" is to be affirmed insofar as its concern is for the wholeness of faith as opposed to partial and one-sided understandings. Just as Christian faith is not a smorgasbord of beliefs, so Christian theology is not a disparate bundle of symbols and doctrines from which one can select at will or organize into any pattern one pleases. The cross of Jesus Christ cannot be understood apart from his life and his resurrection, nor can either of these be properly understood apart from the cross. God's work of reconciliation cannot be rightly understood apart from the work of creation or the hope in the consummation of all things. Christian doctrines form a coherent whole. They are deeply intertwined. They constitute a world. They tell a coherent story. Even expressions of faith that laudably aim to be "christocentric" would be seriously defective if, for example, they neglected the goodness of creation or minimized the reality of evil in the world or marginalized Christian hope in the kingdom of God.

The quest for the wholeness and coherence of Christian faith goes back to the New Testament beginnings of the church. The Bible is a very diverse book. Modern scholarship continues to uncover the immense diversity of the earliest Christian communities. Today we are conscious as perhaps never before of the plurality of Christian theologies, traditions, and priorities in Christian witness and service. The question What is the whole gospel? has thus become inescapable for us. What is that rich unity and wholeness of the Christian faith that not only permits but insists on our diversity, our heterogeneity, our priceless differences as human beings made in the image of God, and yet holds us together in the bonds of acceptance and love? What is the whole gospel that includes the correction and enrichment of faith made by the sometimes angry and always unsettling witness of blacks, Hispanics, women, the handicapped, and the unemployed? When a deaf ear is turned to these disturbing voices, is it not because we assume that we are already in possession of the whole truth? What is the whole gospel that frees us to engage in a process of mutual correction and mutual enrichment in our understanding of the faith and of our vocation as Christians? The church is always threatened by a false unity that does not allow for rich inclusivity. Theology exists to keep alive the quest for the whole gospel that alone can bring unity without loss of enriching diversity, community without loss of personal or cultural integrity, peace without compromise of justice. Theology must ask not only what is the true gospel but also what is the whole gospel: What is the breadth and length and height and depth of the love of God in Christ (Eph. 3:18-19)?

3. *Do the proclamation and practice of the community of faith represent the God of Jesus Christ as a living reality in the present context?* The Christian message must be interpreted again and again in new situations and in concepts and images that are understandable to people in those situations. Who is Christ for us *today?* asked Bonhoeffer.

The questions What is the present gospel? and Who is Christ for us today? may sound shocking at first. Is there a different gospel then and now, there and here? The answer is that there is indeed only one gospel of the triune God who has acted redemptively for the world in Christ and who is still renewing and transforming all things by the power of the Holy Spirit. Yet it is necessary to reinterpret the language of Christian faith — its stories, doctrines, and symbols — for our own time and place if we are faithfully to serve the gospel rather than uncritically endorse the cultural forms in which it has been mediated to us. Responsible theology is not an exercise in the repristination of an earlier culture. It is not a simple repetition of the faith of our fathers and mothers. On the contrary, the work of theology involves creativity and imagination; it is a *constructive* task. It involves the risk of re-presenting the Christian faith in new concepts and in new actions. It demands thinking through and living out the faith in relation to new experiences, new problems, and new possibilities. The Bible itself is a model of this process of dynamic re-presentation of the faith of the community in new times and situations.

4. *Does the proclamation of the community of faith lead to transforming praxis in personal and social life?* This fourth basic question of systematic theology addresses the concrete and responsible embodiment

of faith and discipleship in particular contexts. Christian faith calls people to freedom and responsibility in every sphere of life. Thus an indispensable task of theology is to ask how the gospel might reform and transform human life in concrete ways in our own time and in our own situation. What bearing does the gospel have on the everyday decisions and actions of the community of faith and its individual members? What patterns of our own life, what institutional structures that we may have long taken for granted, must now be called in question by the gospel? What structures of evil must be named and challenged if the gospel is to have any concrete impact on human life in the present? Where can we discern the signs of new beginnings in a world marked by terror, apathy, and injustice?

All these questions presuppose an inseparable bond between our trust in God's grace and our call to God's service. The gospel of Jesus Christ proclaims God's gift of forgiveness, reconciliation, freedom, and new life. But the gift of God enables and commands our free, glad, and courageous discipleship. Theology and ethics are thus conjoined. As James Cone writes, "Theological concepts have meaning only as they are translated into theological praxis, that is, the Church living in the world on the basis of what it proclaims."[11] True faith works through love (Gal. 5:6). We cannot seriously receive God's gift of new life without asking equally seriously what God commands us to do. Theology exists to remind us of God's gift *and* command, and thus to keep alive the question: What would it mean for us personally and corporately to bear a faithful and concrete witness to the crucified and risen Lord in our world today?

These four central questions of systematic theology must be asked not once but continuously. Theology never achieves more than partial success in answering them. And however important it is to respect and learn from the answers given to these questions in the past, there is no guarantee that theology can simply build upon past answers. For this reason, theology must always have the freedom and courage to "begin again at the beginning."[12] Since such freedom and courage are gifts of the Spirit of God, prayer is the inseparable companion of theological inquiry: *Veni Creator Spiritus,* "Come, Creator Spirit!"

11. Cone, *God of the Oppressed* (New York: Seabury Press, 1975), p. 36.
12. Barth, *Evangelical Theology,* p. 146.

Methods of Asking Theological Questions

THEOLOGY not only asks questions but must be self-conscious about the way it does so. This is, in brief, the problem of theological method. While much has been written about theological method in recent years, we are far from any clear consensus. No doubt differences in theological method reflect fundamental differences in understandings of revelation and the mode of God's presence in the world. They also show the limitations of any single method to do all the tasks of theology.

An important factor affecting theological method is the social location in which a particular theology is pursued. The concrete situation of a theology helps to shape the questions that are raised and the priorities that are set. David Tracy contends that the plurality of theologies today can be understood in part as a result of their various primary locations in church, academy, or society. In each setting, different aims and criteria come into play. Each social location of theology imposes its own set of questions, its own relative criteria of truth and adequacy, and its own special emphases. Theology in the academic context naturally tends to be apologetically oriented; theology in the church is interested primarily in the clarification and interpretation of the church's message; theology in the wider society is concerned about the practical realization of God's new justice and peace.[13] With the help of Tracy's analysis, we can readily identify three important types of theological method, three different ways of asking theological questions, in the twentieth century.

1. One influential method of theology is Karl Barth's *Christocentric theology*, or the theology of the Word of God. Barth describes theology as a discipline of the church in which the church continuously tests itself and its proclamation by its own norm, which is Jesus Christ as attested in Scripture. For Barth, to say that theology is a discipline of the church is not to say that its task is simply to repeat church doctrines or traditions. Barth's *Church Dogmatics* is a thoroughly critical inquiry even if he claims that its method and norms are independent of other university disciplines. Theology for Barth is the process of subjecting the church and its proclamation to questioning and testing by reference to the living Word of God in Jesus Christ. The primary questions with which theology has to do are the questions the Word of God addresses to us here and now

13. Tracy, *The Analogical Imagination: Christian Theology and the Culture of Pluralism* (New York: Crossroad, 1981), pp. 3-98.

rather than the questions that arise out of our experience or situation. In spite of popular misrepresentations of his method, Barth does not say that we must suppress our own questions in the study of Scripture and in theological inquiry generally; nor does he argue that theology should work in isolation from philosophy, the social sciences, and other disciplines. His overriding emphasis, however, is that the questions of theology, no less than its answers, must be disciplined by theology's own subject matter and norm. In short, Barth's theological method underscores the priority of the Word of God and the unsettling questions that it continuously puts to all human life, but most especially to the church in regard to the faithfulness of its proclamation and life.

2. A second very influential method of theology is the *correlation method*, or apologetic theology of Paul Tillich.[14] In this method, existential questions are formulated by an analysis of the human situation in a given period as seen in its philosophy, literature, art, science, and social institutions. These questions are then correlated with the "answers" of the Christian message. The aim is to create genuine conversation between human culture and revelation rather than driving a wedge between them. From Tillich's perspective, Barth's theological method is more of a soliloquy than a conversation. It moves only from revelation to culture and experience rather than back and forth. Tillich does not believe that the method of correlation surrenders the normativity of revelation to general culture and human experience. Revelation is not normed *by* the situation but it must speak *to* it, and it can do this only if the actual questions of the situation are attended to. David Tracy's revisionary theology is a modification of Tillich's method of correlation. He stresses more fully and explicitly than Tillich that correlation involves mutual correction and mutual enrichment of the partners in the conversation. Only in this way, he argues, is it possible to open theology to the important contributions of culture and to approach culture with genuine concern for the intelligibility and credibility of the truth claims of faith.

3. A third method of theology is the *praxis approach* of liberation theology. This method is represented by African-American, feminist, black South African, and many other Third World liberation theologians, most notably in Latin America. Gustavo Gutiérrez, a pioneer of Latin American liberation theology, recognizes that theology in the past has

14. See Tillich, *Systematic Theology,* especially 1: 3-68; 2: 13-16.

taken the forms of spiritual wisdom and rational knowledge, and he allows that these are "permanent and indispensable functions of all theological thinking." But he defends the importance of a new form of theology as "critical reflection on praxis."[15] In this method of theology, praxis comes first. It is out of praxis, or the real struggle for human freedom and justice in the world, that the pertinent questions of theology are raised. A new way of reading and interpreting Scripture results when praxis is taken as the point of departure for critical theological reflection. The first step is "real charity, action and commitment to the service of men. Theology is reflection, a critical attitude. Theology follows; it is the second step."[16] So understood, theology promotes justice rather than serving as an ideology that justifies a given social or ecclesial order. Beginning with participation in the struggle for change, theology helps to deepen and direct this struggle by recourse to the sources of revelation. Thus "the theology of liberation offers us not so much a new theme for reflection as a *new way* to do theology."[17] Liberation theologians are not satisfied with either Barth's *Church Dogmatics* or Tillich's *Systematic Theology*. Theology and the questions that it pursues must arise "from below," from the praxis of solidarity with the poor and their struggle for justice and freedom.

It will become fairly obvious to the reader that the method and content of theology presented in the following chapters is considerably influenced by Karl Barth's approach to theology and by his creative reinterpretation of the Reformed theological tradition. At the same time, contributions from both the theologies of correlation and praxis will also be apparent. The ecumenical church has learned — and will no doubt continue to learn — from the methods of christocentric and correlational theologies. It has, however, only begun to learn from the method of liberation theology. Writing from a prison cell and reflecting on what theology and the church should have learned from having been compelled to live for ten years through the horrors and suffering of the Nazi regime, Dietrich Bonhoeffer observed, "There remains (for us) an experience of incomparable value. We have for once learnt to see the great events of world history from below, from the perspective of the outcast, the sus-

15. Gutiérrez, *A Theology of Liberation* (Maryknoll, N.Y.: Orbis Books, 1973), p. 6.

16. Gutiérrez, *A Theology of Liberation*, p. 11.

17. Gutiérrez, *A Theology of Liberation*, p. 15.

pects, the maltreated, the powerless, the oppressed, the reviled — in short, from the perspective of those who suffer."[18]

Bonhoeffer tells us that he had to *learn* to view life and the gospel from below. And so I suspect do most of us in the church in North America. We are learning slowly that it makes a difference whether the Bible is read and the gospel is apprehended only from the standpoint of relatively well-to-do people or "from below," through the eyes of those who are weak and who don't count for much by the standards of successful people and institutions. As Gustavo Gutiérrez has noted, much depends on whether the effort of theology is to help make the proclamation and practice of the gospel more understandable and credible to the First World nonbeliever or to test itself against the situation of the forgotten nonpersons of the Third World.

It would, of course, be a mistake for theology to take up one of these tasks and totally reject the other. The questions about Christian faith raised by the heirs of the Enlightenment deserve a hearing and a response, even if the presuppositions of these questions must be challenged more vigorously than has been the case in much modern theology. Yet it is equally true that theology has for too long ignored the questions raised by the weak and powerless of the earth. What is the true gospel? What is the whole gospel? What is the present gospel? What concrete practice of the gospel is called for today? These inescapable questions of faith and theology need to be asked also "from below," from the vantage point of what Bonhoeffer called "the incomparable experience" of solidarity with the afflicted. This should not be construed as a summons to anti-intellectualism or romanticism. It concerns finally the kind of theology one intends to pursue: a theology that accompanies those who cry "out of the depths" (Ps. 130:1) and that finds its center in the message of "Christ crucified" (1 Cor. 1:23), or a triumphalist theology that serves only the interests of the powerful.

To summarize these introductory reflections, I have contended that asking questions is part of what it means to be human, and that asking questions in the light of the grace of God in Jesus Christ is part of what it means to be Christian. What is theology? It is faith asking questions, seeking understanding. It is disciplined yet bold reflection on Christian faith in the God of the gospel. It is willingness to take rational trouble over the mystery of God revealed in Jesus Christ as attested by Scripture.

18. Bonhoeffer, *Letters and Papers from Prison* (New York: Macmillan, 1971), p. 17.

It is inquiry yoked to prayer. When theology is neglected or becomes distracted, the community of faith may drift aimlessly, or be captured by spirits alien to its own. However difficult the theological task today, there is no escaping the questions about the truth, the wholeness, the present intelligibility, and the practical expression of the gospel. And there is no escaping the issue of whether all these questions of theology will be asked not only from the locations of church, academy, and society familiar to most North Americans but also "from below."

2

The Meaning of Revelation

EVERY THEOLOGY HAS TO OFFER SOME ACCOUNT OF THE BASIS OF its affirmations. It has to say on what grounds believers claim to have knowledge of God and of all creatures in relation to God. Questions of this sort are not ordinarily addressed in the hymns, prayers, and creeds of the church. These primary expressions of faith do not attempt to give a reasoned account of the truth claims that they make. The most familiar and the most widely used of Christian creeds — the Apostles' and the Nicene — simply begin with the words, "I (or We) believe . . ." Theological reflection on such confessions, however, is compelled to ask how the community of faith has come to know these things. What is the source of our knowledge of God and of all things in relation to God? What place do human reason and imagination have in our knowledge of God? Such questions have usually been discussed in theology, especially in the modern period, under the topic of revelation.

What Is Revelation?

THE word *revelation* literally means an "unveiling" or "disclosure" of something previously hidden. While the term has distinctive meanings when it refers to our knowledge of God, there is a sense in which every experience of knowing presupposes openness to a kind of "revelation." There is a gift-like quality to many of our experiences of knowing. Every knower must be receptive as well as active if true knowledge is to be attained. We must let the object to be known "speak" to us rather than

19

forcing it to conform to our preconceptions. Moreover, when new knowledge is received, it may come with life-transforming effect rather than as merely additional information that does not basically change the way we think or live. As these remarks suggest, what is called revelation in theology is not entirely without analogy in our other experiences of knowing.[1]

Yet the meaning of revelation in Christian theology is much more specific. It refers to the self-disclosure of God in the creation, in the history of the people of Israel, and above all in the person of Jesus. Revelation is not the transmission of a body of knowledge but the personal disclosure of one subject to other subjects. God has taken the initiative and has freely made known the divine identity and purpose. In brief, the knowledge given in revelation is not simply knowledge *that,* or knowledge *about,* but knowledge *of.*[2]

The claim that God has acted to disclose who God is and what God wills is deeply etched in the biblical traditions. In the Hebrew Bible, the revelation of God is centered in the history of the gracious covenant of Yahweh with the people of Israel. This includes the promise of God to Abraham and Sarah (Gen. 17), the disclosure of the divine name to Moses (Exod. 3:14), the liberation of Israel from bondage in Egypt, the giving of the Torah, and the preaching of God's judgment and grace by the prophets. While God is truly disclosed in these events, the divine freedom or hiddenness is never dissolved. *God does not cease to be a mystery in the event of revelation.* The self-revealing God never becomes a controllable object or a manipulable possession. This is vividly expressed in many biblical narratives: Moses is permitted to see only the back of God (Exod. 33:12-23); Elijah hears the voice of God not in the wind, earthquake, or fire, but in a small voice (1 Kings 19:11ff.).

In the New Testament the revelation of God is still more sharply focused. What God has done in the covenantal history with the people of Israel is not abrogated but confirmed and surprisingly enlarged in the new covenant in Jesus Christ. In the proclamation, ministry, death, and resurrection of Jesus, and in the renewing work of the Holy Spirit, a new relationship between God and all humanity is established. For

---

1. See John Baillie, *The Idea of Revelation in Recent Thought* (New York: Columbia University Press, 1956), pp. 19ff.; and John Macquarrie, *Principles of Christian Theology,* 2d ed. (New York: Scribner's, 1977), pp. 84ff.
2. Baillie, *The Idea of Revelation in Recent Thought,* p. 47.

Christian faith, Jesus Christ is the decisive revelation of the sovereign and holy love of God. The New Testament authors express the uniqueness of this revelation of God in Christ in various ways. They confess that in this person God has spoken not only through a prophet but through a Son (Heb. 1:1-2), that the eternal divine Word has become incarnate in a human life (John 1:14), that the Spirit-anointed Liberator of all the oppressed has appeared (Luke 4:18ff.). As in the Old Testament, however, the revelation of God is also, paradoxically, the hiddenness of God. That God is revealed in a humble servant who suffers and is crucified is sheer scandal and folly to the wise and powerful of this world (1 Cor. 1:22-23).

While the idea of revelation has been a centerpiece of much modern theology, some theologians are convinced that its importance has been greatly exaggerated. They claim that this concept is actually quite peripheral within the Bible. Their primary argument is that the notion of revelation tends to focus attention on the sorts of epistemological questions that are prominent in modern philosophy and science (e.g., Are our claims to knowledge well-grounded?), rather than on the question of salvation.[3] If we concentrate on the theme of revelation, do we not suggest that the basic human predicament is ignorance rather than sin? In the Bible people do not ask What must I *know?* but Who must I *be* and what must I *do* to be saved? (see Mark 10:17; John 3:3).

There is some truth in this criticism of inflated talk about revelation in modern theology. If revelation is equated with divinely given information, the danger of the concept is obvious. According to the Bible, faith is primarily a matter of personal trust in and obedience to God rather than mere intellectual assent to a set of authoritative doctrines. By "knowledge of God" the biblical tradition does not mean simply information about one of the myriad objects whose existence we may more or less indifferently concede, but rather a saving knowledge, a knowledge that bears decisively on the meaning, wholeness, and fulfillment of our life in relationship to God and others. In the same vein, as we noted in the preceding chapter, Calvin states that knowledge of God is far more than conceiving that God exists; properly speaking, God is known only where there is piety, where knowledge is fused with love of God and the desire to do God's will.[4]

---

3. See F. Gerald Downing, *Has Christianity a Revelation?* (London: SCM Press, 1964).

4. John Calvin, *Institutes of the Christian Religion,* 1.2.1.

But if it is a mistake to equate knowledge of God with mere information, it is no less a mistake to think of faith as a desperate leap in the dark. Believers claim that what they affirm is true. How could we trust God if we did not have any knowledge of God's trustworthiness? How could we obey the will of God if we had no knowledge of what that will is? How could we rightly worship or pray or serve a God who is totally unknown and unknowable? Christian faith and life are inseparable from reliable knowledge of the character and purpose of God. If we do not want to call the source of this knowledge revelation, then we will have to invent some other term to take its place.

An issue repeatedly debated by theologians is whether we are to think of revelation as an *objective occurrence* or a *subjective experience*. Some doctrines of revelation emphasize the objective and others emphasize the subjective aspects of revelation. But surely both sides of the process of revelation are important and must be held together. Revelation is God's free and gracious self-disclosure through particular events that are attested and interpreted by people of faith. In Paul Tillich's words, "Revelation always is a subjective and an objective event in strict interdependence."[5] What is called revelation includes both God's self-disclosing activity through particular persons and events and the working of God's Spirit, who enables people to appropriate and bear witness to this activity.

Probably the most frequently discussed issue in recent reflection on the doctrine of revelation is what part human reason and imagination play in the revelatory process. A number of theologians have noted that the experience of revelation as described in theology is similar to other experiences of fresh insight or "paradigm shifts," as in artistic creation or in scientific inquiry.[6] Their work shows that the idea of revelation is distorted when it is seen as a supernatural substitute for the use of human reason and the play of human imagination. Revelation does not destroy or disable human capacities; to the contrary, the concrete love of God in Jesus Christ captures the allegiance of the heart, brings new vision to human imagination, and provides new direction to human reason.

According to Garrett Green, the revelation of God in the history of Israel and supremely in the person of Jesus Christ takes effect in human

---

5. Tillich, *Systematic Theology,* 1: 111.

6. On the idea of "paradigm shift" in scientific inquiry, see Thomas Kuhn, *The Structure of Scientific Revolutions,* 2d ed. (Chicago: University of Chicago Press, 1970).

life by releasing our powers of imagination from the bondage of false idols. It provides us with a new model or paradigm of who God is and what it means to live according to God's will. Revelation and faith help us to see and thus to live differently; the whole of reality is reinterpreted in the light of the pattern of divine and human life embodied in the person of Christ.[7] This is the point of the Apostle Paul's appeal to his readers to have the mind of Christ (Phil. 2:5) and to let their minds be transformed by the revelation of God in Christ rather than being conformed to ways of thinking and living characteristic of worldly powers (Rom. 12:2). In John Calvin's striking metaphor, the biblical witness to revelation is like a pair of spectacles that enable us to see God, the world, and ourselves in a radically new manner.[8]

Reality can be seen and interpreted in many different ways, of course. The revelation of God is not coercive. It frees us to see the world as created and reconciled by God, but this does not eliminate other possible ways of seeing. In the light of Christ as the true image of God (Col. 1:15), we are enabled to know and imagine God as a holy and beneficent Deity whose intentions toward us are gracious and to understand ourselves as people created in God's image and destined for communion with God and each other. Thus while believers are aware of other ways of seeing and interpreting reality, and can even recognize the partial truth of these other interpretations, they nevertheless affirm that the revelation of God in Christ is the truth that sets humanity free (John 8:32), the light that illumines all of life (John 8:12).

One of the most influential modern analyses of the meaning of revelation is that of H. Richard Niebuhr. He speaks of the event of revelation as like a "luminous sentence" that we come across in a difficult book, "from which we can go forward and backward and so attain to some understanding of the whole."[9] It is like a "special occasion" (Alfred North Whitehead) in the life of a person or community that provides them with a central clue for the interpretation of all occasions of their experience. "The special occasion to which we appeal in the Christian church is called Jesus Christ, in whom we see the righteousness of God,

---

7. See Green, *Imagining God: Theology and the Religious Imagination* (San Francisco: Harper & Row, 1989).

8. Calvin, *Institutes of the Christian Religion*, 1.6.1.

9. Niebuhr, *The Meaning of Revelation* (New York: Macmillan, 1941), p. 93. See also Green, *Imagining God*, p. 61.

his power and wisdom," says Niebuhr. "But from that special occasion we also derive the concepts which make possible the elucidation of all the events in our history. Revelation means this intelligible event which makes all other events intelligible."[10]

My introductory comments on the meaning of revelation as used in Christian theology may be summarized in the following theses:

First, revelation refers to *God's own self-disclosure.* Apart from this act, the character and intention of God would remain a matter of guesswork. To speak of revelation is to declare that God graciously takes the initiative and freely communicates with us. Revelation thus means a gift that comes to us rather than some discovery about God, the world, or ourselves that we might have made entirely on our own.

Second, the term revelation points to *particular events and particular people* through whom God has communicated in decisive ways with humanity. Above all, the revelation of God means Jesus Christ. There is a relentless specificity and an inexpungible particularity about the Christian understanding of revelation.

Third, the revelation of God calls for our *personal response and appropriation.* As God's personal approach to us, revelation seeks the response of the whole person. True knowledge of God is a practical rather than a merely theoretical knowledge. The goal of the event of revelation is not the possession of secret doctrines but the generation of a new sensibility, a new way of seeing, new dispositions and affections, a transformed way of life.

Fourth, the revelation of God is *always a disturbing, even shocking event.* It disrupts the way we have previously understood God, the world, and ourselves. If it is truly God who is revealed, the hiddenness of God is never dissolved.[11] For the revealed God is the free and ever-surprising God. We know this to be true mainly because of God's revelation in Jesus Christ. In his person, revelation means the presence of God in the least expected place, in the midst of sinners, in the company of the poor, in the deep hiddenness of the cross. The dimension of the hidden and the unexpected — even of the outrageous — belongs to the revelation of God as Christian faith and theology employ this term.

Fifth, revelation becomes the *new interpretative focus* for our under-

---

10. Niebuhr, *The Meaning of Revelation*, p. 93.

11. See Douglas John Hall, *Thinking the Faith: Christian Theology in a North American Context* (Minneapolis: Augsburg, 1989), pp. 404-9.

standing of God, the world, and ourselves. Revelation does not narrow our vision or constrict our search for understanding. It transforms the imagination. In the light of the "special occasion" called Jesus Christ, we see God and all things anew and seek to act in accordance with this new vision. Consequently, far from being narrow and obscurantist, revelation is an inexhaustible source of creative human imagination and of transforming human action in the world. ✓

General and Special Revelation

IN the above summary of the meaning of revelation, I have emphasized the particularity and distinctiveness of the revelation of God as understood by Christian faith and theology. My emphasis on particularity, however, is not meant to deny the presence and activity of God in all of nature and history. The Word of God incarnate in Jesus Christ (John 1:14) is present and at work in all creation (John 1:9). What then is the relationship between the biblical witness to the revelation of God that culminates in Christ and what has been revealed of God in the natural order and in universal history?

Christian theology has traditionally distinguished two channels of knowledge of God: general revelation and special revelation. There can be little doubt that the Bible teaches and experience confirms a revelation of God in the created order, in the human conscience, and in religions other than Christianity. "The heavens are telling the glory of God, and the firmament proclaims his handiwork," writes the Psalmist (19:1). The Apostle Paul contends that God's eternal power and deity have been clearly shown in the things that have been created (Rom. 1:20). When Paul speaks to the Athenians on the Areopagus, he proclaims to them the identity of the unknown God that they have been worshiping (Acts 17:22ff.).

If there can be little doubt that the Bible teaches that God gives knowledge of Godself in many ways and in many times and places, there can also be little question of the many advantages of acknowledging this fact. For one thing, it provides the basis of presenting the Christian message with some assurance of common ground between the believer and the nonbeliever or non-Christian. It also encourages Christians to be receptive to knowledge acquired by the human sciences and to be respectful of and open to the teachings of other religious traditions. On the other hand, a preoccupation with general revelation poses problems. It may lead to the idea that special revelation is superfluous, or at least that it lacks the critical significance that Christians have always attached to it.

Christian theologians and theological schools have related general and special revelation in a variety of ways. At one end of the spectrum are philosophers and theologians who claim that religions based on allegedly special revelation are only different symbolic expressions of a universally available knowledge of God. At the other end of the spectrum is the argument that revelation in Christ alone provides true knowledge of God and that all other claims to know God are simply false. Somewhere in the middle range of the spectrum are those who insist on the importance of general revelation as providing a broad foundation for morality and religion, even if what is known on this basis is incomplete and in need of the fuller knowledge of God given in the special revelation attested in Scripture. According to the First Vatican Council (1870), for example, God's existence can be demonstrated and some things known of God by human reason apart from any appeal to special revelation. The relation between general and special revelation in this view is like the relationship between part and whole, the incomplete and the complete.

John Calvin's position on this issue, while not without ambiguity, offers a distinctive emphasis. He insists that there is a natural knowledge of God. He speaks of a universal "sense of divinity" and a universally implanted "seed of religion." Not only do the liberal arts assist us in entering into the secrets of the divine wisdom, but even the uneducated are aware of the evidence of the divine workmanship in the creation. Hence Calvin concludes that "there is within the human mind and by natural instinct an awareness of divinity. This we take to be beyond controversy."[12]

All this sounds unambiguous enough, but it is important to follow the further course of Calvin's argument. In the first place, Calvin thinks of the universal "sense of divinity" as weakened by sin and thus "insufficient," "confused," vague, and dim by comparison with the special revelation in Scripture. The relative dimness of the revelation in creation and in human conscience is, in Calvin's view, a source of danger. What ordinarily follows from the dark and indefinite knowledge of God is not

---

12. Calvin, *Institutes of the Christian Religion*, 1.3.1.

what Vatican I optimistically depicted in its statement on natural theology. Instead, Calvin emphasizes that the knowledge of God that is in fact available to humanity in the world of nature and in the universal moral and religious awareness is regularly corrupted, often being turned into something sinister and destructive. Calvin's contention, then, following the Apostle Paul in Romans 1:18-23, is that while there is a universal revelation that renders all people responsible, the habit of sinful human beings is to turn this general knowledge of God into idolatry. Religion is often put to the service of evil human purposes.

Most Christians today would be far more generous than Calvin in finding truth and value in what can be known of God in the created order and in the different religions of humanity. As a renaissance scholar, Calvin honored the arts and sciences, but when assessing religions other than the Reformed faith, he tended to highlight only their distortions. By contrast, many Christian theologians today would emphasize that all religions must be approached with openness and respect, and they would recognize the presence of God's gracious initiative and faithful human responses in other religious traditions.

However, we should not allow Calvin's exaggerations to obscure the important point he is making — namely, that a vague and superficial religiosity, when it does not lead simply to indifference or despair, is continuously vulnerable to idolatrous manipulation.[13] One thinks of the ominous coupling of a shadowy religiosity with a militant nationalism or racism in such slogans as "God and Fatherland" or "God, family, and country." The ideology of the German Christians during the Third Reich, the mixture of religion and apartheid in South Africa, and the vague references to God and religious values in jingoistic movements in the United States and other countries are vivid reminders of the essential correctness of Calvin's (and later, Barth's) warning that we are repeatedly inclined to control and manipulate the knowledge of God that goes under the name of general revelation.

It is a familiar charge of critics of the Christian faith that concentration on the distinctive and specific revelation of God attested in Scripture and centered above all in Jesus Christ must necessarily lead to a narrow and arrogant attitude. Narrowness and arrogance have, to be sure, all too frequently found a home in the church, and on this account the church

13. For some of the ideas in this paragraph, I am indebted to Prof. Michael Welker of the University of Münster.

needs to be called to repentance. It is a mistake, however, to lay the blame for this on the appeal to special revelation. On the contrary, provincialism and exclusivism are often the result of losing touch with what is specifically Christian rather than excessive loyalty to it. Hence the familiar criticism of emphasis on the particularity of Christian revelation may be reversed, and the argument advanced that a vague and amorphous religious commitment is far more vulnerable to ideological manipulation than the specific witness of the biblical tradition to the revelation of God. Indeterminate religiosity is easily co-opted by self-interested individuals, groups, and nations. It offers unlimited potential for pretension and self-righteousness. Admittedly, the Bible has also been used for ideological purposes, as the appeal to certain biblical texts to legitimize slavery and the subordination of women makes clear enough. Still, the danger that resides in vague religiosity is especially acute since the resources of self-criticism are considerably weaker than in a community of faith that claims to recognize the authority of the prophetic tradition of the Bible.

A capacity for criticism, including self-criticism, is essential to the Christian experience of revelation. Revelation and the critique of all forms of idolatry go hand in hand. We should not equate special revelation, then, with the mere denial of general revelation. Nor should we think of it, equally simplistically, as the tranquil continuation and completion of general ideas of divinity. Rather, special revelation repeatedly challenges, corrects, and transcends all of our earlier knowledge of God, from whatever source, as well as confirming what is good and true in it. The revelation of God in Jesus Christ is a continual disturbance to all religious life, including and beginning with the Christian religion.[14]

Prophetic criticism belongs necessarily to a revelation of God that finds its center in the activity of one who takes up the cause of the poor, forgives sinners, and is finally crucified between two criminals. If we take the cross of Christ seriously as God's decisive revelation, we will not pretend to have revelation in our possession and under our control. Revelation always means the surprising, unexpected, scandalous activity of God. The proclamation of the cross of Christ as the supreme revelation of the person and purpose of God brings a continual revolution in our understanding of God, the world, and ourselves.[15]

---

14. See the Confession of 1967 in the Presbyterian Church (U.S.A.) *Book of Confessions* (Louisville: Office of the General Assembly, 1983), 9.41-42.

15. See Niebuhr, *The Meaning of Revelation*, pp. 185-91.

Thus while it is important to distinguish between general and special revelation, we should avoid all simplistic dichotomies. The distinction should not be employed to compartmentalize our knowledge or to portray as eternal opposites revelation and reason, Christ and culture, nature and history, or Christianity and all other religions. The point of the distinction is to acknowledge the need for continuous conversion in every dimension of human life. The surprising self-disclosure of God in the ministry and cross of Jesus calls for the transformation of our personal and interpersonal relations, our attitude toward nature, our cultural activity, and, most basically, our ways of imagining and relating to God.[16] √

Revelation as God's Self-Disclosure

WE have said that Christian theology looks primarily to the revelation in Christ for an understanding of God and of all things in relation to God. While God is present and active in all of nature and history, for Christian faith and theology the fullness of revelation can come only in a personal life. Only revelation through a person can be fully intelligible to us, who are persons, and only personal revelation can adequately disclose the reality of God, who is supremely personal.[17]

Thus when we seek for further clarification of the meaning of revelation, we are drawn to the sphere of *interpersonal communication* for the most appropriate analogies. As Basil Mitchell notes, "the basic analogy involved in all talk of revelation is that of communication between persons."[18] Of course, this is not the only analogy that might be employed in a doctrine of revelation. In fact, a number of different analogies or models have been used in theological reflection on this theme.[19]

According to one view, revelation is like the *transmission of accurate or even infallible information* in the form of propositions of Scripture or doctrines of the church. This propositionalist model of revelation was

16. See H. Richard Niebuhr, *Christ and Culture* (New York: Harper, 1951).
17. See William Temple, *Nature, Man and God* (London: Macmillan, 1956), p. 80.
18. Mitchell, "Does Christianity Need a Revelation?" *Theology* 83 (1980): 105.
19. Avery Dulles analyzes five types of revelation in *Models of Revelation* (New York: Doubleday, 1983): doctrine, history, inner experience, dialectical presence, and new awareness.

typical of pre–Vatican II Catholic theology and is still represented by some Protestant fundamentalist theologies.

A second model of revelation compares it to *turning points in our personal or corporate history.* Revelation is not identified directly with the biblical text or with church teachings but is located in momentous events or figures of the past. Thus the more we learn from historical research about the exodus of Israel from Egypt or about the trial and execution of Jesus, the closer to revelation we come. Among the most influential expressions of this historicist model of revelation was the "life of Jesus" theology of the nineteenth century.

According to a third model, revelation is like a *crucial experience of new insight and self-discovery.* In this view, the locus of revelation is not the Bible or tradition or historical facts but a present liberating and renewing experience. Some contemporary liberation theologians espouse this model of revelation.[20]

If we consider interpersonal communication as the most satisfactory analogy of what is meant by the revelation of God, there will be some elements in common with each of the aforementioned models, but the focus will be different. Our reflection will center not on propositions (although propositions have their place), nor on historical facts (although they are important), nor on our present experiences of liberation and renewal (although these are certainly part of the meaning of revelation). Instead, we will attempt to understand God's self-revelation as being like the personal knowledge human beings share with each other. The most adequate model of revelation in the Christian sense of the term is the event of interpersonal knowledge.

Some theologians who hold this view reject the strictly propositionalist interpretation of revelation and contend that what is important to Christians is not the transmission of propositional truths as such but a "personal encounter" with Christ.[21] While I think this view is correct in emphasizing the personal character of faith knowledge, I think the "encounter" language remains extremely vague and lacks compelling

---

20. According to Elisabeth Schüssler Fiorenza, "the locus or place of divine revelation and grace is . . . not the Bible or tradition of a patriarchal church but the *ecclesia* of women who live the 'option for our women's selves'" (*Feminist Interpretation of the Bible,* ed. Letty M. Russell [Philadelphia: Westminster Press, 1985], p. 28).

21. Among the twentieth-century theologians espousing this view are Emil Brunner, Karl Barth, and, in an earlier phase of his work, Gordon Kaufman (see *Systematic Theology: A Historicist Perspective* [New York: Scribner's, 1968]).

power because the analogy from the knowledge of persons that is being assumed is not carefully developed.[22]

How are persons known? One way of answering this question that at first seems promising for an analogy to a doctrine of revelation is to say that we can know very little of importance about other persons unless they speak directly to us. Knowledge of other persons based on their behavior, the argument would run, is far from adequate, let alone incorrigible. Unless others tell us what they intend by their actions, we may very easily come to the wrong conclusion about their motives and purposes. According to this view, the self is completely hidden behind its actions.

The problem with this interpretation of personal knowledge is that it rests on a dualistic view of the human person. It assumes that who we are has little connection with what we do. This view of human identity has been widely criticized in modern philosophy and theology. Our knowledge of a person's identity and intentions is much more closely bound to the person's actions than the dualistic viewpoint allows. While verbal communication is valuable, we should not underestimate the importance of personal self-disclosure through action.

If we begin not with the assumption that we are selves hidden in bodies but agents who manifest their identity and intentions in actions, then the analogy between personal knowledge and the revelation of God to us can be developed in a different, nondualistic way.

In the first place, our knowledge of persons requires *attention to persistent patterns* in their actions that manifest, as we might say, who they really are, what is in their heart, what their true character is. Not everything that we do reveals our identity and our deepest intentions and dispositions. John and Mary, for example, may be ornery people often a bit irritable, and now and then hard to get along with. But i times of crisis we note that they are always the first at the side of person in need, asking what they can do to help. By virtue of t consistent pattern of activity, we feel justified in describing the t character of John and Mary as sensitive and caring. What they are r like has been revealed to us by a persistent pattern of behavior, and may radically change our ideas of them that were based on rela unimportant facts.

22. The argument presented in the following paragraphs is indebted to T Tracy's *God, Action, and Embodiment* (Grand Rapids: William B. Eerdmans, 1

If in our knowledge of others we look for particularly disclosive patterns of action to determine what sorts of people they are and what their true characters are like, then the revelation of God can also be understood as self-disclosure through particular actions. The character and intentions of God are not immediately evident in every event of nature or history but are focused in the particular event named Jesus of Nazareth — and not just in every detail that might be mentioned about this person (height, hair color, taste in music) but in the persistent patterns of his action, distilled in the Gospel stories and climaxed in the passion narrative.

Second, while a person's identity is disclosed in his or her persistent behavioral patterns, it is not exhausted in them. People are more than the sum total of their actions, even those actions that we call characteristic. A person is *free to do new and surprising things,* not because a person is a self hidden inside a body, a kind of ghost in a machine, but because people are not imprisoned by their past actions. While not necessarily arbitrary, there is an element of spontaneity and unpredictability about human action.

Similarly, while never speaking of God's action as arbitrary, the Bible always respects divine freedom. God is faithful but does new and surprising things. To the extent that we neglect this freedom of God, we turn the knowledge of God based on what God has done in the past into idolatry and manipulate it to serve our own interests. As often as Israel was called by the prophets to remember what God had done and commanded them to do in the past, Israel was also summoned to be open to the new actions of God (see Isa. 43:18-19).

Third, knowledge of persons involves a continuous *invitation to trust and to live in response to promises.* This is connected with the freedom of personal knowledge — freedom both on the side of the subject who is known and on the side of the knower. In giving ourselves to others we remain free, unless our self-giving has been in fact a process of losing our identity and being absorbed by the other. Hence there is always something new, surprising, and unpredictable about personal knowledge. This is why promising is such an important dimension of personal relationships. We cannot promise our friend, nor can our friend promise us, to be absolutely the same tomorrow as today. But we can promise to be there for each other, even if differently than we were there for each other today.

Here again the analogy holds true for the biblical description of God's self-disclosure. The revelation of God in the history of Israel and

in the life and death of Jesus Christ is also characterized by promises and calls to faithfulness.[23] The Gospel narratives contain many promises of Jesus: "your sins are forgiven" (Luke 7:48); "blessed are you poor, for yours is the kingdom of God" (Luke 6:20); "come to me, and you will no longer be hungry" (John 6:35); "believe in me, and you will never thirst again" (John 4:14); "those who want to save their life will lose it, and those who lose their life for my sake will save it" (Luke 9:24); "behold, I am with you always to the close of the age" (Matt. 28:20).

A final and decisive element of the analogy of personal self-disclosure through action is the *importance of narrative for identifying persons*. Because God's personal self-communication occurs through the persistent patterns of action of a personal agent who promises to be faithful and summons us to trust, narrative is among the primary literary forms by which the event of revelation is attested. As F. Michael McLain writes, "If God is an agent who acts in the world so as to disclose divine character and purpose, then narrative is the appropriate form in which to render God's identity."[24]

There are, of course, many literary forms in Scripture: prophetic oracles, proverbs, commands, and hymns, to mention the most obvious. But Scripture is also replete with narratives depicting the agency and intentionality of God and of human beings in relation to God. Narrative is an apt vehicle for describing character because it can effectively convey the persistent patterns that define a particular person's identity. At the same time, good narrative appropriately depicts personal action in all its freedom, unpredictability, and promissory character. It is therefore understandable that narrative plays an exceedingly important role in the biblical witness to the identity and purpose of God and also in the subsequent and dependent witness of the Christian community to this revelation.[25] I return to this topic in my discussion of Scripture in Chapter 3.

As media of the revelation of God, the biblical narratives and the retelling of these narratives in the proclamation and actions of the church

---

23. See Ronald F. Thiemann, *Revelation and Theology: The Gospel as Narrated Promise* (Notre Dame, Ind.: University of Notre Dame Press, 1985).

24. McLain, "Narrative Interpretation and the Problem of Double Agency," in *Divine Action*, ed. Brian Hebblethwaite and Edward Henderson (Edinburgh: T. & T. Clark, 1990), p. 143.

25. See George Stroup, *The Promise of Narrative Theology* (Atlanta: John Knox Press, 1981); see also Stroup, "Revelation," in *Christian Theology: An Introduction to Its Traditions and Tasks*, rev. ed. (Philadelphia: Fortress Press, 1985), pp. 114-40.

are not simply interesting stories of what happened in the distant past. As Rowan Williams puts it, "All good stories change us if we hear them attentively; the most serious stories change us radically."[26] The biblical narratives do not aim to entertain but to engage us, to liberate and transform us. Their purpose is to tell us what God has done for us and to invite us to enter into the new freedom that is ours in Christ. They make truth claims about God and about the world in relation to God, and they invoke our response. Only as these narratives of the activity of God intersect our own lives, personally and corporately, giving us a new relationship to God, a new identity, a new life, and a new mission, do they become for us genuine media of the revelation of God.[27]

Revelation, Scripture, and Church

IN Christian theology the word *revelation* refers first of all not to the Bible, or to a creed, or to a set of doctrines, or to some ecclesiastical authority but to God's activity in Jesus Christ. His life, death, and resurrection are the supreme manifestation of the nature and purpose of God. The free grace of God in Jesus Christ is the core of the Christian message.

Yet we would know nothing of the good news of the reconciliation of the world with God through Christ (2 Cor. 5:19) apart from the witness of Scripture and the proclamation and life of the church. The Spirit of God works through particular human witnesses, with all their limitations and flaws, to lead us to a right knowledge of God and ourselves. Where the witness of Scripture or church or both is ignored or disparaged, the meaning of revelation in the Christian sense is also threatened.

In his doctrine of the three forms of the Word of God, Karl Barth clarifies the relationship between revelation and the concrete media that it employs. According to Barth, the Word of God is threefold: revealed, written, and proclaimed.[28] These distinct but inseparable forms of the one

---

26. Williams, "Postmodern Theology and the Judgment of the World," in *Postmodern Theology: Christian Faith in a Pluralistic World*, ed. Robert N. Bellah et al. (San Francisco: Harper & Row, 1989), p. 109.

27. For a discussion of the "collision" between the biblical narrative and our personal narratives, see Stroup, *The Promise of Narrative Theology*, pp. 171-75.

28. Barth, *Church Dogmatics*, I/1 (2d ed., 1975): 88-124.

Word of God are related to each other like three concentric circles. The innermost circle is the revealed Word of God in Jesus Christ. We have access to this circle only through a second circle of prophetic and apostolic witness. The biblical witness in turn is the basis of a third circle, constituted by the continuing proclamation and life of the community of faith.

If the Word of God has this threefold structure, it is clear that God has chosen to give human beings an important part in the event of revelation. The Word became flesh (John 1:14). God is revealed in particular human words and deeds. This is singularly true of the incarnation of God in Jesus Christ. But every other witness to this event is also in a sense "incarnational." The good news of God comes to us not directly but indirectly, through the fully human witness, memory, hope, and practice of a community of believers.

The light of God that shines in Jesus Christ is transmitted, first of all, through the prism of the biblical witnesses. As long as the church remains faithful, it will acknowledge the priority and authority of the scriptural witness in its life and mission. At the same time, the definite humanity of the biblical witnesses will also be recognized without apology or embarrassment. It is not a weakness but a strength of the Christian understanding of revelation that its original witnesses are unmistakably historically conditioned and remarkably diverse human beings. That we have the treasure of the gospel in clay jars (2 Cor. 4:7) is as true of Scripture as it is of all subsequent Christian witness based on Scripture. Hence not everything found in the Bible is to be taken as a direct word of God to us. Some texts of the Bible may stand in utmost tension with revelation. We cannot deny, for example, that Scripture contains militaristic and patriarchal ideas. Scripture witnesses to revelation but is not identical with it. Even Calvin acknowledged this, although not as boldly as Luther.[29] Today it is essential that a Christian doctrine of revelation distinguish clearly between Scripture's witness to the personal self-disclosure of God that culminates in Jesus Christ and the historical contingencies and ambiguities of this witness.

But, secondly, the original witness of Scripture to God's revelation in Jesus Christ is itself mediated to us through the witness of the church. We hear and understand the message of Scripture with the help of many interpreters near and far. Like the Ethiopian official, we need guidance

---

29. On the one hand, Calvin speaks of God as the "author" of all of Scripture (*Institutes of the Christian Religion,* 1.3.4); on the other hand, he contends that it is only when Scripture "shows forth Christ" that it conveys the word of life (1.9.3).

in the understanding of Scripture (Acts 8:30-31). If we were to cut ourselves off from the proclamation and life of the church as the medium through which we receive the biblical message, our understanding of the revelation of God would not be purer, as biblicists mistakenly imagine, but greatly impoverished. Yet while we are always indebted to the witness of the church, we must also recognize that the revelation of God attested in Scripture often stands in judgment on the church and calls it to repent of the ways in which it has obscured and distorted revelation.

Sensitive to the fallibility of church teaching and practice and aware of the need for continuous reform within the church, Protestant theology has tended to look for revelation in the biblical text alone, in isolation from the witness of the church past and present. But this is as barren as the attempt to set the church on the same level with or even above Scripture. While the Reformers were right in insisting that the central witness of Scripture is normative for the faith and life of the church, this witness does not exist in a vacuum. The truth is that it is neither "Scripture alone" nor "Scripture plus church tradition" that is sufficient to communicate the gospel of Christ effectively: it is the Spirit of God, who freely uses the witness of Scripture in the context of the witness and life of the church to evoke faith in and obedience to Christ.[30]

Although the relationship between revelation, Scripture, and the teachings and traditions of the church continues to be a point of contention between Protestant, Roman Catholic, and Eastern Orthodox theologies, most would agree that Scripture and church doctrine are not two independent media of revelation. Church doctrines are what the church confesses and teaches on the basis of the revelation of God attested. in Scripture.[31] Church teachings have a relative authority in the life of faith. Always subordinate to Scripture, the church's common creeds and contemporary confessions provide important hermeneutical keys to what is central in Scripture and give succinct summaries of the mighty acts of

---

30. See George S. Hendry, *The Holy Spirit in Christian Theology* (Philadelphia: Westminster Press, 1956). Hendry notes that "Luther says the Word is the cradle in which Christ lies; we may also say that the church is the nursery in which the cradle lies" (p. 95).

31. Jaroslav Pelikan defines Christian doctrine as "what the church of Jesus Christ believes, teaches, and confesses on the basis of the word of God" (*The Christian Tradition: A History of the Development of Doctrine*, vol. 1: *The Emergence of the Catholic Tradition, 100-600* [Chicago: University of Chicago Press, 1971], p. 1).

God. According to Calvin, ecumenical confessions such as the Apostles' Creed are to be highly valued because they "sum up in a few words the main points of our redemption."[32] Creeds and confessions play an important role in the life of the church as "primary commentaries" on Scripture, not as independent channels of revelation.[33]

Recent liberation theologies have underscored the social and cultural factors at work in every mediation of revelation.[34] They also emphasize far more than the classical theological tradition that both the Bible and church teaching have often been used in ways that have contributed to the oppression of people rather than to their liberation. For this reason they insist that a privileged hearing should be given to the interpretations of the Bible by the marginalized and the poor of the world. Whatever criticisms may be made of liberation theologies, it should be noted that their intent is to seek not a revelation apart from the Bible but a new reading of the Bible; they wish not to abandon the church as the matrix of Christian faith but to discover the reality of the church among the poor and those who struggle for justice.

Recognition that there are flaws and distortions in all witnesses to revelation is disturbing to many Christians. But if we remember that God's grace and power are made perfect in human weakness (2 Cor. 12:9), we will have little difficulty in seeing the grace of God at work in the fact that fallible human beings are taken into the service of God's revelation. By communicating indirectly with us, God's revelation is accommodated to our creaturely condition. God respects our humanity and seeks our free response.[35] The light of revelation does not descend on us perpendicularly from above; it comes through worldly media by the power of God's Spirit, who enlists our participation in the process of responsible interpretation and critical appropriation.

Because all human witnesses to revelation are subject to ambiguity and distortion, it is necessary to understand the reception of revelation as a dialectical process. On the one hand, there can be no reception of

32. Calvin, *Institutes of the Christian Religion*, 2.16.18.

33. On the place of the church's creeds and confessions in relation to Scripture, see Barth, *Church Dogmatics*, I/2: 585-660.

34. This point is well made in *Lift Every Voice: Constructing Christian Theologies from the Underside*, ed. Susan Brooks Thistlethwaite and Mary Potter Engel (San Francisco: Harper & Row, 1990).

35. Cf. Søren Kierkegaard, *Concluding Unscientific Postscript* (Princeton: Princeton University Press, 1941), pp. 216ff.

the revelation of God in Christ apart from attentive and trustful reading
and hearing of the witness of Scripture in company with other members
of the people of God. Only in the context of the faith, prayer, proclamation, sacramental life, and service of the church does the transforming
power of Jesus Christ attested by Scripture become effective for us.

On the other hand, there is need for critical appropriation of the
revelation of God in Christ as mediated to us by Scripture and by the
proclamation and life of the church. Only as we enter into the new
freedom in Christ that resists every form of bondage, including those
that may be supported by certain elements of Scripture and church
teaching, do we become active and responsible recipients of the revelation
of God. Neither the witness of Scripture nor that of the church is more
than a servant of the living God. They point beyond themselves to
Another, to a transforming and renewing reality at work in our midst
but never under our control.

A doctrine of revelation will thus take account of the fact that
inasmuch as we are human beings, our lives are shaped by the particular
communities to which we belong, by the values they espouse, the stories
they tell, the doctrines they teach. Reception of the revelation of God
and the reformation of human life in its light also occur in a communal
context. Yet faithfulness to the revelation of God requires far more than
a process of socialization into the beliefs and practices of a religious group.
Becoming Christian involves far more than absorbing and repeating a
tradition. To respond in faith to the revelation of the living God mediated
through Scripture and the witness of the church is to undertake the risk
of becoming an accountable witness of the good news one has received
and to share responsibility with others for interpreting and living it out.

An important conclusion to be drawn from these reflections is that
while the revelation of God draws a people into its service, the community must never presume to have control of the revelation that it attests.
If that were to happen, revelation would be replaced by ideology, and
theology by idolatry. Revelation is never simply identical with a book, a
system of doctrine, a particular tradition, or the special experience of an
individual or group. It is God's free and gracious act of self-disclosure in
Jesus Christ mediated through the witness of Scripture and the testimony
of the community of faith by the power of the Spirit. Revelation can
never be taken for granted; it is an event for which the church must
continually pray: "Come, Holy Spirit! Speak once again to your people
through your Word." In acknowledging a revelation of God, the Chris-

tian community confesses that it is not its own master, that God alone is Lord, that this community is called to proclaim Jesus Christ and not itself (2 Cor. 4:5), and that it must expect to be addressed and reformed again and again by the living Word of God.

3

The Authority of Scripture

SINCE THE BEGINNING OF THE CHURCH, EVERY CHRISTIAN THEOL-
ogy has implicitly or explicitly acknowledged the authority of Scripture.
The serious question has never been *whether* Scripture is a primary
authority for Christian faith and life but *what sort of* authority it is.[1]

For the sixteenth-century Reformers, the authority of Scripture was
rooted in its liberating message, in the good news of God's gracious
acceptance of sinners offered in Jesus Christ. The Bible was experienced
not as an arbitrary or despotic authority but as a source of renewal,
freedom, and joy.

This is not the way everyone, or even every Christian, understands
the meaning of scriptural authority today. Many people inside and outside the church equate the idea of the authority of the Bible with coercion
rather than liberty, with terror rather than joy. They know all too well
how the authority of the Bible has been invoked to suppress free inquiry
and to legitimize such practices as slavery and patriarchy.

Thus a major task of theology today is to develop a liberative
understanding of the authority of Scripture. Toward this end I will
contend that the authority of Scripture has to be understood in relation
to its particular function within the community of faith. Scripture is the
unique and irreplaceable witness to the liberating and reconciling activity
of God in the history of Israel and supremely in Jesus Christ. By the

1. Portions of this chapter are based on my earlier discussion of the authority of
Scripture in chap. 1 of *Called to Freedom: Liberation Theology and the Future of Christian
Doctrine* (Philadelphia: Westminster Press, 1980).

power of the Holy Spirit, Scripture serves the purpose of relating us to God and transforming our life.

The Problem of Authority in Modern Culture

THE problem of the authority of Scripture is part of the wider crisis of authority in modern Western culture. Since the Enlightenment, every claim to authority has had to justify itself before the bar of autonomous reason. In this process of critical examination, much that was previously considered authoritative is dismissed as arbitrary and groundless.

Kant's famous dictum "Dare to think for yourself" is the motto of Enlightenment mentality. In the name of autonomous reason and the freedom of the individual, every established "house of authority"[2] — whether of state, church, or society — is placed in question. As heirs of Enlightenment rationality, we have acquired a strong and persistent allergy to the notion of authority.

Applied in every field of inquiry, the modern critical mentality has undoubtedly enriched the meaning and task of being human. In all areas of modern culture, the summons to give up infantile dependencies and become mature people who think and decide for themselves continues to make its mark. The development of modern democratic systems of government, for example, owes much to Enlightenment philosophy. Christian faith and theology should honor the good that has accompanied this modern critical spirit as well as reject the pretensions. Christian faith is not nostalgia for a world undisturbed by the critical mentality; it is not a secret ally of the state authoritarianisms of Hitler, Stalin, Duvalier, and Marcos, nor of ecclesiastical authoritarianisms that refuse to allow any dissent whatever to their established teachings. While there are deep ambiguities in the critique of authority of modern culture in the name of autonomous human reason that should be exposed, mere rejection of the Enlightenment critique of oppressive authority would be a failure to understand the Christian message. The gospel also wants to proclaim a new freedom from bondage.

Many Christians are willing to accept the modern spirit of critical reason and its radical questioning of traditional authority up to the

2. See Edward Farley, *Ecclesial Reflection* (Philadelphia: Fortress Press, 1982).

point of the study and interpretation of Scripture. Yet Scripture has no immunity from this wider cultural critique of authority. There is no turning back from the vigorous pursuit of critical methods of biblical study that have shattered many traditional ways of thinking and speaking of biblical authority. While it is true that the application of critical reason to the Bible has not been without its own distorting ideologies, the imperative that this places on theology is to be not *less* but *more* critical.

The real question that is raised for theology by the modern critical mentality is whether the authority of Scripture is properly understood as oppressive. Is its authority an arbitrary datum simply to be accepted by a sacrifice of the intellect, or is it inseparable from the scriptural proclamation of the liberating grace of God in Jesus Christ? Put differently, the question is whether the church has forgotten that its own scriptural tradition contains a powerful critique of arbitrary authority and a distinctive message of freedom.

Within the biblical witness, there is relentless criticism of every authority that identifies itself with the ultimate authority of God. Jesus refused to ascribe ultimacy either to religious doctrines and traditions (Matt. 5:21ff.; Mark 11:28ff.) or to the claims of the state (Mark 12:13-17). The Apostle Paul distinguished between written codes that kill and the Spirit that gives life (2 Cor. 3:6). This remarkable biblical heritage of freedom from all idolatry, including bibliolatry, was vigorously upheld by Martin Luther, who used the term "straw" to describe all scriptural texts that failed to express clearly the liberating message of Christ. John Calvin was not as bold as Luther in his doctrine of Scripture; nevertheless, in his own way, he also refused to separate the authority of Scripture from "that which shows forth Christ" and insisted that it is "the internal testimony of the Holy Spirit" that finally persuades us of the truth of Scripture.[3] In short, the Reformers' view of the authority of Scripture was intimately bound to its proclamation of freedom in Christ.

Occasioned by the modern crisis of authority, but under the primary impulse of the gospel, it has been a major effort of modern theologians to divest theology of authoritarian ways of thinking about God, the church — and Scripture. Gerhard Ebeling argues that there is a "deep, inner connection" between the historical-critical reading of Scripture and

3. Calvin, *Institutes of the Christian Religion,* 1.9.3; 1.7.4.

the Reformers' doctrine of justification by grace through faith in that both function to remove all false securities.[4]

Thus, while Christian theology takes issue with the Enlightenment assumption that the only true authority is that of the independent and isolated self (an assumption also under attack by "postmodern" philosophy), it nevertheless engages in its own critique of oppressive authority, including versions of such authority that appear in doctrines of Scripture. In the God of the gospel attested in Scripture, Christian faith finds the authority of liberating love that creates new community rather than an authority that works by coercive power. The gracious reign of God manifest in Jesus Christ is characterized not by authoritarian rule but by the "authoring" of new life and freedom in relationship with God and others.

Inadequate Approaches to the Authority of Scripture

BEFORE developing further this understanding of the liberative function of Scripture in the life of the community of faith, it may be helpful to identify several inadequate approaches to scriptural authority.

1. In the biblicist view, the Bible is authoritative by virtue of its *supernatural origin*. This theory arose out of the church's efforts to defend its faith against the acids of modernity. Anxious to protect the insights of the Reformation, Protestant theologians became increasingly defensive and strident in their claims about the supernatural character of Scripture. They insisted that every book, every chapter, every verse, every word was directly inspired by God. The doctrine of inspiration became a theory of the supernatural origin of Scripture. Various ideas about how this took place were advanced, including the proposal that God dictated the words of Scripture to the biblical writers, who acted as secretaries. Such theories of inspiration held two points in common.

First, inspiration meant inspiredness. It referred to an inherent property of Scripture resulting from its supernatural origin. The effect of this doctrine of inspiration was to focus attention on the alleged miraculous origin of the Bible rather than on its central message and its

---

4. Ebeling, "The Significance of the Critical Historical Method for Church and Theology in Protestantism," in *Word and Faith* (Philadelphia: Fortress Press, 1963), pp. 17-61.

role in eliciting and nourishing faith. Scripture was viewed as a closed system of inspired statements.

Second, inspiration meant infallibility. Since God was the author of Scripture, it was without error. It was perfect to the smallest detail, and "free from all error whether of doctrine, fact, or precept" (Hodge), at least in its original Hebrew and Greek texts (Warfield). Thus, to the Roman Catholic dogma of the infallibility of the pope (1870), directed against the rising tide of modernity, there corresponded the Protestant doctrine of the infallibility of the Bible. The true basis of Christian confidence was thereby obscured. The church wanted an absolute guarantee of its faith and proclamation; it found this in the parallel doctrines of biblical and papal infallibility. But a church with an infallible teaching office or an infallible Bible no longer allows Scripture to work as liberating word in its own way.

This biblicist doctrine of the authority of Scripture is a perfect target of the critique of heteronomy characteristic of the modern period. The Bible is to be taken as authority not because of *what* it says, or because of the transforming *effect* it has on human life, but simply because its words are identified without qualification with God's words. One result of this identification is that biblical texts are leveled in importance so that, for example, the instruction that women should be silent in the church (1 Tim. 2:12) carries the same authority as the proclamation of the new equality and inclusive community in Christ (Gal. 3:28). In this way biblicism turns the authority of Scripture into a deadening authoritarianism.

2. With the rise of the modern historical consciousness, a new approach to Scripture was introduced. The Bible was read simply as a *historical source*. This has brought many gains to our understanding of Scripture. It has helped to break the chains of scholastic and dogmatic readings of Scripture. It has helped us to understand the biblical writings in their own historical contexts.

Yet alongside its achievements, the historical method also created a new potential for taking Scripture captive. The interest of the historian focused primarily on establishing "what really happened," what could be validated as "factual." What was authoritative was not the text in its received form but the "facts" behind the text as reconstructed by the historian.

A serious consequence of this historicist interpretation was "the eclipse of biblical narrative."[5] When attention focuses on the facts behind

---

5. See Hans Frei, *The Eclipse of Biblical Narrative* (New Haven: Yale University Press, 1974).

the text, the meaning of the Bible is separated from its literary form. These facts are then necessarily set within a new interpretative framework provided by the biblical scholar. Thus the historicist approach allows the Bible to speak only within the limits of the assumptions about the nature of history brought by the interpreter to the texts.

3. Another approach to the authority of Scripture views it as a *religious classic.* Typically, Scripture is here described as great (or at least important) literature, and its authority is seen as analogous to that of "classics" in the literary tradition and other spheres of human culture. The approach to the Bible as literature is very popular in university courses in religion. And since there is so much sheer ignorance of the Bible in American culture today, it may seem inappropriate to say anything critical about this approach to the Bible. But though a knowledge of the Bible as literature is a laudable goal, it cannot substitute for the function of the Bible in the community of faith. The Bible is not just great literature for the faith community. God is not just a character in a story, however captivating and well told. Jesus Christ is not just an impressive if somewhat puzzling literary figure. As James Barr notes, no one doubts that Jesus was raised from the dead in the gospel story; the question that really matters for faith is whether Jesus was really raised and is alive today.[6] The believing community approaches the Bible not only as literature, great or not so great, but as Scripture, as normative witness to the acts of the living God for our salvation.[7]

4. Still another approach to Scripture sees it as a *private devotional text* whose authority is located in the saving meaning it has for the individual. There is, of course, a legitimate concern that prompts this emphasis. Against the speculation of scholastic theology, the obsession with past facts in modern historicism, and the aestheticism of detached literary readings, piety concentrates on the meaning of the Bible for the individual's salvation. The Bible speaks to me and assures me of God's forgiveness and mercy in Jesus Christ. What is significant for faith is not the crucifixion of Jesus as a bare historical fact but the message that Christ died for me.

While it is always important to read and hear the message of

6. Barr, quoted by John Barton, in *People of the Book? The Authority of the Bible in Christianity* (Louisville: Westminster/John Knox, 1988), p. 49.

7. See Krister Stendahl, "The Bible as a Classic and the Bible as Holy Scripture," *Journal of Biblical Literature* 103 (1984): 3-10.

Scripture "for me," this emphasis becomes distorted when it is separated from the meaning of Scripture "for us" and "for the world." A reduction of Scripture occurs when it serves only to illumine my own experience and struggle as a pilgrim of faith. The individualistic interpretation of Scripture represents a retreat of the church and theology. The public realm is abandoned in favor of the private realm of life, where faith can be secure from attack.

The Indispensability of Scripture in Relating Us, by the Power of the Spirit, to the Living God Revealed in Jesus Christ

BEYOND the dead letter of biblicism, the uncritical assumptions of historicism, the narrowness of bourgeois privatism, and the detachment of aestheticism lies the real authority of Scripture in the life of the community of faith. Christians do not believe *in* the Bible; they believe in the living God attested by the Bible. Scripture is indispensable in bringing us into a new relationship with the living God through Christ by the power of the Holy Spirit, and thus into new relationship with others and with the entire creation. To speak of the authority of the Bible rightly is to speak of its power by God's Spirit to help create and nourish this new life in relationship with God and with others.

The Bible is a unique witness to the sovereign grace of God at work in the history of Israel and above all in the life, death, and resurrection of Jesus. As witness, the Bible does not call attention to itself. "A real witness," Karl Barth insisted, "is not identical with that to which it witnesses, but it sets it before us."[8] An authentic witness directs our attention to some other reality. Thus the Bible is the Word of God only in a derivative sense. The living Word of God is Jesus Christ, and it is with him that we are brought into relationship by the witness of Scripture. Scripture is thus authoritative not in itself but, as the Reformers insisted, as it "sets forth Christ," as it functions in the community of faith by the power of the Spirit to create a liberating and renewing relationship with God through Christ.

Barth was fond of describing the function of the scriptural witness as like that of the figure of John the Baptist in the Isenheim altarpiece by the painter Matthias Grünewald. With his abnormally long index

---

8. Barth, *Church Dogmatics*, I/2: 463.

finger, John points to the crucified Lord. The inscription on the painting reads: "He must increase, but I must decrease."[9]

The witness of Scripture accomplishes its purpose in a polyphonic rather than homophonic manner. Its faith discourse is extraordinarily rich. As Paul Ricoeur has argued, the literary genres of the scriptural witness are fittingly diverse ways of bringing us into relationship with God. The narrative form is required if God is to be identified as a living, personal agent who acts as creator, reconciler, and redeemer. Prophetic discourse is a fitting medium to call in question the complacency and arrogance of the people of God who recite and celebrate the great acts of God in the past but who do not live justly, love mercy, and walk humbly with God. Wisdom literature aptly gives expression not only to the presence of God in everyday experience but also to the radical hiddenness of God in the experience of suffering and evil. In short, the various literary forms of the biblical witness are irreducible media of revelation and mutually complement and correct each other. The church should not ignore or collapse this literary diversity into an artificial unity any more than it should anxiously try to harmonize the theological differences in the scriptural witness between the Old and the New Testaments, between Paul and James, or between John and the Synoptics. The scriptural witness is extraordinarily rich and diverse.[10]

Yet there is a coherence in this diversity of the scriptural witness that is provided largely by its overall narrative framework. An extensive literature has developed around this theme in recent theology. As Charles Wood writes, "When one regards the biblical canon as a whole, the centrality to it of a narrative element is difficult to overlook: not only the chronological sweep of the whole, from creation to new creation . . . but also the way the large narrative portions interweave, and provide a context for the remaining materials so that they, too, have a place in the ongoing story, while these other materials — parables, hymns, prayers, summaries, theological expositions — serve in different ways to enable readers to get hold of the story and to live their way into it."[11]

9. See Barth, "Biblical Questions, Insights, and Vistas," in *The Word of God and the Word of Man* (New York: Harper, 1957), p. 65.

10. See Ricoeur, "Toward a Hermeneutic of the Idea of Revelation," in *Essays on Biblical Interpretation,* ed. L. S. Mudge (Philadelphia: Fortress Press, 1980), pp. 73-118.

11. Wood, *The Formation of Christian Understanding: An Essay in Theological Hermeneutics* (Philadelphia: Westminster Press, 1981), p. 100. See also *Scriptural Author-*

My primary point is that biblical authority has a different basis and works in a different way from that described by traditional theories. Through the biblical witness, and especially through its narratives of God's gracious, liberating activity in Jesus Christ, God is newly identified for us and we are led into a new way of life in communion with God and with others. If our attention is focused on the larger pattern of the biblical story, with its climax in the life, death, and resurrection of the unsubstitutable person Jesus of Nazareth, we shall have little doubt about the indispensability of the Bible to Christian faith and life.[12]

The Bible is a witness, and at its center it attests the sovereign, liberating grace of God in Christ. As described by the biblical narratives, God is always greater than we imagine. Scripture not only declares the coming of the Christ but tells the story of the crucified Christ; it not only praises the eternally rich God but proclaims that this God became one of the poor; it not only speaks of God's judgment and grace but declares that God stands on the side of the poor and the oppressed and judges the exalted and the powerful. This is the ever-disturbing, even revolutionary witness of the Bible.

Scripture witnesses to God's world-transforming activity. Of course, the coming reign of God inaugurated in Jesus Christ includes personal transformation. The liberation of the individual from the egocentrism, isolation, apathy, and hopelessness of existence in bondage to sin and death is of fundamental importance. Nevertheless, the "strange, new world of the Bible" (Barth) cannot be limited to the individual, nor to a private zone of life. It reaches out to all people and to the whole creation. It announces the beginning of a new world, new relationships, new politics, in which justice prevails over injustice, friendship over hostility, mutual service over domination of some by others, and life over death.[13]

---

ity and Narrative Interpretation, ed. Garrett Green (Philadelphia: Fortress Press, 1987); George Lindbeck, *The Nature of Doctrine: Religion and Theology in a Postliberal Age* (Philadelphia: Westminster Press, 1984).

12. On the Bible as a means of grace by which we are brought into communion with God, see James Barr, *The Scope and Authority of the Bible* (Philadelphia: Westminster Press, 1980), especially chap. 4. On the "unsubstitutable identity" of Jesus Christ as rendered by the gospel narrative, see Hans Frei, *The Identity of Jesus Christ* (Philadelphia: Fortress Press, 1975), p. 136.

13. See Karl Barth, "The Strange New World within the Bible," in *The Word of God and the Word of Man,* pp. 28-50.

Principles of the Interpretation of Scripture

IF the authority of Scripture is understood primarily in terms of its indispensable witness to the sovereign, liberating, and reconciling love of God in Jesus Christ, the following principles of interpretation may be proposed.

1. *Scripture must be interpreted with the help of literary and historical criticism; yet Scripture's unique witness to the living God resists its reduction to pious fiction or its imprisonment in the past.* Interpretation of Scripture within the community of faith is not driven merely by antiquarian or aesthetic interests. Believers turn to Scripture to hear the word of God and to hold to the promise of liberation and salvation in Christ. Historical and literary criticism can serve a better hearing of this word.

Historical study of the Bible is important for many reasons. To begin with, it compels us to take seriously the particularity of God's actions. If God becomes known through events at particular times and places, then the historical study of the Bible is one way we respect the historical particularity of revelation. The Bible proclaims the liberating acts of God by naming particular places, events, and persons. Of course, historical investigation cannot prove that this or that event is an act of God, but it can clarify the specific context of the events in which faith discerns God's actions.

Historical study of the Bible also reminds us that the narrative of the Bible refers to realities outside the text. The central narrative is not to be construed as a mere construct of the imagination of the community of faith. If the Gospels refer to the living God acting and suffering in Christ for our salvation, if the story they tell is not simply pious fiction, then historical study can never be *irrelevant* for Christian faith. The faith of the church does not stand or fall with the accuracy of every detail of the gospel story, as Calvin noted,[14] but faith does stand or fall with the truthfulness of the gospel portrayal of the central events of the ministry, death, and resurrection of Christ. It matters to faith whether Jesus really befriended sinners, blessed the poor, and gave his life willingly for others.

Historical study of the Bible serves still another theologically important function. It not only helps us to recognize the historical con-

14. See the Calvin texts quoted by William C. Placher, in "Contemporary Confession and Biblical Authority," in *To Confess the Faith Today,* ed. Jack L. Stotts and Jane Dempsey Douglass (Louisville: Westminster/John Knox, 1990), p. 71.

creteness of revelation but also continually reminds us that the biblical writers were limited, fallible human beings. To deny their finitude is to rob them of their humanity. Contrary to some doctrines of Scripture, the Spirit of God does not have to destroy the humanity of the biblical witnesses in order to work through them. The grace of God does not destroy human freedom but renews and empowers it for partnership with God.

If we are embarrassed by the humanity of the biblical writers, we are also probably embarrassed by the humanity of Jesus the Jew from Nazareth and by our own humanity. Just as we are Docetists if we deny the full humanity of Jesus, so we are Docetists in our doctrine and interpretation of Scripture if we claim that the biblical witnesses were mere automatons set in motion by the Spirit of God. If we affirm the full humanity of Jesus, we will also respect the humanity of the biblical witnesses.

Of course, to engage in historical study of the Bible is to accept risk. Some things that we previously held to be factual will be called in question. The difference between the thought world of the Bible and our own will widen. This is the risk of the historical study of the Bible, and it disturbs us. But the risk cannot be evaded because it is implied in the event of God's decisive presence and action in a finite human life. "The Word became flesh" (John 1:14). This means that the Word of God entered into the ambiguity and relativity of historical reality. The incarnation involved risk and vulnerability, and no doctrine of biblical authority is acceptable that denies or minimizes that risk.[15]

Yet our emphasis on the importance of historical interpretation of Scripture is far from an endorsement of a positivistic understanding of the historical task. To interpret the Bible historically is not simply to remember past events but to anticipate the fulfillment of promises contained in these events. The narratives of Scripture are told and retold by Israel and the church because the history of God's liberation that they recount is not yet finished. It is still open. The liberation begun in Jesus Christ points to a final liberation in which the whole creation will be set free (Rom. 8:21).

No event can be fully understood apart from the future that it engenders. As a general principle of the interpretation of history, this thesis may be debatable. But such a principle is surely necessary in the

---

15. Cf. Walter Kreck, *Grundfragen der Dogmatik* (München: Chr. Kaiser, 1970).

interpretation of Scripture for those who believe in the resurrection of the crucified Jesus and his living lordship. To read the Bible historically in the deepest sense is to read it with an eye to the extension of its story of God's liberating activity in Christ into our own time and beyond it. We must ask of Scripture not only what past it calls us to remember but also what promises it wants us to claim and what future it wants us to pray and work for.

This means that we should not pretend that the full meaning of the new freedom in Christ was already actualized in the early church. This is evident, for example, in some of Paul's statements about the place of women in the church (1 Cor. 14:34). Still, the ferment and transforming power of the story of Christ the liberator are undoubtedly if imperfectly at work in the attitude of the New Testament church toward women. Episodes in the Gospels depict Jesus' new openness to and friendship with women. Paul himself composed a magna charta of freedom: "There is neither Jew nor Greek, there is neither slave nor free, there is neither male nor female: for you are all one in Christ Jesus" (Gal. 3:28) — a passage Krister Stendahl rightly describes as a "breakthrough," a radical new beginning of freedom incompletely realized in the early church, yet full of promise for the future under the guidance of God's Spirit.[16]

To read Scripture historically is to read it both critically and with sensitivity to the direction in which it moves rather than with nostalgia for New Testament times. Our interpretation of Scripture must therefore include both a hermeneutics of trust and a hermeneutics of suspicion. This is not a contradiction. If Scripture is viewed primarily as a witness to God's liberating love in Christ, as an earthen vessel that contains a great treasure (2 Cor. 4:7), then the passing on of its liberating and transforming message must be a creative and critical process rather than a mechanical repetition. This is apparent in the history of the transmission of tradition within the Bible itself. As liberation theologians have emphasized in recent years, the Bible is faithfully interpreted when it is read as a source of freedom in Christ to overcome every bondage, including the use of the Bible itself as a weapon of oppression.[17]

---

16. Stendahl, *The Bible and the Role of Women: A Case Study in Hermeneutics* (Philadelphia: Fortress-Facet, 1966).

17. Cf. Mary Ann Tolbert: "One must defeat the Bible as patriarchal authority by using the Bible as liberator" (quoted by Letty M. Russell in *Feminist Interpretation of the Bible* [Philadelphia: Westminster Press, 1985], p. 140).

2. Scripture must be interpreted theocentrically; however, the meaning of "God" is radically redefined in the biblical story of liberation. The central actor in the biblical drama is God. Scripture witnesses to the reality of God, to the purposes of God, to the kingdom of God. The content of the biblical story is God's faithfulness in acts of judgment and mercy in the covenant with the people of Israel and in the history of Jesus. The biblical narrative has many aspects, but the central theme is the work of the faithful God who takes up the cause of justice, freedom, and peace on behalf of the creation oppressed by sin and misery. Even in judgment the work of grace and promise is heard: "While we were yet sinners Christ died for us" (Rom. 5:8). In the resurrection of the crucified Jesus all of God's promises are decisively ratified. "All the promises of God find their Yes in him" (2 Cor. 1:20).

Who is the God of the scriptural witness? The answer is surely the God who acts, who is not an abstract value or a lifeless ideal but the creator, liberator, and reconciler. Yet the God of Scripture who does mighty deeds, creates the heavens and the earth, and delivers Israel from bondage, is also the God who suffers. If God is triumphantly present in the exodus of Israel from bondage, God is also present with Israel as it makes its bitter pilgrimage through the wilderness and suffers humiliation in exile.

Who is more majestic and powerful than the God of Scripture, the one who does wondrous things (Ps. 86:10) and whose glory the heavens declare (Ps. 19:1)? What power is comparable to that of God, who gives life to the dead and calls into existence the things that do not exist (Rom. 4:17)? Yet the power of the God depicted by Scripture is strange power. It is not the power of force but the power of Spirit (Zech. 4:6), and it is made known above all in the weakness of the cross of Jesus (1 Cor. 1:18ff.).

Again, whose freedom exceeds that of the God of Scripture, who is unlimited by any outside power? Yet the freedom of this God is far greater than the idea of absolute independence from others. The free, self-determined God is free *for* others. God is free to take the form of a servant without ceasing to be God (Phil. 2:5ff.), free to become poor to make others rich, to suffer death to give others life (2 Cor. 8:9; John 3:16).

Thus a theocentric reading of the biblical story of liberation does more than provoke us to a new self-understanding or provide us with a new communal identity.[18] To be sure, it does these things. But

---

18. Cf. David Kelsey, *The Uses of Scripture in Recent Theology* (Philadelphia: Fortress Press, 1975).

primarily the witness of Scripture to God's activity newly identifies God. Scripture revolutionizes our understanding of our own identity, power, and freedom as creatures made in the image of God because it first overturns our understanding of the true identity, power, and freedom of God.

A theocentric reading of Scripture is christocentric, but it is not christomonistic. *Christians read Scripture as witness to the activity of the triune God.* The God of the biblical witness is God the Father who has created the heavens and the earth, God the Son who has become the mediator for the whole world, God the Holy Spirit who brings new life and new freedom. In response to the activity of the triune God, men and women are called to repentance and faith. They are summoned and empowered to become partners in God's liberating and reconciling activity in the world. They are called to the living hope that the whole creation will be freed from all enslaving powers and will enjoy "the glorious liberty of the children of God" (Rom. 8:21).

If a consistently trinitarian interpretation of Scripture prompts a continuous revolution in our understanding of God, it also challenges the many ways we try to make God useful for our own cultural and political projects. The biblical story of God's liberating activity is both an authorization and a continual criticism of our various liberation movements. When the church automatically reacts to liberation theology and liberation movements with alarm, it merely shows that it no longer understands the message of Scripture. At the same time, all liberation movements are exposed to powerful temptations. They are tempted to identify God with particular groups and to equate liberation with the acquisition of power over others. The God of the biblical story, whose way of liberation is self-giving love, is always surprisingly different from what we imagine or wish divinity to be.

3. *Scripture must be interpreted contextually; however, the context of our interpretation must be increasingly open to and inclusive of the yearning of the whole creation for justice, freedom, and peace.*

Every interpretation of Scripture is driven by certain interests. These interests are shaped by our personal and social contexts of life. The context of our interpretation of Scripture will always include and will frequently begin with our own personal needs: our awareness of our own captivity, of our own anxiety, guilt, frustration, alienation, loneliness, and despair, and of our yearning for freedom and new life. In no way is this personal context of understanding Scripture as liberating word to be denigrated. Unfortunately, the context of the interpretation of the Bible for many Christians never extends beyond this sphere.

The larger context for interpreting Scripture is the community of believers. The Bible is the book of the church.[19] Thus, to interpret Scripture contextually means to listen to its story in and with the community of faith, remembering that this community has declared these writings to be canonical (i.e., that they measure up to the rule or norm for identifying the Word of God) and confidently expecting that the Spirit of God will again speak to us through the biblical witness. To interpret Scripture contextually is to interpret it in the context of the memory and hope of the Christian community.

Those who stand within the community of faith in their reading and interpretation of Scripture will be open to the instruction and insights of the larger community of faith, past and present. We interpret Scripture contextually by allowing ourselves to be guided by the church's confessions and worship, and by the wisdom and experience of the whole community of faith, which can deepen and correct our own understandings of sin and salvation, captivity and liberation. While Scripture is not subordinate to the creeds and confessions of the church, they often provide exemplary interpretations of Scripture. They articulate in their own time and place the "rule of faith," declaring how the central message of Scripture is to be understood in a particular moment of controversy and confusion in the life of the church. Among the other functions they serve, the ecumenical doctrines of the church are communally tested and approved rules for the interpretation of Scripture.[20] The function of doctrines in the church is not primarily legalistic but hermeneutical: they lead us to the central and living truth of the biblical witness.

But interpreting Scripture contextually means still more. Since Scripture is in fact read in many different ecclesial and social contexts, all interpretations of Scripture must be open to and tested by other interpretations that arise out of experiences, circumstances, needs, and hopes that may be very different from our own. In particular, our interpretation of Scripture needs to be tested and deepened by readings of its

19. See Phyllis A. Bird, *The Bible as the Church's Book* (Philadelphia: Westminster Press, 1982); Darrell Jodock, *The Church's Bible: Its Contemporary Authority* (Philadelphia: Fortress Press, 1990).

20. For a discussion of the similarities of doctrines and rules of grammar, see George Lindbeck, *The Nature of Doctrine,* especially chaps. 1, 4, and 5.

message that arise out of communities of suffering and struggle for justice and freedom. Because of their long history of suffering, Jews approach Scripture with a sensitivity to the reality of evil and suffering in the world that is all too easily neglected by many Christians in dominant cultures. Blacks, Hispanics, women, and other oppressed or marginalized peoples read Scripture through Third World eyes, and this presents a deep challenge to First World readers, who all too often expect that Scripture will endorse their comfortable white, middle-class values. Training in a rich contextual reading of Scripture thus demands an ongoing ecumenical conversation and the Spirit-given courage "to hear the voices of people long silenced."[21] If we listen carefully to these voices, we will hear echoes of the cry for justice so central in the message of the prophets (Isa. 1:16-17; Jer. 5:1; Amos 5:23-24; Mic. 6:8).

That the experience of suffering and solidarity with oppressed people is the necessary context for responsible interpretation of Scripture is sometimes summarized in the phrase "the hermeneutical privilege of the poor." Properly understood, this phrase does not imply the moral or religious superiority of the poor. The poor, like the rich, are radically dependent on the grace of God for life itself, for new life, and for full life. What the hermeneutical privilege of the poor means is that the experience of suffering and poverty provides an opportunity for understanding the message of the Bible that is frequently obscured for those who insulate themselves from the suffering of others and from their own suffering. The reidentification of God in the scriptural narrative of God's new and surprising work in Christ culminates in God's voluntary journey into solidarity with sinners, the poor, and the victims of injustice, and God's free acceptance of the way of suffering love for the redemption of all who are in bondage. "You know the grace of our Lord Jesus Christ, that though he was rich, yet for your sake he became poor, so that by his poverty you might become rich" (2 Cor. 8:9).

From this perspective, the necessary context for interpreting Scripture is practical engagement in the living of Christian faith, love, and hope in a still unredeemed world. The noncoercive authority of the biblical witness finds its awaited hearing in gratitude for God's grace, in a new solidarity with the poor, in a commitment to justice, and in a new sensitivity to the eager expectation of the whole groaning creation.

---

21. See the Presbyterian Church (U.S.A.) Brief Statement of Faith, l. 70.

4

The Triune God

CHRISTIAN THEOLOGY BEGINS, CONTINUES, AND ENDS WITH THE inexhaustible mystery of God. It speaks of God, however, not in vague and general terms but on the basis of the particular actions of God attested in Scripture. The central task of a Christian theology, therefore, is to attempt to clarify the understanding of God that is proper to the Christian faith, to describe its own peculiar "logic" of God. To the questions Who is God? What is God like? How does God relate to us? a Christian doctrine of God responds in the light of the scriptural witness to God's history with the people of Israel and God's new covenant with all humanity in Jesus Christ. Since, as John Calvin insisted, our knowledge of God and our knowledge of ourselves are always inextricably intertwined,[1] the route that we take and the conclusions that we reach in the doctrine of God will profoundly influence everything else that we say about Christian faith and life.

The Problem of God in Modern Theology

TALK of God has become a problem for many people today. While criticisms of traditional doctrines of God arise from various sources and take very different forms, they often focus on the human experience of domination by some coercive power and on the human quest for freedom and fulfillment.

---

1. Calvin, *Institutes of the Christian Religion*, 1.1.1.

56

Perhaps foremost among these criticisms, especially among people influenced by the principles of the Enlightenment, is the charge that belief in God and affirmation of human freedom are incompatible. Critics of religious belief argue that it is sustained only by uncritical and authoritarian habits of mind. According to Feuerbach, humanity impoverishes itself in religion, since God is simply the projection of our own hidden potential. In a similar vein, Freud called belief in God an infantile illusion that our needs will be met by an omnipotent parent.

Traditional theologies and church teachings are also called in question by those who speak for victims of injustice and oppression. Official doctrines of God, they contend, serve to justify and sanction existing conditions of misery and exploitation. In classical Marxist theory, religion is described as the opiate of the people.

Again, profound questions about the presence of God in history are raised for many people today by events of overwhelming evil. The long and torturous history of black slavery in North America compels some thinkers to ask whether God is a white racist;[2] the holocaust of six million Jews during World War II gives credence to the conviction that God is dead; the possibility of a world-encompassing nuclear holocaust seems to render all inherited claims about the sovereignty and goodness of God glib and even blasphemous.

The problem of God is also a continuing topic of philosophical discussion in our time. An important critique is advanced by process philosophers and theologians, who argue that traditional doctrines of God are hopelessly inadequate because they view God as absolute and unaffected by the events of history. They charge that the tradition portrays the relationship of God and the world as unilateral and coercive rather than reciprocal and persuasive. The traditional view is considered utterly incompatible with the modern experience of reality as dynamic, processive, and relational; it is also said to be insensitive to the enormity of suffering in the world.

Among the most devastating criticisms of traditional doctrines of God is that of feminist theology. Representatives of this perspective charge that traditional thinking and imagery of God are bound up with patriarchal attitudes and structures that endorse and perpetuate relationships of domination. By patriarchy is meant "the male pyramid of graded

2. See William Jones, *Is God a White Racist?* (Garden City, N.Y.: Doubleday, 1973).

subordinations and exploitations"[3] in which men lord it over women, white people over people of color, and humanity over nature. Unchallenged patriarchalism erodes the credibility of Christian faith. As Shug, a black woman in one of Alice Walker's novels, puts it: "When I found out I thought God was white and a man, I lost interest."[4] Sallie McFague summarizes the feminist critique of patriarchalism and its legitimating theology by contending that at the heart of our most pressing issues today is the misuse of power. Whether we think of the exploitation of the natural environment or of political, economic, racial, cultural, and gender oppressions or of the development of weapons of incalculable destruction, the fundamental problem is "the question of power; who wields it and what sort it is. . . . Is power always domination?"[5]

The above list of charges against traditional doctrines of God is not meant to be exhaustive. It is intended simply to remind us of what are perhaps the most fundamental questions of theology: Who is the God worshiped and proclaimed by the Christian community? Is this God the enemy or the friend of human maturity and freedom? Is the sovereignty of God exercised in brute power or in costly love?

In seeking to address these questions, we must first decide what route we shall follow. Shall we begin by developing a doctrine of God general enough to fit every religious conviction? Shall we argue, on the basis of common religious experience and allegedly universal principles that God — whatever else this word might designate — is surely the one perfect, omnipotent, wise, good, and eternal being? If we were to follow this approach, we would postpone to some later point our thinking and speaking of God on the basis of the biblical witness, and particularly of its witness to God's revelation in Jesus Christ. Although this approach to the doctrine of God has a long and distinguished history in Christian theology, I think we should follow a different path.

While it is true that everyone begins an inquiry about the reality and identity of God with some prior ideas or unexpressed assumptions, a Christian theology should not uncritically adopt these often general and inchoate notions about God and should certainly not attempt to

---

3. Elisabeth Schüssler Fiorenza, *Bread Not Stone: The Challenge of Feminist Biblical Interpretation* (Boston: Beacon Press, 1984), p. xiv.

4. Walker, *The Color Purple* (New York: Washington Square Press, 1982), p. 177.

5. McFague, *Models of God: Theology for an Ecological, Nuclear Age* (Philadelphia: Fortress Press, 1987), pp. 15-16.

make them normative. Christian faith and theology do not speak of God in a general and indefinite way; they speak of God concretely and specifically. Christians affirm their faith in God as the sovereign Lord of all creation who has done a new and gracious work in Jesus Christ and who continues to be active in the world through the power of the Spirit. On the basis of this particular history of revelation and redemption, the Christian community confesses God to be the source, the mediator, and the power of new life. God is the majestic creator of the heavens and the earth, the servant redeemer of a world gone astray, and the transforming Spirit who empowers new beginnings of human life and anticipatory realizations of a new heaven and a new earth. To use the familiar terms of the biblical and classical theological tradition, God is "the Father, the Son, and the Holy Spirit." In brief, Christians confess the triune identity of God.

The Christian *confession* of God as triune is a summary description of the witness of Scripture to God's unfathomable love incarnate in Jesus Christ and experienced and celebrated in the community of faith. The *doctrine* of the Trinity is the always inadequate attempt to interpret this witness in the most suitable images and concepts available to the church in a particular era. Rightly understood, the doctrine of the Trinity is not an arcane, speculative doctrine; rather, it is that understanding of God which is appropriate to and congruent with the gospel message. In applying the terms "appropriate" and "congruent" to this understanding of God, I am saying, negatively, that the doctrine of the Trinity is not a revealed doctrine. It did not fall down from heaven, nor was it etched in tablets of stone. It is the product of the reflection of the church on the gospel message over many centuries. The doctrine of the Trinity is second-order reflection on the workings of divine love attested in Scripture and experienced by the Christian community. In other words, the starting point of trinitarian faith is the good news of the love of God in Christ that continues to work transformingly in the world by the Holy Spirit. The doctrine of the Trinity is the church's effort to give coherent expression to this mystery of God's free grace announced in the gospel and experienced in Christian faith.

But isn't it simply preposterous to focus on the doctrine of the Trinity in constructing a Christian doctrine of God today? Isn't a trinitarian understanding of God a prime example of the *problem* of thinking and speaking of God rather than in any sense a credible response to that problem? While trinitarian language is still found in liturgy, prayers, and theological textbooks, is not this language for many Christians as well as non-Christians surrounded today by an impenetrable cloud? Is not this doctrine a paradigm of sterile theological speculation? Is it not both lacking in any practical significance and riddled with mathematical non-sense that demands a sacrifice of our reason and a demeaning submission to arbitrary church authority? Can this doctrine serve any other purpose than to obscure and obstruct the important causes to which enlightened people should dedicate themselves? And on top of all this, does not the language of "Father, Son, and Holy Spirit" simply prove that the Christian doctrine of the triune God is inescapably and irreformably sexist?

These questions show that the problem of God in modern theology confronts us in its most urgent and intractable form precisely in what we have called the distinctively Christian understanding of God: the doctrine of the Trinity. Is it possible to retrieve and re-present the Christian doctrine of the Trinity in a contemporary idiom and in all its revolutionary significance?

The Biblical Roots of the Doctrine of the Trinity

THE biblical basis of the doctrine of the Trinity is not to be found in a few "proof texts" (e.g., Matt. 28:19) but in the pervasive trinitarian pattern of the New Testament description of the revelation and activity of God.

On the one hand, the Bible affirms that there is but one God (both Old and New Testaments share this faith in the sole sovereignty of God — Deut. 6:4, Mark 12:29-30). On the other hand, a trinitarian understanding of the reality of God is implied in the history of God's love for the world in Jesus Christ by the Holy Spirit. In the New Testament account of this history, there are three centers of divine activity. The love of God comes originally from the one called "Father," is humanly enacted for the world in the sacrificial love of the one called "Son," and becomes a present and vital reality in Christian life by the one called "Spirit." In Jürgen Moltmann's words, the story of the gospel is "the great love story of the Father, the Son, and the Holy Spirit, a divine love story in which we are all involved together with heaven and earth."[6]

6. Elisabeth Moltmann-Wendel and Jürgen Moltmann, *Humanity in God* (New York: Pilgrim Press, 1983), p. 88.

Thus Christians call God triune because this way of speaking accords with the biblical witness and with the experience of the church rooted in this witness. The God known in Jesus Christ is God over us, God for us, and God in us — the loving God, the gracious Lord Jesus Christ, and the community-creating Spirit of God (2 Cor. 13:14). These are not three Gods but distinct personal expressions of the one yet differentiated love of God. The biblical narrative of God's coming to the world in Jesus Christ by the Holy Spirit implies a trinitarian understanding of God (cf. Rom. 5:1-5; 8:9-11).

If talk of the triune God is not to be wild speculation, it will always find its basis and its limit in the biblical narration of the love of God for the world. This means that responsible trinitarian thinking must always begin with the so-called *economic Trinity* (i.e., the differentiated agency of Father, Son, and Spirit in the "economy" of salvation). All reference to the life of the *immanent Trinity* (i.e., the eternal distinctions of persons within the being of God) rests on this basis. In the gospel story, God is active as "Father," "Son," and "Holy Spirit" as the source, the medium, and the effective promise of liberating and reconciling love. To this beginning point trinitarian theology must return again and again. When Christians speak of God as eternally triune, they simply affirm that the love of God that is extended to the world in Jesus Christ by the Holy Spirit is proper to God's own life.

When the doctrine of the Trinity is turned into a purely speculative ontology of divinity, it is rightly criticized as arbitrary. We should not pretend that the revelation in Christ has given us exhaustive knowledge of the mystery of God. But Christians do not believe they are engaging in arbitrary speculation when they confess that what God has revealed of Godself in Jesus Christ and the Holy Spirit corresponds to God's innermost life. If God is expressed to us in three distinct personal ways, then there is a basis of this structure of divine love in God's own immanent, eternal being. God's own life cannot contradict what God is in relation to the world. In God's own life there is an activity of mutual self-giving, a community of sharing, a "society of love" (Augustine) that is the basis of God's history of love for the world narrated in Scripture. Hence proper trinitarian theology does not first speculatively posit a Trinity in eternity and afterward search for evidence of the Trinity in revelation and Christian experience. Rather, it begins concretely from the history of revelation and salvation attested by Scripture and experienced by Christians from the beginning of the church. Only on this basis do faith and theology declare that trinitarian communion belongs to God's own eternal being as well as to God's relation to the world. The logic of trinitarian theology moves from the differentiated love of Father, Son, and Holy Spirit in the economy of salvation (the economic Trinity) to the ultimate ground of this threefold love in the depths of the divine being (the immanent Trinity).[7]

Classical Trinitarian Doctrine

OVER the course of several centuries, the church formulated an explicit doctrine of the Trinity. Two milestones in the development of this doctrine were the Councils of Nicea (A.D. 325) and Constantinople (A.D. 381). The crux of the classical Niceno-Constantinopolitan teaching is that God is "one in essence, distinguished in three persons." While this technical language of fourth-century metaphysics *(mia ousia, tres hypostases)* is strange to us, the intent is to describe the reality of the living God in conformity with the gospel story. The negative meaning of this affirmation of the unity and threefold self-differentiation of God is evident in its opposition to the doctrines of subordinationism, modalism, and tritheism.

According to subordinationism, the names "Father, Son, and Spirit" describe different ranks or orders of deity. There is one great God — the eternal Father — and two exalted creatures or inferior divinities. Subordinationism is a strategy to protect God from contact with matter, suffering, mutability, and death. But such a strategy conflicts with the gospel message. How can Christ be the Savior, and how can the Spirit be the power of divine transformation here and now if they are not "very God of very God" but only exalted creatures or second-rank divinities?

According to modalism, the names "Father, Son, and Spirit" refer to mere masks of God that do not necessarily manifest God's inmost being. This would mean that the events of Jesus' ministry among the poor, of his crucifixion and resurrection, and of the outpouring of the Spirit were mere appearances and possibly unreliable indicators of the true nature of God. But how can believers be sure of what God is really like if all they know of God are these external masks that keep God's real identity deeply hidden?

---

7. See Karl Barth, *Church Dogmatics,* I/1 (2d ed., 1975): 384-489.

According to tritheism, the names "Father, Son, and Spirit" refer to three individual and separate deities who collectively constitute the object of Christian faith. This view flatly contradicts the command of the Old Testament and of Jesus to love God, the one and only Lord. How can the object of Christian trust, loyalty, and worship be three different Gods?

Classical trinitarian doctrine, with its carefully conceived but now mostly puzzling formulation, "one in essence, distinguished in three persons," intends to guard against the misunderstandings of subordinationism, modalism, and tritheism. But what does all this technical conceptuality want to say *positively?* It wants to redescribe God in the light of the event of Jesus Christ and the outpouring of God's transforming Spirit. It wants to say that God is sovereign, costly love that liberates and renews life. It wants to say that God's love for the world in Christ now at work by the power of the Spirit is nothing accidental or capricious or temporary. It wants to say that there is no sinister or even demonic side of God altogether different from what we know in the story of Jesus who befriended the poor and forgave sinners. God *is* self-expending, other-affirming, community-building love. The exchange of love that constitutes the eternal life of God is expressed outwardly in the history of costly love that liberates and reconciles. Only *this* God who "loves in freedom" (Barth), both eternally and in relation to the world, can be worshiped and served as the ultimate power in full confidence and total trust.

To speak thus of God as triune is to set all of our prior understandings of what is divine in question. God is not a solitary monad but free, self-communicating love. God is not the supreme will-to-power over others but the supreme will-to-community in which power and life are shared. To speak of God as that ultimate power whose being is in giving, receiving, and sharing love, who gives life to others and wills to live in community, is to turn upside down our understandings of both divine and human power. The reign of the triune God is the rule of sovereign love rather than the rule of force. A revolution in our understanding of the true power of God and of fruitful human power is thus implied when God is described as triune. God is *not* absolute power, *not* infinite egocentrism, *not* majestic solitariness. The power of the triune God is not coercive but creative, sacrificial, and empowering love; and the glory of the triune God consists not in dominating others but in sharing life with others. In this sense, confession of the triune God is the only understanding of God that is appropriate to and consistent with the New Testament declaration that God is love (1 John 4:8).

In so interpreting classical trinitarian doctrine, our aim is to get beneath the surface grammar, to penetrate to the intention, rather than remaining stuck in the ancient conceptuality with all of its strange terminology. We do not truly respect doctrines if we simply repeat them as trained parrots might. Indeed, such mindless repetition often results in the subversion of the real intent of church teachings. Thus the important question for us is what was then, and what is now, at stake in affirming that God is triune, that God communicates Godself to us in Jesus Christ by the Holy Spirit. The answer to this question is that trinitarian doctrine describes God in terms of shared life and love rather than in terms of domineering power. God loves in freedom, lives in community, and wills creatures to live in community. God is self-sharing, other-regarding, community-forming love. This is what might be called the "depth grammar" of the doctrine of the Trinity that lies beneath all the "surface grammar" and all of the particular, and always inadequate, names and images that we employ when we speak of the God of the gospel.

Distortions in the Doctrine of God

WHEN attention to the doctrine of the Trinity declines, distortions of the Christian understanding of God appear. The demise of vital trinitarian faith is followed by a variety of unitarianisms.[8]

1. One distortion takes the form of the *unitarianism of the Creator,* or the first person of the Trinity. Here God is viewed as the first principle of the universe, the origin of all things, and not infrequently the "Father Creator" of a particular ethnic or national group. American civil religion is by and large a unitarianism of the Creator. God is acknowledged as the source of life, of certain inalienable rights, and of the providential guidance of American destiny. There is little awareness of sin in this understanding of our relationship to God and consequently little sense of the need for forgiveness, repentance, or radical transformation of life. American civil religion is, of course, not the only form of the unitarianism

---

8. Cf. H. Richard Niebuhr, "Theological Unitarianisms," *Theology Today* 40 (July 1983): 150-57.

of the Creator. It also finds expression in other national religions and in the vague theism espoused by many educated people whose doctrine of God must be cut to the specifications of religion according to the limits of Enlightenment reason.

2. Another distortion assumes the form of the *unitarianism of the Redeemer,* or the second person of the Trinity. Jesus is the exclusive concern of this kind of piety. Jesus alone is the object of trust and allegiance, but the unitarian Jesus is a cult figure of some sort or other rather than the Jesus proclaimed in the Gospels. Little connection can be found between this cult of Jesus my Savior and the biblical affirmation of the lordship of God over all nature and history. Salvation is defined in terms of the welfare of me and my little group. Nothing else is of real concern. If all that counts is that you "Honk if you love Jesus," what does it matter if our environment is poisoned or if people are treated brutally because of their race, religion, or sex? The unitarianism of the second person is unable to discern any necessary connection between its cozy and sentimental Jesusolatry and passionate concern for the coming of justice for all people and for the renewal of the ravaged earth.

3. A third distortion in the Christian understanding of God appears as the *unitarianism of the Spirit,* or the third person of the Trinity. Here the experiences and gifts of the Spirit are everything. Little effort is made to test the spirits to see whether they are the Spirit of God's Christ, the Spirit who builds up the community and commissions it for service of God and others. Some "charismatic" groups skate dangerously close to a unitarianism of the Spirit. In saying this, I do not mean to denigrate the movements of spiritual renewal in the church today or undervalue their importance. The increased emphasis in recent years on the experience of the Spirit and the new attention to the doctrine of the Spirit in theology are no doubt legitimate protests against a Christianity that so often gives the appearance of lifeless antiquarianism or bureaucratized religiosity incapable of arousing and redirecting our feelings, affections, and dispositions. But the solution to this problem is not mere revelry in intense religious experiences. The point that I want to make here is simply that in the Christian church the experience of the Spirit is either the experience of the Spirit of the triune God or it is a divisive and even destructive experience. The Spirit who empowers reconciliation and liberation is the Spirit of Christ and of the one he called "Abba, Father."

Restatement of the Meaning of the Doctrine of the Trinity

I HAVE contended that the doctrine of the Trinity expresses the distinctively Christian understanding of God and that where this understanding of God declines, the church is in danger of losing its identity. Rather than becoming mired in the surface grammar of trinitarian faith, I have tried to penetrate to its depth grammar.

From the earliest centuries of the church, discerning theologians have stressed the inadequacy and relativity of all our language about God — including the trinitarian symbols. Today we are even more aware of how imperfect and historically burdened all language about God is. The search for new and more inclusive metaphors of God that correct and complement the old one-sided, patriarchal metaphors is an important development in recent theology. This search will doubtless help us to retrieve much suppressed imagery of God in the biblical tradition. As the church's hymns and prayers employ a wide range of images of God, the spiritual life and theological sensitivity of both men and women in the church will be enriched.

At present the church has not arrived at any consensus on how to expand the exclusive masculine imagery of God in the tradition. Some urge doing away with all gender-specific imagery of God by restricting our theological language to impersonal metaphors; others propose speaking of the Spirit as feminine; and still others argue that it is both appropriate and necessary to use masculine and feminine images of each member of the Trinity.

The argument against the first-mentioned option is the fact that in the Bible God is described most frequently in personal imagery. Of course, the biblical repertoire also includes impersonal metaphors of God such as rock, fire, and water, and our understanding and worship of God would be poorer without these images. Nevertheless, much would be lost if the church departed from the biblical practice of addressing God primarily as personal, as some*one* rather than some*thing*.

In favor of the other two options mentioned is the fact that the Bible depicts God not only as a father who cares for and protects his chosen people (1 Chron. 22:10; Ps. 103:13; Matt. 6:6-9) but also as a mother who gives birth to, feeds, and defends her children (Isa. 49:15; 66:12-13; Matt. 23:37). In view of this richness of biblical imagery of God — all the more remarkable considering the patriarchal setting of the biblical witness — the language of Father, Son, and Holy Spirit must not be absolutized in the theology and liturgy of the church. The search for other imagery to speak of the triune God should be affirmed.[9] At the same time, new images of God should be considered complements to rather than replacements for the traditional images. And it must be remembered that all of our images of God, old and new, masculine and feminine, personal and impersonal, receive a new and deeper meaning from the gospel story beyond the meanings that they have in the contexts in which they are ordinarily used. When we speak of God as father or mother, the meaning of these designations is determined finally not by our cultural or familial history but by the history of God's steadfast love for the world that stands at the center of the biblical witness.

As theologians and local congregations explore new images of God, it is utterly crucial, as some feminist theologians recognize, that we not lose the trinitarian depth grammar.[10] I have defined this depth grammar of trinitarian faith as the grammar of wondrous divine love that freely gives of itself to others and creates community, mutuality, and shared life. God creates and relates to the world this way because this is the way God is eternally God. I want to expand this thesis by offering three additional interpretive statements about the doctrine of the Trinity.[11]

1. To confess that God is triune is to affirm that *the eternal life of God is personal life in relationship*. The Bible speaks of God as "the living God" (Matt. 16:16). God is not like the dead idols who can neither speak nor act. God speaks and acts creatively, redemptively, transformatively. The God of the biblical witness is not impersonal but personal reality and enters into living relationship with creatures. Yet according to trinitarian faith, God does not first come to life, begin to love, and attain to personhood by relating to the world. In all eternity God lives and loves as Father, Son, and Holy Spirit. In God's own eternal being there

---

9. See Brian Wren, *What Language Shall I Borrow? God-Talk in Worship: A Male Response to Feminist Theology* (New York: Crossroad, 1989). The strongly trinitarian Presbyterian Church (U.S.A.) Brief Statement of Faith describes God as "like a mother who will not forsake her nursing child, like a father who runs to welcome the prodigal home" (ll. 49-50).

10. See Patricia Wilson-Kastner, *Faith, Feminism and the Christ* (Philadelphia: Fortress Press, 1983), pp. 121-37; Catherine Mowry LaCugna, "The Baptismal Formula, Feminist Objections, and Trinitarian Theology," *Journal of Ecumenical Studies* 26 (Spring 1989): 235-50. LaCugna contends that "the trinitarian God is eminently God for us, whereas the unitarian God is eminently for himself alone" (p. 243).

11. Cf. Jan Milič Lochman, "The Trinity and Human Life," *Theology* 78 (April 1975): 173-83.

is movement, life, personal relationship, and the giving and receiving of love.

God is one, but the unity of God is not undifferentiated, dead unity. The Trinity is essentially a *koinonia* of persons in love. Some twentieth-century theologians, preeminently Karl Barth and Karl Rahner, are reluctant to speak of three persons in God because of modern philosophical conceptions of personhood. Their recommendation is to speak instead of "three modes of being" in God or "three distinct ways of subsisting."[12] However, instead of relinquishing the concept of person in reference to Father, Son, and Holy Spirit, trinitarian theology does far better to challenge regnant understandings of the meaning of personhood. The trinitarian persons are not isolated and independent selves but have their personal identity in relationship. A trinitarian understanding of personal life questions modern theories that equate personal existence with absolute autonomy and isolated self-consciousness. In such definitions there is no reference to relationship with others as intrinsic to personal life. The trinitarian persons are not self-enclosed subjects who define themselves in total separation from others. Instead, in God "persons" are relational realities and are defined by intersubjectivity, shared consciousness, faithful relationships, and the mutual giving and receiving of love.[13]

If in the New Testament witness the one God is described as the faithful Father, the servant Son, and the enlivening Spirit, then according to the doctrine of the Trinity, these distinct ways of God's being present in the world and acting for our salvation are rooted in the eternal being of God. In the fecundity and dynamism of the eternal triune life there is differentiation and otherness rather than sheer mathematical oneness. Otherness is the presupposition of personal relationship; it is the sine qua non of the event of love. In contrast to sinful human attitudes and practices that rest on fear or hatred of the other and seek to remove or conquer the other, the triune God generates and includes otherness in the inner dynamism of the divine life. That God's own being is a being in personal differentiation and relationship is expressed outwardly in the creation of a world filled with an extravagance of different creatures. So much of the spirit of conquest that manifests itself in our relationships

---

12. See Barth, *Church Dogmatics*, I/1 (2d ed., 1975): 348ff.; Rahner, *The Trinity* (London: Herder, 1970), pp. 103-15. Cf. Tillich, *Systematic Theology*, 3: 286-94.

13. See John J. O'Donnell, *The Mystery of the Triune God* (London: Sheed & Ward, 1988), pp. 100-111.

with the natural world and with people of other nations, cultures, races, and gender stems from a fear of the other that ultimately betrays a monarchical rather than a trinitarian conception of God.[14]

2. To confess that God is triune is to affirm that *God exists in community*. The divine life is social and is thus the source and power of inclusive community among creatures. Two kinds of analogy have been used in trinitarian theology to depict the trinitarian life: the psychological analogy that is based on the individual human person as a subject with the faculties of memory, understanding, and will, and the social analogy that takes the human experience of community as the best clue to an understanding of the triune life of God (a favorite triad being lover, beloved, and their mutual love). The Western church has given primary emphasis to the psychological analogy,[15] while the Eastern church has preferred the social analogy.[16]

While both of these analogies have their strengths, and neither can claim to comprehend the whole mystery of God, it is the judgment of many theologians today (and mine as well) that much greater attention should be given to the social analogy of the Trinity.[17] According to this analogy, trinitarian faith attests the sociality of God. The God of the Bible establishes and maintains community. God is no supreme monad existing in eternal solitude. God is the covenantal God. God's will for community with and among the creatures is an expression of God's faithfulness to God's own eternal life, which is essentially communal. According to classical trinitarian theology, the three persons of the Trinity have their distinctive identity only in their deepest relationship with each

---

14. Susan Thistlethwaite rightly observes that "the resistance to diversity . . . can be noted in the lack of consideration given the Trinity in modern theology" (*Sex, Race and God: Christian Feminism in Black and White* [New York: Crossroad, 1989], p. 122).

15. The classic statement of Western trinitarianism is Augustine's *On the Trinity*. For criticism of the primacy of the psychological analogy in Augustine's trinitarianism, see Colin Gunton, "Augustine, the Trinity, and the Theological Crisis of the West," *Scottish Journal of Theology* 43 (1990): 33-58.

16. The most influential Eastern trinitarian theologians are the Cappadocians, especially Gregory of Nyssa. See Cornelius Plantinga, Jr., "Gregory of Nyssa and the Social Analogy of the Trinity," *The Thomist* 50 (1986): 325-52.

17. Cf. Jürgen Moltmann, *The Trinity and the Kingdom* (San Francisco: Harper & Row, 1981); David Brown, *The Divine Trinity* (London: Duckworth, 1985); and Cornelius Plantinga, Jr., "Social Trinity and Tritheism," in *Trinity, Incarnation and Atonement: Philosophical and Theological Essays* (Notre Dame, Ind.: University of Notre Dame Press, 1989).

other. They "indwell" each other (as the technical trinitarian concept *perichoresis* suggests); they "make room" for each other, are incomparably hospitable to each other;[18] or, to use still another metaphor, they are united in an exquisite divine dance.

That God's life can be described in the light of the gospel with the beautiful metaphors of trinitarian hospitality and the dance of trinitarian love has far-reaching implications. It points to experiences of friendship, caring family relationships, and the inclusive community of free and equal persons as intimations of the eternal life of God and of the reign of God that Jesus proclaimed. That God is a trinity of love means that concern for new community in which there is a just sharing of the resources of the earth and in which relationships of domination are replaced by relationships of honor and respect among equals has its basis in the divine way of life. In the words of Leonardo Boff, "the Trinity understood in human terms as a communion of Persons lays the foundations for a society of brothers and sisters, of equals, in which dialogue and consensus are the basic constituents of living together in both the world and the church."[19]

Christian social ethics is thus grounded in trinitarian theology. The Christian hope for peace with justice and freedom in community among peoples of diverse cultures, races, and gender corresponds to the trinitarian logic of God. Confession of the triune God radically calls in question all totalitarianisms that deny the freedom and rights of all people and resists all idolatrous individualisms that subvert the common welfare. The doctrine of the Trinity seeks to describe God's "being in love" as the source of all genuine community, beyond all sexism, racism, and classism.[20] Trinitarian theology, when it rightly understands its own depth grammar, offers a profoundly relational and communal view both of God and of life created and redeemed by God.

3. To confess that God is triune is to affirm that *the life of God is essentially self-giving love.* However scandalous the idea, the gospel narrative identifies God as the power of compassionate love that is stronger than sin and death.[21] To have compassion means to suffer with another.

---

18. For the metaphor of trinitarian hospitality I am indebted to Cornelius Plantinga, Jr.

19. Boff, *Trinity and Society* (Maryknoll, N.Y.: Orbis Books, 1988), pp. 118-20.

20. See Anthony Kelly, *The Trinity of Love: A Theology of the Christian God* (Wilmington, Del.: Michael Glazier, 1989), pp. 147-49, 157-59.

21. See Eberhard Jüngel, *God as the Mystery of the World* (Grand Rapids: William B. Eerdmans, 1983), pp. 299-396.

According to the biblical witness, God suffers with and for the creatures out of love for them. Above all in Jesus Christ, God goes the way of suffering, alienation, and death for the salvation of the world. It is this compassionate journey of God into the far country of human brokenness and misery that prompts the revolution in the understanding of God that is articulated — although never fully adequately — in the doctrine of the Trinity. God loves in freedom not episodically but eternally. God can enter into vulnerable interaction with the world, even to the depths of temporality, deprivation, suffering, and death, because as Father, Son, and Holy Spirit God is essentially a living process of mutual self-surrendering love.[22] This boundless love of the triune God is decisively revealed in the cross of Christ and is the eternal source and energy of human friendship, compassion, sacrificial love, and inclusive community.

A trinitarian understanding of God thus coheres with the witness of the Old and New Testaments, with the suffering love of the God of the prophets (see Hos. 11:8-9), and with all aspects of the gospel story: the compassion of Jesus for the sick, his solidarity with the poor, his parables, and above all his passion and resurrection. Moreover, a trinitarian faith redefines the meaning of salvation. If the triune God is self-giving love that liberates life and creates new community, then there is no salvation for the creature apart from its sharing in God's agapic way of life in solidarity and hope for the whole creation (cf. Rom. 8:18-39). Thus a trinitarian understanding of God and salvation gives new depth and direction to our still fragile sense of the interdependence of life and our half-hearted commitment to the struggles for justice and freedom for all people.

If the triune God is understood as a continuing history of compassionate and victorious love, it follows that we must not, like so much of the tradition, think of the Trinity primarily in retrospect, looking backward from God's dealings with the world to the Trinity before creation. We must also think of the Trinity prospectively, looking ahead to the glorious completion of the history of divine love. The trinitarian history of God moves forward to a consummation symbolized as the reign or commonwealth of God. The glory of the triune God will be complete only when the creation is set free from all bondage and God is praised as "all in all" (1 Cor. 15:28). Trinitarian faith thus appropriately

---

22. See Hans Urs von Balthasar, *Credo: Meditations on the Apostles' Creed* (New York: Crossroad, 1990).

culminates not in doctrinal definitions but in doxology, praise, and adoration.[23]

The Attributes of God

OUR reflections on the triune reality of God point to the need for a thorough rethinking of the doctrine of the attributes of God, which have all too often been presented and debated without any reference to the life, death, and resurrection of Jesus Christ or to the doctrine of the Trinity, which is simply a summary redescription of the God of the gospel.

The Christian theological tradition has frequently been ambiguous and confused in speaking of the attributes of God. It has tried to synthesize the confession that God is compassionate, suffering, victorious love revealed decisively in Jesus Christ with a number of speculative ideas about what constitutes true divinity, such as immutability, impassibility, and apathy. According to Augustine, for example, God does not truly grieve over the suffering of the world; according to Anselm, God does not experience compassion within Godself; according to Calvin, when Scripture speaks of God's compassion it employs a figure of speech that accommodates to our finite understanding. Even the gospel witness to the suffering of Christ on the cross was not able to dislodge the ancient philosophical presuppositions of divine immutability and impassibility from theological reflection. Numerous theologians, including Calvin, attempted to reconcile God's presence in Christ with the conviction that God does not suffer. Looking for support in classical two-natures Christology, they affirmed that while the human nature of Jesus suffered, the divine nature remained impassible.[24]

Protestant and Catholic scholastic theology tended to treat the attributes of God in two virtually separate sets: one set containing the so-called absolute or incommunicable attributes (simplicity, immutability, eternity, omnipresence, self-existence, etc.) and the other containing the so-called relative or communicable attributes (holiness, love, mercy, justice, patience, wisdom, etc.). The first set was reached by the *via*

23. See Jürgen Moltmann, *The Church in the Power of the Spirit* (New York: Harper & Row, 1977), pp. 56-60; and *The Trinity and the Kingdom*, pp. 151-54.

24. Calvin, *Institutes of the Christian Religion*, 2.14.2. See also Paul S. Fiddes, *The Creative Suffering of God* (New York: Oxford University Press, 1988), pp. 25ff.

negativa, or negative knowledge of God, while the second set was reached by the *via eminentiae,* or knowledge of God that begins with the virtues of creatures and then infers their perfect or eminent realization in God.[25]

This division in the doctrine of the attributes of God creates many problems from a biblical perspective and leads to serious consequences both in the imaging of God and in the ethical realm. If the traditional attributes of God — apathy, immutability, omnipotence — are not thoroughly rethought and reformed in the light of the exercise of power by the living God of the gospel narrative, the result is a theological justification of the status quo and of the arbitrary and unlimited exercise of power by some creatures over others.

No wonder Pascal expressed a preference for the "God of Abraham, Isaac, and Jacob . . . God of Jesus Christ, not the God of the philosophers and scholars." How can Christians talk about the apathy of the God who "so loved the world that he gave his only begotten Son" for its salvation (John 3:16)? How can Christians talk about the immutability of God if God is the living God who acts and suffers, who speaks and listens, who affects others and is affected by them? How can Christians who know of God's weakness in the cross of Christ allow the divine omnipotence to be identified with tyrannical power? And yet this is what so much of the Christian theological tradition and especially the old dogmatic textbooks seemed unable to avoid. Of course God is "immutable" in the sense that God is steadfast and faithful in character and purpose. Of course God is "apathetic" in the sense that the life of God is not controlled by the sorts of passions that rule and destroy human life in its alienation from God and from others. Of course God is "omnipotent" in the sense that the sovereign love of God has no equal. But the problem is that immutability, apathy, omnipotence, and other attributes were often predicated of God not in these very specific senses but in an unqualified manner that undermined the biblical witness to the living and loving God of the gospel. God is the One who loves in freedom, and there is no love without vulnerability and risk. There is no love without openness to rejection, suffering, and loss. To believe in the triune God is to believe in a God who shares in our suffering, whose suffering is not a sign of impotence but of strength, who promises the final victory of compassionate love.

25. For the Reformed scholastic treatment of the divine attributes, see Heinrich Heppe, *Reformed Dogmatics* (London: George Allen & Unwin, 1950).

In explicit contrast to the scholastic tradition, a number of modern theologians have labored at the reconstruction of the doctrine of the attributes of God.[26] Instead of discussing the attributes of God independently of the doctrine of the Trinity, they maintain that that doctrine is the context in which all that is said Christianly of God is rightly to be set. In a trinitarian context, the attributes of God are held together as mutually qualifying descriptions of the living God whose being is in free, self-giving love.

Thus the unity of the triune God is not mere mathematical oneness but a *living unity* which includes diversity; the steadfastness of the triune God is not a dead immutability but a *dynamic constancy* of character and purpose that includes movement and change; the power of the triune God is not raw omnipotence but the *sovereignty of love* that is incomparably strong even in weakness; the *grace* of the triune God is *righteous,* and the righteousness of this God is gracious; the omniscience of the triune God is not trivial "know-it-allness," but the deep *wisdom* of God that includes the foolishness of the cross.

Karl Barth, the most consistent trinitarian theologian of the modern era, calls for a reconstruction of Christian thinking about the attributes of God in these words: "Who God is and what it is to be divine is something we have to learn where God has revealed [God]self. . . . We may believe that God can and must only be absolute in contrast to all that is relative, exalted in contrast to all that is lowly, active in contrast to all suffering, inviolable in contrast to all temptation, transcendent in contrast to all immanence, and therefore divine in contrast to everything human, in short that [God] can and must be only the 'Wholly Other.' But such beliefs are shown to be quite untenable, and corrupt and pagan, by the fact that God does in fact be and do this in Jesus Christ."[27]

The Electing Grace of God

IF the Christian understanding of God follows a trinitarian logic, we will have to rethink not only the doctrine of divine attributes but also the doctrine of election or predestination.

---

26. See, for example, Jürgen Moltmann, *The Crucified God* (New York: Harper, 1974); Daniel L. Migliore, *The Power of God* (Philadelphia: Westminster Press, 1983).
27. Barth, *Church Dogmatics*, IV/1: 186.

Few doctrines in the history of Christian theology have been as misunderstood and distorted, and few have caused as much controversy and distress, as the doctrine of the eternal decrees of God or double predestination. Although taught in some form by many classical theologians — Augustine, Aquinas, Luther, Calvin — this doctrine has often been a distinctive mark of the Reformed theological tradition. The Westminster Confession, for example, states that by God's secret decrees and for the manifestation of God's glory, from all eternity "some men and angels are predestined unto everlasting life, and others foreordained to everlasting death."[28] Thus stated, the doctrine of election seems to make God an arbitrary tyrant and an enemy of human freedom. The result of this teaching appears to be virtually indistinguishable from fatalism. Far from good news, the doctrine that from eternity God has decreed some to salvation and others to damnation is "dreadful," as Calvin himself described it.[29]

According to the biblical witness, the electing grace of God is astonishing but not dreadful. In the Bible election means that the God who freely chose Israel as covenant partner and who freely established a new covenant in Jesus Christ with Jew and Gentile alike is the God of free grace. Just as in the Old Testament Israel is chosen to be God's people not because of their power or virtue but solely by God's freely given love (Deut. 7:7-8), so in the New Testament the favor of God is surprisingly directed to sinners, the poor, and the outcast. The mystery of God's will is that in Jesus Christ, God chooses to be freely gracious to both Jew and Gentile (Rom. 11:25-36). Even the faith by which this grace is received is considered a free gift of God (Eph. 2:8). Thus the biblical theme of election is doxological; it praises the free grace of God as the only basis of creation, reconciliation, and redemption: "God chose us in Christ before the foundation of the world to be holy and blameless before him in love" (Eph. 1:4).

The development of the doctrine of election in Christian theology went awry when it was made to serve purposes that it was never intended to serve. The doxological intention of the doctrine has been obscured by a variety of motives: the desire to explain why some hearers accept while others reject the gospel message (Augustine); the determination to follow

---

28. The Presbyterian Church (U.S.A.) *Book of Confessions* (Louisville: Office of the General Assembly, 1983), 6.016.

29. Calvin, *Institutes of the Christian Religion*, 3.23.7.

rigorously what appeared to be the logical implications of God's omnipotence and providential governance of the world (Aquinas); the insistence that the righteousness of God is evident in the damnation of the reprobate just as God's mercy is displayed in the salvation of the elect (Westminster Confession).

Within a trinitarian context, however, the doctrine of election has one central purpose: it declares that all of the works of God — creation, reconciliation, and redemption — have their beginning in the free grace of God. It affirms that the triune God who lives eternally in communion graciously wills to include others in that communion. A trinitarian doctrine of election would therefore include the following affirmations:

1. *The subject of election is the triune God.* The electing God is not an arbitrary deity who exercises naked power and whose eternal decrees unalterably fix human destiny in advance. Just as God's attributes are predicates of the triune God decisively revealed in Jesus Christ rather than free-floating ideas about what divinity must be like, so God's election of human beings to be covenant partners corresponds to God's eternal triune love in freedom. It is the decision of God to be God for the world, the divine determination to be God in relationship not only ad intra but also ad extra. Election means that God chooses to share with others God's life in communion. Thus the superabundant grace of God (Rom. 5:20) manifest in Jesus Christ and in the gift of the Holy Spirit represents God's primary intention from all eternity; it is the very foundation and starting point of all the works of God. Because election is God's decision to be God for the world, it is appropriately included in the doctrine of God.

2. *Our knowledge of election has no other basis than the unfathomable love of God for the world in Jesus Christ which we share in the community of the Holy Spirit.* What is the content of the knowledge of election when it is riveted to this basis? Having been chosen in Christ "before the foundation of the world," we know that we have no claim on God, that our salvation depends solely on God's grace, and that we can live in the confidence that nothing can separate us from the love of God in Christ Jesus (Rom. 8:39). Moreover, because the subject of election is the triune God who loves in freedom, and because in Christ we are called to freedom (Gal. 5:13) and given the Spirit of freedom (2 Cor. 3:17), we know that God's election, far from negating human freedom, intends our free service of God and our glad participation in the new life of communion with God and others. In addition, because God desires that everyone be saved

(1 Tim. 2:4) and commissions the church to proclaim the gospel to all peoples (Matt. 28:19), we know that we must not set any a priori limits to the electing grace of God.

3. *The goal of election is the creation of a people of God and not, in the first instance, the salvation of solitary individuals.* The doctrine of election is not intended to cater to excessive self-concern but precisely to open us to the blessings and responsibilities of life in community. Election is the expression of God's will to create a community that serves and glorifies God. In the Old Testament, the people of Israel are the object of election (Lev. 26:12); in the New Testament, the object of election is Jesus Christ and all who are united with him. God purposes a new humanity in Christ in which individuals are free from preoccupation with themselves and free for thankful service to God and solidarity with others. Thus the doctrine of election must have a place not only in the doctrine of God but also in the doctrine of the Christian life and the vocation of the Christian community.

4. *The electing grace of God is accompanied by the righteous judgment of God, but these are not related like two parallel lines as has been suggested in many traditional doctrines of double predestination.* Election and rejection do not stand in equilibrium in the biblical witness; rather, God's judgment operates in the service of God's gracious will. If this is the case, we must not separate God's grace and justice, and certainly must not posit an eternal decree of rejection alongside God's electing grace. God's word to the world in Jesus Christ is not ambiguous: in him all of the promises of God are Yes and Amen (2 Cor. 1:20). But neither are we allowed to reduce the message that Jesus Christ has lived and died and been raised for all into an abstract guarantee of universal salvation. Grace is not cheap, and faith can never be separated from obedience. This is the clear teaching of Romans 9–11, the locus classicus of the biblical understanding of the relationship of grace and judgment, election and rejection. In this passage, the Apostle Paul does not teach that some human beings (Jews) are eternally rejected while others (Christians) are eternally elected by God. Nor does he contend that glad and faithful human response to God's free grace is a matter of indifference since in the end all will be saved. Rather his point is that God's mercy is a free gift (Rom. 9:18), that God judges human sin and unfaithfulness but that this judgment is not necessarily final, for God wills to have mercy on all (Rom. 11:32). If any are excluded from the community of grace at the end, it is because they have persisted in opposition to God's grace, not

because they were excluded before the foundation of the world (cf. Matt. 25:34, 41).

Although Calvin's position has been interpreted in various ways, his decision to locate the doctrine of election in the context of the discussion of the life of faith rather than in an abstract consideration of the decrees of God (as happened in later Calvinism) shows that he intended to look to Christ as the "mirror of election."[30] He rightly warned against viewing the doctrine of election in an arrogant, fearful, or merely curious manner, presenting it instead as a doctrine that gives assurance and confidence to believers as they serve God and others. Moving boldly beyond Calvin, Barth developed a still more radically Christocentric doctrine of election according to which Jesus Christ is both the Elected *and* the Rejected, and all others are strictly to understand their election *and* rejection as real only in him. This is why Barth can say of the doctrine of election that it is "the sum of the gospel" and that it is the best of all words that can be said or heard: that in Christ, God elects humanity as covenant partner, that apart from any need or constraint the freely gracious God chooses to be God for humanity.[31]

When the doctrine of election is rethought in a trinitarian context, the meaning and goal of election are clarified. The content of this doctrine is not the "dreadful" news that the purpose of God from all eternity is to save a certain number of elect and condemn a certain number of reprobate. The mystery of election is the mystery of God's will from the foundation of the world to share with others God's own life in communion to the praise of God's glorious grace.

The doctrines of the Trinity, the divine attributes, and the electing grace of God aim to identify God not in general terms but with Christian specificity. As suggested at the outset of this chapter, our knowledge of God and our knowledge of ourselves go hand in hand. Every view of what it means to be truly human implies a certain understanding of what God is, and every understanding of what is divine issues in a particular view of what it means to be human. If the doctrine of the Trinity is the distinctively Christian understanding of God, and if this understanding is to give direction and form to the Christian way of being in the world, the question that has to be put to the church today is obvious: Is the God of Christian devotion and practice the God who is the basis of

30. Calvin, *Institutes of the Christian Religion*, 3.24.5.
31. Barth, *Church Dogmatics*, II/2: 3-194.

personal life in relationship, the foundation of richly diverse human community, and the hope of the transformation of the world by the power of compassionate love? In short, do the personal and corporate lives of Christians give evidence of commitment to the triune God, the sovereignly gracious God who has come to the world in Jesus Christ and continues the work of renewal and transformation by the power of the Holy Spirit?

5

The Good Creation

THE BIBLE PROCLAIMS GOOD NEWS IN ITS VERY FIRST VERSE: "IN THE beginning God created the heavens and the earth" (Gen. 1:1). The creation of the world is the first of the majestic and gracious acts of the triune God. It is God's calling "into existence the things that do not exist" (Rom. 4:17). While the good news of God's free grace has its center in the liberating and reconciling work of Jesus Christ and will have its final and victorious realization when God "makes all things new" (Rev. 21:5), the sovereign goodness of God is already at work in the act of creation. The triune God who eternally dwells in loving community also welcomes into existence a world of creatures different from God. The creation of the world, its reconciliation in Jesus Christ, and its promised renewal and consummation are all acts of the one triune God, and they all exhibit the astonishing generosity and beneficence of this God.

Christian Faith and the Ecological Crisis

ALTHOUGH the doctrine of creation has always had a place in Christian theology, primary if not exclusive attention has been given to the creation of the human species. That there were other beings created by God was certainly acknowledged, but they were often treated, as Alan Lewis notes, more like stage props than like important participants in the drama of salvation whose central protagonists were God and humanity.[1]

1. Lewis, *Theatre of the Gospel* (Edinburgh: Handsel Press, 1984).

80

However, a shift in emphasis in the doctrine of creation has occurred in recent decades as both church and society have begun to awaken to the worldwide ecological crisis. In the view of some experts, the damage to the environment is already severe and in some cases probably irreversible. Hardly a day goes by without a report of a Bhopal, a Three Mile Island, a Chernobyl, or of new oil spills, leaking chemical dump sites, ominous increases in rain acidity, and the reckless pollution of streams, fields, and forests. The scope and gravity of the ecological crisis give new urgency to the task of rethinking the Christian doctrine of creation. Any neglect, marginalization, or distortion of the doctrine of creation in our time would only contribute to impending disaster. Development of a strong and comprehensive theology of the first article of the Apostles' Creed, in which the church confesses its faith in God as "Maker of heaven and earth," must be a major part of every Christian theology today.

We have to recognize at once, however, that critics of the Christian tradition see matters very differently. They contend that the real source of the rapacious attitudes toward the natural environment characteristic of the modern era is to be found precisely in the Christian tradition and its scriptures. In the view of these critics, the teaching that human beings alone are created in the image of God and are commanded by God to exercise "dominion" over all the other creatures has given Western civilization religious justification for treating the natural environment in a ruthless and brutal manner. All of our wanton destruction of nature is sanctioned in the name of fulfilling the divine command. Thus historian Lynn White, Jr., concludes that Christianity bears a "huge burden of guilt" for our present ecological crisis.[2]

It would be a mistake to react in a purely defensive way to this criticism of the Christian theological tradition. As numerous studies have shown, negative and domineering attitudes toward the body and the physical world are present in many strands of Christian theology and even in the Bible itself.[3] Feminist theologians have underscored the link between the hierarchy of male over female and that of humanity over nature.[4] Such attitudes have offered little theological resistance to the

---

2. White, "The Historical Roots of Our Ecologic Crisis," *Science* 155 (1967): 1203-7.

3. See H. Paul Santmire, *The Travail of Nature: The Ambiguous Ecological Promise of Christian Theology* (Philadelphia: Fortress Press, 1985).

4. See Rosemary Radford Ruether, *Sexism and God-Talk: Toward a Feminist Theology* (Boston: Beacon Press, 1983).

spirit of conquest that has characterized the relationship of humanity to the natural environment in Western history. Torn out of its biblical context, the divine command to humanity to "have dominion" over the earth (Gen. 1:26) has been twisted into an ideology of mastery. There is, therefore, ample reason for Christians to repent of their complicity in the abuse of the environment and for Christian theology to engage in serious self-criticism.

Nevertheless, White's argument is based on a caricature of biblical teaching and the classical Christian doctrine of creation. We can identify elements of the biblical witness that are strongly supportive of an ecological theology. The Bible presents the nonhuman creatures as the inseparable companions of humanity in creation, reconciliation, and redemption. According to the first creation narrative in Genesis, God declares "very good" all that has been made (Gen. 1:31). When the narrative states that human beings are created in the image of God and are given the command to have dominion over the earth, this must be understood in the context of the distinctive identification of God — not only in this passage but throughout the Bible — as the God not of arbitrary power but of free grace and covenantal love.

While it is undeniable that there are passages of the Bible, particularly of the Old Testament, where God is described as exercising fierce suzerainty over the nations and nature, calling for acts of vengeance and even slaughter of the innocents (e.g., 1 Sam. 15:3), Christian faith does not find in such passages the central clue to the power and purpose of God. Certainly the reign of God proclaimed by Jesus and enacted in his life and death turns upside down every view of sovereignty as mastery over others: "You know that among the Gentiles those whom they recognize as their rulers lord it over them, and their great ones are tyrants over them. But it is not so among you; but whoever wishes to become great among you must be your servant, and whoever wishes to be first among you must be slave of all" (Mark 10:42-44). Seen in the light of what Christians hold to be the central biblical message, the command of God to humanity to have dominion calls for respect, love, and care for the good creation. It is a summons to wise stewardship rather than selfish indulgence, to leadership within the commonwealth of creatures rather than a license for exploitation. We might paraphrase the divine command to humanity as follows: "Let your faithful ordering of the world image the way in which the gracious God exercises dominion." According to the witness of Scripture at its deepest level, therefore, there is no absolute right of humanity over nature; on the contrary, human beings are entrusted with its care and protection.[5]

That God values and takes delight in all creatures is highlighted in the biblical assertion that not just humans but all creatures are able in some way to give glory to God their creator. "The heavens are telling the glory of God, and the firmament proclaims his handiwork" (Ps. 19:1). While the stars, the trees, and the animals do not speak or sing of the glory of God in the same way that humans do, in their own way they too lift up their praises to God, and for all we know, they do this with a spontaneity and consistency far greater than our own. The book of Job describes strange and wondrous creatures (Job 39–41) who seem to have no purpose other than to show the fecundity of God's grace. If God takes delight in all the creatures, and if they are all called in their own distinctive way to praise and glorify God, nonhuman creatures cannot be mere ancillary figures in a Christian doctrine of creation.

The Bible not only presents the nonhuman world as part of God's good creation but also views the whole creation as mysteriously entangled in the drama of sin and redemption and included in the hope of God's coming kingdom. Humanity and the other creatures are bound together in suffering and hope. If both experience divine judgment (Gen. 3), both are recipients of the divine promise (Gen. 9).

Under the present conditions of life, humanity and nature are caught in a web of mutual alienation and abuse. The separation of human beings from God insinuates itself into all other relationships, including that between humanity and nature. On the one side, there is brutal human exploitation and destruction of the natural environment; on the other side, there is tragic human suffering at the hands of destructive forces of nature, as such phenomena as cancers, earthquakes, hurricanes, and drought remind us. So the Apostle Paul speaks of the natural world as groaning like a woman in childbirth, even as humanity also groans for its final liberation from suffering and death (Rom. 8:22-23). According to the biblical witness, we human beings exist in a solidarity of life and death with the whole groaning and expectant creation.

This inseparability of humanity and nature in the biblical view extends to their final destiny. The Bible includes the natural world in the promise and hope of redemption. Evidence of this is the divine covenant

---

5. The Presbyterian Church (U.S.A.) Brief Statement of Faith speaks of planet earth as "entrusted to our care" by God the Creator (l. 38).

with Noah, symbolized in the rainbow after the flood (Gen. 9), which explicitly embraces all creatures. There are numerous visions of future redemption in the Bible, and they are staggeringly inclusive. They speak of a transformed, resurrected body (1 Cor. 15), of a new heaven and a new earth (Rev. 21), of the wolf dwelling in peace with the lamb and children playing with scorpions (Isa. 11), of a time of universal shalom when all creatures will live together in harmonious and joyful community.

If with the biblical witnesses we see ourselves as fellow creatures in company with all the inhabitants of the world of nature, if we understand ourselves as trustees rather than as masters of the earth, if we see nature as entangled with us in the drama of sin and redemption, and if we include nature in our hope for justice, freedom, and peace throughout God's creation, we will no longer want to rationalize our abuse of nature by alleging a God-given right to rule over the rest of creation as we please. Criticisms of the use of the Bible and Christian doctrine to justify arrogant and exploitative relationships to the world of nature are to be taken seriously; they call for reform of faith and theology. While there is certainly distortion in these criticisms, the summons to a new ecological consciousness in Christian proclamation and practice must not be passed over.

Themes of the Doctrine of Creation

A CHRISTIAN doctrine of creation must be developed in the light of the revelation of God in Christ, and it must attend to several closely related themes.

1. To speak of the world as God's creation is first of all to make an affirmation about God. By calling God the "creator" and everything that constitutes the world "creatures," Christian faith affirms the *radical otherness, transcendence, and lordship of God.* There is, in other words, an ontological difference between God and the world, creator and creation. According to classical Christian doctrine, God creates *ex nihilo,* "out of nothing." "Nothing" is not a primordial stuff out of which the world was created. Creation "out of nothing" means that God alone is the source of all that exists. The creation of the world is an act of sovereign freedom. God is not like the craftsman of Plato's *Timaeus* who imposes form and order on pre-existing matter. Nor is creation an emanation of the divine reality and thus partially divine. For Christian faith God is

not a part of the world, and the world is not partly or secretly God. God is creator of all things — "the heavens and the earth" — and that means, as Langdon Gilkey puts it, "the nebulae, the amoebae, the dinosaurs, the early Picts and Scots, the Chinese, the Kremlin, You, I, our two dogs, and the cat."[6] God is the mysterious other on which all that exists radically and totally depends.

But to confess that God is creator is to say more. It is to say that *the free, transcendent God is generous and welcoming.* God was not compelled to create the world. It is an act of free grace. Creation is a gift, a benefit. When we confess God as the creator, we are saying something about the character of God. We are confessing that God is good, that God gives life to others, that God lets others exist alongside and in fellowship with God, that God makes room for others. No outside necessity compelled God to create. Nor did God create because of some inner deficiency in the divine life that had to be satisfied. If creation is a necessity in either of these meanings, it is not grace.

In another sense, however, creation may be called "necessary" — that is, in the sense that God creates in total consistency with God's nature. Creation fittingly expresses the true character of God, who is love. Creation is not an arbitrary act, something God just decided to do on a whim, as it were. On the contrary, God is true and faithful to God's own nature in the act of creation. To speak of God as the creator is to speak of a beneficent, generous God, whose love and will-to-community are freely, consistently, and fittingly displayed in the act of creation. The grace of God did not first become active in the calling of Abraham or in the sending of Jesus. In the act of creation, God already manifests the self-communicating, other-affirming, community-forming love that defines God's eternal triune reality and that is decisively disclosed in the ministry and sacrificial death of Jesus Christ. God is love, and this eternal love of the triune God constitutes, in Jonathan Edwards' words, a "disposition to abundant communication."[7] Already in God's own trinitarian life of shared love, God aims at the coming into being of created community.[8] God is eternally disposed to create, to give and share life with

---

6. Gilkey, *Message and Existence: An Introduction to Theology* (New York: Seabury Press, 1979), p. 87.

7. Jonathan Edwards, *The End for Which God Created the World*, chap. 1, sec. 3.

8. Eberhard Jüngel, *God as the Mystery of the World* (Grand Rapids: William B. Eerdmans, 1983), p. 384.

others. The welcome to others that is rooted in the triune life of God spills over, so to speak, in the act of creation.

God's work of creation is not only aptly described as grace but also, in a sense, as "costly grace." It is an act of divine *kenosis*. Although the metaphor of divine kenosis is usually restricted to the "emptying" or self-humbling of the Son of God for our salvation (Phil. 2:5-6), there is a sense in which the act of creation is already a kind of divine kenosis — a self-humiliation or self-limitation — that others may have life, may have a relatively independent existence alongside God. As Emil Brunner writes, "The kenosis, which reaches its [highest] expression in the cross of Christ, began with the creation of the world."[9]

2. The doctrine of creation is at once an affirmation about God and an affirmation about the world and ourselves. So a second theme of this doctrine is that *the world as a whole and all beings individually are radically dependent on God.* Such radical dependence is far more than a sense of partial dependence on God in some regions of our experience or at some especially difficult moments of our life. In confessing that God is creator and that we are creatures, we acknowledge that we are finite, contingent, radically dependent beings. We express our awareness that we might not have been, that our very existence and every moment of our experience is a gift received from a source beyond ourselves.

The realization of this radical contingency, of our awareness of being primarily recipients of life, is what some philosophers and theologians have called the "shock of nonbeing." You and I are not necessary. We are creatures who exist at the pleasure of our creator. As contingent beings, our existence is precarious, and we are frequently reminded of this by sickness and failure and anxiety and the death of loved ones, and even by the positive experiences of joy, happiness, contentment — all of which come and go so quickly. Experiencing a moment of intense beauty that we would like to possess forever, feeling impotent in the face of injustice, witnessing the birth of a child, or being present at the funeral of a child — all this and so much more is taken up into our confession of our creatureliness. Our hold on life is fragile. Like the grass that withers and dies (Isa. 40:6), we live on the edge of nonbeing. We did not bring ourselves into existence, and we cannot guarantee our continued existence. Friedrich Schleiermacher described the

---

9. Brunner, *The Christian Doctrine of Creation and Redemption* (Philadelphia: Westminster Press, 1952), p. 20. See also John Polkinghorne, *Science and Creation: The Search for Understanding* (Boston: New Science Library, 1988), pp. 62-63.

universal feeling of "absolute dependence" on God, and Rudolf Otto spoke of our "creature feeling." This is not simply a feeling about an event in the distant past called the creation of the world. It is a sense of being dependent here and now, always and everywhere, on the creative power of God. "Know that the Lord is God! It is God that has made us and not we ourselves" (Ps. 100:3).

This sense of being radically dependent on God for our very existence is closely related to the Christian awareness of salvation in Christ by grace alone. We are created and justified by grace alone. As creatures and as forgiven sinners, we are recipients of grace. In neither case is it a status that we have achieved through our own doing. Luther summarizes this faith awareness in his remark that "we are all beggars"; Calvin expresses the same conviction in the words "we are not our own, we belong to God."[10] It is, then, no coincidence that the Apostle Paul brings together faith in the God who raises the dead (our dependence on God for future life), faith in God who justifies sinners (our dependence on God for present life), and faith in God who brings into existence things which were not (our dependence on God for the creation and preservation of life) (cf. Rom. 4:17; 5:1). We are utterly dependent on God for the gift of life, for new life, and for the final fulfillment of life. This is what we confess when we call God our creator.

Radical dependence on God as a theme of the doctrine of creation must be properly interpreted, especially today when it is charged that Christian theology has often inculcated a spirit of passivity and servile dependence. The God on whom we are radically dependent is the God who wills us to be free. Reliance on the God of the gospel is radical liberation from all servile dependencies. Thus, far from being a theological put-down, the doctrine of creation is the magna charta of human freedom. God our creator, the triune God, is the graciously liberating God who wills community in freedom.

3. A third theme of the doctrine of creation is that *in all of its contingency, finitude, and limitation, creation is good* (although not "perfect"). If God is good, then for all its limitations and precariousness the gift of life which God gives is good. This is emphasized in the Genesis creation narrative where the refrain is repeated: "And God saw that it was good" (Gen. 1:10, 18, 21, 25, 31).

10. Calvin, *Institutes of the Christian Religion*, 3.7.1.

The biblical affirmation that creation is good is easily turned into an ideology that obscures the brokenness of life and the reality of evil. This happens when this article of faith is separated from other faith affirmations about the actual fallenness of the world God has created — about sin, the work of reconciliation, and the hope in God's final victory over all those forces in the world that deform and distort God's good creation. When spoken casually and carelessly, the claim that God's creation is good can become an outrageous and even blasphemous assertion that every present state of affairs is good or that everything that happens is good. Hence what Christian theology does and does not say in affirming the goodness of creation must be briefly noted.

a. To say that creation is good is to reject every metaphysical dualism, to deny that some aspect or sphere of what God has created is inherently evil. Dualism in some form or other has insinuated itself into the theology and life of the church from its beginnings to the present. Consider some of the forms it has taken and continues to take: the spiritual is good, the physical is evil; the intellectual is good, the sexual is evil; the masculine is good, the feminine is evil; white is good, black is evil; human beings are good, the natural environment is evil. Over against all such dualisms, Christian faith declares that all that God has created is good. To regard any part of the creation as inherently evil — the Manichean heresy — is both slanderous and destructive.

b. Saying that creation is good is very different from saying that the world around us is useful to satisfy whatever purposes we have in mind. It is to say that God values all creatures whether or not we consider them useful. The affirmation that creation is good is the ground of respect and admiration for all beings. Not only humans but the animals — including the strange and frightening animals (cf. Job 39–41) — are God's creatures and deserve our respect. The inanimate as well as the animate world is God's creation and has its place within God's purposes and as such is to be honored. As already noted, human beings have no God-given right to exploit or deface or destroy the creation. The arrogant assumption of so much of our modern technocratic way of life — namely, that God loves only human beings (and usually only a fraction of them) — is an anthropocentric distortion of the Christian doctrine of creation.

c. To say that the world as created by God is good is not to say that it is "perfect" in some pollyannaish sense. The Bible is not especially interested in a past golden age when there was no need to struggle, no experience of suffering, and no death whatever. If all creatures are finite, limited, and vulnerable and if challenge, risk, and growth are part of creaturely existence as intended by God, then there is no reason to suppose that *all forms* of suffering are inherently evil. There is, as Karl Barth puts it, a "shadow side" of the good creation.

d. To say that creation is good is not to deny that the world, as we know and experience it, is "fallen" and in need of redemption. There is much in the world that should *not* be. While creaturely existence entails finitude and limitations, the powers of disease, destruction, and oppression are not part of the creator's intention. God is not the cause but the opponent of evil forces in their individual and corporate expressions. I will say more about the mystery of evil in God's good creation in subsequent chapters; in this context, it is sufficient to note that when faith speaks of the goodness of creation, it refers not simply to the value of the reality brought into being at the beginning but also to the additional value this reality is given by virtue of God's continuing and costly love for it. The value of human life is determined not simply by the dignity the creator originally gave it but also by what divine love can do with it and intends for it. Thus Christian affirmation of the "good creation" encompasses the entire history of God's relation to the world from its beginning to its final consummation.

4. A fourth theme of the doctrine of creation is *the coexistence and interdependence of all created beings.* Luther is surely right in saying that one meaning of speaking of God as creator of heaven and earth is that "God has created me." And yet clearly God has created more than me. So Luther correctly goes on to say, "God has created me and all that exists."[11] In other words, creaturehood means radical coexistence, mutual interdependence, rather than solitary or monarchic existence. The creation of human beings with each other and with other creatures is an unmistakable theme of the Genesis creation stories. For all their differences, both narratives of creation in Genesis portray human beings as standing in organic relation to each other and to the world of nature.[12] Yahweh sets humanity in a garden and declares that "it is not good that the *adam* (human creature) should be alone" (Gen. 2:18).

11. Luther, "The Small Catechism," 2.2, in *The Book of Concord,* ed. Theodore G. Tappert (Philadelphia: Fortress Press, 1959), p. 345.
12. See George S. Hendry, "On Being a Creature," *Theology Today* 33 (April 1981): 64.

Karl Barth speaks of coexistence as the "basic form" of humanity, by which he means that we are human only in relation to God and to each other. Barth also contends that our essential relationality, or existence-in-coexistence, extends beyond the circle of human life. Human beings exist with the animals, with the soil, sun, and water and all the forms of life that they produce.[13] God is creator of a world whose inhabitants are profoundly interdependent. The world was created by God not as an assemblage of solitary units but for life together, and its structure of existence-in-community reflects God's own eternal life in triune community. This is an extremely important theme, and I develop it more fully in Chapter 7, on the doctrine of humanity in the image of God.

5. A fifth theme of the doctrine of creation is that *God the creator is purposive, and the world that has been created is dynamic and purposeful.* God continues to act as creator and preserver. To limit the work of God the creator to a single moment of the past would be, as Calvin said, "cold and barren."[14] The creative activity of God continues and has a goal. To be sure, this purposive activity of the creator and the purposefulness of the world cannot be directly "read off" what we perceive and experience. It is an affirmation of faith, not an empirical observation. There are clearly elements both of order and disorder, rationality and indeterminacy, cosmos and chaos in the world known to modern science. While the world described by scientific investigation is open to a faith interpretation, the evidence does not require that it be interpreted in this way.

Yet if we take as our central clue God's way with the people of Israel and the decisive confirmation of that way in Jesus Christ, we are led to confess that creation has a purpose. God creates not by accident, nor by caprice, but by and for the Word of God. According to Scripture, Jesus Christ is the Word who was with God in the beginning and through whom all things were created (John 1:1-3; Heb. 11:3). He is the goal toward which the whole creation moves, and it is this divine goal that makes of the world a cosmos rather than a chaos. In Christ "all things hold together" (Col. 1:17). The purpose for which God created the world is decisively disclosed in the life, death, and resurrection of Jesus Christ. With God the Father and the Holy Spirit, the

13. See Barth, *Church Dogmatics,* III/1.
14. Calvin, *Institutes of the Christian Religion,* 1.16.1.

Word of God is present and active in the creation, redemption, and consummation of the world.

In a trinitarian theology of creation, the Spirit of God, like the eternal Word, is at work in the world from its beginning, moving over the primeval waters (Gen. 1:2), giving life and breath to creatures (Ps. 104:30). The creative and re-creative Spirit of God continues to act everywhere, extending justice, building and restoring community, renewing all things. The Spirit acts freely, like the wind (John 3:8). Believers, however, recognize the Spirit mainly as the transforming power who comes from the Father and the Son and who liberates people for participation in the divine re-creative activity. Led by the Spirit, we are called to be God's partners — God's co-workers (cf. 1 Cor. 3:9) — in conducting creation to its appointed goal, called the reign of God.

The promised goal of redeemed creation is described in the New Testament as a time of freedom, peace, and festivity. This messianic time of peace and festivity is prefigured in the sabbath rest that completes God's creative activity. Just as the first story of creation in Genesis moves toward its goal in the sabbath rest and enjoyment of the creator, so the history of the new creation finds its goal in the celebration and festivity of perfectly realized and fully enjoyed fellowship with God and other creatures in the new heaven and new earth. According to Jürgen Moltmann, "Israel has given the nations two archetypal images of liberation: the exodus and the sabbath."[15] The goal of the liberation of creation is both "external" freedom from bondage and "internal" freedom for the peace and joy of life in community with God and other creatures.

When the creation of the world by God is set in the context of the whole activity of the triune God, we are able to describe creation not as something past and finished but as still open to the future. And the future for which creation is open is not only the coming of Christ to renew the creation but the participation of the creation in the end-time glory of God. Moltmann makes this point with a helpful revision of a medieval theological axiom. According to the scholastic theologians, "Grace does not destroy, but presupposes and perfects nature"; according to Moltmann, "Grace neither destroys nor perfects, but prepares nature for eternal glory."[16]

---

15. Moltmann, *God in Creation: A New Theology of Creation and the Spirit of God* (San Francisco: Harper & Row, 1985), p. 287.

16. Moltmann, *God in Creation*, p. 8.

Models of Creation

THE major possibilities of understanding the relationship between God and the world are often said to be theism, pantheism, and panentheism. Theism is the belief that God is the transcendent creator of the world, pantheism is the belief that the world is a mode of God's being, and panentheism is the belief that the world and God are mutually dependent. Since none of these positions, as stated, is entirely adequate to a trinitarian doctrine of God and creation, a different inventory of models and metaphors for understanding this relationship is desirable. While the creation of the world is a unique act, there is no reason why we should not expect *analogies* to this event in our own experience. We must remember, of course, that all analogies, metaphors, and models are imperfect when they are employed with reference to the divine life and activity. They never exhaust what we are seeking to understand. As Sallie McFague reminds us, our language about God is inescapably metaphorical, and a metaphor says both that "it is, and it is not."[17]

George Hendry identifies several models or analogies used in Christian theology to speak of the divine act of creation. Each would claim some biblical support, and each has roots in common human experience.[18]

1. One obvious analogy is *generation*. We speak of procreation with reference to the human act of giving life to another. There are some hints of this analogy in the Bible. God is described as being like a "father" or "mother" to Israel. Yet while the procreational metaphor is present in the Bible, it is remarkably subdued by comparison with other religions of the ancient Near East. When the prophets of Israel, and later Jesus, speak of God as "father" or "mother," the metaphor points not primarily to an act of sexual procreation but to God's creative love and parental care.

2. Another analogy of creation is *fabrication* or *formation*. The idea of fabrication is evident in the depiction of God as a builder (Ps. 127:1), and the idea of formation is evident in the depiction of God as a potter who forms clay into vessels (Jer. 18; Rom. 9:21) and when God is said to have formed human beings from the dust of the ground (Gen. 2:7). These analogies of fabrication and formation underscore the intention-

---

17. McFague, *Metaphorical Theology* (Philadelphia: Fortress Press, 1982), p. 13.
18. See George S. Hendry, *Theology of Nature* (Philadelphia: Westminster Press, 1980), pp. 147-62. See also Ian Barbour, *Religion in an Age of Science*, vol. 1 (San Francisco: Harper & Row, 1990), pp. 176ff.

ality and purposefulness of God the Creator, but they have two distinct disadvantages. They both presuppose a given material that is worked upon (thus obscuring the radicality of God's creation of the world "out of nothing"), and they both assign a subpersonal status to what God brings into being.

3. Still a third analogy is that of *emanation,* which means literally a "sending out," in the sense of water flowing from a spring, or light and heat radiating from the sun or a fire. According to this analogy, creation is an overflowing of God's fullness; it has its origin in the richness and abundance of deity. Earlier in this chapter I myself made some use of this imagery. However, the metaphor of emanation can suggest an impersonal and even involuntary process. Hendry points out that while the analogy of emanation is used in classical theology with reference to the intertrinitarian relations — "light from light" in the Nicene Creed, for example — it did not gain wide acceptance as an analogy for God's creation of the world.

4. An analogy widely discussed today but not mentioned by Hendry is the *mind/body* relationship. In an effort to provide an alternative to oppressive hierarchical models, some theologians have proposed that the world be described as the body of God. They argue that this analogy best expresses the intimacy and reciprocity of the relationship between God and the world.[19] The problem with this analogy, of course, is that it is incapable of articulating the gracious, nonnecessary, asymmetrical relationship of God to the world described in the Bible.

5. Finally, there is the analogy of what Hendry calls *artistic expression,* or what might also be called *play.* We often speak of the creation as a "work" of God. That way of speaking has its place, but it may connote something routine and mostly unpleasant, which is unfortunately the way work is often experienced in human life. It may be more helpful, therefore, to think of the creation of the world as the "play" of God, as a kind of free artistic expression whose origin must be sought ultimately in God's good pleasure.

According to the Bible, the creation is brought into being by the Word and Spirit of God. God speaks and the world is given existence (Gen. 1). The Spirit of God moves over the primordial chaos (Gen. 1:2) and gives life to all creatures (Ps. 104:30). This divine creative activity

19. See Sallie McFague, *Models of God: Theology for an Ecological, Nuclear Age* (Philadelphia: Fortress Press, 1987).

occurs freely and spontaneously and thus displays features of play and artistic expression.

What are some of these features? First, true play is always free and uncoerced activity. All artistic expression — whether in music, drama, dance, painting, or sculpture — is creative, free, expressive, playful. While such playful activity has its own rules, they are not experienced as arbitrary but as defining a particular field of freedom. Second, there is free self-limitation in all artistic activity. Artists must respect the integrity of the medium with which they work, and for this reason some voluntary self-limitation is required. Third, when artists express themselves, they bring forth something really different from themselves yet with their own image stamped upon it. And these artistic creations often acquire a life of their own. A classic piece of music or a classic literary text "speaks for itself." The characters of a novel or a drama acquire a personality and profile of their own and cannot be made to say or do just anything without the appearance of authorial violence or artificiality. Artistic creations are born in freedom, and they acquire a certain independence from their creators. Finally, while the artist needs certain materials, the result of artistic activity is of a different order from the materials used. A Mozart concerto or a Rembrandt painting is not simply a reassemblage of given materials but a "new creation."

The model of creation as artistic expression seems particularly appropriate for a trinitarian theology. The idea of God as an uninvolved and distant creator (a typical characterization in the Western philosophical tradition) is totally inadequate from a biblical perspective. On the other hand, the newly revived panentheistic description of the world as God's body, while emphasizing the intimacy of the relationship between God and the world, fails to depict appropriately either the freedom of God in relation to the world or the real otherness and freedom of the world. The model of artistic expression is attractive because it combines the elements of creative freedom and intimacy of relation between artist and artistic creation. Just as the love of God is freely expressed and shared in intertrinitarian community, so in the act of creation God brings forth in love a world of free creatures that bear the mark of the divine creativity.

Our failure to explore the metaphor of artistic activity or play in the doctrine of creation may be due in part to an unfortunate cleavage between theology and the arts in the modern period. And in part, as Moltmann suggests, it may be due to theology's regrettable disregard of the significance of the sabbath day of rest in the first creation narrative in Genesis. God's creativity comes to its conclusion in this story not in the making of humanity but in the rest, celebration, and festivity of the sabbath. As the completion and crown of creation, the sabbath is a reminder of the playful dimension of the divine creativity and a foretaste of the joy, freedom, and peace for which the world was created.[20]

The Doctrine of Creation and Modern Science

THE preceding exposition should have made it clear that the Christian doctrine of creation is not a quasiscientific theory about how the world came into being. It is a deeply religious affirmation, shaped by the experience of the grace of God in Jesus Christ. It gives expression to our faith awareness that we are contingent, finite beings whose very existence is a gift from God. The stories of Genesis 1 and 2 are not scientific descriptions competing with modern cosmological theories but rather poetic, doxological declarations of faith in God, who has created and reconciled the world and each one of us.

In discussions of the relation between faith in God the creator and modern science, several principles should be recognized. First, we should note that science and theology employ two very distinct languages, are two different "language games" (Wittgenstein). On the one hand, there is the language that speaks of data, empirical evidence, causal connections, and probable theories; on the other hand, there is the language that speaks in rich symbols, images, and poetic cadences. To try to equate the scientific description of the origin of the world with the symbolic and metaphorical affirmations of biblical faith and theology is, as Karl Barth once put it, like trying to compare the sound of a vacuum cleaner with that of an organ. The language of science and the language of faith must be recognized in their distinctiveness rather than collapsing one into the other. The claim that only one of these languages is the voice of truth is simply unfounded and arrogant.

But we must go on to say, secondly, that the two languages of science and theology are not totally different or mutually exclusive.[21]

---

20. Moltmann, *God in Creation*, pp. 5-7, 276-96, 310-12.

21. Ian Barbour insists that "we cannot remain content with a plurality of unrelated languages if they are languages about the same world" (*Religion in an Age of Science,* p. 16).

They certainly need not be at war with each other. Of course, if the Bible is asserted to be an infallible textbook of natural science, that is the equivalent of a declaration of war on science by faith. And conversely, if evolutionary theory is coupled with explicit atheism, that is the equivalent of a declaration of war on faith by science. There have indeed been several centuries of warfare between science and theology. When Galileo was forced to renounce his scientific judgment that the earth moves, his case became a symbol of the enmity between science and faith. In the nineteenth and early twentieth centuries, the conflict focused on the theory of evolution. The Wilberforce-Huxley debate, the Scopes trial, and recent arguments for "creation science" remind us of how widespread the confusion has been and continues to be on both sides about the relationship of science and faith.

Despite the confusion, there is nothing inherently inconsistent in holding both to evolutionary theory and to faith in God the creator. However extensively we may have to revise our previous assumptions about the time span, stages, and processes of God's creative activity, this does not substantively affect the central claim of faith in God the creator. If some defenders of evolutionary theory think that faith is disproved by modern science, their conclusions are no more warranted by the theory itself than "creation science" is a required or even appropriate conclusion to be drawn from faith's affirmation of the creation of the world by God. Both reductionism in science and imperialism in theology must be avoided. There are multiple levels in the world of our experience (physical, chemical, biological, personal, social, moral, religious), and each level is intelligible on its own terms as well as open to new understanding at a higher level.[22] This means that we can explore the congruence of scientific and theological understandings of the world without insisting on a proof or disproof of the one by the other.

Third, there is growing consensus among many theologians and scientists that science and faith not only need not be at war with each other but that they can and should influence and enrich each other. Scientists increasingly recognize the dimension of personal participation and creative imagination in scientific inquiry.[23] They also emphasize that the scientific

22. On levels of cognitional activity, see Bernard Lonergan, *Insight: A Study of Human Understanding* (London: Longmans, Green, 1957), pp. 271-78.
23. See Michael Polanyi, *Personal Knowledge* (Chicago: University of Chicago Press, 1958).

enterprise itself rests on assumptions and root metaphors that cannot be strictly proved. Stanley L. Jaki argues persuasively that assumptions which make modern science possible — that observed entities are objectively real, that they possess an inherent rationality, that they are contingent, and that the universe is a coherent whole — are entirely congruent with the Christian doctrine of creation.[24] A philosopher of science remarks that today it is not only the case that theology seeks understanding, but that scientific understanding is in search of faith.[25]

On the other side of the coin, Christian faith and theology have much to learn from modern biological research and scientific cosmology: that God has indeed created a dynamic and open rather than a static and closed universe; that God has created a highly differentiated rather than a monolithic universe; and that God has created a universe in which there is change, novelty, and indeterminacy as well as continuity, order, and coherence.[26] The pendulum may even have begun to swing too far in the opposite direction of expecting science to make clear what faith and theology only dimly intuit. This is at least the case in some popular writings which argue that quantum physics and the Big-Bang cosmology offer a surer path to God than faith. Careless claims of this sort will not advance the conversation between modern science and theology.

What will assist progress is a new openness on both sides: of science to the dimension of mystery in its own work, and of faith and theology to a vision of God's purposeful activity that transcends the narrow framework of anthropocentrism. Theological anthropocentrism must be overcome by a new theocentrism and by a doctrine of creation that is not fixated on the past but oriented to a future consummation embracing the whole creation of God. This does not mean a devaluation of human life but a revaluation of all creation. As Jürgen Moltmann writes, "The enduring meaning of human existence lies in its participation in [the] joyful paean of God's creation. This song of praise was sung *before* the appearance of human beings, is sung *outside* the sphere of human beings, and will be sung even *after* human beings have — perhaps — disappeared from this planet."[27]

24. Jaki, *Cosmos and Creator* (Edinburgh: Scottish Academic Press, 1980).

25. Polkinghorne, *Science and Creation*, p. 32.

26. See A. R. Peacocke, *Creation and the World of Science* (Oxford: Clarendon Press, 1979).

27. Moltmann, *God in Creation*, p. 197.

In view of the ecological crisis that we face today, it is imperative that we put the old warfare between Christian faith and science behind us. A natural theology, at least of the traditional sort, is not what is needed or desired. But a theology of nature is of crucial importance.[28] It is time to move beyond a policy of total separation or mutual indifference between scientists and their discoveries on the one hand and theologians and the vision of faith on the other. It is imperative that scientists and theologians talk and work together toward a new understanding of the complex and fragile beauty of the interrelated world created by God.

28. Cf. Barbour, *Religion in an Age of Science*, p. 183.

6

The Providence of God and the Mystery of Evil

IN CHAPTER 1, I DEFINED THEOLOGY AS FAITH SEEKING UNDER-standing and said that one aspect of this task is the quest for wholeness and coherence in our thinking about God, ourselves, and the world in the light of God's revelation in Jesus Christ. Our quest for coherence, however, must resist the temptation to build a system of ideas that pretends to know more than we do and thereby loses touch with both faith and lived reality. While we can have confidence in the truth of God revealed to us in Christ, our knowledge of God is not exhaustive. Just as the condition of faith is that of seeing only dimly (1 Cor. 13:12), so all theology is necessarily "broken thought" (Barth). This fact comes home to us nowhere more forcefully than when we affirm the providence of God in the face of the reality of radical evil in the world. In relation to divine providence and the "problem of evil," the efforts of theology to clarify the claims of faith seem pitifully weak and unsatisfying. All grandiose theological systems that purport to have an answer to every question are exposed as illusory by the monstrous presence of evil and suffering in the world. Radical evil is the disturbing "interruption" (Cohen) of all theological thinking and speaking about God and especially about the providential rule of God.

Belief in Providence and the Reality of Evil

CHRISTIANS confess the lordship and providential care of God over the world. God the creator does not abandon the creation, leaving it to run on its own, as deism teaches. The true God is no absentee landlord but remains ever faithful, upholding, blessing, and guiding the creation to its appointed goal. God's continuing care for all creatures is attested in many passages of Scripture (e.g., Ps. 104:27-30), perhaps the most familiar being the teaching of Jesus that God sends rain on both the just and the unjust (Matt. 5:45), feeds the birds of the air, clothes the lilies of the field (Matt. 6:26-30), and knows every hair on our head (Matt. 10:30).

A brief but pointed definition of providence is offered by the Heidelberg Catechism of 1563: providence is "the almighty and ever-present power of God whereby he still upholds, as it were by his own hand, heaven and earth together with all creatures, and rules in such a way that leaves and grass, rain and drought, fruitful and unfruitful years, food and drink, health and sickness, riches and poverty, and everything else, come to us not by chance but by his fatherly hand."[1]

This affirmation of God's providential activity is most severely tested by the reality and power of evil. As that which opposes the will of God and distorts the good creation, evil is neither illusion nor mere appearance nor a gradually disappearing force in the world. All theories that deny the reality of evil or minimize its power have been exposed as fantastic and worthless by events of the twentieth century. An earlier era might have thought of evil as the result of cultural lag or inadequate education or insufficient social planning, and might have been convinced of the gradual and inevitable progress that the cosmos and humankind were making toward a paradise in which all suffering and evil would be eliminated. But in the twentieth century, in the wake of horrendously destructive wars, acts of genocide, and the grim possibility of nuclear annihilation, all such easy faith in progress has been discredited.

If evil cannot be explained away but confronts us with immense reality on the pages of our newspaper, in the cancer ward, and in "the brutal facts of modern historical life,"[2] theology cannot avoid the

---

1. Heidelberg Catechism, A. 27, in the Presbyterian Church (U.S.A.) *Book of Confessions* (Louisville: Office of the General Assembly, 1983), 4.027.
2. Arthur A. Cohen, *The Tremendum: A Theological Interpretation of the Holocaust* (New York: Crossroad, 1981), p. 81.

theodicy question: How can we continue to affirm the lordship of God in the face of such horrendous evil? Or, as the question is often formulated: If God is both omnipotent and good, why is there so much evil in the world? This question presses itself on us with respect both to what is sometimes called natural evil — the suffering and evil that human beings experience at the hands of nature — and to what is described as moral evil — the suffering and evil that sinful human beings inflict on each other and on the world they inhabit. In both spheres of experience, we soon find that our effort to relate our faith in God to the brutal facts of life leads into a labyrinth of unanswered questions.

1. "Natural evil" refers to injury and suffering caused by diseases, accidents, earthquakes, fires, and floods. We may think of a young mother mortally stricken by cancer, of an infant born with AIDS, of a young child who is killed by a runaway automobile, of thousands buried in a mud slide caused by a volcanic eruption, of hundreds killed in a plane crash in dense fog. Every pastor who makes hospital visitations and counsels with the bereaved knows that the pain and misery caused by such events are profound and sometimes devastating.

In seeking to cope with experiences of natural evil, we may be tempted to view vulnerability, finitude, and mortality as evil in themselves. But this would be a mistake. As we noted in the previous chapter, some limits and vulnerabilities belong to the goodness of life as created by God. Human beings are part of the natural order established by God and, like other creatures, are subject to its laws. Being a finite creature includes the possibility of pain, illness, grief, failure, incapacity, and the certainty of aging and eventual death. Creaturely life is transient; it has a beginning and an end (Ps. 90:10). God has created a world in which there is both birth and death, both rationality and contingency, both order and freedom, both risk and vulnerability. In such a world, challenge, struggle, and *some* forms of suffering belong to the very structure of life. To wish the world were immune from *every* form of struggle and *every* form of suffering would be to wish not to have been created at all.[3] To insist that believers should be immune from the limits and risks of all creaturely existence would be petty and self-indulgent. Thus while finitude and mortality constitute the "shadow side" of life as created by God, they cannot be called inherently evil.

3. Cf. Douglas John Hall, *God and Human Suffering* (Minneapolis: Augsburg, 1986), pp. 49-71.

But even if we are careful to distinguish between finitude and evil, we are nevertheless confronted by an abysmal form of suffering in the natural order that appears to be absurd, excessive, and entirely out of proportion to any good that might arise from it. While the death of a person "in good old age and full of years" (Gen. 25:8) brings sorrow but usually does not threaten our faith, the death of a single child or young adult by leukemia or some other disease is more than sufficient to prompt the theodicy question.

Furthermore, the impulse to question God's providential guidance within the natural order is not confined to individual experiences of tragedy. It forces itself on us in the interpretation of cosmic process as well as personal experience. Are not violent death and wasted life constitutive elements of the entire natural order? John Macquarrie comments on the "waste" present in the evolutionary process: "The process of evolution on the earth's surface looks more like a groping procedure of trial and error, with fantastic waste, than like the carrying through of a preconceived plan."[4]

The abysmal side of nature has led some to deny God or to equate God with destruction and evil. In Tennessee Williams's play *Suddenly Last Summer*, Sebastian, who is searching for God, is driven to delirium by seeing the large birds over the Encantadas Islands swoop down to devour all but a few of the newly hatched sea turtles as they struggle to reach the sea. Having witnessed this carnage, Sebastian tells his mother: " 'Well, now I have seen Him!' and he meant God."[5] The shocking cruelty, terrible wastefulness, and apparent arbitrariness of the manifold occurrences of evil in nature can lead to doubt and even despair about the providential care and goodness of God.

2. The mystery of evil is equally impenetrable when we turn from the natural to the historical sphere of its operation. Whereas for the eighteenth century, the symbol of the theodicy question was the Lisbon earthquake, for the twentieth century it is the memory of such places as Auschwitz that interrupts all traditional theological reflection. The Holocaust of European Jewry during World War II by Nazi Germany has come to serve as the prime example of radical evil in an unredeemed world.

---

4. Macquarrie, *Principles of Christian Theology*, 2d ed. (New York: Scribner's, 1977), p. 257.

5. Williams, quoted by Gordon D. Kaufman, in *Systematic Theology: A Historicist Perspective* (New York: Scribner's, 1968), pp. 310-11.

We are indebted to Jewish writers who have taken the lead in reflecting theologically about this thought-paralyzing experience. The massacre of six million Jews constitutes a scale of evil in history that numbs the mind and soul. With machine guns and gas ovens, Nazis destroyed millions of innocent people in the death camps for no other reason than their Jewish ancestry. The only motive behind this consummate act of genocide was sheer hatred. This gives the event an utterly diabolical character. The fact that it was perpetrated by a society that represented the very pinnacle of modern Western culture only underscores its horror. Nazis could not even claim that their demonic work was helpful to the German war effort, since there is abundant evidence that the opposite was the case. Jewish men, women, and children were senselessly and brutally annihilated not because of their unfaithfulness to the God of the covenant but precisely because of their membership in the covenant people.

A moment of the horror of the Holocaust is captured in a single episode from the death camp Auschwitz, told by Elie Wiesel in his book *Night.* On one occasion, a young boy was hanged before all the prisoners for a minor infraction of the camp rules. As his body dangled from the rope, Wiesel was asked by someone, "Where is God now?" and a voice within him replied, "Where is He? Here He is — He is hanging here on this gallows. . . ."[6] The power of Wiesel's story comes from its focus on the profound crisis of faith in the experience of terrible affliction. Every experience of innocent suffering has an inescapable theological dimension. As Simone Weil shows in a valuable essay, affliction has many dimensions. It includes not only physical pain but also social rejection and self-hatred. Above all, however, "Affliction makes God appear to be absent for a time."[7] The experience of the absence — or death — of God is closely coupled with the experience of radical evil.

The event of the Holocaust is particular and unique. And yet the witness to what happened there is joined by the witness of innocent sufferers everywhere: the black victims of slavery and apartheid, the prisoners in the Stalin concentration camps, the killed and the survivors of Hiroshima, the starving children of Ethiopia, the countless civilian victims of American and Soviet militaristic policies. The list is endless. Arthur Cohen writes: "When Jews insist that the *tremendum* of the death

6. Wiesel, *Night* (New York: Bantam Books, 1982), p. 62.
7. Weil, *Waiting for God* (New York: Harper & Row, 1976), p. 120.

camps is unique, they speak correctly, but no less the other butchered people of the earth, butchered no less in their being and hence no less irrationally and absolutely."[8]

What the *tremendum*, by whatever name it is known, discloses is that evil is real and powerful, that it must be resisted, and that those who suffer under its weight sooner or later ask the Psalmist's question, "How long, O Lord?" (Ps. 13:1), or the even more terrible question of Jesus, "My God, my God, why have you forsaken me?" (Mark 15:34).

Providence and Evil in the Theological Tradition

THE classical doctrine of providence was not constructed by theologians insensitive to the reality of evil in the world. When they spoke of providence as God's work of preserving the world in existence, ruling over all events, and directing the world to its final end, they did not ignore the power of the negation of God's will present in both individuals and in societies and nations. This is evident in the impressive doctrines of providence developed by Augustine and Calvin.[9]

According to Augustine, God's providence is at work both in the lives of individuals and in history even though it is largely hidden. In his *Confessions* Augustine recounts how God secretly but surely guided his life through many twists and turns toward faith in Christ and entrance into the church. The divine purpose was worked out not coercively, or from the outside as it were, but precisely in and through Augustine's own free decisions and actions. Later in the *City of God* he tries to help his readers see the providential hand of God at work amidst the disintegration of the Roman empire. Tyranny, injustice, social breakdown, war, and other evil events are not caused by God but have their origin in the creatures' misuse of their freedom. Nevertheless, God permits these events to occur and uses them to accomplish the divine purpose. God exercises sovereignty over evil by bringing good out of what by itself is only negative and destructive.[10]

---

8. Cohen, *The Tremendum,* p. 36.

9. See Langdon Gilkey, *Reaping the Whirlwind: A Christian Interpretation of History* (New York: Seabury Press, 1976), pp. 159-87.

10. See Augustine, *City of God,* 13.4: "By the ineffable mercy of God even the penalty of man's offense is turned into an instrument of virtue."

Calvin's doctrine of providence affirms God's governance over all events even more emphatically. Among his central aims is to oppose the idea that any event occurs by fortune, chance, or caprice. "All events are governed by God's secret plan," says Calvin; "nothing happens except what is knowingly and willingly decreed by God."[11] Holding that it is insufficient to affirm a "bare foreknowledge" of God, Calvin declares that God governs the course of nature and history down to the smallest details. God "directs everything by his incomprehensible wisdom and disposes it to his own end."[12]

Despite his emphasis on God's sovereign control, Calvin does not equate providence with fatalism; on the contrary, he teaches that while we are to look to God as the "first cause" of all things, we are also to give attention to the "secondary causes" in their proper place.[13] God has given human beings reason to foresee dangers and to exercise prudence. If danger is evident, we are not to plunge headlong into it; if remedies for suffering are available, we are not to neglect them. Like other classical theologians of divine providence, Calvin walks a tightrope between ascribing everything to God at the expense of the freedom and responsibility of creatures and compromising the omnipotence of God by allowing some autonomy to creaturely activity.

For both Augustine and Calvin, divine providence is less a speculative doctrine than a practical truth. We can be confident that God reigns and that evil is firmly under God's control. This is a teaching with important benefits for the life of faith. In the first place, it teaches us the humility to receive adversity from God's hand even though we cannot understand the reason. Second, we are taught by the doctrine of providence to give thanks for the times when we prosper. And finally, trust in God's providence sets us free from all undue anxiety and care. Calvin sums up these points by saying that "gratitude of mind for the favorable outcome of things, patience in adversity, and an incredible freedom from anxiety about the future, all necessarily follow from this knowledge [of providence]."[14]

Within the framework of traditional doctrines of providence, there are at least three prominent answers to the theodicy question.

11. Calvin, *Institutes of the Christian Religion*, 1.16.2, 3.
12. Calvin, *Institutes of the Christian Religion*, 1.16.4.
13. Calvin, *Institutes of the Christian Religion*, 1.17.6.
14. Calvin, *Institutes of the Christian Religion*, 1.17.7.

1. One familiar theodicy argument underscores the *incomprehensibility of God.* We do not know why there is so much evil in the world, or why it is distributed so unevenly, but we are nevertheless to trust God and have patience. This is a response to evil with considerable biblical support. Out of the whirlwind, God replies to Job's questions with a series of counterquestions that are intended to remind Job of his finitude and inability to grasp the ways of God with the world (see Job 38–41). "The story of Job," Calvin writes, "in its description of God's wisdom, power, and purity, always expresses a powerful argument that overwhelms men with the realization of their own stupidity, impotence, and corruption."[15]

We must surely agree that our knowledge of God's ways is limited and that sometimes silence is a far more appropriate response to the enormity of suffering than feeble attempts to answer the question why. A problem associated with this response, however, is that it may tend to suppress all questions and to encourage the unchallenged acceptance of *all* suffering. When used in this way, the theme of divine incomprehensibility does not have unanimous biblical warrant. Indeed, the book of Job itself is the most striking biblical example of permission to remonstrate with God and to call into question the divine governance. Although the picture of the pious, patient Job of the prologue and epilogue of the book is deeply imprinted in Christian consciousness, the rebellious and questioning Job of the poetic section is far less familiar. At the end of the book, it should be remembered, it is Job rather than his orthodox critics who is commended by God for having spoken what is right (42:7). There is both theological and pastoral significance in the permission to question the justice of God in the face of outrageous suffering and evil.

2. Another traditional theodicy argument interprets the experience of adversity as evidence of divine *punishment* (of the wicked) or *chastisement* (of the people of God). According to this view, God so governs the world that both the good and the wicked receive what they deserve, if not in this life, then in the life to come.[16] Calvin contends that "the scriptures teach us that pestilence, war, and other calamities of this kind are chastisements of God, which he inflicts on our sins."[17]

15. Calvin, *Institutes of the Christian Religion,* 1.1.3.
16. Calvin, *Institutes of the Christian Religion,* 1.5.10.
17. Calvin, quoted by Dorothee Sölle, in *Suffering* (Philadelphia: Fortress Press, 1975), p. 24.

While there are some strands of the Bible that lend support to this conviction (e.g., the Deuteronomic tradition, the defenders of God in the book of Job), Jesus explicitly calls it in question. He teaches that the blind man was not born blind on account of his own or his parents' sins (John 9:1-3), and he claims that it was not because of their special wickedness that people in Siloam were killed when a tower fell upon them (Luke 13:4). The theodicy of divine punishment, which so easily blames the victim and often ignores the victimizers, becomes especially repulsive and destructive when it is implied that God is punishing people who have incurable diseases or are murdered by the millions in the holocausts of history. Human deeds do have consequences, and sometimes a person's reckless or sinful behavior brings suffering in its train. But the theodicy of punishment sees the relationship between sin and suffering too simplistically. Not all suffering can be causally related to sin, and certainly not to the sin of the sufferer. To add guilt to the burden of suffering carried by the victims of natural evil or of human injustice is unconscionable.

3. Still another argument of traditional theodicy centers on the *divine pedagogy* that makes use of earthly sufferings to turn us to God. Christians are to view all suffering as an opportunity for spiritual growth. They are to learn to have contempt for the present life and to meditate on the future life. God sends poverty, bereavement, diseases, and other perils to wean us away from this earth, to cause us to fix our eyes on heaven rather than on the goods of the present life.[18] The Apostle Paul might be cited in support of this view: "I consider that the sufferings of this present time are not worth comparing with the glory that is to be revealed to us" (Rom. 8:18).

It should be noted, however, that the Apostle is thinking primarily of sufferings that are willingly assumed by the Christian for the sake of Christ and the gospel. His statement ought not to be used to obscure the distinction between suffering that is willingly accepted for the sake of God's reign and suffering that arises from conditions that can and should be changed. While few Christians would want to contest the main point of the Apostle — that hope in the final victory of God over evil gives meaning to innocent suffering — there is surely reason to question any interpretation of his teaching that would lead to ethical quietism or a depreciation of this life. Like Jesus, we can learn from our suffering

18. Calvin, *Institutes of the Christian Religion,* 3.9.1.

(Heb. 5:8), but this is not to be converted into the general truth that suffering is good. The cries of victims must not be suppressed in this way, and any theodicy that suggests otherwise is dealing in mystifications.

The traditional theodicies summarized above have undoubtedly offered comfort and support to countless believers in particular situations. An element of truth is present in each of them. But they are all marked by a lack of sustained attention to the gospel story in their thinking about divine lordship and in their response to the reality of evil. In the late twentieth century, all theodicy must be tested both by "the brutal facts of modern historical life" and by the biblical witness to the love of God in Jesus the crucified. This situation compels faith to rethink all inherited understandings of God, and in particular the ideas of divine omnipotence and omnicausality that are often presupposed in traditional doctrines of providence.

Rethinking Providence and Evil

TWENTIETH-CENTURY theologians have attempted to rethink the doctrine of providence in a way that respects both divine power and creaturely freedom. Divine and human activity are not mutually exclusive. God regularly works in and through creaturely agency to accomplish the divine purpose (Rom. 8:28).

Even a theologian as deeply respectful of his own classical Reformed theological tradition as Karl Barth could nevertheless say that its doctrine of providence was tragically flawed by a conception of divine omnicausality. Barth grants that the activity of God is "as sovereign as Calvinist teaching describes it,"[19] but he insists that the divine sovereignty must always be understood in the light of God's revelation in Christ. In practice, Barth contends, belief in providence in orthodox Reformed theology was indistinguishable from Stoic resignation, an acceptance of whatever happens as ordained by God. The consequence of such a teaching within modern culture was an inevitable "revolt against a capricious sovereign rule."[20] Failing to apply to the doctrine of providence the proper norm of Christian knowledge of God — namely, the revelation in Christ — the tradition became the herald of a "sinister deity."

19. Karl Barth, *Church Dogmatics*, III/3: 148.
20. Barth, *Church Dogmatics*, III/3: 116.

Hence Barth called for a "radical rethinking of the whole matter." The Christian doctrine of providence is not a mere logical deduction from abstract claims about the omnipotence and goodness of God. It must be worked out in the light of a genuinely Christian (i.e., christocentric and trinitarian) understanding of God as the One who loves in freedom, who wills to live in community, and who from all eternity elects Jesus Christ and in him the people of God and all of creation.

Barth himself took important steps in this direction in his own doctrine of providence. Employing the categories of traditional theology, he describes divine providence as including God's preservation *(conservatio)*, accompaniment *(concursus)*, and governance *(gubernatio)* of all creatures. But he redefines each of these aspects of divine providence in the light of God's ways with the world in Jesus Christ. The God of creation and providence is none other than the God of the covenant whose faithfulness and grace are manifest in the person and work of Jesus Christ.

Thus God's preservation of creation is not an arbitrary exercise of almightiness but an expression of God's faithfulness to the creation elected in Jesus Christ from all eternity to be God's covenant partner. God's act of preserving is thus an act of serving, an act of free grace to the creature, empowering and sustaining it for participation in the covenant of grace. God is not the impersonal or mechanical "first cause" of all that happens but the one whom Jesus revealed as the heavenly Father.

Moreover, God accompanies creatures in the exercise of their own vitality and freedom. That God accompanies the creatures means that God recognizes and respects the free activity of creatures and does not play the part of a tyrant. The creature is not a mere puppet or tool in the hands of the creator. God rules and overrules creatures, always respecting their finite autonomy "in a way that is congruous to and worthy of" God as revealed in Jesus Christ.[21]

Finally, God rules over all things by guiding creation to its goal, but accomplishes this by God's Word and Spirit and not by unilateral and coercive power. "God rules," Barth insists, "in and over a world of freedom."[22] God is present everywhere, always, and in all things, but God is not the sole actor. The God who wills to have communion with

---

21. Barth, *Church Dogmatics*, III/3: 90.
22. Barth, *Church Dogmatics*, III/3: 93.

creatures gives them freedom to return love for love. In providence no less than in creation and redemption, God is the gracious Lord. All this shows that Barth clearly wanted to break free from a doctrine of providence based on a "logic of control" or domination (Farley).

While offering new direction for a Christian doctrine of providence that refuses to adopt a priori definitions of deity and omnipotence and concentrates instead on the grace of God as revealed in Jesus Christ, Barth's treatment of the reality of evil and of our part in the struggle against it leaves many questions unresolved. Evil for Barth is the alien power of "nothingness" that arises mysteriously from what God does *not* will in the act of creation. As Barth understands it, "nothingness" is not nothing. While neither willed by God nor an equal of God, it has its own formidable and threatening power. It is that which contradicts the will of God manifested in Jesus Christ. God alone is able to conquer the power of nothingness. "The power of nothingness should be rated as low as possible in relation to God and as high as possible in relation to ourselves."[23]

A number of Barth's critics view his doctrine of nothingness as a lapse into metaphysical speculation.[24] They charge that Barth sometimes seems to treat the reality of evil and its conquest by God as a transcendental conflict that leaves unclear in what ways human beings are to be understood as not only helpless slaves of evil but also as active subjects in the struggle against it. If evil is viewed as an alien sphere of power within the creation that God alone can overcome, will we not be disinclined to unmask proximate sources of human suffering and oppression and to take up the struggle against them?

It would be mistaken, however, to understand Barth's view of God's struggle against nothingness as an invitation to passivity. For Barth it is precisely confidence in the superiority of God's grace that empowers believers to fight against evil and suffering in the world against seemingly impossible odds. Barth himself was very active in the church struggle during the Nazi period in Germany, and his theology has been an inspiration to many who have struggled against evil structures such as apartheid in South Africa.

Nevertheless, the criticisms of Barth have some validity. While a pioneer in the modern reconstruction of the doctrine of providence, he

---

23. Barth, *Church Dogmatics*, III/3: 295.

24. See, e.g., G. C. Berkouwer, *The Triumph of Grace in the Theology of Karl Barth* (Grand Rapids: William B. Eerdmans, 1956).

did not sufficiently clarify the relationship between the activity of God and human activity in the struggle against evil. Nor did he sufficiently explore the relationship between patience and protest in a Christian doctrine of providence and in a Christian response to the reality of suffering and evil. These remain among the open questions in contemporary theological discussion.

Recent Theodicies

NUMEROUS theologians after Barth have shared his criticism of the traditional doctrines of providence and evil but have proposed widely differing approaches to the task of rethinking these themes. Any review of recent theodicies and their corresponding understandings of providence would have to include the following.

1. *Protest theodicy.* This is the name given by John Roth to his own position, which has its basis and inspiration in the witness and reflection of the Holocaust survivor and author Elie Wiesel.[25] Jewish theologians Richard Rubenstein and Arthur Cohen may also be considered representatives of a protest theodicy. Assuming with the Bible a very strong view of the sovereignty of God, the tendency of this theodicy is to question the total goodness of God. There is simply too much tragedy, injustice, and murder in history. We must be honest to our experience and to God and thus quarrel with the all-too-familiar refrain that God is love. In the tradition of Jacob, who wrestled all night with a divine adversary and who was renamed Israel or "He who strives with God" (Gen. 32:22-32); in the tradition of the Psalmist who asks, "How long, O Lord?" (Pss. 13, 35, 74, 82, 89, 90, 94); in the tradition of Job, who defends his innocence, and of Jesus' cry of dereliction from the cross (Mark 15:34), we are compelled to protest against the silence and inaction of God, to remind God of the promises of the covenant even though God seems to have forgotten them. The reality that faith confronts forces it to "put God on trial," to be "for God by being against God."[26]

This is a theodicy with no easy answers but with the honesty to

---

25. See Roth, "A Theodicy of Protest," in *Encountering Evil: Live Options in Theodicy,* ed. Stephen T. Davis (Atlanta: John Knox, 1981), pp. 7-22.

26. Roth, "A Theodicy of Protest," pp. 11, 19.

raise what earlier believers would have considered unthinkable questions and with a determination to be faithful to God even when it appears that God has ceased to be faithful. One might well demur from the theological conclusions that protest theodicy derives from the persistence of evil in nature and history while at the same time acknowledging the legitimacy of the protest as part of a faithful response to God.

2. *Process theodicy.* John Cobb, David Griffin, and Marjorie Suchocki are well-known representatives of process theodicy.[27] They approach the problem of evil from the perspective of process metaphysics. Refusing to compromise on the divine goodness, process thought argues that the solution lies instead in a radical restriction of divine power.

For the process theologians, God's power is essentially limited. The power of God is persuasive rather than coercive. Persuasion is the only way one power can influence another without violating the freedom of the other. God creates not ex nihilo but more like the Platonic demiurge who persuades recalcitrant matter as best he can. The world is a plurality of beings, all of which have some freedom and power of their own. God does not have, and never had, a monopoly on power. Thus there are some things God is simply unable to do — such as prevent the Holocaust, or stop a runaway car from killing a child in its path, or eliminate the possibility of cancerous growths in human beings.

In an indirect sense, God is responsible for evil because God has persuaded the world to bring forth forms of life that have the potential not only of great good but also of great evil. While indirectly responsible, however, God is not blameworthy. God always intends the good and always shares the suffering of the creatures in a world in which beauty and tragedy are interwoven.

Process theodicy is arguably the most comprehensive and consistent of modern theodicies, but at the same time it may also be the one most distant from the biblical witness. This is perhaps best seen in the fact that process theodicy, with its teaching that the sovereignty of God's love is metaphysically limited, can make no sense whatever either of the doctrine of creation out of nothing or of the biblical hope in a definitive eschatological victory over suffering and evil.

27. Cobb, *God and the World* (Philadelphia: Westminster Press, 1969), pp. 87-102; Griffin, "Creation out of Chaos and the Problem of Evil," in *Encountering Evil*, pp. 101-19; Suchocki, *The End of Evil: Process Eschatology in Historical Perspective* (Albany: State University of New York Press, 1988).

3. *Person-making theodicy.* This is one of the most influential of modern theodicies, and John Hick is perhaps its ablest representative.[28] He distinguishes between the Augustinian and the Irenaean types of theodicy. In the former, evil is represented as the consequence of sin; in the latter, the possibility and experience of evil are conditions of the possibility of growth toward free and mature humanity in the image of God. The freedom and potential for growth with which human life is endowed can be abused, but without the real choice between good and evil, and without the possibility of learning through hard experience, the formation of character is simply impossible. According to Hick, God desires not puppets but persons who freely render their worship and adoration. Hence human beings are created incomplete and must freely participate in the process by which they come to be what God intends them to be.

Unlike process thinkers, Hick refuses to qualify the power of God working as love. He postulates the existence of worlds beyond this world in which persons continue their movement toward the fullness of life in love that God intends for all creatures. This latter feature of Hick's theodicy underscores its speculative bent.

While person-making theodicy does not entirely lack a social-ethical dimension, its weakness in this area is conspicuous. The stress has been on growth through acceptance of suffering rather than on resistance to suffering that can and should be removed. To be sure, the idea of learning from and growing in suffering is deeply ingrained in the Bible (Jesus "learned obedience through what he suffered," Heb. 5:8). Moreover, many individuals and groups in the history of the church and of other religious communities have borne powerful witness to the working of grace even in the darkest of experiences. Still, it must not be overlooked that there are events of suffering and evil that in their immensity virtually consume their victims and thus resist the interpretation of suffering as always the opportunity for spiritual development. In brief, despite its strengths, this theodicy proves to be less than satisfactory when it is tested by the experience of the *tremendum.*

4. *Liberation theodicy.* Liberation theology in its many forms must come to terms with the theodicy question because the continuing reality of the suffering of the poor and the oppressed appears to stand in

---

28. See Hick, *Evil and the God of Love* (New York: Harper & Row, 1966); and "An Irenaean Theodicy," in *Encountering Evil,* pp. 39-52.

contradiction to the claim of this theology that God is at work in the world liberating the poor.

James Cone has addressed this problem. He refuses to diminish either the divine power or the divine goodness in order to arrive at an intellectually satisfying resolution of the dilemma. He acknowledges the plurality of responses to the mystery of evil in the Bible. He finds the deepest response in the theme of redemptive suffering (the Servant Songs of Isaiah) and in the history of Jesus Christ. Cone interprets this tradition, however, as supporting not the passive acquiescence in suffering but courageous human participation in God's struggle *against* suffering. The black religious tradition does not focus on the question of the origin of evil or on the submission of the victims of injustice to their masters. It is a faith tradition that sees in the cross God's struggle against evil and in the resurrection God's promise of the final victory of God over evil. God grants "power to the powerless to fight here and now for the freedom they know to be theirs in Jesus' cross and resurrection."[29]

When placed alongside much classical theodicy, with its tendency to passivity in the face of evil, the important truth of liberation theodicy is readily apparent. If there is a one-sidedness in its emphasis, the tradition has been no less one-sided.

The Triune God and Human Suffering

IF we honestly acknowledge the persistence and power of evil in the world, can we still speak responsibly of divine providence? For Christians this question can be answered affirmatively if the lordship of God is consistently redescribed in terms of the gospel narrative whose center is the ministry, crucifixion, and resurrection of Jesus Christ. A Christian approach to the lordship of God in relation to the reality of suffering must therefore be explicitly christocentric and trinitarian.

A trinitarian understanding of God, rooted in the revelation of God in Christ, gives expression to the rich and differentiated expressions of God's relationship with the world as Father, Son, and Holy Spirit. God relates to creatures in ways appropriate to their own nature — to rocks and stones in one way, to plants in another way, to animals in another

29. Cone, *God of the Oppressed* (New York: Seabury Press, 1974), p. 183.

way, and to human creatures in still another way. God is present with the creatures both as co-agent and as co-sufferer.

As noted in an earlier chapter, subordinationism and modalism both cringe at the notion that God experiences struggle, suffering, and death. Trinitarian faith, however, recognizes that God's eternal being-in-love reaches out to the world. Far from being aloof, apathetic, and immutable, God freely becomes vulnerable out of faithful love for the world. The destructiveness of evil in creation can be overcome not by divine fiat but only by a costly history of divine love in which the suffering of the world is really experienced and overcome by God.

In an often-quoted passage Dietrich Bonhoeffer wrote, "The Bible directs us to God's powerlessness and suffering; only the suffering God can help."[30] When turned into a slogan that is thoughtlessly repeated, the profound meaning of this statement is obscured. Only a suffering God can help us, but the suffering God is the triune God whose holy, self-giving, victorious love is at work from the creation of the world to its completion.

Perhaps more than any other modern theologian, Jürgen Moltmann has emphasized the deep connection between the event of the cross and a trinitarian understanding of God. What transpires in this event can be grasped theologically only in trinitarian terms. According to Moltmann, in his passion and death the Son of God experiences suffering and death out of love for the world. But the Father who sent him on his salvific mission also experiences the grief of loss of the beloved Son. And from this event of shared suffering love comes the Spirit of new life and world transformation. All of the suffering of the world is encompassed in the affliction of the Son, the grief of the Father, and the comfort of the Spirit, who inspires courage and hope to pray and work for the renewal of all things.[31] Some of Moltmann's critics charge that he comes close to eternalizing suffering in God and thus to turning theodicy into ideology. But Moltmann's intention is clearly to couple emphasis on the suffering of the triune God with hope in the eschatological victory of divine love over all evil and the participation of creation in God's eternal joy.

The crucial point is that a trinitarian understanding of divine providence and the reality of evil is marked not by a pagan notion of

---

30. Bonhoeffer, *Letters and Papers from Prison* (New York: Macmillan, 1972), p. 361.

31. See Moltmann, *The Crucified God* (New York: Harper, 1974).

God as sheer almightiness but by the power of love at work in the ministry, cross, and resurrection of Jesus. Such a theology is centered not in a triumphalistic "logic of control" but in the "logic of trinitarian love" of the creator, redeemer, and consummator of the world. The power of the triune God is not raw omnipotence but the power of suffering, liberating, reconciling love. An emphasis on God as Trinity gives providence a different face. The God who creates and preserves the world is not an abstract omnipotence but the heavenly Father; the God who accompanies us is the incarnate, crucified, risen Lord; the God who rules all things works by Word and Spirit rather than by coercive force.

1. *The love of God the creator and provider is at work not only where life is sustained and enhanced but also where all that jeopardizes life and its fulfillment is resisted and set under judgment.*

According to the biblical witness, the God who created the heavens and the earth is the primary combatant in the struggle against all that threatens life. This is evident in the story of the exodus, the giving of the law, and the sending of the prophets to declare God's judgment on injustice and violence.

In the Gospels, Jesus' message of the coming reign of God and his ministry of liberation are presented as necessarily involving from the very outset conflict with forces that threaten to enslave and destroy human life. Jesus does the work of the one who sent him, healing the sick, blessing the poor, having table fellowship with social outcasts, and calling all people to repent and turn from the way of death to the way of life. Thus his journey to the cross is not a resignation to blind fate but a loving consent to the righteous will of the Father that evil be resisted to the bitter end. Far from being a basis for a Christian masochism, the passion story is, in J. B. Metz's words, a "dangerous memory" of God's passionate protest against the evil powers that resist the will of God and hold human life in bondage.[32]

Traditional theology has one-sidedly linked faith in providence with patience. It has often counseled the poor to accept their lot as ordained by God.[33] It has sometimes failed to help the sick and those who minister to them to distinguish between mere resignation and faithful resistance to disease. The providence of the triune God does not foster fatalism.

---

32. Metz, *Faith in History and Society: Towards a Practical Fundamental Theology* (New York: Seabury Press, 1980), pp. 65-67, 88ff.

33. See Calvin, *Institutes of the Christian Religion*, 1.16.6.

The divine *conservatio* works not only through our patience but also through our impatience and our courageous resistance to evil. For the Christian, evil is not to be resisted with evil, but it *is* to be resisted (cf. Rom. 12:21).

2. *The love of God the redeemer is at work both in the heights and in the depths of creaturely experience, both when the creature is strong and active and when it is weak and passive.* To confess that "in everything God works for good" (Rom. 8:28) is to affirm that God is ever faithful. Whether healthy or sick, whether sufferers or those who enter into solidarity with sufferers, we are not alone.

According to a Christian doctrine of providence, God does more than work for the preservation of life and against all that threatens it; God also intimately accompanies the creatures in their activity and in their suffering. The God of free grace does not will to act alone and does not will that the creatures should suffer alone. Although often overlooked by traditional theology, the divine *concursus* includes the fellow-suffering of God.

The Bible portrays God as mourning with the people of Israel in their affliction. According to the Psalmist, God is even present in the depths of Sheol (Ps. 139:8), an affirmation echoed in the statement of the Apostles' Creed that Christ descended into hell for us. In the Gospels Jesus is described as being moved with compassion for the crowds because they were harassed and helpless (Matt. 9:36). He healed the sick, had table fellowship with sinners, and associated freely with women and other marginalized people of his time. It is thus fully congruent with the biblical witness to say that God is present as co-sufferer with all the wretched of the earth, whether in cancer wards or in concentration camps. As revealed in the covenantal history with Israel and supremely in the history of Jesus Christ, God accompanies the creature not only in its activity but also in its agony and death.

God's accompanying of the creatures in their suffering is sheer grace, unexpected companionship in the depths of affliction. The presence of another in the experience of suffering is a gift; the presence of the compassionate God in the experience of suffering is a gift precious beyond words. In God's companionship with sufferers, they are affirmed in their dignity and value in spite of the assault on their being by disease or their victimization by others.

People who suffer are under attack not only by physical pain and social oppression but also by a sense of worthlessness and abandonment.

To speak of God's solidarity with victims is thus no mere rhetorical consolation but a life-renewing affirmation. The message that Jesus the Son of God has companionship with sinners and social outcasts, has compassion on the sick and the poor, and is finally crucified between two criminals outside the city gates has saving power because it overcomes the hopelessness and self-hatred that suffering at the hands of nature or our fellow creatures instills. Thus in the face of the fierce reality of evil, God's solidarity with victims is both judgment and grace — judgment on all insensitivity and inhumanity, and grace to all who are afflicted. God's companionship with the suffering is a touchstone of a Christian doctrine of providence as well as an apt description of the call to Christian discipleship.

3. *The love of God the sanctifier is at work everywhere, preparing for the reign of God, planting seeds of hope, renewing and transforming all things.* Wherever a new freedom breaks the chains of bondage in an individual life or in the experience of an entire people, wherever new community in love and freedom takes shape, wherever hope is inspired against all odds, the Spirit of God who changes all things is present and active. The appearance of new life in the midst of death, wherever it may occur, is a sign that God's Spirit is still at work, transforming the groaning creation and moving it toward the completion of God's purpose in Christ.

God does indeed rule and overrule the events of each human life and all of history. But the way in which God rules and overrules a world of freedom, sin, and suffering is by the power of Word and Spirit, the power of sacrificial love that is stronger than death. This is the way of the divine *gubernatio* in the light of the ministry, cross, and resurrection of Christ.

To be in Christ and to walk by the Spirit is to participate in the energy of God's liberating, sacrificial love and to be given new courage and hope by it. Only such love — the greatest gift of the Spirit (1 Cor. 13) — can transform a broken world and bring healing and renewal. Only such love can persist in the struggle against disease and devastation and resist the bitterness they can engender. Only such love can forgive sins — and without God's forgiveness of our sins and our forgiveness of the sins of others against us, no hope of real transformation of life is possible. Only the divine love that aims at new life and new community where all are free and all are affirmed can sustain the struggle for healing, justice, and peace without being captured by the spirit of hatred and revenge. Only a love that moves through the suffering of the cross to the promise of new life confirmed in the resurrection of Christ can be the basis of hope that does not despair in the face of personal and corporate disappointment and death. The Spirit is at work wherever there are such eruptions of new life, new community, and new hope in the midst of death, separation, and hopelessness.

At the conclusion of this chapter it is necessary to return to the point made at the beginning. All our reflections on providence and evil remain broken and incomplete. They do not amount to a theoretical solution to the "problem of evil." What I have proposed can be no more than a prolegomenon to a reconstructed doctrine of providence grounded in the christocentric and trinitarian faith of the church.

What is certain is that the biblical witness is far less interested in speculation on the origin of evil than on resistance to it in confidence of the superiority and ultimate victory of God's love. The solution to the problem of evil is more practical than intellectual. Here as elsewhere the real task of theology is to interpret the tradition of faith from its center in Jesus Christ so as to allow it to become once again a transforming power in human life. New Testament faith in the power of God's love in Jesus Christ is neither arrogant nor speculative. Its confessions that "in everything God works for good" (Rom. 8:28) and that "nothing can separate us from the love of God in Christ Jesus" (Rom. 8:38-39) are best understood not by ivory-tower theologians but by those who know what it means to suffer deeply. Evil is not yet conquered. Nevertheless, faith holds to the promise of God ratified in the resurrection of the crucified: "God will wipe away every tear from their eyes. Death will be no more; mourning and crying and pain will be no more" (Rev. 21:4). While the inauguration of the reign of God has happened "once for all" (Rom. 6:10) in Jesus Christ, believers know that they must continue to watch, pray, and struggle for God's new world in the company of all who are afflicted and cry for deliverance.

7

Humanity in the Image of God

WE HUMAN BEINGS ARE A MYSTERY TO OURSELVES. WE ARE RATIONAL and irrational, civilized and savage, capable of deep friendship and murderous hostility, free and in bondage, the pinnacle of creation and its greatest danger. We are Rembrandt and Hitler, Mozart and Stalin, Antigone and Lady Macbeth, Ruth and Jezebel. "What a work of art," says Shakespeare of humanity. "We are very dangerous," says Arthur Miller in *After the Fall.* "We meet . . . not in some garden of wax fruit and painted leaves that lies East of Eden, but after, after the Fall, after many, many deaths." The Bible and Christian theology give expression to this mystery of the honor and terror of human identity in three related affirmations: we are created in the image of God; we are sinners who deny and distort our created being; and we are forgiven sinners, surprisingly enabled to begin life anew by the grace of God and to move toward the final transformation of life promised in the resurrection of the crucified Jesus. Knowledge of God and knowledge of ourselves, we recall, are intertwined. We cannot know God without being shocked into new self-recognition, and we cannot know our true humanity without new awareness of who God is. In the following reflections I shall try to adhere to this fundamental principle of all theological reflection.

Interpretations of "Image of God"

ACCORDING to the first creation narrative in Genesis, God said, "Let us make humankind in our image, according to our likeness; and let

120

them have dominion over the fish of the sea, and over the birds of the air, and over the cattle, and over all the earth, and over every creeping thing that creeps upon the earth. So God created humankind in his image; in the image of God he created them; male and female he created them" (Gen. 1:26-27). The evocative phrase "the image of God" has been interpreted in a number of different ways in the history of Christian theology.

According to some interpreters, human beings in their upright stature have a *physical resemblance* to God. Some passages of the Bible are strikingly anthropomorphic in their depiction of God (e.g., Gen. 3:8ff.). However, with its more characteristic emphasis on the transcendence and hiddenness of God, the Old Testament lends little support to the notion of a physical resemblance between God and humanity and indeed explicitly forbids the making of all images of God (Exod. 20:4). Similarly, while the New Testament community speaks of beholding the glory of God in the face of Christ (2 Cor. 4:6; John 1:14), it is not Jesus' physical correspondence to God that is meant but the correspondence of his intention and action to that of God. John Calvin, while not flatly rejecting the interpretation of the image of God as physical resemblance, is obviously concerned about excessive anthropomorphism.[1]

Perhaps the dominant Western interpretation of the image of God has been that it resides in the *capacity to reason*. In the view of many classical theologians, including Thomas Aquinas, human rationality is a participation in and reflection of the divine logos or reason by which the world was created. This high valuation of human reason has an element of truth in it, but it has fostered an intellectualization of Christian anthropology. If the essence of being human is seen primarily in the process of abstract reasoning by which the physical dimension of life is transcended, a corresponding depreciation of the emotional and physical dimensions of human existence results.

A related but different interpretation focuses on the reference of the Genesis text to humanity's being given *dominion over the earth*. Humanity resembles God in its exercise of power and dominion over the other creatures. This interpretation of the image of God is often associated with a worldview in which all relationships are construed in hierarchical patterns: God rules over the world; the soul controls the body; men are the masters of women; and humanity dominates the other

---

1. Calvin, *Institutes of the Christian Religion,* 1.15.3.

creatures. As we have seen, this interpretation of the image of God in the modern era has often been used to legitimize the reckless exploitation of nature. Patriarchy, racism, and colonialism are other forms of this spirit of mastery over others. Against these views, I have contended that, rightly understood, the dominion entrusted to humanity, like God's own exercise of dominion, involves respect and care for others rather than mastery and manipulation of them.

Still other interpreters have emphasized *human freedom* as the meaning of the image of God. Modern philosophers and theologians have described the human being as free, self-determining, and self-transcending. Humans are both self-creators and creators of a world of culture that they superimpose upon the order of nature. In this free creative activity humans reflect the free creativity of God and thus become the image of God in the world. There is surely a measure of truth in this interpretation. But its serious limitations become evident in the frequency with which modern culture identifies the idea of freedom with mere independence from others or even self-gratification.

In agreement with numerous twentieth-century theologians, I would contend that the symbol "image of God" describes *human life in relationship* with God and with the other creatures. In the first story of creation in Genesis, the statement "God created humankind in his own image" is followed by "male and female he created them" (Gen. 1:27). To be human is to live freely and gladly in relationships of mutual respect and love. The existence of human creatures in relationship — the paradigmatic form of which is the coexistence of male and female — reflects the life of God who eternally lives not in solitary existence but in community. Thus the image of God is not to be construed primarily as a set of human faculties, possessions, or endowments. It expresses self-transcending life in relationship with others — with the "wholly other" we call God, and with all those different "others" who need our help and whose help we also need in order to be what God intends us to be.

The image of God is not like an image permanently stamped on a coin. It is more like an image reflected in a mirror. That is, human beings are created for life in relationships that mirror or correspond to God's own life in relationship. In light of the history of Jesus Christ, Christian faith and theology are led to interpret the *imago Dei* as an *imago Christi* and an *imago trinitatis*. Just as the incarnate Lord lived in utmost solidarity with sinners and the poor, and just as the eternal life of God is a triune society of love that is open to the world, so humanity in its coexistence with others is intended to be a creaturely reflection of the living God.

From the last few statements, it should be clear that the understanding of the image of God in Christian theology cannot be restricted to an exegesis of the first chapter of Genesis. The witness of this biblical text acquires new depths of meaning in the light of the gospel story. For Christian faith, Jesus Christ is the fullest expression of what God intends humanity to be. *This* human being is the "image of God" (2 Cor. 4:4; Col. 1:15). Hence the form of human life that we meet in Jesus the Christ will surely be the decisive factor in any Christian statement of what it means to be genuinely human.[2] That is not to say, of course, that a Christian understanding of human life can disregard other experiences and understandings of human existence. A theological anthropology cannot ignore the findings of cultural anthropology, psychology, sociology, and other disciplines. I mean simply that for Christian faith and theology, the life, death, and resurrection of Jesus will constitute the decisive norm of both true divinity *and* true humanity.

Created Humanity

I SHALL now attempt to describe the structures of human being in relationship with God and others under the headings of created humanity, fallen humanity, and new humanity in Christ.[3] In each case, I view the phenomena of human life from the perspective of Christian faith. I begin with three theses regarding human life as created by God.

1. *Human beings, created in God's image, are beings freely addressed by God and free to respond to God.* Although modern anthropologies, both philosophical and scientific, have cut themselves loose from traditional Christian doctrine, they have nevertheless had to wrestle with the question of the distinctiveness of humanity. Understandings of human life have often oscillated between an angelism on the one hand and a natu-

---

2. "In a sense," writes José Comblin, "the whole contribution of Christianity to a comprehension of the human consists of a single datum: Jesus Christ" (*Retrieving the Human: A Christian Anthropology* [Maryknoll, N.Y.: Orbis Books, 1990], p. 223). For Karl Barth's attempt to develop a rigorously christocentric anthropology, see *Church Dogmatics*, III/2.

3. Cf. Peter C. Hodgson, *New Birth of Freedom: A Theology of Bondage and Liberation* (Philadelphia: Fortress Press, 1976).

ralism on the other. By *angelism* I mean the tendency to view human beings as disembodied minds, and by *naturalism* I mean the tendency to consider human beings as creatures whose behavior is entirely predictable and requires no reference to such intangibles as free will, the soul, or relationship to God.

In the twentieth century, philosophical and cultural anthropologists have sought to identify and describe the uniqueness of being human without falling victim to either angelism or materialism. Thus they have spoken of the "self-transcendence" of humanity or its "world-openness" or its peculiar linguistic, cultural, and religious capacities and activities. To a far greater extent than other animals, human beings exist "exocentrically": they are drawn outside themselves by the objects of their experience and especially by their relations with other human beings. According to Wolfhart Pannenberg, "the concept of self-transcendence — like the concept of openness to the world which is to a great extent its equivalent — summarizes a broad consensus among contemporary anthropologists in their effort to define the special character of the human."[4]

The self-transcending freedom or openness to the world that is characteristic of human beings is, of course, not absolute but finite and conditioned. Human existence is embodied existence. We are psychophysical unities, not disembodied spirits. We do not simply *have* bodies: we *are* our bodies. Human flourishing cannot be separated from the satisfaction of bodily needs.

Moreover, human life is socially and historically embedded. We belong to particular societies, cultures, and historical epochs, and these help to define our human identity. What is most important to recognize, however, is that our particular embodiment and our historical embeddedness are not mere negative boundaries of human life; they are the condition of our finite but real freedom. No doubt genetics, history, and culture shape us in very definite ways: we did not choose to be born male or female, black or white, Russian or American. Nevertheless, we can choose to make something of these contingencies by turning them into occasions for the enrichment of life. While never absolute or unlimited, human freedom does involve the possibility of reshaping and redirecting the given of our experience.

From a Christian perspective, what I have been describing are

4. See Wolfhart Pannenberg, *Anthropology in Theological Perspective* (Philadelphia: Westminster Press, 1985), p. 63.

symptoms or signs of human life as created by God. Our embodied existence is no obstacle to fellowship with God. On the contrary, in its affirmation of the goodness of embodied life as created by God, in its teaching that the Word became flesh in Jesus Christ, and in its hope in the resurrection of the body, Christian faith shows itself to be "the most avowedly materialistic" of the world religions.[5]

According to Christian faith, our "exocentricity" and our finite but real freedom arise from the fact that, as embodied, historically conditioned beings, we are created for fellowship with God and are addressed by God. Our creator freely gives us life, calls us, covenants with us, and wants our response. God addresses human beings in their psychophysical totality and in their particular historical situations. God wants the free response of the whole person.

While the entire biblical witness portrays human beings as creatures to whom God speaks and from whom a response is awaited, this dialogical nature of human life in relation to God is made most explicit in the gospel story. Jesus is fully responsive to the will of God and the needs of others. His whole being and ministry are defined by total trust in and free obedience to the One he calls Abba and to the Spirit who commissions and empowers him for ministry. In the light of the humanity of Jesus, it becomes clear that being truly human means living in faithful response to the grace of God. God calls human beings out of isolation and into life in relationship. What God wants from human beings is not a mere echo or a mechanical reflex but a free and glad response. Human beings become free agents and historical subjects through being addressed by the living God who calls them to life in partnership and service. To be human is to live in response to the gracious initiative of God.

2. *Being created in the image of God means that humans find their true identity in coexistence with each other and with all other creatures.* Once again, the findings of modern philosophy, anthropology, and psychology can offer help to theological anthropology. They emphasize that human existence is not individualistic but communal. We become and stay human in the tension between personal identity and communal participation. We exercise our freedom not in complete isolation but in continuous interaction.

Human life depends upon ecological systems and structures of

5. William Temple, *Nature, Man and God* (London: Macmillan, 1956), p. 478. See also chap. 2 of Comblin's *Retrieving the Human.*

interrelationship. Stated briefly, we live in dialogue.[6] Long before we are conscious of the fact, we exist in response to and interaction with others. We have to learn to trust others even before we take a single step on our own. What is true for individual development is also true for life in the political order. When Aristotle defined human beings as "political" animals, he meant that human beings must live and develop their capacities in the intricate relationships and interdependencies of the *polis,* or city. Being truly human and living in community are inseparable. This wisdom is beautifully captured in an African proverb: "I am human only because you are human."[7]

When we read the biblical accounts of creation with care, we are struck by the importance of interrelatedness in the depiction of the creation as a whole and of human beings in particular. In the first creation story (Gen. 1), humanity is part of a cosmic order established by God; in the second creation story (Gen. 2), humanity is created out of earth and placed in a garden inhabited by many other creatures.

Most strikingly, according to the biblical witness, human beings are created in the image of God not as solitary beings but in the duality of male and female (Gen. 1:27). As created by God, we are essentially relational, social beings, and this essential sociality and co-humanity is unalterably concretized by our coexistence as men and women. We are created for life in community with others, to exist in relationships of mutual fidelity and mutual freedom in fellowship. This is the theological context of a Christian understanding of human sexuality.[8]

No theologian of the twentieth century has been more influential in the development of a theology of human relationality than Karl Barth. For Barth human existence is coexistence, and this fact is paradigmatically expressed in the coexistence of man and woman. Barth contends that if we ignore this particular expression of our co-humanity, if we obscure the significance of our existence in the mutual and reciprocal relationship of man and woman, we are likely to be tempted in every sphere of life by an inhuman vision of *homo solitarius.*

Barth makes three fundamental assertions in his elaboration of this

6. The classic modern statement of dialogical personalism is Martin Buber, *I and Thou* (Edinburgh: T. & T. Clark, 1958).

7. Allan Boesak, *Black and Reformed* (Maryknoll, N.Y.: Orbis Books, 1984), p. 51.

8. Barth uses the memorable phrase "Coitus without co-existence is demonic" (*Church Dogmatics,* III/4: 133).

theme: that human beings are *either* male *or* female and are called by God to affirm their particular sexual identity; that human beings are male *and* female and are called to find their human identity in mutual coordination with others who are both similar and yet also very different; and that human beings as male and female coexist in a definite and irreversible *order*.[9]

Each of Barth's assertions prompts questions. One might agree wholeheartedly that every human being should rejoice in his or her sexuality rather than deny or be ashamed or it, yet wonder whether Barth's first assertion must not be immediately qualified by warnings against all stereotypical descriptions of the differences between male and female. Again, Barth's second assertion must be carefully qualified to avoid the suggestion that unmarried individuals are any less called to a life in relationship with others than are those who marry.

But the most problematic of Barth's assertions is the third, which posits an irreversible order in the relationship between man and woman. Barth acknowledges that every word used to describe this order is "dangerous" because of the possibility of stereotype and ideology.[10] Nevertheless, he speaks of the man in this relationship as "A," as "leader," as "superordinate," as "above," and the woman as "B," as "follower," as "subordinate," as "below." Despite the many qualifications he makes, Barth's depiction of this irreversible order of the relationship of man and woman has been widely and rightly rejected.[11] It is not only unacceptable to contemporary sensibilities but profoundly incompatible with Barth's own basic methodological principle of rethinking all Christian doctrine in the light of Jesus Christ and the new community of mutual love and mutual service that has its basis in him.

Contrary to Barth, it should be noted that in the first creation story there is no mention of hierarchy, of superiority or inferiority, or an above and a below, of a first or a second in the relationship between man and woman. We are simply told that male and female together constitute the image of God. The implication is that human beings are to live in "partnership," as Letty Russell puts it, speaking, listening, living, and

9. Barth, *Church Dogmatics*, III/4: 149-81.
10. Barth, *Church Dogmatics*, III/4: 169.
11. See Paul Jewett, *Man as Male and Female* (Grand Rapids: William B. Eerdmans, 1975); Jürgen Moltmann, *God in Creation* (San Francisco: Harper & Row, 1985); Rosemary Radford Ruether, *Sexism and God-Talk: Toward a Feminist Theology* (Boston: Beacon Press, 1983).

working with each other.[12] The appropriate order of the relationship of man and woman in the light of the God of the gospel is not hierarchy but mutual love and mutual service (Gal. 3:28; Eph. 5:21). To employ a trinitarian analogy, the relationship of man and woman is "perichoretic," a life of mutual indwelling and reciprocal love.[13]

The Old Testament teaching that life-in-community is the clue to our human identity is confirmed and deepened by the gospel narrative. Jesus is depicted as the human-being-for-others, as someone who lives in the utmost solidarity with other men and women, especially with those who are defined by social and religious conventions as being outside community with God and God's chosen people. So to exist, says Christian faith, is to be the image of God, whose eternal triune love makes room for others and establishes richly diverse community.

3. *Being created in the image of God is not a state or condition but a movement with a goal: human beings are restless for a fulfillment of life not yet realized.* Human life is dynamic. It is propelled forward. Men and women are seeking, inquiring, expectant beings. In a familiar prayer, Augustine speaks of human life as ever on the move: "You have made us *toward* yourself, and our hearts are restless until they rest in you." This restlessness of the heart, the always unsatisfied drive in the human creature toward an ever-elusive goal, can be described phenomenologically, in the language of Wolfhart Pannenberg, as "world openness" or "openness to the future."

Whereas animals other than humans have drives or instincts that are triggered by definite needs or particular objects, in the case of human beings there is a restlessness that is virtually boundless. Humans have a surplus of drives. They search not only for physical and emotional satisfaction but for a meaning in life that is very difficult to define or pin down. Human restlessness finds no goal in this world that is satisfying for very long. Moreover, the nonhuman animals are rather strictly confined to their environment. By contrast, human beings readily transcend given environments, both natural and cultural. They create worlds of meaning that they continually transform, yet without ever finding full satisfaction. Humanity is created with a radical openness to the future, to the not-yet, to a fullness of life beyond every

12. Russell, *The Future of Partnership* (Philadelphia: Westminster Press, 1979).

13. Cf. Alexander McKelway, "Perichoretic Possibilities in Barth's Doctrine of Male and Female," *Princeton Seminary Bulletin* 7 (1986): 231-43.

personal, social, or cultural achievement.[14] Humans are radically temporal beings, never content merely to preserve the past or to endorse the present without reservation. Being human means being open to a future that we cannot definitively envisage and certainly cannot fully actualize. There is at work in all creation, but especially in human life, a "call forward" to new freedom.[15]

This dynamism of human life is a signal of what theology speaks of as human freedom for the coming reign of God. There are only hints of this dynamism of creaturely freedom in the Genesis creation narratives. God gives human creatures a commission or vocation. They are to have dominion over the earth which, I have contended, is rightly interpreted as a charge to responsible stewardship. To be a steward is to be a partner with God in caring for the world that God has created.

The witness of the prophets enriches the Genesis narrative by describing human life in relation to the future as a choice — either to enter into partnership with God to establish greater justice and peace in the world, or to court judgment and destruction. In the messianic tradition of the Old Testament, human life is to be lived in defiant expectancy of the time when God will make all things new. The gospel of Jesus Christ deepens this pervasive human expectation of fulfilled life. In proclaiming the coming of God's reign, in prophetic acts that boldly inaugurate its arrival, and above all in his cross and resurrection, Jesus brings new intensity to the orientation of human life to God's future and its promise of fulfilled and abundant life. Human beings have a destiny; they are created and redeemed to glorify and enjoy God forever.[16]

The structures of created freedom that I have outlined — responsibility before God, relationship to others, and openness to God's promise — are tightly bound to each other. Our created freedom is awakened by God's address to us, expanded by our coexistence with others very different from us, and directed toward a future fulfillment in the coming reign of God.

14. Cf. Wolfhart Pannenberg, *What Is Man? Contemporary Anthropology in Theological Perspective* (Philadelphia: Fortress Press, 1970).

15. See John B. Cobb, Jr., *God and the World* (Philadelphia: Westminster Press, 1969), pp. 42-66.

16. When allowances are made for its time-bound language, the answer to the first question of the Westminster Shorter Catechism remains valid: "Man's chief end is to glorify God and to enjoy him forever" (the Presbyterian Church [U.S.A.] *Book of Confessions* [Louisville: Office of the General Assembly, 1983], 7.001).

Fallen Humanity

THE Christian doctrine of human nature is starkly realistic. While affirming the good possibilities of human existence as created by God, theological anthropology takes with utter seriousness the profound disruption, disorder, alienation, brutality, and oppression that characterize the actual human condition. This condition is described in the assertion that we are "fallen," sinful creatures. Our alienation not only from God but also from our fellow creatures and ourselves is vividly portrayed in the Yahwist account of creation and fall (Gen. 2–3). The image of God in which humans were created is obscured and distorted by sin.

Our next task, then, is to describe in greater detail this condition of sin as a disruption of the created structures of human existence. If we are created for relationship with God who is wholly different from us and for relationship with other creatures who are relatively different from us, sin is a denial of our essential relatedness to those who are genuinely "other." We deny our dependence on the Other who is God and reject our need for our fellow creatures, most particularly those who seem so totally strange and "other" to us — the victim, the poor, the "leftover person."[17] Seen in this perspective, sin is "the depth of human intolerance for difference."[18] As in the case of the discussion of humanity as created, so in the description of fallen humanity, the embodiment of the image of God in Jesus Christ is our primary norm.

1. If being human in the image of God means life in free response to God who freely and graciously addresses us, then sin can be described as the denial of our relatedness to God and our need for God's grace. From this vantage point, sin is fundamentally *opposition to grace,* saying No to the invitation to be human in grateful service to God and in friendship with our fellow creatures. Sin is the great refusal to live thankfully and gladly by the grace of God that makes personal life in community with diverse others possible.

Thus we misunderstand the depth of sin if we see it only as a violation of a moral code; it is, instead, primarily the disruption of our relationship with God. As the Psalmist writes, "against you, you alone, have I sinned" (Ps. 51:4). This disruption of our relationship with God

17. See Comblin, *Retrieving the Human,* p. 55.
18. Susan Thistlethwaite, *Sex, Race and God: Christian Feminism in Black and White* (New York: Crossroad, 1989), p. 59.

that is the essence of sin appears in vastly different forms. Two warrant special mention. Sin may take the form of rejecting God's grace and absolutizing ourselves. Declaring our freedom to be infinite, we proclaim ourselves God. This is the sin of the prideful, titanic, egocentric self. Often referred to simply as the sin of pride, it is an *active and self-centered idolatry.* It is the refusal to recognize the limits of the self and the need that the self has of others. Finitude and limitation are not evil in themselves, but they are often the occasion of anxiety and insecurity. Instead of living by a grace whose source is beyond ourselves, in our insecurity we seek to be our own God.

But the disruption of our relationship with God may take a very different form. Rejecting God's grace, we may negate ourselves and may allow other creatures to take the place of God in our lives. This is the sin of self-rejection, and it frequently leads to a *passive and other-centered idolatry.* Sin as pride gets more than its share of attention in sermons and theological textbooks. Sin as self-hatred is often ignored. But while less sensational, this form of sin is no less a turning from the gracious God who calls us to freedom, maturity, and responsibility in community. In our self-loss we deliver ourselves over to shabby little idols and thus make of ourselves pitiful caricatures of what God intends for human life.

In recent years, feminist and other liberation theologians have rightly exposed the gross one-sidedness of traditional theology in its preoccupation with sin as pride.[19] They have insisted that, as human denial of grace, sin is not only insurrectionary and sensational but is also banal, mediocre, and totally uninventive. An adequate doctrine of sin will recognize that sin against the grace of God is not only titanic, Luciferian rebellion but also the timid, obsequious refusal to dare to be fully human by God's grace. Judas's act of betrayal is sin in its aggressive form; the fear and cowardice of the other disciples is sin in its passive form.

2. If being human in the image of God means responding to God's call to accept our freedom as a gift and to live freely with and for others, then sin in dealings with fellow creatures takes the dual form of *domination and servility,* self-exaltation and self-destruction. As in the description of sin in relation to God, so in the interpretation of sin in the relationship of human beings to each other, we must note the duality of

---

19. See Judith Plaskow, *Sex, Sin and Grace: Women's Experience and the Theologies of Reinhold Niebuhr and Paul Tillich* (Lanham, Md.: University Press of America, 1980).

forms. The description of sin as domination and mastery over others is familiar to many people. They may quickly identify as sinful the technocratic spirit that uses people and the world of nature merely to serve its own ends, the spirit of racial or national superiority that is prepared to go to any lengths to get rid of the obnoxious presence of those considered inferior, the spirit of boundless will-to-power that culminates in holocausts, genocidal war, and the destruction of entire species of creatures.

But sin in relation to others manifests itself not only in this will-to-power but also in the slide-into-powerlessness, in unquestioning passivity, self-dissipation, diffuseness, triviality, lethargy, and fear of initiative. "Sin," writes Rosemary Ruether, "has to be seen both in the capacity to set up prideful, antagonistic relations to others and in the passivity of men and women who acquiesce to the group ego."[20] We must be very careful here not to engage in the practice of "blaming the victim." The point is not, for example, to heap guilt upon battered women who feel helpless or to say that the poor are poor because they are lazy, as we hear so often from right-wing politicians. The point is that distorted interpretations of sin can help to lock victims into their victimization by undermining their will to break free.

Feminist psychiatrists and theologians have rightly objected to traditional doctrines of sin that focus exclusively on the experience of "making it," rising to positions of power, being assertive and aggressive. Such a description of sin is often curiously off-target for many women in all cultures but most especially for desperately poor and exploited peoples, women and men, of the Third World. The proper theological response to this distortion in the tradition is not the simplistic device of distributing the two forms of sin — domination and servility, self-exaltation and self-abnegation — to the masculine and feminine populations respectively. That would be a new kind of ideology that would cover up rather than expose the insidious workings of sin in concrete human experience. What is essential to see is that sin has many faces, that it is, as Mary Potter Engel observes, a kind of hydra, a monster that grows two new heads for every one that is severed.[21]

---

20. Ruether, *Sexism and God-Talk,* p. 164.

21. Engel, "Evil, Sin, and Violation of the Vulnerable," in *Lift Every Voice: Constructing Christian Theologies from the Underside,* ed. Susan Brooks Thistlethwaite and Mary Potter Engel (San Francisco: Harper & Row, 1990), p. 163.

As recent studies show, gender difference is not the only factor that needs to be taken into account in thinking about the many faces of sin. Race and class are also important factors. Thus what sin means in relation to the "survival" issues of most black women is different from what it means in relation to the "fulfillment" issues of white middle-class women.[22]

Although differences of sex, race, and class should inform our doctrines of sin, it remains true that human life as created and reconciled by God is denied not only by brutal domination of others but also by supine passivity, always letting the agenda be set by others, doing what everyone else wants you to do or tells you to do. Mere passivity is the breeding ground of totalitarianism and inhumanity no less than outrageous pride. Both men and women of all races and classes are to some extent vulnerable to both forms of sin. Neither the inordinate love of self nor the secret hatred of self is the exclusive property of any sex, race, or class of people. Still, given the one-sided emphases of traditional theologies of sin, the major effort in any rethinking of the doctrine of sin today must be to dismantle those interpretations that serve as a religious ideology inculcating passivity in the face of injustice. The human freedom and maturity intended by God is destroyed both where one lords it over another and where one fails to resist being lorded over.

3. If being human in the image of God means being open to the coming of God's kingdom, then sin is *the denial of human destiny as appointed by God.* Once again, to grasp rightly the assault on human openness to God's future, we must attend to its two contrary forms, analogous to pride and sloth, to domination and servility.

There is, on the one hand, the sin of indifference, apathy, and *resignation.* The kind of resignation I have in mind is an unqualified acquiescence to the hellish forces of human history. It is total doubt and cynicism about the possibility of anything really changing, or rather of any real change for the better. What's the use of talking, let alone trying to do something about the injustice, war, and oppression that we or others may be experiencing? Don't we simply have to get used to the fact that these things are the inevitable and triumphant realities

22. See Jacquelyn Grant, *White Women's Christ and Black Women's Jesus: Feminist Christology and Womanist Response* (Atlanta: Scholars Press, 1989), pp. 195-201; Thistlethwaite, *Sex, Race, and God,* pp. 77-91.

of the world? And so we become resigned to our fate. The future will be the same as today. As a result of this spirit of resignation, the little opportunities for greater justice, the small steps in the direction of peace and reconciliation, are mostly ignored or cynically dismissed. This attitude is false testimony because it denies our destiny as created in God's image and as heirs of God's promise in Jesus Christ.[23]

But on the other hand, no less a contradiction of our human openness to God's future is the sin of *presumption*, the violent effort to bring in God's kingdom with or without God. In this spirit of presumption and violence, there is limitless confidence in ourselves and our goodness, and a secret or open despair about the effectiveness of the gracious God who works through suffering love and whose power appears so weak and unpromising in comparison with guns and tanks.

The world today, and Christians within it, are caught between apathy about the evils that confront us and coercive ways of achieving our ends that seriously compromise or even destroy what we are struggling for. Either way we can close off the future to which we are directed by God our creator and redeemer.

4. The vexing question of the *origin of sin* has been a preoccupation of much traditional theological anthropology. Several of the proposed answers to this question are clearly in contradiction to the primary biblical emphasis on sin as rooted in the misuse or corruption of human freedom. The origin of sin is not to be traced back to bodily existence or human sexuality or some other natural condition of life, as has been the tendency in some strands of Christian theology. Nor is the origin of sin to be found in ignorance or underdeveloped rationality, as much Protestant liberal theology of the nineteenth century believed. Nor is the origin of sin to be located in a simplistic fashion in unjust social conditions, as is assumed by many social reform movements. Conditions of injustice are more properly seen as corporate expressions of human sinfulness rather than as its ultimate cause.

The biblical stories of the Garden of Eden and the "fall" of humanity (Gen. 2–3) are imaginative portrayals of the goodness of creation and the universality of sin rather than historical accounts of sin's origin. In the theological tradition there has been much fantasizing about the splendor of human existence in the golden age before the fall, but such

23. Cf. Karl Barth's description of the three primary forms of human sin: pride, sloth, and falsehood (*Church Dogmatics,* IV/1-3).

thinking is not encouraged by the biblical witness. The Bible is far more interested in affirming the reality of sin, the need of repentance, and the divine promise of redemption than in longing for the recovery of a lost paradise. As Paul's discussion of Adam and Christ in Romans 5:12ff. shows, the Bible is eschatologically rather than protologically oriented in its thinking about sin and redemption.

In the wake of the catastrophic evils of the twentieth century, all optimistic understandings of the origins and remedies of sin have been exposed as superficial. As much twentieth-century theological anthropology has emphasized — especially the still-powerful writings of Reinhold Niebuhr[24] — the origin and nature of sin cannot be adequately depicted without recourse to paradoxical statements. Among the most important of these paradoxes are the following.

a. Sin is a *universal condition,* but it is also a *self-chosen act* for which we are responsible. The traditional doctrine of original sin that stems from Augustine has frequently lost hold of this tensive relationship between universality and personal responsibility in the biblical portrayal of sin. When this happens, sin is reduced to fate and is no longer something for which all human beings are accountable.

b. Sin insinuates itself into all human action, including not only what is widely condemned as *evil* but also what is commonly praised as *good.* This is not to say that distinctions between good and evil are unimportant; instead, it is to emphasize that sin may be most seductively and demonically at work under the guise of doing good. Again it is Reinhold Niebuhr more than any other modern theologian who has emphasized this point.

c. Sin is a corruption of the *individual* person, but it is also active and powerful in public and *corporate* structures of life. In modern society there is an increasing tendency to privatize sin and to restrict it to the behavior of individuals. Against this tendency stands the biblical witness with its emphasis on an encompassing reign of evil and the solidarity of all humanity in the old "Adam" of sin and alienation.

While these paradoxes do not provide a rational explanation of the origin of sin, they more adequately characterize the reality of sin than theories that attempt such an explanation.

---

24. See especially Niebuhr's *The Nature and Destiny of Man* (New York: Scribner's, 1955).

New Humanity in Christ

CHRISTIAN freedom is the beginning of a new freedom from the bondage of sin and for partnership with God and others. This fresh start has its basis in the grace of God present in the new humanity of Jesus. He is the perfect realization of being human in undistorted relationship with God. He is also the human being for others, living in utmost solidarity with all people, and especially with sinners, strangers, the poor, the disadvantaged, and the handicapped. He is, furthermore, the great pioneer (Heb. 12:2) of a new humanity that lives in radical openness to God's promised reign of justice, freedom, and peace. In his total trust in God, Jesus acts as our great priest mediating God's grace and forgiveness to us; in his startling solidarity with all people, and especially with the poor and outcast, Jesus acts as our king, bringing us into the new realm of justice and companionship with the "others" from whom we have long been alienated; and in his bold proclamation and enactment of God's in-breaking reign, Jesus is the prophet par excellence who leads the way toward the future for which all creation yearns. To be Christian is to participate by faith, love, and hope in the new humanity present in Jesus.

1. If being in the image of God means living by the grace of God, and if such a relationship with God is denied by the sins of self-glorification and self-abnegation, *faith* is that simple trust and confidence in the benevolence of God extended to us in Jesus Christ by the Holy Spirit.[25]

As a free act of entrusting oneself to God, faith is the end of all idolatry, whether the idolatry of self or the idolatry of others in place of self. It is the glad response to the first commandment to love God with all our heart and mind and soul. Faith is the opposite of the will to absolute power that wants to lord it over others, but it is no less opposed to the indifferent slide into powerlessness that is coupled with total doubt about one's ability or right to have any power. As a free response to a trustworthy and gracious God who exercises power by making room for others, faith differs both from centering the world around oneself and

---

25. Cf. Calvin's definition of faith as "a firm and certain knowledge of God's benevolence toward us, founded upon the truth of the freely given promise in Christ, both revealed to our minds and sealed upon our hearts through the Holy Spirit" (*Institutes of the Christian Religion*, 3.2.7).

from rejecting oneself. The God of Christian faith does not envy human freedom. To the contrary, the gracious God empowers freedom, sets human beings on their feet, and calls them to maturity and responsibility. When freedom is based on God's grace, people are liberated both from the drive to absolutize their freedom and from the desire to escape from the responsibility of freedom by merely going along with the seductive currents of history and culture around them.

2. If being in the image of God means life in mutual, helpful relations with others, and if this created structure of human life is distorted both by despising others and by hating ourselves, both by a lust for power and by a spirit of servility, then *love* is that new way to be human with and for others supremely expressed in Jesus Christ and awakened in us by the Spirit.

Christian love is strong and free self-giving. It may express itself sacrificially, but it must be distinguished from destructive selflessness, passivity, or mere acquiescence to whatever pressures are at work in a situation. Like faith, Christian love is an act of freedom. It is the free practice of self-limitation and regard for the other. It is the willingness to assist others, especially those others called enemies, and to take the first step in promoting justice, mutuality, and friendship.

According to the biblical witness, love is not first of all a duty to be discharged; it is the joyful practice of a new freedom for others that we have received. Christian love is always preceded by God's surprising love for us. "We love because [God] first loved us" (1 John 4:19). We become and stay human when we acknowledge our solidarity with brothers and sisters everywhere, because this is the way we were created to live — not in self-important isolation from others but in deep and often costly solidarity with others. To be in Christ is to enter into an inclusive family where there are no more hierarchical orderings of Jews and Greeks, masters and slaves, males and females, but all are brothers and sisters (Gal. 3:28).[26] People whose freedom is rooted in God's grace and who are therefore surprisingly free to be with and for others — especially others called strangers and undesirables — will always be disturbing presences in a world that knows all too well both the coercive power of "masters" and the unresisting servility of "slaves" but scarcely can imagine the meaning of the "freedom of the glory of the children of God" (Rom. 8:21).

26. See the interpretation of this text by Elisabeth Schüssler Fiorenza, *In Memory of Her* (New York: Crossroad, 1983), p. 212.

3. If being in the image of God means a hunger for the coming of God's kingdom, and if this hunger is denied or distorted by the sins of despair and presumption, then *hope* is that new freedom toward God's future in which we live in the expectation of the fulfillment of the gracious promise of God in Jesus Christ by the power of the Holy Spirit.

The Spirit of Christ makes us restless for God's great conclusion of the work of creation and redemption. No less than faith and love, hope is an exercise of human freedom. It is using our creative imagination to envision a more just society. It is discerning the real possibilities for friendship and peace, and working as best we can to realize them. Christian hope is not utopian in the sense that we try to bring in God's kingdom ourselves. It is living and acting in a way that expresses confidence in God as Lord not only of the past and the present but also of the future. To live in Christian hope is to live in the expectation that by God's grace things can change, disease and death do not have the last word about human destiny, peace is possible, and reconciliation between enemies can occur, and we are called to pray and work toward these ends. To live in hope means to persevere in the struggle for justice and peace in the world even though good projects and noble causes will often meet with resistance and defeat. While never arrogant, Christian hope is confident in the ultimate victory of God.

Faith, love, and hope are thus the expressions of a new human freedom in relationship, a new way of being human in solidarity with others, made possible by the grace of God in Jesus Christ.

8

The Person and Work of Jesus Christ

WHILE A CHRISTIAN THEOLOGY MUST INCLUDE MANY TOPICS, THE decisive basis and criterion of all that it says is the person and work of Jesus Christ. This explains why in preceding chapters when I spoke of God, creation, humanity, sin, and evil, I looked to the revelation of God in Christ as the decisive clue. Likewise, when in subsequent chapters I take up the doctrines of the Holy Spirit, Christian life, the church, and Christian hope, it will again be my intent to anchor my thinking in the biblical witness to the purpose and activity of God made known in Christ. Theological reflection on any topic is *Christian* to the extent that it recognizes the centrality of Jesus Christ and the salvation he brings. For good reason the second article of the Apostles' Creed (which begins, "And [I believe] in Jesus Christ, [God's] only Son, our Lord . . .") is by far the longest. Neither the first article on God the creator nor the third article on the Holy Spirit and the church has any distinctively Christian content apart from its relationship to the second article. For Christian faith "the Father Almighty, Maker of Heaven and Earth" is identified as the Father of our Lord Jesus Christ, and "the Holy Spirit" is primarily defined as the Spirit that empowered Jesus and continues his work in the world. Christology is not the whole of Christian doctrine, but it is the point from which all else is illumined.

Problems in Christology

WHO is Jesus? How does he help us? Stated as simply as possible, these are the questions that have traditionally been discussed in theology under

139

the headings of Christology (the doctrine of the person of Jesus Christ) and soteriology (the doctrine of his saving work). In every age the church has confessed that Jesus is Lord and that he brings salvation. Many Christians today, however, are far from certain about the meaning and truth of these affirmations. Among the hard questions that every serious Christology must face in our time are the following.

1. One question concerns the intelligibility of the ancient Christological creeds. The Nicene Creed speaks of the Son as being "of one substance" *(homoousios)* with God the Father, and Chalcedon affirms that Jesus Christ is "fully divine and fully human," two natures united in one person *(hypostasis)* without confusion, change, division, or separation. For many scholars as well as laypeople these classical Christological formulas are cast in a conceptuality that is obscure, abstract, and far removed from the experience of faith. In addition, critics say that the Christology of the old creeds comes close to losing sight of the concrete historical reality of Jesus of Nazareth in a maze of speculation. Even theologians who disagree with these critics will acknowledge that classical Christology must be reinterpreted and not merely repeated.

2. Another challenge to Christology comes from the rise of historical consciousness and the application of the historical-critical method to the Gospels. During the nineteenth century, historical-critical exegesis confidently expected to discover the "real Jesus" behind the encrusted dogmas of the church and the allegedly biased faith confessions of the New Testament community. Albert Schweitzer, who wrote the history of this movement, declared it a tremendous act of courage that nevertheless had to be judged a failure. Schweitzer concluded that Jesus could not be made attractive and accessible to the modern age as so many biblical historians attempted to do. When these investigators peered down into the well of history, they managed to see only their own faces reflected in the water below. According to Schweitzer, Jesus was an eschatological prophet whose message of the imminent coming of the reign of God is utterly strange to the modern world.[1]

In recent decades, more sophisticated and chastened "quests of the historical Jesus" have been launched. While agreeing that a biography of Jesus is impossible — given the nature of the Gospels as documents of faith and proclamation — many New Testament scholars now hold that an attitude of complete skepticism regarding historical knowledge of Jesus

---

1. Schweitzer, *The Quest of the Historical Jesus* (New York: Macmillan, 1961).

is both unjustified and dangerous. Such skepticism easily slips into docetism or into a total identification of Jesus with the life and teaching of the church. An important part of the general agreement among these scholars, which will inform my later constructive position, is that the center of Jesus' proclamation is the coming reign of God and that he enacts this reign in an anticipatory way by his own love of God and his astonishing freedom to bless the poor, heal the sick, and extend forgiveness and table fellowship to sinners.

3. A third problem of modern Christology, closely related to the second, is the awareness of the remarkable variety of pictures of Jesus in the New Testament. Added to this are the practically limitless interpretations of Jesus in the history of Christian theology and in Western culture generally. This plurality of Christologies is both blessing and bane. It is a blessing because we now have available a far richer array of understandings of Jesus Christ and his saving work than the church of the past had. This gives us a greater appreciation of the fullness of salvation in Christ and heightens our awareness of our freedom and responsibility to reinterpret the meaning of Christ for our own time and place.

But there is another, more problematic side to the proliferation of modern pictures of Christ. As Hans Küng has noted, there are so many different Christs — the Christs of piety and secularity, of ancient dogma and modern ideology, of dominant culture and counterculture, of political reaction and social revolution, of classical and popular literature, of religious art and kitsch — that the question Which Christ is the true Christ? becomes unavoidable and urgent.[2] If it is true that diversity in Christology is not something to be feared, since it has its basis in the New Testament witness itself, nevertheless enriching diversity must be distinguished from an anything-goes relativism. The latter would mean the loss of Christian identity and the inability to distinguish authentic faith in Christ from ideological distortions.

4. A fourth problem of Christology today is what often goes under the name of the scandal of particularity. In one form or another this problem has always confronted Christian faith and theology. The Apostle Paul speaks of the message of Christ crucified as scandalous and foolish to most of its hearers (1 Cor. 1:23). In addition to this perennial scandal of the cross, however, other scandals of particularity confront the church and Christology today. Feminist theologians, for example, contend that

---

2. Küng, *On Being a Christian* (New York: Doubleday, 1976), pp. 126ff.

patriarchal theology has in effect replaced the true scandal of the gospel with the scandal of the ontological necessity of Jesus' maleness.[3] Black and Third World theologians ask whether the church in the First World — mostly white and relatively affluent — takes at all seriously the scandal of Jesus' ministry to the poor and the oppressed.[4] Other theologians, concerned to foster new understanding and cooperation among the world religions, insist that we must renounce the false scandal of Christological imperialism and develop a "nonexclusive" and even a "nonnormative" Christology.[5]

Principles of Christology

As a guide to our exploration of the doctrine of the person and work of Christ in relation to the problems just outlined, we offer the following working principles:

1. *Knowledge of Jesus Christ is not simply "academic" or historical knowledge; it is faith knowledge.* It has to do with human salvation. Faith in this person is not just knowing about him but trusting in him and being ready to follow him.[6] The biblical witness and the proclamation of the church do not intend simply to inform us about the fact that a man named Jesus once lived a noble life, taught precious truths, and died a tragic death. When reference is made in the Bible and in church proclamation to Jesus, it is to declare that his life, death, and resurrection are "for us," "for many," "for all" (Mark 10:45; Rom. 5:8; 8:32; 1 Cor. 15:22). What the Bible and the church want primarily to affirm about this person is that in him God brings forgiveness, liberation, reconciliation, and new life to the world. A soteriological dimension is present in every layer of New Testament tradition and in all the classical Christological affirmations of the church. The real "point" of Christology, therefore, is neither to satisfy historical curiosity nor to engage in idle specu-

---

3. See Rosemary Radford Ruether, *To Change the World: Christology and Cultural Criticism* (New York: Crossroad, 1981), pp. 45-56.

4. See Jon Sobrino, *Jesus in Latin America* (Maryknoll, N.Y.: Orbis Books, 1987).

5. See Paul F. Knitter, *No Other Name? A Critical Survey of Christian Attitudes toward the World Religions* (Maryknoll, N.Y.: Orbis Books, 1985).

6. Calvin asserts that the faith that embraces Christ is "more of the heart than of the brain, and more of the disposition than of the understanding" (*Institutes of the Christian Religion,* 3.2.8).

lation; it is to affirm that in this Jesus, God is decisively present and graciously active for the salvation of the world.[7]

2. *Jesus Christ cannot be properly understood in a vacuum; he can be rightly identified only within the context of God's purpose and activity in the history of the people of Israel and throughout the cosmos.* The New Testament proclaims that Jesus is the fulfillment of the covenant of God with his people and thus presupposes an understanding of the history and hope of Israel.[8] Still more comprehensively, Jesus is seen as the decisive embodiment of the eternal Logos of God who everywhere and always impinges upon human life in the world both in grace and in judgment (cf. John 1:1-14). Christology has a cosmic as well as a historical setting.[9] It must not be reduced to a concern simply for "my salvation," although it certainly includes that concern. Nor should its cosmic dimensions be smothered by ecclesiocentric attitudes. In this sense, a "nonexclusive" Christology is demanded by the scriptural witness itself.

3. *The doctrines of the person and work of Christ are inseparable.* While this distinction is used for convenience, it can be seriously misleading. We cannot speak meaningfully of anyone's identity, and certainly not of Jesus' identity, apart from that person's life act.[10] Personal identity is constituted by a person's history, by his or her life story. The early church proclaimed who Jesus is by telling his story. It is in the telling of the story of Jesus, in the narration of the whole gospel — his message, ministry, passion, and resurrection — that we hold together the person and work of Jesus. That the New Testament does not split apart his person and work is evident in its interpretation of his name: "Call his name Jesus, for he will save his people from their sins" (Matt. 1:21).

4. *Every understanding and confession of Jesus Christ grows out of a particular situation and both reflects and speaks to particular needs and aspirations.* We must learn from understandings of Christ that are shaped by histories of suffering and hope very different from our own.[11] In the

---

7. Cf. Schubert Ogden, *The Point of Christology* (New York: Harper & Row, 1982).

8. Cf. Paul Van Buren, *Christ in Context* (San Francisco: Harper & Row, 1986).

9. The cosmic context of Christology has been given special attention in process theology. See W. Norman Pittenger, *The Word Incarnate* (New York: Harper, 1959); and N. M. Wildiers, "Cosmology and Christology," in *Process Theology,* ed. Ewert H. Cousins (New York: Newman Press, 1971), pp. 269-82.

10. This is a prominent feature of Barth's christology (see *Church Dogmatics,* IV/1-3) and of recent narrative Christology.

11. This is a major emphasis of liberation Christologies. See James H. Cone, *God*

New Testament, there is already a plurality of Christologies, some emphasizing more the teaching of Jesus (e.g., the Q document, the Gospel of Matthew), some emphasizing more the passion of Jesus (e.g., the Gospel of Mark, the letters of Paul), some emphasizing more the glory and triumph of the resurrected Lord (e.g., the Gospel of John). The one unsubstitutable Christ is inexhaustibly rich and gathers the whole range of human need and experience to himself. New situations call for new confessions of Christ, for he wills to be acknowledged as Lord and Savior in every time and place. Christians have both the freedom and the obligation to confess Christ in appropriate and relevant ways in their own specific contexts, in continuity with the New Testament witness and in conversation with the particular experiences, needs, and hopes of people here and now.

5. *The living Jesus Christ is greater than all of our confessions and creeds and surpasses all of our theological reflection on him.* The risen Lord continually upsets our neat categories and classifications of him and the salvation he brings. "Who do you say that I am?" Jesus asks. "You are the Christ," Peter correctly replies. But in the next moment, when Jesus says that he must suffer and die to do the Father's will, Peter resists Jesus and shows that his previous understanding of him as the Christ is far from adequate (see Mark 8:27-35). Jesus Christ not only has come, and is present, but is also still to come (Rev. 1:4). No Christology can claim to have exhausted the breadth and depth of the mystery of Christ. While the Christological creeds of the ecumenical church are milestones of the tradition and deserve our serious attention and respect, they are not absolute. As Karl Rahner states — with the two-natures Christology of the Creed of Chalcedon (A.D. 451) in mind — the church's creeds are not the final word for our theological reflection but points of departure.[12] We may have to quarrel with the language and conceptuality of the classical creeds even while, as members of the same community in which these creeds arose, we will certainly want to be instructed by them. Our faith is in God revealed in Christ and not in a particular theological

---

of the Oppressed (New York: Seabury Press, 1975), pp. 108-37; Jon Sobrino, *Christology at the Crossroads* (Maryknoll, N.Y.: Orbis Books, 1978); Rosemary Radford Ruether, *Sexism and God-Talk: Toward a Feminist Theology* (Boston: Beacon Press, 1983), pp. 116-38; Jacquelyn Grant, *White Women's Christ and Black Women's Jesus: Feminist Christology and Womanist Response* (Atlanta: Scholars Press, 1989), pp. 195-222.

12. Rahner, "Current Problems in Christology," in *Theological Investigations,* vol. 1 (Baltimore: Helicon Press, 1965), pp. 149-200.

system or Christological formulation. We are to trust and obey Christ in life and in death, but that is something very different from absolutizing a particular doctrine of Christ, whether ancient or modern.

Classical Affirmations of the Person of Christ

IN every Christological affirmation, reference is made to the historical person Jesus of Nazareth, and some theological claim is made about him, often in the form of a special title. The earliest Christian confessions took the form "Jesus is the Christ" (Mark 8:29) and "Jesus is Lord" (1 Cor. 12:3). In these confessions, Jesus is recognized as genuinely human, and he is said to have a special relation to God and a special role in the work of salvation. In the following presentation, I remain in broad agreement with these early Christological confessions and with the intent of Chalcedon's affirmations of Jesus Christ as "fully human, fully divine." But I shall also recognize some important deficiencies of the classical Christological tradition and shall make proposals for its reformulation.

1. Jesus is *fully human*. While the New Testament does not give us materials for a biography of Jesus, there can be no doubt that it refers to a concrete human being who is like us in all respects, except in that alienation from and hostility to the grace of God which is the essence of sin. This means, for example, that Jesus did not know everything. Like every human being, he experienced finitude and limitation. As a first-century Jew, he was deeply influenced by the culture and religious heritage of his people. He grew and matured physically, intellectually, and spiritually. An itinerant preacher of the coming kingdom of God, he had no home of his own. He experienced hunger and thirst. He became tired. He knew from experience the pain of grief when a loved one dies. He had real, rather than make-believe, temptations. He knew both acclaim and rejection. In the end he was betrayed, arrested, humiliated, tortured, and finally crucified.

If we acknowledge that confession of the full humanity of Jesus necessarily implies, among other things, his intellectual and physical limitations, his experience of the strong emotions of anger, grief, and compassion, his suffering, and finally his death, we thereby refuse to go the way of the Docetists who were embarrassed by all this. In their view, Jesus' humanity was only an "appearance": he did not really suffer or die. While some Docetists even contended that Jesus never left footprints and never blinked his eyes, the mainstream of the Christian community has resisted all such denials of the full humanity of Jesus. The basic objection to any crass or subtle qualification or reduction of the full humanity of Jesus is soteriological. In the memorable phrase of Gregory of Nazianzus, "That which he has not assumed, he has not healed."[13] If God in Christ is not present to us in the depths of our human finitude, misery, and godforsakenness, then all that this person said and did cannot be a saving event for us who know finitude, misery, and godforsakenness all too well. If God in Christ does not enter into solidarity with the hell of our human condition, we remain without deliverance and without hope. For the classical tradition the full humanity of Jesus is the precondition of the inclusiveness of his salvation.

To this point, however, our affirmation of the full humanity of Jesus has been, like the classical tradition, very general and insufficiently informed by the gospel narrative. According to that narrative, Jesus was a *disturbing* and revolutionary human being. He proclaimed the coming reign of God and acted in God's name with an astonishing freedom. He spoke of God as *Abba,* "dear father," taught his hearers to love their enemies, and announced God's grace to sinners and the poor. He summarized his mission by saying, "the Spirit of the Lord is upon me, because he has anointed me to bring good news to the poor; he has sent me to proclaim release to the captives, and recovery of sight to the blind, to let the oppressed go free, to proclaim the year of the Lord's favor" (Luke 4:18-19).

Jesus' proclamation and ministry transgressed the supposed boundaries of God's grace and thus shocked the sensibilities of the guardians of religious tradition. He blessed the poor, healed the sick, befriended women, and had table fellowship with sinners. His words and actions seemed blasphemous to his critics. Further, his announcement of the in-breaking reign of God made him vulnerable to the charge of being a political conspirator. The disturbing ministry of Jesus thus led to his crucifixion as a blasphemer and a possible threat to imperial rule.[14]

Jesus is indeed fully human, but his is a new humanity. The inti-

---

13. Gregory of Nazianzus, Epistle 101, in *Christology of the Later Fathers,* Library of Christian Classics, vol. 3, ed. Edward R. Hardy (Philadelphia: Westminster Press, 1954), p. 218.

14. Cf. ll. 19-20 of the Presbyterian Church (U.S.A.) Brief Statement of Faith: "Unjustly condemned for blasphemy and sedition, Jesus was crucified. . . ."

macy of his relation with God and his solidarity with sinners and the oppressed are unique and shocking. He is the human being radically free for God's coming kingdom and therefore radically free for communion with and service to the neighbor. Like the father in the parable of the prodigal child, Jesus extends the welcoming love of God to those who are thought least deserving of it (Luke 15:11ff.). Thus when Christians call Jesus fully human, the claim is not simply that he is *a* human being but that he is the norm and promise of a new humanity in relation to God and to others.

It is with this understanding of the full humanity of Jesus that we should take up the serious questions that have been raised for Christology by feminist theologians. Can a male be the savior of women, or does the particularity of Jesus' sex preclude him from being a universal savior? This question obviously grows out of the history of oppression that women have experienced and that has all too often been supported in the church by direct or indirect reference to the maleness of the one who is said to be the norm of full humanity. If true humanity is by definition masculine, then women must always be less than fully human. A response to this concern must emphasize, as a number of feminist theologians do, that the New Testament sees the full humanity of Jesus not in his maleness but in his shocking love, his prophetic criticism, his inclusive freedom for God and for others.

No doubt the assumptions of patriarchal culture more or less pervade the biblical witness as a whole. While the message and ministry of Jesus are not immune from this influence, they also contain profound challenges to patriarchy. In his parables of the reign of God (which include not only the story of the forgiving father [Luke 15:11ff.] but also the story of the woman who searches for her lost coin [Luke 15:8ff.]), in the new imagery he uses of God and of his own ministry (Luke 13:34), in his friendship with women, and in his advocacy of the cause of the poor and the oppressed, Jesus' proclamation, life, and death were prophetic and scandalous. Hence, a Christology faithful to the biblical witness will always have a critical and subversive dimension; it will be iconoclastic in relation to conventional understandings of God and the support that these understandings give to oppressive attitudes and relationships.

More specifically, it is a complete distortion of the humanity of Jesus as depicted in the gospel story to claim that maleness is an onto-logical necessity of the incarnation of the Word of God or that because

Jesus was male women should not be ordained to the office of ministry.[15] If we follow the description of Jesus in the gospel story, we will surely agree that the theological significance of the humanity of Jesus resides not in his masculine gender but in his unconditional love of God and his shockingly inclusive love of others. This and this alone makes the life and death of Jesus a radiant expression of the eternally self-giving, other-affirming, community-forming love of the triune God.

2. Jesus is not only fully human but also *fully divine*. Classical Christology asserts the divinity of Jesus Christ without reservation and does so in faithfulness to the New Testament witness: "God was in Christ reconciling the world to himself" (2 Cor. 5:19). If this affirmation means anything, it means that what Jesus does and suffers is also the doing and suffering of God. The preaching of Jesus is more than the word of a prophet; in this preaching God decisively addresses us. When Jesus forgives sinners, this is not just the pardon of a human being; it is also God's forgiveness expressed and embodied in this human being. Jesus' companionship with the poor and sick is not just a caring human being's companionship with suffering fellow creatures; it is God's solidarity with these people made concrete in what this human being does and suffers. Jesus' passion and death for us is not just the martyrdom of another innocent victim in an unjust world; it is also God's suffering, God's taking death into the being of God and there overcoming it for our salvation. The resurrection of Jesus from the dead is not the victory of a solitary human being over death; it is God's victory over sin and death for us all in the raising up of this man Jesus.

God acts, suffers, and triumphs in and through Jesus. In Jesus Christ we do not have less than God's own presence in our humanity. In this person the eternal God suffers and acts for our salvation. However strange their language, this is the point of the ancient creeds of Nicea and Chalcedon, which declare that Jesus Christ is "of one substance" with the Father and that he is "fully God, fully human." The concern is again soteriological. No human being alone can save us. If Jesus Christ is not God with us, if the life and forgiveness that he offers are not God's own

---

15. "An understanding of the incarnation in terms of biological gender positivism does not square with the tradition according to which the *humanity* and not the *masculinity* of Jesus has saving significance," says Elisabeth Schüssler Fiorenza ("Lk. 13:10-17: Interpretation for Liberation and Transformation," *Theology Digest* 36 [Winter 1989]: 303-19). Jacquelyn Grant contends that "The significance of Christ is not his maleness but his humanity" (*White Women's Christ and Black Women's Jesus*, p. 220).

life and forgiveness, if his self-giving, sacrificial love poured out for our sake is not *God's* own love, then he cannot be Savior and Lord. Christian faith cannot compromise either on the full humanity or on the full deity of Jesus Christ.

But if this Jesus is God with us, then a radical conversion of our ordinary understandings of the words "God" and "Lord" is required. This is not made explicit by the Chalcedon creed. As in the case of the confession of Christ's full humanity, Chalcedon speaks of his divinity in a rather formal and abstract manner that fails to bear the specific imprint of the gospel narrative. This narrative does not invite us to think first of what everyone knows divinity to be and then to recognize in Jesus the presence of divinity. Instead, it describes the coming of God's Word, or God's Son, in the actions and sufferings of a servant who humbles himself and becomes obedient even to the death on a cross (Phil. 2:5ff.). Just as the gospel story surprisingly redefines the meaning of true humanity by describing Jesus' intimate relation with God and his shocking fellowship with sinners and the poor, so this story unexpectedly redefines the meaning of true divinity and genuine lordship by depicting the actions and sufferings of a humble servant who gives his life unconditionally for the renewal of the world. Christian faith sees no less than God in the transforming, suffering, and victorious love at work in Jesus' ministry, cross, and resurrection. But precisely in this person divinity and lordship are radically redefined in terms of a surprising love that welcomes sinners, makes itself vulnerable, and is shockingly partisan toward the weak, the poor, and the outcast.[16]

3. The affirmation that Jesus is fully human and fully divine points to the *mystery of the unity of his person*. According to classical Christological doctrine, the two natures of Christ are "hypostatically" united in one person without confusion, change, division, or separation. Critics have charged that this doctrine leaves us with the impression of the artificial joining of two discrete objects or things, like two boards that are glued together. Even theologians who are in basic agreement with Chalcedon have called for a rethinking and restatement of its teaching.

Perhaps it would help if we were to speak not of static "natures"

---

16. In *White Women's Christ and Black Women's Jesus*, Jacquelyn Grant argues that black Christians do not have the white liberal's problems with confessing Jesus as God and Lord. For blacks Jesus is "the divine co-sufferer, who empowers [black people] in situations of oppression" (p. 212).

but of living subjects in relationship. Then the question of Christology could be rephrased: How can two subjects be perfectly united? How can there be two agents of the same act? In his book *God Was in Christ,* Donald Baillie makes the point that while the personal unity of the humanity and divinity of Christ is a "paradox" that we can never fully grasp, nevertheless we can know something of its reality by analogy from our own Christian experience. At the heart of Christian existence is the experience of divine grace that precedes and enables human freedom. In every age Christians have testified that we are most truly human, most fully ourselves, most profoundly free when we live in response to God's grace. Divine grace and human freedom are not mutually exclusive.[17]

Baillie's paradox of grace emphasizes the prevenience of God's activity yet also underscores its person-making and freedom-granting power. Other analogies for thinking about the union of God and humanity in Christ might be suggested. We might think, for example, of a close friendship, or of a loving marital relationship, in which a deep unity of will, understanding, and disposition may sometimes be experienced. Such experiences fall far short of the unique union of God and humanity in Christ, but they may serve to remind us that personal existence is life in depth of relationship, not in being closed within oneself. The most appropriate, yet always inadequate, analogies for the union of God and humanity in Christ come from the sphere of personal relationships where there is mutual love and mutual self-limitation for the sake of the other.

Pursuing this line of thought, we might speak of the "kenotic unity" of God and humanity in Jesus Christ.[18] The idea of *kenosis* comes from the Christological hymn of Philippians 2:5ff. *Kenosis* (literally, "emptying") is the action of free self-limitation and free self-expenditure. In Jesus Christ, God and humanity are united in mutual self-giving love. It is a union of the Spirit in which there is reciprocal self-limitation and total openness of each to the other. The divinity and humanity of Jesus are neither confused (monophysitism) nor separated (Nestorianism). As the Word of God and the man Jesus are totally oriented to each other in love, a unique unity of free divine grace and free human service occurs.

17. Baillie, *God Was in Christ* (New York: Scribner's, 1948), pp. 106-32. "Human nature, at the contact of God, does not disappear," writes John Meyendorff; "on the contrary, it becomes fully human" (*Christ in Eastern Christian Thought* [Washington: Corpus Books, 1969], p. 64).

18. See Lucien J. Richard, *A Kenotic Christology* (Lanham, MD.: University Press of America, 1982).

Taking Philippians 2:5ff. as our guide, the unity of divinity and humanity in Jesus Christ is best described as a "kenotic" union rooted in the Spirit of mutual self-surrendering love.

It must be emphasized that the act of *kenosis* as described above does not entail a negation or diminution of God's nature (as earlier kenotic Christologies mistakenly taught). As I stressed in my discussion of the doctrine of the Trinity, it is the very nature of God to be self-giving, other-affirming, and community-creating. Life in mutuality and fellowship does not diminish but defines the reality of God. In the eternal life of God there is interaction and exchange between "Father" and "Son" in the uniting love of the "Spirit." The unity of the triune God is a union of reciprocal, self-giving love.

The trinitarian communion of love is thus both ground and prototype of the union of true God and true humanity in Jesus Christ.[19] In the incarnation, God and humanity are fully free and fully united in love. Each is totally free for and unconditionally faithful to the other. God elects Jesus as God's "chosen," God's "beloved" (Matt. 12:18); in turn, Jesus is entirely devoted to God and freely subordinates his will to God's (Luke 22:42). In perfect mutual love, divinity and humanity are distinct yet united in Jesus Christ. In him the perfect love of God and a perfect human response to that love are united. While faint analogies of the unity of divinity and humanity in the incarnate Lord may be found in what Baillie calls the "paradox of grace" in Christian life, or in our experiences of intimate personal relationship, the identity of Jesus Christ as described by Scripture and creed is unique and unsubstitutable. The relationship of God to Jesus and of Jesus to God has its basis and fullest analogy in the eternal exchange of love in the life of the triune God.

Classical Interpretations of the Work of Christ

WHILE the ministry, death, and resurrection of Christ are all essential aspects of his liberating and reconciling work, the cross has been the center of attention in most doctrines of atonement in Western theology. The New Testament uses many different metaphors to express what

---

19. According to Walter Kasper, "In the last resort, the mediation of God and man in Jesus Christ can only be understood in the light of Trinitarian theology" (*Jesus the Christ* [New York: Paulist Press, 1976], p. 249).

happened in Christ's death for us. We find financial, legal, military, sacrificial, and other metaphors, all of which contain treasures of meaning. Despite the familiarity of these metaphors, they can still surprise us with fresh insight.[20] Some of the New Testament metaphors of the work of Christ have been expanded into elaborate theories of atonement. While no single atonement doctrine has received ecumenical approval, there have been several prominent theories of atonement in Christian theology.[21]

1. One of these is called the cosmic conflict or *Christ the Victor* theory. This theory develops the military metaphor found in some New Testament passages (e.g., Col. 2:15). According to this view, the work of atonement is a dramatic struggle between God and the forces of evil in the world. In the incarnate Lord, divinity is deeply hidden. Under the veil of his humanity, Christ battles with the demons, the devil, and all the principalities and powers that hold human beings captive. By his cross and resurrection, Christ decisively defeats these powers and thus frees their captives.

While this theory helpfully emphasizes the reality and power of evil forces that hold humanity in bondage, and while it correctly stresses the costliness and assurance of God's victory, its limitations are equally evident. It is especially misleading if its imagery is taken literally. This results in reducing the humanity of Jesus to a mere disguise to fool the evil powers, in making believers mere spectators of a cosmic struggle that takes place over their heads, and in denying the persistence of the power of evil and sin in history and in our own lives.

2. Another influential theory of atonement is the Anselmian or *satisfaction* theory. It is rooted in biblical passages that suggest vicarious suffering as the way by which humankind is redeemed (e.g., Isa. 53; Gal. 3:13). The theory finds classic expression in Anselm's *Cur Deus Homo?* ("Why Did God Become Human?"). Anselm's reflections on this question arise out of the medieval thought world and presuppose then-current understandings of law, offense, reparations, and social obligations. God and humans are related like feudal lords and their serfs. Any act of disobedience dishonors the lord, and satisfaction must be given. The

20. See Colin E. Gunton, *The Actuality of Atonement: A Study of Metaphor, Rationality, and the Christian Tradition* (Grand Rapids: William B. Eerdmans, 1989).

21. On what follows, see Gustav Aulén, *Christus Victor* (New York: Macmillan, 1951).

satisfaction that is due to God on account of the offense of sin is infinite. While humanity *must* provide this satisfaction, only God *can* provide it. Therefore God has become human in Christ. In his perfect obedience unto death, satisfaction is rendered, justice is done, and God's honor is restored. As a result, sinners are forgiven.

The humanity of Christ is given a more significant role in this theory of atonement than in the cosmic conflict theory. In addition, the seriousness of sin and the costliness of redemption are expressed in a way that was intelligible to the church in the medieval period. But the satisfaction theory as traditionally presented raises serious questions. Most important of all, it seems to set God in contradiction to Godself. It draws upon the juridical metaphors of the New Testament in a way that brings mercy and justice into collision. In other words, the Anselmian theory makes the act of forgiveness something of a problem for God. Grace is made conditional on satisfaction. But is conditional grace still grace? According to the New Testament, it is not God but humanity who needs to be reconciled. In the New Testament God is not so much the object as the subject of reconciliation in Christ.

In addition, the satisfaction theory, as developed by the tradition, does not adequately distinguish between a substitute and a representative. Dorothee Sölle has made this point rather convincingly. The world of substitution is the impersonal world of replaceable things. When a part of a machine wears out, a new part can be substituted. Representation, however, belongs in the world of persons and personal relationships. The representative stands in for us provisionally but does not divest us of responsibility. Parents can represent their children until their maturity, when they are able to speak and act for themselves. The atoning work of Christ is more faithfully and understandably interpreted as an act of personal representation rather than a work of mechanical substitution.[22]

3. A third prominent theory of atonement is often called the liberal or *moral influence* theory. It is also spoken of as a "subjective" theory, in contrast to the "objective" emphases of the two theories already outlined. In the moral influence theory Christ reconciles humanity not by some cosmic battle nor by some legal transaction — both of which would appear to be complete apart from any participation of those on behalf of whom the action is performed — but by showing God's love to us in

22. Sölle, *Christ Our Representative* (Philadelphia: Fortress Press, 1967).

such a compelling way that we are constrained to respond in wonder and gratitude.

The moral influence theory has its strength in emphasizing the unconditionality of God's love and in stressing the importance of our human response. While attending primarily to the "subjective" side of atonement, the theory might be developed in a way that recognized the objective web of illusions and self-deceptions that constitute our sinful condition as well as the objective power of the revelation of God's sacrificial love that shines into our sin-darkened world. However, it is doubtless true that many versions of the moral influence theory have had serious weaknesses. They have tended toward a sentimentalization of God's love, underestimated the power and tenacity of evil in the world, and depicted Jesus as merely a good example for people to follow. Still relevant is H. Richard Niebuhr's critique of a naive form of liberal theology in America: "A God without wrath brought people without sin into a kingdom without judgment through the ministrations of a Christ without a cross."[23]

These theories of atonement, and the New Testament metaphors on which they are based, are not mutually exclusive. Of course, at various times in the history of theology there have been those who have asserted that one or another of them embodies total and exclusive truth. When such absolutization of one image or one theory occurs, there is a loss of the richness of the New Testament proclamation and the centuries-long meditation of the church on the meaning of the atoning work of Christ.

Moreover, each of the three theories can be reclaimed and reinterpreted for our own time with its particular sense of bondage and cry for liberation. Through the ministry and cross of Christ, God does something decisive on behalf of oppressed humanity, liberating us from evil forces that enslave us, freeing us from our burden of guilt, and restoring moral order in a disordered world, setting us free from the illusions and self-deceptions that bring destruction on our neighbors as well as ourselves. It is instructive that in the current hymnody of the church all three theories of atonement are represented, as can be seen, for example, in the three hymns "A Mighty Fortress Is Our God" (Christ the victor), "O Sacred Head Now Wounded" (satisfaction), and "God of Grace and God of Glory" (moral influence).

23. Niebuhr, *The Kingdom of God in America* (New York: Harper Torchbook, 1959), p. 193.

John Calvin's doctrine of the three offices of Christ offers help in keeping our understanding of the atonement open and inclusive. Calvin says that Christ acts as our prophet, priest, and king.[24] In this doctrine of the *munus triplex,* Calvin is able to include the teaching of Jesus, his sacrificial death, and his lordly rule. We might restate Calvin's teaching of the three offices of Christ as follows: Christ as prophet proclaims the coming reign of God and instructs us in the form of life appropriate to that reign (moral influence); Christ as priest renders to God the perfect sacrifice of love and obedience on our behalf (satisfaction); Christ as designated king rules the world despite the recalcitrance of evil and promises the ultimate victory of God's reign of righteousness and peace (Christ the victor).

In his elaborate doctrine of reconciliation, Karl Barth also makes use of the idea of three offices of Christ, imaginatively weaving them together with the classical doctrines of two natures (divinity and humanity) and two states (humiliation and exaltation). This yields the themes of "The Lord as Servant" (God in Jesus Christ acts humbly as our priest, redeeming us from our sin of pride), "The Servant as Lord" (humanity in Jesus Christ is exalted by grace to royal partnership with God, liberating us from our sin of sloth), and "The True Witness" (the union of God and humanity in Jesus Christ carries its own prophetic power, dispelling our sin of falsehood).[25] Calvin's and Barth's theologies of the person and work of Christ are richer for their inclusive approach to the multiple metaphors of the New Testament witness and the mutually corrective motifs of classical theology.

Our reflections on several prominent theories of atonement suggest that fruitful interpretations of the work of Christ should be guided in our time by the following principles.[26] (1) We should respect the richness of the New Testament metaphors of atonement and the diversity of classical formulations rather than seeking to reduce everything to one common denominator. (2) The atoning work of Christ encompasses the whole gospel story: the ministry, teaching, cross, and resurrection. None of these should be omitted or isolated from the others. (3) The work of atonement is based on God's gracious initiative, but it also calls for a

24. See Calvin, *Institutes of the Christian Religion,* 2.15.

25. Barth, *Church Dogmatics,* IV/1-3.

26. Cf. Paul Tillich's summary of principles of the doctrine of atonement in *Systematic Theology,* 2: 173-76.

human response. An adequate doctrine of atonement will give both factors their appropriate attention. (4) The grace of God includes judgment, and the judgment of God serves the purpose of grace. A doctrine of atonement should not present the grace and judgment of God as conflicting with each other. (5) The atoning work of God in Christ has significance for individuals, society, and the entire cosmos.

Liberation Christology

SOME of the most creative work in Christology today is that of Latin American liberation theologians, as found in the recent books of Jon Sobrino and Leonardo Boff and the five-volume project of Juan Luis Segundo.[27] While Latin American Christology is by no means a monolithic perspective, there are several common emphases that have already had a wide impact and no doubt will continue to influence the work of Christology throughout the ecumenical church.

1. *God in Christ enters into utmost solidarity with the poor.* The liberation theologians intend to do Christology "from below" (i.e., starting with the concrete historical ministry of Jesus) rather than "from above" (i.e., starting from the doctrines of the Trinity and the incarnation of the eternal Logos). If we begin with the human Jesus and his ministry in first-century Palestine, we are confronted by one who proclaimed the near advent of God's kingdom of justice and freedom, who blessed the poor, forgave sinners, had table fellowship with the outcast, befriended women, collided with the self-righteous custodians of the law, and evoked the suspicion and anger of the Roman authorities with his message of liberty to the captives. The clearer all this becomes for us, the more disturbing and even shocking becomes the Christian affirmation that "God was in Christ reconciling the world." If we focus on the concrete ministry, life, and death of Jesus, then when we speak of God in this light, we cannot avoid the conclusion that God indeed enters into the

27. Sobrino, *Christology at the Crossroads* (Maryknoll, N.Y.: Orbis Books, 1978); and *Jesus in Latin America* (Maryknoll, N.Y.: Orbis Books, 1986); Boff, *Jesus Christ Liberator* (Maryknoll, N.Y.: Orbis Books, 1978); Segundo, *Jesus of Nazareth Yesterday and Today,* trans. John Drury (Maryknoll, N.Y.: Orbis Books, 1984-88): vol. 1, *Faith and Ideologies;* vol. 2, *The Historical Jesus of the Synoptics;* vol. 3, *The Humanist Christology of Paul;* vol. 4, *The Christ of the Ignatian Exercises;* vol. 5, *An Evolutionary Approach to Jesus of Nazareth.*

utmost solidarity with the poor. Critics of this emphasis contend that it distorts the universal offer of salvation in the biblical proclamation. Rightly understood, however, the theme of God's solidarity with the poor is an expression of inclusivity, not exclusivity. It is the poor who are being unjustly excluded, and thus it must be the poor who are first and explicitly included in the salvific activity of God.

2. *The sin that keeps people in bondage and the salvation that frees them have both personal and political dimensions.* Liberation Christology not only includes but underscores the corporate, political dimension of sin and salvation. This emphasis is a response to the entrenched and damaging privatization of sin and salvation. While this privatization may fit well with the dualism endemic to modern Western culture, it is a distortion of the biblical message. There are corporate structures of sin and injustice. Jesus did not simply come up against sinful individuals but a sinful structure of life. Similarly, salvation is not just the rescue of isolated souls to fellowship with God. Jesus proclaimed and inaugurated the rule of the gracious and righteous God that encompasses the whole of life.

3. *When Christology is done self-consciously in a situation of oppression, it becomes imperative and urgent to distinguish faith from dehumanizing ideologies.* The political significance of the ministry of Jesus is not to be sought in simplistic parallels between the actions of Jesus and what Christians should do today in their particular situations. The attempt, for example, to find a link between Jesus and the Jewish revolutionaries called Zealots so that revolutionary action can be endorsed by Christians today is misguided. It is rather Jesus' prophetic exposure of an idolatrous conception of God and its alliance with a dehumanizing order of life that constitutes the political dimension of his ministry.

The danger of ideology in Christian teaching is perhaps most pronounced in the interpretation of the cross. The cross is not an event disclosing that God wants us all to suffer as much as possible. The message of the cross has repeatedly been used to undercut resistance to injustice and to help keep the oppressed in their place. There is a world of difference, however, between suffering that is imposed on others and suffering that is willingly assumed for the sake of assisting others to gain release from their bondage. The cross as a sign of the suffering of God in the passion of Christ is a protest against unjust suffering as well as a promise of God's companionship with the oppressed. The resurrection of Christ is not to be construed as the sign of despair over the impossibility of a real transformation of the world but precisely as the divine promise of the comprehensive transformation of life and the universal triumph of God's righteousness.

4. *Christology is inseparably linked to Christian praxis.* We will never understand Christ, his proclamation, his ministry, his cross, or his resurrection until we find ourselves where he placed himself — in the company of those who are afflicted and unjustly treated and who cry out for justice and freedom that they have lost or never known. Sobrino argues that "the only way to get to know Jesus is to follow after him in one's own life; to try to identify oneself with his own historical concerns; and to try to fashion his kingdom in our midst. In other words, only through Christian praxis is it possible for us to draw close to Jesus. Following Jesus is the precondition for knowing Jesus."[28] Sobrino's axiom of Christology can and should also be reversed. Surely we must also say that knowing Jesus is the precondition of following him. But Sobrino's version is a much-needed reminder to the church in his situation and elsewhere that the pursuit of Christology apart from the dangerous practice of following Christ is bound to miss the point.

Violence and the Cross

THE Scriptures and the tradition unanimously affirm that the death of Jesus was "for us," "for our sins," "for many," "for the world." "Christ died for our sins in accordance with the Scriptures" (1 Cor. 15:3). How can we understand this today?

Perhaps the primary reason we have such difficulty in making sense of the death of Jesus for us is that it is an event of violence, and we are experts in covering up the violence that pervades our lives and the workings of our society.[29] In failing to acknowledge the violence of the event that stands at the center of the gospel drama, we turn the message of the love of God into sentimentality, or we project the violence onto others (often the Jews) or onto God (as in theories of atonement that say the cross was necessary to appease the wrath of God) or onto ourselves.

---

28. Sobrino, *Christology at the Crossroads*, p. xiii.

29. I am indebted in the following paragraphs to the work of René Girard (*Violence and the Sacred*) and Gerhard Forde's reflections on his work in *Christian Dogmatics*, vol. 2 (Philadelphia: Fortress Press, 1984), pp. 79-99.

No less than the world of antiquity, ours is a world of violence. As studies show, the domestic sphere is often not an arena of harmony and tranquillity but a field of violence, where wives are battered and parents abuse their children. In the social and economic spheres competition is glorified even if it means advancing one's fame and fortune at the expense of others. The international sphere is an arena of conflict and the construction of systems of mutually assured destruction. Violence is a structural element of our social and domestic life.

God in Christ enters into a world saturated with violence, a world in which people are victimized again and again — the poor neglected, women beaten and raped, children abused, the earth plundered, prophets murdered — so that the order of our society and our world may not be disturbed. When Jesus disturbs that order — announces God's forgiveness of sinners, promises the future to the poor, welcomes outcasts and strangers, calls all to repentance and a new way of life characterized by love of God and others — when Jesus does this in a world built from its very foundation stone upon violence, then it is no arbitrary religious doctrine but profoundest truth that Jesus *must* suffer, the boundless love of God must clash with a world built on hostility and violence. As the risen Jesus explains to the disciples on the way to Emmaus, did not the Christ have to suffer all this and enter into his glory? (Luke 24:26). It was divine necessity — the necessity of God's gracious and nonviolent love — that the love of God be fully expressed in all its vulnerability in Jesus Christ. It was human necessity — the necessity of the world order of our own making — that this one who mediated God's forgiveness and inaugurated the reign of God characterized by justice, freedom, and peace should become the victim of our violence because he threatened the whole world of violence that we inhabit and will to maintain.

We are not all equally blameworthy for the systems of violence and death that envelop our personal lives, our society, and our world. But we are all caught up in vicious circles of violence, whether as victims or victimizers or some of both.

Jesus lived and died for us all. But God raised the crucified Jesus and made him the chief cornerstone of a new humanity that no longer espouses the way of violence, that no longer needs scapegoats, that no longer wills to live at the expense of victims, that no longer imagines or worships a bloodthirsty God, that is no longer interested in legitimations of violence, but that follows Jesus in the power of a new Spirit. We may briefly identify three aspects of Christ's death for us as it impinges upon our world of violence.

1. *Christ died for us in order to expose our world of violence for what it is — a world that stands under God's judgment, a world based on coercion and leading to death.* The cross is the revelation of the nonviolent love of God that sets us all, individually and corporately, under judgment. Nietzsche once said that because God is dead, everything is permitted. The claim of this message to be good news is a lie. The freedom that is born of deicide is bound up with homicide, genocide, and biocide. "Christ died so that we might know that *not* everything is permitted."[30]

2. *Christ died for us in order to enter into utmost solidarity with us as victims of violence and to mediate God's forgiveness to us as perpetrators of violence.* The cross of Christ is God's own gift of costly love, mediating God's forgiveness and friendship in the midst of a violent world. Contrary to some interpretations, the cross is no legitimation of the suffering of victims. It does not signify some power of necessity or fate to which both God and human victims must simply bow. By freely taking up the cross, God in Christ forgives sinners and enters into solidarity with all the wretched of the earth. The message of the cross has nothing to do with resignation to the forces of violence and nothing to do with the spirit of revenge. Wherever the cross of Christ is rightly preached and heard, the deadly circle of violence and counterviolence is broken, and the rule of violence begins to yield to a new world of compassion and solidarity.

3. *Christ died for us in order to open a new future for a new humanity in the midst of our violent world.* Seen in the light of the resurrection, the cross is the indelible promise of the victory of the nonviolent love of God. There is good news in the message of the cross that becomes radiantly clear in God's resurrection of the crucified: "God has not undergone the cross in order to eternalize it and deprive us of all hope. On the contrary, God has assumed it because God means to put an end to all the crosses of history."[31] The cross of Christ etches deeply into human history the truth that God's compassion is greater than the murderous passions of our world, that God's glory can and does shine even in the deepest night of human savagery, that God's free forgiveness

---

30. José Porfiro Miranda *(Being and the Messiah)*, quoted by Leonardo Boff, in *Passion of Christ, Passion of the World* (Maryknoll, N.Y.: Orbis Books, 1988), p. vii.

31. Boff, *Passion of Christ, Passion of the World*, p. 144.

is greater than our paralyzing recognition of guilt, that God's way of life is greater than our way of death.

The Finality of Jesus Christ

THE unconditionality of Christian commitment to Jesus Christ as the unique and definitive presence of God in human life is sometimes expressed by the phrase "the finality of Christ." Can Christians continue to affirm the "finality" of Christ in a world where the plurality of cultures and religions increasingly points to the need for a spirit of openness and dialogue?

Several ways of relating faith in Jesus Christ to other faiths may be distinguished. Each of them involves a distinctive understanding of the sense in which the disclosure of God in Jesus Christ is "final."

1. The *exclusivist* way asserts that other religions and faith commitments are simply false; Christian faith alone is true. According to this view, openness to and dialogue with other faiths is a betrayal of God's revelation in Christ, since it assumes that Christians may have something to learn from these other faiths as well. In this view, finality means closure. Of the many reasons why this position must be called mistaken and untenable, two may be mentioned that are especially important. The first is that we must always distinguish between Jesus Christ and *our* ideas and understandings of Jesus Christ. Christ is the living Lord; he is not reducible to a formula that we can manipulate and control. To confess Christ as our Lord is not to say that we are in possession of all that Christ is and means. Openness to the truth that has not yet dawned upon us is ingredient to authentic commitment to Christ. Second, it has been part of Christian proclamation and teaching from the very beginning that God is never left without a witness, that the Word of God that was incarnate in Jesus of Nazareth is the light that enlightens every human life (John 1:9).

2. Another way of relating Christian faith to other faiths is to speak of them as preparations for the acceptance of Christ. According to this *developmentalist* view of the religions, all the faiths of humanity find their fulfillment in the gospel of Jesus Christ. The finality of the revelation in Christ is to be understood as the highest member in an ascending series. The modern form of this view was first worked out by Schleiermacher in the nineteenth century, and it continued to be dominant in theology

and missiology until well into the twentieth century. The most serious weakness of this view is its gradualistic or evolutionary assumptions about the relation of the world religions to each other. Deeper studies of the religions have shown that they cannot be ordered in a neat hierarchical series, since they turn on different axes. Each religion must be understood on its own terms. It must be appreciated from the inside, as it were, and not simply as a preparatory step toward Christian faith. For example, Christianity's relation to Judaism has been distorted by the idea that the Hebrew Bible and Judaism have no significance beyond serving as a preparation for Christian faith.

3. A third view is that the grace and judgment of God is present and active "transcendentally" throughout creation and in all human experience, even if it is explicitly and definitively (i.e., finally) revealed in the historical ministry and death of Jesus Christ. According to this *transcendentalist* view, represented most ably by Karl Rahner, believers of other faiths have access to God's transcendental grace although they may know nothing of Christ or for various reasons reject the Christian message. In Rahner's view, all who sincerely live according to the light that has been given them are "anonymous Christians." This position has been criticized by many as a subtle form of theological imperialism. Some have asked why a Buddhist might not turn Rahner's doctrine of anonymous Christianity upside down and speak of Christians as "anonymous Buddhists." Others have asked whether the moralistic tone of this position, which is accepting of all people who observe the law, are sincere, and show good will does not contradict the gospel proclamation of God's acceptance of sinners and lawbreakers.[32]

4. A fourth way is perhaps best called *dialogical.* It says that Christians and people of other faiths must *both* take their own faith commitments with utmost seriousness *and* enter into open dialogue with others. Paul Tillich, Hans Küng, and Jürgen Moltmann are three representatives of this position. Tillich proposed the way of "dynamic typology," by which he meant that in conversation with other religions, believers would rediscover latent or recessive dimensions in their own tradition; in such dialogue all would be enriched.[33] Hans Küng holds that all religions are

---

32. See Lesslie Newbigin, *The Open Secret: Sketches for a Missionary Theology* (Grand Rapids: William B. Eerdmans, 1978), p. 196.

33. See Tillich, *Christianity and the Encounter of the World Religions* (New York: Columbia University Press, 1963).

"ways of salvation" but that all contain a mixture of truth and falsehood. Christian faith in dialogue may serve as a "critical catalyst" for the other religions, helping to bring out in them what is deepest and best; and conversely, Christian faith will be challenged and clarified in the dialogue inasmuch as it will have to discover the specificity and the fullness of God's revelation in Jesus Christ.[34] Jürgen Moltmann insists on dialogue with other faiths as a concrete expression of life in love. If Christians believe in a God who is love and who aims at community in the creation, they cannot wish to be closed and invulnerable. They "live in a God who can suffer and who in the power of his love desires to suffer in order to redeem. Therefore, in their dialogue with people of a different faith, Christians cannot testify through their behavior to an unalterable, apathetic and aggressive God. By giving love and showing interest in others, they also become receptive to the other and vulnerable through what is alien to them. They can bear the otherness of the other without becoming insecure and hardening their hearts. The right thing is not to carry on the dialogue according to superficial rules of communication, but to enter into it out of the depths of the understanding of God."[35] On this view, the finality of Christ is not something we possess but a promise that we are given.

5. A fifth way seeks to radically *relativize* the historical particularities of the individual religions and tries to identify the "theocentric" core in all of them. John Hick, for example, calls for a "copernican revolution" in theology involving "a shift from the dogma that Christianity or Christ is at the center to the realization that it is God who is at the center, and that all the religions of humanity, including our own, serve and revolve around that God."[36] Having identified the reality and goodness of a Supreme Being as the essential core of all religions, Hick interprets Christian affirmations about Christ not as ontological truth claims but as the poetic or exaggerated language of love for the one through whom Christians have come to know God. This approach is reminiscent of the Enlightenment rationalism that sought to identify the natural or universal religion behind all historical religions. Neither then nor now does such

34. See Küng, *On Being a Christian*, pp. 89-116.
35. Moltmann, *The Church in the Power of the Spirit* (New York: Harper & Row, 1977), pp. 160-61.
36. Hick, *God and the Universe of Faiths* (New York: St. Martin's Press, 1973), p. 131.

abstraction from the concrete understandings of God in the world religions seem very helpful.[37] For Christians, it is not a Supreme or Transcendent Being as such who is spoken of as God but the One who freely became a humble servant in Jesus Christ.

The path of responsible Christology today must surely negotiate between the extremes of exclusivism on the one hand and relativism on the other. Dialogue between Christianity and the other religions is right and necessary because a proper understanding of the biblical message demands it and the search for peace in the world requires it. The "finality" of Jesus Christ, therefore, should not be understood by Christian believers as their present possession of the full truth. Jesus Christ is far greater than any Christology. The confession of Christ must therefore be expectant rather than overly defensive, prospective rather than only backward-looking. While Christians are confident that no future revelation of God will contradict what has been revealed in Christ, they readily acknowledge the incompleteness of their present knowledge of God. Thus while commitment to Jesus as the definitive expression of God's character and purpose belongs to the nonnegotiable core of Christian faith, Christians humbly acknowledge that they are far from comprehending the mystery of God in Christ. Like all people of faith, Christians await the completion of God's purposes. In the meantime, they seek to be faithful to the light that shines in Jesus Christ and are confident that the brightness of this light increases rather than decreases when they venture to enter into dialogue with believers of other religions.

37. Harvey Cox emphasizes "the indispensable element of particularity" in all interfaith dialogue in *Many Mansions: A Christian's Encounter with Other Faiths* (Boston, Beacon Press, 1988).

9

The Holy Spirit and the Christian Life

CHRISTIANS AFFIRM THAT GOD IS THE CREATOR WHO HAS GRA-
ciously called the world into existence and made human beings in the
image of God. They also confess that God was decisively present in
the person and work of Jesus Christ to reconcile the world and to
liberate humanity from its bondage to sin, death, and all other evil
powers that threaten to ruin God's good creation. If the creed of the
church ended abruptly with these first two articles of faith in God as
creator and reconciler, it would speak of an abstract, distant, and
ineffectual deity. In John Calvin's words, "As long as Christ remains
outside of us, and we are separated from him, all that he has done and
suffered for the salvation of the human race remains useless and of no
value to us."[1]

The third article of the creed affirms that God is not only *over* us
and *for* us but also at work *in* us. It speaks of the Holy Spirit and the
new humanity in Christ. How do men and women participate in the
great drama of creation, reconciliation, and transformation? What power
enables humanity to have a share in the life and activity of the triune
God? What new attitudes, practices, and relationships are to characterize
those who have encountered God's grace in Jesus? To what goal does our
history and the history of the whole creation move? A reply to these
questions must begin, as the third article of the creed begins, with an
affirmation of faith in the Holy Spirit.

---

1. Calvin, *Institutes of the Christian Religion*, 3.1.1.

Neglect and Recovery of the Doctrine of the Holy Spirit

THE doctrine of the Holy Spirit has seldom received the attention given to other doctrines of the faith such as Christology and the authority of Scripture. Some theologians have even spoken of the early creedal definitions of the doctrine of the Holy Spirit as almost "slipshod."[2] Even more disturbing than the church's neglect of the Spirit are many instances of official church opposition to movements that have stressed the presence and power of the Spirit, such as the Montanists of the second century, the Waldensians of the twelfth century, the radical reformers of the sixteenth century, and the Christian base communities of our own time.

Neglect and suspicion of the work of the Holy Spirit has damaging effects on both Christian life and Christian theology. It can lead to distortions in the understanding of God, the doctrine of Scripture, the significance of the natural order, the value of human culture, the interpretation of Christ and his work, the nature of the church, the freedom of the Christian, and the hope for the final fulfillment of life. When the work of the Holy Spirit is forgotten or suppressed, the power of God is apt to be understood as distant, hierarchical, and coercive; Christocentric faith deteriorates into Christomonism; the authority of Scripture becomes heteronomous; the church is seen as a rigid power structure in which some members rule over others; and the sacraments degenerate into almost magical rites under the control of a clerical elite.

In recent years, however, there has been a resurgence of interest in the Holy Spirit and Christian spirituality.[3] A number of factors have contributed to this development.

1. Viewed in broad cultural perspective, the new interest in the Holy Spirit is a protest against depersonalization and bureaucratization in both modern society and the church. It is a protest against the domination of form over vitality, structure over purpose, external authority over free consent. When questions are settled simply by quoting passages from the Bible or citing the doctrines of the church, this is rightly judged by many people as but another instance of the ethos of control and

2. See George S. Hendry, *The Holy Spirit in Christian Theology* (Philadephia: Westminster Press, 1956), p. 13.

3. This is reflected in the theme chosen for the seventh assembly of the World Council of Churches in Canberra, Australia, in 1990: "Come, Holy Spirit — Renew the Whole Creation." For a helpful recent discussion of the doctrine of the Holy Spirit, see Alasdair I. C. Heron, *The Holy Spirit* (Philadelphia: Westminster Press, 1983).

coercion. To know God as Spirit is to experience God as a liberating rather than a coercive power.

2. The new interest in the Holy Spirit may also be seen as a hunger for a deeper faith, for a new relationship with God, for the experience of love and friendship, and for the spiritual resources to deal with the personal and corporate crises of our time. Many people in modern technological society feel lonely and ignored. They often experience utter helplessness in the face of the impersonal forces that affect their lives. Cultural institutions that once provided meaning, support, and companionship are disintegrating. Help in dealing with these personal and cultural crises can scarcely be found in secular philosophies that exalt self-reliance and the spirit of individualism. The hunger for new life, new community, new joy finds expression in the renewed interest in the Spirit and in the search for a new spirituality.

3. Recent interest in the Holy Spirit may also be connected with the sense of historical distance and cold objectivity that seems endemic to modern consciousness. Even a so-called Christocentric theology is not immune to the acids of historical distance and objectivistic ways of thinking. What is the significance of the objective reality of salvation in Christ if there is no personal appropriation of this reality and no actual participation in its transforming power?[4]

4. Renewed interest in the Holy Spirit may also be related to the experience of emptiness and "burn-out" of many pastors, church leaders, and countless other people who have taken part in the various social and political movements of reform in recent years. The spiritual life has sometimes been neglected or even denigrated by social activists as an unnecessary vestige of the past. But it has now become apparent that perseverance in struggles for justice, peace, and freedom cannot be sustained apart from a vital spirituality.

5. The new interest in the Holy Spirit is also clearly associated with developments in the ecumenical church. Among the more important of these are the remarkable expansion of the Pentecostal churches that have historically placed great emphasis on the Spirit, the growing influence of

4. Yves Congar states as the most important conclusion of his extensive writings on the Holy Spirit that there can be "no Christology without pneumatology and no pneumatology without Christology" (*The Word and the Spirit* [San Francisco: Harper & Row, 1986], p. 1). See also his trilogy *I Believe in the Holy Spirit* (New York: Seabury Press, 1983).

the Eastern Orthodox Churches which have argued for centuries that the Western church's theology of the Spirit is defective, and above all the emergence of the Christian base communities in Latin America and in other parts of the world.

6. Not least of the factors promoting recent interest in the Holy Spirit is a better appreciation of the importance of the experience of the Spirit in both the Old and New Testaments. In the Old Testament the Spirit is the creative breath of God giving life to all creatures (Ps. 104:29-30). The Spirit offers assurance of forgiveness of sins (Ps. 51:10-12), gives courage to the downtrodden (Hag. 2:4-5), brings new life out of death (Ezek. 37), restores hope (Joel 2:28-29), and promotes justice in the land (Isa. 11:1ff.). A special feature of the Old Testament understanding of the Spirit is that the Spirit of God is given to God's chosen servants, commissioning and empowering them to restore justice in the land when the weak and the poor are oppressed (cf. Isa. 42:1-4a; 61:1-4).

The early church understood itself as living in the time of the long-promised outpouring of the Spirit (Joel 2:28-32; Acts 2:17-21). The Synoptic Gospels describe the life and ministry of Jesus as empowered by the Spirit from beginning to end (Luke 4:18ff.). The special prominence of the work of the Holy Spirit for the evangelist Luke is indicated by the fact that he begins his Gospel with the story of the birth of Jesus to Mary by the power of the Spirit and starts his sequel to the Gospel (the Acts of the Apostles) with the account of the coming of the Spirit to the disciples at Pentecost. Paul thinks of the Spirit in the closest possible relation to the risen Christ and interprets the work of the Spirit as the firstfruits of the harvest of God's coming reign (Rom. 8:23). For the evangelist John, the Spirit is sent to bear witness to Christ and to lead the disciples into the fullness of truth in him (John 14:26).

After a long period of concentration on Christology in Western theology, is it now time for attention to shift in the direction of pneumatology? This question has been raised in our time even by Karl Barth, the greatest advocate of Christocentric theology in the twentieth century.[5]

5. See Barth, "Concluding Unscientific Postscript on Schleiermacher," in *The Theology of Schleiermacher* (Grand Rapids: William B. Eerdmans, 1982).

A Sketch of a Theology of the Holy Spirit

WHATEVER the various factors at work in the resurgence of interest in the person and work of the Holy Spirit, the principal elements of this doctrine are in need of rethinking today.

1. *To speak of the Holy Spirit in Christian theology is to speak not just of any spirit but of the Spirit of the triune God.* As we have seen, according to trinitarian Christian faith, God is the living God whose eternal being is a dynamic communion of love. God's being is the act of mutual sharing of life and love among Father, Son, and Holy Spirit. The three persons of the Trinity are not separate selves living in isolation from each other. Rather, they are so intimately united that they "indwell" each other in a society of love. Their personhood is defined in terms of their relationship with each other. The Spirit is the uniting love of the Trinity, the power of community in diversity, of mutual love and friendship.

The relation of the Holy Spirit to the Father and the Son has been the topic of a long-standing controversy in the trinitarian theologies of the Eastern and Western churches. What are we to say about the Spirit? Is the Spirit personal? Is the Spirit fully equal to the Father and the Son, or in some way subordinate to them? Such questions are prompted by the New Testament texts themselves, which rather less amply describe the deity and personhood of the Holy Spirit than they do that of the Father and the Son. The consensus of the church, which developed gradually and was eventually registered in the classical creeds, is that if the Holy Spirit is the agent of the liberation and transformation of life, then, like the Father and the Son, the Spirit is both personal and divine.

In classical trinitarian theology a distinction is made between the "missions" and the "processions" of the Son and the Spirit. The "missions" refer to the activities of the Son and the Spirit in the creation, reconciliation, and redemption of the world. Eastern and Western theologies are agreed that every work of God involves the cooperation of all three persons of the Trinity. Corresponding to the missions of the triune God in relation to the world are the eternal "processions" of the Son and the Spirit within the Trinity. On this point a doctrinal divergence has developed between East and West.

In the Western church the phrase *filioque* was added to the text of the Nicene Creed in the sixth century. According to the revised Creed, the Holy Spirit is said to proceed from the Father "and from the Son." The church in the East has rejected this addition and has affirmed that the Spirit proceeds only from the Father (cf. John 15:26). According to Western theology, the *filioque* doctrine declares that Christ and the Spirit are inseparable. It emphasizes the unity of God as well as providing a criterion for testing the spirits. If the work of the Spirit were separated from that of Christ, the church would be unable to make responsible judgments about various spiritual movements and would be vulnerable to all sorts of natural theologies that do not look to Christ as the decisive revelation of God.[6]

According to Eastern theologians, however, the *filioque* has the effect of subordinating the Spirit to Christ and thus promotes a Spirit-deficient Christology and an ecclesiology in which power is divorced from spiritual presence. Furthermore, in the Eastern view the *filioque* obscures the uniqueness of the Father as the source of Christ and the Spirit and makes it difficult to affirm the activity of the Spirit in all creation and history rather than only where the Word incarnate is explicitly proclaimed and confessed.

Some progress toward a resolution of this ancient controversy might be made if both sides could agree on at least two points. (1) Neither the Western nor the Eastern model of the procession of the Spirit fully captures all forms of the relationships of Father, Son, and Spirit depicted in the New Testament witness. (2) In addition to a "procession model" of the Trinity that describes the movement of the Spirit from Father and Son to the world, we also need an "eschatological model" that speaks of the Spirit's activity in the ministry of Jesus and in that of his followers to draw all creation into the loving communion and eschatological glory of the triune God.[7]

In the New Testament, the Spirit is intimately related to Jesus and his ministry. More precisely, Jesus and the Spirit are interdependent.[8] Jesus is both the receiver and the giver of the Spirit. On the one hand, Jesus is the gift of the Spirit. He is, according to the infancy narratives, conceived by the Spirit (Matt. 1:20; Luke 1:35). At his baptism the Spirit descends and remains on him (John 1:32). Jesus is the one anointed by

---

6. For a vigorous defense of the *filioque*, see Karl Barth, *Church Dogmatics*, I/1 (2d ed., 1975): 448-89.

7. See Jürgen Moltmann, *The Trinity and the Kingdom* (San Francisco: Harper & Row, 1984); and David Coffey, "The Holy Spirit as the Mutual Love of the Father and the Son," *Theological Studies* 51 (1990): 193-229.

8. Cf. Hendrikus Berkhof, *The Doctrine of the Holy Spirit* (Grand Rapids: William B. Eerdmans, 1965).

the Spirit for the ministry of good news to the poor and liberation to those in bondage (Luke 4:18ff.), the one who casts out demonic forces in the power of the Spirit (Matt. 12:28), the one who is himself raised from the dead by the Spirit (Rom. 1:4). On the other hand, the Spirit is the gift of the risen Christ, the power who teaches us what is the mind of Christ (1 Cor. 2:16), pours the love of God into our hearts (Rom. 5:5), empowers our new life in Christ (Rom. 8:11), and motivates and equips us for discipleship and service (Rom. 8:14). The intimacy of the relation of Christ and the Spirit in the New Testament is such that a test of the authenticity of the presence of the Spirit is whether it enables the confession "Jesus is Lord" (1 Cor. 12:3).

2. In comparison with the extensive debates in classical theology about the status of the Spirit as person and about the relationship of the Spirit to the Father and the Son in the eternal triune life, the doctrine of *the work of the Spirit* in the world and especially in relation to the transformation of human life has been accurately described as under-developed.[9] In sharp contrast, the New Testament contains a multi-dimensional description of the work of the Holy Spirit.

a. One aspect of this work may be called re-presentative. The Spirit makes Christ present to believers — *re-presents Christ*. The Spirit unites believers to Christ and thus spans the gap between the then and there and the here and now. By the power of the Spirit, the Christ attested in Scripture and proclaimed in the church does not remain a mere object outside of us or a distant event of the past from which we are separated by a broad, ugly ditch of space and time. Christ is not merely a memory of someone long gone or someone who may arrive in the future; he is present here and now to us — in the power of the Spirit. As Calvin writes, it is through the "energy of the Spirit" that we come to "enjoy Christ and all his benefits."[10]

b. A second aspect of the work of the Spirit is the *creation of new life*. According to John's theology, the Spirit is the agent of our second birth. Just as we are born from our natural mother's womb in our first birth, so we must be born anew by the power of the Spirit. The Nicene Creed follows 1 Corinthians 15:45 in naming the Spirit the "life giver." While this designation refers primarily to the new life in Christ, it

9. See Heron, *The Holy Spirit*, p. 99; Berkhof, *The Doctrine of the Holy Spirit*, pp. 94-108.

10. Calvin, *Institutes of the Christian Religion*, 3.1.1.

probably also has in mind the activity of the Spirit at the creation of the world (Gen. 1:2). The Spirit is the power of transformation from the old to the new, from enslavement to the powers of sin and death to a new life in communion with God and others.

As recipients of new life from the Spirit, Christians are enabled both to speak of God's mercy and righteousness and to act as co-workers with God in the renewal of creation. The disciples' new power of speech given by the Spirit is dramatically depicted in Acts 2. And the new empowerment to act by those who are filled with the Spirit is underscored in the description by Paul of the gifts of the Spirit that equip all members of the community for significant service. Gifted by the Spirit, all become contributors to the common welfare, partners in the creative and redemptive work of God.

c. Another aspect of the work of the Holy Spirit is *liberative.* "Where the Spirit of the Lord is, there is freedom" (2 Cor. 3:17). The Spirit energizes resistance to injustice and sets people free (cf. Isa. 42:1ff., 61:1ff.). The New Testament associates the coming of the Spirit with the liberation of life from bondage and with a new freedom for the service of God. Inasmuch as the work of Christ is essentially one of liberation ("For freedom Christ has set us free," Gal. 5:1), the activity of the Spirit is a continuation of the work begun by Christ. The Spirit brings freedom for new and abundant life in communion with God and others. The liberating work of the Spirit is present not only in human life but throughout the creation that groans and longs to participate in "the freedom of the glory of the children of God" (Rom. 8:21).

d. Still another aspect of the work of the Holy Spirit is the *communal.* As the Spirit is the bond of love and friendship between Father and Son in the Trinity, the Spirit is also the power who unites us to Christ and to each other. The unitive power of the Spirit is not mere togetherness of the like-minded or the kinship of people of the same family, race, economic class, or nation. It is a power of new community that unites strangers and even former enemies. It creates community where formerly there were insuperable barriers. "There is no longer Jew or Greek, there is no longer slave or free, there is no longer male and female; for all of you are one in Christ Jesus" (Gal. 3:28). In Christ and by the power of the Spirit we are one community; we are members of one body and mutually dependent on one another. By drawing us into new solidarity with others, the Spirit remakes us as persons-in-community who no longer live as isolated, self-centered individuals.

e. Also of great importance is the *promise* associated with the work of the Holy Spirit and the anticipation this evokes. The Spirit at work in the Christian community is said to be the "firstfruits" (Rom. 8:23) or, in another metaphor, the "first installment" and "guarantee" (2 Cor. 1:22; 5:5) of the future that God is bringing. As the power of God's promised future, the Spirit awakens hope, yearning, and restlessness for the completion of God's redemptive work and the establishment of justice and peace throughout the creation. The Spirit sighs in us and in all the creation for God's coming kingdom. The Spirit keeps hope alive and incites fresh visions of God's new world. Where there is no vision or hope, no discontent or protest against present injustice and evil, there is assuredly no presence of the Spirit in the biblical understanding of this term.

f. A further brief comment should be made about *the gifts of the Spirit.* According to the biblical witness, there are many diverse gifts of the Spirit, and each should be respected. In celebrating the diversity of spiritual gifts, we recognize our mutual dependence and encourage mutual support. As the Apostle Paul teaches in 1 Corinthians 12–14, however, the most important gifts are not the sensational ones, such as speaking in tongues, but the gifts of faith, hope, and above all love. While Paul does not want to outlaw speaking in tongues within the Christian community, it is clear that neither he nor any other New Testament witness considers this phenomenon crucial for Christian spirituality. The primary criterion of life in the Spirit is an unconditional love of God and a correlative love of others, especially those who are commonly considered strangers and even enemies. Such love is motivated by God's love for sinners and the poor in Christ.

Thus while we should not denigrate any of the various gifts that the Spirit gives to members of the church, we should test their authenticity by the criterion of whether they serve the common good rather than promoting division and contention in the community. A true gift of the Spirit builds up the community and contributes to the common good rather than serving only the self-aggrandizement of a few.

g. Finally, we should say something about the appropriateness of *female imagery of the Spirit.* We can begin by noting that the word for Spirit is feminine in Hebrew *(ruach),* although it is neuter in Greek *(pneuma)* and masculine in Latin *(spiritus).* More pertinent, however, are New Testament descriptions of the nurturing and empowering activities of the Spirit and the fact that in the conversation with Nicodemus in the Gospel of John, Jesus speaks of the work of the Spirit as like that of a mother (John 3:5-6).[11]

Some theologians suggest that the Holy Spirit is the feminine counterpart to the incarnate Son of God. Following Irenaeus, José Comblin proposes that we think of the Word and the Spirit as the two hands of God that are equally divine. If one hand of God is the Word of God incarnate in a single human being, the other hand of God is the Spirit who is intimately present in one inclusive community, bringing to birth and nurturing God's new humanity. Comblin suggests that a theology of the maternity of the Spirit could have counterbalanced the excessive masculinity of the church's traditional imaging of God and its understanding of power.[12] Modifying Comblin's proposal somewhat, it might be suggested that the Word and Spirit of God can be described respectively as the Son and Daughter of God, working together to make us all adopted children of God.

But while speaking of the Spirit of God in feminine imagery is suggested by some biblical passages and should be welcomed in both theology and liturgy, the name "Spirit" should also serve to remind us that God is beyond gender and that we must avoid the danger of making idols of our images and metaphors of God. The triune God is neither an exclusive fraternity nor a divine company composed of two males and one female. That the triune God is also called Spirit teaches us to think and speak of God as uniquely personal, allowing gender-specific imagery, yet far transcending all such imagery. God is Spirit and lives in perfect love and mutual interrelationships.[13]

The Christian Life: Justification

WHILE the Spirit of God is the source and renewer of all life, it is also and in particular the energy of the new life in Christ.

Christian life is grounded in the grace of God. It is based in our union with Christ and is empowered and directed by the Holy Spirit.

11. See Virginia Ramey Mollenkott, *The Divine Feminine: The Biblical Imagery of God as Female* (New York: Crossroad, 1984).

12. Comblin, *The Holy Spirit and Liberation* (Maryknoll, N.Y.: Orbis, 1989), p. 39.

13. Cf. Krister Stendahl, *Energy for Life: Reflections on the Theme "Come, Holy Spirit — Renew the Whole Creation"* (Geneva: WCC Publications, 1990), pp. 6-8.

On its objective side, Christian life is founded on God's transforming work of justification, sanctification, and vocation. On its subjective side, Christian life is the free personal appropriation of God's grace in faith, love, and hope.[14]

Christian life in the power of the Spirit is a dynamic process of transformation into the likeness of Christ that is set in motion by the gracious initiative of God. It begins with justification, continues in sanctification, and moves to its goal in vocation. Christian life is patterned after the life, death, and resurrection of Jesus Christ and thus is a continuous dying to an old way of life and a rising to a new way of life. It is both mortification and vivification, both receiving and responding, both passive and active, both gift and task, both being freed and exercising new freedom, both being loved and loving others. Christian life is the process of entering increasingly into the fullness of the new humanity in Christ.

As the first moment of this process, *justification is God's forgiveness of sins that is received by faith alone* (Rom. 3:23-28). Accomplished and manifested in Jesus Christ, it is God's free, unconditional, and unmerited acceptance of us in spite of our sin and alienation from God, from others, and from ourselves. *Justification* is a term from the judicial sphere and means "acquitting" or "making right." That we are justified means that our broken relationship with God has been restored by an act of free grace and forgiveness. What God does for us is sheer grace *(sola gratia)* and is received by simple faith and trust alone *(sola fide)*.

This doctrine of justification is sometimes expressed in the abbreviated form: we are justified by faith. However, a major distortion of the doctrine occurs if it is taken to mean that faith is the human act by which we merit justification. God's act of justification is a free gift and is in no way dependent upon us although it calls for our response. Thus a more adequate brief statement of the doctrine is that we are justified by grace through faith. We cannot merit justification even by our act of faith. Faith is simply the appropriate response of trust and acceptance of God's unconditional affirmation of us.

While the doctrine of justification was the centerpiece of the theology of Luther and has been called "the article by which the church

---

14. I am here following the broad outline of Barth's treatment of the Christian life in terms of justification, sanctification, and vocation in his *Church Dogmatics*, IV/1-3. Cf. Tillich, *Systematic Theology*, 2: 176-80.

stands or falls,"[15] it would be a mistake to suggest that all Christian doctrine can be reduced to this single truth. The fullness of the event of Jesus Christ does not find expression simply in the doctrine of justification. At the same time, it would be folly to think that this doctrine is an outmoded teaching. On the contrary, it continues to have enormous relevance for our own time. Consider the multiple ways in which we try to justify ourselves, render our lives acceptable and meaningful, perhaps not by "good works" but by plain hard work or by acts that we think will win the approval of others. Who is entirely immune from this desire for approval and not anxious about being rejected? In modern society, we are all to some degree continuously on trial, not unlike the accused in Franz Kafka's story *The Trial*, who is tormented by the fear of being condemned by an anonymous judge. The quest for acceptance and the drive to succeed border on idolatry in our competitive society. Both as individuals and as a people, we are terrified by the prospect of failing to win the recognition and love that we crave.

The desperate search for acceptance is no doubt at work in the epidemic of drug addiction in American society. While the motivations for using drugs are complex, the sense of hopelessness and worthlessness and the absence of significant affirmation by others are important factors. The turn to drugs exposes the heartlessness of our social structures and relationships as well as the universal human vulnerability to the self-imposed bondages that we call addictions.

Although not often noted, our consumerist way of life is also an addiction. Modern societies create artificial needs through advertising and seduce us into seeking identity and meaning in accumulating material possessions. Whether captured by the spirit of possession or success, we are driven by the desire to "make it," to feel valued, accepted, and loved. In view of all this, anyone who thinks that the doctrine of justification has no relevance for people in our sophisticated society captive to many kinds of addictions — whether of money, work, leisure, fame, sex, or the more frequently mentioned forms of substance abuse — is simply out of touch with common experience.

One of the most impressive twentieth-century restatements of the doctrine of justification by grace through faith was offered by Paul Tillich in a sermon entitled "You Are Accepted." "Just accept the fact that you

15. See Carl E. Braaten, *Justification: The Article by Which the Church Stands or Falls* (Minneapolis: Fortress Press, 1990).

are accepted," said Tillich, "accepted by a power that is greater than you."[16]

But perhaps an even more powerful expression of the doctrine of justification comes out of the struggle of blacks for justice and freedom in North America and South Africa. An important element of the message of such eloquent preachers as Martin Luther King, Jr., Jesse Jackson, and Allan Boesak could be summarized in the affirmation that "we are somebodies." Interpreted in light of its gospel roots, this affirmation means that we are of worth despite the negative evaluation of the society in which we live or even our own negative self-evaluation. We are of worth not because our employers or teachers say so; not even because the president of the United States or the American constitution says so. We are somebodies because God our creator and our redeemer says so. It is because we are creatures made in the divine image, because we are children of God, persons for whom Jesus Christ suffered, died, and was raised again, persons in whom the Spirit of God is at work — because of all this, we are somebodies. That is the basis of our dignity, our worth, our human rights, and our human responsibilities.

A similar discovery is made by a character in Alice Walker's novel *The Color Purple*. When Celie expresses surprise that her friend Shug thinks that God loves her even if she doesn't do things like go to church, sing in the choir, and feed the preacher, Shug replies: "But if God love me, Celie, I don't have to do all that. Unless I want to."[17] Far from being irrelevant, such rediscoveries of the biblical message of justification by grace have revolutionary potency. We can be certain that the Caesars of history tremble when people discover that, just as they are — female, black, poor, or whatever their identity — they are loved by God and hence are not "nobodies" but "somebodies."

The Christian Life: Sanctification

IF justification by grace through faith is the foundation of the Christian life, *sanctification is the process of growth in Christian love.* The word *sanctification* means "to make holy," but that definition may be more a hindrance than a help. We should not understand holiness here in the

16. Tillich, *The Shaking of the Foundations* (New York: Scribner's, 1948), p. 162.
17. Walker, *The Color Purple* (New York: Washington Square Press, 1982), p. 176.

sense of moral flawlessness or religious otherworldliness. It certainly has little to do with the smug attitudes of the so-called Moral Majority. Becoming holy or sanctified in the New Testament sense means being conformed to the image of Christ by the working of the Holy Spirit in our lives. The essential mark of this Christ-likeness is that free self-giving, other-regarding love that the New Testament calls *agape*. Released from the compulsive power of self-centeredness, we are enabled to love God and our neighbors.

It is a mistake to think of sanctification as solely what *we* do in contrast to justification as solely *God's* work. Just as faith is properly understood as a response to the divine justification of human life, so love of God and our fellow creatures is properly understood as a response to the divine sanctification of human life in Jesus Christ. It is first of all the gift of God, and then also a human task.

The term *growth* must be used with care in reference to the Christian life. Any suggestion of an organic process of development or an ordered sequence of stages should be avoided. There is real movement in Christian life, but it is not predictable and does not take place in neatly identifiable stages. If we respect the freedom of God's grace and the limitless disguises that sin assumes, we will avoid oversimplification in our portrayals of the process of growth in Christian life. Still, in the environment of the Spirit of God, growth in Christian faith, love, and hope does occur. Several criteria or marks of growth in Christian life may be briefly mentioned.[18]

1. The first is *maturing as hearers of the Word of God.* Christian life is shaped and normed by the Word of God whose unique and primary witness is the Scripture of the Old and New Testaments. This Word proclaims God's grace and judgment and calls its hearers to repentance, conversion, and new life. Maturing as hearers of the Word means approaching Scripture not as a magical answer book but as the church's primary witness to the sovereign love of God supremely revealed in Jesus Christ. The Spirit of God uses the witness of Scripture to form and reform Christian life and to build and strengthen Christian character.

Mature hearing of the scriptural witness involves opening oneself

---

18. Cf. Paul Tillich's discussion of marks of growth in the Spirit in his *Systematic Theology*, 3: 231-37.

to all its formative influences: its narratives, poetry, parables, songs of praise, directives, promises, and warnings. Mature hearing also involves listening to this witness not as an isolated individual but in community. And it means allowing ourselves to be opened to new and surprising readings of Scripture by Christian communities in very different contexts from our own. The interpretations of Scripture by the poor and the afflicted especially will correct and deepen interpretations with which we are more familiar. When this kind of listening to Scripture occurs, we can be sure that the Spirit of God is at work.

What we are calling mature hearing of the Word of God will involve our readiness to assume responsibility for the fresh interpretation and praxis of the witness of Scripture in the present situation. Above all, mature hearing of the Word of God issues in a continuing transformation of life by the concrete practice of love of God and love of neighbor.

2. A second mark of Christian growth is *maturing in prayer.* Prayer is a concrete expression of our love of God. It is personal communication with God, calling upon God as a strong and caring father or mother (cf. Matt. 6:9; Rom. 8:15; Isa. 66:13). For the Christian, God is not some-*thing* but some*one* — and primarily someone who is spoken *to,* rather than only spoken *about.* Moreover, this someone addressed in prayer is not feared as a tyrant but genuinely loved as the sovereign and free God who exercises dominion with astonishing goodness and mercy. Prayer is thus our acceptance of the invitation to call upon God in confidence. Maturing in prayer does not mean mastering certain techniques or becoming virtuosos of the spiritual life. It means, on the contrary, being open and honest to God, praising God but also crying to God in our need, and even sometimes crying out against God.

Prayer is the fundamental exercise of the new human freedom in partnership with the Spirit of God. Calvin calls prayer "the chief exercise of faith."[19] While it includes adoration and thanksgiving, prayer is essentially bold petition. As instructed by Jesus, we are to pray for the hallowing of God's name, for the coming of God's reign, for the doing of God's will, for daily bread, for forgiveness, for deliverance from temptation (Matt. 6:9-13). Maturing in prayer means being ready to learn, in the presence of the God of costly grace, the difference between what we want and what we need. It means learning that at the beginning,

19. Calvin, *Institutes of the Christian Religion,* 3.20.

middle, and end of every fruitful human action is prayerful recognition of the prevenient and sustaining grace of God.[20]

3. A third mark of Christian growth is *maturing in freedom.* The Spirit of God is known by the fact that where it is at work, freedom flourishes (2 Cor. 3:17). The power of the Spirit does not work like a steamroller: it does not crush but rather empowers human life. It liberates from bondage rather than sanctioning old bondages or introducing new ones. The life of the Christian thus involves liberation from every legalism that strains at a gnat and swallows a camel (Matt. 23:24). While there is a "law of Christ" (Gal. 6:2) that is summed up in the command to love God and others, it is not a law that produces anxiety about our standing before God but a law that provides guidance for the exercise of new freedom in Christ.[21]

If Christian freedom can be described negatively as freedom *from* the terror of having to win God's favor, it can be described positively as freedom *for* the service of God and others. Augustine aptly characterizes Christian freedom in the statement "Love God, and do what you will."[22] The point of this remark is that if we love God above all else, we will freely do what God wills. Freedom in Christ is utterly different from self-indulgence. God's liberating grace sets in motion a struggle with the forces of evil within us and around us. The gospel is good news and bestows freedom, but when the good news breaks into human life, it exposes that life in all its ambiguity and questionableness. Struggle against evil, both within us and around us, is the inseparable companion of Christian freedom.

Christian growth thus means increasing freedom *from* the ideologies that prevent us from acknowledging and repenting of the injustice and inhumanity that we and our society promote, and increasing freedom *for* new opportunities of Christ-like service. Such service is costly, and in this sense suffering is a component of the process of sanctification. This has nothing to do with the idea of suffering for suffering's sake; it has

20. See Karl Barth, *The Christian Life* (Grand Rapids: William B. Eerdmans, 1981), and Jan Milič Lochman, *The Lord's Prayer* (Grand Rapids: William B. Eerdmans, 1990).

21. Calvin speaks of "three parts" of Christian liberty: freedom from the law, freedom for obedience, and freedom in indifferent matters (*Institutes of the Christian Religion,* 3.19).

22. Augustine, *Homilies on 1 John,* VII.8, in *Augustine: Later Works,* ed. John Burnaby (Philadelphia: Westminster Press, 1955), p. 316.

everything to do with the freedom to face suffering for the sake of the coming reign of God. As Moltmann notes, in a superficial, apathetic, and dehumanized society, willingness to risk suffering can be a sign of spiritual health.[23]

4. A fourth mark of Christian growth is *maturing in solidarity.* By "solidarity" I mean regard for and love of all our fellow creatures. This means in the first place love of our fellow human beings, and especially the poor and the neglected.[24] Growth in Christian life is a process of entering into solidarity with ever wider circles of community that are created and nourished by the Spirit. This new spirit of solidarity presupposes a *metanoia,* a repentance or renewal of the mind, whereby we cease to be attentive only to ourselves and become increasingly conscious of and sensitive to the needs of others.

Hearing the Word of God and partaking of the sacraments are concrete and regular practices of the community of faith that help to engender this new way of thinking, feeling, and living in the new solidarity in Christ with the whole groaning creation. If they do not serve this purpose, they are empty religious rites.

Christian life in many congregations is stifled by the fact that membership is all too homogeneous. Too many congregations are birds of a feather who have flocked together. Christian growth involves openness to and a search for heterogeneous and inclusive community. Church membership and mission should not be mere reflections of the socio-economic, cultural, racial, and gender divisions of secular society. Increasing solidarity with strangers, people commonly considered undesirables, and even enemies is a criterion of growth in Christian life.

But maturing in solidarity for the Christian also entails solidarity with the whole realm of nonhuman creatures. Regnant anthropocentrism in our everyday attitudes, our lifestyles, and our economic and political decisions is an obstacle to growth in Christian life. Growth in solidarity always comes at a cost. It is costly both in the sense of requiring us to give up self-centered ways of thinking and living and in the sense of arousing opposition and perhaps even persecution from those who see the movement toward solidarity as a deadly threat rather than a blessing.

---

23. Moltmann, *The Crucified God* (New York: Harper & Row, 1974), p. 115.

24. Solidarity with the poor is the central theme of Latin American liberation spirituality. See Gustavo Gutiérrez, *A Theology of Liberation* (Maryknoll, N.Y.: Orbis Books, 1973), and *We Drink from Our Own Wells* (Maryknoll, N.Y.: Orbis Books, 1984).

Classical theological descriptions of the Christian life, following Scripture, have rightly always emphasized the inescapability of cross-bearing in the life of the disciples of the crucified Lord.[25]

5. A final mark of growth in Christian life is *maturing in thankfulness and joy.* The Heidelberg Catechism sums up the Christian life under the term *thanksgiving.* In the same confessional tradition, the Presbyterian Church (U.S.A.) Brief Statement of Faith includes these lines: "In gratitude to God, empowered by the Spirit, we strive to serve Christ in our daily tasks, and to live holy and joyful lives" (ll. 72-74). Of course, the joy and thanksgiving that belong essentially to Christian life are very different from superficial optimism or artificial cheeriness. We are speaking of a thankfulness and an impulse to celebrate that come from the heart and express themselves in prayer and eucharist, new friendship and joyful service. This thanksgiving, praise, and joy grow out of confidence in God, who by the Spirit has already begun the renewal of life in Christ and whose grace will ultimately triumph over all evil, sin, and death. Grace generates thanksgiving; *charis* brings forth eucharist. For this reason, the eucharistic meal — anticipation of the joyful messianic banquet — will always be the central act of Christian worship. There is much to protest and much to struggle against in the church and in society, in one's own life and in the life of the body politic. As Calvin and all great theologians of the Christian life have emphasized, cross-bearing is a signature of growth in grace. Still, in the midst of struggle and cross-bearing, Christians grow as they continue to give thanks. We show ourselves to be maturing Christians as our capacity for thanksgiving, praise, and joy go hand in hand with our readiness for costly discipleship.

The Christian Life: Vocation

CHRISTIAN life is a movement toward a goal. God not only justifies and sanctifies human life in the power of the Spirit but also gives it a particular vocation and a great hope. When this aspect of God's work of liberation and reconciliation is neglected, a certain narrowness and even narcissism creeps into the life of faith and the work of theology.[26]

25. Cf. Calvin, *Institutes of the Christian Religion*, 3.8.

26. As Karl Barth writes, "The *articulus stantis et cadentis ecclesiae* is not the doctrine of justification as such, but its basis and culmination: the confession of Jesus Christ in

The themes of election and vocation are deeply embedded in the biblical witness. God calls Abraham, chooses the people of Israel, summons the prophets, sends Jesus of Nazareth, and commissions the followers of Jesus for service in the world. Indeed, Scripture speaks of the election of the people of God in Jesus Christ before the foundation of the world (Eph. 1:4). But in spite of the pervasive presence of the themes of election and vocation in the Bible, they are virtually forgotten or unintelligible doctrines for many Christians today.

God freely elects creatures to be partners in the mending of creation. Election is a call not to privilege but to service. Israel is chosen by God to be a blessing to all the nations of the earth (Gen. 12:2-3). The servant of God is to be a light to the nations (Isa. 42:6; 49:6). Jesus Christ is the chosen Son of God who obediently does the work of God and calls others to take part in this work (John 4:34; 15:16). Human beings are called to be co-workers with God in the mission of liberation and reconciliation. They receive new dignity and purpose when they are given this task. Every gift of the Spirit of God includes a responsibility. As Dietrich Bonhoeffer writes, the grace of God is freely given, but it is not cheap. We have been called and commissioned to costly service.[27]

The vocation of a Christian is not to be confused with having a job by which one earns one's livelihood. Whatever one's job or profession, as a Christian one is called to be a partner in God's mission in the world. Christian life involves inward growth and renewal, but it does not turn in on itself. It participates in a movement outward to others and forward to the future of the completion of God's redemptive activity. The Christian vocation is the ministry of liberative reconciliation, the call to invite all into a new community where justice is done and where freedom and love flourish, a community that is grounded in Christ, empowered by the Spirit, and destined for participation in the eternal communion of the triune God. Universal participation in the love of the triune God made known in Christ and effectively at work in the activity of the Holy Spirit is the goal of Christian mission.

Christians live by the promise of God and thus in creative hope. There is work to be done, a message to be proclaimed, service to be rendered, hostility to be overcome, injustice to be rectified. Guided by

---

whom are hid all the treasures of wisdom and knowledge (Col. 2:3); the knowledge of his being and activity for us and to us and in us" (*Church Dogmatics,* IV/1: 527).

27. Bonhoeffer, *The Cost of Discipleship* (London: SCM Press, 1959), p. 45.

the Word and Spirit of God, Christians take up these tasks in confidence and hope in the final fulfillment of God's promise of a new humanity in a new heaven and a new earth. Christian life is more than acceptance of the forgiveness of sins and more than personal transformation. It is also the vocation to participate in the preparation of all creation for the coming of the new community of justice, freedom, and peace in partnership with the triune God.

10

The New Community

For many Christians the doctrine of the church, or ecclesiology, is perhaps the least interesting and the most irritating topic of Christian theology. "Jesus yes, church no" nicely summarizes the anger and frustration that discussion of the church frequently arouses. Faith in God the creator, trust in Christ and his reconciling work, and experience of the transforming power of the Holy Spirit are all recognized as vital aspects of Christian faith and theology. While these doctrines may prompt numerous questions, as a rule their importance is not doubted. However, this is not the case with the doctrine of the church, a subject many associate with the politics of organization and management but hardly with realities indispensable to Christian faith and life. Such an attitude contrasts sharply with the understanding of the church in the Bible and in classical Christian confessions. The Nicene Creed contains the familiar words, "I believe in . . . one, holy, catholic and apostolic church." Augustine declared that he would not have believed except for the church, and John Calvin spoke of the church as the "mother" of believers.[1]

My thesis in this chapter will be that if the very nature of God is communal, if God enters into covenant with creatures and seeks their

---

1. Calvin, *Institutes of the Christian Religion,* 4.1.4. The entire passage is worth quoting: "Because it is now our intention to discuss the visible church, let us learn even from the simple title 'mother' how useful, indeed how necessary it is that we should know her. For there is no other way to enter into life unless this mother conceive us in her womb, give us birth, nourish us at her breast, and lastly unless she keep us under her care and guidance until, putting off mortal flesh, we become like the angels. Our weakness does not allow us to be dismissed from her school until we have been pupils all our lives."

partnership, then questions regarding the nature of the church and its mission in the world today, far from being matters of secondary importance to the understanding of Christian faith, are quite central. The end for which the world was created and redeemed is deep and lasting communion between God and creation, a commonwealth of justice, reconciliation, and freedom based on the grace of God. While flawed and always in need of reform and renewal, the church is nonetheless the real beginning of God's new and inclusive community of liberated creatures reconciled to God and to each other and called to God's service in the world.

The Problem of the Church

WHILE there are many problems that people have with the church today, several are widespread and deep-seated.

1. A great deal of misunderstanding and even hostility to the church results from the *individualism* that saturates American culture. Some of our most powerful cultural myths and images center on the self-made and independent individual who achieves success in life without assistance from others. Independence rather than interdependence is our cultural bias, and this has an impact on the prevailing understandings of Christian faith and life. A sense of the importance of community is, of course, not entirely absent from modern Western society. Characteristically, however, the groups to which the self-sufficient individual or private person belongs are "voluntary societies," groups one chooses to join and in which one remains a member for as long as they meet one's needs and serve one's purposes. In much white North American Christianity, this translates into a self-centered piety in which the church is quite secondary and frankly unnecessary. Being a Christian is an individual matter and is not essentially bound to life with others. This individualism hides the profound hunger for companionship and community that runs beneath the surface of life in America.[2]

2. Not only is religious belief and practice individualized in modern culture; it also assumes a *privatized* form. That is, the world of work and public affairs is separated from the world of domesticity, leisure, personal

2. See Robert N. Bellah et al., *Habits of the Heart: Individualism and Commitment in American Life* (Berkeley and Los Angeles: University of California Press, 1985).

nurture, and religion. The process of privatization severs the message and mission of the church from the larger questions and struggles of life. If any purpose of the church is recognized, it is to serve the needs of private individuals and small homogeneous groups.

3. Still another obstacle to a proper understanding of the church is its accommodation to *bureaucratic organization*. Bureaucracy is a system of administration marked by anonymity, adherence to fixed rules, hierarchy of authority, and the proliferation of officials. The ultimate in modern bureaucracy is the reduction of relationships between people to communication with a machine. The church is subject, like all organizations, to bureaucratic pressures. Out of forgetfulness of its own essence, the church attempts to mimic the organizational structures and managerial techniques of profitable corporations. When the church succumbs to these pressures, it loses its true identity and its distinctive mission in the world.

4. Another major source of the problems that many people have with the church is to be found in the conspicuous and disturbing discrepancy between the expressed faith of the church and its *actual practice*. As Nietzsche wrote, "They would have to sing better songs to make me believe in their Redeemer: his disciples would have to look more redeemed!"[3] There is a chasm between what is proclaimed and what is practiced. As a result, the language about the community called *church* sounds shamelessly triumphalistic and unreal. The church is one (Does it only appear to be broken into countless racial, national, and class factions?); the church is holy (Does it only seem to be a community of very fallible and sinful people?); the church is catholic (Is it merely an illusion that the church is often provincial and hypocritically self-interested?); the church is apostolic (Does it only appear to have frequently set itself above the apostles?).

As Joseph Haroutunian points out, statements like these embarrass and upset us because we know that the church is different from what we say it is.[4] To the extent that Israel and the early church were a people up against the wall — poor, weak, and in peril — their language about the reality of the people of God had a dignity. It was intended to comfort

---

3. Nietzsche *(Thus Spake Zarathustra)*, quoted by Hans Küng, in *The Church* (New York: Sheed & Ward, 1967), p. 150.

4. Haroutunian, "The Realization of the Church," *Theology Today* 17 (1960): 137-43.

and support God's little, marginal, often persecuted people. But when the same language is used to describe the church as we know it, the language goes false on us. We know that the language is only cosmetic, and we become embarrassed or angry. Because of their sensitivity to this predicament, a favorite motto of ecumenical church leaders in this century has been "Let the church be the church!" (John Mackay). Let the church live and act like the body of Christ, the temple of the Spirit, and the servant people of God. This is a summons to the church to stop preening itself with all sorts of metaphysical compliments without any corresponding social reality and praxis.

Missing in the individualized, privatized, bureaucratic, and cosmetic forms of Christianity today is any real understanding of the interconnectedness of life that is expressed in all the basic doctrines and symbols of classical Christian faith. Christians confess their faith in the triune God whose reality is constituted by the welcoming love of Father, Son, and Holy Spirit. Christians believe in God the creator, who wills not to be alone but to have a covenant partner; in God the liberator and reconciler, whose costly grace in Jesus Christ inaugurates a new freedom for relationship with God and with others; and in God the Holy Spirit, who is the power of new community-in-freedom that anticipates the redemption of all creation. The Christian understanding of God as trinitarian communion and of salvation as the free participation of creatures in God's society of love highlights the importance of the church for Christian faith and theology.

Thus the call for the reform and renewal of the church today does not derive from a "craze for modernity" but from a fresh apprehension of the gospel that gave the church life.[5] When we honestly admit the problems of the church — which have their roots in our forgetfulness of the profoundly social meanings of all the articles of the faith as well as in our failure to hold together faith and praxis — we may begin to catch sight of the mystery of the church. The mystery is that through the free grace of God in Jesus Christ at work in the world by the power of the Holy Spirit, God is breaking down all walls of separation and making "one new humanity" (Eph. 2:15). The mystery of the church is that it is called to share in the trinitarian love of God, the God who gives existence to others, shares life and power, and lives in the mutual giving and receiving of love. The church is called to be the beginning of new

5. See Küng, *The Church,* p. xi.

human life in relationship, solidarity, and friendship beyond all privatism, classism, racism, and sexism.

New Testament Images of the Church

IN the New Testament the *ecclesia,* or church, refers to the new community of believers gathered to praise and serve God in response to the ministry, death, and resurrection of Jesus and in the power of the Holy Spirit. The word *church* can designate either local assemblies of Christians or the universal Christian community.

If we probe somewhat deeper, we find that the *ecclesia* as described in the New Testament refers to a unique and transformed way of being human in relationship with God and with other persons. It designates a distinctive form of human community characterized by mutuality, interdependence, forgiveness, and friendship. In the *ecclesia* power and responsibility are shared and there is always a special concern for the poor, the weak, and the despised. Ecclesial life is a new community of free persons centered on God's love in Jesus Christ and empowered to service by the Holy Spirit.[6]

In the New Testament the church and its ecclesial form of life are related to but never identified with the coming reign of God. The church is a sign and provisional manifestation of the reign of God. The triumphalistic identification of the church with the reign of God has been the source of much arrogance and destructiveness in church history. The church anticipates and serves the coming reign of God but does not fully realize it.

The New Testament describes the church, or *ecclesia* (literally, "those called out"), in many different images and metaphors. In his book *Images of the Church in the New Testament,* Paul Minear lists some ninety-six different images or analogies of the church found in the New Testament.[7] Clearly, there is a surplus of biblical images in regard to the church as there is also in regard to God and the person and work of Jesus Christ.

---

6. For a penetrating analysis of the sociality of the life of faith, see Edward Farley, *Ecclesial Man: A Social Phenomenology of Faith and Reality* (Philadelphia: Fortress Press, 1975).

7. Minear, *Images of the Church in the New Testament* (Philadelphia: Westminister Press, 1960).

Among the many images of the church are: "the body of Christ" (1 Cor. 12:27), "the salt of the earth" (Matt. 5:13), "a letter of Christ" (2 Cor. 3:2-3), "fishers for people" (Mark 1:17), "branches of the vine" (John 15:5), "the field of God," "the building of God" (1 Cor. 3:9), a building on a rock (Matt. 16:18), "the bride of Christ" (Eph. 5:23-32), "God's own people" (1 Pet. 2:9), a "new Jerusalem" (Rev. 21:2), "the household of God" (Eph. 2:19), "strangers and foreigners" (Heb. 11:13), and "the poor" (Luke 6:20).

From the rich inventory of New Testament imagery of the church, four major clusters may be identified.[8]

1. One set of images centers in the description of the church as the *people of God,* and especially the exodus people of God. The theme of the covenant between God and God's elect people is deeply embedded in both the Old and the New Testaments. "I . . . will be your God, and you shall be my people" (Lev. 26:12). "You are . . . God's own people, in order that you may proclaim the mighty acts of him who called you out of darkness into his marvelous light" (1 Pet. 2:9). According to this cluster of images, the church is not primarily a building or an organization but a people, a community, and specifically the people of God who have been called by God. Related to this image of the church as the people of God are images such as chosen race, holy nation, new Israel, sons and daughters of Abraham, remnant, and the elect. A basic function of this constellation of images is to connect the Christian community to the historic Israelite community of God based on the covenant promises and to describe this people as an exodus, pilgrim community, a people called out for a special task and set on the way toward a new homeland. One of the great achievements of the Second Vatican Council was to give renewed prominence to this image of the church as the people of God.

2. A second set of images describes this people of God as a *servant people.* This is a very prominent motif of the Old Testament. Repeatedly, Yahweh calls for the liberation of the people of Israel "that they may serve me" (Exod. 8:1; 9:1; 10:3). The theme of a servant people is no less important in the New Testament. Just as the Lord of this community is a servant Lord, so the community called by God is to be a community of servants. "The Son of Man came not to be served but to serve and to give

8. Cf. Peter C. Hodgson, *Revisioning the Church: Ecclesial Freedom in the New Paradigm* (Philadelphia: Fortress Press, 1988). I am indebted to Hodgson's study at a number of points in this chapter.

his life a ransom for many" (Mark 10:45). Christians are likewise to be servants — "servants for Jesus' sake" (2 Cor. 4:5). Called to serve God and others, the church is not to exercise power in a self-centered way or to lord it over others but to be ready for costly service (Matt. 20:25-26). There are many images that cluster around this service image. The people of God are co-workers, helpers, ambassadors, and witnesses. All of these images suggest that this particular community has its reason for being not in itself but in its task, which is to serve God and the world created by God. The church's service of God finds expression in its worship, prayer, and praise; the church's service to the world takes the form of witness in word and in deed to God's grace and God's call for justice. These two aspects of the service of the church are integrally related, as in Jesus' twofold commandment to love God and our neighbors.

3. A third set of images focuses on the metaphor of the church as the *body of Christ*. This description of the church occurs in the Pauline letters (above all, 1 Cor. 12:12-31). The community participates in one Lord, one Spirit, one baptism, and thus becomes "one body." This organic image of the church as a body whose head is Christ has been enormously influential in Christian theology and in the history of the church. The image conveys the mutual dependence of all members of the community on one another, their variety of gifts which are for the enrichment and edification of the whole community, and the common dependence of all members of the body on the one head who is Christ (cf. Col. 1:15-20; Eph. 5:23). The unity of the church as one body is indispensable if it is to be effective in carrying out its mission in the world.

4. A final set of images portrays the activity of God in creating a community of the end-time, a *community of the Spirit*, filled by the gifts of the Spirit. In the renewing experience of the Spirit of God, the New Testament church sees important evidence of the fulfillment of the promises of the prophets (Acts 2:17ff.). Racial, gender, and class divisions are broken down (Gal. 3:28); strangers are welcomed; the sharing of power replaces domination. Empowered and guided by the Spirit, the community is God's "new creation," the first signs of God's new humanity, the "firstfruits" of a glorious new age. This cluster of eschatological symbols of the church all point to the radical new beginning of life realized in the coming of Christ and his Spirit and the promise of still more comprehensive renewal and transformation to come. The church serves and suffers but also celebrates and hopes, because it already experiences a foretaste of new life and joy in the *koinonia*, the fellowship of the Holy

Spirit. The church is thus a sign of the kingdom of God. As an "alternative community" in which a new Spirit of freedom reigns and in which the most wretched are included and even enemies are welcome, the church gives the world reason to hope.[9]

Critique of Current Models of the Church

INSTRUCTED by these New Testament images of the church, it is possible to review critically some models of the church both past and present. Whereas images and symbols constitute the more immediate language of faith, the term *model* refers to a theoretical construct that is employed to deepen our understanding of a complex reality. Avery Dulles identifies several models of the church: institution, mystical communion, sacrament, herald, and servant.[10] In the following paragraphs I will make use of his categories but develop them in my own way.

1. Among the most influential models of the church is that of an *institution of salvation*. This view defines the church primarily in terms of divinely authorized structures, officers, procedures, and traditions. As institution, the church has a definite form and organization. The chain of power and authority is precisely determined. Some organizational features — structures of leadership, patterns of worship, authoritative writings — are, of course, already evident in the church of the New Testament period. Within a century or two, the structures of canon, bishop, and doctrine had become well developed and provided stability and coherence to the community. But an institutional view of the church was characteristic neither of the patristic period nor of the Middle Ages; it achieved dominance only in the nineteenth century.

Institutional structure belongs to the humanity of the church. Some kind of structure and order is a necessity in any historical community. It is sheer romanticism to suggest otherwise. But the institutionalist view of the church, especially when it has entered into alliance with state power, has done far more harm than good. It has not resisted the temptation to see the purpose of the church as institutional survival and domination rather than costly service. One might describe the

9. See David J. Bosch, *The Church as Alternative Community* (Potschefstroom: Instituut vir Reformatoriese Studie, 1982).

10. Dulles, *Models of the Church* (New York: Doubleday Image Books, 1974).

characteristics of the church according to the institutional model as being rather like those of an imperial state. Typically, order in this church is hierarchical rather than representative or interactional. Power always flows from the top to the bottom. Furthermore, power is centralized in the hands of the few who are supposedly ordained by God to rule over the silent and powerless masses of believers. Above all, there is the mentality of maintenance of the institution and, if possible, extension of its power.

While all this is portrayed in Protestant polemics as the typically Roman Catholic version of the church, the truth is that the tendency of the institutional structures of the church to grow and harden into institutionalism has proved to be very real in both Catholic and Protestant ecclesial life. When this happens, hierarchy triumphs over community, and the mentality of survival supplants the spirit of service. In the Reformed churches, there has been much emphasis on the priesthood of all believers, on ordained ministry as functional rather than metaphysical, and on the stirring motto *ecclesia reformata semper reformanda* — "The church reformed, always in need of being reformed." Such principles fight against the tendency toward institutional sclerosis, but they have often been honored more in word than in practice. Whereas Roman Catholic institutionalism identifies the church with the hierarchy, Protestant institutionalism identifies the church with its own patterns of organization and tests of orthodoxy.

The strongest criticism of the over-institutionalized church comes today neither from liberal Catholic nor classical Protestant sources but from Latin American liberation theology. We do not rightly understand this theology unless we recognize that one of its important concerns is critique and reformation of a hierarchical, over-centralized, and anxious institutional church. In the judgment of liberation theologians, the institutional church all too often exercises power in a manner resembling that of totalitarian governments and exploitative corporations. Leonardo Boff even compares the institutional church to a business enterprise with an elite in charge of the capital (the sacraments) and with the masses reduced to mere consumers.[11] Because the church is not immune to the temptation to seize and abuse power, the structures of the church must be continuously challenged and converted by the gospel and its summons to risk-taking service.

11. See Boff, *The Church: Charism and Power* (New York: Crossroad, 1985), p. 43.

2. Another model of the church portrays it as *intimate community of the Spirit.* According to this view, the church is not so much a formal organization as it is a closely knit group whose members share a common experience of God's revivifying Spirit. Whereas the church in its traditional form is large, hierarchically organized, impersonal, and often insensitive to the needs of individuals, the typical spiritual community is small, personal, loosely organized, and develops a strong sense of belonging and mutual support among its members.

The principal task of the church so conceived becomes the facilitation of spiritual experiences and the promotion of interpersonal relationships. The church as intimate community takes different forms. In Catholicism, an ecclesiology of mystical communion, developed partly in reaction to deadening institutional and hierarchical structures, has encouraged a more personalistic understanding of the church and has recognized the importance of the gifts of the Spirit to all the people of God. Protestantism has produced a variety of understandings of the church as spiritual community. One appears in the charismatic movement, which emphasizes the gifts of the Spirit and special experiences of spiritual healing and renewal. Individuals who have had these experiences often form close, mutually supportive groups.

The model of the church as intimate community undoubtedly addresses real human needs. Many people in modern society are desperately lonely and battle-scarred. They seek a safe refuge and a community where they can feel at home. Some are physically and spiritually broken by their efforts to survive in a depersonalized and indifferent social order, and they cry out for spiritual healing and new meaning for their lives. With its emphasis on prayer, meditation, spiritual exercises, and exchange of personal experiences, the church as intimate community cultivates a more personal and egalitarian experience of life in community than does the institutional model of the church. Whatever its limitations, such ministry to individuals in need is an essential element of the mission of the church. Much of Jesus' ministry, it may be noted, was devoted to the healing of the sick in body and spirit (Mark 1:32-34).

But there are some weaknesses in this model as well. These become especially evident when the understanding of Christian community is uncritically borrowed from movements in contemporary culture and ecclesial life becomes indistinguishable from encounter sessions, sensitivity groups, and other kinds of therapeutic-religious communities that are so popular today. It is not always clear what distinguishes such communities as specifically Christian. An ecstatic experience of the holy or an experience of intimacy and bonding with another does not necessarily constitute an experience of Christian faith. Moreover, therapy-oriented communities tend to concentrate on the individual's growth at the expense of the larger social responsibilities of the community. Currently popular New Age spirituality provides evidence of this fact. A church that copies such patterns of spirituality and intimate community becomes simply a haven from an insensitive and bureaucratic society and its depersonalizing effects. It becomes, in other words, an escape from, rather than a renewing critique of, the larger society that is in need of transformation. While the church is indeed the community of the Spirit in which all have gifts and in which power is shared, the New Testament views this new Spirit-guided community as called to serve God's purpose of both personal and world transformation.

3. Another current model of the church is that of *sacrament of salvation.* Increasingly prominent in Roman Catholic theology since Vatican II, the model of the church as sacrament emphasizes that in its worship, witness, and service, the church is the sign of the continuing presence of the grace of God in Jesus Christ in history. As interpreted by some theologians, the model draws attention primarily to the church's own sacramental life, and particularly to participation in the eucharist. In the community nourished and renewed by eucharistic action, the redemptive work of Christ is extended to all humanity. One of the strengths of the sacramental model is its combination of the objective and subjective aspects of the life of the church, which tend to be separated in the institutional and mystical models.

But the model of the church as sacrament also has its weaknesses. It can lean toward ecclesiocentrism, often in the form of liturgism. Christ and the Spirit are thought to be at work primarily in the rites of the church. This may result in a decline of emphasis on the social responsibility of the faith community. While some Latin American liberation theologians have adopted the model of the church as sacrament, they use the phrase to refer to the church's embodiment of God's redemptive activity in history through the praxis of solidarity with the poor. As a sacramental community, the church should signify both in its internal structures and in its social praxis the liberation of life that it announces.[12]

12. Cf. Gustavo Gutiérrez, *A Theology of Liberation* (Maryknoll, N.Y.: Orbis Books, 1988), pp. 143ff.

4. A fourth prominent model of the church is that of *herald of good news.* This is the understanding of the church that has been primary in the Protestant traditions. It is based on the conviction that the church's mission is above all to proclaim the Word of God and to call the nations to repentance and new life. Men and women are to be summoned to put their faith in Jesus as Savior and Lord. All matters of institutional structure and satisfaction of personal needs are to be subordinated to the task of proclamation and evangelization.

An evaluation of this model of the church as herald must begin with the acknowledgment that the proclamation of the gospel is indeed a primary task of the community of faith. However, this task has often been construed in rather narrow terms. When the model of the church as herald dominates or even excludes other models, it is easy for the church to take a patronizing and self-righteous attitude toward people and cultures to whom the Word is to be proclaimed. Then the church only speaks and never listens. If the church as herald is not to be an instrument of domination, it must be willing to be instructed by others how it might best be of service to them and, equally important, what they may have to give as well as receive. Moreover, a holistic understanding of service is often missing from this model. Preoccupation with the delivery of the message may override the concern to meet concrete human needs for food, shelter, medical care, education, and other basics of dignified human life.

5. A fifth current model of the church portrays it as *servant* of the servant Lord. This may also be called the diaconal model. According to this view, the church is not primarily an institution whose purpose is survival and expansion, nor an intimate community designed to foster the personal growth of individuals who feel neglected and depersonalized by modern society, nor merely the herald of a message. The church is a servant community called to minister in God's name on behalf of fullness of life for all of God's creatures.

According to this model, the church serves God by serving the world in its struggle for emancipation, justice, and peace. Dietrich Bonhoeffer defined the church as the community that exists for others. "The church," he wrote, "must share in the secular problems of ordinary human life, not dominating but helping and serving."[13] This model of

13. Bonhoeffer, *Letters and Papers from Prison* (New York: Macmillan, 1967), p. 204.

the church for others, a church that is servant rather than master of the world, has been influential in many modern ecclesiologies. It plays an important role both in the emphasis on the church's mission of reconciliation in the midst of conflict and in the call to the church to participate in the struggle for the liberation of the oppressed.

In the Presbyterian Church (U.S.A.) Confession of 1967, which takes as its primary theme God's work of reconciliation in Jesus Christ, the service of the church is described in terms of the ministry of reconciliation within every sphere of life. The ministry of reconciliation includes both proclamation of God's grace and forgiveness and struggle for reconciliation in societies torn by racism, international conflict, indifference to poverty, and sexual exploitation.

Liberation theologies, suspicious of premature calls to reconciliation that often bypass the reality of oppression and the need to struggle against it,[14] understand the proper service of the church as participating in God's liberating activity in the world, exposing conditions of bondage, calling for the conversion of people and corporate structures, prompting prophetic action on behalf of justice and freedom, and sustaining believers in their struggle against the power of evil and in their solidarity with the poor.

The concrete form of ecclesial life that helped to give birth to liberation theology is the "Christian base community."[15] These base communities, especially prominent in Latin America but a growing phenomenon throughout the Third World, are often in the thick of movements for social change. Made up of small groups of poor people in particular localities who gather to pray, interpret the Bible together, and relate their faith to their common, everyday problems, the Christian base communities understand themselves as experiments in a new way of being the church. Often led by laity, the base communities are far more communitarian than hierarchical. Power is shared rather than centralized. In the light of the gospel, the people analyze such problems as water or electricity shortages, inadequate sewers, widespread unemployment, low wages, lack of schools, police harassment, and state persecution. They

14. The *Kairos Document*, which was written in the context of the struggle against apartheid in South Africa, criticizes both a "state theology" that endorses apartheid and a "church theology" that avoids real struggle with injustice with talk of reconciliation.

15. See *The Challenge of Basic Christian Communities*, ed. John Eagleson and Sergio Torres (Maryknoll, N.Y.: Orbis Books, 1982).

consider strategies of change and offer support to each other in their various tasks.[16] Yet the Christian base communities cannot be reduced to mere political action groups. While it is true that they are decidedly oriented to the praxis of faith in the world, they find strength in a distinctive spirituality of prayer, Bible reading, and eucharistic fellowship.

The servant model of the church has much to contribute. At its best, it helps to overcome the split between the spiritual and the mundane, between concern for evangelization and struggle for justice, a split all too frequent in other models of the church. Like Bonhoeffer, Karl Barth insists that the church exists for the world. Because God first and supremely exists for the world, the church is to exist not for itself but for others.[17] The missionary character of the church is not incidental but quite essential to its very being as the people of God.

There are also dangers of distortion in the servant model, of course. Many feminist theologians doubt that the idea of service by itself is the most appropriate way to characterize the new life in Christ.[18] They argue that for women in particular, service has meant always being submissive and allowing others to dominate one's life rather than entering into new freedom and friendship in Christ (John 15:15) that empowers service of others. While service of God and others is central to Christian identity, its meaning must be carefully distinguished from servitude and self-negation.

Other dangers may threaten the servant model of the church. The church may forget what the basis and goal of its service is, with the result that ecclesiology is reduced to social function. Further, the church that understands itself as servant of the world may tend to subordinate nurture of the spiritual life to zeal for political action. Closely related to this is the ever-present danger of an uncritical identification of the reign of God with a particular program of social and political change. This is frequently accompanied by a loss of self-criticism and openness to reform. Social activism may overlook the many forms of bondage from which human

16. See Carl Mesters, *Defenseless Little Flower* (Maryknoll, N.Y.: Orbis Books, 1989).

17. Says Barth, "As the people created by Jesus Christ and obedient to him, it is not subsequently or incidentally but originally, essentially, and *per definitionem* summoned and impelled to exist for God and therefore for the world and men" (*Church Dogmatics*, IV/3.2: 762).

18. See, e.g., Susan Nelson Dunfee, *Beyond Servanthood: Christianity and the Liberation of Women* (Lanham, Md.: University Press of America, 1989).

beings need to be liberated: the sins of pride, greed, apathy, presumption, and self-indulgence, no less than such structural forms of sin as economic exploitation, racism, sexism, and domestic and state-sponsored violence. It makes little sense to set these various liberation concerns against each other.

Perhaps the greatest obstacle to a proper understanding of the church is the absolutization of any of its historical forms or of any particular ecclesiology. The gospel of the crucified and risen Jesus Christ is always greater than our theologies, including our theologies of the church. When the church keeps its eyes on Christ, it is in touch with the one necessary power of continuous reform and renewal of ecclesial life. The ever-present danger of triumphalistic ecclesiocentrism may even be aggravated by the search for a supermodel of the church that would somehow combine the virtues of all other models without showing any of their limitations. No doubt every ecclesiology, while needing to remain open to the insights of all models, will in fact have to choose one working model. But it will then have the responsibility to show how this particular understanding of the church coheres with the biblical witness to Jesus Christ in whom God's kingdom has dawned — and how it helps Christians here and now to grasp their identity as a new people in Christ who are called to participate in his liberating and reconciling mission in the world.

Consistent with the trinitarian emphases throughout this book, I am convinced that ecclesiology needs to be developed in closer relationship with trinitarian doctrine.[19] A trinitarian ecclesiology would take its basic clue from the fact that the most fundamental Christian affirmation about the God who has been revealed in Jesus Christ through the continuing activity of the Holy Spirit is that God is extravagant, outreaching love. The triune God is a missionary God, and the mission of the church is rooted in the trinitarian missions.[20] Furthermore, according to trinitarian doctrine, the very nature of God is communal, and the end for

19. According to Colin E. Gunton, "the manifest inadequacy of the theology of the church derives from the fact that it has never seriously and consistently been rooted in a conception of the being of God as triune" ("The Church on Earth: The Roots of Community," in *On Being the Church: Essays on the Christian Community*, ed. Colin E. Gunton and Daniel W. Hardy [Edinburgh: T. & T. Clark, 1990], p. 48).

20. On the basis of Christian mission in trinitarian theology, see Lesslie Newbigin, *The Open Secret: Sketches for a Missionary Theology* (Grand Rapids: William B. Eerdmans, 1978).

which God created and reconciled the world is depth of communion between God and creatures. The church is the community called into being, built up, and sent into the world to serve in the name and power of the triune God.[21] When the church is true to its own being and mission, it offers an earthly correspondence to God's own unity in diversity, to the inclusive and welcoming love of the other that characterizes the communion of the triune God.

Classical Marks of the Church

SINCE the church is not identical with the reign of God but is only its witness and anticipatory realization, it should not be surprising that the life of the people of God is filled with dynamic tensions. When these tensive elements are no longer held together in such a way that they are mutually corrective and mutually enriching, they become polar opposites that struggle against each other and threaten to destroy the integrity of the church.

It is destructive to drive a wedge between the church as a charismatic community and the church as an institution with order and structure. Spiritual vitality without some form and structure is chaotic, just as institutional form without spiritual vitality is empty and deadening. Order in the church should be understood functionally, not ontologically; provisionally, not permanently; interactionally, not hierarchically. The order of the church must always be subject to reform by God's Word and Spirit.

It is destructive to compel people to choose between the worshiping church and the socially involved church. Praise and prayer must not be set against service and action in the name of Christ, or vice versa. What kind of prayer is it that fails to open people to the service of God in the world? And what kind of Christian action is it that is not rooted in the prayer for forgiveness and in all the other petitions of the Lord's Prayer?

It is destructive to play off the church of the Word and the church of the sacraments, or vice versa. A good Reformed church, according to the stereotype, is a church of the Word and not a sacramental church; and a good Catholic church, the stereotype continues, is a sacramental church and not a church of the Word. This is a deeply injurious dichot-

---

21. See Karl Barth's doctrine of the church in *Church Dogmatics*, IV/1-3.

omy. What is the Word that is not accompanied by its concrete enactment in the sacraments? What is a sacrament that is unaccompanied by the strong and clear Word of God?

It is destructive to permit a split to develop between an inclusive church and a partisan church. We must not so interpret the inclusiveness of the church that we are afraid ever to take sides on crucial issues of justice and peace. Otherwise reconciliation becomes a cheap word for avoiding all conflict and lacking the courage to take a stand. On the other hand, the partisanship of the church must always have a catholic or inclusive intention. If the universality of the church is achieved only through particularity, the church's commitment to particular people and their needs aims at universality.

The dynamic tensions of ecclesial existence must be kept in mind in any helpful reinterpretation of the classical "marks" of the church. According to the Nicene Creed, the church is "one, holy, catholic, and apostolic." These are often cited in the theological tradition as the marks or essential characteristics of the true church.[22]

1. What is meant by the *unity* of the church? The unity of the church is not to be found primarily in structures, offices, doctrines, or programs. It is a distinctive unity rooted in new fellowship with God through Christ in the Spirit. The unity of the church is a fragmentary and provisional participation in the costly love of the triune God. Unity in the love of this God cannot possibly mean lifeless uniformity or deadening sameness. The unity of the church is a unity of love that enters into relationship with others and finds identity in relationship.

The love of God, and the unity of the church which is grounded in it, is a lavish celebration of the communion of the different. As creator of heaven and earth, God gives existence to a vast diversity of beings. As reconciler, God unites in new fellowship those who were once estranged from God and from each other. As sanctifier, God the Holy Spirit brings together a community made up of people of many nations, cultures, and ethnic groups and empowers them with many gifts for mutual service in the church and in the world. The New Testament speaks of the unity of the church as an expression of the unity of the triune God. It is a unity that is to reflect the communion of Father and Son in the Spirit (John 17:21). It is a unity of those previously estranged who, having been

22. In the following reflections I am indebted to the work of Jürgen Moltmann, *The Church in the Power of the Spirit* (New York: Harper & Row, 1977).

reconciled by the cross of Christ, now have access in one Spirit to the Father (Eph. 2:18). The unity generated by the triune God is thus no stifling, suffocating unity. It is a differentiated and rich unity that is confessed by faith, awaited in hope, and experienced now only in part. The one church is *in via,* on the way toward the fulfillment of the promises of God in Christ. It is the pilgrim church, celebrating now a new unity of humanity around the Lord's table, but moving toward the great eschatological banquet in which all the people of the earth, from east, west, north, and south, will sit together in peace and joy in the presence of their Lord (Luke 13:29).

2. What is meant by the *holiness* of the church? Holiness does not mean being "holier than thou," developing an attitude of moral superiority leading to separation from those deemed inferior. The church is the community of forgiven sinners. If the church is called holy, it is not meant in a moralistic sense. The holiness of the church is not grounded in itself but in Christ, by whose life, death, and resurrection believers are justified by grace and set on the path of sanctification. The church is holy by participation in the holy love of God. God's love is holy not because it holds itself aloof from sinners and strangers but because it embraces them without reservation. This is God's holiness and justice revealed in Jesus Christ: that God justifies, accepts, and loves sinners despite their unworthiness.

By analogy the true holiness of the church is seen not in impeccable conformity to conventional moral rules but in the courageous criticism of injustice, acts of solidarity with the poor and the outcast, the sharing of friendship and power with the weak and despised. As is true of all the marks of the church, the confession that the church is holy is an utterance of faith and hope. It receives its warrant from the promise of God and not from an empirical description of its life. Yet this confession is not solely about the future. There are or should be signals of a new form of human life taking shape in the community called the church. Men and women of Christian character and discipline should be formed within this community who are able to resist the style of life characteristic of a self-centered consumer society, who lead the way in opting for a simpler way of life, and who show openness to the needs of others, especially the poor.

3. What is meant by the *catholicity* of the church? The classical definition of catholicity is "what is believed everywhere, always, and by all" (Vincent of Lerins). The church is catholic or universal in a number

of senses. It is present in all parts of the world and in all periods of history. It has many parishes, but it is not provincial. These are readily accepted meanings of the church's catholicity. The problem is that catholicity too often is understood as a sort of abstract universality hovering above the particularities of culture and history. A related mistake is the association of catholicity with a noncommittal attitude, a neutrality that strives to please all and offend none.

The church today needs to interpret the meaning of *catholic* as inclusive of all kinds of people. In order to be catholic in this sense, it is, paradoxically, necessary for the church to be partisan. If the gentiles are being excluded from hearing the good news of freedom in Christ, then it becomes necessary to be partisan for the gentiles, as was the Apostle Paul, precisely to affirm the catholicity of the church and the universality of the lordship of Christ. If particular racial groups and certain economic classes are being turned away from the church, either directly or indirectly, because they do not find their concerns and needs taken seriously, then it is necessary to become partisan for these people, as black theology, feminist theology, and other forms of liberation theology do. When the church makes an option for the poor, it demonstrates rather than denies its catholicity. The other side of this coin, however, is that every partisan act of the church must be intentionally universal, or it becomes not the partisanship of God but a divisive and destructive party spirit.

4. What is meant by the *apostolicity* of the church? Apostolicity does not mean being in the chain of apostolic succession in some external and mechanical sense. Nor is apostolicity to be restricted to the ordained clergy. Every baptized person is summoned to be a witness to the good news of God's in-breaking kingdom in Jesus Christ and in this sense to take part in the apostolate of the church. The apostolicity of the church is the church's conformity in all aspects of its life to the gospel of Jesus Christ attested by the prophets and the apostles. This apostolic succession of faithfulness to the gospel should manifest itself both in what the church proclaims and in how the church lives. It should determine the way in which the church seeks to communicate the gospel and carry out every aspect of its mission in the world. Specifically, true apostolic witness to the gospel eschews force, intimidation, and deception as strategies to win adherents, whether this takes the form of a blatant appeal for state power to secure the church's position and influence, or the more covert forms of threat and coercion or narrow appeals to self-interest employed in certain kinds of evangelism,

both on and off television. As the Apostle Paul pointed to his scars and persecutions in order to demonstrate his apostolate (2 Cor. 11:23ff.), so the apostolic church will show its faithfulness to the gospel by carrying out its mission in the weakness and poverty that the grace of God uses to God's glory and humanity's salvation.

While the Nicene marks of the church are commonly affirmed by all Christian traditions, the Protestant Reformers also defined the true church in a different way. They asked, What is the basis of the unity, holiness, catholicity, and apostolicity of the church? Their answer to this question was: the pure preaching and hearing of the Word of God and the right administration of the sacraments. According to Luther, "if the church is without the Word, it ceases to be the church."[23] Calvin and Luther agree on this point: "Whenever we see the Word of God purely preached and heard, and the sacraments administered according to Christ's institution, there, it is not to be doubted, a church of God exists."[24] The Reformers' view was necessary and appropriate to counter the schismatic tendencies in their own reform movement and to respond to the charge of the established church that they were violating the Nicene definition. In fact, the two sets of marks of the church are complementary. Without the Reformation set, the Nicene marks could be interpreted moralistically; without the Nicene set, the Reformation marks could be interpreted schismatically.

It is also important to ask, however, whether these two classical sets of marks of the church are adequate, at least as they have been tradition-ally interpreted. Since the New Testament, it has been a principle of ecclesiology that where Christ is, there is the church. But where is Christ? The answers to this question in the history of doctrine are familiar: Christ is where the bishop is; Christ is in the eucharist; Christ is where the gospel is preached and heard; Christ is where the gifts of the Spirit are manifest. While there is an element of truth in all these responses, none of them explicitly includes the response given in Matthew 25:31ff. Christ is present among the poor, the hungry, the sick, and the imprisoned. Those who minister to the wretched of the earth minister to Christ. The true church is not only the church of the ear (where the gospel is rightly preached and heard), and not only the church of the eye (where the

---

23. Luther, "Concerning the Ministry," in *Luther's Works,* vol. 40, ed. Helmut T. Lehmann (Philadelphia: Fortress Press, 1966), p. 37.

24. Calvin, *Institutes of the Christian Religion,* 4.1.9.

sacraments are enacted for the faithful to see and experience); it is also the church of the outstretched, helping hand. Why has the church neglected the clear answer of Matthew 25:31ff. to the questions: Where is Christ? and How shall we recognize the true church? Christ is among the poor, and the church is the people of God free enough to enter into solidarity with the poor. Let the church be the church!

11

Proclamation, Sacraments, and Ministry

PREACHING OF THE WORD, SACRAMENTS, AND MINISTRY ARE CLOSELY related doctrines that continue to divide Christian churches. Indeed, they are the principal topics on which the efforts toward ecumenical consensus and the reunion of the churches repeatedly stall. Agreement would be easily secured if it were enough to say that, like every human community, the church needs to order its life, choose leaders to guide it, and have regular practices that clarify its identity and support its mission. But such agreement, while valid in sociological terms, would fall short of the theological understanding that faith seeks. Since proclamation of the Word and celebration of the sacraments are vital to Christian faith and life, and since ministerial office and church polity should cohere with the central message and mission of the church, theology must not abdicate its responsibility for critical reflection on these themes.

The Proclamation of the Word

THEOLOGY and preaching are distinct yet mutually related activities. On the one hand, the responsibility of preaching is a major stimulus to theological reflection; on the other hand, a central task of theology is to provoke, criticize, and assist preaching. Theology serves preaching by testing its faithfulness to the gospel, by reminding it of the fullness of God's revelation in Jesus Christ, by urging that preaching be more intelligible, more concrete, more self-critical, less trivial, less intimidated by dominant cultural assumptions.[1]

Proclamation of the Word and celebration of the sacraments belong together. They presuppose and complement each another because in their different ways they both attest and mediate the free grace of God in Jesus Christ. Proclamation may be defined as faithful witness to the Word of God addressed to specific people in a particular time and place. The following theses amplify this definition.

1. Proclamation of the Word of God is *a human act.* The preacher does not become superhuman when he or she mounts the steps of the pulpit. If his or her words truly convey the Word of God, that is due neither to the brilliance nor the eloquence of the preacher but to the sovereign and free grace of God the Holy Spirit, who is able to make effective use of the service of creatures. An honest acknowledgment of human limitations is part of the preparation for the task of proclaiming the gospel. An arrogant or self-serving spirit is especially reprehensible in a preacher. As Karl Barth states, "as ministers we ought to speak of God. We are human, however, and so cannot speak of God. We ought therefore to recognize our obligation and our inability, and by that very recognition give God the glory."[2]

2. Proclamation of the Word of God is an act of *witness to the truth.* Being a witness is among the most solemn of human acts, requiring utmost attention and commitment. As Paul Ricoeur notes, its most familiar location in common human experience is the courtroom, where the truth is at issue and justice is at stake.

Several features of the act of witness stand out. First, the witness is sworn to tell the truth. Second, faithful witnesses draw attention not to themselves but to someone or some event distinct from themselves. Third, the act of witness presupposes that the event attested is singular. The truth that is attested by a witness is thus quite different from a mere example or instance of a truth that is generally known or universally accessible. Fourth, the act of witness is self-involving: it requires personal participation, commitment, and risk-taking. Because the truth is often resisted, the commitment of the witness in its most solemn form may become a commitment unto death. The linkage between witness and

---

1. See Fred B. Craddock, *Preaching* (Nashville: Abingdon Press, 1985); Gerhard O. Forde, *Theology Is for Proclamation* (Minneapolis: Fortress Press, 1990).
2. Barth, *Word of God and Word of Man* (New York: Harper, 1957), p. 186.

risk-taking is preserved in the New Testament word *martus,* "martyr." While not in itself proof that a witness speaks the truth, commitment and risk-taking distinguish what a witness does from detached observation or passive transmission of information.[3]

3. Proclamation of the Word of God is *based on the biblical text.* As used in Christian theology, the phrase "Word of God" has three meanings: (1) the incarnate or living Word of God, who is Jesus Christ; (2) the written Word of God, or Scripture; and (3) the proclaimed Word of God, or the preaching of the gospel in the present. These three forms of the Word are inseparably bound to each other in a definite order. When present proclamation is faithfully based on the original witness of Scripture to the living Word of God incarnate in Jesus Christ, it becomes God's Word to people here and now by the power of the Spirit.

The claim that preaching should be *based* on the witness of Scripture is certainly intended to reject a view of preaching as arbitrary invention. But it also repudiates the idea that preaching is the mere repetition of biblical words or ideas. Proclamation is re-presentation; it requires reflection and imagination. Restatement of the gospel is necessary if the preacher is to be faithful to the apostolic gospel. Proclamation is new witness in the here and now to the promise and claim of God addressed to the world in the covenant history with Israel and supremely in Jesus Christ.

Encountering the Word of God through Scripture is never a matter of course. Just as God is surprisingly revealed in the hiddenness of the cross of Christ, so the Word of God is hidden in the historical contingencies of Scripture. The witness of Scripture must be studied, pondered, questioned, and argued with.[4] Preacher and congregation return again and again to Scripture, now comforted, now disturbed, now strengthened, now infuriated by it, in the expectation that the Spirit will once again address us through the witness of prophets and apostles with a life-giving word.

4. Proclamation of the Word of God employs the medium of *language.* Christian witness is certainly not limited to the linguistic realm. There is a witness of deeds as well as a witness of words. Still, procla-

---

3. Cf. Paul Ricoeur, "The Hermeneutics of Testimony," in *Essays on Biblical Interpretation,* ed. Lewis S. Mudge (Philadelphia: Fortress Press, 1980), pp. 119-54.

4. For a remarkable example of wrestling with the scriptural witness, see Phyllis Trible, *Texts of Terror* (Philadelphia: Fortress Press, 1984).

mation of the living Word of God *also* takes the form of verbal communication.

Human beings have been endowed with the capacity to communicate and to understand through language. For good or ill, language shapes human life. Individuals and communities may be condemned to bondage or invited to freedom by the particular stories that they tell and retell and by the metaphors and parables that they employ to understand the world, themselves, and the ultimate reality called God. We think and speak of God, if at all, in carelessly or carefully chosen words.

The importance of language in human life is recognized and honored by the seriousness with which the church takes up the task of proclaiming the gospel. While the writers of Scripture knew that there are experiences, insights, and sighs of faith too deep for words (Rom. 8:26), they also declared that "faith comes from what is heard, and what is heard comes by the preaching of Christ" (Rom. 10:17).

Christian proclamation necessarily uses language in arresting, disturbing, uncommon ways. This is why metaphor, image, and story are so prominent in Christian talk of God. In proclamation, language is stretched to its limits to point to the reality of the gracious Creator, Redeemer, and Sanctifier. How could the language of proclamation not be jolting, even shocking, when at the heart of the Christian message is the story of Christ crucified for the world? If God's grace is surprisingly present in the midst of our everyday life, how could the language of proclamation, like the literary forms of the Bible, not abound in fresh imagery, startling metaphor, and arresting parable.[5]

While no particular words or forms of speech are inherently adequate to speak of God, some are more fitting than others to identify and describe the being and action of God according to the biblical witness. If, as we have emphasized, the revelation of the living God takes its decisive form not in a set of eternal truths but in the life-act of a person, the proclamation of the church will give a certain priority to realistic narrative that speaks of God as a living, personal, and gracious reality.

5. While the content of the proclamation of the Word of God is rich and deep, it is also fundamentally simple. It is the *gospel*, the "glad tidings" of God's astonishing faithfulness to humanity and the entire creation in all their brokenness. The task of proclamation is to present

5. See Thomas G. Long, *Preaching and the Literary Forms of the Bible* (Philadelphia: Fortress Press, 1989).

this "gospel of God" (Rom. 1:1), this gift of forgiveness and new life from God in Jesus Christ, in all its inner consistency, intelligibility, and clarity, in all its inexhaustible fullness, irresistible appeal, and liberating power. The content of Christian proclamation is not everything in the Bible but rather the central biblical message.

Although the gospel is fundamentally simple, it is not simplistic; while affirmative, it is never trivial or cheap. The gift that it announces is accompanied by a call for disciplined service and by a warning of judgment. Lutheran and Reformed theologies make this point in distinctive ways.

A notable emphasis of Lutheran theology is that if Christian proclamation is to avoid trivializing the grace of God announced in the biblical witness, it must always distinguish between law and gospel and know the importance and place of each. Summarizing the teaching of the Lutheran Confessions on this point, Edmund Schlink writes, "The law terrifies; the Gospel comforts and cheers the terrified person. The law beats a man down; the Gospel raises him up and strengthens him. The law accuses and condemns; the Gospel pardons and bestows. The law punishes and kills; the Gospel makes free and alive."[6]

While these concerns to distinguish Christian proclamation from the announcement of "cheap grace" (Bonhoeffer) and to fight every reduction of the gospel to moralism are crucial, the Reformed theological perspective holds that it is equally important to avoid a dualistic understanding of the Word of God. While Christian proclamation includes both law and gospel, both God's judgment on sin and God's promise of grace, God's word to the world in Jesus Christ is not an equally balanced Yes and No but a strong and unambiguous Yes (2 Cor. 1:20). Thus at the center of Christian preaching is not an abstract law-gospel dialectic but the free grace of God in Jesus Christ crucified and resurrected for the salvation of the world. Only if preaching focuses on the whole Christ of the biblical witness will it avoid both the moralistic preaching rightly criticized by Lutheran theologians and the preaching of a gospel that lacks direction for the new life in Christ rightly criticized by Reformed theologians.[7]

6. Schlink, *Theology of the Lutheran Confessions* (Philadelphia: Fortress Press, 1961), p. 104. See also Carl E. Braaten, *Justification: The Article by Which the Church Stands or Falls* (Minneapolis: Fortress Press, 1990), pp. 143-53.

7. In the Reformed tradition, the proper purpose of the law is to give direction to love and to provide order for the life in community that God intends. See John Calvin on the three uses of the law, and particularly on its chief "third use" to guide believers in the new life in Christ (*Institutes of the Christian Religion*, 3.7.6-14). See also Karl Barth,

6. The proclamation of the Word of God always takes place in particular situations. If Christian witness always has a text, it also always has a particular *context*. It does not deal in general truths about God, the world, and humanity. If that were the case, the content of proclamation would not be the living Word of God but timeless truth that leaves everything as it is. As witness to the living Word of God, Christian proclamation speaks to particular people in a specific time and place. It addresses a particular situation here and now with a specific message. It calls men and women to concrete decision and concrete action. Christian proclamation is not vague, neutral, safe discourse about God but concrete witness to the gospel that aims at a concrete response. Jesus Christ who is attested in Christian proclamation is, to be sure, "the same yesterday, today, and forever" (Heb. 13:8), and loyalty to this person is essential in all Christian witness. But as the living Lord, Jesus Christ comes as the gift and claim of God in ever new and context-specific ways, and his voice must be heard and obeyed anew. When the contextuality of proclamation is lost, so also is the presence of the Spirit, who alone gives life to the letter (2 Cor. 3:6).[8]

What Are Sacraments?

WHILE proclamation of the Word of God is an indispensable means of grace, it does not exhaust the many different ways in which the extravagant love of God is communicated. In addition to proclamation there are sacraments. Sacraments are "visible words,"[9] embodiments of grace, enacted testimonies to the love of God in Jesus Christ.

An often-repeated definition of sacraments was formulated by Augustine, who called them "visible signs of an invisible grace." The definition offered by the Westminster Shorter Catechism is much more specific: A sacrament is "a holy ordinance instituted by Christ wherein by visible signs Christ and the benefits of the new covenant are repre-

"Gospel and Law," in *Community, State, and Church*, ed. Will Herberg (Garden City, N.Y.: Doubleday-Anchor, 1960), pp. 71-100.

8. On the importance of contextuality in preaching, see Justo L. Gonzalez and Catherine G. Gonzalez, *Liberation Preaching: The Pulpit and the Oppressed* (Nashville: Abingdon Press, 1980).

9. See Robert W. Jenson, *Visible Words: The Interpretation and Practice of Christian Sacraments* (Philadelphia: Fortress Press, 1978).

sented, sealed and applied to believers."[10] Sacraments are enactments of the gospel by means of which the Spirit of God communicates to us the forgiving, renewing, and promising love of God in Jesus Christ and enlivens us in faith, hope, and love.

The Bible does not provide a definition of a sacrament, nor does it specify their number. In the New Testament, the Greek word *mysterion* — literally "mystery," later translated in the Latin by *sacramentum,* or "sacrament" — refers to the presence and purpose of God made known in Jesus Christ, not specifically to baptism, the Lord's Supper, or other rites (cf. Eph. 1:9-10). In the early Middle Ages, the number of sacraments varied widely. Since the thirteenth century, their number has been set at seven in the Roman Catholic and Eastern Churches: baptism, confirmation, eucharist, penance, ordination, marriage, and anointing of the sick.

The Reformation churches reduced the number of sacraments to two or three, with baptism and the Lord's Supper always recognized as the most important. It was argued that sacraments were to be limited to those practices clearly instituted by Christ and the Apostles. Even more important than the Reformers' reduction in the number of sacraments, however, was their insistence on two basic points: first, the inseparability of Word and sacrament; and second, the importance in both Word and sacrament of the working of the Spirit and our faithful response. These emphases countered every quasimagical view of the nature and efficacy of the sacraments.[11]

From the earliest times, two tendencies in interpreting the sacraments have been evident. One emphasizes the *objective reality* of God's grace in and through the sacraments. Those who hold to this view see the sacraments as divinely appointed rites that, when properly administered, convey grace and salvation if there are no impediments. The sacraments are said to be efficacious in themselves *(ex opere operato).* This tendency is found in Ignatius, who speaks of the Lord's Supper as the "medicine of immortality"; in Augustine, who held against the

---

10. Westminster Shorter Catechism, in the Presbyterian Church (U.S.A.) *Book of Confessions* (Louisville: Office of the General Assembly, 1983), 7.092.

11. As Martin Luther put it, "it is not the water that produces these effects, but the Word of God connected with the water, and our faith which relies on the Word of God connected with the water. For without the Word of God the water is merely water and no Baptism" (*The Small Catechism,* 4.3, in *The Book of Concord,* ed. Theodore G. Tappert [Philadelphia: Fortress Press, 1959], p. 349).

Donatists that the effectiveness of the sacrament does not depend upon the purity or worthiness of the celebrant; and in the traditional Catholic doctrine of transubstantiation, according to which the substance of the bread and wine is changed into the substance of the body and blood of Christ.

The second tendency in the interpretation of the sacraments emphasizes the *importance of our faith response.* According to this view, the sacraments are dramatic signs of the grace of God and are effective not in themselves but only as they are received by faith. The sacraments are not so much something done to us as something that we do: we repent, we confess our faith, we vow to be faithful. The purpose of the sacraments is to give people the chance to bear public witness to their faith.

These two tendencies struggle with each other in the church and theology up to the present. The danger of the more objective view by itself is that it minimizes the importance of the response of faith and seems to disregard the freedom of the Spirit. Viewed purely objectively, the grace of God mediated by sacramental action is depersonalized and reified. The danger of the more subjective view by itself is that it obscures the unconditional and objective reality of God's grace. These two tendencies are not to be correlated respectively with the Roman Catholic and Reformation traditions. They are present and in tension with each other in both traditions.

Both Catholic and Protestant theologians today increasingly emphasize the personal character of God's self-communication in Word and sacrament. There is an effort to get beyond the impasses of traditional sacramental controversies. One way of doing this is to redefine the meaning of *sacrament* in such a way that Christ becomes the paradigm of what is sacramental and the theology of the sacraments becomes more adequately trinitarian. Thus Karl Barth, Karl Rahner, and Edward Schillebeeckx contend that Jesus Christ is the primordial sacrament: in him takes place the decisive redemptive meeting of God and creaturely life. This christocentric redefinition of sacrament underscores the free, personal presence of God's grace in concrete, worldly form while also insisting that grace, as personal presence, calls for free personal response. If Christ is the primary sacrament, then those rites of the church that are called sacraments will correspond to their archetype. The sacraments are celebrated in Christ and re-present Christ. God comes to human beings personally by the power of the Holy Spirit in the concrete, worldly media of spoken word and enacted sacrament. God's love is both spoken to us and enacted in our midst. Both Word and sacrament re-present in different ways the gift and demand of God's unconditional grace in Jesus Christ by the power of the Holy Spirit.

Since Vatican II it is possible to speak of a growing convergence among Roman Catholic and Protestant theologians in the understanding of the sacraments. This convergence is marked by several features: (1) an emphasis on the inseparability of Word and sacraments, (2) a trinitarian and christocentric interpretation of both the proclamation of the Word and the celebration of the sacraments, (3) an effort to interpret the sacraments in relation to a new understanding of the whole creation as a sacramental universe, and (4) a concern to make as explicit as possible the connection between the sacraments, Christian life, and Christian ethics.

The Meaning of Baptism

CHRISTIAN baptism is the sacrament of *initiation* into the Christian life. It marks the beginning of the journey of faith and discipleship that lasts throughout one's life. In baptism a person is immersed in water, or water is poured or sprinkled upon him or her in the triune name of God.

1. Authorization of baptism is often found in the command of Jesus: "Go therefore and make disciples of all nations, baptizing them in the name of the Father and of the Son and of the Holy Spirit, and teaching them to obey everything that I have commanded you. And remember, I am with you always, to the end of the age" (Matt. 28:19-20).

Important as this passage has been in the history of baptismal practice, baptism is based not only on the *command* of Jesus but on the *act* of Jesus in freely submitting himself to baptism. Jesus commences his vocation, his obedient response to the call of God, by being baptized by John. In this act, Jesus enters into solidarity with lost humanity. He begins the life of costly love and service that eventually leads to his passion, death, and resurrection. Jesus' baptism thus signifies his solidarity with the sinners and outcasts of this world and his complete obedience to his Father's will. As described by the evangelists, this self-identification of Jesus with sinful humanity is met by God's identification of him as the beloved Son and by the descent of the Spirit of God on him (Mark 1:9-11).

Jesus uses the image of baptism in relating the life of his disciples to his own mission of self-expending love. "Are you able to drink the cup that I drink, or be baptized with the baptism that I am baptized with?" (Mark 10:38). The event of baptism thus marks the beginning of the Christian's participation in the life, death, and resurrection of Christ. It signals one's death to an old way of life and one's birth to a new life in Christ. Christians are given a Christian name, and their whole life becomes a journey of faith in which they enter ever more fully into their baptismal identity. They become participants in the life and love of the triune God in whose name they are baptized.

2. The New Testament unfolds the meaning of baptism in many rich images. Each of them is important and complements the others.[12]

a. Baptism is described as a *dying and rising* with Christ. The descent into the water signifies the Christian's identification with the passion and death of Christ, whereby the power that sin has in the old way of life is broken, and the Christian's ascent from the water signifies a participation in the new life based on the power of the resurrection of Christ (Rom. 6:3-4).

b. Baptism is also pictured as the *washing* of a sin-stained life. Just as water washes away the dirt of the body, so God's forgiveness washes away the sins of those who are truly repentant (1 Cor. 6:11). Those who are pardoned and cleansed by Christ receive in baptism a fresh start in life and a new ethical orientation.

c. Baptism is further portrayed as a *rebirth* by the Holy Spirit and a receiving of the Spirit's empowerment (John 3:5; Acts 2:38). While the Holy Spirit is at work everywhere in creation, giving and renewing life, the New Testament closely associates the gift of new life in the Spirit with baptism.

d. *Incorporation* is another image of baptism in the New Testament. By this act we are united with Christ, with each other, and with the people of God in every time and place. Welcomed into the covenant community by baptism, we are no longer solitary individuals but members of a new family and citizens of a new society (Eph. 2:19). This new society is one in which there is neither Jew nor Greek, neither slave nor free, neither male nor female (Gal. 3:28).

e. Baptism is also a *sign of God's coming reign*. It is the beginning of the Christian's movement in faith toward that reign. By baptism Christians receive the Spirit as the "firstfruits" (Rom. 8:23) of the harvest

12. For the following, see *Baptism, Eucharist and Ministry* (Geneva: World Council of Churches, 1982).

to come and are set in solidarity with the whole groaning creation which eagerly awaits the fulfillment of God's purposes and the coming of justice and peace throughout the creation.

3. If baptism is the commencement of Christian life, signifying a dying and rising with Christ, a cleansing from sin, a receiving of the life-giving Spirit, a welcoming into God's new society of love, and the start of a faith journey toward God's coming renewal of all things, what sense does it make to baptize infants?

Strong objections to infant baptism have been raised for centuries by those in the Baptist traditions. More recently, they have been raised within Reformed theology by Karl Barth.[13] Barth's objections to infant baptism can be summarized as follows:

a. Infant baptism has no explicit basis in Scripture. While the possibility that infant baptism was practiced in the apostolic age cannot be excluded, all evidence seems to point to the conclusion that it became a practice of the church only in the postapostolic period.

b. Barth argues further that infant baptism has led to the disastrous assumption that people become Christians virtually by birth. Grace is thus cheapened, and the gospel is spread by subtle and sometimes overt coercion. In Barth's judgment, infant baptism has contributed to the serious sickness and impotence of the church in the modern era.

c. Barth's central theological argument is that infant baptism obscures the meaning of baptism as an entrance into free and responsible Christian discipleship. In baptism there is first an action of God (baptism with the Spirit) and then a corresponding human action (baptism with water): there is a divine gift and a human response. Baptism attests God's grace and marks the beginning of the new life in Christ. If baptism is this free, glad, responsible human answer to God's gracious activity in Jesus Christ, then Barth thinks that there can be no doubt that infant baptism obscures and distorts its meaning.

What can be said in response to Barth's objections? In reply to his first point, reference could be made to the covenantal promises of God given to believers and to their children (Acts 2:39) and to the fact that in the apostolic period sometimes entire households were baptized (Acts 16:33). Still, it must be conceded that the case for infant baptism cannot be made on the grounds that it was undeniably practiced in the New Testament church.

13. See Barth, *Church Dogmatics*, IV/4 (Fragment).

Nor can we deny Barth's second charge that infant baptism has been subject to much abuse in the history of the church. The same criticism, however, could be leveled against virtually every theological doctrine and liturgical practice of the church. The distortion of a doctrine or the abuse of a practice calls for correction and reform but not necessarily elimination.

The real issue, then, is the theological *permissibility* of infant baptism under certain conditions. Should churches baptize only adults or *may* they baptize infants as well as adults?

Common to both infant and adult baptism is the affirmation that we are recipients of the gift of God's love and are claimed for God's service. Just as in the Lord's Supper we are fed by the bread of life and the cup of salvation, so baptism declares that something is done *for* us. Whether baptized as children or adults, our baptism signifies primarily what God has graciously done for us, and it is upon this that faith rests.

It can be argued that the two forms of baptism — infant and adult — together express the full meaning of baptism better than each would alone. In other words, their meanings are complementary rather than mutually exclusive. Adult baptism gives greater play to the conscious and free response of a person to God's forgiving love in Jesus Christ. It stresses explicit public confession and personal commitment to the way of Christ. But if practiced exclusively, adult baptism may tend toward a view of faith as preceding rather than responding to God's initiative. It may also foster a false individualism to the extent that it neglects the importance of the community in the process of growing in faith and Christian discipleship from one's earliest days. The fact that in traditions that baptize adults exclusively there is often a dedication and commitment service for infants and their parents points to the need for some public recognition of the responsibility of the church for nurturing children in the life of faith.

Infant baptism, on the other hand, declares the sovereign grace and initiative of God. It demonstrates that even when they are helpless, human beings are loved and affirmed by God. It proclaims, as Karl Rahner says, that God loves this child.[14] It expresses loving reception into a confessing community that takes responsibility for helping this child to mature in faith as a member of the Christian community. It makes clear that baptism is a beginning of the process of growing into

14. Rahner, *Meditations on the Sacraments* (New York: Seabury Press, 1977), p. 1.

Christ and that this process of growth cannot take place without a supportive community of faith.

Since the chief objection to infant baptism is that it undercuts the necessity of free and conscious acceptance of the life of discipleship, it is imperative that the practice of infant baptism be dissociated from the dispensation of cheap grace. Some kind of "commissioning" service must link together infant baptism and the free, personal response of the person baptized. Baptism and faith *are* inseparably related. The question is simply one of time. Must the response of faith on the part of the baptized be simultaneous with or follow immediately the event of baptism? After all, as Barth would surely agree, God's grace is not coercive but gives humanity time. Of course, the patience of God must not be used as an argument for casually postponing a response; it is appropriate, however, to refer to God's patience in giving children who have been baptized time to come of age, stand on their own feet, and respond freely and gladly to the call to discipleship already at work in their lives. In the meantime, there is a faith that is already responding to the enacted grace of God in the baptism of the infant. It is the faith of the parents and the community in whose midst the child is baptized. While their faith cannot simply substitute for that of the child, it can help prepare the way for the child's eventual free response to baptism. Parents and congregation vow to provide a Christian environment for their children until the day when they are ready to speak for themselves.

Does the Holy Spirit work in infants? Geoffrey Bromiley is surely right to say that it would be shocking to answer this question in the negative. The Holy Spirit can and does work in the lives of infants and children through the ministrations of their parents, guardians, teachers, and friends. Why not also through the proper practice of infant baptism?[15] The working of God's Spirit is not restricted by gender, race, or class. Neither is it restricted by age.

I conclude, therefore, that while the practice of infant baptism is not absolutely necessary in the life of the church, it may be permissible. And whether it is permissible depends on whether it is being practiced as a form of cheap, magical grace or with the clear understanding that it proclaims the unconditional grace of God and calls both parents and community to responsibility for the nurture and upbuilding of the baptized child in the love and instruction of the Lord.

---

15. Cf. Bromiley, *Children of Promise: The Case for Baptizing Infants* (Grand Rapids: William B. Eerdmans, 1970).

Infant baptism, responsibly practiced, is a sign of *God's gracious initiative* in creation and redemption. It is a powerful expression of the fact that God loves us before we begin to respond to God in trust and love. It proclaims the love of God as sheer gift.

Further, infant baptism is a sign of *human solidarity* in the presence of God. At no stage of human life are we isolated from each other or from God. Christian life has a social dimension; it is formative of new community. Because the grace of God aims at the transformation not only of individuals but also of our life together as families and communities, the practice of infant baptism is theologically legitimate and meaningful.

Finally, infant baptism is a sign of *covenantal responsibility* as a community of faith and most especially as parents of this child. If people are indifferent to or negligent of their responsibility as parents to bring up their children in a home and educational environment that guides them toward their own free, personal decision about Christian faith and discipleship, it is unlikely that their sense of social responsibility will be very strong in regard to people beyond the family circle. Especially in our age of broken homes, one-parent families, and many abused and abandoned children, infant baptism could be a strong and unambiguous declaration of the fact that God loves these and all children. When infant baptism is taken with appropriate seriousness, parents and other members of the congregation of Jesus Christ are called to responsibility in the care and nurture of children in the life of faith.

4. A special problem for the theology of baptism today is whether it is permissible to substitute other words for the traditional trinitarian formula in the service of baptism to avoid gender-specific language of God. This question does not have an easy answer. Exclusive masculine imagery of God courts idolatry and must be challenged; at the same time, the classical trinitarian images should not be discarded peremptorily. Proposals to speak of God exclusively in functional terms — for example, as creator, redeemer, and sustainer — are not theologically acceptable because they veer in the direction of modalism. On the other hand, we should eschew liturgical fundamentalism that refuses *any* alternatives to the traditional images. Baptism "in the name of Father, Son, and Holy Spirit" is not a magical incantation. It is a witness to the love of the triune God whose own life is in community and who welcomes all into the new human community founded on grace alone. Brian Wren is doubtless correct in pleading for more serious theological work, more

creative imagination, and more responsible expansion of our language of God in hymn, prayer, and liturgy. Guided by God's Word and Spirit, the church should be open to fresh trinitarian imagery that will complement — not replace — the classical trinitarian images.[16]

The Meaning of the Lord's Supper

THE event of the Lord's Supper is narrated in the Gospels, and the tradition is also passed on by the Apostle Paul in 1 Corinthians 11:23ff. "The Lord Jesus on the night when he was betrayed took bread, and when he had given thanks, he broke it, and said, 'This is my body that is for you. Do this in remembrance of me.' In the same way he took the cup also, after supper, saying, 'This cup is the new covenant in my blood. Do this, as often as you drink it, in remembrance of me.' For as often as you eat this bread and drink the cup, you proclaim the Lord's death until he comes."

1. If baptism is the sacrament of the foundation of Christian life in God's grace, the Lord's Supper is the sacrament of the *sustaining* of Christian life by that same grace. If baptism is the sacrament of the beginning of Christian life, the Lord's Supper is the sacrament of *growth* and nourishment in Christian life. If baptism marks the gift of God's love that welcomes us into new community and confirms our solidarity with Christ and with others, the Lord's Supper marks God's continued *sharing* of life and love that gives strength to the new community and motivates it for service in the world.

The Lord's Supper gathers together the past, the present, and the future of God's creative and redemptive work. It is a vivid reminder of Christ's salvific death and resurrection and also of all of God's lavish gifts in the creation and preservation of the world. But for the community of faith, Christ is no mere memory: he makes himself present here and now through the breaking and eating of the bread and the pouring and drinking of the wine, and those who partake of this meal are made one community in him. Furthermore, in this sacrament Christians are aroused to hope in Christ's coming again. They look eagerly for the consummation of the liberating and reconciling activity of God in which

16. See Wren's arresting suggestions in *What Language Shall I Borrow?* (New York: Crossroad, 1989).

they are now co-workers. Thus in the celebration of the Lord's Supper the whole range of Christian life in time — with its memory of the crucified Lord, its provisional experience of God's Spirit in the present, and its hope for the coming of God's kingdom in fullness — is expressed.

2. Since there has been extensive and often acrimonious dispute among the churches about the nature of Christ's presence in the Lord's Supper, any discussion of this topic should be prefaced by the reminder that all theological formulations are provisional rather than absolute and that "the reality of fellowship in the church always precedes theological understanding."[17] Of the numerous interpretations of the presence of Christ in the Lord's Supper, four have been especially influential.

a. The first is the traditional Roman Catholic doctrine of *transubstantiation*. According to this view, the "substance" of the elements of bread and wine is transformed by the power of God into the substance of the body and blood of Jesus Christ. The "accidents," or outward form, of the elements — those qualities that can be seen, tasted, and felt — remain the same. This view presupposes Aristotelian and Thomistic philosophic concepts and distinctions that are no longer familiar to many people. It can be argued, however, that the intent of this doctrine is actually to avoid magical views, even if its popular versions tend to come very close to this.

In more recent Catholic theology, new interpretations of the doctrine of transubstantiation have been proposed. One is transignification (change of meaning) and another is transfinalization (change of end or purpose). The point of these interpretations is that what something is cannot be separated from its context and use. Changes in context and use entail changes in meaning and identity, as when a piece of paper becomes in another context a letter bearing a message. This way of thinking about the change that occurs in the bread and wine bypasses the older Aristotelian conceptuality and the problems it has created. Although it has not been recognized in official Catholic teaching, it has the potential of overcoming some of the disagreement among the churches about the "changing of the elements."[18]

17. Wolfhart Pannenberg, *The Church* (Philadelphia: Westminster Press, 1983), p. 148.

18. See Edward Schillebeeckx, "Transubstantiation, Transfinalization, Transignification," *Worship* 40 (1966): 366; Alasdair I. C. Heron, *Table and Tradition: Toward an Ecumenical Understanding of the Eucharist* (Philadelphia: Westminster Press, 1983), p. 164.

b. Another view is the Lutheran doctrine of *consubstantiation*. While Luther rejected the Catholic doctrine of transubstantiation, his doctrine of the presence of Christ in the Lord's Supper is emphatically objective and realistic. Christ is present "in, with, and under" the elements of bread and wine, as fire permeates and envelops a glowing ember. The Lutheran doctrine stresses that Christ is present not just "spiritually" but bodily. And he is present even to those who eat unworthily and to their judgment.

c. A third view is found in the central strand of the *Calvinist or Reformed* tradition. This interpretation agrees with Catholics and Lutherans in affirming the real presence of Christ, but its special emphases are that Christ is received by faith through the uniting power of the Spirit. Calvin resists interpretations of the Lord's Supper that would mechanically affix Christ to the elements on the one hand, or that would deny that the whole Christ is really given in the Supper on the other hand. For Calvin, in our faithful eating of the bread and drinking of the wine Christ joins us to himself by the grace and power of his Spirit. Christ is present in the whole eucharistic action rather than in the elements viewed in isolation from the use God makes of them. When Calvin says that Christ is present not corporeally but "spiritually," he means that Christ is present to faith by the power of the Holy Spirit. He does not mean that Christ is present only docetically or as a mere idea. For Calvin there is a Spirit-actualized correspondence between the eating and drinking of the bread and wine and the receiving of the real presence of Christ for the upbuilding of Christian life. "The sacraments," Calvin says, "profit not a whit without the power of the Holy Spirit."[19]

d. Still another interpretation is known as the *memorialist* doctrine. The celebration of the Lord's Supper is essentially a memorial or reminder of what Christ did for human salvation in his passion, death, and resurrection. Lively or vivid "memory" replaces the language of "real presence" in the description of what happens in this sacrament.

3. Two major tendencies in the interpretation of the Lord's Supper continue to struggle with each other. The one tendency sees this sacrament primarily as a sacrifice; the other tendency sees it primarily as a meal. Some Catholic and Anglican theologians have interpreted the mass as a repetition of the sacrifice on Calvary. Over against this view, most Protestants have emphasized the once-for-allness of Christ's sacrifice and

19. Calvin, *Institutes of the Christian Religion*, 4.14.9.

are suspicious of any talk of sacrifice in the Lord's Supper except as this refers to the church's offering of the sacrifice of praise and thanksgiving to God in response to the sacrificial love of God in Jesus Christ.[20]

The sacrament called the Lord's Supper has many other names — holy communion, eucharist, divine liturgy, the breaking of the bread. But by whatever name it is called, it is essentially a meal, a meal of thanksgiving to God the Father, a meal of communion with Christ, a meal of joy and hope in the power of the Spirit who gives us new life and provides a foretaste of the great messianic banquet of the end time, when God's liberating and reconciling activity will be completed. If the trinitarian and eschatological nature of this meal were more fully acknowledged, new possibilities of rapprochement between Roman Catholic and Protestant theologies of the Lord's Supper would follow. In particular, recovery of the importance of the *epiclesis,* the invocation or prayer for the coming of the Holy Spirit in the eucharistic service, would correct the attempt to focus on one particular segment of the service as the moment of consecration and would underscore the church's utter dependence on the Spirit of God for the gift bestowed in this meal.[21]

The Lord's Supper discloses what human life by God's grace is intended to be — a life together in mutual sharing and love. Just as the meaning of Christian baptism is inseparable from Jesus' own baptism as the commencement and epitome of his own singular life of love, obedience, and service, so the meaning of the Lord's Supper is inseparable from Jesus' practice of table fellowship with sinners and the poor throughout his ministry (Mark 2:15; Luke 15:1-2). The Lord's Supper is rightly understood as an anticipation, in the midst of present suffering, of the coming joy of the messianic reign of justice, freedom, and peace. It is a concrete sign and seal of God's promise of a new, liberated, and reconciled humanity in a new heaven and a new earth. To eat and drink

---

20. See Calvin, *Institutes of the Christian Religion,* 4.18.13-16. See also D. M. Baillie, *The Theology of the Sacraments* (New York: Scribner's, 1957), p. 115.

21. Lukas Vischer asserts that "the prayer for the presence of the Spirit shows that the church must always appear before God with empty hands" ("The Epiclesis: Sign of Unity and Renewal," *Studia Liturgica* 6 [1969]: 35). Cf. the agreement of the Roman Catholic and Lutheran dialogue commission: "It is through the Holy Spirit that Christ is at work in the Eucharist. All that the Lord gives us and all that enables us to make it our own is given to us through the Holy Spirit. In the liturgy this becomes particularly clear in the invocation of the Holy Spirit (epiclesis)" (*Das Herrenmahl* [Paderborn: Verlag Bonifacius, 1980], p. 20). See also *Baptism, Eucharist and Ministry,* pp. 10ff.

at this table is to be united with Jesus and to be nourished by the self-giving, other-affirming, community-forming love of the triune God. All are invited to this table, but most especially the poor, the sick, the outcast (cf. Luke 14:15-24). Understood in this way, the Lord's Supper has profound significance for Christian ethics and for the mission of the church in the world today.

Baptism, the Lord's Supper, and Ethics

I HAVE spoken of baptism as the sacrament of solidarity and of the Lord's Supper as the sacrament of sharing. This way of describing the two great sacraments of the Christian community has the advantage of bringing out the essential connection between sacramental action and Christian ethics. Baptism and the Lord's Supper are not practiced merely out of reverence for ancient tradition or because of their aesthetic value. In these symbolic actions Christians receive their identity and their vocation. Together with the proclamation of the Word, the sacraments are means of grace by which God calls, strengthens, and commissions the church for its mission in the world.

Baptism is the sacrament of *God's solidarity with the world* in all its sinfulness and estrangement. In Jesus Christ, God entered into unconditional solidarity with sinful and lost humanity. Christ was baptized for lost humanity, and Christian baptism is the first step of participation in the life, death, and resurrection of Christ. In baptism Christians are given a new identity. They are defined as children and partners of the triune God, who from all eternity wills to live in solidarity with others.

Baptism is the sacrament of *human solidarity in Christ with each other,* and especially with all those who are different, strange, and even frightening to us. There can be no baptism into Christ without a deepening of the sense of solidarity with fellow creatures and with all their needs and yearnings. In Christ there is neither Jew nor Gentile, neither slave nor free, neither male nor female (Gal. 3:28). Apparently an early baptismal confession, this New Testament text declares the unprecedented solidarity of life in Christ. Baptism creates a solidarity that defies and shatters the divisions and barriers that sinful human beings have created. Racism, sexism, and other ideologies of separation are doubly reprehensible when they exist within or are supported by the Christian church, since they are a denial of the solidarity which is God's intention for human life made in the image and reconciled by the activity of the triune God.

Baptism is also the sacrament of *human solidarity with the whole groaning creation*. It is a sign of God's coming reign and of the promised transformation of all things. Nature is present in the act of baptism in the element of water. If God uses water in baptism to signify the cleansing and renewal of humanity in Christ, can the church disregard the implications of this for its stewardship of the natural world? Can Christians who begin a life of new solidarity in baptism remain indifferent to the despoilment of the earth's water, soil, and air by reckless policies of pollution? Ought not baptismal theology, among its many rich meanings and dimensions, also remind us in the closing years of the twentieth century that God is the creator and Lord of the whole cosmos and has appointed human salvation to be inextricably bound together with the call to stewardship and protection of the natural order?

As baptism signifies multidimensional solidarity, so the Lord's Supper signifies multidimensional sharing. The Lord's Supper is, in the first place, the sacrament of the *sharing of the divine life with humanity*. The triune God, who is eternally rich in love and fellowship, freely and graciously shares that life of love with humanity in Jesus Christ. Sharing life with others, whatever the cost, is God's own way of being. That is the identity of God disclosed in the life and death of Jesus Christ and articulated in the doctrine of the Trinity.

The Lord's Supper is therefore also the sacrament of *human participation in the divine life by sharing life with each other*. As a public, open, joyful, hopeful meal, the Lord's Supper is a foretaste of a new humanity. Christians cannot eat and drink at this table — where all are welcome and none goes hungry or thirsty — and continue to condone any form of discrimination or any social or economic policy that results in hunger or other forms of deprivation. The Lord's Supper is the practice of "eucharistic hospitality," in which strangers are welcomed into the household of God.[22] Christians cannot share this bread and wine while refusing to share their daily bread and wine with the millions of hungry

---

22. See L. Gregory Jones, "Eucharistic Hospitality," *The Reformed Journal*, March 1989, pp. 12-17. Jürgen Moltmann makes the same point: "The Lord's Supper takes place on the basis of an invitation which is as open as the outstretched arms of Christ on the cross" (*The Church in the Power of the Spirit* [New York: Harper & Row, 1977], p. 246).

people around the world.[23] There is an intrinsic connection between responsible participation in the Lord's Supper and commitment to a fairer distribution of the goods of the earth to all its people.

The Lord's Supper, whose natural elements are grain and the fruit of the vine, is also a symbolic recognition of *the shared life and common destiny of humanity and nature.* The natural order shares in God's work of giving life to human beings and of granting them new life. And conversely, human beings share in the care and cultivation of the earth and receive with thanksgiving its good gifts. The Lord's Supper is a beautiful portrayal of the interconnection and interdependence of personal, communal, and cosmic salvation.

Ludwig Feuerbach, the great humanist philosopher of the nineteenth century who interpreted all Christian doctrines as simply secret ways of speaking about human potential in a natural environment, concluded his famous book *The Essence of Christianity* with an interpretation of the sacraments. His last words are: "Therefore let bread be sacred for us, let wine be sacred; and also let water be sacred! Amen."[24] A Christian interpretation of baptism and the Lord's Supper will not succumb to Feuerbachian naturalism. We must surely say much more than Feuerbach, but we must not say less. "Let water that symbolizes our new life in solidarity with Christ and with others be kept clean and pure. Let bread and wine that symbolize Christ's sharing of life and love with us also be shared by us with all who are hungry and thirsty."

The Meaning of an Ordained Ministry

IF all Christians are called to participate in God's ministry of liberation and reconciliation through Jesus Christ, and if all have been given the gift of the Holy Spirit, what is the meaning and necessity of an ordained ministry? Does not the office of ordained ministry contradict the vocation of all Christians to service of God and neighbor? Does it not foster elitism

23. Cf. Monika K. Hellwig, *The Eucharist and the Hunger of the World* (New York: Paulist Press, 1976); Anne Primavesi and Jennifer Henderson, *Our God Has No Favourites: A Liberation Theology of the Eucharist* (Turnbridge Wells, England: Burns & Oates, 1989).

24. Feuerbach, *The Essence of Christianity* (New York: Harper Torchbooks, 1957), p. 278.

and hierarchy in the church? A response to these questions may be given in the form of several important distinctions.

1. As used in Christian theology, the word *ministry* has *a broader and a narrower meaning.* In my discussion of Christian vocation in Chapter 9, I emphasize that all Christians are called to the worship and service of the triune God. All are given the vocation of love of God and love of neighbor, all are called to follow Jesus Christ and to be his faithful witnesses in word and deed, all are given gifts by the Spirit to make their unique contribution to the life of the community and its mission to the world. In this *broad* sense of ministry, often expressed in the Reformation tradition as the priesthood of all believers, all Christians are called to ministry and are empowered for this task by the Holy Spirit.

But there is also a *narrower* meaning of the term Christian ministry. Among the diverse gifts of the Spirit to the church is the calling and ordination of certain people to the ministry of Word and sacrament. Ministry in this sense is an office that is ordained by God to provide for regular and responsible preaching of the gospel, celebration of the sacraments, and leadership in the life and service of the church. So crucial are these activities to the life and well-being of the community of faith that they are not left to chance occurrence or haphazard preparation. In every time and place, the church needs leaders who are qualified to preach, teach, administer the sacraments, and offer guidance in Christian faith and life.

2. The call to the ministry of Word and sacrament has both *an inward and an outward aspect.* People are called to this ministry by the Holy Spirit, who bestows special gifts and motivates their recipients to dedicate their lives to the gospel ministry. The Apostle Paul refers to this inward call of God when he says, "Woe to me if I do not proclaim the gospel" (1 Cor. 9:16).

But the call to ordained ministry also has an outward aspect. It is mediated by the community of faith. Since the office of ministry is conducted on behalf of the entire community, it is essential that the will of the Spirit be expressed not only to the individual called but also through the community's acknowledgment of that calling. Hence schools are established to prepare leaders for the church, candidates for the ministry undergo examination, and formal calls to ministry are issued by congregations on behalf of the whole people of God.

People called both inwardly and outwardly by the Spirit of God for leadership responsibilities are set apart by a service of ordination. In this service the ordinand promises to be faithful to Christ and to the whole people of God. Other ordained ministers lay hands on the head of the ordinand as a sign of commission to ministry, and the church prays for the Spirit to empower his or her ministry.

3. Ordination is properly understood *missiologically rather than ontologically.* That is, ordination is not a mysterious change of ontological status elevating the person ordained over other Christians. It is being commissioned and authorized to a particular task in the power of the Spirit. There is no basis in Scripture for thinking of ordination to the ministry of Word and sacrament as a "higher" or "fuller" ministry in comparison with other ministries of Christians. The clergy do not constitute a separate class of Christians. A hierarchical division between clergy and laity is a wound in the life of the church.

This is not to say, however, that ministry can be reduced to mere function. The person of the minister cannot be entirely divorced from the task of ministry. Ministry presupposes not only thorough educational preparation but also deep commitment to God and a sincere desire to serve Christ. Ministry is a form of life and not just a role one plays or a job one does.

Yet ministers of the gospel of Jesus Christ convey a great "treasure in clay jars" (2 Cor. 4:7). Like other believers, ordained ministers are fallible human beings. The people they serve may sometimes expect their pastors to be perfect saints. They may wish for infallible advisors, brilliant preachers, courageous leaders, people who are always in charge of things, with an answer for every question, and a faith that contains no uncertainty or doubt. But the "terrible and happy truth," as Karl Rahner puts it, is that ministers are often weak as well as occasionally strong: they too live in fear and trembling, they too cry, "Lord, I believe, help me in my unbelief" and "Lord, be merciful to me, a sinner." Nevertheless, they preach the gospel that transforms the world. Ministers must therefore continuously remind their people and themselves not to take offense at their humanity. Their plea must be: Do not be offended by our failures. Take our frailty and weakness as a promise that God's grace is victorious even through the ministry of ordinary people. From our inadequacy "learn that God has no horror of human beings."[25]

In sum, theology must avoid both a *sacralizing of ministry* that separates ordained leaders from the rest of the people of God and a

---

25. Karl Rahner, *Meditations on the Sacraments*, pp. 61-62.

demeaning of ministry that trivializes the importance of this office in the life of the church. If it is a caricature of ministry to pretend to be superior to and holier than other Christians, it is equally scandalous when ordained ministers ignore the disciplines of spirit and body requisite to faithful ministry of the gospel in an anxious effort to be trendy or just part of the crowd. The proper perspective on ministerial identity comes not from our idealized views of ministry, nor from secular models of what it means to be a successful leader (e.g., the manager of a corporation or a TV celebrity) but from the biblical witness to Christ and his exercise of ministry.

4. Every ministry of Christ must be characterized by *service rather than domination*. Jesus said that he came to serve rather than to be served (Mark 10:45), and he commanded his disciples to exercise authority differently from those who lord it over others (Mark 10:42-44). Whatever church order is adopted — episcopal, presbyterian, congregational, or some other — it must be clear that any claim by some Christians to possess the power of domination over others is completely out of place. If the church has moderators, superintendents, bishops, or even a pope, all must understand themselves as servants of the servant Lord and should discharge their responsibilities accordingly. The purpose of every ministry is to build up the whole people of God in faith, hope, and love for more effective service in the world. All church orders must therefore be tested continuously by the criterion of basic coherence with the ministry of Christ and by the practical test of whether a particular order in fact helps the church to take part in this ministry.

While ministry is not authoritarian, it does involve the exercise of authority. Servants of Christ are not like leaves blown about by the wind. Christian service is not servile subjection to power structures outside the church or within it. Especially within the Reformed tradition, service of the Word of God includes the freedom and responsibility to speak against the community when it obscures or departs from the gospel and to challenge whatever powers there be when they subvert justice and resist the coming of God's reign. The authority of the ordained minister is based not on his or her person but solely on the gospel of Jesus Christ. It is an authority that is always exercised in partnership with the whole people of God. Ministerial authority is not monarchical but collegial in nature.

While various ministries of leadership have been recognized in the church since its beginning, no particular church order can claim exclusive

New Testament authorization. A threefold pattern of ministry is acknowledged by many churches: bishops to oversee the work of several churches in a particular area; presbyters to lead in the proclamation of the Word and the celebration of the sacraments in a local congregation; and deacons to lead in service of the needy. However familiar this threefold pattern may be, no particular church order should be absolutized. All church orders must be open to reform and should recognize the need for new forms of ministry under the guidance of the Spirit and in response to new situations.

5. Ordination to ministry of Word and sacrament is *inclusive rather than exclusive.* No groups of people should be excluded from the exercise of this office on the basis of such criteria as gender and race. A doctrine of ministerial inclusivity is based not on a theory of natural human rights but on the free grace of God, who summons people of all races, classes, nations, and gender to all ministries of the church.[26]

In our time, the most important development in Christian ministry is the recognition by many churches that the Spirit of God extends the call to ministry of Word and sacrament to women as well as men. This will no doubt be a point of tension among the churches for years to come. From a Reformed perspective, however, it must be stated clearly that the continued exclusion of women from the ministry of Word and sacrament by some churches under the pretext that God is masculine, or that Jesus chose only male apostles, or that only a male can properly represent the person and work of Christ to the people of God is a great scandal to the gospel, a denial of the freedom of the Spirit to work in new and surprising ways among the people of God, and an increasing impoverishment of the church and its mission today.

26. According to the Presbyterian Church (U.S.A.) new Brief Statement of Faith, the Spirit "calls women and men to all ministries of the church" (l. 64).

12

Christian Hope

CHRISTIAN FAITH IS EXPECTANT FAITH. IT EAGERLY AWAITS THE COMpletion of the creative and redemptive activity of God. In the language of Scripture and creed, Christians hope and pray for the coming of "God's kingdom" (Matt. 6:10), for "the resurrection of the body and the life everlasting" (Apostles' Creed), for "a new heaven and a new earth" (Rev. 21:1), for the "final triumph of God" over death and all the forces that resist God's will and disrupt the creation (Presbyterian Church [U.S.A.] Confession of 1967). Eschatology, or the doctrine of the last things, is reflection on the Christian hope for the consummation of God's purposes for all creation and for the completion of our lives in perfect fellowship with God.

The fact that I am taking up the doctrine of hope in my final chapter should not be taken as a suggestion that it has less importance than doctrines discussed earlier. On the contrary, I might just as well have begun this introduction to theology with eschatology as concluded with it. Modifying Anselm's famous definition, I might have described Christian theology at the outset as *spes quaerens intellectum*, "hope seeking understanding."[1] For apart from hope, every Christian doctrine becomes distorted. A doctrine of revelation would be flawed if it did not acknowledge that we now see through a glass darkly and not yet face to face; a doctrine of God would be deficient if it did not recognize the inexhaustible mystery of the triune God whose love is extended to the world

---

1. See Jürgen Moltmann, *The Theology of Hope* (New York: Harper & Row, 1967), p. 33.

in creation, redemption, and consummation; a doctrine of creation would be incomplete if it failed to emphasize that the creation still groans for its liberation and completion; a Christology would be misleading if it did not stress that the Lord is not simply a memory or a present experience but also the One who is coming; our doctrines of the church and its sacraments would be pathetically inadequate if they succumbed to triumphalism and showed no passion for the completion of God's reign of justice, freedom, and peace throughout the creation. Not only at the end but from the very beginning, Christian faith and theology are oriented to the coming glory of God and the fulfillment of the promise of God contained in the gospel of Jesus Christ.

The Crisis of Hope in a Nuclear Age

THE biblical witness is a book of hope. From Abraham and Sarah to the present day, the people of Israel have placed their hope in the promises of God who has entered into covenant with them. Trusting in God's faithfulness, they hope for the fulfillment of the divine promise of a land of their own, for God's blessing of justice and peace upon all those who keep God's commandments, and for deliverance from all evil. The prophets envision a time of universal concord when the Lord shall be glorified in all the earth, when nations "shall beat their swords into plowshares, and their spears into pruning hooks" (Isa. 2:4), when justice and peace shall prevail throughout the creation.

The New Testament, too, is saturated with the spirit of expectation. Jesus proclaims the coming reign of God in word and in deed. In his ministry of forgiveness and healing, and above all in his resurrection from the dead, the beginning of God's victory over all the forces of sin and death in the world is declared (1 Cor. 15:57). As is clear from virtually all New Testament books, the early followers of the crucified and risen Lord eagerly await the final triumph of God when "death will be no more" (Rev. 21:4). They speak of God as the "God of hope" (Rom. 15:13), and their persistent prayer is "*Maranatha* — our Lord, come!" (1 Cor. 16:22).

However, as the church expanded, adapted to its cultural environment, and eventually became the official state religion under Constantine, hope in the glorious coming of Christ and in the transformation of the world was increasingly marginalized. Ecclesiastical triumphalism replaced the passion for God's coming reign. While hope in personal survival beyond death remained, hope for the transformation of all creation waned. To be sure, the embers of a greater hope continued to burn underneath the surface of established Christian doctrine and institutional church life, erupting from time to time like a mighty volcano in various apocalyptic movements — the Montanists in the second century, the followers of Joachim of Fiore in the Middle Ages, the Munzerites during the sixteenth-century Reformation, the black Christian slaves in the American South.[2] But in mainstream, orthodox Christianity the earth-shaking hope of the New Testament was largely forgotten. It is not surprising, then, that in the modern era hopes other than the biblical hope have dominated both secular and religious consciousness.

1. Beginning with the Enlightenment and continuing up to the early twentieth century, critics scorned the apocalyptic hope of the Bible as the product of ignorance and fear. For enlightened society, biblical eschatology was definitely out of style except as it was trimmed to the culturally acceptable form of the *liberal theory of progress*. Human history, like all of life, was a steadily upward-moving process. Education and modern science virtually guaranteed the progress of the human race.

To a considerable extent, Christian theology acquiesced in this reduction of hope to the limits of Enlightenment reason. The teachings of Jesus were seen as encouragements to humanity on its path of moral progress. Eschatology became, as Karl Barth said, a "harmless little chapter at the conclusion of Christian Dogmatics."[3] Even the rediscovery of the utter strangeness of New Testament eschatology by Johannes Weiss and Albert Schweitzer at the beginning of the twentieth century had little immediate impact on Christian doctrine.

What did bring about a change of attitudes toward biblical eschatology were two devastating world wars, the Holocaust, the development of nuclear weapons, the ominous signs of ecological disaster, and powerful movements of social unrest and revolution in many parts of the world. These events have shattered the dreams of liberal humanism and have created a crisis of hope in Western society. All naive dogmas of progress have been eclipsed by the possibility of nuclear destruction and en-

2. See Gayraud S. Wilmore, *Last Things First* (Philadelphia: Westminster Press, 1982).

3. Barth, *The Epistle to the Romans*, trans. Edwyn C. Hoskyns (London: Oxford University Press, 1933), p 500.

vironmental ruin. Ours is a postliberal and postmodern world that is no longer confident that reason, science, and technology are always on the side of life against death or that they will guarantee a golden future for humanity.

2. The liberal theory of progress is not the only modern claimant to supersede the eschatological hope of the Bible. Among modern philosophies of the future, none has been more influential than *Marxist utopianism*. For the past century and a half, it has offered humanity a secularized and militant version of biblical hope.

In his remarkable *Philosophy of Hope,* Ernst Bloch develops a neo-Marxist interpretation of all human experience and cultural activity as moved by a passionate hope for a future that transcends all alienation.[4] Bloch calls his philosophy of hope the legitimate heir of the revolutionary apocalyptic hope of the Bible. His interest is not in demythologizing the biblical hope in order to make it more acceptable to the bourgeois world but in releasing the social critique and prophetic vision conveyed in the dangerous memories and eschatological images of the Bible. The fantastic imagery of cosmic judgment and renewal is no embarrassment to Bloch as it has been so often to acculturated Christianity. In his view, such images are an appropriate language to speak of the incalculable conflict and suffering experienced in history and the radical transformation of life that is required to set things straight. For Bloch, of course, it is not God but the revolutionary proletariat who will execute the "final judgment" on capitalist oppressors and establish "the new heaven and the new earth" of socialism.

In a nuclear age, however, both official and revisionary Marxist hope, no less than the hope of liberal Enlightenment humanism, are in crisis. After decades of Marxist police states and Stalinist concentration camps, the promise of a new humanity created solely through armed revolutionary struggle has become increasingly hollow. Marxist critics may still serve to awaken Christians to dimensions of the biblical hope that they are tempted to forget in affluent consumerist societies. But as recent events in Eastern Europe and the Soviet Union show, the power of Marxist utopianism is on the decline; many who previously held to this ideology have begun to experience the need for a hope beyond hope, for a fulfillment of life that Marxism has promised but has not been able to realize.

4. Bloch, *The Philosophy of Hope,* 3 vols. (Cambridge: MIT, 1985).

3. The crisis of hope in the nuclear age is also evident within the church. This is especially clear in the voices of *fundamentalistic apocalypticism* who claim to represent authentic biblical hope for the world today. Their pictures of the future are dark and terrible. They expect not utopia but dystopia, and they are transfixed by a vision of the future as ending in universal nuclear holocaust. The writings of Hal Lindsey (e.g., *The Late Great Planet Earth*) come immediately to mind.[5] Coupling the biblical symbols of the end of history with the prediction of the destruction of the world by nuclear conflict, this neo-apocalypticism has surged in North American churches in recent years. Every new turmoil in the Middle East heightens the fever of apocalypticism.

Given the threat of nuclear, chemical, and biological warfare, the conflicts among the nations over territory and natural resources, the spread of terrorism, and the sense of powerlessness and impending doom that overwhelms many people today, it is not difficult to understand the appeal of Lindsey's sort of apocalyptic teaching. The failure of the dominant theologies in North America, too domesticated and too complacent to take seriously the disturbing eschatological themes of the Bible, has also helped to create a kind of theological vacuum that is now being filled by fundamentalistic apocalypticism.

The Lindsey version of Christian hope feeds on the fears of people. He offers to allay those fears by describing the exact timetable of the coming awful events of the end as ordained by God and predicted by the Bible. With the reestablishment of the modern state of Israel as a base date, and drawing in a highly selective and tendentious manner from a few obscure texts in Ezekiel, Daniel, and the book of Revelation, Lindsey predicts the outbreak of World War III in the very near future, who the contestants will be, and where it will be centered. He portrays a thermonuclear holocaust that will culminate in the incredibly destructive battle of Armageddon. From this period of terrible tribulation, believers will be rescued or "raptured" — that is, snatched out of a world plunging toward destruction. The return of Jesus Christ and the rapture that will accompany it "is the real hope for the Christian, the blessed hope of true believers." The assertion that the true church will not have to experience the horrors of the tribulation period provides a considerable

5. Hal Lindsey, *The Late Great Planet Earth* (Grand Rapids: Zondervan, 1970); see also Grant Jeffries, *Armageddon — Appointment with Destiny* (New York: Bantam Books, 1990).

incentive for becoming a Christian. By God's plan, the responsibility for evangelizing the earth during those years will be assigned to 144,000 converted Jews. Lindsey predicts that all this will happen in the lifetime of his readers. What is wrong with this brand of apocalypticism?

a. It is a crass manipulation of biblical texts. The life, ministry, death, and resurrection of Christ become quite secondary to Lindsey's arbitrary speculation about the final events of history. Lindsey plays apocalyptic roulette with the Bible, ripping texts out of their historical context and fitting them into his own schema.

b. Lindsey's apocalyptic timetable is highly deterministic. The wheel of apocalyptic destiny spins out of human control. Hence Lindsey's followers have no sense of responsibility for the future. Knowing that they will be exempted from the terrors to come, they can be mere observers of world events and calmly await their rapture.

c. What Christians really hope for in this eschatology is the rapture. Lindsey terrifies his readers with his descriptions of nuclear holocaust, seas of blood running six feet deep, and the like. Then he tells them: "Believe in Jesus Christ and you will be raptured. You will escape all of these horrors." This is nothing less than "apocalyptic terrorism," entirely lacking in any sense of solidarity with creation and with humankind groaning for emancipation from sin, suffering, and death.

d. Lindsey's rendition of Christian hope lacks a theology of the cross. Eschatology and the cross are torn apart. Suffering and hope are severed. The church will be safe in heaven when all hell breaks loose. Witnessing for God on the earth in these coming awful days will be the task of Jews. One can imagine the fully justified sarcasm of death-camp survivors should they be asked to respond to this picture of the future: "The self-centered and complacent church never was around when helpless victims were machine-gunned, men and women gassed, the heads of children bashed in by rifle butts. So it will not be a surprise when this church again is not around when all those things happen once more. Then, as before, faithful Jews and Christians will be left alone to bear a terrible witness to God." The signature of New Testament hope is not the rapture, as in Lindsey's book, but the resurrection of the crucified Jesus.[6]

---

6. My critique of Lindsey, first presented in an unpublished lecture in 1979, was used with my permission by J. Christiaan Beker in *Paul's Apocalyptic Gospel* (Philadelphia: Fortress Press, 1984), pp. 26-27. For a different critique of modern apocalypticism, see Gordon D. Kaufman, *Theology for a Nuclear Age* (Philadelphia; Westminster Press, 1985).

4. Theology must not default on its responsibility to "give an account" of the hope of Christians (1 Pet. 3:15). If not the liberal belief in progress, or Marxist utopianism, or the neo-apocalyptic hope of rapture amidst nuclear holocaust, what is the Christian hope? The answer to this question is not made easier by the often *confusing and contradictory interpretations* of Christian hope in twentieth-century biblical and theological scholarship. While the majority of biblical scholars and theologians of Christian hope would be united in their opposition to the eschatologies of naive liberalism, militant Marxism, and fundamentalistic apocalypticism, their own interpretations of biblical hope are often in conflict with each other. We can identify four such conflicts in modern eschatology.

a. One conflict is between futurist eschatology (Albert Schweitzer) and realized eschatology (C. H. Dodd). Is the kingdom of God proclaimed in the New Testament an already present reality, or is it still entirely in the future?

b. Another conflict is between personal or existential eschatology (Bultmann) on the one hand and corporate eschatology (Moltmann, the liberation theologians) on the other. Does the kingdom of God have to do with fulfillment of life for the individual, or does it concern social, economic, and political fulfillment?

c. Still another conflict takes the form of historical eschatology (modern Western theology) versus cosmic eschatology (Eastern theology, process theology). Is the kingdom of God the fulfillment of human life, or does it comprehend the whole of nature and cosmic process?

d. Finally, there is the conflict between eschatology that focuses on God's activity (neo-orthodoxy) and eschatology that concentrates on human activity (Social Gospel theology, recent theologies of praxis). Is the kingdom of God solely God's work, or are human beings to take it upon themselves to build the kingdom by their own effort?

These conflicts result from one-sided interpretations of biblical eschatology. The reign of God for which Christians hope is already inaugurated in Jesus Christ but is not yet complete. It embraces personal and communal fulfillment. It encompasses history and cosmic process. It is a divine gift yet liberates humanity for partnership with God. Amidst the hopelessness and false hopes of our nuclear age, Christian hope must be expressed anew in all its fullness.

Principles for Interpreting Christian Hope

CHRISTIANS hope in the final victory of the creative, self-expending, community-forming love of the triune God. Hence they hope in the triumph of the love of God over all hate, of the justice of God over all injustice, of God's freedom over all bondage, of community with God over all separation, of life with God over the power of death. Yet this hope becomes indistinguishable from cheap optimism if it fails to recognize and to share the present agony of the world.

In the world as we know it, death seems to have the last word. Each human life, the whole of human history, and the entire cosmos drive inexorably toward death. The death that is at work in our own lives, in history, and in nature is far more than biological termination. It is the power of negativity and destruction that threatens the fulfillment of life created and redeemed by God. Disease, disability, alienation, injustice, oppression, war, and a host of other evils constantly remind us that "in life we are in death." Only those who take with utter seriousness the reality of death and the grave can begin to grasp the meaning of life as a sheer gift of God and the joyous hope of resurrection to new life by the grace of God.[7]

Christian hope amidst the ravages of sin, evil, and death has many dimensions. One of these is, of course, hope for the fulfillment of personal life. Protestant theologians have not written much about this dimension of hope in recent decades. As their emphasis has shifted to the political dimensions of Christian hope, the question of the meaning of hope in relation to the death of individuals has been pushed to the side. Some Catholic theologians (notably Karl Rahner) have developed a theology of death in which the death of each person becomes a final opportunity to give oneself into the gracious hands of God in trusting self-surrender.[8] However one evaluates such a theology of death, the fact remains that theology cannot ignore the death of individuals or their hope for fullness of life. If people are created in the image of God, forgiven and loved by God in Christ, and through the work of the Spirit experience even now the beginnings of new life in relation to God and others, then hope of personal fulfillment is no mere relic of an antiquated piety: it is an integral

---

7. For an example of this sort of seriousness, see the moving book of Nicholas Wolterstorff, *Lament for a Son* (Grand Rapids: William B. Eerdmans, 1987).

8. See Rahner, *On the Theology of Death* (New York: Herder & Herder, 1961).

part of Christian hope. The idea that personal human life is expendable and unimportant to God is alien to the biblical witness.[9]

But Christian hope is not limited to the fulfillment of individual life. It insists that personal and communal fulfillment are inseparable. Christians thus work and hope for the transformation of life in community. As individuals we know that our lives are intimately entangled with those of friends and neighbors near and far. When by grace we rise above our egocentricity, we realize that there can be no salvation for us as persons apart from the transformation of the many communities and institutions to which we belong: family, society, humanity as a whole. The expansion of Christian hope to include new life for societies and economies ruled by the power of death has been a major contribution of liberation theologies in our time. If our hope is in the triune God, it must necessarily be a hope not of the salvation of isolated individuals but of people in community.[10]

Christian hope also has a cosmic dimension. It encompasses the entire creation. The fulfillment for which we yearn cannot be found apart from the renewal and transformation of the heaven and the earth to which we are bound in life and in death.[11] In the last decade of the twentieth century, increasingly surrounded by an environmental wasteland, we are learning how important it is to us as individuals and as societies to be able to hope that by God's grace new blossoms may yet break forth in the desert and that life-giving waters may yet flow in the wilderness (Isa. 35:1-2, 5-7).

Christian hope in God's final triumph over sin, evil, and death is multidimensional — personal, corporate, and cosmic. The final victory belongs to God, not to death (1 Cor. 15). This conviction must guide any restatement of the meaning of the eschatological symbols of the Bible

9. While Jürgen Moltmann is well known for his emphasis on the political significance of Christian hope, he does not discount the importance of hope in personal fulfillment. See his essay "Love, Death, Eternal Life," in *Love: The Foundation of Hope*, ed. Frederic B. Burnham, Charles S. McCoy, and M. Douglas Meeks (San Francisco: Harper & Row, 1988).

10. See Jürgen Moltmann, *The Theology of Hope* (New York: Harper & Row, 1967), and *The Trinity and the Kingdom* (San Francisco: Harper & Row, 1981).

11. Process theologians have placed particular emphasis on this dimension of the Christian hope. See John B. Cobb, Jr., and David Ray Griffin, *Process Theology: An Introductory Exposition* (Philadelphia: Westminster Press, 1976), pp. 111-27; John B. Cobb, Jr., *Is It Too Late? A Theology of Ecology* (Beverly Hills, CA: Bruce, 1972); Norman Pittenger, *"The Last Things" in a Process Perspective* (London: Epworth Press, 1970).

and the Christian creeds. In view of the lack of consensus in Christian eschatology today, it is important to establish basic hermeneutical principles for interpreting Christian hope.[12]

1. *The language of Christian hope is language stretched to the limits, language rich in symbol and image.* We should not pretend to have precise and detailed information about the future. The symbolic language of hope is to be taken seriously but not literalistically. When we speak of life beyond death, or of a resurrected body, or of a new heaven and a new earth, we speak in images, metaphors, and parables.[13] We must have the humility to recognize with Luther that "as little as children know in their mother's womb about their birth, so little do we know about life everlasting."[14]

2. *Christian hope is centered on the glory of the triune God that is revealed above all in the resurrection of the crucified Jesus and that contains the promise of new life for all creation.* The God of Christian hope is the triune God, the creator, redeemer, and consummator. From the very beginning, the purpose of the triune God has been to share life with others, to create a community of love in which all are united without loss of enriching differences. Through the work of Christ and by the power of the Spirit, we are invited to participate in the eternal life and glory of the triune God. As the power of self-giving, other-affirming, community-forming love, the triune God is the God whose glory is in the triumph of life over death, of mutuality and friendship over isolation and separation.

3. *Christian eschatological symbols must be interpreted nondualistically and must be shown to encompass the quest for fulfillment and wholeness in all dimensions of life.* It is necessary to exercise a hermeneutics of suspicion and to dismantle all the harmful dualisms in the interpretation of Christian hope — between the spiritual and the physical, between personal and communal fulfillment, between hope for humanity and hope for the

---

12. Cf. Karl Rahner, "The Hermeneutics of Eschatological Assertions," in *Theological Investigations*, vol. 4 (New York: Seabury Press, 1974), pp. 323-46.

13. John Calvin recognized this in his sober and restrained writings on eschatology: "Though the Scripture teaches that the kingdom of God is full of light, joy, felicity, and glory, nevertheless all that is said about it is far above our intelligence, and as though wrapped in imagery until the day shall come when the Savior will explain himself to us face to face" (*Institutes of the Christian Religion*, 3.25.10).

14. Luther, quoted by Hans Schwarz, in *Christian Dogmatics*, vol. 2, ed. Carl Braaten and Robert Jenson (Philadelphia: Fortress Press, 1984), p. 586.

whole creation. The activity of God always finds its consummation in embodiment.[15]

4. *Christian eschatological symbols, rightly understood, relativize all historical and cultural achievements of humanity.* Christian hope differs from all utopianisms that eventually capitulate to the ideas that the end justifies the means and that the present must be sacrificed for the future. Authentic Christian hope will certainly stand in opposition to present injustice and to every effort to absolutize the status quo. However, in the struggle for justice, equality, and human rights, Christians will always insist on something more, something greater than what is ever achievable by human effort alone, a hope beyond hope. Utopian hope finds in humanity itself the resources and capacities to remove all suffering, establish universal justice, and complete history. A Christian theology of hope, by contrast, knows that the fulfillment we seek is an incalculable gift of God. Consequently, Christian hope will generate criticism both of the status quo and of all absolutized programs of progress and strategies of revolution. Christian symbols of the end are symbols of total and permanent revolution.[16]

5. *Christian hope and its rich symbols are immensely evocative and give birth to creative human activity.* When properly interpreted, Christian hope incites the imagination to dream new dreams and motivates individuals and societies to fresh effort to find ways of helping to "make and keep human life human in the world" (Paul Lehmann). This may seem to contradict what I just said about the critical, relativizing function of Christian hope and eschatology, but the point of differentiating between what only God can do and what human beings are called to do is not to minimize the importance of the latter but to free us from ultimately stultifying presumption. Christian symbols of the end do indeed speak of the coming reign of God as a gift. Yet to acknowledge

15. For a discussion of this thesis, see Jürgen Moltmann, *God in Creation* (San Francisco: Harper & Row, 1985), pp. 244ff. The critique of dualism in Christian eschatology, as in other areas of Christian doctrine, has been a major contribution of feminist theology. See Rosemary Radford Ruether, "Eschatology and Feminism," in *Lift Every Voice: Constructing Christian Theologies from the Underside*, ed. Susan Brooks Thistlethwaite and Mary Potter Engel (San Francisco: Harper & Row, 1990), pp. 111-24.

16. Writing in a revolutionary context, Karl Barth called attention to "the revolution of God" that sets in motion a spirit of "permanent revolution." See Paul L. Lehmann, "Karl Barth, Theologian of Permanent Revolution," *Union Seminary Quarterly Review* 28 (Fall 1972): 67-81.

the gift of grace is also to be commissioned to a task. We cannot bring in God's reign by our own efforts, but we can and should be encouraged by our hope in God to work for a world of greater justice, freedom, and peace. In brief, Christian hope ignites rather than paralyzes human imagination and action in the direction of God's coming new heaven and new earth.[17]

Classical Symbols of Christian Hope

ESCHATOLOGY has traditionally focused on four clusters of symbols of the end of history and the completion of human life. Every Christian understanding of these symbols will be guided by the history of Jesus Christ as the decisive expression of the triune God's sovereign love for the world. As I have emphasized throughout this survey of Christian doctrine, God's love is eternally shared in freedom, is graciously open to the world in creation and incarnation, and moves toward the consummation when God will be fully glorified by a liberated and redeemed creation.

1. One cluster of Christian symbols of hope centers on the *parousia* of Christ. *Parousia* means "arrival" or "coming" and refers in the New Testament to the coming of the crucified and risen Jesus in glory. In expectation of this final coming, the church prays: "Come, Lord Jesus" (Rev. 22:20).

Hope in the parousia of Christ emphasizes, first of all, that Christian hope is hope in *someone,* not just in many *things,* however valuable they may be. Christians do not simply hope for life, joy, freedom, justice, and peace in the abstract. They hope in the coming of Jesus Christ, in whom all good things have their basis and meaning and without whom they would be empty and worthless. Christians hope not simply to survive, but to participate with all creatures in the praise of Jesus Christ and in the glorification of the triune God.

But, secondly, hope in the parousia of Christ is not blind hope in an unknown Christ. The Christ whose arrival is awaited is the Christ who has come before. He has come in ministry to sinners and the poor, in his passion and resurrection, in the outpouring of the Holy Spirit, in

17. See Carl E. Braaten, *Eschatology and Ethics* (Minneapolis: Augsburg Press, 1974).

his presence in Word and sacrament, and in his surprising presence among the hungry, the thirsty, the sick, the naked, and the imprisoned who cry out for help. Christians do not hope for the coming of a Lord who is now absent and entirely unknown. The one whose parousia is awaited is the very same one whose proleptic comings have sparked our hope in a final coming.

But, thirdly, all these present experiences of the coming of the Lord are fragmentary and provisional. God's justice and peace are not yet realities throughout the creation. The world is not yet redeemed; God's work of salvation is still unfinished. Sin and suffering, alienation and death still mar the creation and are still present in the lives of believers. The final act of the drama of redemption has not been played out. So the church prays: "Your kingdom come" (Matt. 6:9), and "Come, Lord Jesus" (Rev. 22:20).

In their hope for the final arrival of Jesus Christ and his consummated reign, Christians make no claim to know either the date or the manner of this coming. They have been told not to spend their time speculating about the timetable of the last events but simply to keep alert (Mark 13:32-33). They are confident simply that the very same crucified and risen Lord who is at the center of the church's memory and present experience of God's liberating and reconciling activity will also be at the center of the final act of the drama of redemption. Whatever the ultimate future of humanity and the cosmos may hold, God's action then will be fully congruent with what God has done in the history of the covenant decisively confirmed for the world in Jesus Christ.

2. Another cluster of hope symbols centers on the *resurrection* of the dead, and the companion symbol of the resurrection of the body. These symbols acquire their Christian meaning, of course, from the event of the resurrection of Christ. Resurrection is an apocalyptic image symbolizing the holistic and inclusive character of Christian hope. The inclusivity of hope in resurrection has several aspects.

In the first place, the symbol of resurrection encompasses soul and body. The ancient doctrine of the immortality of the soul is, from a Christian perspective, inadequate on at least two counts.[18] The belief in the immortality of the soul posits an inherently indestructible element of human life which is separable from the mortal, corruptible body that

---

18. Cf. Oscar Cullmann, *Immortality of the Soul or Resurrection of the Dead?* (New York: Macmillan, 1958).

it temporarily inhabits. Christian hope in the resurrection of the body does not rest on an immortality that is supposedly an inherent possession of at least some segment of human existence. Instead, Christians hope in the resurrection as a gift of God analogous to the creation at the beginning and to the event of reconciliation in Christ. Moreover, God wills to give new life to the whole person, not merely to a disembodied soul. Even if we cannot adequately conceive of a resurrection body, the symbol stands as a bold and even defiant affirmation of God's total, inclusive, holistic redemption.

The second aspect of inclusive hope in the resurrection power of God is closely connected with the first. If God's promise includes the body, then it also embraces society, the body politic, and indeed the entire cosmos with which our bodies are so intimately bound up. In contrast to the individualism and anthropocentrism of the doctrine of the immortality of the soul, resurrection hope envisions not simply a future for me or for the human species but for the whole cosmos. Christians hope for a changed, transformed world, for a "new heaven and a new earth."

The third aspect of the inclusivity of hope in resurrection is that it embraces those who have already died as well as those now living and those still unborn. Rightly understood, Christian hope is breathtakingly inclusive. It is not narrower but broader than secular hopes for a golden age of the future in which only those living at that time will participate.[19] There is no more emphatic expression of resistance to all the forces of disease, negativity, evil, and death in the world than the hope in God's resurrection of the dead. All of the ways of God — the triune God — begin and end in inclusive community.

3. The symbol of the *last judgment* is an awesome and, to many people, terrible element of Christian eschatology. They may think of the famous *Dies Irae* (day of wrath) that became a part of the Catholic mass for the dead. Or they may think of Michelangelo's somber painting of the last judgment on the wall of the Sistine Chapel, in which Christ the irate judge gestures rejection to the damned who are lying at his feet, their faces distorted with despair and their bodies mangled with pain. The martyrs of the faith who surround Christ seem to take satisfaction in the torment of the damned.

---

19. For a discussion of the resurrection power of God with reference to the victims of injustice, see Peter C. Hodgson, *God in History: Shapes of Freedom* (Nashville: Abingdon Press, 1989), pp. 224ff.

Christian hope in the last judgment must be sharply distinguished from all self-righteousness and resentment. The gospel of Jesus Christ and the motive of resentment and revenge are absolutely incompatible. The God who is decisively revealed in the cross of Christ does not exercise vindictive judgment.

In reaction to the doctrine of judgment as vengefulness, liberal Protestantism rather too quickly dismissed the symbol of the last judgment altogether. The result was a sentimentalizing of Christian faith, hope, and love. God is indeed a "consuming fire" (Heb. 12:28-29), not a doting grandfather. But the fire of God is the fire of a loving judgment and a judging love that we know in the cross of Christ to be for our salvation rather than our destruction.

In distinction from both lurid portrayals of the last judgment in the tradition of the church on the one hand and superficial liberal dismissals of the reality of divine judgment on the other, a faithful and adequate interpretation of the symbol of the last judgment will have three primary emphases. First, we shall *all* be judged by God. Hence we must never assume, or act as if we assumed, that the sins of others will be exposed and condemned while only ours will be forgiven. Second, the very same Christ who was crucified and raised for us will also be our judge on the final day. We do not have to do now with a gracious, forgiving Lord but then with a different, vengeful, vindictive judge. Third, the criterion of judgment, now and then, is nothing other than the self-giving, other-including love of God decisively made known in Jesus Christ. We will not be judged by whether we have said, "Lord, Lord" (Matt. 7:21) or whether we have subscribed to certain orthodox doctrines. If we are guided by the scene of the final judgment in Matthew 25, the question we will have to answer will be something like this: In response to God's superabundant mercy to us, have we shown mercy, or only loved ourselves?[20] Orthodox belief and petty legalism are not the criteria by which human lives are measured. The criteria are simple trust in God's grace and glad but usually quite unspectacular participation in Christ's agapic way of life that manifests itself in the service of others, and especially of the poor, the sick, and the outcast.

4. A final set of Christian symbols of hope center on the promise of *eternal life* ("heaven") and the possibility of *eternal death* ("hell"). In

---

20. See Hans Urs von Balthasar, *Credo: Meditations on the Apostles' Creed* (New York: Crossroad, 1990), pp. 70-71.

considering these symbols, we are not to focus on such matters as "the shape of the furniture of heaven or the temperature of the fire of hell." And we should note that they are not ascribed equal weight in the biblical witness. The coming of the kingdom of God is promised; the references to final destruction and hell constitute a warning that is not to be ignored.

The symbols of the consummated reign of God, or heaven, point to everlasting life in depth of fellowship with the triune God. Eternal life is unbroken and unending communion, the sharing of life with others in the God whose being is in community. When the reign of God is interpreted as the reign of the triune God, it is seen at once to be the fulfillment of both personal life and life in community. The biblical images of eternal life are profoundly communal — the kingdom of God, the new Jerusalem coming down from heaven, the great banquet. Eternal life is no endless extension of the existence of isolated selves, no perpetuation of individualism into infinity. Eternal life means unending participation in God's eternal community of love. As Zachary Hayes writes, "the social nature of humanity finds its historical fulfillment in the mystery of the church, and its final fulfillment in the sharing of life with all others who together share the life of God."[21] Such life in communion is not the loss but the fulfillment of personal identity in relationship with God and others.

The everlasting life of God is inexhaustibly rich. We will never be sated or bored by it, never feel we have gotten to the bottom of it. In the praise and service of the triune God there will be ever new surprises and adventures as God's gift of life and love "goes on unfolding boundlessly."[22]

By contrast, hell is simply wanting to be oneself apart from others and even in disregard of others. Hell is that condition in which, in opposition to God's agapic love and the call to a life of mutual service and friendship, individuals barricade themselves from others. Hell is the terrible weariness and incredible boredom of a life focused entirely on itself. Hell is not an arbitrary divine punishment at the end of history; it is not the conclusive retaliation of a vindictive deity. Hell is self-destructive resistance to the eternal love of God. It symbolizes the truth that the meaning and intention of life can be missed. Repentance is

---

21. Hayes, *Visions of a Future: A Study of Christian Eschatology* (Wilmington, Del.: Michael Glazier, 1989), p. 196.
22. Urs von Balthasar, *Credo*, p. 103.

urgent. Our choices and actions are important. God ever seeks to lead us out of our hell of self-glorification and lovelessness, but God will not coerce us.[23]

Will there be universal salvation? Will God's love prevail even over the most recalcitrant of creatures? This is not a question that Christian faith and theology can answer with a presumptuous guarantee of yes or no. There are biblical passages that issue sharp warnings (e.g., Matt. 24:36-42), and passages that point toward the redemption of all things (e.g., 1 Cor. 15:22). It is best, as Karl Barth has suggested, not to try to resolve this tension theoretically, but to hope and pray, on the basis of the astonishing love of God in Jesus Christ, for a redemption of the world far greater than we are inclined to desire or even able to imagine.[24]

Eschatology and Ethics

THE symbols of Christian hope — the coming of Christ in glory, the resurrection of the dead, the last judgment, the promise of eternal life, and the warning of eternal death — are both spiritually and ethically profound. By comparison the banal hope of bourgeois Christianity and the apocalyptic terrorisms of political and religious groups on the right and the left are shallow and destructive.

Unfortunately, the church has lost the link between Christian hope and Christian ethics, and it is a matter of urgency that this link be recovered in our time. Our hope is in God alone, but precisely for that reason we are empowered to engage in ministries of consolation and transformation. Rightly understood and practiced, Christian hope brings to our activities and struggles in this life the passionate expectation of all-encompassing renewal. Conversely, only in the life of discipleship is the true meaning of Christian hope grasped. The dialectical relationship of Christian hope and Christian discipleship — that eschatology prompts ethics, and ethics needs eschatology — can be expressed in the following statements:

1. *Hope empowers us to enter into solidarity with the groaning creation and to persist in the struggle for the renewal of all things.*

---

23. See Hans Küng, *Eternal Life: Life after Death as a Medical, Philosophical and Theological Problem* (New York: Doubleday Image Books, 1985), pp. 129-42.

24. Barth, *The Humanity of God* (Richmond: John Knox Press, 1960), pp. 61-62. Cf. Tillich, *Systematic Theology,* 3: 406-9.

Genuine Christian hope — hope in the final triumph of God, in the completion of God's redemptive work in Christ, in God's promise of resurrection — empowers believers to enter into real solidarity with afflicted humanity and with the whole groaning creation. Based solely on the grace of God, Christian hope liberates us for the praise and service of God in a needy world.

Christian hope does not close our eyes to the suffering of the world. On the contrary, Christians believe that God cherishes the world, has created and redeemed it, and wills to have abiding communion with it. If we hope in fulfilled life after death, we cannot be indifferent to suffering life before death. As Jürgen Moltmann has put it, "those who hope in Christ can no longer put up with reality as it is, but begin to suffer under it, to contradict it. Peace with God means conflict with the world, for the goad of the promised future stabs inexorably into the flesh of every unfulfilled present."[25]

Surely one of the most pressing needs of people inside and outside the church today is to acquire a greatly widened sense of solidarity with all who suffer.[26] We tend to be ethical individualists, or perhaps ethically sensitive family members, or people with a sense of solidarity with our particular class, sex, race, or nation. The Christian gospel of the self-expending, other-regarding, community-forming love of the triune God frees us to enter into solidarity with all creatures. We are thus liberated by grace to become hopeful not only for a narrow clique but for the whole human family, not only for the human family but for the whole cosmos, not only for the whole cosmos as it has existed and presently exists but for the cosmos as it will continue to exist if we do not destroy it. Our hope as Christians embraces not only our present generation but generations past and those yet to come. Any society whose policies callously neglect the present needs of the poor or recklessly disregard the health and welfare of future generations is deeply anti-Christian.

In saying that Christian hope should stretch our imagination, widen our visions of salvation, and deepen our solidarity with other people and with the whole groaning creation, we are not arguing that the visions and symbols of Christian hope are to be espoused merely because they are useful to us. On the contrary, we are claiming that the biblical visions

25. Moltmann, *The Theology of Hope*, p. 21.
26. For a moving statement of this concern in strictly humanist terms, see Jonathan Schell, *The Fate of the Earth* (New York: Alfred A. Knopf, 1982).

of hope give expression to the truth that God purposes to liberate and reconcile all creation and is faithful to that purpose. Only the truth can really free us for costly service (John 8:32). Human beings will not long struggle and hope for that which they know to be merely make-believe.

As we approach the end of the second millennium since the gospel of Jesus Christ was first proclaimed, the world still groans for freedom from many bondages. If we have cause to rejoice that the long cold war between East and West appears to be over, many divisions of peoples and nations nevertheless remain. Nuclear, chemical, and biological weapons continue to proliferate. The gap between rich and poor peoples of the earth is widening. Racism and sexism are virulent in all parts of the globe. Our despoliation of the environment proceeds at a reckless pace. A new solidarity among people of diverse races, gender, and cultures and a new sense of common destiny with all of God's creatures are desperately needed. The Christian gospel frees us to include friends, strangers, and enemies — all the "others" — in our hope. We are called to unrestricted solidarity because the triune God loves in freedom, lives in community, and wills to be glorified by the participation of all creation in God's own life of shared love.

2. *In the midst of our struggle for a renewed world in which life flourishes and the forces of evil, death, and destruction are overcome, we learn the meaning of hoping in God rather than in our own abilities and achievements.*

If Christian hope cultivates a new spirit of solidarity, it is also true that the life of costly discipleship reminds us again and again that our hope is finally based on nothing else than the sovereign grace of God. All is grace: that is a brief summary of Christian theology from prolegomena to eschatology.

Christians learn the meaning of hope in the grace of God only in the practice of discipleship. That practice includes proclaiming the gospel and sharing with others the forgiveness, peace, reconciliation, liberation, and hope that are the gifts of God. It includes passing on to others the apostolic benediction of the grace of the Lord Jesus Christ, the love of God, and the communion of the Holy Spirit (2 Cor. 13:14). As the church waits and prays, it also acts. Christian hope, I have insisted, does not immobilize people but makes them eager to get to work. It is not escapist hope but creative hope. It encourages anticipatory realizations of God's new world of justice and peace.

Yet while anticipatory signs of God's reign are to be found in every triumph over disease and suffering and in every victory for justice and peace, we are also reminded, personally and corporately, of the incompleteness of these victories. We cannot perfect the world. We are unable to heal every disease or right every wrong. We cannot raise the dead. As Edward Schillebeeckx writes, "There is human hurt for which no social or political cure exists."[27] We are a pilgrim people, and there is a "homeland," a "better country," that our hearts seek (Heb. 11:14, 16). Therefore Christians are never to equate their efforts and achievements with what Karl Barth calls the "great hope," the "great righteousness," the "great peace," by which he means the kingdom of God that comes as a gift from God. Instead, Christians are to proclaim the gospel and work with imagination and energy for the realization of many "little hopes," for more justice, more peace, more compassion in our families, our communities, our churches, our nations, and our international relationships.[28] We are most loyal to the earth when our ultimate loyalty is to God alone.

In reliance on the "God of hope" (Rom. 15:13), Christians dare to persist in a life of service and costly discipleship when others have given up the task as useless. There is so much pain and suffering in the world, so much destruction and death, that we become weary and are tempted to despair. Yet hope in God sustains us. While avoiding every foolish confusion between God's coming reign and their always meager, inadequate, and flawed efforts to prepare its way, Christians are nevertheless called to struggle against apathy and resignation and to plant seeds of hope and new life that God will water and bring to fruition.

Christian hope offers no guarantee of quick or easy success. It remembers that Christ was crucified. True hope is thus learned only in companionship with the crucified Christ and those whose suffering he shares.[29] Only in that location is it possible to discover that God's grace is sufficient. Only at Calvary and in all the many places of suffering in the world that remind us of the one who suffered there can we begin to repent and learn to love and to hope. In these places of darkness and pain, North American Christians might learn to ask elementary but

27. Schillebeeckx, *Jesus: An Experiment in Christology* (New York: Seabury Press, 1977), p. 624.
28. See Barth, *The Christian Life* (Grand Rapids: William B. Eerdmans, 1981), pp. 205-13, 260-71.
29. See Nicholas Lash, *Theology on the Way to Emmaus* (London: SCM Press, 1986).

necessary questions: Will we continue to squander our wealth on armaments instead of using it to feed the poor and heal the sick? Will we persist in a way of life that makes it difficult or even impossible for others — the poor, the oppressed, future generations — to have enough food, sufficient supplies of energy, drinkable water, arable land? Must not Christians in more affluent countries understand their responsibility as Christian disciples today to resist the spirit of limitless consumption so widespread in North Atlantic societies? Would not the cultivation of a new Christian ascesis, a simpler way of life, be one practical expression of authentic Christian hope in our time?

This is the spirit of Christian hope: to struggle and to take risks for justice, freedom, and peace for all people; to be zealous for the completion of God's redemptive activity for the world; to live in the confidence that nothing can ever separate us from the love of God in Christ Jesus our Lord (Rom. 8:38-39); and to discover ever new reasons to give thanks and glory to God. Provoking love and service of the world yet without elevating the world to ultimate reality, Christian hope time and again infuriates the Caesars of this world and confounds the ideologues of the right and the left. Hope in the triumph of the love of God made known in the crucified and resurrected Lord differs radically from hope in the triumph of our version of Christianity, not to mention the triumph of our culture or our nation.

Christians hope in the steadfast love of God that raises the dead and brings a transformed heaven and earth filled with God's righteousness, freedom, and peace. They hope for the coming of God's glory, for the final "healing of the nations" (Rev. 22:2), for the end of all crying and all death (Rev. 21:4), for everlasting life in God's society of love. They hope not only to see God but to serve, glorify, and enjoy God forever. Christian hope is hope in fulfillment beyond all that we deserve or can even imagine — hope in the consummation of life in the joyful community of the triune God.

Thus Christian theology, like Christian faith, hope, and love, appropriately ends in doxology:

"For from God, and through God, and to God are all things.
To God be the glory forever" (Rom. 11:36).

APPENDIX A

Natural Theology: A Dialogue

THE INITIAL DIVISION OF MANY STANDARD TEXTBOOKS IN THEOLOGY goes under the name of "natural theology." While it assumes different forms, the purpose of natural theology is to establish a knowledge of God, or at least a readiness for knowledge of God, common to all people. To clarify the possibility and limits of natural theology, distinctions are sometimes made between common grace and extraordinary grace, and between general revelation and special revelation. According to natural theology, common grace and general revelation make possible a knowledge of God that is plain everywhere and always through "the things that have been made" (Rom. 1:20), and is apprehensible through human reason, conscience, and common experience. Extraordinary grace and special revelation, by contrast, refer to the unique action and self-disclosure of God in relation to the people of Israel and in the history of Jesus Christ as made known through the witness of Scripture. The expectation is that once natural theology has prepared the way, a theology based on special revelation can do its job of refining and deepening the understanding of God.

The project of natural theology has been the topic of vigorous and complex controversy for centuries both among philosophers and theologians. For our purposes, it is sufficient to identify briefly three positions taken in this controversy. (1) According to one tradition of natural theology, the existence of God can be demonstrated by reason. Shared by both Protestant and Catholic scholastic theologies, this view was made an official teaching of the Roman Catholic Church at Vatican I in 1870. (2) According to a more recent understanding of natural theology, while a strict proof of the existence of God is not possible, and while the revelation of God in Christ is normative, there is nevertheless an important religious dimension in all human experience and genuine knowledge of God in all religions. Different versions of this position are held by such influential theologians as Paul Tillich, Karl Rahner, and Hans Küng. (3) According to a third view, all efforts to formulate a natural theology, old or new, are misguided; they invariably obscure the distinctiveness of God's revelation in Jesus Christ, which is the supreme norm of Christian theology and of Christian faith and life. Karl Barth, the best-known representative of this position, does not deny that there are other little lights and other good words than the great light and the decisive Word of God in Jesus Christ. But while insisting that Christians should be open to these other lights and words, Barth distinguishes this attitude from a program of natural theology.

This will do as a rough introduction to the problem. If we use our imagination, we can listen in to an agitated conversation about natural theology among the following four theologians.

Karl Barth. Barth's theology, presented in his *Church Dogmatics* (13 vols.), is rigorously Christocentric.

Paul Tillich. Tillich's magnum opus is his *Systematic Theology* (3 vols.), in which he develops a "method of correlation" between existential questions and theological answers.

Karl Rahner. Perhaps the most prolific and influential of twentieth-century Roman Catholic theologians, Rahner is the author of *Theological Investigations* (20 vols.). His method is based on transcendental philosophy and attempts to expose the dimension of mystery in all human experience.

Ecumenist. This figure represents some of the concerns of such contemporary theologians as the Roman Catholic Hans Küng (*Christianity and the World Religions*) and the Protestant John B. Cobb, Jr. (*Beyond Dialogue: Toward a Mutual Transformation of Christianity and Buddhism*), whose goal is to foster mutual understanding and respect among the world religions.

An Unusual Meeting

BARTH: Paul Tillich, you old rascal! Imagine meeting you here. What have you been up to since we last met in Basel? I hope you have stopped all that method-of-correlation nonsense since you went to heaven. You did go to heaven, didn't you, Paul?

TILLICH: Karl, you haven't changed a bit. I see that you're still smoking that old pipe of yours as if it were your ultimate concern, and still wise-cracking your way through uncomfortable situations. Yes, I did make it to heaven, but no, I haven't stopped advocating my method of correlation. What I *have* tried to get stopped are those endless performances of *The Magic Flute* that you and Mozart keep organizing. I am not sleeping well with all the racket you make.

BARTH: Sorry about your insomnia, Paul, although as I recall you were quite a night owl on earth. But you know my weakness for Mozart's music; it is the passion of my life second only to the passion for good theology.

TILLICH: We're both passionate theologians, Karl. Do you remember the time I boxed your ears by saying that your Word of God theology was too wordy?

BARTH: Yes, and I gave you a good kick in the shins by replying that your abysmal God beyond God was an abomination. But enough of this friendly chatter. We have obviously been summoned here for some important reason, and if I'm not mistaken, we are about to be joined by our two Catholic friends, Karl Rahner and Ecumenist.

ECUMENIST: Greetings, gentlemen, and thank you all for coming. I tried to have John Calvin join us, too, but he is taking a required seminar on inclusive language and sends his regrets. Let me come directly to the point. The reason we have been brought together is that theology today seems to be afflicted by an epidemic of confusion about method. My hope is that after talking with each other a bit, we could issue an impressive consensus statement. It wouldn't take us very long, and it would be a great ecumenical event.

BARTH: Splendid idea, Ecumenist. And I have just the right strategy. Why don't I write the document while the rest of you take a little nap? Then when you wake up, you can all sign it, and we can get back to where we came from. Where did you say you came from, Paul?

RAHNER: Karl, I don't think your plan is quite what Ecumenist had in mind. You see, the chief theological confusion today is about what used to be called natural theology, about how our knowledge of mystery and transcendence which arises out of common human experience and is expressed in all the religions relates to our knowledge of God based on the particular revelation in Christ. What we would like to accomplish at this meeting is the preparation of a manifesto for a new way of viewing natural theology. We want to vindicate the value and necessity of an analysis of human existence — its possibilities, limitations, and hidden dimensions — that would be based simply on common reason and common human experience and would form an essential, if preliminary, ingredient in all theological work.

BARTH: What!? Someone please pinch me. Did I hear right? Do you honestly think I will be party to a consensus statement with you people on the reconstruction of natural theology? Haven't I made my position plain enough in a little essay titled "Nein!" and in thirteen fat volumes of the *Church Dogmatics?* And Ecumenist, shame on you! The odds at this meeting are scandalous. It's three against one.

RAHNER: Now wait a moment, Karl. We all know how absolutely opposed you are to what has been called natural theology in the past. But each of us — Paul, Ecumenist, and I — are just as opposed as you are to some of the things that have traditionally been called natural theology.

TILLICH: No doubt about it. For instance, none of us here is in the least interested in trying to rejuvenate the classical proofs of the existence of God. They are in my judgment failures as rational arguments, and theology is ill advised to try to use them today to convince people of God's existence. At the same time, however, I think these classical arguments are remarkable expressions of the *question* of God implied in human existence. "Natural theology," or as I would prefer to call it, "philosophical theology," does not give answers about God that compete with Christian revelation; it simply analyzes the existential question of God to which the Christian revelation is addressed.

RAHNER: I might add to what Paul has said that the proofs for the existence of God are really reflexive elaborations of a more basic and original knowledge. The point is that we all live surrounded by mystery. All of our knowing and doing presuppose an infinite horizon of mystery. At a primordial and preconceptual level, we human beings are oriented to the inexhaustible mystery we call God. What I call "foundational theology" — I do not use the term *natural theology* — is the attempt to clarify this primordial and universal human experience of the holy mystery called God.

ECUMENIST: All this makes good sense to me. I also refuse to practice natural theology in the traditional scholastic sense. I do not think that we can prove the existence of God by a purely rational thought sequence. On the other hand, I do not think we can limit knowledge of God to the biblical revelation. This would lead to disaster for theology and the church. I think we can and must carry on a discussion about God with everyone who is willing to listen and to speak about the matter — humanists, atheists, Marxists, and most certainly people of other religions. I think we can show that human life requires a fundamental trust in reality which is re-presented and thematized in the great religions of humanity. I don't think we are left with the unhappy alternative of *either* a purely authoritarian assertion of God *or* a purely rational proof in the sense of the old natural theology.

BARTH: Well, well, well. You all seem to be convinced that you are not engaged in anything so tasteless as natural theology. I do get the uneasy feeling, however, that I am standing before three wolves in sheep's clothing who are all loudly declaiming "We are not wolves." Brother Paul talks of the necessity of analyzing the questions implied in the modern human situation so that the Christian message may then be addressed to those questions. Father Karl wants to speak of a primordial experience of God that is presupposed by the special categorial knowledge of God contained in the Christian proclamation. And courageous Ecumenist — *et tu*, Ecumenist? — wants to show that all human life presupposes fundamental trust in reality, however inarticulate, and that the specifically Christian understanding of God both corrects and completes what we dimly may know of God apart from God's revelation in Jesus Christ. Do I understand you all correctly so far?

Tillich and Barth

TILLICH: Yes, I think you do. But if we are to get beyond this point in our discussion, I think it would be least confusing if the three of us, whom you have identified as crypto-natural theologians, had an opportunity to go one-on-one with you. And since I have the floor at the moment, I will begin by saying that you, Karl, are an ass.

BARTH: Paul, thank you for the delightful compliment. I take you to mean that I am like Balaam's ass — one who speaks for the Lord.

TILLICH: No, not Balaam's ass, Karl, just a plain old stubborn ass who refuses to concede the obvious. No matter how many fat volumes you write to the contrary, you simply cannot disregard the actual questions people have without ending up talking only to yourself. You cannot give people answers if they are not aware of the questions those answers are supposed to address. The only people your theology of revelation will ever speak to are those who respond to all the familiar words like Pavlov's dogs drooling every time they hear the right bells.

BARTH: You have a delightful menagerie in your imagery, Paul — asses, dogs, and who knows what else. Well, let me add another beast to your zoo — the ostrich — and ask you to get your head above the ground of being long enough to hear my position as *I* state it. I do indeed think that all Christian theology must have its center in God's self-revelation in Jesus Christ. We will, of course, have all kinds of questions when we start, continue, and end with this revelation. But we must not elevate our existential questions to systematic importance such that the revelation in Christ is allowed to speak only to these questions and only so far as it meets our prior criteria of meaningful communication. If we are attentive, open, and responsible as theologians, we will discover that revelation questions us, reformulates the questions that we may have thought were so important at the beginning. If we center on Christ, all of our questions will be included and addressed. If we insist on starting with our own urgent and often self-serving questions, we will probably end up with our own predictable and probably self-serving answers. That's not revelation.

TILLICH: What you have just described seems to me a closed circle. If you are in the circle, fine. But if you are outside the circle, the whole thing sounds about as intelligible as the beeps of R2D2. We have to help people see that faith in God is not just the experience of a little religious clique but that all people are human insofar as they experience a "depth dimension" in life, insofar as they have some "ultimate concern." When we understand faith as ultimate concern, we break out of all closed circles.

BARTH: I am amused to be told that my theology creates a closed circle, since many of my sharpest critics charge that my understanding of the grace of God in Jesus Christ leads irresistibly toward universalism. Be that as it may, I see that you are still sawing away on that old theme of ultimate concern. You must know that I have always found your approach to faith much too general and abstract. With all these generalizations about ultimate concern, one is bound to miss the uniqueness and particularity of Christian faith in God made known in Jesus Christ as attested in Scripture.

TILLICH: But even in its uniqueness, Christian faith bears *some* resemblances to other faiths. There are common elements that can be discovered and that make comparison and contrast possible. In other words, there are at least some formal similarities among all world religions and quasireligions. They are all expressions of what I call ultimate concern, and they are all quests for human salvation — that is, for our human well-being as opposed to nonbeing.

BARTH: I do not deny that common features can always be seen among faiths, but this process usually results in a lot of bloodless generalities. If you want to know what Christian faith is, start with its hard particularities. Don't assume in advance that it is simply one instance of faith in general. I rather suspect, by the way, that the same procedure would also be helpful in trying to understand Islam or Hinduism. In any case, I contend that the method of concentrating on the particular event of revelation is basic for a right understanding of Christian faith. Do you recall the astonishing precision and specificity of Calvin's definition of faith: "a firm and confident knowledge of God's benevolence to us, founded on the gracious promise of Christ, illumined to our minds and sealed in our hearts by the Holy Spirit"?

TILLICH: But surely the particular knowledge of God in Christian faith presupposes some prior knowledge of God, just as surely as the New Testament proclamation of the in-breaking of God's kingdom in Jesus presupposes the Old Testament understanding of God. Do I need to remind you that Calvin did not *begin* his *Institutes* with the definition of faith you have just cited; he began with a recognition of a "seed of religion" present in every human heart. The particular presupposes the general. I can know something about baking a pie regardless of the particular pie to be baked. There are common elements: pie pan, crust, oven, and so on, and certain rules governing the process of pie-making in every case.

BARTH: Have you ever baked a pie in general? I would prefer eating an apple pie to one of your pies in general.

TILLICH: No, I haven't baked a pie in general, but I can *understand* something about baking pies without baking this or that particular pie.

BARTH: As you know, Paul, Christian theology has always insisted that God cannot be confined to any of our categories, and certainly not the category of pies. So let's drop the analogy. My point is simply that faith is created by and oriented to the incarnate love of God in a very particular person named Jesus of Nazareth. The particular nature of

Christian faith is determined by the distinctive and unsubstitutable person who is the object of faith.

TILLICH: True enough, but why can't I make you see that we can still have some understanding of faith or ultimate concern as a possibility of human existence regardless of its concrete manifestation?

BARTH: I suspect it is because you want to talk about faith as a general human possibility, while I want to talk about revelation as a particular gift received by faith.

TILLICH: You are a victim of your own false dichotomy. Of course revelation is a gift, but a gift can be accepted or rejected. To talk about a gift rightly is to talk about the possibility of accepting or rejecting it. If faith is not an always-present human possibility, then it is something thrown at people like a stone. Some gift that is.

BARTH: There you go again, making a complete caricature of my position with your analogy of stone-throwing. I do not doubt the importance of receiving a gift, but it is sheer folly to confuse the gift with the reception. When children open their packages on Christmas morning, their attention is entirely upon the content of their gifts and not upon their remarkable capacity to receive. My concern is that we allow Christian faith to be openness to something genuinely new rather than accommodating it to our previous knowledge and experience.

TILLICH: How can we ever know anything if we do not already know something about it? There must be some basis for recognizing the new. Otherwise we couldn't even ask questions about it.

BARTH: I think that line of reasoning is suspicious. Maybe we could take a little clue from the history of science, where great discoveries have been made not when the old has been presupposed as a condition for recognizing the new but when the new has broken into all our previous assumptions and demanded a new understanding of everything we thought we were so certain of before. The coming of the genuinely new compels us to raise questions we hadn't dreamed of before. In this sense, maybe theology will win recognition as an exemplary science just to the extent that it faithfully acknowledges the utter *novum* of its object.

TILLICH: I call this breaking in of the new a *kairos*. And as you yourself have now admitted, the experience of a *kairos,* an opportune moment when the old foundations are shaken, occurs in some form or other not only in relation to Christian revelation and faith but in many spheres and dimensions of human life. Revelation indeed shakes the foundations of our knowledge and experience, but there can be no shaking if there are are no foundations.

Ecumenist and Barth

ECUMENIST: I'm simply going to interrupt here. Since you two are in a rut, let me see if I can recast the issue.

BARTH: Ecumenist, my good friend and, after Pope John XXIII, my favorite Catholic theologian — do they ever greet you at the Vatican like that, Ecumenist? Before we lock horns, let me ask you a little question. Have you told Pope John Paul II that he is not infallible? Do it, Ecumenist, but do it gently. Make it easy for him; tell him Barth wasn't infallible either.

ECUMENIST: I'm glad to hear your confession of fallibility, Karl, especially since there are a lot of your followers — Barthians, we call them — who sure talk as if they were infallible.

BARTH: Ecumenist, how many times have you heard me say "I am not a Barthian"? Why just the other day, I jumped out in front of a very serious-looking Presbyterian theologian and said, "Boo! I'm not a Barthian. Why do you want to be one?" You should have seen how scared he was.

ECUMENIST: Well, let's see whether you are a Barthian or not. Do you still insist on that sharp distinction between religion and revelation? Do you still insist on seeing all human religion as the pinnacle of human arrogance and unbelief?

BARTH: The answer is yes to both questions. Revelation is God's self-manifestation and self-communication in Jesus Christ. In the light of Jesus Christ, all human religion — and I emphasize, Ecumenist, that includes also our Christian religiousness — stands under the judgment of God. We take our religion, our dogmas, our rituals, our institutions, our moralities with frightful seriousness. But invariably at work in all this is our arbitrary attempt to storm heaven, our secret urge to justify and sanctify ourselves, to strengthen our conviction that we are able to master life and to bring it to fulfillment by ourselves.

ECUMENIST: Yes, yes, we are well acquainted with your theological criticism of religion, and I will admit that the whole church is deeply indebted to you for it. You have helped to liberate the gospel from thoughtless entanglements with bourgeois Western culture and nationalistic ideologies. You have helped us — at least indirectly — to enter into conversation with humanists, atheists, and Marxists, because your insistence on theological criticism of religion recognized the element of truth in all the secular critiques. You dared to argue that the modern atheistic critique of religion is only an echo of God's far more potent criticism of it. Moreover, your criticism of the identification of Christian faith with Western culture has helped the younger churches of the world — in Asia, Africa, and South America — to claim their freedom and responsibility to interpret the Word of God in their own time and culture.

BARTH: Ecumenist, this is supposed to be a dialogue, not a testimonial. But I hear a qualification beginning to surface.

ECUMENIST: Indeed, there is. Your theological critique of religion played an important role in its time, but it was always one-sided, and its continuation today would simply be a tragedy. We find ourselves in a new situation that calls for a new kind of Christian apologetics. We need to argue for the reasonableness of faith in God, to show that our development as individuals, our confidence in the worthwhileness of life, and our sense of the importance of ethical activity all presuppose a fundamental trust in a reality beyond ourselves. Furthermore, your diatribe against religion is simply too indiscriminate and too vague to be adequate for the church in our time. We live in an age when close and frequent contact between the world religions is a fact that we can no longer ignore. Christian theology today simply cannot be done responsibly in splendid isolation from the other religions.

BARTH: Well, you know that I have nothing against fundamental trust, but surely it makes a big difference in what or whom you place this trust. If I was one-sided when I said "Nein!" to every open or covert support for the German Christians who wanted the church to place at least part of its fundamental trust in Hitler and the German Third Reich, then so be it. After the horrors of this century, anyone who talks about fundamental trust as something unambiguously good is simply naive. On the other point you mentioned, if you have read carefully what I have written on the subject of religion, you know that I have always insisted that our evaluations of the non-Christian religions must be characterized by charity and great modesty. Not because of some liberal doctrine of "tolerance" — which all too often hides an arrogant and patronizing attitude — but because of the freedom of the grace of God in Jesus Christ who has reconciled us all, in all of our religiousness.

ECUMENIST: Your reply is a good example of what I mean by the evasive-
ness and vagueness of your teaching on the religions. On the one hand,
all religion stands under God's judgment; on the other hand, we are
all, regardless of our religion, and whether we recognize it or not,
already reconciled to God through the grace of Christ. This is a
curiously ambiguous approach. You criticize Tillich for what you call
his vague talk about faith as ultimate concern, but then you deal with
the subject of religion as though Buddhism, Hinduism, Islam, and all
the other religions could be lumped into a single laundry bag called
religion. I see here a fatal lapse in your insistence on beginning with
the particular and the concrete in our theological work. Why doesn't
that hold for our understanding of the other religions as well?

BARTH: My point is simply that Christian theological reflection on world
religions must always be from the standpoint of revelation in Christ,
or it ceases to be Christian. There may indeed be important words
and, yes, revelations that other religions have to convey to us, and we
must be open to hear what they have to say that may deepen or correct
our understanding of the Word of God in Jesus Christ. But as Christians we can recognize and honor the truth of these words only as
they reflect some aspect of *the* Word of God. If you can speak of the
religions more concretely, more discriminately than I did, by all means
do so, but unless you give up your task as a Christian theologian, your
study will be guided by the light of the revelation of God in Christ.

ECUMENIST: I have no quarrel with the insistence that our theological
work as Christians must never dodge the normative question of truth.
Nor do I contest for a moment that our conversations with people of
other faiths will seek to lift up the specificity of God's self-revelation
in Jesus Christ. As I have said over and again, we must always be
asking what constitutes the specifically Christian, what is unique about
Christian faith in relation to the other religions. But frankly, Karl,
there is a chasm between us. I don't think the differences among the
religions have much significance for you, and I suspect that means
that religions other than Christianity have no constitutive significance
for you. You never allow the religions to come into conversation with
you on their own terms. Let me put it sharply. You refuse, a priori
and systematically, to allow the religions not only to stand under the
judgment of revelation but to be bearers of truth about God and hence
also media of revelation and ways of salvation in their own right.

BARTH: Surely you don't think that I bind God's grace to the Christian church. God is freely and graciously at work everywhere in the world, including in the world of religions. But we Christians can only speak of what God is doing in the world in the light of the history of revelation and reconciliation in Jesus Christ. Otherwise, we are on the slippery slope of relativism.

ECUMENIST: I don't endorse relativism or syncretism any more than you do. I am only saying that we can learn from our encounter with the non-Christian religions as also ways of salvation, just as they will be better and richer for their encounter with an honest, open, humble, and faithful witness to Jesus Christ. I am saying that we should approach our non-Christian brothers and sisters not as though God were completely alien to them, not as though God's grace were entirely strange to them, not as though we were bringing the re-creative love of God into their lives for the very first time. Rather we should approach them as people among whom God has already been at work, both in judgment *and* in grace. This does not mean that we should abandon Christian mission; on the contrary, it means that our missionary task should be carried out in a new spirit of openness, self-criticism, and thankfulness for what is true, good, and beautiful in other religions, without compromising on our allegiance to what God has revealed in Jesus Christ.

BARTH: That's a long speech, Ecumenist. And there's much in it that I agree with. Have I not emphasized repeatedly that God has objectively reconciled the whole world in Jesus Christ? He is the way of salvation! And just for that reason the question of whether religions other than Christianity are *also* ways of salvation is a terribly misleading question, since it assumes that *Christianity* or the *Christian church* is the way of salvation. You are certainly correct in saying that we must not relate to non-Christians as though God were not already for them. Jesus Christ has died and been raised for them as well as for us. That ontological fact determines their lives no less than ours. All this talk about being "inside" or "outside" the church is very relative and never more than provisional. What we may offer, if anything, to those provisionally "outside" is the good news of their and our reconciliation in Christ.

ECUMENIST: Your position is a conundrum. On the one hand, you say that God's revelation places all religion under judgment. On the other hand, you have working for you a kind of Christocentric ontology of universal scope which declares that all people are already reconciled in Jesus Christ. If we took only the first affirmation seriously, what you call revelation in Jesus Christ would be utterly dehistoricized and would be no more closely related to historical Christianity than to any other historical phenomenon. If we took only the second affirmation seriously, we would seem to be committed to a kind of a priori universalism. What in the world *is* your theology of world religions?

BARTH: I am not sure that I have a "theology of world religions," if by that is meant some way of systematically relating Christian faith to all the other faiths of humanity by including them all under some general explanatory theory. Why can we not say *both* that every religion stands under judgment, is in need of new light and reformation, *and* that God is graciously at work long before we come on the scene to bear our witness to Jesus Christ or to enter into dialogue with people of other faiths? Let the call to mission and dialogue be motivated by joy and thanksgiving rather than by either arrogance or fear.

ECUMENIST: I honestly do not think you have shown us how to do this, Karl, and that is why I believe we are in need of a post-Barthian approach to the question of the relationship between revelation and the religions.

BARTH: Don't forget, Ecumenist, to tell them that I'm not a Barthian!

Rahner and Barth

RAHNER: I think it's time for our tête-à-tête, Karl. I hope the fact that we have the same first name is a sign of a much deeper bond between us. I have learned much from your theology.

BARTH: And I have admired your creative theological activity from afar. Your volumes of *Theological Investigations* must be almost as large now as the *Church Dogmatics*. Or have you already surpassed me? No matter, we both know now that they won't let you bring them into heaven. You have to leave them in the cloakroom.

RAHNER: Like Paul and Ecumenist, I have no zeal for the traditional natural theology. What I am concerned to show is that the holy and gracious mystery of God is present as the milieu in which we live and move and have our being. In all our striving after truth, we confront an unfathomable mystery that ever eludes us. We reach out to the future to shape it by our actions, and we are in the presence of the absolute future that we cannot control.

BARTH: I have not read your theology carefully, so pardon me if I say that it sounds to me faintly similar to what we Protestants have heard ad nauseum from the school of Schleiermacher and Bultmann. [To ECUMENIST:] Why didn't you invite them?

RAHNER: I am well aware of your criticisms of anthropocentric theology, but I think that whole debate is trapped in hopeless dichotomies — nature *or* grace, philosophy *or* theology, experience *or* revelation. I speak of my anthropology as a christocentric anthropology. I see human life as surrounded and moved by grace before we become conceptually clear about that grace through the decisive self-revelation of God in Jesus Christ.

BARTH: In other words, you are going to make a distinction between a universal, primordial, preconceptual knowledge of God and the particular, categorical knowledge of God mediated to us through historical revelation. I find this distinction troublesome. I think you are going to end up saying that the Christian gospel tells us what we knew deep down all along. That really worries me.

RAHNER: Perhaps you misunderstand me. I sometimes think that what I am after is not so far from your own claim that all human beings are embraced by the love of God in Jesus Christ even if they do not know it. My way of saying this is that indeed many people do not know it — conceptually, categorically, with "the top of their minds." Still, they may experience something of the holy mystery of God in everyday things and may surrender themselves to that mystery. This act of surrender is an act of faith, and I would call a person who freely surrenders herself to the holy mystery that encompasses all human life an "anonymous Christian." In other words, people may have an experience of judgment and grace even though they do not articulate this experience in terms of the knowledge of God mediated by the particular historical revelation in Christ.

BARTH: Then what you call explicit Christian faith is nothing more than the use of a definite set of religious symbols to express a universal religious experience. The churches with declining membership should really take to your idea of "anonymous Christians." It will do immediate marvels for church roles and General Assembly reports. Just imagine one such report: 246 "confessing Christians" and, at last count, 7,259 "anonymous Christians."

RAHNER: That's a flippant response, and you know it, Karl. I could just as easily say that your theology provides an elixir for exhausted Christians and their flagging programs of evangelism: "No need to panic; everyone is already reconciled even if they don't yet know it." I am not downgrading the importance of historical revelation, the proclamation of the Word, and the celebration of the sacraments. I am saying that there is a condition of the possibility of our hearing and understanding the proclaimed Word. This possibility is itself a gift of grace. Perhaps an example of what I mean by the experience presupposed by the proclaimed Word would be helpful.

BARTH: I'm all ears.

RAHNER: Sleeping is a regular part of our everyday experience. We take it for granted. Yet it is, when we pause to think about it, an exceedingly mysterious phenomenon. Human creatures who are so distinguished by their freedom and who engage most of their waking energy in the effort to master the world and provide security for themselves, let go of themselves in falling asleep, give up control of themselves, commit themselves to the mystery that enfolds them in sleep — a mystery that they do not understand and that they have not created. If we ponder the matter, we may see that falling asleep is an act of confidence in the reliability and goodness of a power greater than ourselves, an act of faith in and surrender to what is beyond our control. You see, we do know something about surrender and trust to a nameless mystery, and it is this primordial knowing that makes it possible for us to receive the gospel message in freedom. In faith we surrender ourselves freely into the hands of the gracious God, who is not an alien power altogether extrinsic to our being but, as you might put it, Karl, a friendly mystery at work in us.

BARTH: There is something peculiar going on here. Karl, if you are saying that in the light of the gospel, in the light of Christ's dying and rising for us and of our dying and promise of rising in him, we are liberated to see the whole range of human phenomena, including the familiar act of sleeping, in a completely new way, I agree entirely and wish you well in your further theological investigations. But I would not call this natural theology, old, new, or otherwise. I would say that what you are doing is discovering parables or analogies of the concrete grace of God in Jesus Christ in the wide field of nature, history, and human experience. Bravo, I would say to this agenda. It is precisely what I myself substituted for so-called natural theology. If we view the act of sleeping and many other events and phenomena through the spectacles of the gospel, we may arrive at your conclusions. But I'm afraid this is not what you are doing, or that it is not only what you are doing, or that neither of us is completely sure what you are doing. You seem to want to move both from revelation to experience and from experience to revelation. Can you have it both ways?

RAHNER: Why not? Are both ways not in some sense included in the reality of the incarnation? And have you yourself not expounded at length on the two inseparable movements of the incarnation: the movement of God from above to below and the movement of a free human being from below to above?

A Final Exchange

ECUMENIST: I'm not going to give Karl a chance to answer that question. Our time is up, and, gentlemen, we have failed to capitalize on an extraordinary ecumenical opportunity. We are obviously not going to be able to produce a consensus statement on natural theology as I had hoped. Theological students will have to continue to suffer in the present theological confusion.

TILLICH: Take heart, Ecumenist. We can each leave our own document stating our own position on the issue. I just happen to have a copy of mine in my pocket. The first sentence reads: "The purpose of every sermon is to expose the depth dimension of our life and to awaken infinite concern."

ECUMENIST: Well, I must confess that I, too, brought a document of my own along. It is entitled: "Peace on Earth and Peace among the Religions," and its central appeal to all Christians is this: in the emerging dialogue of the world religions, expect to enrich others with your faith, and expect to be enriched by theirs.

RAHNER: My definitive statement on the subject will require at least two volumes, but I do happen to have with me a draft of a new essay, "On Discerning the Presence of God in the Everyday."

BARTH: Yes, of course, I brought one, too. It begins: "Are there *parables* of the kingdom of God in nature, experience, culture, and religion? — Yes. Shall we pursue a new *natural theology?* — No." And there is only one footnote in the whole text. It reads: "Don't forget, I am not a Barthian!"

APPENDIX B

The Resurrection: A Dialogue

NO ISSUE HAS BEEN MORE WIDELY DEBATED IN MODERN THEOLOGY than the relationship of Christian faith and history. This issue comes to a sharp focus in the various interpretations of the New Testament witness to the resurrection of Jesus of Nazareth. The affirmation that God raised the crucified Jesus from the dead, far from being peripheral, stands at the very center of the New Testament proclamation. Without the Easter witness, Christian faith would either not exist at all or would be something very different — perhaps a religious sect that recalled the tragic death of its great founder and teacher. On this point there would be virtually universal agreement among Christian theologians. According to Rudolf Bultmann, the New Testament documents are so permeated with the Easter faith that all attempts to reconstruct the history behind the texts are exceedingly shaky. Karl Barth goes so far as to say that while we might imagine a New Testament that had only the resurrection narratives, we certainly could not imagine a New Testament without them. Wolfhart Pannenberg and Jürgen Moltmann place the resurrection of Jesus at the very center of their eschatological reinterpretations of Christian faith.

But while Christian theologians agree on the importance of the Easter witness, they interpret it in very different ways. Interpretations of the resurrection are like windows through which we may gain a glimpse of the salient features of a theology — most especially its particular understanding of the relation of faith and historical inquiry, the authority of Scripture, the sense in which God is said to act, and the hope Christians

An earlier version of this dialogue appeared in *Theology Today* 33 (April 1976): 5-14.

have for personal, political, and cosmic renewal. We may be able to get a better sense of the possibilities and problems of different theologies of the resurrection if we are allowed to eavesdrop on an imaginary conversation among four theologians. The participants are:

Rudolf Bultmann. A noted New Testament scholar, Bultmann is best known for his program of the demythologization and existential interpretation of the New Testament. His many writings include *Theology of the New Testament* and a commentary on the Gospel of John.

Karl Barth. Barth, introduced in Appendix A, engaged in a long-term controversy with Bultmann concerning the relationship of faith and history and the proper interpretation of the New Testament. Barth contended that Bultmann dissolved Christian faith and theology into anthropology, and Bultmann charged that Barth was philosophically and hermeneutically naive.

Pannenbergian. This speaker may be considered a more or less faithful disciple of the contemporary theologian Wolfhart Pannenberg, who emphasizes the reasonableness of faith, the need for a new Christian apologetic to be developed in relation to modern science, and the inseparable link between Christian faith and the results of historical inquiry. Pannenberg's writings include *Revelation as History; Jesus — God and Man; Theology and the Philosophy of Science;* and *Anthropology in Theological Perspective.*

Moltmannian. This member of the dialogue has obviously been greatly influenced by eschatological theology, or the theology of hope, whose primary voice in recent decades has been that of Jürgen Moltmann. The position represented is also akin to many political and liberation theologies. Moltmann's writings include *Theology of Hope; The Crucified God;* and *The Trinity and the Kingdom.*

Resurrection and Historical Reason

BARTH: Have I ever told you my joke about modern theologians? Bonhoeffer is good beer; Tillich is beer; Bultmann is foam.

BULTMANN: Your attempt at humor is no more successful than your attempt to understand me. But I do share your view of Bonhoeffer. His theological sophistication was never more evident than when he called *your* theology a positivism of revelation. You throw doctrines indiscriminately at people: Virgin Birth, the Trinity, and all the rest. Then you say, in effect, "Like it or lump it."

MOLTMANNIAN: Well, now that you two have had a chance to greet each other, maybe we can get on with our conversation. Did you all see the big news in the Sunday *New York Times?* Front page story! "Archaeologists have uncovered the skeleton of a young man crucified and buried outside the walls of Jerusalem some two thousand years ago."

BULTMANN: Yes, and as might have been expected, the journalists and TV anchormen concluded their coverage with the comment: "And some people are raising the question whether this skeleton might be that of You-Know-Who." I must say that I feel rather fortunate that I demythologized my theology some years back.

PANNENBERGIAN: If that remark was supposed to be funny, I find your sense of humor rather tasteless. Your attitude toward history and its relation to faith is thoroughly cavalier. Just for openers, there is not a shred of evidence this skeleton might be that of Jesus of Nazareth. If anything, such an archaeological find gives support to the historicity of the gospel narratives. It shows that criminals were crucified by the Romans during the time of Jesus in precisely the manner described by the Gospels.

BULTMANN: Faith is not dependent on the results of historical inquiry, as you seem to be suggesting. Of course, faith presupposes the fact that Jesus of Nazareth really lived and died. But the Easter *kerygma* is independent of the claims and counterclaims about the historicity of the traditions of the New Testament.

Mostly Barth and Bultmann

BARTH: I suspect, Pannenbergian, that I am closer to you than to Bultmann on this issue. But let's not forget that the heart of Christian faith — that Jesus was raised from the dead by God — can neither be refuted nor supported by historical evidence of the sort you mentioned. The resurrection is an act of God, and this makes it historical in a unique sense.

PANNENBERGIAN: After that comment, I'm not so sure you *are* closer to my position than to Bultmann's. You seem to be tearing the resurrection out of history and locating it in some nebulous theological domain where God acts, a domain far removed from the nitty-gritty of actual human history. The resurrection of Jesus is a historical event.

It is a public fact, if you like. If it isn't something that really took place in history, then the message of the church is a deception, and we are still in bondage to sin and death.

BARTH: I think you misunderstood what I said. My point is simply that the resurrection, while an event that really happened, is not historical in the same sense as, say, Caesar's crossing of the Rubicon, or even the crucifixion. The resurrection is a historical event in the sense that it really happened in space and time. But I should willingly concede that it is not a historical event in the sense that it can be shown to have occurred or not to have occurred by the modern historian with his critical method and assumptions. I do not subscribe to the weak-headed idea that the resurrection was merely a change of mind on the part of the disciples. The idea that nothing has happened except what modern historians by their critical procedures can establish to have happened is pure myth and deserves to be demythologized.

BULTMANN: I suppose these pontifical comments about weak-headed people and myth were spoken for my benefit, so let me try to make my position clear. I also think that the Easter faith is historical. But this does not mean that Christian faith asserts that the resurrection can be historically demonstrated, which it obviously cannot. Nor does it mean that, as Barth says, the resurrection is an event that happened in space and in time, even though historical science has no access to this event. In my judgment, this is a completely unintelligible claim. We cannot disregard what Ernst Troeltsch has taught us about the principle of analogy in modern historical reasoning without bringing Christian faith into a disastrous clash with the ethics of modern critical inquiry. It is an axiom of critical historical reason that we can understand the past only on the basis of some analogy with present knowledge and experience.

BARTH: Now who's pontificating? Your principle of analogy is going to compel you to reduce the event of the resurrection to a subjective experience of the disciples.

BULTMANN: To believe in the resurrection is not to commit oneself to unintelligible and nonsensical claims. To believe in the resurrection is to believe in the redemptive significance of the cross of Jesus for one's own life. The believer says, "When I am confronted with the message of Jesus crucified, I know that faith means radical dependence on the grace of God." To make that confession is to accept a completely new self-understanding. As a historian, I am interested in the archaeologist's discovery of a skeleton of a crucified Jew. As a Christian, I couldn't care less.

BARTH: Talk about unintelligibility! Your interpretation of the resurrection seems to me completely incoherent. What you appear to be saying is that the resurrection didn't really occur at all and that the rise of faith in the disciples and in us *is* the resurrection. You rob the Easter faith of an objective basis and put it in the category of an hallucination. Unlike you, when I say that the resurrection is an act of God, an event of revelation, I do not empty this act of its objectivity and concreteness. I do not reduce it to a mere cipher for a change of mind by the disciples.

Mostly Pannenbergian

PANNENBERGIAN: Hold on, you two. Don't you see that you are both equivocating? You both talk about the resurrection as historical in some very strange sense — an inaccessible event of revelation or new self-understanding. This is utterly out of touch with what the word *historical* ordinarily means. Thus you both end up divorcing faith from concrete history. You are both prisoners of the principle of analogy. To speak of history is to speak of the singular, the particular, the unique. The modern historian does not say: This could not have happened because it is not part of my experience. He says: What is the evidence? This is the question that in different ways both of you want to bypass.

MOLTMANNIAN: I agree with you, Pannenbergian, that the principle of analogy, as Bultmann apparently insists on using it, should not be allowed to go unquestioned. If we demand that something can be considered historically real only if it can be conformed to our present experience, history is closed a priori, and our understanding of it can never allow for the coming of the genuinely new and unexpected. I prefer to speak of the resurrection as an "event of promise," an event that makes history, that opens it up, that disturbs all our so-called established facts, and that makes us dissatisfied with the status quo of human alienation, suffering, and injustice. If this is the direction in which you are moving, Pannenbergian, then I am with you. But you seem so preoccupied with verifying the resurrection as an event of the past that I wonder if you will do justice to its future-orientation, its promissory character. I could subscribe to the idea of the "eschato-logical verification" of the resurrection, but I simply do not think we are now in a position to offer proof of the historicity of the resurrection witness.

PANNENBERGIAN: Then you are also engaging in a lot of woolly thinking. All of you want to claim that the Easter faith is historical, but from that point on you *all* engage in systematic ambiguity. This results in a de facto divorce of the resurrection from history. Barth says that the resurrection takes place in history, but the history it takes place in is not accessible to ordinary historical investigation. What is this supra-history? Faith and theology are brought into total disrepute by this talk of suprahistory, *Heilsgeschichte,* and *Horsegeschichte.* If historical evi-dence is not relevant to the affirmation or denial of the alleged event of Jesus' resurrection, then what we call the resurrection is no more historical than the dying and rising of the ancient Egyptian god Osiris.

MOLTMANNIAN: Your criticisms are appropriate if they are directed against Barth, but you can't seriously lay these charges against me. I am just as concerned as you are to engage in critical conversation with modern historical reason.

PANNENBERGIAN: Well, Moltmannian, even though I much prefer your description of the resurrection as an event of promise to Barth's talk of it as an event of revelation, I think your disregard of the factual evidence for the Easter faith finally puts you in the same position as Barth. I, too, have spoken of an "eschatological verification" of faith affirmations, but if this sort of language is not to remain mythological and meaningless — in short, a cop-out — we will have to engage in some hard-nosed analysis of historical reasoning. We will have to show that history is open, that the meaning of an event cannot be separated from the interpretative context in which it originally occurred, and that the full meaning of any event can finally be determined only at the end of history, when it can be seen in the context of universal history. The openness of history and of historical reason has to be shown convincingly to the modern world. Otherwise the proclamation of the resurrection will get a hearing only in the church, and Chris-tianity will retreat more and more into a pocket of unintelligibility and irrelevance.

BULTMANN: You don't have a corner on the concern about the intelligi-bility of the Christian message. I have spent my entire scholarly career on the issue of faith and understanding.

PANNENBERGIAN: Sure you have, but you say in effect that the resurrection was not something that happened *to Jesus* but is something that happens *in us*. We understand ourselves anew as we discover the redemptive meaning of the cross of Jesus for us. Well, read the New Testament accounts. If they say anything at all, they say that the resurrection was something that happened first to Jesus and was subsequently made known or revealed to the disciples. So you see, I find myself disagreeing with all of you. You all disengage the resurrection from the domain of public history, the history that we live, the history that critical historians deal with. Whether you locate the resurrection in some suprahistorical sphere and call it "event of revelation" or "event of promise" or place it in some existential domain and call it a "new self-understanding" really makes little difference. There's more than a touch of Docetism in all of your positions.

BARTH: I do hope that this discussion isn't going to degenerate into a name-throwing contest, though I've got a pretty good arsenal if you want to try me out. Let's get one point straight: *I* did not say that the resurrection takes place in some suprahistorical sphere. Those are your words, Pannenbergian, and they do not represent my position. What I did say was that the resurrection of Jesus took place in space and time and in this sense is like every other event. In addition, I said that there could be no historical demonstration that this event occurred in space and time, at least short of the conclusive and universal revelation of Jesus' lordship at the parousia. The Easter faith of the disciples was not a conclusion reached by reasoning from facts on which everyone could agree. The resurrection really happened, but *that* it happened was revealed. Jesus himself appeared to the disciples. This act of his appearance is quite beyond modern historical inquiry and its procedures of proof.

PANNENBERGIAN: But that is what I emphatically reject. You are splitting apart revelation and reason, faith and history. Of course the historian cannot *demonstrate* that the resurrection occurred in the same way that the chemist can demonstrate that water is composed of two parts hydrogen and one part oxygen. You are assuming a positivistic notion of historical knowledge that has long been abandoned by most historians. The historian does not provide conclusive demonstrations in this positivistic sense. I have said that each historical event can be fully known only at the end of history, and this obviously precludes the positivistic model of what is involved in historical interpretation. Still, we are not excused from the task of offering the most reasonable interpretation of the evidence at hand. We make inferences on the basis of available evidence. We then make informed judgments that we are prepared to support with arguments. Historical judgments cannot be arbitrary and capricious; they must be reasonable and arguable. When we say "Jesus is risen," we are making a truth claim. We are advancing a claim to the historicity of this event. We are claiming that the judgment that this event took place in space and time is the most reasonable historical explanation of the evidence, and we must remain open to correction on the basis of additional evidence or more convincing interpretations of the evidence. The Apostle Paul, at least, was not squeamish about citing eyewitnesses to the resurrection to support the claims of faith.

BULTMANN: You know, of course, that I think Paul undercut his message with that list of eyewitnesses to the risen Jesus in 1 Corinthians 15. As for the traditions of the empty tomb, they are clearly later legendary accretions.

PANNENBERGIAN: I am not arguing that we have to accept all the New Testament traditions uncritically. Of course, the tradition of Easter faith underwent a development and some legendary additions were made. But we will only understand the meaning of the claim "Jesus is risen" as we enter into the horizon of interpretation of the early Christian community instead of prematurely judging that *this* can't happen or *that* is simply impossible. We won't even know what in the world we are talking about when we use the word *resurrection* until we grasp what meaning it had in the context of Jewish and Christian apocalyptic. For apocalyptic all of history is oriented toward the eschatological future of God. The early disciples believed that the resurrection of Jesus signaled and anticipated the general resurrection and final judgment toward which universal history moves. Neither for New Testament believers nor for us can affirmation of the resurrection of Jesus be separated from one's understanding of the whole of reality. My main point is that we have to be reasonable, rather than irrational, in our effort to communicate the faith to the modern mentality. Unless we are able to offer reasons for our belief in the resurrection of Jesus, as the early church itself tried to do, we render Christian faith completely arbitrary and authoritarian. We evacuate the Easter message of all intelligibility and truth claim.

BULTMANN: Now listen, Pannenbergian, your position strikes me as fantastically naive and presumptuous. You take upon yourself the task of telling historians how to do their job. I am not sure you really appreciate the critical rigor of historical investigation. You speak of historians as if they could never pose a threat to the historicity of the biblical narratives. Critical historians interrogate their sources like a prosecuting attorney interrogates a witness in a courtroom. They say: "This is what we are told happened. But did it really happen that way, or at all?" And historians carry out this inquiry on the basis of presuppositions rooted in common human experience.

PANNENBERGIAN: "Common human experience" is a pretty vague notion.

BULTMANN: Is it? I don't accept as historical fact reports of a person walking on water, because this completely contravenes our present knowledge and experience of reality. Suppose someone who tried to assassinate the President of the United States were brought to trial and said to the court: "I didn't fire the gun at the President. It was an 'act of God.' The Holy Spirit pulled the trigger." What would you do, Pannenbergian? Would you say: "Let's look at the evidence. Check the FBI files and see what we have on this Holy Spirit character." My point is that we often argue from the analogy of common experience. This is why I simply can't see how a resurrection from the dead could function as an historical explanation.

PANNENBERGIAN: That's because you have an incredibly narrow idea of what historians do. History is precisely the arena of the unique, the singular, the once-for-all. There are no a priori laws of history that can be used to answer historical questions or exclude certain possibilities without first looking at the evidence. The resurrection of Christ from the dead cannot be called unhistorical simply because it violates some general law like "resurrections from the dead don't happen."

BARTH: Well, I certainly agree with that. Bultmann has always seemed to me to take his radical skepticism much too seriously. But I must say, Pannenbergian, that what bothers me about your line of argument is that you seem to make faith dependent on the conclusions of historical-critical reason. Your approach seems to be: first knowledge, then faith. As you know, I simply reject this as the proper method of theological inquiry. *Fides quaerens intellectum,* "faith seeking understanding" — this is the right procedure for theology. Otherwise faith ceases to be faith and becomes the conclusion of a historical or metaphysical argument. We simply have to begin with the reality of the resurrection of Jesus. We do not establish the truth of the risen Lord; his truth establishes us as forgiven and liberated persons.

Mostly Moltmannian

MOLTMANNIAN: OK, Barth, we have heard this line from you before, and up to a certain point it makes sense. But I think that Pannenbergian has grasped something about the resurrection that is missing in your theology of revelation, and that is the proleptic, anticipatory, promissory nature of this event. If we are rightly oriented to the resurrection of Christ, we should not be facing the past but should be moving into the future of righteousness, peace, and new life promised by God in this event of the raising of the one who was crucified. The resurrection is the ground of Christian hope and the basis of the commission of the church. If we really believe in the resurrection of Jesus, this will manifest itself in our being a pilgrim people, an exodus community, a people called to take part in the struggle against injustice and for the liberation and transformation of all things from the chains of the law and of death.

PANNENBERGIAN: Since I interpret the resurrection as a proleptic event as you also seem to want to do, I am not sure what you find objectionable in my approach.

MOLTMANNIAN: I am afraid that your preoccupation with a new interpretation of history and historical reason means a loss of the sense of liberation for service that is inextricably connected with the apprehension of the resurrection in the New Testament church. If I may baptize a saying of Marx, the real task of theology is not to provide a new interpretation of the world but to take part in its transformation. The proclamation of the resurrection of the *crucified* Jesus does more than create anticipation; it sets us in contradiction to present injustice.

BULTMANN: Well, without trying to baptize Marx, let me say that I too want to talk about freedom from the past, openness to the future, and the transformation of life by the gospel of the crucifixion and resurrection of Jesus. This is precisely why I find the abstract way in which all of you speak of this message to be completely sterile and boring. You are so anxious about preserving its "objectivity." Barth wants to make sure that we remember to say that it happened in space and time. But he doesn't feel compelled to give any support to this statement. It just hangs in mid-air, and believing in the resurrection of Jesus comes to involve assenting to some unintelligible claim. This is dishonest. I don't think that Christian faith is this sort of sacrifice of moral and intellectual integrity. So, perhaps surprisingly, I have considerable admiration for Pannenbergian's refusal to allow faith to be equated with intellectual irresponsibility. The problem is that he ends up identifying faith with assent to objective historical statements. The New Testament has a different texture. It is a summons to you and to me to accept the crucified Jesus as God's redemptive act for us, a summons to us to say, Yes, God's presence in the world is realized in the paradoxical form of the crucified one — a summons therefore to live entirely in dependence upon God's forgiveness. This involves dying to my old anxious and grasping self and allowing God alone to be my future and my hope.

MOLTMANNIAN: *My* future and *my* hope! That's just the problem with your interpretation of the Easter message, Bultmann. You individualize and privatize the message. Sure, you talk about transformation and new life. But what you mean is transformation of *my* consciousness. You have split self and world apart. I don't think the early church did that. When they proclaimed the resurrection of Jesus from the dead, they understood this to be the beginning of *world* transformation. I appreciate your criticism of a false kind of objectivism and an anxious searching after proofs and demonstrations in theology. But your interpretation of transformation is much too narrow, too provincial, too individualistic. To believe in the resurrection of the crucified is not just to have a new *self*-understanding. It is to understand and relate to *God* differently. It is to understand and act in the social and political *world* differently. It is to believe in the faithfulness of God in the face of personal and political structures of death. The confession that the crucified one has been raised always has been and continues to be the expression of a subversive faith with revolutionary implications for our social-political as well as personal spheres of life.

PANNENBERGIAN: Well, Moltmannian, I am certainly impressed by the way you have demolished Bultmann, and of course I agree with much of what you have said. I am interested in a public theology with all its attendant difficulties rather than a theology that simply caresses the convictions of an insulated community. But, Moltmannian, you're evading the real issue of this conversation. We're talking about the historicity of the resurrection of Jesus. Stop trying to play the role of junior social prophet and recognize that the real task of theology is to provide a responsible account of the claims of Christian faith.

BARTH: The real question is what theological responsibility means. When you say responsible, Pannenbergian, I think you mean engaging in apologetics, vindicating Christian truth claims before the bar of reason. However aggressive it may seem, apologetics is always theology that has lost its nerve. Real theological responsibility means being responsive to the one concrete and living center of the biblical witness, Jesus Christ, the crucified and risen Lord. Bultmann says that I have no support for the claim I make that the resurrection is an event in space and time. The New Testament texts are my support! Surely they present the resurrection as an event in space and time, as a real happening to which the disciples responded.

BULTMANN: But the texts need to be interpreted! Your simple appeal to the fact that the texts say so would land us in biblicism and fundamentalism.

BARTH: That was a low blow. You know full well that I am no fundamentalist. I fought that mentality for forty years. Of course the texts need to be interpreted. But if you think you can skirt around the claim that the resurrection was an objective event, an event that happened in space and time, you are not interpreting the texts: you are manipulating them to say what you want them to say.

BULTMANN: I see that the elderly Barth still possesses a volatile temper.

BARTH: You bet I do, particularly when there is as much at stake as there is here. We're arguing about the heart of the gospel. You say that the message of the resurrection challenges people to understand themselves anew in the light of the saving significance of the cross. And I say that this will not do. The New Testament speaks of a second and victorious act of God beyond the cross of Jesus. You make the apostolic message a mere summons to realize what has become possible because of the cross. And I say that the apostolic message proclaims not the *possibility* of new life but the *realization* of new life in Jesus the risen Lord. The new world of God created in the resurrection of Christ is objectively true, even if only believers acknowledge it subjectively as true.

PANNENBERGIAN: The way you two knock your heads together amuses me. You have so many things in common: a positivistic notion of historical inquiry, a fear of engaging in apologetics vigorously and unashamedly, a suspicion of every attempt to provide reason and evidence for the claims of faith, and, naturally resulting from all this, a curious ambiguity about the sense in which the resurrection can be said to be a historical event. You know, when I read the New Testament accounts of the resurrection, I don't get the impression, as Bultmann does, that the biblical witnesses thought that the desire for evidence of the resurrection was illegitimate. When you disparage such evidence, you make faith in Jesus and his claims for himself completely arbitrary and authoritarian. The resurrection is God's vindication of Jesus' claims to authority. It is God's certification that Jesus was who he said he was. It is that event in history which proleptically realizes the goal of history.

MOLTMANNIAN: In my judgment, Pannenbergian, we must emphasize that the resurrection of Jesus is *God's* vindication, *God's* proof, *God's* promise. Otherwise we will be pursuing a theology of glory separated from a theology of the cross. In my view, it is really the identity of God that is the basic issue of the resurrection narratives. Who is the God made known in the raising of the crucified Jesus? The God present in the cross and resurrection of Jesus is the triune God. To speak of God as triune is to say that the event of cross and resurrection defines God as the Father who in love surrenders the Son, as the Son who in love is obedient to the Father's will, and as the Spirit of love who holds Father and Son in communion in their greatest distance from each other and who opens this communion to the world. On the cross God takes suffering and death into the divine life for the sake of the salvation of the world. In the resurrection the joy of God's final victory over evil is promised.

PANNENBERGIAN: You are surely aware that my theology of the resurrection is also eschatologically oriented and that I am as thoroughly trinitarian in my theology as you try to be in yours. So I still don't see what you find so objectionable in my theological work.

MOLTMANNIAN: I suspect that it has to do with the lack of attention to the significance of the cross in your theology and to the consistently conservative political implications that you draw from your interpretation of the biblical witness. As I understand the gospel message, to know this God of cross and resurrection is to take part in the suffering and joy of the history of divine love which wants to transform all things. We continue to live in the brokenness and incompleteness of history under the signature of the cross. The cries of the oppressed and the groaning of creation have not ceased. Authentic Easter faith manifests itself, therefore, not in impressive intellectual or historical proofs but in the spirit of sacrifice and service that comes from God's own history of suffering, liberating, and reconciling love for the world. I see you, Pannenbergian, as advancing a theology of the resurrection that is continually tempted to become a theology of glory. My theology of the resurrection tries to avoid this by consistently emphasizing that God raised the *crucified* Jesus from the dead and calls us to solidarity with the victims of history in the hope of the renewal of all things.

Summations

BARTH: Since that last speech is probably going to require an interpretation as long as my *Church Dogmatics,* we had better call it a day. But before we do, I want to challenge each of you to say on what text you would preach your next Easter sermon. I have always believed that theology is for the sake of better, more faithful preaching. So what I am asking is this: How would our interpretations of the resurrection work themselves out in our Easter sermons? For my part, I would like to preach on the text in which the angel announces to the disciples at the tomb, "He has risen. He is not here" (Mark 16:6). I think I would emphasize that an angel brought this message, that it was revelation, and that above all else it was good and joyful news.

BULTMANN: I have always been especially attached to the Gospel of John. I think I would preach on the word of the risen Lord to Thomas: "Have you believed because you have seen me? Blessed are those who have not seen and yet believe" (John 20:29). In light of our previous discussion, I think my emphasis in this sermon would be pretty self-evident. Easter faith is an existential response to the scandal of the cross; it is not a matter of being a privileged eyewitness of a spectacular event in history called the resurrection.

PANNENBERGIAN: I would want to preach a sermon emphasizing the centrality of the fact of the resurrection for our faith. A good text would be the Pauline claim: "If there is no resurrection of the dead, then Christ has not been raised; if Christ has not been raised, then our preaching is in vain and your faith is in vain" (1 Cor. 15:13-14). I would try to bring out both sides of Paul's argument: that the intelligibility of the resurrection of Christ depends on an understanding of reality as radically open to the new, and that the actuality of the resurrection is the basis of the Christian interpretation of reality and of the whole of Christian faith and life.

MOLTMANNIAN: My choice for an Easter text is perhaps a little unexpected, but that is surely appropriate for the subject matter. I would preach on the text from the Apocalypse: "Behold I make all things new" (Rev. 21:5). I would emphasize that only the church that risks itself in the service of the crucified and risen Christ, attending to the pain and suffering of the world, will hear that word of promise.

APPENDIX C

Political Theology: A Dialogue

THE RELATIONSHIP BETWEEN CHRISTIAN FAITH AND CURRENT struggles for justice, freedom, and peace has become one of the central issues in theology today. In recent decades, Christians have not only been involved but have offered theological justifications for their involvement in the civil rights movement, the black liberation struggle in the United States, the women's liberation movement, the struggle against apartheid in South Africa, the praxis of solidarity with the poor and the formation of Christian base communities in Latin America, the protest against totalitarian rule and oppression in Poland, Haiti, and the Philippines, the worldwide opposition to the nuclear arms race, resistance to American military intervention in the 1960s in Vietnam and in the 1980s in Central America, participation in the sanctuary movement — the list could be extended almost indefinitely.

Some critics have condemned such activity as a damaging politicization of the church that has diverted it from its true mission. However, for most Christians it has become increasingly clear that the real issue is not *whether* there is an inseparable link between faith and political practice but *how* this link is to be understood. What follows is an imaginary exchange among several political theologians who seek to clarify their positions on this issue. The participants are:

Karl Barth. Since he has been introduced in the preceding two appendices, it is sufficient to say here that he was a leader of the German confessing Church in its resistance to Nazism, that his early participation in the socialist movement has become a focal point in some recent interpretations of his theology, and that he wrote a number of occasional

283

essays on theology and political issues, some of which are collected in *Community, State and Church* and *Against the Stream.*

Reinhold Niebuhr. Far and away the most influential American ethicist and political theologian of the twentieth century, Niebuhr addressed national and international issues with prophetic insight and analytical power for four decades. Among his many writings are *Moral Man and Immoral Society, The Nature and Destiny of Man, The Irony of American History,* and *The Children of Light and the Children of Darkness.*

Liberationist. This is a composite figure who does not speak for any single Latin American liberation theologian but who obviously is influenced by such writers as Gustavo Gutiérrez *(A Theology of Liberation; We Drink from Our Own Wells)* and Leonardo Boff *(The Church: Charism and Power).*

Feminist. This speaker, too, is a composite figure and should not be identified without qualification with any particular contemporary feminist theologian. Among the most widely read feminist theologians today are Rosemary Ruether *(Sexism and God-Talk)*, Phyllis Trible *(God and the Rhetoric of Sexuality)*, Sallie McFague *(Models of God)*, Elisabeth Schüssler Fiorenza *(In Memory of Her)*, and Letty Russell *(The Future of Partnership).*

A Gathering of Political Theologians

BARTH: Since I don't believe in chance, an invisible hand must have been at work in arranging another of these unlikely conversations. The dear Lord must have a marvelous sense of humor.

LIBERATIONIST: I can assure you that the Vatican had nothing to do with it. As you know, they're a little nervous about all this free-wheeling debate among theologians. They think it usually leads to confusion among the faithful as to what the church teaches. While I do not share this view, I have my own reasons for not being very optimistic about what will come of our meeting.

NIEBUHR: That we have gotten together at all, even if only in someone's imagination, is one of those impossible possibilities about which I have written. The surprises and twists of history defy rational explanation. The fact is that we are here, political theologians all, with the opportunity of discovering, if not where we agree, at least where, why, and to what extent we disagree.

FEMINIST: I've been trying to figure out why the four of us were selected. True, we have all been involved in political struggles as theologians and have written more or less extensively on the relationship of Christian faith and political responsibility, but for goodness' sake, so have lots of other people — Joseph Ratzinger, Michael Novak, and Pat Robertson, to mention a few. What a conversation about political theology we might have had with any or all of them!

NIEBUHR: I am not sure it would have been a conversation; more likely it would have turned into a shouting match or even a riot. Maybe there's some value in four clearly left-of-center political theologians like us finding out how much ground we share, if any. We all have been tagged as liberals, radicals, or even "commies" at some time or other.

BARTH: Indeed, we have, Reinie. In fact, I think you were responsible for stuffing me in a bag like that once or twice. But never mind. Even if we can't hope for a Barmen-like Declaration to result from this meeting, that is no reason we cannot engage in an open and friendly conversation. Part of the problem of most theologians is their lack of a sense of humor; they take themselves and what they call the present situation with such frightful seriousness.

FEMINIST: That is a rather predictable and gratuitous remark, Karl. As some of us see the matter, the church and theology are not nearly serious enough about the oppression and exploitation of people around the world. It's all so cozy to be reminded to be friendly and to keep a sense of humor, but the fact is that millions of people are dying because of the apathy and complicity of the church. I honor your prophetic leadership of the church in the struggle against Nazism, but what you lost sight of in those infinite expanses of the *Church Dogmatics* is that there are forces at work in the world today that are as sinister and destructive as Nazism.

LIBERATIONIST: Olé! The question of the church's political commitment and responsibility is not a topic for friendly conversation in the safety and decorum of an academic seminar. It is a life-and-death issue for millions of people, at least in Latin America and other parts of the Third World. My guess, Feminist, is that what happened in the cases of our friends Karl and Reinie is that their work became increasingly detached from pastoral and political praxis. As their theology and ethics became ever more theoretical — however concrete or even pragmatic it claimed to be — they were tolerated, and perhaps to some extent co-opted, by the ruling powers. When Karl was the "red pastor" of Safenwil, or involved in the German Church Struggle, and when Reinie was a Detroit pastor forced to speak out against the exploitative policies of the auto magnates, or incensed by the ravages of the Great Depression, their theology had social critical power. In those days they spoke out of the social struggle and in solidarity with suffering people.

BARTH: I was involved in the religious socialist movement early on. But I was never really caught up in its ideology. What was important to me as a pastor was union organizing and helping the working people struggle for their rights. I do not believe I ever abandoned the commitment to justice and peace that animated my early ministry. I *do* think I later put that commitment on a firmer theological foundation and guarded better against confusion of the kingdom of God with any human politics — whether right, center, or left.

FEMINIST: But Karl, that's precisely my point, and I think Liberationist's, too. Your theology, which is *usually* impeccably orthodox, tries to walk a tightrope between a desire for pure Word-of-God theology and occasional pronouncements and actions in relation to particular social and political issues and movements. But that is simply not possible — or rather it is possible only at the expense of serious and sustained involvement of the church and theology in the most vital political struggles of our time. By the way, I hope you noticed that I said your theology was "usually" impeccably orthodox, since at least in the case of your teaching about the ordered relationship of man and woman in the image of God — according to which man always is the leader and woman always the follower — you are both dead wrong and, in the only sense that counts, terribly heretical. If you had remained a theologian of praxis instead of pontificating about what God says from your safe professorial chair in Basel, you might have learned from some of your female comrades in the struggle for justice that Galatians 3:28 rather than Ephesians 5 is the important clue for a genuinely Christian understanding of the relationship of man and woman.

BARTH: After that tongue-lashing, I am more persuaded than ever that the charge to women to keep silent in the church (1 Cor. 14:34), while by no means to be construed as a general rule, may well be a necessary command in exceptional cases. As far as I am concerned, the question is not whether faith and theology are to hover above history or whether concrete decisions are to be risked in the praxis of faith. My position is that the church never speaks or acts "on principle." It makes its evaluations and judgments spiritually and by individual cases. The real question for me is what norm or criterion finally guides our political decisions and praxis. I am far more respectful of the contextuality of Christian decision making than you suggest, but I am even more passionately concerned that the political decisions of Christians be guided by the Word of God attested in Scripture.

Niebuhr and Barth

NIEBUHR: Well, Karl, even if you do insist on the concrete risk-taking of Christians, Feminist and Liberationist are right in pointing out the folly of trying to develop a political theology that is based on the Word of God alone and that does not interact with, and stand corrected by, the concrete experiences of individuals and societies. As you will recall, I warned you long ago about this business of turning theology into a kind of airplane that soars so high above the world of experience and history that it can no longer make discriminating judgments regarding the persons and events below, which appear so tiny and insignificant from that distance. I think responsible theology and ethics should refuse to ride in this high-altitude airplane. We are human beings, not God, and we must form our judgments and make our decisions as finite, fallible human beings.

BARTH: Where in the world do I deny that? Should I laugh or cry at your charge that I think we fly to heaven in some kind of eschatological airplane and play God? My point is simply that our political decisions as Christians, which must always be as concrete and well informed as possible, must always be disciplined and directed by exegetical attention to the Bible. "Exegesis, exegesis, exegesis!" I told my students in Bonn before being expelled from Germany by the Nazis. I still think that is sound advice for all theology and ethics. It is bad theology and bad Christian ethics to argue that the Christian view on any particular social or political issue is settled by appeal to some vague notion like the Judeo-Christian tradition, the perennial philosophy, the mind of Christ, or whatever.

NIEBUHR: Your obsession with biblical exegesis makes theology captive to biblical literalism. You want to establish biblical authority in all matters of Christian faith and practice with as little recourse as possible to sources of truth and right that come from common reason, universal conscience, or cultural history. That way of thinking drives us straight into theological obscurantism.

BARTH: So in your eyes I am a literalist and an obscurantist. I have learned not to be intimidated by these bogeyman slogans substituting for arguments. I happen to believe, as I thought you did too, that the Word of God is like a sword that cuts through our self-righteous confidence that God is always on our side. I am unalterably opposed to any identification of the biblical message with the going cultural values of Western society, whether these are focused on the infinite worth of the individual, as with the old liberal school, or on the glory of free enterprise, as with our present so-called neoconservatives. You're not one of them, are you Reinie?

NIEBUHR: You know darn well I'm not. You are absolutely right about the substitution of self-righteous civil religion for prophetic biblical teaching and the easy replacement of the hard truths of classical Christian faith with the naive creeds of modern culture. I have no quarrel with you in your effort to extricate Christian faith from the idolatries of our day. What I do object to is your remedy, which is almost as bad as the disease. You destroy all commerce between Christian faith and the philosophical, ethical, and anthropological disciplines. You refuse to enter into a debate with modern culture to show that its analysis of the human situation is superficial and its expected redemptions are illusory. Your isolationist theology belies your claim that the political decisions of Christians should be as well informed as possible. Where do you enlist the help of social scientists and politicians in describing the dynamics of specific political issues? All you want to do is preach the gospel and wait for the Holy Spirit to validate it.

BARTH: In one sense, at least, that is just what I think we should do, but it is a preposterous reading of my theology and a complete distortion of my lifelong engagement in political issues to charge me with isolationism and otherworldly quietism. Have you ever heard of Barmen?

NIEBUHR: Yes, I have, and it illustrates the point I am making. Your brand of political theology is strictly for the church in the most extreme crises, where the issues of good and evil are obvious. In these circumstances, your theology can arouse Christians to heroic action. However, in situations of great complexity and ambiguity, where the devil is not so obvious, your eschatological extremism is impotent.

That is why you never found yourself able to make a clear decision against the threat of communist totalitarianism as you had against Nazi totalitarianism. So when Hungary was invaded by the Soviet Union, we heard only silence from the Barth who once roared like a lion against Nazism.

BARTH: As you should know by now, that "silence" in relation to the invasion of Hungary was a careful and painful response to a particular and very complex situation that you and some other Western church leaders tried to oversimplify for your own propagandistic purposes. Anyone who knows anything about me and my theology knows my strong support of democratic government. But I did not then, and I do not now, see Russia as the evil empire and the United States as the incarnation of goodness and innocence. In relation to the conflict between these two superpowers that developed after World War II, a different response from the church was and is needed in comparison with the one which I helped to mobilize against Hitler. The church needs to search for and promote a third option rather than allow itself to become the religious echo of one or the other of these superpowers. It seems to me that in this case it is *you* who refused to recognize the importance of the particular situation in which Christians have to make their political decisions with a "nicely calculated more or less." Instead, you simply waved the flags of Western self-righteousness which came to haunt you in the 1950s with the McCarthy witch-hunt and in the 1960s with the terrible war in Vietnam. I think you have written something about the irony of history?

NIEBUHR: I see that we both have warrior's instincts and go for the jugular. I will not deny that your perception of the myth of American innocence and the pretensions of American power may have been sharper than mine in that period when I argued a little too one-sidedly for the legitimate exercise of limited power to counter the Soviet threat. While I regret not having criticized the American Vietnam war policy earlier than I did, that still does not alter my fundamental rejection of your feeble and obscure efforts to assist the church to make enlightened and discriminating judgments in the political sphere. You have only your spiritual intuition to offer, and of course in the case of Nazism it was brilliant. But the church needs something more than intuition robed in the garments of the Word of God.

BARTH: I have never rested my case on so-called intuition. I have argued that Christian political decision making must follow the direction and line of God's own political action in Jesus Christ. We may discern parables or analogies of the kingdom of God in every protection of human rights, in preferential care for the poor and the oppressed, and in open societies that have fundamental freedoms of speech, assembly, and the like. While God's action in Jesus Christ does not supply blueprints for Christian political actions, it points in a definite and unswerving direction. Among the political options open to the Christian community in a particular situation, it will choose the one that most suggests an analogy or correspondence with the gospel of Jesus Christ. This is not "intuition," and it is not biblicism, at least not in the sense of thinking we can find the biblical "answers" to our particular political problems ready-made for us.

NIEBUHR: Your attempt to develop a political theology based solely on the Word of God by the device of reasoning analogically from the gospel story just doesn't work. It amounts to a tour de force. Your clever analogies are designed to protect the sole authority of the Word of God and to claim independence of the insights of cultural history, natural law, the moral conscience, political theory, or social analysis. But the whole process is simply an illusion. To begin with the obvious, your references to the Bible are bound to be selective. Other interpreters might come up with analogies very different from yours. For example, one might argue from the biblical description of God as Lord and King and of God's people as servants that a monarchy or even dictatorship is an appropriate way of ordering human life in accordance with God's action. Admit it, Karl, your preference for democracy and a system of law that protects human rights owes much more to general cultural history than you are willing to say.

BARTH: It is now very clear to me that you have a thoroughly mistaken notion of what I think biblical interpretation involves. Whatever may be the case with your American fundamentalists, for me the Bible is to be interpreted in the light of its central testimony to God's covenant history with Israel fulfilled in Jesus Christ. That covenant history discloses both the true identity of God and the true identity of humanity as God's covenant partner. All of the terms that we ascribe to God and all that we think we know about God's purposes must be reexamined, corrected, and transformed in the light of the covenantal activity of God. In terms of this history, God is not just any Lord but a Lord who becomes a servant. God is not just any king but a king who humbles himself and exalts humanity to royal partnership with

God. If you can find in monarchy and even dictatorship an analogy to *this* history of *this* God, you are close to desperation.

NIEBUHR: It all seems to me to be a very devious and dubious way of trying to circumvent the fact that the Christian faith owes something to general culture. To ignore this fact, especially in our ethical analyses and political decisions, can only lead to self-deception and a ghetto mentality. Instead of engaging in exegetical gymnastics to display these kingdom-like analogies of yours that are supposed to guide our political action, political theology should take as its task a realistic analysis of a particular political situation informed by an interpretation of the classical Christian symbols of sin, the Christ, the cross, and so on. In the interaction of concrete political analysis and the interpretation of symbols like the cross, in which God's justice and love intersect, depth is given to our political theory and realism and hope to our political proposals. As a political ethicist, I take Christian symbols not literally but with utmost seriousness.

BARTH: Again, you misrepresent my approach. I do not advocate or practice ignorance of cultural history, philosophy, social and political analysis, or anthropological studies. I believe that there are many little lights of creation, culture, and history that we would be not only foolish but disobedient to ignore. These lights must be honored, but they are little lights which for the Christian never substitute for the one great light of God's revelation in Jesus Christ. In other words, that great light of Jesus Christ is the criterion by which we recognize and affirm the truth that is present in all the little lights of our experience, cultural history, and common sense.

NIEBUHR: What you have just said may be a significant step beyond the impression of a cleavage between faith and culture that many of your earlier writings left. Still, I am not satisfied with this latest version of your position. For you the little lights of creation, experience, and cultural history can be in the last analysis only reflections of the great light of revelation in Jesus Christ. I see the relationship as much more dialectical. Our knowledge of God's revelation in Jesus Christ is continually tested, corrected, or verified by common experience and general culture. It is, for example, unfortunate that the confessing church did not allow its opposition to Nazism to embrace the inviolability of Jews as human beings rather than limiting its concern to the church and the freedom of its proclamation. A Christian approach to political theory, social criticism, and the struggle for justice must recognize that the church is heir to both the prophetic biblical tradition and the Enlightenment tradition of political rights. These two traditions constitute a creative synthesis — Christian realism, I call it — the elements of which must be kept in mutually corrective and mutually enriching interaction.

Liberationist and Niebuhr

LIBERATIONIST: Reinie, I share a number of your misgivings about Barth's approach to the relationship of faith and politics. Despite his courageous leadership of the Confessing Church, I find it difficult to grasp the connection between his explicit biblicism and his professed contextualism. He is of course right when he says that we all move by some process of analogy between the proclamation of the kingdom of God in the Bible and the present situation. But there is a lot of residual idealism in his failure to begin with concrete situations and reflect critically on them in the light of revelation. I am, therefore, much closer to you than to him on the matter of the positive interaction of human experience and social analysis with what is called *revelation* or *Word of God.* Barth's analogies of the kingdom of God seem to me well intentioned but terribly vulnerable to all sorts of ideological manipulation.

NIEBUHR: But, if I am not mistaken, you also have a number of reservations about my work. Well, it so happens that I have some questions for you, too, so why not fire away?

LIBERATIONIST: All right. For starters, I question the social location of your theology no less than Barth's. You value what you call the wisdom of experience and general cultural history as a means of testing, correcting, or confirming the teachings of the Bible and the Christian tradition. But precisely whose experience and whose cultural history do you have in mind? As far as I can see, you don't even try to break out of the model of theology as primarily an apologetic enterprise designed to convince enlightened nonbelievers of Europe and North America of the limitations of their understandings of human life and the depth dimensions that they overlook because of their disdain of the profound symbols of the Judeo-Christian tradition. My theology of liberation, however, is aimed not at the sophisticated and usually well-to-do nonbeliever of the Western world but at the nonperson of so much of the Third World. It begins with the experience of the poor and their struggle for justice and freedom.

NIEBUHR: I am surprised that you would consider me insensitive to the concern of God for the poor. What I call Christian realism is to a large extent a retrieval of the prophetic tradition of the Old Testament — with its word of judgment on the abuse of the poor by the wealthy and powerful — as well as a reclaiming of the apostolic teaching: "God chose what is low and despised in the world, even things that are not, to bring to nothing things that are" (1 Cor. 1:28).

LIBERATIONIST: Advocacy of the cause of the poor is one thing, but solidarity with the struggle of the poor — with which liberation theology begins — is something else. It presupposes a clear and unqualified commitment to the cause of the poor, and out of this experience the biblical message is heard and understood in a new way. By comparison, your prophetic theology retains many of the features of complacent North American liberalism.

NIEBUHR: I happen to think that there are elements of the liberal tradition well worth preserving. What bothers me about your call to an unconditional commitment to and struggle with oppressed people is the danger of identifying particular political strategies and commitments with the kingdom of God or the absolute good. I would have thought that the lesson of history in the twentieth century is that a reign of terror is not far away when *any* people claim unequivocally that they are the privileged bearers of God's will. A reservation about this sort of presumption is a very important element in Christian realism.

LIBERATIONIST: I find your Christian realism a very slippery concept. It is presumably supposed to mean living by God's grace without illusions and denials of the finitude and sinfulness of all human activity. It is clearly targeted against all utopian thinking. But whether you like it or not, your Christian realism has become in many cases indistinguishable from a hard-nosed pragmatism that uniformly defends the existing state of affairs. It has the effect of blaming the victims of oppression if they take action to overcome their bondage and become subjects of their own history.

NIEBUHR: Don't put that reactionary label on me. You know I am far from denying the legitimacy of revolution in certain circumstances. What I am arguing is that God is more mysterious and hidden than either the self-righteous possessors of power or the unselfcritical leaders of revolutionary movements allow. They both illicitly claim to be the guardians or executors of God's will. The point of the eschatological biblical symbols, in my judgment, is that the final meaning of history cannot be realized by humanity's own effort. History cannot complete itself, but depends for its completion on a power beyond itself. The eschatological symbols thus mitigate our pride without destroying our hope.

LIBERATIONIST: I think you see the relationship between biblical eschatology and politics primarily in a negative way. I see the relationship more positively. Historical action presupposes confidence in the future. Biblical eschatology — especially Jesus' proclamation of the coming kingdom of God — ignites rather than suffocates hope and effort at historical transformation. I am therefore much more appreciative than you of the importance of utopian thinking. True utopian thinking involves both a denunciation of the existing order and an annunciation of what may yet be in contrast to what is. The effective denunciation and annunciation of utopian thinking can be achieved only in concrete praxis. You too quickly identify utopian thinking with the ideology that masks rather than discloses real possibilities of change.

NIEBUHR: I am well aware of the utopian mentality and how the failure of its schemes leads invariably to disillusionment and brutality. The basic error of this way of thinking is its pretentious conviction that always someone or some institution outside the self is solely responsible for all injustice and evil in the world. The profound truth of the symbol of original sin is thereby ignored. Marxism is the greatest of modern utopias, and its historical failures are such that I would have thought it would not be quite the temptation to you liberation theologians as it appears to be. Have you kept up with recent events in eastern Europe and the Soviet Union?

LIBERATIONIST: We in Latin America have not and do not intend to adopt Marxism uncritically, any more than we intend to be mesmerized by the European and North American ideology of "democratic capitalism." We seek our own third way (here I applaud the insight and independence of Barth), and that way may indeed be a form — but *our own form* — of democratic socialism.

NIEBUHR: I am happy to hear that. You may know that I was once very active in the Christian socialist movement, but I gradually moved away from it as its principles seemed helpless before the harsh realities and dark ambiguities of modern history. It was caught up, for example, in a naive pacifism that ignored the urgency of resistance to the demonic movement of Nazism. My own endorsement of democracy sums up my Christian realism: the creation of humanity in the image of God makes democracy possible; the sinfulness of humanity makes democracy necessary.

LIBERATIONIST: Even this wise saying can so easily become a mask that covers reality rather than a light that shines on it. It may hide a sophomoric confidence in the electoral process and in the system of checks and balances within "democratic" societies that ignores actual control of government by moneyed interests and that is totally ignorant of the experience of the poor within and outside those societies. The cry for transformation arises from the experience of suffering, and without attending to that experience even our best democratic theories and systems become masks of injustice. This is why for me the purely theoretical debate for or against democracy, or capitalism versus socialism, has an unreal quality. A paradigm shift is required if we are to avoid this unreality in our theology and our political commitments. We must enter into solidarity with the poor on the wager that it is this experience in which the coincidence of the transforming grace of God and the struggle for justice and freedom becomes evident.

NIEBUHR: You have not understood me rightly if you think I am interested only in minimal and undisturbing advances in justice and not in radical transformation. On the contrary, it is precisely when we recognize the impossible but relevant ideal of sacrificial love as disclosed in the cross of Christ that all of our relative achievements of justice are questioned. The call for relative justice and mutual love in all our social relations is the historical approximation to the impossible ideal of sacrificial love. But God's suffering love symbolized by the cross defines the limits of history and points to a completion of human life and history by resources that are not our own. For this reason I think that the Christian's engagement in political struggle is most responsible when it is de-absolutized, unburdened of all its pretensions. I am deeply concerned that the loss of emphasis in liberation theology on some of the central symbols of the faith — atonement, justification, Trinity — or that the transmutation of these symbols into a code language for uncritical participation in all liberation struggles may result in a politicization of the church and its theology no less disastrous than that of neoconservative political theology on the other end of the spectrum.

LIBERATIONIST: There is an old adage of scholastic theology, *abusus non tollit usum,* which I believe is relevant here. Of course, liberation theology and its social expression — the basic Christian communities — are subject to distortion and can be made into fronts for the recruitment of members for a strictly secular liberation movement. But no fair-minded reading of my books, which deal at length with the need for a spirituality of liberation to sustain and continually convert the liberation commitment, could charge my theology with the sort of abuse of which you speak.

Feminist and Liberationist

FEMINIST: Liberationist, I think an understandable nervousness is evident in what we've heard from both Karl, with his appeal for a pure theology of the Word, and from Reinie, with his summons to tough-minded Christian realism. These are probably the two greatest theologians of Europe and North America in the twentieth century, but the relationship of their theological reflection to concrete praxis remains more or less ambiguous. In this regard they represent rather than transcend the approach of academic theology with which the method of liberation theology fundamentally disagrees. The church of the future will remember their work with gratitude but will not be able to follow in their steps.

BARTH [to NIEBUHR]: See, Reinie, we're already passé.

LIBERATIONIST: I agree, Feminist, and that means that the church and theology must take up a new agenda focused on the experience of genuine solidarity with the suffering of the poor. Can we expect an alliance of at least some segments of the church in both the First and the Third World on this agenda?

FEMINIST: I hope so, but it won't be easy. Representatives of various liberation theologies will have to have a lot of patience and listen to each other carefully, and that will sometimes prove painful. For example, from my own feminist perspective, I have some pretty hard words to address to your project of liberation theology.

LIBERATIONIST: Well, if you give me the chance to tell you what's on my mind that I think you need to hear, I'm willing to listen for the moment.

FEMINIST: Your theology of liberation is sharply critical of the praxis of the church, but in my judgment, quite uncritical and even naive in regard to the traditional doctrine of the church. You fail to explore in any depth the connection between the doctrinal tradition, with which you seldom express disagreement, and the actual practice of the church that you challenge.

LIBERATIONIST: I'm startled to hear you say that. Don't I criticize the separation of the spiritual and the material, and every purely other-worldly interpretation of Christian hope, to mention only a few points?

FEMINIST: Yes, of course. But your method of doing theology does not seem to me to recognize sufficiently the necessity both of prophetically denouncing injustice in the present situation in the light of the biblical tradition, and of critically engaging the tradition in the light of our new experience of God's work in the world. I hear a great deal of the former in your work but rather little of the latter. We are both Catholics, and deeply committed to the church, so that's not the issue. The issue is whether loyalty to what the tradition is really about must not include, if it is to be honest and free, criticism of many aspects of the tradition.

LIBERATIONIST: Are you speaking in particular about patriarchal language about God and the question of the ordination of women?

FEMINIST: Those are merely symptoms of a much larger issue. I am asking whether you are prepared to approach the biblical texts and the history of Christian doctrine with a hermeneutics of suspicion, ready to expose and criticize those elements of the tradition that enter into complicity with attitudes and practices of injustice in society and in the church. I do not see how any responsible political theology or theology of liberation can avoid this task.

LIBERATIONIST: My own effort, I suppose, has been concentrated on the retrieval of the power and illumination of the Word of God in relation to the suffering of the poor and their struggle for liberation. That for me has been an all-consuming task. Anything else would be — well, a harmful distraction. Note, please, I do not say that what you are asking for is unimportant. Indeed, I am happy to see that some of my fellow liberation theologians are doing the sort of thing you want, but I have not found that to be my most pressing task.

FEMINIST: But surely, the way the church itself exercises its power, the kind of leadership and extent of participation that it fosters, the freedoms that it cultivates or denies in its own life, the honesty or dishonesty with which it treats its own history of complicity with oppression — these matters are hardly peripheral to the quest for integral liberation. The church cannot call for freedom in the institutions and relationships of society while it represents in its own life a rigid, hierarchical, closed society.

LIBERATIONIST: I certainly cannot quarrel with that, but why do I have the feeling that you have still not expressed your central concern, which has to do with the sexism of the whole tradition, as well as its present manifestations in the church and society?

FEMINIST: That is indeed my central, although not my only, concern in the struggle for integral liberation. And I am frankly distressed that it is all but absent from your own analysis of oppression and exploitation in your writings. Sexism is deeply embedded in the Christian tradition, including the biblical tradition. The very best theological minds of this century — Niebuhr, Barth, Rahner — have hardly been able to recognize it as a problem. We will never come to terms with this sexism — which is the oldest and most virulent form of oppression — until we expose and denounce it in our own tradition of faith. It is certainly part of political theology, as I understand it, to uncover the sexism in Barth's theology of man and woman in which woman is by divine ordination set in subordination to man; to uncover the inadequacy of Niebuhr's description of human sin as predominantly pride, thus showing his own masculine bias and his disconnection from the experience of women and minority peoples, whose temptations to self-hatred and resignation are far greater than to pride; and to expose the lack of attention to the special plight of Latin American women in your own liberation theology. Have you ever examined the consistently sexist character of your language about God?

LIBERATIONIST: I have been helped by the contribution of women like yourself to a deeper understanding of oppression and liberation. My experience is that women assume a significant leadership role in all aspects of the life, reflection, and service of the base communities, and I would certainly want to do all that I can to encourage this. If I have showed insensitivity to the plight of Latin American women in my earlier writings, I regret this. I do now see far better than before how traditional structures of the church and certain interpretations of traditional doctrines serve to strengthen and perpetuate the system of *machismo* in our societies. Sentimentalized portraits of the Blessed Virgin would be an obvious example. It is chilling to consider that our macho attitudes simply reflect in our own man/woman relationships something of the abuse and exploitation that our whole society experiences at the hands of imperialist powers.

FEMINIST: Nor should we overlook the fact that in the Christian tradition this exploitative attitude toward women goes hand in hand with a similar attitude toward nature. In patriarchal societies, nature is viewed simply as raw material to be used by human beings to satisfy not only their needs but their every desire. A liberation theology that does not expand its concern to the cosmic scale is inadequate for our age of nuclear weaponry and runaway industrial pollution. The whole earth is groaning for liberation.

LIBERATIONIST: All right, but now I must be permitted the opportunity to address you with my concerns. I am disturbed, first of all, that women, and especially North American women, seem rather inattentive to the danger of supplanting the question of economic oppression with the issues of linguistic sexism and environmental abuse. I agree that liberation must be integral and comprehensive, but my impression is that we have some way to go before we can be mutually confident that our various liberation agendas are not simply fighting each other. That would be truly tragic. It would simply fall into the long-established strategy of the powerful: divide and conquer.

FEMINIST: You are entirely right about this, and I must express my embarrassment when a North American woman indiscriminately attacks the masculine ego without any attempt to understand the special experiences of suffering of men in oppressed minorities or in poor countries, or when a middle-class North American woman fails to distinguish her own situation from that of her sisters in Latin America.

LIBERATIONIST: Not only in Latin America. There are rather strikingly different experiences of oppression represented in North America by white middle-class women and most black women. I believe you are now beginning to hear from these black women, who call themselves *womanist* rather than *feminist* theologians and who insist that their primary struggle is for survival rather than self-fulfillment. My guess is that much of Latin American liberation theology will find itself closer to black womanist than to liberal feminist theology.

FEMINIST: I see womanist theology as a challenge and a radicalization of the feminist movement, and I think that it will serve to deepen and strengthen it.

LIBERATIONIST: Then, too, you must forgive us if we smile when we are told that we neglect concern for the natural environment in our theology of liberation. The traditional cultures of the Third World have a deeply reverent attitude toward nature. It is precisely the colonialization and neocolonialization of our societies that has brought ecological havoc. So again, you see, I am still inclined to consider the economic factor as more important than either the sexual or the ecological or the racial, although with regard to the latter I have learned much from my black friends in North America and South Africa. I am prepared to listen further to others so long as they speak out of real experiences of suffering and are not just advancing theoretical constructs to entertain themselves and those who debate with them.

Prayer and Politics

BARTH: We must conclude our conversation for the time being. The earlier predictions of a lack of a clear consensus appear to have been accurate. Before we part, may I suggest that we strike a little blow against the popular opinion that we political theologians have no use for prayer. I for one want it to be carefully noted that my final reflections on Christian ethics in the *Church Dogmatics* are an extended meditation on the first two petitions of the Lord's prayer: "Hallowed be Thy name. Thy kingdom come." Prayer and political responsibility are thoroughly intertwined in the Christian life.

NIEBUHR: Neither of us, Karl, could ever be accused of being soft on pietism when it is mixed with political irresponsibility. But I entirely agree with your point about the inseparability of political action and prayer for the kingdom. My political theology is summed up in the prayer I have used so often: "Lord, give me the courage to change what I can change, the serenity to accept what I cannot change, and the wisdom to know the difference."

LIBERATIONIST: I am not so sure that in the situation in which I do theology it is appropriate to balance so nicely the prayer for courage to work for change and the prayer for serenity to accept the unchangeable. Perhaps you will allow me to modify your prayer: "Lord, give us the courage to change what we can change even though we have been taught for so long that we must accept our hunger, poverty, and disease as things which you will. And give us the wisdom to distinguish courage from arrogance." With this modification, I can express agreement with the point that you and Karl have made. I have long contended that we need not only new theological concepts but a new spirituality that informs our thought and action. In the context of the liberation struggle, prayer is far from "useless." My friends, the poor are teaching the church to pray in a new way, which, if my reading of the Gospels is correct, is also a very old way.

FEMINIST: I will simply call to mind the Song of Mary: "My soul magnifies the Lord, and my spirit rejoices in God my savior. . . . God has put down the mighty from their thrones and exalted those of low degree" (Luke 1:46-47, 52).

Index of Scripture References

Index of Names and Subjects

ON NATURE

BOSTON UNIVERSITY STUDIES IN PHILOSOPHY AND RELIGION

General Editor: Leroy S. Rouner

Volume Six

Volume Five
Religious Pluralism
Leroy S. Rouner, Editor

Volume Four
Foundations of Ethics
Leroy S. Rouner, Editor

Volume Three
Meaning, Truth, and God
Leroy S. Rouner, Editor

Volume Two
Transcendence and the Sacred
Alan M. Olson and Leroy S. Rouner, Editors

Volume One
Myth, Symbol, and Reality
Alan M. Olson, Editor

On Nature

Edited by
Leroy S. Rouner

UNIVERSITY OF NOTRE DAME PRESS
Notre Dame, Indiana 46556

BD581
.05
1984

Library of Congress Cataloging in Publication Data

Main entry under title:

On nature.

(Boston University studies in philosophy and religion ;
v. 6)
Includes index.
Contents: Of sticks and stones / W.V. Quine — Cosmology
as science and religion / Stephen Toulmin — Two
evolutions / Huston Smith — [etc.]
1. Philosophy of nature—Addresses, essays, lectures.
2. Nature—Religious aspects—Addresses, essays, lectures.
I. Rouner, Leroy S.   II. Series.
BD581.05 1984   113   84-7502
ISBN 0-268-01499-X

Contents

Preface

Boston University Studies in Philosophy and Religion is a joint project of the Boston University Institute for Philosophy and Religion and the University of Notre Dame Press. While these Studies may eventually include occasional volumes by individual authors dealing with critical issues in the philosophy of religion, it is presently focused on an annual volume edited from the previous year's Institute lecture program. The Director of the Institute, who also serves as editor of these Studies, chooses a theme and invites participants to lecture at Boston University in the course of the academic year. These public lectures are on Wednesday evenings, chaired by faculty from the various schools and departments within the university which jointly sponsor the Institute. There is a critical respondent to each paper and general discussion by the audience. The papers are then revised by their authors, and the editor selects and edits the papers to be included in these Studies. In preparation are volumes on problems of religious knowledge, and on civil religion/political theology.

The Boston University Institute for Philosophy and Religion is sponsored jointly by the Graduate School, the School of Theology, the Department of Philosophy, and the Department of Religion at Boston University. As an interdisciplinary and ecumenical forum it does not represent any philosophical school or religious tradition. Within the academic community it is committed to open interchange on questions of value, truth, reality, and meaning which transcend the narrow specializations of academic life. Outside the university community it seeks to recover the public tradition of philosophical discourse which was a lively part of American intellectual life in the early years of this century before the professionalization of both philosophy and religious studies.

Our themes are intentionally broad and inclusive in order to provide a home for a variety of views and projects. Our essays focus on the analysis of quite specific issues within the theme, however, and we encourage our authors to make an autobiographical connection with their analysis. We also emphasize the need for comparative studies. Religious and cultural pluralism is now the inescapable context for all work in the philosophy of religion.

The administration of Boston University and Deans Geoffrey Bannister, Michael Mendillo, and William Carroll of the Graduate School provide continuing budget support, which makes the Institute program possible. Bill Carroll, in his role as Director of the Humanities Foundation at the university, has helped arrange for a special grant to the Institute program from the Foundation. To all these friends and supporters we wish to express our continuing appreciation.

It is our hope that these volumes will provide a resource for critical reflection on fundamental human issues of meaning and value both within academic communities and beyond.

For Jürgen Moltmann
Protestantism's premier theologian, and one of the Institute's most unpretentious friends. His Institute lectures have brought theology out of the ivory tower, and his counsel has encouraged us to engage critical issues of contemporary life.

Acknowledgments

Many have helped in the preparation of this book, most particularly the authors of our lectures, who have been prompt in getting their essays to the editor and gracious in accepting editorial revisions. When these revisions are done the manuscripts go to Irena Makarushka for copy editing. Irena has not yet memorized the entire *Chicago Manual of Style*, but she is getting closer with each volume in the series. Barbara Darling Smith, my omnicompetent Assistant, takes responsibility for the final form of the manuscript before it is sent to our friends at Notre Dame, and with this volume she had additional help from Rosalind Carey. Barbara's combination of speed, efficiency, and good cheer are blessings I have come to count on.

Jim Langford is Director of the University of Notre Dame Press, and the author of a major scholarly study of Galileo and a major league study of the Chicago Cubs. He knows science from Galileo, and suffering from the Cubs, and these among other gifts help make him the publisher *par excellence*. I am increasingly grateful for his professional expertise and encouragement, but especially for his friendship. Ann Rice, as Executive Editor of the Press, continues to oversee the publication of these volumes. Working against the deadline of a publication party which must be scheduled well before the manuscript even gets to the printer, she has been unflappably relaxed, and both professional and personable at the same time. She is the person who transforms the manuscript into a book, and the Institute is full of admiration and gratitude for her and her staff.

Contributors

JOHN C. BENNETT, President, *Emeritus*, of Union Theological Seminary, New York, was educated at Williams College, Oxford University, and Union Theological Seminary. He taught at the Pacific School of Religion at Berkeley and was Professor of Social Ethics at Union Theological Seminary for most of his long career. He has been Alden Tuthill Lecturer at Chicago Theological Seminary, Alexander Graham Bell Lecturer at Boston University, and Birks Lecturer at McGill University. Honorary degrees have been conferred on him by Oberlin College, Columbia University, Harvard University, Fordham University, and the Jewish Theological Seminary. Among his many books are: *Christianity and Our World* (1936); *Christianity and Communism* (1948, 1960, 1970); *Foreign Policy in Christian Perspective* (1966), and *The Radical Imperative* (1975).

J. N. FINDLAY is University Professor and Borden Parker Bowne Professor of Philosophy at Boston University. He has studied at Transvaal University College, South Africa; and at Balliol College, Oxford. His doctorate is from the University of Graz, Austria, in 1933. Professor Findlay has written numerous books, including *Meinong's Theory of Objects* (1933); *Hegel: A Reexamination* (1958); *Values and Intentions* (1961); two series of Gifford Lectures entitled *The Discipline of the Cave* (1966) and *The Transcendence of the Cave* (1967); *Ascent to the Absolute* (1970); *Plato: The Written and Unwritten Doctrines* (1974); and *Kant and the Transcendental Object* (1981). At present he is writing a book on Wittgenstein.

CHARLES HARTSHORNE is a Fellow of the American Academy of Arts and Sciences. Educated at Harvard, he received his Ph.D. there in 1923. Honorary degrees have been conferred on him by Haverford College (1967), Emory University (1969), Episcopal Seminary of the Southwest (1977), and the University of Louvain, Belgium (1978). Professor Hartshorne is the author of over four hundred articles and his books include *The Philosophy and Psychology of Sensation* (1934); *The Divine Relativity* (1948); *Reality as Social Process* (1953); *The Logic of Perfection* (1962), for which he won the Lecomte du Noüy Award; and *Aquinas to Whitehead: Seven Centuries of Metaphysics of Religion* (1976). He is also the editor (with Paul Weiss) of *The Collected Papers of Charles S. Peirce.*

LYNN MARGULIS is Professor of Biology at Boston University. She received her A.B. from the University of Chicago in 1957, M.S. from the University of Wisconsin in 1960, and Ph.D. from the University of California at Berkeley in 1965. In 1983 she was elected to the National Academy of Sciences. Her many guest lectureships abroad include the Twenty-Fourth International Geological Conference in Montreal (1972); the Royal Society, London (1978); Universidad de Barcelona (1982); and the Marine Biological Association in Plymouth, England (1983). Author of over one hundred articles of both a technical and a nontechnical nature, reviews, booklets, and films, her books include *Origin of Eukaryotic Cells* (1970), *Symbiosis in Cell Evolution* (1981), *Early Life* (1982), and (with Dorion Sagan) *An Inquiry into the Evolutionary Origins of Sex* (in press). Her many awards include the Guggenheim Fellowship in 1979.

JÜRGEN MOLTMANN was educated at the University of Göttingen where he received his Ph.D. in 1955 and his Habilitation in 1957. He is also the recipient of several honorary degrees and the Elba Library Prize. Currently he is Professor of Systematic Theology at Tübingen University and the Woodruff Distinguished Visiting Professor at the Candler School

of Theology at Emory University. Among his many books are *Theology of Hope* (1967), *The Crucified God* (1974), *The Church in the Power of the Spirit* (1977), *The Future of Creation* (1979), and *The Trinity and the Kingdom* (1981). Professor Moltmann will present the Gifford Lectures at Edinburgh in 1984–85.

W. V. QUINE is a Fellow of the American Academy of Arts and Sciences and of the British Academy. Professor of Philosophy, *Emeritus*, at Harvard University, he was educated at Oberlin College and Harvard where he received his Ph.D. in 1932. Honorary degrees have been conferred on him by Oxford University, Cambridge University, Oberlin College, the University of Chicago, Université de Lille, and the University of Uppsala, among others. Professor Quine has written over one hundred articles and his books include *Mathematical Logic* (1940, 1951), *Methods of Logic* (1950, 1959, 1972, 1982), *The Ways of Paradox and Other Essays* (1969), and, most recently, *Theories and Things* (1981). In 1970 Professor Quine was the recipient of the Nicholas Murray Butler Gold Medal at Columbia University.

LEROY S. ROUNER is Professor of Philosophical Theology at Boston University, Director of the Institute for Philosophy and Religion, and general editor of Boston University Studies in Philosophy and Religion. He graduated from Harvard College (A.B., 1953), Union Theological Seminary (B.D., *summa cum laude*, 1958), and Columbia University (Ph.D., 1961). He was Assistant Professor of Philosophy and Theology at the United Theological College, Bangalore, India, from 1961 to 1966. He is editor of the Hocking Festschrift, *Philosophy, Religion, and the Coming World Civilization* (1969), and (with John Howie) of *The Wisdom of William Ernest Hocking* (1978), as well as author of *Within Human Experience: The Philosophy of William Ernest Hocking* (1969). A member of Phi Beta Kappa, he has published a number of papers on philosophy of religion and theology in scholarly journals.

CARL A. P. RUCK is Professor of Classical Studies at Boston University. He received his A.B. from Yale University, M.A. from the University of Michigan, and Ph.D. from Harvard University. Among his many articles, reviews, and books are: (with W. H. Matheson) *Pindar: Selected Odes* (1968); *Ancient Greek: A New Approach* (1968, 1979); and (with R. Gordon Wasson and Albert Hofmann) *The Road to Eleusis: Unveiling the Secret of the Mysteries* (1978), which appears in translation in French, Spanish, and Italian. At present he is working on *Latin: A New Approach.* Professor Ruck has been the recipient of the Fulbright Fellowship and the Woodrow Wilson Fellowship.

DORION SAGAN received his B.A. from the University of Massachusetts, Amherst, in 1981. He has studied in summer programs at Trinity College, Oxford; and at Harvard University. He has worked as an illustrator for *The Sciences, The Expanding Microcosm: Four Billion Years of Evolution* (in press), and *Coevolution.* He has collaborated with his mother, Lynn Margulis, on several projects. Among the books he has edited and indexed are: *Five Kingdoms* by Lynn Margulis and Karlene V. Schwartz (1982), *Early Life* by Lynn Margulis (1982), and *An Inquiry into the Evolutionary Origins of Sex* (in press). Aside from his interest in science, Mr. Sagan is also a professional magician.

HUSTON SMITH was born in Soochow, China, and took his doctorate at the University of Chicago in 1945. He was Thomas J. Watson Professor of Religion and Distinguished Adjunct Professor of Philosophy at Syracuse University from 1973 to 1983. His books include *The Religions of Man* (1958), *Forgotten Truth: The Primordial Tradition* (1976), and *Beyond the Post-Modern Mind* (1982). Author of over forty articles, he has also produced three film series on world religions for National Educational Television. Professor Smith has been the recipient of many honorary degrees and awards including the E. Harris Harbison Teachers Award (1964) and the Bronze

Medal at the New York International Film and Television Festival (1968).

ROBERT A. F. THURMAN is the author of *The Holy Teaching of Vimalakīrti* (1976), *The Life and Teachings of Tsong Khapa* (1982), *Speech of Gold: Tsong Khapa's Central Way Critical Philosophy* (1984), and *The Buddhism of Tibet: The Vajra and the Lotus* (in press), as well as numerous articles and essays in Buddhist studies. He has also translated a significant number of Buddhist texts. Having studied at Namgyal College in India, he was ordained as *bhikṣu* in 1965, and received his doctorate in Buddhology from Harvard in 1972. Recipient of many awards, Professor Thurman was Senior Fellow at the American Institute for Indian Studies in 1979–80 and is now teaching at Amherst College.

STEPHEN TOULMIN is the author of numerous books including *Reason and Ethics* (1949); *Philosophy of Science* (1953); *Foresight and Understanding* (1961); (with June Goodfield) *The Discovery of Time* (1965); (with Allen Janik) *Wittgenstein's Vienna* (1973); and (with Richard Rieke and Allen Janik) *Introduction to Reasoning* (1979). Born and educated in England, he received his Ph.D. from Cambridge University in 1948. Currently Professor of Social Thought and Philosophy at the University of Chicago, Professor Toulmin has also taught at Oxford University; Leeds University; Brandeis University; Michigan State University; and Crown College, University of California at Santa Cruz. His many guest lectureships and awards include the Guggenheim Fellowship which he received in 1977.

TU WEI-MING is Professor of Chinese History and Philosophy at Harvard University and was previously Professor of History at the University of California at Berkeley. Born in Kunming, China, he was educated at Tunghai University and Harvard University where he received his Ph.D. in 1968. His

fields of interest include Confucianism, Chinese intellectual history, and religious philosophies of Asia. Among his publications are *Neo-Confucian Thought in Action* (1976), *Centrality and Commonality: An Essay on the Chung-yung* (1976), and *Humanity and Self-Cultivation: Essays in Confucian Thought* (1980). Currently he is working on Chu Hsi and Neo-Confucian humanism.

Introduction

LEROY S. ROUNER

JUDAISM, CHRISTIANITY, AND ISLAM — the world religions of the West — tend to regard nature as the stage for God's historical drama. For Western religion, history is therefore the fundamental reality for human experience. However, the dominant schools of modern Western philosophy — our rationalisms, empiricisms, realisms, and naturalisms — tend to regard nature as the fundamental reality of our experience. For our scientific philosophies, therefore, history is a natural phenomenon. This contrast between scientific and religious views of nature has been softened in recent years as both have become less dogmatic. Scientific thinkers are now more modest in their claims to know the causes of the cosmos. Religious thinkers, for their part, recognize that nature has been neglected or denigrated in much religious reflection.

The decline of dogmatism led to a new interest in integrating the personal and spiritual values of historicism with the physical and operational values of naturalism. That new common interest is the dominant theme in the essays which follow. Since the great cultures of the East never made the modern West's radical distinction between mind and matter, history and nature, their holism has a long tradition, as Tu Wei-Ming shows in his essay on China's "continuity of being" in Part II. Most of our authors are Western, however, and their essays are often original adventures in the philosophy of nature. Stephen Toulmin, for example, makes a case for the authority of religious insight in understanding the cosmos; Huston Smith argues that Darwinism is dying; Lynn Margulis makes a microbiologist's case for the biosphere as a life force responding to its internal life needs; Jürgen Moltmann makes a

1

theological case for what might be called a Christian naturalism; and so forth.

We begin, however, with a dissenter from this consensus. When I first invited Willard Quine he demurred, since he has no interest in religion and felt himself out of place in this series. I persuaded him that any serious book on the philosophy of nature ought to include a defense of the natural realism which has so influenced modern Western culture. So he gives it in his paper on the "ins and outs of existence," which is a synopsis of his tightly logical realistic empiricism. For Quine philosophy is part of natural science. He accepts the external world as we know it. What you see is what you get. What he wants to examine is the relation between the input of sense data through the triggering of our nerve endings and our subsequent claims to knowledge of the whole. These interpretations, our output, he calls our "descriptions of faraway things and theories of the inner workings of nature." How do we come to these theories, and what is their relation to the objects they theorize about? Surely the right strategy, Quine tells us, is to analyze the descriptive use of language. He begins with expressions learned by direct association with nonverbal stimulations, as when a child says "Milk" in order to get milk, or to recognize milk. These "observation sentences," as he calls them, are only occasional. Science, on the other hand, is about regular occurrence, or what Quine calls "standing sentences." The connection comes in observation categoricals in which one finds a *whenever* or *wherever* construction, as in "Where there's smoke there's fire." Here is the beginning of rudimentary science. Scientific theory is the distinction between true and false observation categoricals. The mid-section of Quine's paper is a careful explication of this process. But what of the eventual theory? All evidence stems from sensory stimulation and enters language through observation sentences, Quine reminds us, so that whether one is interpreting sticks and stones or quarks, numbers, and classes, what matters is structure rather than ontology. We discover the truth about nature by looking to the stimulatory input and the structure of scientific theory. Even if presented with a different set of objects for interpretation, the network of logical implications connecting theory with observation will remain undisturbed.

The bare prose and logical intensity of Quine's argument con-

trasts with Stephen Toulmin's robust wit in fashioning a case for religious interpretations of nature. We have all thought of cosmology as a branch of physics, but Toulmin argues that the idea of the world as an ordered whole originally went well beyond the bounds of physical astronomy and viewed nature as making sense to the human mind, and intrinsically hospitable to human life and the human heart. This sense of human beings linked in harmony with the scheme of natural things is medieval as well as ancient, but it begins to break down by the time of John Donne's famous lament (1610) that the cosmic order "is all in peeces, all cohaerance gone." The new science was objectively detached from one's object of study, and inherently value-neutral, as with Laplace's Omniscient Calculator. The originating geniuses of the new method knew that its scope was limited, but as its successes accumulated it became virtually universal, whereas it had originally been fashioned to deal only with a subclass of scientific inquiries during a particular phase of history.

Toulmin's concern is with the idea that the universe is a fit home for humanity, and he finds a revived interest in older cosmological issues in postmodern fields like ecology and psychiatry. In popular philosophy Toulmin finds two views interacting; a green philosophy, espoused by ecologists; and a white philosophy, espoused by psychiatry. The white philosophy is concerned with fulfillment of the human potential and teaches the ethical doctrines of self-command and self-detachment. Practical wisdom is to learn Epicurus' discipline of staying cool and not letting things get to you. The green philosophy, on the other hand, is Stoic, rooted in ecological science, achieving contentment through a life lived with the grain of nature. These two positions were antagonists in the ancient world but now come together. They revive the older natural religion in the intense commitment of their adherents. The piety of the environmentalists and the devotion of humanistic psychologists are evidence, for Toulmin, that a new religiously oriented view of the cosmos as a human home may be in the making.

Willard Quine is a scientific logician; Stephen Toulmin's field is the history and philosophy of science. Huston Smith is principally a philosopher of religion, but his interest in science was sharpened during his years teaching philosophy at the Massachusetts Institute of Technology. Smith is experimental; and in the

fearless tradition of William James, who often found himself in odd
philosophic company, Smith regularly finds himself learning from
those with irregular views. In his paper on "Two Evolutions" he
contrasts the view backed by modern science, that the human self
can be understood naturalistically as an organism in an environment, with the Judeo-Christian view that humankind is created
in God's image with an immortal soul, occupying a place in nature between the beasts and the angels. He finds these two views
incompatible but notes that most of us accept parts of both, and
he sets out to fashion some resolution. En route, he challenges
Darwinism, and finds himself in the uncomfortable company of
the Creationists. That they have muddied the waters with simplistic theology and sometimes bogus science he has no doubt. He admits that in some ways they have his respect, because they have
sensed that Darwinism is not compatible with what Toulmin called
a universe "intrinsically hospitable to human life and the human
heart," but Smith is no Creationist. His proposal is much broader.
His Great Origins thesis argues simply that humankind has derived
from that which exceeds us. Since such metaphysical propositions
do not admit of proof, he takes the negative path of showing that
Darwinism does not serve our need for feeling at home in the universe, and that such felt need is a scientifically legitimate way of
approaching the metaphysical issue. Like Toulmin he is concerned
to overcome the self/world divide of modern Western thought, and
he points out that the Great Origins thesis, in answering the question about the origins of humankind, must include the answer to
the origins of everything else. "Reality and the life that is set within
it are charged with meaning throughout by virtue of being, at
heart, whole."

   This first section concludes with a landmark essay by Lynn
Margulis and her son, Dorion Sagan, detailing Margulis's work on
the Gaia hypothesis. Margulis is a microbiologist who has supported
the theory first proposed by the British atmospheric chemist James
Lovelock. Margulis and Sagan note that the world does not work
the way science expects it to. For example, astronomers generally
agree that the sun's output of energy has increased during the past
4 billion years, and they infer from this that the mean temperature of the Earth's surface ought to have risen correspondingly. The
Earth's fossil record shows, however, that the Earth's temperature

has remained relatively stable. The Gaia hypothesis in its most general form therefore states that the temperature and composition of the Earth's atmosphere are actively regulated by the sum of life on the planet — the biota.

Toulmin and Smith have issued philosophers' calls for a view of humankind integrated with nature. Margulis now provides such a view. It is noteworthy that, like Quine, she has no interest in traditional religion, and has explored the philosophical implications of the Gaia hypothesis only after some urging. Her basic interest in the hypothesis is purely scientific, but for a scientist to theorize that the Earth in some sense feels and responds marks a new age of postmodern scientific theory. However, it continues the Copernican and Darwinian attack on anthropocentrism. Margulis and Sagan end their essay with the comment that "we should rejoice in the new truths of our essential belonging, our relative unimportance, and our complete dependence upon a biosphere which has always had a life entirely its own."

Our second group of essays turn back in historical time to premodern traditions and world views which already integrated humankind with nature. Whether these traditions are recoverable without first passing them through the acids of modernity is a question on which there will be shades of varied opinion. It is clear, however, that any new integration of humankind with the natural world must take account of these traditional views. We begin this section with Carl Ruck's original and iconoclastic interpretation of classical Greek religion. Ruck is a classicist specializing in linguistics and etymology. Through his work on mystery religions, however, he has developed an interest in sacred plants and their vision-inducing role in shamanism. He notes that ancient religious literature such as the Hindu *Ṛg Veda* regularly refers to the use of drugs in inducing religious experience. His attention in this paper, however, focuses on the Eleusinian Mysteries. All scholarship is detective work to an extent, but Ruck's analysis is particularly intriguing since it deals with an event surrounded by extraordinarily well-guarded secrecy. Ruck uses this contrast between the wild and the cultivated as a way of assessing the integration of Indo-European culture with that of pre-Hellenic Mediterranean peoples in making up the culture of classical Greece. His point is that the Greeks, unlike their later admirers, never ignored the primitive *persona* that

lurks in nature behind the sublime cultured development of classical Greek philosophy and religion.

Robert Thurman's essay on Buddhist views of nature is a thematic examination of ways in which Buddhist culture has understood nature as a symbol of reality. Thurman notes that the teaching concerning suffering is too often mistaken for the whole of the Buddhist attitude toward nature. He argues, on the contrary, that the luminous contemplation of nature is at the very heart of the Buddhist experience, and he quotes numerous passages from Buddhist scripture in which the teaching of the Buddha can appropriately be described as a vision of ecological splendor. Having countered the view that Buddhism is somehow anti-nature, Thurman then sets forth a carefully compiled assessment of Buddhist nature affirmation interacting with elements of nature rejection. Thurman's theme is that Buddhism is a broad middle way on many levels, not least the relation of humankind to the natural environment. The ideal is an interpenetration of culture and nature, body and mind, absolute and relative. Unlike Margulis and Sagan, however, Thurman's concern for nature does not celebrate the decline of anthropocentrism. In fact, "the bottom line of all Buddhist views of nature" is the celebration of human life as the highest development of nature. Buddhist culture considers human life so precious that they enshrine nonviolence as the highest virtue.

Tu Wei-Ming focuses on a central theme of Chinese culture, the belief in the continuity of being. The Chinese are apparently unique in having no creation myth. Chinese cosmogony is that of an organismic process which is self-generating and in which all parts are interactive participants. Here, then, is another response to Toulmin and Smith's call for an integrated universe. However, the prospect of an uncreated world raises a new question. Precisely what kind of natural/human integration are we looking for? We began with no such views available, and now we discover that we must choose among several, or integrate them in some way. Tu clarifies the issue by pointing out that what China rejects is the view that creation is the work of an external intelligence and will radically different from human thinking and willing. Since the universe is larger than we, Smith's Great Origins criterion that we come from that which exceeds us seems to be met; and surely Margulis and Sagan would find much in common with Tu. But Smith

talks much of creation, and seems to imply some sort of transcendent creator. What is meant by Smith's verb *to exceed*? Transcendence of any religiously recognizable sort seems excluded from Margulis's Gaia. And here she and Tu are at least speaking a different language. Gaia is not a metaphysical theory; it is a scientific hypothesis. And Tu is specifically concerned with an epistemological model which is not empirical and scientific, but rather "a metaphorical mode of knowing, an epistemological attempt to address the multidimensional nature of reality by comparison, allusion, and suggestion."

Tu presents the Chinese view of nature as *ch'i*, which he translates as "vital force," creating an all-enfolding harmony. Nature is therefore continuous, holistic, and dynamic. Its enduring pattern is union rather than disunion, integration rather than disintegration, and synthesis rather than separation. Human life is part of the continuous flow of this cosmic process. Nothing is totally fixed, and Chinese painters show mountains flowing like rivers. The human goal is to form one body with the universe, and to participate in the dynamic energy of *ch'i*.

Our third group of essays is more specifically concerned with questions of human nature and traditional religious values. Jürgen Moltmann heads this section on "Human Nature in the Natural World" with an essay on "The Alienation and Liberation of Nature." He begins with Karl Marx's view of the alienation of nature and then examines his friend Ernst Bloch's attempt to tie Marx's dialectical materialism to Schelling's nature philosophy through the idea of the naturalization of humanity. For Bloch nature is a subject with its own history, independent of the history of humans. Humanity is the "highest bloom" of nature for Bloch, but nature remains subject and does not become the object of the human subject. Moltmann is a Reformed theologian much influenced by Karl Barth. Like Barth, his convictions concerning the Lordship of Jesus Christ are givens upon which his entire work rests; but also like Barth, he is well schooled and much involved in the critical cultural issues of the day. Moltmann uses Marx and Bloch as preparation for his own reflection on the human concern for nature both as a place in which to work and a place in which to be at home.

For Moltmann, as for our other authors, the critical question

is nature as a place to be at home. He notes that the natural environment contributes to the sense of relaxation, balance, acceptance, and recognition which are all part of being at home. Our present centralized industrialization has done much to destroy the livability of our natural home. He agrees with Bloch that humanity is part of nature. "The nature-being of humanity is the original given; nature-domination and nature-possession are secondary facts. They remain dependent upon the original given because they build upon it and live from it."

John Findlay is also concerned to redress the values of the Mind/Matter split in modern Western philosophy whereby Mind was highly valued and Matter accorded a rather low estate. He begins with a brief sketch of classical views, and comes away keenly disappointed. Hellenic thought characterizes Matter as having no character at all; "an inert substrate, a mere something or other, which owes all its positive attributes to the imposition on it of organizing pattern or Form." Medieval thought is no better. Findlay mutters through clenched philosophic teeth that "these miserable views of materiality persisted" even in the High Middle Ages. In Kant, he notes, "there is some mercy shown toward Matter," but Fichte undoes this good work. With Hegel "Matter is treated with a little more ceremony," and this gives Findlay an opportunity to sketch his own view.

The higher life of the Spirit, which is admittedly Findlay's principal concern, nevertheless needs the body. He hazards the view that there is something wonderful and admirable about the resistant simplicity of things. He rejoices in the fact that "they are simply and solidly what they are. . . . Carbon, hydrogen, and oxygen join or separate in countless ways consistent with their sort where there are fitting confrontations between them. They do not dither or consider the effect of their interactions, nor wonder whether they will be doing quite the right thing. It is the invariance of Matter which makes it admirable." Findlay concludes with reflections on the religious significance of Matter. While the center of things is spiritual, it can often best be described in material terms — the Rock of Ages and the burning bush. And the virtue of invariance in material things must always humble us dissembling humans.

Charles Hartshorne takes up the specific challenge which science has regularly posed to religion, and that is irrelevance. As a

focus for this challenge, Hartshorne gives an extended analysis of Robert Nozick's *Philosophical Explanations*. Nozick argued that life can have meaning without a religious notion of God. Hartshorne takes the scientific challenge of irrelevance seriously. God cannot be optional equipment for human life. Either God is necessary for meaning in life, or God is entirely unnecessary for us all. Nozick raised the question of death, arguing that an endless immortality for humanity would not solve the problem of meaning. Hartshorne agrees but points out that the problem of transience is deeper than death; it is forgetfulness. Only God can assimilate an infinitely prolonged experience without monotony. Our lives can have meaning only if they exist whole. Neither we nor anyone else can remember our lives in anything like their whole detail, so our lived lives are always fragmentary as well as fallible. "We look to the divine life as adequately, infallibly treasuring forevermore all that happens, all achieved values, and as thus being in itself the inclusive good by which all lesser goods are given their due."

Hartshorne concludes by presenting a summary of his theistic arguments. The meaning of life is love in a generalized sense. God loves us better than we can love ourselves, and is the inclusive object of love. Without this sustaining power of love, through which the substance of our lives gains immortality, there can be no meaning to life at all.

We conclude with John Bennett's reflections on human nature and the human condition in the period since the rise of liberal progressivism. Bennett is an experienced representative of American Protestantism, a close colleague of Reinhold Niebuhr on the faculty of Union Theological Seminary in New York. He writes appreciatively of Niebuhr's influence both in fulfilling many goals of liberalism and in criticizing many others. Bennett's concern for nature is that we may create an atomic holocaust which could destroy humanity. For those who found Jonathan Schell's book *The Fate of the Earth* extreme, he quotes Jerome Wiesner of the Massachusetts Institute of Technology, saying that the separate effects of nuclear war noted by Schell amounted to a degree of destructiveness not appreciated even by the experts. Lynn Margulis would counter that the microbes will probably survive even an atomic holocaust, and that Gaia would therefore continue. But Bennett has struggled through the earlier liberal assessment of human good-

ness to a profound sense of human sin. Given the immensity of the period of cosmic and biological preparation for human life, "for our human history to be cut short now would be a tragic failure beyond words to express."

Bennett highlights a critical issue for many of our authors in their search for an integration of humanity with the natural world. Lynn Margulis and Dorion Sagan reject anthropomorphism. Many of our other authors set that issue aside in trying to overcome the humanity/nature division. Bennett, however, implies that the death of humanity is a natural disaster which calls into question the meaning of the natural process itself. Whether created or uncreated, is the development of humankind really higher than the beasts, as Huston Smith put it? To have been split off from nature is to separate humankind from what Moltmann and others poignantly refer to as home. Bennett's jarring question is simply, If humankind is gone, what would nature mean?

Natural Science and the Philosophy of Nature

1

Sticks and Stones; or, the Ins and Outs of Existence

W. V. QUINE

THE BRAIN IS OFTEN compared to a computer. Philosophers disagree on how far the analogy can be carried, but a limited analogy is obvious and useful. It is useful to talk of cognition in terms of input and output.

We are organisms in the physical world, and are bombarded with waves and particles. This is input. In the fullness of time we emit descriptions of faraway things and theories of the inner workings of nature. This is output. We, in between, are the information processor, the black box.

Our way of processing current input is influenced by earlier input, by theories that we have devised in consequence of earlier input, and by other people's testimony. That testimony likewise reached us in sound waves, or in rays from pages, and our ability to understand it was acquired through earlier instruction that consisted again in our reacting to sound waves and other sensory input. In short, our objective information about the world passes through our sensory receptors and is transmuted into science according to our subjective way of processing the information—a complex way, in which the processing of later input depends on intermediate effects of processing earlier input.

That our objective information about the world comes solely through the sensory receptors was the insight of the old empiricists, except that they talked of sense data, not nerve endings. Talk of nerve endings would have trapped them in a vicious circle, for they were trying to justify our talk of nerve endings and other physi-

cal objects. I am not. I am accepting the external world as we know it, and then proceeding to examine the relation of one part — the triggering of our nerve endings — to our knowledge of the whole.

The principle of empiricism — *nihil in mente quod non prius in sensu* — is itself properly seen as a discovery of natural science. Science affirms the slenderness of its own data, finding any channel of information other than the sensory to be physically inexplicable. There is no plausible physical mechanism for telepathy, much less for clairvoyance. Clairvoyance would contravene basic physical principles of time and causality.

Natural science is fallible, I grant, and subject to revision. The ban against action at a distance gave way under Newton's theory of gravitation, and the absoluteness of time and the law of conservation of mass gave way under Einstein. But the ban against nonsensory channels of information is where science now stands and has stood for a long time. If the principle of empiricism has been the bulwark of science, science is equally the bulwark of empiricism.

The traditional epistemological problem of our knowledge of the external world emerges now, or something like it, as a problem within natural science. It becomes the question how we manage to project our elaborate and powerful theory of the world on the strength of this slender input in the way of triggering of nerve endings. How much is our subjective contribution? How much is revisable, and how far, without violating the data? Science raises the problem by the limitations upon data that science itself imposes, and we can pursue the question by means of science, within the limits that science imposes. Cartesian doubt is not involved. Our question concerns relations between events in the external world: between input, the impacts on our nerve endings, and output, our discourse about the world.

For traditional epistemology the empirical content of science consisted of sense data. They give way now to the triggering of nerve endings. We were aware of our sense data, according to the old epistemology, and we somehow reasoned from them to the external world. We are not aware of the triggering; it is rather what makes us aware of our surroundings.

The relation of stimulatory input to scientific output mediates all the empirical content of science, and all the evidence there

can ever be for scientific pronouncements. But it is a bafflingly complex relation, and no mere matter of the direct conditioning of scientific sentences to stimuli. How are we to untangle it? Certainly the right strategy is investigation of how the descriptive use of language is learned and progressively modified; for language acquires its empirical meaning only as we acquire the language.

We learn some expressions derivatively through other expressions, but there has to be a beginning. Some expressions are learned by direct association with nonverbal stimulations. The child is conditioned to utter them in response to those stimulations, or to utter them as a means of inducing those stimulations — he may say "Milk" to get milk. At an early stage children learn to assent and dissent — to say "Yes" and "No." They learn to assent to a queried expression when stimulated in a way that would have inclined them to volunteer the expression themselves, and to dissent when stimulated in a way that would have inhibited such an utterance. When children have learned assent and dissent, they can acquire new expressions by leaps and bounds.

What expressions can be learned by direct association with nonverbal stimulations? "Milk" was our example. Others are "It's raining," "Dog," "Fido," "Red." They are best thought of to begin with not as terms but as sentences, even when they are single words; for terms connote reference to objects, and that belongs to a more sophisticated stage of language, to be considered later. These early expressions are best thought of holophrastically, moreover, as indissoluble little sentences even when they contain several words. Each is simply an expression learned intact by association with a stimulation and, derivatively, with similar stimulations.

The similarity involved here is subjective similarity. It is central to the subject's programming. It is the avenue of so-called stimulus generalization, and hence of habit formation. The similarity of two stimulations for a given subject is measured by the likelihood of his responding to the one in the way in which he has been conditioned to respond to the other. Similarity, so defined, will change as the subject continues to learn things, but there have to be some unlearned standards of similarity to begin with, if learning is to get started. They are somehow in the genes.

Sentences that can be learned thus are what I call *observation sentences*. They do not *need* to be learned in that way. One

person may acquire a given observation sentence in that way and another person may acquire it through other sentences by explanation or context. A sentence still counts as observational for a subject if nonverbal stimulations that are subjectively very similar always agree with each other in prompting one's assent to the sentence, or in prompting one's dissent, or in prompting neither. The point is that the present stimulation can be depended on to settle the verdict independently of what may have been going on in the subject's mind or in the vicinity at the time. The subject could have acquired these habits by associating the sentence directly with a nonverbal stimulation, whether he happens to have done so or not.

Observation sentences are not sentences about observations, nor sense data, nor stimulations, nor nerve endings. I gave examples: "Milk," "It's raining," "Dog." It is inappropriate initially to regard them as about anything. Retrospectively we construe them as about milk, rain, dogs, anything.

I have explained that an observation sentence for an individual is one on which his verdict is uniform under subjectively similar nonverbal stimulation. Granted now that verbal behavior conforms to that of the community in which it is learned, and granted further a substantial intersubjective conformity of similar standards, it follows that witnesses will generally agree in their verdicts on observation sentences. Thus it is that observation sentences serve in arbitrating scientific disagreements.

Our concern was with the relation of input, the stimulation, to output, scientific discourse. We have now considered the relation of stimulation to observation sentences. We have still to deal with the logical connections between observation sentences and scientific theory. Now observation sentences are occasion sentences, whereas science is couched in standing sentences. What this means is that an observation sentence may be true on one occasion and false on another; "It's raining" is true at some times and places and false at others. Scientific pronouncements, on the other hand, purport to be true once for all. How can one forge a connection?

A plausible first step from occasion sentences to standing sentences is the *whenever* or *wherever* construction: "When it rains it pours"; "Where there's smoke there's fire"; "When it thunders there is lightning." It joins observation sentences in pairs to form stand-

ing sentences which I call *observation categoricals*. They express conditional expectation. Children master the component observation sentences and at length come to appreciate that on assenting to the first they are regularly prepared to assent to the second.

In the observation categorical we already encounter rudimentary science, at an extremely empirical level. Prediction, the test of natural science, already figures here. Children may, in the case of smoke and fire, be caught short; they may quite properly assent to the query "Smoke?" and then find themselves constrained to dissent from the query "Fire?", seeing no fire. They thereupon learn, we hope, to dissent from the observation categorical "Where there's smoke there's fire." It has been refuted. The conditioning has been extinguished. Find yourself so stimulated as to be prompted to assent to the first component of an observation categorical and to dissent from the second, and you have refuted the categorical.

Even here, where science is in the bud, there is no talk of past or future, nor is there any call to impute references to objects of any sort. The key idiom that clinches reference to objects is still in the offing.

We have now connected observation sentences with some standing sentences, namely, the observation categoricals that contain them. It remains to relate the observation categoricals to more serious science. I suggest that scientific theory is related to observation categoricals by implying some of them and the negations of others. This is surely an oversimplified schema, but it provides the right sort of connection. When a theory is said to be refuted by a failed prediction, what has happened is that an observation categorical implied by the theory has been refuted. Refutation of an observation categorical consists, we saw, in our being so stimulated as to assent to its first part and to dissent from its second part.

The observation categorical represents a prediction paired with its initial condition, but with no lapse of time between them. This is as it should be. If there is a lapse of time, what has to be set over against the predicted observation is not the remote initial condition, but the present observable record or other evidence that the condition had been met; and the relation of this evidence to the initial condition is the business of the scientific theory that is being tested. Time and talk of past events belong to the web of scientific theory along with forces, electrons, numbers, and the rest.

When I represent the empirical content of a theory as comprising the implied observation categoricals and negations of observation categoricals, I leave two loose ends conspicuously dangling: implication and negation. How do we learn these?

Let us begin with negation. I represented the child as somehow learning at an early stage how to assent to or dissent from a queried sentence. Thereupon negation is an easy second-order acquisition. The child comes to appreciate that people are prepared to assent to the negation of a sentence when and only when they are prepared to dissent from the sentence itself, and to dissent from the one when and only when prepared to assent to the other.

The learning of the *and* of logical conjunction can be accounted for similarly. Children learn to assent to the conjunction"*p* and *q*" in all and only those circumstances in which they are prepared to assent to "*p*" and also to "*q*," and they learn to dissent from "*p* and *q*" in all those circumstances, at least, in which they are prepared to dissent from "*p*" or to dissent from "*q*." This affords them some cases of implication. They have learned that a conjunction implies each of its clauses and that the negation of each clause implies the negation of the conjunction.

The learning of the *or* of alternation is parallel to that of *and*. The child learns that the alternation is implied by each of its clauses and that the negation of the alternation implies the negation of each clause.

Let us turn now to objective reference. Some expressions are said to name objects, one apiece. Some expressions, general terms, are said to denote many objects apiece. Some expressions are said to purport to name or denote, but to fail; thus "Pegasus" and "unicorn." Some expressions, such as prepositions, conjunctions, and articles, are said not even to purport to name or denote.

Questions abound. Does our use of the term "dog" commit us to admitting to our universe an object which this term names, perhaps the property of being a dog or perhaps the class of dogs, or may we merely regard the term as denoting each dog? Does our use of the term "sake"—"for my sake," "for God's sake"— commit us to recognizing various objects for the term to denote, various sakes, and what would they be like?

One soon appreciates that merely looking to one's terms is not the way to settle one's ontology: what objects one wants or needs

to admit. Looking to the words "everything" and "something" is more to the point. If we affirm a sentence governed by "something," there had better be an object in our universe that meets the condition that the sentence imposes. If we affirm a sentence governed by "everything," there had better not be among the objects of our universe any that violate the condition that the sentence imposes.

In the notation of modern logic the work of "everything" and "something" is accomplished in familiar fashion by means of bound variables and quantifiers: "$\forall x$" and "$\exists x$" mean "everything x is such that" and "something x is such that." The objects that we reckon to our universe, then, are the objects that we admit as values of the variables.

Matters of reference stand forth vividly, we see, in the notation of bound variables. Not so in ordinary language, for those matters are not an everyday concern. However, the illumination gained from the logical notation can be reflected back into ordinary language, revealing a prototype of the bound variable. It is the relative pronoun, and any auxiliary pronouns that refer back to the relative pronoun.

So let us look into relative clauses. Here, to begin with, is a sentence about someone named Alex:

(1) I visited Alex at his country home.

We can think of it as "Fa," where a is Alex. But what is F? Now the business of the relative clause is abstraction of the F:

(2) (one) whom I visited at his country home.

If we predicate (2) of Alex, thus: Alex is one whom I visited at his country home, we recover (1).

Here is a more awkward example:

(3) If I see Bobby, I'll phone his mother.

What does this say Bobby is?

(4) one whom, if I see, I'll phone his mother.

Awkward cases involve us in contortions. Mathematicians, who spend their days among awkward cases, cut the Gordian knot by switching to the "such that" idiom:

(5) one such that, if I see him, I'll phone his mother.

For (2) we get:

(6) one such that I visited him at his country home.

The grammar thus becomes simple: we just prefix "one such that" to the original sentence, (1) or (3), and put a pronoun in place of the name, "Alex" or "Bobby," from which we are abstracting.

But what about bound variables? They come next. Try this example:

(7) I bought Fido from one who found him.

This says that Fido is

(8) one such that I bought him from one who found him.

Putting the part "one who found him" likewise into the "such that" idiom, we get:

(9) one such that I bought him from one such that he found him.

Yes, but who found whom? The latter the former. The mathematician handles the matter of former and latter, or more complex cases such as first, second, and third, by using distinctive letters instead of the pronouns. (9) becomes:

(10) x such that I bought x from y such that y found x.

So (5) and (6) become:

(5) x such that if I see x I'll phone x's mother.
(6) x such that I visited x at x's country home.

Here, logically if not historically, is the root of the bound variable in all its uses. Its work is combinatorial. It accomplishes what would otherwise be accomplished by focusing on some singular term of particular interest in a sentence, nailing it with a "whom," and contorting the rest of the sentence to give the "whom" initial position, incidentally relabeling cross-references to avoid ambiguity. Quantification is not logically at the root of the bound variable; it is independent. In saying that there are wombats, $\exists F$, or that all human beings are mortal, $\forall(F \rightarrow G)$, there is no call for

bound variables. The familiar quantification, with its bound variable, amounts simply to "∃" or "∀" followed by a general term that happens to be an "x such that" clause.

I pointed out some cases of implication, at the level of conjunction and alternation. Now that the full power of quantification is at hand in one form or another, there is the whole predicate calculus to draw upon. Simple implications would be learned, here as before, in the process of learning to use the logical words. More complex implications would be learned by chain reasoning from the simple ones.

My speculations on language learning have brought us to the point where the learner can be said to be referring to objects. To posit an object, to recognize it as existing, is to admit it as a value of bound variables — or, where ordinary language is concerned, to admit it as the reference of a relative pronoun. When we abstract the relative clause (2) from the sentence (1), we thereby recognize Alex as an element of our ontology.

I lately asked whether the term "dog," which denotes each separate dog, should in addition be taken to name a single abstract object, the property of being a dog or perhaps the class of dogs. We now see that it is a question whether to admit the term in the position of a bound variable, as warranting inference by existential generalization — for example,

Dog is a species, $\therefore \exists x(x$ is a species$)$.

The step is indeed commonly made; properties or classes are posited. It comes of a confusion, perhaps, between general and singular terms, but this does not condemn it. Science has profited from happy accidents.

If we look merely to the relative clauses of every day, or if we translate everyday discourse as literally as we can into quantifier notation, we are apt to find lavish positing of gratuitous and dubious entities. This is all very well; ontology is not the everyday game. Scientists and philosophers are interested in a more explicit accounting of what there may be said to be, and they put a premium also on economy. They put their theories over into ontologically clearer form, perhaps using bound variables, and in such a way as not to admit any values of variables without reason.

At that point, what about classes and properties? Both are

abstract objects, and there is only this difference between them: classes are identical when they have the same members, whereas properties are sometimes distinguished even when they are properties of all the same things. What conditions do suffice for identity of properties is never made clear. The services that properties offer are offered equally by classes, so in a considered scientific ontology we do well to take the classes and let the properties go, even though the everyday idiom leans decidedly to properties.

Quantification over classes is a powerful and versatile tool. A familiar illustration of its utility is Gottlob Frege's definition of ancestor in terms of parent. My ancestors are the members shared by all classes that contain me and contain also all parents of their own members.

A more conspicuous case where abstract objects figure as values of bound variables is the case of numbers. Quantitative laws are central to serious science, for they embody what John Stuart Mill called the method of concomitant variation, which is far and away the most powerful method of induction.

The glories of number, in the service of science, are further to the glory of classes; for it is known that numbers of all kinds — integers, ratios, reals, imaginaries — can be reconstructed as classes within set theory, where the ontology comprises just individuals of some sort, and classes of them, and classes of those classes, and so on up. Other objects of classical mathematics — functions, relations — can be reconstructed there as well. This hierarchy of classes, with concrete individuals of appropriate sorts at the bottom, evidently suffices for all of science. It is all there need be said to be. The rub is at the bottom: the individuals. The present point is just that no abstract objects need be posited except the hierarchy of classes rising from the chosen domain of individuals.

What then of that domain? Bodies, animate and inanimate, abound as values of variables as a matter of course. Unobservable individuals come to be posited too when it is found that our system of statements about the world can thereby be tightened and simplified without detriment to its empirical content, that is, the observation categoricals that the theory implies.

I see no difference in kind between these artful posits and the common sense posits of sticks and stones, the macroscopic ontology that stems, one would say, from the dawn of humankind. Many

philosophers view the two sorts of objects as fundamentally un-like, these being observed and those being invented or conjectured. I have been urging rather that observation sentences, unformed in respect of reference to objects of any sort, are the best we can muster in the way of direct linguistic response to sensory stimulation. The positing of objects of any sort, from sticks and stones on up or down, is a sophisticated move that makes sense only after the mastery of the relative clause.

I speak in the parochial confines of our own language, for it is not clear what sense it would make to speak of reference on the part of a radically alien language. We think of our stone-age forebears as referring at least to sticks and stones, but this is a projection of our own linguistic habits. True, they reacted to sticks and stones; so do cats and dogs; but what does it mean to say that sticks and stones rather than qualities, or temporal stages of sticks and stones, or anything at all, are assumed as objects of reference in their language? I see how to make parochial sense of reference in our language, and in other languages relative to proposed translations into our language, and no more.

Nothing, one would have thought, could be more fundamental and objective than the fact of the matter of what there is, what exists, what is real. I seem now to derogate from its solidity and objectivity by making no sense of the question outside our own and related languages. I propose now to go farther and raise related doubts within the limits of our own language.

Imagine an aggregate scientific theory, an overall system of the world. Or you may just as well imagine a more limited theory, if in isolation from supplementary theories. The imagined theory has its ontology, the objects over which its variables range. Now choose a one-to-one mapping, any one you like, that carries each of these objects into another. It may simply permute the objects among themselves, or it may map them into a new domain. The mapping is what I call a proxy function. Now let us reconstrue every term in the theory to accommodate the proxy function. If a term meant "dog," or "prime number," we reinterpret it to mean "f of a dog" or "f of a prime number," where f is the proxy function. If we transform the old ontology by the proxy function and then reconstrue the terms in this compensatory way, all true statements remain true and all false ones false.

Furthermore, all the old empirical evidence for the theory continues to support the theory when the ontology and terms are reinterpreted in this way. For all evidence stems from sensory stimulation and enters language through observation sentences. These are the final arbiter, and are neutral in point of objective reference. They are associated with stimulation as unanalyzed strings of phonemes. The proxy function has changed no word of them, nor any word elsewhere. It has changed only our eventual choice of what objects to think of as values of the variables when they emerge, and as named and denoted by the singular and general terms with which the variables consort. The network of logical implication that connects the sentences of the scientific theory ultimately with observation sentences, through the mediation of observation categoricals or whatever, is independent of these interpretations and hinges only on the logical structure of the sentences concerned. The logical links are thus undisturbed, and the sensory links as well.

The whole cosmic upheaval, the reshuffling or transformation of ontology and exhaustive reinterpretation of terms, has disturbed nothing. What matters to science and all discourse is structure rather than ontology. The objects serve as mere nodes in the structure, and this is true of the sticks and stones no less than the electrons, quarks, numbers, and classes.

What can it mean, then, to hold one ontology rather than another onto which it can be mapped? I say that it makes sense only relative to proposed translations. We translate *pierre* as "stone" and *nombre* as "number," and we mean no more than this in saying that we interpret the French as treating of stones and numbers. Domestically it is simply true and trivial to say that "stone" denotes the stones and "number" denotes the numbers.

We are at the point where some of my readers sense a certain tension in my views, which is their charitable word for self-contradiction. I have professed a robust realism, ascribing full reality to sticks, stones, electrons, and the rest pending advice from natural science itself to the contrary. How can I then hold that evidence is indifferent to what there is said to be?

My answer, in a word, is naturalism. The question about what there is, what objects there are, is for me a question to be answered within our total empirical, scientific system of the world and not

outside it in some first philosophy prior to science. We say in so many words, in the name of science, that there are sticks, stones, electrons, and classes, and that there are no unicorns. The sentences thus uttered are part of a network that enjoys good logical relations with observation sentences that are sustained by sensory stimulation. We cannot ask better than that. Science is fallible, but scientific evidence is all we have to go on.

My point about proxy functions, then, is not to be seen as casting doubt on sticks, stones, and the rest, but as having to do with the theory of evidence. It belongs not to ontology but to the epistemology of ontology. It tells us that the evidence on which we base our theory of sticks, stones, electrons, and the rest would equally well sustain a theory whose objects were other things altogether. But the evidence is none the worse for that.

In retreating thus from ontology into its epistemology, am I retreating into a first philosophy prior to science after all? Not so. My epistemology is likewise naturalistic and of a piece with natural science. It is concerned with the relation between the triggering of our nerve endings and our eventual discourse about the world. It is as integral to science as is the scientist's discourse about sticks, stones, and electrons. These are merely different topics.

Even so, there is a carry-over that gives one pause. Consider what happens if we apply a proxy function to our ontology and actually rewrite all our terms accordingly, instead of just reinterpreting them. Suppose we rewrite them everywhere, even back in the observation sentences where they initially played no referential role. All the sentences, thus rewritten, still retain their old logical relations to one another, and all the empirical evidence remains in force. Yet many of these sentences will contradict sentences of our original theory, not just in interpretation but verbally and explicitly. We must declare them false, for we have only our science to go by; our naturalism allows us no prior philosophy. At the same time we could appreciate, thanks to our naturalistic epistemology, that the deviant theory is empirically equivalent to our own and hence that in declaring it false we are betraying our empiricism.

We can escape this fanciful dilemma by treating the deviant theory, despite appearances, as couched in a foreign language. We can then proceed to translate it into our language by applying the converse of the proxy function that we had used in devising it. The

apparent conflict of the two theories, we can thus conclude, was merely verbal.

However, save the surface as we will, I see a lasting lesson here: look to the stimulatory input and the structure of scientific theory, and let the objects, the values of the variables, fall where they may.

2

Cosmology As Science and As Religion

STEPHEN TOULMIN

MOST PEOPLE WHO GREW UP and formed their ideas within the world of the twentieth-century natural sciences understand the term *cosmology* as referring to a subbranch of physics, and more specifically of astronomy. In this sense, cosmological investigations and discussions are concerned with questions about the overall form and historical development of the astronomical universe as a whole: notably with cosmogony, pertaining to the question of its origin. Anyone who wishes to be quite precise may call this field of inquiry, more specifically, *physical cosmology*; but, since few scientists today think of cosmology as including any other kind, that phrase has become something of a tautology. Nowadays, *cosmology* tends to mean physical cosmology, and little more.

This remains the case, even when the physicists who work in this field stray beyond its narrow scientific limits and address broader issues. Thus, as a five-hundredth birthday tribute to Copernicus, John Archibald Wheeler gave an address to the National Academy of Sciences and the Smithsonian Institution with the ringing (and not yet sexist) title, "The Universe as a Home for Man." Given the celebratory nature of the occasion, nobody challenged his right to do so; on the contrary, many of his hearers probably assumed that this was just the kind of hot-air title such a quincentennial birthday party called for. Nor did many people stop to think, either, that here at last a physical cosmologist was bringing himself to address truly cosmological issues, in a much older and more traditional sense of the term: that John Wheeler was going beyond the sheer physical makeup of the astronomical universe,

and was asking how far that universe, and the human race of which we are members, are well matched to one another.

In short, the focus of cosmological attention has shifted away from questions about the place of humanity in nature, and toward questions about the overall structure of the physical world itself. The purpose of this paper will be to swim against this tide: to suggest that we should look again at the case for reinstating *cosmology*, in its older and broader sense as a field of discussion that overlaps the boundaries of science, philosophy, and religion; and for regarding physical cosmology as a subbranch, not just of physics but also of general cosmology in this older and broader sense. The interest of physical cosmology for cosmology proper will then, precisely, be the light that physicists such as John Wheeler can throw on the rootedness of humanity within nature.

A brief etymological excursion will begin the discussion. We owe the term *cosmology* to the Greeks of the fifth and fourth centuries B.C., who constructed the word on the basis of the standard Greek word *kosmos*, which meant — roughly — "order." (The modern English word *cosmetics* reflects this original notion: the cosmetic arts are concerned with the appearance of being well ordered or well turned out.) The Greek word for the physical universe, by contrast, was not *kosmos* but *ouranos*, and so it remains today. Pedantically, therefore, one may refer to the scientific study of the physical world as a whole, not as *cosmology* but rather as *ouranology*.

From the start, then, the thesis that the world (*ouranos*) forms an ordered whole (*kosmos*) went beyond the intellectual reach of astronomy alone. For at its heart lies a claim that the physical and biological things in nature are of such kinds, and are set up in such ways, that not only do they make sense to the human mind, they also are intrinsically hospitable to human life and the human heart. To view the world of nature as mere observers, purely from the outside, would be to set aside the deepest and most significant questions about it; such as those that throw light on the harmony between nature and humanity. Far from being a strictly factual and value-neutral enterprise, the study of natural philosophy in antiquity was repeatedly concerned with the question how far, and in what respects, it is good for human beings that the world of nature should be as it in fact is. And, eventually, the Stoic philoso-

phers of late antiquity broadened that issue further, and argued that cosmology should make room not just for anthropology but also for political theory. In a well-ordered universe, the *kosmos* would be matched with the *polis* so as to form a single, integrated *kosmopolis*.

We should keep this point in mind whenever we think about the role that cosmic ideas and cosmological images played within the overall world picture, right up to the end of the sixteenth century A.D. From the time of the ancient Babylonians (approximately 1000 to 700 B.C.) right up to the high point of medieval Europe, the authoritative and established ways of thinking about the world of nature represented multi-purpose modes of thought: designed to tell us, at one and the same time, what the structure of nature was, how humanity and human affairs fitted into that structure, and even what relations nature and humanity bore to the gods.

From the beginning, the gods themselves were considered as natural powers; and one mark of the harmonious interaction of human beings with their natural world lay in their ability to master the operation of those powers. From this point of view, to devise a reliable calendar was to read the divine mind; to fathom the mysteries of the seas was to be on good terms with Poseidon; and so on. The cycles of the seasons, agriculture, and the tides were evidences of divine power and action; so human beings who mastered these cycles were keeping in step with both the forces of nature and also the associated divinities. Conversely, the fact that the natural cycles lend themselves to human mastery was further evidence that humanity is indeed at home within and in harmony with nature, and through nature with the divinities that lay behind the powers of nature.

This sense that human beings are linked in harmony with the scheme of natural things, and that they have their own distinct place within its overall orderedness, made the medieval world picture a true cosmology in the traditional sense of the term. And this same sense began to break down, at first piecemeal but later more comprehensively, in the years around A.D. 1600. For an evocative expression of this breakdown, one need only look at John Donne's poem "An Anatomie of the World," usually dated around 1610 or 1611. Donne uses the death of a young girl as an occasion to lament "the frailty and decay of the whole world"; and this subtitle

(it soon appears) refers, quite as much, to the decay of the whole traditional world picture. Ranging across human experience, from astronomy and matter theory to political authority and personal relations, Donne sees signs of collapse everywhere he looks; to recall his much-quoted couplet:

> 'Tis all in peeces, all cohaerance gone,
> All just supply, and all Relation.[1]

In this couplet, furthermore, Donne's word *all* referred not only to the astronomical relationships that he had discussed in the dozen or so lines immediately preceding this couplet:

> The Sun is lost, and th' earth, and no mans wit
> Can well direct him where to looke for it. . . .[2]

It embraced also many of the other relationships that had been woven together in the comprehensive traditional *kosmos*, for example, the relations of political and social super- and subordination:

> Prince, Subject, Father, Sonne, are things forgot
> For every man alone thinkes he hath got
> To be a Phoenix. . . .[3]

Individualism had seized the public mind; no natural authority was recognized any longer; and the autocratic reign of Thomas Hobbes's *Leviathan* was just around the corner.

Despite their extraordinary achievements, then, seventeenth-century thinkers did not enjoy great intellectual confidence. On the contrary, theirs was a time of spiritual and ideological disarray. If their scientific ideas were drastically novel, that is because the crisis to which they responded struck them as new and drastic. For half a dozen different sets of reasons, they gave up the key feature of the traditional world picture, its multi-purpose, integrated character, and developed in its place a new and basically dualistic view of the world. This view dichotomized not only mind from matter, and thought from extension, but also rational arguments from causal forces, values from facts, and finally humanity from nature.

True, physiological processes going on within the bodies of human beings could not be distinguished in principle from other physical and chemical processes, so the emotions that spring from

adrenalin secretion were to be thought of as things that our bodies do to us; but all the most essentially human activities and thoughts must take place mentally, outside the mechanistic framework of the physical world of nature.

Meanwhile, institutional reasons also helped to keep the discussion of scientific issues on a strictly factual level, and encouraged seventeenth-century scientific thinkers to steer clear of questions of grave human moment or passion. As bitter experience had taught them, such issues too easily became violent and divisive: Europeans had spent, not just thirty, but sixty or more years embroiled in Wars of Religion, and could not afford to go on in the same way. So, from 1650 on, those people who joined together to found the new national academies, like the Royal Society of London, took care to confine their proceedings to isolated and uncontentious topics, about which some collective rational agreement might be expected.

On the one hand, it was necessary to avoid the trap that had awaited the Alchemists, who were never sure that the outcomes of their experiments were wholly independent of the mental states of those who conducted them. On the other hand, one should try to make quiet but steady progress in studying the properties of crystals, or building up a system of mechanics; and to avoid insisting from the outset on the imperative need for one's crystallography to have a Catholic *imprimatur* or for one's physical theories to be certifiably Protestant.

Hence arose the intellectual strategy, method, or research program characteristic of Modern Science, as the mathematical and experimental philosophy of Galileo and Descartes, Newton and Huygens, came to be called. The crucial features of this program were, firstly, the demand for a new kind of objectivity, based on systematic detachment of observers from their objects of study; and secondly, an insistence on the need for scientific inquiry to be value-neutral.

The presuppositions of this program were, in due course, crystallized in Laplace's image of the Omniscient Calculator, the detached thinker who, given only the initial positions and velocities of all the particles in the universe at the moment of the creation, could in principle apply Newton's laws of motion to compute the entire subsequent history of the physical world. For such a thinker,

that history would be a matter of purely factual concern, which in no way implicated one's own interests. In addition, this computation could be made in the first place only to the extent that the Calculator was looking in on the universe from the outside, being influenced by it without in any way affecting its operations in return.

At the outset, of course, Descartes, Newton, and the other founders of the new method recognized that its scope was limited: that it could be used in the study of passive material objects but was not appropriate in dealing with active mental agents. Before long, however, this strategy was enormously fruitful, spreading over from physics into chemistry and physiology; and, as its successes accumulated, its limitations were overlooked. By the middle of the nineteenth century, many people had come to see the method of Modern Science as providing a universal recipe, not just for the study of inanimate nature but for rational inquiries of all kinds. So were born the notions of objectivity, value neutrality, and detachment that have recently been called into question, on the mistaken assumption that they are intrinsic to scientific thought rather than being exaggerations of the method appropriate to a particular subclass of scientific inquiries during a particular phase of history.

Once the reach of science expanded far enough, of course, it overflowed the boundaries that Descartes and Newton had initially imposed on it. The coupling between the Omniscient Calculator and the world might be a purely one-way affair, as required by the strictly detached posture of a rational scientific spectator, or theorist. But in this respect the interactions between, for example, psychiatrists and patients whose afflictions are being studied are entirely different. If psychiatrists insist on viewing patients from a hiding place, like birdwatchers anxious to avoid disturbing courtship or nesting behavior, the psychiatrists deprive themselves of much of the understanding that would be available if they engaged in conversation, or other mutual interchange, with patients. In the human sciences, in short, the detached methodology of Newtonian science is inappropriate to the subject matter and problems of the field.

Similarly, an ecologist who experiments on the factors involved in changes of population in natural environments needs to recognize how far the experiment will itself be implicated in the phe-

nomena being studied. In scientific ecology the subject matter under investigation embraces the actions of the human beings who share in the habitats concerned, and the effects of their actions on those habitats. In this case, too, the traditional Newtonian strategy has only a limited relevance and applicability; and it is better to rethink the methods of scientific investigation so as to take account of the unavoidably reciprocal character of all these interactions.

Even in fundamental physics, as it has finally turned out, the Newtonian presuppositions hold good only up to a point. Once the delicacy of our interaction with the physical world increases far enough, we can no longer continue to reduce still further our influence on the processes we are studying; on the contrary, beyond that point those interactions are two-way ones, quite as much as they are in ecology or psychiatry. This fact, as John Dewey rightly pointed out, is the real philosophical moral of Werner Heisenberg's uncertainty principle.

In the twentieth century, Modern Science reached a point at which it radically outgrew the scaffolding within which it was originally constructed. From now on, all scientists were exposed once again to the Alchemists' problem, which the initial strategy of seventeenth-century science had been designed to overcome. In studying nature, they had always to ask how far, and in what respects, their investigations might affect, and even alter, the natural processes they were studying. Their rational objectivity had to become less purely detached, and more like the objectivity of an entirely just arbitrator, who must always take care to recognize and discount personal interest in, or reactions to, the issues in question. So the ideal of objectivity operative in science today is no longer that of Laplace's Omniscient Calculator, and has become instead that of the scrupulous psychoanalyst, continually on the lookout for countertransference and aware of the dangers that this poses to one's interpretations.

The new phase in the historical development of the sciences that has been inaugurated as an outcome of these changes is so different in its central ideals and methods from that which held good from the 1620s to the 1920s that it may even deserve a new name. It is no accident, therefore, that writers like Frederick Ferre choose to contrast the new phase in the sciences with its Cartesian and

Newtonian forerunner by calling it the age of postmodern rather than modern science. I shall argue that it is a period in which all the main victories of the seventeenth-century scientific revolution have been called in question, not least the divorce of humanity from nature. And once this "bifurcation of nature," as Whitehead called it, is successfully overcome, we are free to reconsider the separation of scientific cosmology from its religious aspects, which was one central consequence of that divorce.

Let me sharpen up the point of my argument. The fundamental dualism which underlay the Cartesian and Newtonian view of nature was not simply operative on an intellectual level alone. It not only exhorted scientists to use different explanatory methods and categories in dealing with the phenomena of nature and the activities of human beings, respectively. If that had been all there was to it, the divorce between humanity and nature would not have had such deep effects. Rather, this new intellectual program was all of a piece with a larger reordering of human ideas and feelings about the natural world, and about the place of human beings in that world.

Around A.D. 1610, for instance, John Donne could deplore the fact that "New Philosophy calls all in doubt"; yet it would be anachronistic to suppose that the skepticism to which he referred was merely René Descartes's maxim of systematic doubt. On the contrary, Donne was sensitive to those much wider challenges which had already begun, in the years before 1600, to erode people's sense of the natural world as a place hospitable to humanity, and so as embodying a "just supply and Relation" matching natural provisions and human needs. It was no part of Donne's purpose to be a scientific obstructionist. Rather, he was distressed by the way in which this larger erosion was destroying the values of the traditional cosmology, with its built-in harmony between natural, social, and human affairs, and encouraging not merely an intellectual insight but also a feeling that human beings are not truly a part of nature, or at home in the world of nature.

In due course this larger consequence became a key element in the general philosophy of Descartes, Newton, and their colleagues. The moral ideas prevalent among sixteenth-century French thinkers had been Stoic in tone; they regarded acting rightly as acting in accordance with the demands of nature. But this option was

no longer open to Descartes. For him the world of nature was a piece of deterministic machinery, and its operations left no room for moral reflection and action. Hence, even on a narrowly philosophical level, the matter-mind division implied the removal of moral reflection from the natural realm. The detachment of rational thought from the world of material extension was not just an intellectual dodge, aimed at speeding up the advancement of scientific learning. It was also one element in a whole new religious sense about the relations between humanity and nature.

This new world view was as much the heir of Epicureanism as the sixteenth-century view had been the heir of Stoicism. For Descartes, intellectual and moral thinking went on in a rational realm, quite detached and distinct from the causal realm of mechanical phenomena and physical forces. To live aright thus meant remaining aloof from the deterministic processes of material, extended nature, and conforming entirely to the demands of mental, extensionless reason. Once mind and humanity were separated from matter and nature, moral thought became purely calculative, and the emotions became an obstacle to living either a rational or a truly moral life. Here are echoes of the Epicurean doctrine of *ataraxia*.

Conversely, any reintegration of humanity into nature that becomes possible for us now in the late twentieth century, as a consequence of the shift from modern to postmodern science, should be considered not merely with an eye to the new modes of explanation that open up as a result of this reintegration. It needs to be considered, also, as holding out the possibility of healing the emotional and even the religious wounds that were created when the Cartesian surgery of the seventeenth-century natural philosophers separated the two halves of their bifurcated world and, by doing so, set the mental lives of human beings apart from and in opposition to the natural phenomena and physical processes of the material realm.

It is time to return to cosmology. To recall: from the start, the focus of cosmology was the question, "What makes the universe a *kosmos*, a harmonious, well-ordered whole?" For the classical Greeks, this question arose about all aspects of nature and humanity also. It embraced the phenomena of astronomy, but the Greeks did not give *ta meteora*, "things up there," a unique cos-

mological role. The heavenly bodies were important because they traditionally possessed a divine status. With some reservations, Plato, Aristotle, and the Stoics all maintained this tradition, either by equating the material substance of the heavens with that of the soul or the reason, or by crediting the heavens with an eternal motion, quite unlike the transitory motion of terrestrial things. (Here again, Epicurus was at odds with such thought.) Rather, they assumed that all aspects of the world were linked together in a cosmic whole. This made nature a model of the *logos*, or "rational law," on which human beings could learn to pattern their social and individual lives.

Our situation today is quite different. Whatever significance we may allot to the heavenly bodies, and to their putative origin in a Big Bang some ten or twenty thousand million years ago, the astrotheological beliefs of the Babylonians are dead, even in the qualified forms in which they survived in the minds of the classical Greeks, and so into the medieval world picture. When scientific issues arise today, about the match between human beings and the natural world in which they live, those questions must be raised nearer to home, and belong not to astronomy but to other sciences. Specifically, they belong to those fields of science like ecology which study the relations between human beings and their natural habitats directly. So it will be no surprise to discover in such postmodern fields as ecology and psychiatry the clearest evidence of a revived interest in older cosmological issues and even a revival of earlier traditions in natural religion.

It is no accident, for instance, that the term *ecology* embodies the same kind of ambiguity as *cosmology* itself. On the one hand, we have ecology the science, involving the study of the food chains and other natural systems that link together the fauna and flora of small ponds, and so maintain the harmonious equilibria on which their continued lives depend. On the other hand, there is ecology the movement, involving the defense of natural habitats and systems against disruption as a result of ill-considered industrial and social policies, and campaigns of public education and political action to promote that defense.

The significance of this ambiguity lies in one fact. The two wings of ecology, the science and the movement, are far more closely linked than, for example, the intellectual and political wings

of nuclear physics. One can pursue an intellectual concern with
the structure of the atomic nucleus, or the properties of subatomic
particles, without being drawn into the political campaign for a
freeze on nuclear weapons. Conversely, those who make the nuclear freeze a focus of political action need have only the sketchi-
est understanding of nuclear theory. In ecology, by contrast, this
detachment of the scientific aspects of nuclear issues from their
political implications has no counterpart. Just because ecology the
science is essentially postmodern, and concerned with the interaction of human beings with one another and with their environments, its intellectual aspects are inseparably linked with the practical concerns of ecological politics and administration.

Scientific ecologists unhesitatingly draw on the work of the
U.S. Fish and Wildlife Service for data and new problems, while
those who work at the management of natural habitats and systems continually draw on scientific ecologists for necessary data
and counsel. So the ideas of ecological science and the practices
of ecological management are two faces of a coin. In principle, it
may be possible for a graduate student in biology to be drawn into
ecology for purely intellectual reasons, unmixed with any practical or political concerns. But it is not likely that this will actually
happen in real life. The two aspects of ecology, intellectual and
practical, are so closely connected that one can hardly be pursued
in isolation from the other.

There are also other, deeper reasons why this should be so.
In the realm of popular philosophy or natural theology, two views
currently engage the public mind. These two views I call the white
philosophy and the green philosophy. The white philosophy is
rooted in the psychotherapy movement. Intellectually, it bases itself on all the new insights about human motivation and self-
fulfillment that have entered public discussion during the last fifty
years. Ethically, it teaches a doctrine of self-command and self-
detachment. If we experience difficulties in our personal lives, that
is because we allow ourselves to be exposed to aggravation from
outside, whether from other people or from our personal situations.
Practical wisdom then consists in learning to avoid aggravation,
by facing and mastering the sources that lie within our psyches and
by educating ourselves to remain cool and avoid letting things get
to us. In this, the white philosophy once again echoes Epicurus'

doctrine of *ataraxia*, which similarly emphasized avoiding letting things *tarassein*, or "bother you."

By the same standards, the green philosophy echoes the teaching of the Stoics. Intellectually, it is rooted in ecology the science, and bases itself on all its insights about the human species as one element in the larger world of natural things. Ethically, it advocates living a natural life, one lived in harmony with the natural world of which humanity is one part. If we experience difficulties in our individual or collective lives, that is because we are acting in ways that go against the grain of nature, and so expose us to aggravation from outside. Practical wisdom then consists in learning to avoid aggravation, by mastering the human place in the natural world and by learning to avoid dealing with the other creatures and systems in that world in ways that will recoil on us. We shall then be able to live in contentment (*eudaimonia*) and without disturbing passions (*apatheia*), because our lives are being lived with the grain of nature.

One thing is new about the present situation. In antiquity, the Stoic and Epicurean schools were rivals, and held different views about the overall history of things. The Stoics held a cyclical or repetitive view, in which the same basic sequence of historical phases recurred time after time. The Epicureans, by contrast, saw history as unilinear. For them, the passage of time was capable of generating real novelty, especially in the field of human customs and institutions. At the present time, these two general positions are much easier to reconcile. The green, Stoic revival position has to take the Darwinian view of biological history into account, and is therefore now as historical as the neo-Epicurean position. It is quite common today to find people who combine a commitment to psychotherapy as the basis of their inner lives with a commitment to ecology as the basis of their public or outer lives.

Why do I suggest that these positions involve a revival of an apparently outdated natural religion? This suggestion rests on the character and intensity of the commitment that one finds in the adherents of these positions. True, some supporters of the ecology movement are prepared to rationalize their views in utilitarian terms. They argue that we must take care of the environment we share with other creatures and systems, because our failure to do so will deplete the gene pool, and so impoverish our descendants. But other supporters of the same environmental positions dismiss

these utilitarian positions as shallow and irrelevant. From their standpoint, we must defend the redwoods because, and merely because, the redwoods do not deserve to become extinct.

In short, many environmentalists display a kind of piety toward nature which owes nothing to any utilitarian calculations. For them, the fundamental scientific insight is that the world of nature forms a marvelously harmonious system, a *kosmos,* and the right way of ordering our lives is to ensure that we maintain, rather than disrupt, the *kosmos* of the creation. If that creation came into existence bit by bit, as an outcome of evolutionary history, this makes it none the less marvelous, and none the less deserving of respect, than it did for Charles Darwin himself. The system of nature revealed by the science of ecology thus takes the same cosmological place in their minds and in their hearts that God's created system took in the minds and hearts of their ancestors in earlier centuries. For them the task of figuring out the scheme of things has the same priority, intellectual and emotional alike, that the task of reading "God's book of nature" had for Robert Boyle and other natural theologians in the seventeenth century.

We find ourselves, accordingly, faced with an intriguing challenge and an opportunity. From now on, the central and most typical fields of scientific inquiry will be postmodern ones, sciences that focus on the relationships between humanity and the rest of nature or among human beings themselves. The issues they raise will no longer be merely factual, to say nothing of value-neutral. On the contrary, all of them will raise questions of wider kinds, moral and political, philosophical and religious. And the opportunity that faces scientists and theologians, philosophers and political theorists is to sit down together and see whether they can reach any common agreement about the cosmological scheme implicit in the findings of those new fields of science.

Yet, if they do so, will they not be condemned to the kind of irresoluble Babel the founders of the Royal Society feared in the aftermath of the Religious Wars? Will not such sciences as psychiatry and ecology prove to be fields in which differences of religious belief will breed irresoluble disagreements, in ways they do not do in chemistry? That is the challenge. Though the initial prospects may not look good, second thoughts suggest rather more grounds for hope.

It is, of course, possible that fanatical Shia Muslims and fun-

damentalist Protestant Christians will continue for a long time to stand outside the broader consensus about such issues. Still, if we leave aside the *frondes,* there is reason to foresee more in the way of general agreement emerging about the insights of these postmodern sciences. It is all very well to say, like a popular Cambridge preacher of my undergraduate days, that all the activities, intellectual and emotional — even the arithmetic — of a Christian must be Christian. But that, as Leibniz was quick to insist, cannot mean that Christians are free to believe, as a matter of faith, that three times three makes ten, or that the square root of two is a rational number. Nor does it mean that religious doctrines can provide substantial warrants for theoretical positions in physics or physiology in significant conflict with those that scientists of other persuasions accept.

Is this a respect in which postmodern sciences inevitably differ from the modern sciences? Must we learn to live with the idea that Calvinist psychiatrists are entitled for doctrinal reasons to hold different views from those of their Jewish or Catholic colleagues even within psychiatry? Or that Southern Baptist biologists may, for good doctrinal reasons, reject all the Darwinian hypotheses that more mainline believers have learned to accept? Those questions are still open. But there are good practical reasons, as well as doctrinal ones, for hoping that the argument will not shipwreck in this way. The ecological problems facing Siberians at Lake Baikal, or Africans living around Lakes Chad and Nyasa, do not significantly differ in their origins or their effects from those that arise in North America over Lake Erie, or in Europe over the Lake of Geneva. When the public representatives of all these nations come together to talk over such environmental issues, one must assume that they can share a common language and framework of analysis when they do so.

This general consensus is not likely to commend itself to uncompromising critics of modern biology among Protestant fundamentalists, but that need not be a reason to despair, either of arriving at a broad consensus in matters of theoretical analysis or at an ecumenical alliance over matters of practical policy. The sufficient reasons that Leibniz hoped, in the years after 1660, would have the power to quiet the fanatics and lead to an ecumenical agreement in matters of natural philosophy, have a relevance not

just to mechanics and physiology but to ecology, psychiatry, and cosmology also. It is time for philosophers and theologians to sit down alongside the scientists with this hope in mind, and to see what agreement is open to us, across disciplinary and doctrinal boundaries, over the content of the natural scheme of things, as the sciences reveal it to us, and as it bears on the task of learning, once again, to embrace the basic cosmological vision that the natural universe is, indeed, a fit home for humanity.

NOTES

1. John Donne, *An Anatomie of the World,* lines 213–14.
2. Ibid., lines 207–8.
3. Ibid., lines 215–17.

3

Two Evolutions

HUSTON SMITH

WALKER PERCY IN HIS *Message in the Bottle* points out that we do not know who we are. There exists in the contemporary West no coherent theory of human nature, no consensus view such as prevailed in thirteenth-century Europe, in seventeenth-century New England, or in traditional societies still. Whether these views were true or false, they were viable beliefs. They animated their cultures and gave life its meaning. They were outlooks people tried to live by.

In contrast to such embracing theories, what we have today is a miscellany of *notions* as to who we are. These notions do not cohere, but they do fall into two rather clearly demarcated camps. On the one hand is the view backed by modern science, that the human self can be understood as an organism in an environment, endowed genetically like other organisms with needs and drives, who through evolution — natural selection working on chance mutations — has developed strategies for learning and surviving by means of certain adaptive transactions with the environment. Over and against this is the Judeo-Christian view that the human being was created in the image of God with an immortal soul and occupies a place in nature somewhere between the beasts and the angels. At some point humankind suffered a catastrophic fall in consequence of which we have lost our way and, unlike the beasts, become capable of sin and seek after salvation. The clue to this second scenario derives not from science or philosophy, but from two historical events — the Exodus and the Incarnation — which produced respectively a people, the Jews; and an institution, the Christian Church.

Not only do these views not mesh; they are in head-on opposition, for according to science we are the more who have derived from the less, whereas our religions teach that we are the less who have derived from the more. In thus contradicting each other, our two views — one taught by our schools, the other by our churches and synagogues — cancel each other out, leaving us without a clear self-image or identity. It is impossible for both views to be true, yet simply by having been born into today's West, all of us believe parts of both of them. Even those who have abandoned the theological specifics of the religious view continue to affirm the afterglow that lingers from its light: the belief that human beings are endowed with certain unique properties — inherent dignity and inalienable rights — that other organisms do not possess, and that as a consequence the highest value a democratic society can set for itself is respect for the sacredness and worth of the individual.

How does one live one's life if one tries to take these two contradictory propositions seriously? The standard way is to see oneself as an organism that has evolved enough to have developed certain values. What is not noticed, as Walker Percy points out, is that the moment the sanctity of the individual is turned into a "value," an act of devaluation has already occurred.

An age comes to a close when people discover that they can no longer understand themselves by the theory their age professes. For a while its denizens will continue to think that they believe it, but they feel otherwise and cannot understand their feelings. This has now happened to us. We continue to believe Darwinism, even though it no longer feels right to us. Darwinism is in fact dying, and its death signals the close of our age.

My rationale for a negative project — deflating Darwinism — is this: with respect to the problem at hand (our point of origin as it bears on who we are), our need is not just to relieve an inconsistency but to do so in the right way, with the better of the two hypotheses triumphing. By the better hypothesis I mean the one that is closer to the truth and more serviceable. Darwinism is obscuring what I believe to be this doubly better answer to the question at stake. If I could prove that we have derived from what exceeds us I would naturally take that direct route, but metaphysical propositions do not admit of proof, so I resort to this *via negativa*. Rabbis say that if we cannot believe in God, we might

at least try to stop believing in idols. Less faith in the Darwinian idol might help to clear a space in which the divine might appear more regularly than it now does.

We would be better off if we could believe that our origin is momentous, and Darwinism counters that belief. Peter Drucker, the industrial consultant, says he never tells managers anything they don't know. He gets them to see that what they have been discounting as incidental information is actually critical information. So it is here. Not being a scientist, I obviously have nothing to contribute to evolutionary theory in its technical aspects. My own thrust takes a different turn. I want to work on the way the entire Darwinian theory looks to us and to change that look by *gestalting* it in a different way; specifically, by placing it in the context of the premises with which this paragraph began. When it is thus placed, my project can be visualized as a triangle, as follows:

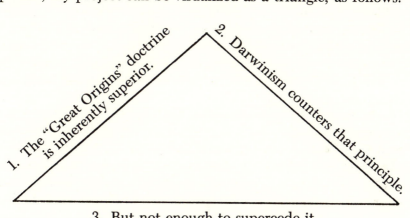

3. But not enough to supercede it.

I derive the phrase "Great Origins" from Joseph Addison's "Ode" in *The Spectator:*

> The spacious firmament on high,
> With all the blue ethereal sky,
> And spangled heavens, a shining frame,
> Their great Original proclaim.

But the point here is this: the force of my critique of Darwinism turns on its position in this triangle. There are some, to be sure, who conclude that it should be shelved for scientific reasons alone,

but my point is a different one: Even if it remains useful as a working hypothesis in science, that is not sufficient reason for us to believe that its basic delivery, the Small Origins hypothesis, is true. For the game of evidence which Darwinism as a scientific theory plays is an idiosyncratic one that introduces both contraction and inflation. Contraction occurs when Darwinism sees itself as answerable only to empirical evidence; other considerations, such as metaphysical ones relating to first and final causes or the intuitive ones with which this paper will close, are discounted from the start. This reduction of the field of evidence in which it stands already exaggerates its stature. An inflationary move follows hard on its heels. To gain acceptance in science a working hypothesis does not need to show much in the way of proof; all it need do is stay ahead of its competitors. If its competitors are weak, the lead hypothesis can look strong without actually being so. And if it has no competitors? There was a period when the evidence turned against Darwinism conclusively; it didn't matter — its rating barely slipped. I refer to that pre-Mendelian moment — it extended for thirty-three years, actually — when an Edinburgh professor showed that by the mechanisms of heredity as they were then understood the emergence of new species from chance variations was logically impossible. For through admixture with the standard hereditary equipment of its mating partner, the strength of a promising evolutionary mutation would be reduced to one-half in its children, to one-quarter in its grandchildren, and so on until it vanished completely. Mendel rescinded this refutation with his discovery that genes do not blend and thus become diluted, but for a third of a century this categorical disproof scarcely tarnished Darwin's star. One is tempted to conclude with Julius Caesar that people believe what they want to believe, and there is much to this; the nineteenth and twentieth centuries wanted to believe Darwinism for its Social Darwinism and its prospect that progress would continue forever. But from the scientific standpoint there was something that was right about this tenacious clinging to a disproven theory. For Darwinism seemed (as it still seems) to be the only possible scientific explanation for life's origin and development, so it was appropriate to see how far it could succeed. That it has not succeeded enough to displace its Great Origins competitor is my conclusion, and it is time to proceed with the argument that leads up to it.

1. The Great Origins thesis is inherently superior.

Underlying this first proposition, naturally, is the supposition that notions regarding origins are important whatever their kind. Sociologically we see this in the search for roots that is cropping up in our highly mobile, transient society, while on a larger scale we find it in the cosmogonic myths that legitimize every known culture. The care with which these myths are transmitted from generation to generation and ritualistically rehearsed proves that more than curiosity is at stake in their origin. They came forward to meet a fundamental human need: the need to sense oneself as grounded in the cosmos and thereby oriented. Without orientation confusion sets in; if it persists, life loses its radar. Being ungrounded is part and parcel of this, for to be without grounding is to be adrift in ever shifting contexts that are unstable. The warning "not good if detached" applies not only to ticket stubs but to life as well. But is one surmise as good as another on this subject?

It seems unlikely. Self-image affects behavior, and to see oneself as descended from noble stock is to assume that one is made of noble stuff. This in turn disposes one to behave nobly, though of course it does not guarantee such behavior. Something like generational rub-off occurs, for where there is noble ancestry there are noble role models; also, shoddy conduct cannot be blamed on shoddy genes. Traditional societies may have sensed such things, for Marshall Sahlins tells us that "we are the only people who think themselves risen from savages; everyone else believes they descended from gods."[1]

What is difficult is to pass from everyday considerations like these to ones that are metaphysical. Two difficulties are involved. First, in our empiricistic age the metaphysical imagination has to a large extent atrophied. The scientific account of origins, with its consistent theme of the qualitatively *more* deriving from the qualitatively *less*, so dominates our horizon that it is difficult to take seriously the opposite outlook which until five hundred years ago everyone took for granted. The second problem is of the opposite sort. The version of the Great Origins hypothesis that is most bandied about today puts that hypothesis in a bad light. I refer, of course, to Creationism, whose apostles have so muddied the waters with simplistic readings of the Scriptures, and scientific claims

that are sometimes bogus, that it is next to impossible for the Great Origins thesis to gain a fair hearing.[2]

Let me take this second obstacle to the Great Origins thesis first. As the precise way to characterize the opposite of the Darwinian thesis I have chosen the phrase "the less from the more" for its generality and abstractness. As Adam and the animals were less than God, a literalist biblical account of how we got here fits the Great Origins hypothesis, but it is far from the only one that does so. All that the thesis requires is that we derive from Something that is superior to ourselves by every measure of worth we know. These transcendent objects include the ultimates of the great religious traditions — Allah, God, Brahman, Śūnyatā, the Tao, the Great Spirit — as well as philosophical ultimates, provided that they exceed human beings in intrinsic worth. Clearly included, for example, is the Neoplatonic One from which beings proceed by emanation rather than creation, and the Whiteheadian God whose primordial and consequent natures conspire to work upon the world their everlasting lure. I hope this latitude in the Great Origins thesis will keep it from being dismissed as Creationism.

The other bar to the Great Origins thesis, the poverty of the metaphysical imagination, is more difficult to deal with. Scientists who by virtue of their sensitivity are equally humanists are rhapsodic in hymning the grandeur of the universe. Einstein referred to its "radiant beauty which our dull faculties can comprehend only in their most primitive forms."[3] What is lacking is anything resembling Aristotle's Prime Mover, a first and final cause which in its very essence is luminously conscious and good. And if one does not sense the decisive difference these attributes make to a world view, this is the atrophy of which I speak.

How does one revive an ailing organ? Art might help if it were not itself at sea metaphysically; Walker Percy says that writers help us to understand the plight he cited but have no remedy to offer.[4] The energy that enters life through the Great Origins hypothesis does not derive solely from the heightened self-image that results from the discovery of royal pedigree. It also derives from the fact that there is in the Great Origins thesis no answer to the question of human origins that does not include the answer to the origin of everything. Here humankind and world conspire. They issue from a single source, and as that source is good beyond all conceiv-

ing, it is impossible that its offspring not be kin. In a single stroke
the self/world divide, laid wide by Descartes' mind/matter disjunc-
tion and the slash between primary and secondary qualities, is
mended.

In favoring small origins, Darwinism challenges the Great
Origins thesis. I shall argue that the evidence for Darwinism fails,
but that demonstration is needed only if Darwinism and the Great
Origins thesis are incompatible. Are they? Yes.

2. *Darwinism and the Great Origins hypothesis are incompatible.*

Darwinism and the Great Origins doctrine cannot be squared.
This needs to be argued, for it runs counter to the current drift
of mainline theology which sees Darwin as assimilatable. Vatican
II instructs the faithful to combine modern scientific theories with
Christian doctrine. It is widely held that evolutionary theory poses
no contradiction to Catholic belief. Except for fundamentalists,
Protestants concur, but scientists seem to feel that they are being
co-opted. Darwin saw his discovery as strongly resistant to admixture with belief in God, while Jacques Monod goes further. "The
mechanism of evolution as now understood," he tells us, "rules out
any claim that there are final causes, or purposes being realized.
[This] disposes of any philosophy or religion that believes in cosmic . . . purpose."[5] Realizing that this conclusion could be colored
by Monod's personal philosophy, I turn to the entry on "Evolution"
in *The New Encyclopaedia Britannica* for a statement that might
reflect, as well as any, consensus in the field. It tells me that "Darwin showed that evolution's cause, natural selection, was automatic
with no room for divine guidance or design."[6]

Which side is right? The question is complex, for a whole
swarm of issues is involved, including the way two important intellectual currents and the institutions they represent are competing for the mind of our age. I spent fifteen years at the Massachusetts Institute of Technology without seeing what a few paragraphs
in E. F. Schumacher's *Guide for the Perplexed* showed me clearly.
There is not one science. There are two, which Schumacher dubs
descriptive and instructional.[7]

Descriptive science is as old as the human race. Pivoting as
it does on careful observation and the organization of data thus
derived, no society could have survived without a touch of it,

though the quantity can vary enormously. When in the seventeenth century John Ray took the first steps toward creating a suitable system of classifying species in the plant world, he provided a good example of this first kind of science, as did Carolus Linnaeus whose naming of life forms in orderly classification established a context in which botanical studies could take place in a sustained fashion. Descriptive science is not confined to the study of nature; it is a part of every cognitive discipline. Even today in continental Europe, words for science tend to have this descriptive ring. *Wissenschaft* is an example. On the Continent, history is a science.

In the English-speaking world it is not, the reason being that here the word has come to denote modern science which turns on science in Schumacher's instructional mode. Instructional science takes the form: Do *X*, and *Y* will follow. In the formal, conceptual sphere we have geometry, mathematics, and logic, where we can issue instructions that work and thereby establish proof. Equally in the empirical, material world: our hands can manipulate objects, so again we can issue instructions as to what manipulations will achieve which ends and again establish proof. An important insight comes to view. Only through instructional science, which is to say, only in what we can ourselves do, can we truly explain and prove.

Applied to evolutionary theory, this distinction gives us descriptive evolution which tries to tell us *what* happened in life's ascent, and instructional evolution which takes up from there to explain *how* and *why* it happened. The ideal of descriptive evolution would be a complete cinematographic record of what has occurred in life's sojourn on this planet. We might think of it as a videotape which, accelerated enormously, PBS could run as a mind-boggling spectacular. It should be a silent film, in keeping with the eerie silence of the fossil record from which it would be primarily derived. Darwinism, on the other hand, is instructional evolution.

Descriptive evolution is essentially the fossil record. Fossils found in the earth's crust show that there have been changes in the constitution of plants and animals, and with the help of radioactive and potassium-argon dating these have been placed in historical sequence. Drawing primarily on this data, descriptive evolution weaves a story the chief features of which are: (a) that higher, more complex forms of life appeared later than simpler ones (much later); (b) that all organisms after the initial self-replicating protein molecule(s) issued from parents; and (c) that all species of life on earth can be traced back through their pedigrees to the simplest forms in which life initially appeared. Darwin contributed to descriptive evolution as just summarized, but his importance lies in his proposal for how it all happened: through natural selection working on chance mutations. It is this explanatory side of his work that I am calling Darwinism in this essay.

It is at once apparent that descriptive evolution is more compatible with the Great Origins hypothesis than is Darwinism, for, being silent on the question of causes, it leaves room for the possibility that God scripted and directs the entire production; if the heavens declare the glory of God, why not the fossil record? If we ponder the matter, though, we can see that psychologically, if not logically, descriptive evolution veils God's glory considerably.

Descriptive evolution works psychologically against the Great Origins concept. For on the one hand, though it brackets the question of *how* the more derives from the less, it nonetheless depicts it as so deriving. And it presents changes as occurring so gradually that nothing extraordinary seems to happen; miracle is reduced to microscopic, incremental accretions. Because these two features of descriptive evolution run psychologically counter to the Great Origins thesis, it is useful to remind ourselves that even descriptive evolution is not indubitable. Materially there are more anomalies, not to mention wide gaps, in the fossil record than the public recognizes, while formally the entire scenario rests on a postulate, uniformitarianism, which holds that the laws of nature do not change. Charles Lyell fixed this postulate into place in the 1830s with his three-volume *Principles of Geology*. As a geologist put it to me recently, "It's impossible to prove uniformitarianism; it's just that you can't be a geologist without it. We now know as Lyell did not that natural processes change — rates of erosion, for example. But natural laws must remain constant or geology isn't a science."

To his children's question, "Who made us, God or evolution?" a British theologian, Don Cupitt, found himself answering, "Both"; which answer, as we saw, is the one that most theologians are giving today. On reflection, though, Cupitt tells us, he concluded that his answer was "diplomatic, orthodox, and shallow."[8] For Darwin-

ism does not purport to describe the instrumentalities through which God works. It is the scientific account for how we and other creatures got here, and as such it must, on pain of begging the question, proceed without recourse to anything remotely resembling divine intention or design. Monod has it exactly right when he writes: "The cornerstone of scientific method is . . . the *systematic* denial that 'true' knowledge can be got at by interpreting phenomena in terms of final causes — that is to say, of 'purpose.'"[9] It is important to see exactly what is being said here. As purposes and final causes entail realities that are greater than ourselves, Monod's dictum translates into saying that Small Origins accounts of how we got here are the only accounts that instructional science — on this point Darwinism — will allow. Darwinism qualifies as being scientific because its working principles are strictly nonteleological: natural selection is purely mechanical, and the mutations on which it works arrive solely by chance. But by the same token, if Darwinism is accepted as true, the Great Origins hypothesis is replaced by the Small Origins one.

3. *In the face of its Great Origins rival, Darwinism fails.*

I am not the first to call the claims for Darwinism into question, of course. A recent issue of *Environment* tells us that Darwin's ideas

> have long been under successful attack not just by religious fundamentalists or "scientific creationists" but by many biologists and such popularizers as the late Arthur Koestler . . . and Norman Macbeth. That this will be news to most educated laypersons and to many biologists is simply an example of cultural lag and the ability of dogmas to dominate not only religion but science as well.[10]

Macbeth's *Darwin Retried* (and in its author's eyes found wanting) has been out for over a decade now.[11] Asked on the November 1, 1981, PBS *Nova* program what his qualifications were for writing on a scientific subject, Macbeth answered that as a professional lawyer he considered himself an expert on evidence, and that it was in their handling of evidence that he faulted Darwin's defenders. More recently Jeremy Rifkin has published his *Algeny*, the central chapter of which is titled "The Darwinian Sunset." "Our

children will not think of the world in a Darwinian way," he writes. "Darwin's theory of evolution will be remembered in centuries to come as a cosmological bridge between two world epochs."[12]

These are all lay verdicts, however, so we should go on to what the biologists themselves are saying. It came as a surprise to find that Darwinism has never gained much of a hearing in western Europe; *The New Encyclopaedia Britannica* notes that "natural selection is . . . not widely . . . recognized in western continental Europe" as evolution's cause.[13] Pierre Grassé for thirty years occupied the chair for evolution at the Sorbonne and edited the twenty-eight volume *Encyclopedia of Zoology*. In his *Evolution of Living Forms*, Grassé has this to say:

> The explanatory doctrines of biological evolution do not stand up to an objective, in-depth criticism. They prove to be either in conflict with reality or else incapable of solving the major problems involved. . . . Through use and abuse of hidden postulates, of bold, often ill-founded extrapolations, a pseudoscience has been created. It is taking root in the very heart of biology and is leading astray many biochemists and biologists, who sincerely believe that the accuracy of fundamental concepts has been demonstrated, which is not the case.[14]

Edwin Conklin, late professor of biology at Princeton, writes, "Religious devotion . . . is probably the reason why severe methodological criticism employed in other departments of biology has not yet been brought to bear on evolutionary speculation."[15] And in making the distinction between descriptive and explanatory evolution David Raup of the University of Chicago writes: "The record . . . pretty clearly demonstrates that evolution has occurred if we define evolution simply as change; but it does not tell us how this change took place, and that's really the question."[16]

A. THE FOSSIL RECORD

The only evidence that we have concerning the past history of life on our planet is found in fossils embedded in rock formations. Darwin admitted that in his day they did little to support his theory. "Geology . . . does not reveal . . . finely graded organic change," he wrote, "and this, perhaps, is the most obvious and grav-

est objection which can be urged against [my] theory."[17] He trusted, of course, that time would fill in the gaps, but how little it has done so Raup again attests. "We are now about 120 years after Darwin . . . and, ironically, we have even fewer examples of evolutionary transition than we had in Darwin's time," inasmuch as many that were thought to be valid are now known not to be.[18] Concerning links between species, an eerie silence prevails. "Evolution requires intermediate forms between species," says David Kitts, professor of geology at the University of Oklahoma, "and paleontology does not provide them."[19] The punctuated equilibrium theory — eons of invariance punctuated by quick (perhaps five- to fifty-thousand-year) spurts in isolated ecological niches — has emerged to account for the fact that, as Stephen Gould says, "phyletic gradualism [which would have left evidences of transitional links] is never seen in the rocks."[20] But does that theory amount to more than justification for continuing to believe in transitional forms when we have no traces of them?

B. POPULATION BREEDING

The breeding of domestic plants and animals which had begun in England in the 1760s had by Darwin's day produced famous breeds of Leicestershire sheep and Dishley cattle. Darwin was immensely impressed with this art and adopted it as a metaphor for his theory, not knowing that in the end it would work against him. For though mutations can effect changes within species (microevolution), with respect to species as wholes they insure stability rather than change. Species-continuity is insured by a constant barrage of subtle variations that allow the species to adapt if the environment should change; concomitantly, species-change (macroevolution) is blocked by the law of reversion to the mean. Beyond a certain point deviations become unstable and, instead of cresting into new species, die out. In a typical experiment that began with fruit flies that averaged thirty-six bristles, it was possible to raise the number to fifty-six or lower it to twenty-five, but beyond those numbers the lines became sterile and expired. As Luther Burbank noted early on, "there is a pull toward the mean which keeps all living things within some more or less fixed limitations."[21] Loren Eiseley is not the only one to have noted the unhappy consequences for Darwinian theory when he writes, "There is great irony in this

situation, for more than almost any other single factor, domestic breeding has been used as an argument for evolution."[22]

C. NATURAL SELECTION

Darwin saw natural selection as his central discovery; he believed that he had found in it the engine of change that had brought higher forms of life into being. But problems have arisen.

If the fittest survive, why don't the less fit disappear? Gertrude Himmelfarb asks. If the hive bee's efficiency in containing a maximum of honey with a minimum of wax gives it a Darwinian edge, why are bumbling, inefficient bumble bees still around?[23]

Natural selection makes no room for long-range considerations; every new trait has to be immediately useful or it is discarded. How then are we to account for the emergence of complex organs or limbs which are made up of myriads of parts that would have had to have developed independently of one another through thousands of generations during which they had no utility? Stephen Gould reduces the problem to its simplest proportions when he asks, "What good is half a jaw or half a wing?"[24]

If novel faculties emerge because of their adaptive edge, why are some of them overqualified for that purpose, as Darwin and Wallace both conceded the human brain to be? Gould takes such points seriously, saying that it is time to free ourselves "from the need to interpret all our basic skills as adaptations for specific purposes."[25]

As no definition of fitness other than survival has been (or can be) proposed, the reasoning on this topic is circular. "Natural selection . . . amounts to the statement that the individuals which leave the most offspring are those which leave the most offspring. It is a tautology."[26] "The survivors, having survived, are thence judged to be the fittest."[27]

Finally, Darwin thought that natural selection accounts for the creativity in evolution — how life forms that are clearly higher emerged. Stephen Gould does not see that it does.[28]

D. EMBRYOLOGY AND VESTIGIAL ORGANS.

I was taught that the human embryo in the course of its development in the womb rehearses the entire evolutionary sequence — in Ernst Haeckel's catchy slogan, "ontogeny recapitulates phy-

logeny." Our useless tailbones, for their part, were cited as vestigial remains of the tails our ancestors had swung from. When I mentioned these matters in presenting an early draft of this paper, a biologist expressed surprise at my bringing them up. "We haven't taught those things in years," he said. It turns out that what I had been taught were incipient gills in the embryo are not gills at all, and that the coccygeal vertebrae — tailbone is a clear misnomer — are in no wise vestigial. Without the muscles they support, our pelvic organs would drop out.

E. BIOGENESIS

Darwin occupied himself only with the living world, but his followers extended his theory to explain how life originated from nonlife. In the early 1950s it was thought that experiments performed by Stanley Miller and Harold Urey had shown this to be possible, but it is now recognized, first, that the atmospheric conditions in which life arose were probably prohibitively different from those in the scientists' laboratory, and second, that the kind of amino acids that they produced — racemates — are not the kind that can support life.

F. MATHEMATICAL IMPROBABILITY

It used to be thought that geological time was immense enough to allow almost anything to happen, and so it is if we are thinking of isolated events like the number nineteen turning up on a roulette wheel precisely when it is needed. Now, though, attention has turned to the extent to which innumerable precise components must converge, each making its appearance exactly on schedule. This is more like the number twenty-three coming up on all the tables at Monte Carlo simultaneously, followed by the numbers twenty-four, twenty-five, twenty-six, and so on, still all appearing simultaneously. For things like this to happen, even four billion years is insufficient. Again a personal anecdote can make the point. At yet another presentation of this paper in progress it happened that the president of the International Association for Mathematical Biology was in the audience. He did not enter into the discussion, but at its close he came forward and identified himself. Then, very quietly, he said, "There wasn't enough time." It is for this reason that Fred Hoyle, Francis Crick, and others are

turning to outer space, deeming it more probable that our planet was "seeded" with life from elsewhere than that it developed here.

"What is not in doubt," says Stephen Gould, "is the fact of evolution," or what I have called descriptive evolution. "But as to its mechanism [here called Darwinism], there is observational evidence for natural selection [true, but outside of microevolution?], but it could be false that it [that is, Darwinism in its distinctive claim] is as strong a determinant of evolution as we think."[29] More recent statements in which Gould associated adaptationism with Voltaire's joke—"Why do people have noses? To support their glasses!"—suggest that his own confidence in it is waning. *The New York Times Magazine* reported that "this forty-two-year-old paleontologist is putting himself more and more at odds with orthodox Darwinism,"[30] but the alternatives he is toying with—constraints imposed by developmental trends and anatomical architecture—are at this stage little more than conjectures.

The point of this critique of Darwinism has been to show how little (in the way of hard evidence) has been allowed to eclipse so much (the Great Origins principle). This is the more so when to the paucity of firm empirical evidence we add intuitive considerations which can only be listed.

—Max Muller, according to Nirad Chaudhuri's book *Scholar Extraordinary*, wrote to Darwin saying that he found it quite possible to believe that the human physique has evolved from simpler bodies, but the idea that human language emerged from grunts and brays struck him as out of the question.

—Can something emerge from nothing? Can a stream rise higher than its source? When I ask my students these questions they almost inevitably answer no. Yet William Bartley, the biographer and foremost interpreter of Karl Popper, tells us that the foundation of Popper's philosophy is the claim that something can come from nothing. What are we to make of these opposite answers? My personal reading of the matter is that Popper, having steeped his life in the philosophy of science, saw clearly the fundamental point. Only if we grant science the counterintuitive, something-from-nothing assumption can we look to it to explain anything above the material plane.

—The going word for that something-from-nothing legerdemain is *emergence,* and in countering reductionism by insisting

that higher forms have ontological components that were not in their precursors, it looks in the right direction. But as an explanation for those novel components it is worthless; it recognizes their arrival while doing nothing to explain it. There would be nothing wrong with this if it did not presume to explain it, which it does by riding analogies that are spurious. The standard one is the liquidity of water which emerges from the convergence of two gases, hydrogen and oxygen. This, though, overlooks the fact that apart from the way water looks and feels to us (which introduces an issue the analogy finesses, namely, the emergence of sentience and awareness) its liquidity is simply a different arrangement of molecules in motion, or primary qualities only. Nothing new in kind has appeared at all. The same old primary qualities have merely been reshuffled.

Conclusion

Is it impertinent for someone untrained in science to tamper with a theory as technical as evolution has become? Who owns this issue?

It has been my contention that more than technicalities are involved. My basic question has been whether we should believe that Darwinism explains how we got here, and my negative answer is predicated on the claim that beliefs take shape on an unrestricted horizon which in this case includes considerations in addition to ones that are paleobiological.

It brings to mind the story of the ill-fated sky diver who, plummeting toward earth in a parachute that refuses to open, passes a hot-air balloonist whose blow torch won't shut off. "Know anything about parachutes?" he shouts, to which the balloonist counters, "No, but what about you? Know anything about gas stoves?" Whitehead predicted that, more than by any other factor, the future will be shaped by the way the two most powerful forces in history—science and religion—settle into relation with each other. That relationship has been my root concern. Though I have openly registered my perception that the Darwinian parachute has not opened very far, I know no more about such devices than the next person. I do know something about gas stoves, here representing convictions that can make the spirit soar. It is as Walker Percy says. Plummeting through sidereal time, we moderns under poor acous-

tical conditions shout across the expanses that divide our special-
ties, "Know anything about this? About that?"

The speaker who has the best grasp of both is the one who
most merits our attention.

NOTES

1. Marshall Sahlins, *Culture and Practical Reason* (Chicago: University of Chicago Press, 1976), p. 17.

2. I find myself in an awkward position here, for though I wish
to extricate the Great Origins thesis from the Creationists' clutches, in
ways they have my respect. Their deep commitment to one version of the
Great Origins doctrine has made them more vigilant than other theologians in spotting places where Darwinism rides on faith rather than fact.

An important chapter in the sociology of knowledge is being written; one in which establishment forces as represented by the university,
the American Civil Liberties Union, and mainline churches will not, in
the eyes of history, emerge as heroes. I touch on these issues in Huston
Smith, "Scientism in Sole Command," *Christianity and Crisis*, 21 Janu-
ary 1982; and in Huston Smith, "Evolution and Evolutionism," *The Christian Century*, 7–14 July 1982.

3. Albert Einstein, *Living Philosophies* (New York: Simon &
Schuster, 1931), pp. 6–7.

4. See also Saul Bellow's 1976 Nobel Laureate Address: "The intelligent public is waiting to hear from art what it does not hear from
theology, philosophy, and social theory, and what it cannot hear from
pure science: a broader, fuller, more coherent, more comprehensive account of what we human beings are, who we are, and what this life is
for. If writers do not come into the center it will not be because the center is preempted. It is not."

5. The conclusion of Jacques Monod, *Chance and Necessity* (New
York: Vintage Books, 1972), as summarized in Don Cupitt, *Worlds of Science and Religion* (New York: Hawthorne Books, 1976), p. 12.

6. *The New Encyclopaedia Britannica*, s.v. "Evolution."

7. E. F. Schumacher, *Guide for the Perplexed* (New York: Harper
& Row, 1976), pp. 100–10.

8. Cupitt, *Worlds of Science and Religion*, p. 1.

9. Monod, *Chance and Necessity*, p. 21, emphasis his.

10. Victor Ferkiss, review of *Algeny* by Jeremy Rifkin, *Environment*
25 (July–August 1983): 44.

11. Norman Macbeth, *Darwin Retried* (Boston: Gambit, 1971).

12. Jeremy Rifkin, *Algeny* (New York: Viking Press, 1983), p. 130.

13. *The New Encyclopaedia Britannica*, s.v. "Evolution."

14. Pierre Grassé, *Evolution of Living Forms* (New York: Academic Press, 1977), pp. 202, 206.

15. Edwin Conklin, *Man Real and Ideal* (New York: Scribner's, 1943), p. 52.

16. David Raup, "Conflicts between Darwin and Paleontology," *Field Museum of Natural History Bulletin* 50 (1979): 24.

17. Charles Darwin, *The Origin of Species* (London: J. M. Dent, 1971), p. 239.

18. Raup, "Conflicts between Darwin and Paleontology," p. 26.

19. David Kitts, "Paleontology and Evolutionary Theory," *Evolution* 28 (1974): 467. Darwinists must produce a family tree, a pedigree, Norman Macbeth observed on the *Nova* program earlier referred to, "and I regret to say that after 120 years they haven't produced a single solid phylogeny."

20. Stephen Jay Gould, with Niles Eldredge, "Punctuated Equilibria," *Paleobiology* 3 (1977): 115.

21. Luther Burbank, quoted in Macbeth, *Darwin Retried*, p. 35.

22. Loren Eiseley, quoted in Macbeth, *Darwin Retried*, p. 36.

23. Gertrude Himmelfarb, *Darwin and the Darwinian Revolution* (New York: W. W. Norton, 1959), pp. 341–42.

24. Stephen Jay Gould, "The Return of Hopeful Monsters," *Natural History* 86 (June–July 1977): 24.

25. Stephen Jay Gould, "The Evolutionary Biology of Constraint," *Daedalus* 29 (1980): 46.

26. C. H. Waddington, *The Strategy of Genes* (London: Allen & Unwin, 1957), pp. 64–65.

27. Himmelfarb, *Darwin and the Darwinian Revolution*, p. 316.

28. *Unitarian-Universalist World*, 2 February 1982.

29. Ibid.

30. James Gleick, "Stephen Jay Gould: Breaking Tradition with Darwin," *New York Times Magazine*, 20 November 1983, p. 50.

4

Gaia and Philosophy

DORION SAGAN AND LYNN MARGULIS

THE GAIA HYPOTHESIS IS a scientific view of life on Earth that represents one aspect of a new biological world view. In philosophical terms this new world view is more Aristotelian than Platonic. It is predicated on the earthly factual, not the ideal abstract, but there are some metaphysical connotations. The new biological world view, and Gaia as a major part of it, embraces the circular logic of life and engineering systems, shunning the Greek-Western heritage of final syllogisms.

Gaia is a theory of the atmosphere and surface sediments of the planet Earth taken as a whole. The Gaia hypothesis in its most general form states that the temperature and composition of the Earth's atmosphere are actively regulated by the sum of life on the planet — the biota. This regulation of the Earth's surface by the biota and for the biota has been in continuous existence since the earliest appearance of widespread life. The assurance of continued global habitability according to the Gaian hypothesis is not a matter merely of chance. The Gaian view of the atmosphere is a radical departure from the former scientific concept that life on Earth is surrounded by and adapts to an essentially static environment. That life interacts with and eventually becomes its own environment; that the atmosphere is an extension of the biosphere in nearly the same sense that the human mind is an extension of DNA; that life interacts with and controls physical attributes of the Earth on a global scale — all these things resonate strongly with the ancient magico-religious sentiment that all is one. On a more practical plane, Gaia holds important implications not only for understanding life's past but for engineering its future.

60

The Gaia hypothesis, presently a concern only for certain interdisciplinarians, may someday provide a basis for a new ecology — and even become a household word. Already it is becoming the basis for a rich new world view. Let us first examine the scientific basis for the hypothesis and then explore some of the metaphysical implications. Innovated by the atmospheric chemist James Lovelock, supported by microbiologist Lynn Margulis, and named by novelist William Golding, the Gaia hypothesis states that the composition of all the reactive gases as well as the temperature of the lower atmosphere have remained relatively constant over eons. (An eon is approximately a billion years.) In spite of many external perturbations from the solar system in the last several eons, the surface of the Earth has remained habitable by many kinds of life. The Gaian idea is that life makes and remakes its own environment to a great extent. Life reacts to global and cosmic crises, such as increasing radiation from the sun or the appearance for the first time of oxygen in the atmosphere, and dynamically responds to insure its own preservation such that the crises are endured or negated. Both scientifically and philosophically the Gaia hypothesis provides a clear and important theoretical window for what Lovelock calls "a new look at life on earth."[1]

Astronomers generally agree that the sun's total luminosity (output of energy as light) has increased during the past 4 billion years. They infer from this that the mean temperature of the surface of the Earth ought to have risen correspondingly. But there is evidence from the fossil record of life that the Earth's temperature has remained relatively stable.[2] The Gaia hypothesis recognizes this stability as a property of life on the Earth's surface. We shall see how the hypothesis explains the regulation of temperature as one of many factors whose modulation may be attributed to Gaia. The temperature of the lower atmosphere is steered by life within bounds set by physical factors. With a simple model that applies cybernetic concepts to the growth, behavior, and diversity of populations of living organisms, Lovelock has most recently shown how, in principle, the intrinsic properties of life lead to active regulation of Earth's surface temperature. There is nothing mystical in the process at all. By examining in some detail the life of a mythical world containing only daisies (about which, more later), even skeptical readers can be convinced that it is theoreti-

cally possible for living, growing, responding communities of organisms to exert control over factors concerning their own survival. No unknown conscious forces need be invoked; temperature regulation becomes a consequence of the well-known properties of life's responsiveness and growth. In fact, perhaps the most striking philosophical conclusion is that the cybernetic control of the Earth's surface by unintelligent organisms calls into question the alleged uniqueness of human intelligent consciousness.

In exploring the regulatory properties of living beings it seems most likely that atmospheric regulation can be attributed to the combined metabolic and growth activities of organisms, especially of microbes. Microbes (or microorganisms) are those living beings seen only with a microscope. They display impressive capabilities for transforming the nitrogen-, sulfur-, and carbon-containing gases of the atmosphere.[3] Animals and plants, on the other hand, show few such abilities. All or nearly all chemical transformations present in animals and plants were already widespread in microbes before animals and plants evolved. Until the development of Lovelock's Daisy World the discussion of control of atmospheric methane (a gas which indirectly affects temperature and is produced only by certain microbes known as methanogenic bacteria) has provided the most detailed exposition of the maintenance of atmospheric temperature stability.[4] The concentration of water vapor in the air correlates with certain climatic features, including the temperature at the Earth's surface. The details of the relationship between temperature and forest trees, determining the production and transport of huge quantities of water in a process called evapotranspiration, was recently presented by meteorologists in a quantitative model.[5] Although these scientists did not discuss their work in a Gaian context they have inadvertently provided a further Gaian example. Indeed, as Hutchinson originally recognized when he described the geological consequences of feces and, as the new ecology book by Botkin and Keller shows, many observations concerning the effects of the biota in maintaining the environment can be reinterpreted in a Gaian context.[6]

How can the gas composition and temperature of the atmosphere be actively regulated by organisms? Although willing to believe that atmospheric methane is of biological origin and that the

process of evapotranspiration moves enormous quantities of water from the soil through trees into the atmosphere, several critics have rejected the Gaia hypothesis as such because they fail to see how the temperature and gas composition of an entire planetary surface could be regulated for several billion years by an evolving biota that lacks foresight or planning of any kind.[7]

Primarily in response to these critics Dr. Lovelock and his former graduate student Dr. Andrew Watson formulated a general model of temperature modulation by the biota, to which they pleasantly refer as "Daisy World." Daisy World uses surface temperature rather than gas composition to demonstrate the possible kinds of regulating mechanisms that are consistent with how populations of organisms behave. Daisy World exemplifies the kind of Gaian mechanisms we would expect to find, based as it is on an analogy between cybernetic systems and the growth properties of organisms. In an admittedly simplified fashion it shows that temperature regulation can emerge as a logical consequence of life's well-known properties. These include potential for exponential growth, and growth rates varying with temperature such that the highest rate occurs at the optimal temperature for each population, decreasing around the optimum until growth is limited by extreme upper and lower temperatures. We will describe the Daisy World in detail shortly.

Some such model, explaining the regulation of surface temperature, is required to explain several observations. For example, the oldest rocks not metamorphosed by high temperatures and pressures, both from the Swaziland System of southern Africa[8] and from the Warrawoona Formation of western Australia,[9] contain evidence of early life. Both sedimentary sequences are over 3 billion years old. From 3 billion years ago until the present we have a continuous record of life on Earth, implying that the mean surface temperature has reached neither the boiling nor the freezing point of water. Given that an ice age involves less than a 10° C drop in mean midlatitude temperature and that even ice ages are relatively rare in the fossil record, the mean temperature at the surface of the Earth probably has stayed well within the range from 5° to 25° C during at least the last 3 billion years. Solar luminosity during the last 4 billion years is thought, by many astronomers, to have increased by at least 10 percent.[10] Thus life on Earth seems to have

acted as a global thermostat. Any current estimate for the increase of solar luminosity, which varies from less than 30 to more than 70 percent,[11] does not alter the outcome of Daisy World's conclusions. A relative increase of solar luminosity from values of 0.6 to 2.2 (its present value is 1.0) is consistent with Daisy World assumptions since a range of values has been plotted by Lovelock and his collaborator Watson.

Cybernetic systems, as is well known to science and engineering, are steered. They actively maintain specified variables at a constant in spite of perturbing influences. Such systems are said to be homeostatic if their variables, such as temperature, direction traveled, pressure, light intensity, and so forth, are regulated around a fixed set point. Examples of such set points might be $22°$ C for a room thermostat or 40 percent relative humidity for a room humidifier. If the set point itself is not constant but changes with time it is called an operating point. Systems with operating points rather than set points are said to be homeorrhetic rather than homeostatic. Gaian regulatory systems, like the embryological ones described by C. H. Waddington,[12] are more properly described as homeorrhetic rather than homeostatic. Fascinatingly enough, both homeorrhetic and homeostatic systems defy the most basic statutes of Western syllogistic thought, although not thought itself, since most people do not think syllogistically but in an associative fashion. For instance, if a person — surely a homeorrhetic entity — is hungry, he or she will eat. Thereupon hunger ceases. Put syllogistically the sense of such a series becomes nullified: I am hungry; therefore I eat; therefore I am not hungry. The thesis leads to an antithesis without ever being synthetically resolved. This circular, tautological mode of operations is characteristic of cybernetic systems, including of course all organisms and organismic combinations. It is consonant with the emotive poetic power of contradictory statements, dichotomous personalities, and oxymoronic lyrics, such as references to a midnight sun.

Even minimal cybernetic systems have certain defining properties: a sensor, an input, a gain (the amount of amplification in the system), and an output. In order to achieve stability or increase complexity the output is compared with the set or operating point so that errors are corrected. Error correction means that the output must in some way feed back to the sensor so that the new in-

put can compensate for the change in output. Positive or negative feedback, usually both, are involved in error correction. A first attempt to apply this sort of cybernetic analysis to the Gaia hypothesis involved development of the Daisy World mathematical model, first by Lovelock[13] and later by Watson and Lovelock together.[14] We turn now to the description of the model.

The Daisy World model is used to demonstrate how planetary surface temperature might be regulated. It makes simple assumptions: the world's surface harbors a population of living organisms consisting only of dark and light daisies. These organisms always breed true. Each light daisy produces only light offspring daisies and each dark daisy produces only its kind. Totally black daisies absorb all of the light coming on them from the sun and totally white daisies reflect all of the light. The best temperatures for growth for both dark and light daisies are considered to be the same: no growth below 5°, increasing growth as a function of temperature to an optimum at 20° C, and decreasing growth rate above the optimum to 40° C, at which temperature all growth ceases.

At lower temperatures darker daisies are assumed to absorb more heat, and thus grow more rapidly in their local area than lighter daisies. At higher temperatures lighter daisies reflect and thus lose more heat, leading to a greater rate of growth in their local area. The details have been published in technical journals,[15] and have recently been explained in a more popular way by us in the British magazine *The Ecologist: Journal of the Post-Industrial Age.*[16] In summary, the graphs generated by models using these assumptions show that dark and light daisy life can, because of growth and interaction with light, influence the temperature of the planet's surface on a global scale. What is remarkable about the various forms of Lovelock and Watson's model is that the amplification properties of the rapid growth of organisms (here daisies) under changing temperatures are enough in themselves to provide the beginning of a mechanism for global thermal homeorrhesis, a phenomenon which some would rather see credited only to a mysterious life force. In general, in these models an increase in diversity of organisms, such as a greater difference between the light and darkness of the daisies, leads to an increase in regulatory ability as well as an increase in total population size.

Daisy World is only a mathematical model. Even with its oversimplification, however, the Daisy World model shows quite clearly that temperature homeorrhesis of the biosphere is not something which is too mysterious to have a mechanism. By implication it suggests that other observed anomalies, such as the near constant salinity of the oceans over vast periods of time and the coexistence of chemically reactive gases in the atmosphere, may have solutions which actively involve life forms. The radical insight delivered by Daisy World is that global homeorrhesis is in principle possible without the introduction of any but well-known tenets of biology. The Gaian system does not have to plan in advance or be foresighted in any way in order to show homeorrhetic tendencies. A biological system acting cybernetically gives the impression of teleology. If only the results and not the feedback processes were stated it would look as if the organisms had conspired to insure their own survival.

The Gaia hypothesis says in essence that the entire Earth functions as a massive machine or responsive organism. While many ancient and folk beliefs have often expressed similar sentiments, Lovelock's modern formulation is alluring because it is a modern amalgam of information derived from several different scientific disciplines. Perhaps the strongest single body of evidence for Gaia comes not from the evidence of thermal regulation which is modeled in Daisy World but from Lovelock's own field, atmospheric chemistry.[17]

From a chemical point of view the atmosphere of the Earth is anomalous. Not only major gases such as nitrogen but also minor gases such as methane, ammonia, and carbon dioxide are present at levels many orders of magnitude greater than they should be on a planet with 20 percent free oxygen in its atmosphere. It was this persistent overabundance of gases that react with oxygen, persisting in the presence of oxygen, that initially convinced Lovelock when he worked at NASA in the late 60s and early 70s that it was not necessary for the Viking spacecraft to go to Mars to see if life was there. Lovelock felt he could tell simply from the Martian atmosphere, an atmosphere consistent with the dicta of equilibrium chemistry, that life did not exist there.[18] The Earth's atmosphere, in fact, is not at all what one would expect from a simple interpolation of the atmospheres of our neighboring planets, Mars and Venus. Mars and Venus have mostly carbon dioxide

in their atmosphere and nearly no free oxygen, while on Earth the major atmospheric component is nitrogen and breathable oxygen comprises a good one-fifth of the air.

Lovelock has compared the Earth's atmosphere with life to the way the atmosphere would be without any life on Earth. A lifeless Earth would be cold, engulfed in carbon dioxide, and lacking in breathable oxygen. In a chemically stable system we would expect nitrogen and oxygen to react and form large quantities of poisonous nitrogen oxides as well as the soluble nitrate ion. The fact that gases unstable in each other's presence, such as oxygen, nitrogen, hydrogen, and methane, are maintained on Earth in huge quantities should persuade all rational thinkers to reexamine the scientific status quo taught in textbooks of a largely passive atmosphere that just happens, on chemical grounds, to contain violently reactive gases in an appropriate concentration for most of life.

In the Gaian theory of the atmosphere, life continually synthesizes and removes the gases necessary for its own survival. Life controls the composition of the reactive atmospheric gases. Mars and Venus, and the hypothetical dead Earth devoid of life, all have chemically stable atmospheres composed of over 95 percent carbon dioxide. Earth as we live on it, however, has only 0.03 percent of this stable gas in its atmosphere. The anomaly is largely due to one facet of Gaia's operations, namely the process of photosynthesis. Bacteria, algae, and plants continuously remove carbon dioxide from the air via photosynthesis and incorporate the carbon from the gas into solid structures such as limestone reefs and eventually animal shells. Much of the carbon in the air as carbon dioxide becomes incorporated into organisms that are eventually buried. The bodies of deceased photosynthetic microbes and plants, as well as of all other living forms which consume photosynthetic organisms, are buried in soil in the form of carbon compounds of various kinds. By using solar energy to turn carbon dioxide into calcium carbonates or organic compounds of living organisms, and then dying, plants, photosynthetic bacteria, and algae have trapped and buried the once-atmospheric carbon dioxide which geochemists agree was the major gas in the Earth's early atmosphere. If not for life, and Gaia's cyclical *modus operandi,* our Earth's atmosphere would be more like those of Venus and Mars. Carbon dioxide would be its major gas even now.

Microbes, the first forms of life to evolve, seem in fact to be

at the very center of the Gaian phenomenon. Photosynthetic bacteria were burying carbon and releasing waste oxygen millions of years before the development of plants and animals. Methanogens and some sulfur-transforming bacteria, which do not tolerate any free oxygen, have been involved with the Gaian regulation of atmospheric gases from the very beginning. From a Gaian point of view animals, all of which are covered with and invaded by gas-exchanging microbes, may be simply a convenient way to distribute these microbes more numerously and evenly over the surface of the globe. Animals and even plants are late-comers to the Gaian scene. The earliest communities of organisms that removed atmospheric carbon dioxide on a large scale must have been microbes. In fact we have a direct record of their activities in the form of fossils. These members of the ancient microbial world constructed complex microbial mats, some of which were preserved as stromatolites, layered rocks whose genesis both now and billions of years ago is due to microbial activities. Although such carbon-dioxide-removing communities of microbes still flourish today, they have been supplemented and camouflaged by more conspicuous communities of organisms such as forests and coral reefs.

To maintain temperature and gas composition at livable values, microbial life reacts to threats in a controlled, seemingly purposeful manner. Gas composition and temperature must have been stable over long periods of time. For instance, if atmospheric oxygen were to decrease only a few percentage points, all animal life dependent on higher concentrations would perish. On the other hand, as Andrew Watson showed, increases in the level of atmospheric oxygen would lead to dangerous forest fires.[19] Small increases of oxygen would lead to forest fires even in soggy rain forests due to ignition by lightning. Thus the quantity of oxygen in the atmosphere must have remained relatively constant since the time that air-breathing animals have been living in forests — which has been over 300 million years. Just as bees and termites control the temperature and humidity of the air in their hives and nests, so the biota somehow controls the concentration of oxygen and other gases in the Earth's atmosphere.

It is this *somehow* which worries and infuriates some of the more traditional Darwinian biologists. The most serious general problems confronting widespread acceptance of the Gaia hypothe-

sis are the perceived implications of foreknowledge and planning in Gaia's purported abilities to react to impending crisis and ward off ecological doom. How can the struggling mass of genes inside the cells of organisms at the Earth's surface know, ask these biologists, how to regulate macro-conditions like global gas composition and temperature? The molecular biologist W. Ford Doolittle, for example, a man who because of his work is perhaps predisposed toward viewing evolution at smaller rather than larger levels, sees the Gaia hypothesis as untenable, a motherly theory of nature without a mechanism.[20]

Another scientist, the Oxford University evolutionist Richard Dawkins, is even more forceful in his rejection of the theory. Likening it to the BBC Theorem (a pejorative reference to the television documentary notion of nature as wonderful balance and harmony), Dawkins has extreme difficulty in imagining a realistic situation in which the Gaian mechanism for the perpetuation of life as a planetary phenomenon could ever have evolved. Dawkins, author of *The Selfish Gene*, can only conceive of the evolution of planetary homeorrhetic in relation to interplanetary selection: "The universe would have to be full of dead planets whose homeostatic regulation systems had failed, with, dotted around, a handful of successful, well-regulated planets of which Earth is one."[21]

These sound like forceful arguments, yet if the critics of Gaia cannot accept the notion of a planet as an amorphic, but viable, biological entity, they must have equal if not greater cause to dismiss the origin of life. Surely at one point in the history of the Earth a single homeostatic bacterial cell existed which did not have to struggle with other cells in order to survive, since there were no other cells. The genesis of the first cell can no more be explained from a strict Darwinian standpoint of competition among selfish individuals than can the present regulation of the atmosphere. While the first cell and the present planet may both be correctly seen as individuals, they are equally alone, and as such they both fall outside the province of modern population genetics.

Nonetheless, Lovelock, a sensitive man with a deep sense of intellectual mischief, has answered his critics with one of their own favorite weapons: mathematical model-making in the form of the aforementioned Daisy World.[22] Not believing that the Earth's temperature and gases can be regulated with machine-like precision

for billions of years, because organisms cannot possibly plan ahead, Lovelock's critics reject his personification of the planet into a conscious female entity named Gaia. Originally lacking an explicit mechanism and falling outside the major Darwinian paradigm of selfish individualism, it was and still sometimes is difficult for trained evolutionists to refrain from regarding Gaia as the latest deification of Earth by nature nuts. How can an entangled mass of disjointed struggling microbes, they ask, effect global concert of any kind, let alone to such an extent that we are permitted to think about the Earth as a single organism? The answer of course is the kind of analysis explored in Daisy World, and one still waits to see how those who accuse Lovelock of conscious mysticism and pop-ecology will respond to it in all its mathematical intricacy.

Perhaps the greatest psychological stumbling block in the way of widespread scholarly acceptance of Gaia is the implicit shadow of doubt it throws over the concept of the uniqueness of humanity in nature. Gaia denies the sanctity of human attributes. If intricate planning, for instance, can be mimicked by cunning arrays of subvisible entities, what is so special about *Homo sapiens* and our most prized congenital possession, the human intellect? The Gaian answer to this is probably that nothing is so very special about the human species or mind. Indeed, recent research points suggestively to the possibility that the physical attributes and capacities of the brain may be a special case of symbiosis among modified bacteria.[23]

In real life, as opposed to Daisy World, microbes, not daisies, play the crucial role in the continual production and control of rare and reactive compounds. Microbial growth is also responsible, possibly through the production of heat-retaining gases as well as the changing colored surfaces, for the continuing thermostasis of the Earth. Evolutionarily, microbes were responsible for the establishment of the Gaian system. Insofar as larger forms of animal and plant life are essentially collections of interacting microbes, Gaia may be thought of as still primarily a microbial phenomenon.[24] We human beings, made of microbes, are part of Gaia no less than our bones, made from the calcium from our cells, are part of ourselves.

In his recent article on classical views of Gaia, J. D. Hughes quoted the ancient Greek work *Economics* by Xenophon: "Earth

is a goddess and teaches justice to those who can learn, for the better she is served, the more good things she gives in return." In the classical view, that is, of the Greek Gaia or Earth Goddess and the Latin Tellus, the Earth is a vast living organism. The homeric hymn sings:

> Gaia, mother of all, I sing oldest of gods.
> Firm of foundation, who feeds all creatures living
>   on earth.
> As many as move on the radiant land and swim in
>   the sea
> And fly through the air—all these does she feed
>   with her bounty.
> Mistress, from you come our fine children and
>   bountiful harvests.
> Yours is the power to give mortals life and to take
>   it away.[25]

Although Gaia is reappearing in modern dress, the modern scientific formulation of the Gaian idea is quite different from the ancient one. Gaia is not the nurturing mother or fertility doll of the human race. Rather, human beings, in spite of our raging anthropocentrism, are relegated to a tiny and unessential part of the Gaian system. People, like *Brontosaurus* and grasslands, are merely one of the many weedy components of an enormous living system dominated by microbes. Gaia has antecedents not only among the classical poets but even among scientists, most notably in the work of the Russian V. I. Vernadsky (1863–1945).[26] But Lovelock's Gaia hypothesis is a modern piece of science: it is subject to observational and experimental verification and modification.

There is something fresh, new, and yet mythologically appealing about Gaia, however. A scientific theory of an Earth that in some sense feels and responds is welcome. The Gaian blending of organisms and environment into one, wherein the atmosphere is an extension of the biosphere, is a modern rationalist formulation of an ancient intuitive sentiment. One implication is that there may be a strong biogeological precedent for the time-honored political and mystical goal of peaceful coexistence and world unity.

Contrary to possible first impressions, however, the Gaia hypothesis, especially in the hands of its innovator, does not protect

all the moral sanctions of popular ecology. Lovelock himself is no admirer of most environmentalists. He expresses nothing but disdain for those technological critics he characterizes as misanthropes or Luddites, people who are "more concerned with destructive action than with constructive thought."[27] He claims, "If by pollution we mean the dumping of waste matter there is indeed ample evidence that pollution is as natural to Gaia as is breathing to ourselves and most other animals."[28] We breathe oxygen, originally and essentially a microbial waste product. Lovelock, employed at one time by the DuPont Corporation, believes that biological toxins are in the main more dangerous than technological ones, and he adds sardonically that they would probably be sold in health food stores if not for their toxicity. Yet there is no clear division between the technological and the biological. In the end all technological toxins are natural, biological by-products which, though via human beings, are elements in the Gaian system. Similarly, legislation and lobbying attempts, such as the recent furor in the United States over the mismanagement of the Environmental Protection Agency, are nothing more or less than part of Gaian feedback cycles.

Ecologically speaking, the Gaia hypothesis hardly reserves a special place in the pantheon of life for human beings. Recently evolved, and therefore immature in a fundamental Gaian sense, human beings have only recently been integrated into the global biological scene. Our relationship with Gaia is still superficial. On the other hand, our ultimate potential as a nervous early warning system for Gaia remains unsurpassed. Deflecting oncoming asteroids into space and spearheading the colonization of life on other planets represent additions to the Gaian repertoire that our species must initiate. On the one hand, Gaia was an early and crucial development in the history of life's evolutionary past. Without the Gaian environmental modulating system life probably would not have persisted. Now, only by comprehending the intricacies of Gaia can we hope to discover how the biota has created and regulated the surface environment of the planet for the last 3 billion years. On the other hand, the full scientific exploration of Gaian control mechanisms is probably the surest single road leading to the successful implementation of self-supporting living habitats in space. If we are ever to engineer large space stations that replen-

ish their own vital supplies, then we must study the natural technology of Gaia. Still more ambitiously, the *terraformation* of another planet, for example, of Mars, so that it can actually support human beings living out in the open, is a gigantic task and one that becomes thinkable only from the Gaian perspective.

In terms of the metaphysics of inner space, acceptance of the Gaian view leads almost precipitously to a change in philosophical perspective. As just one example, human artifacts, such as machines, pollution, and even works of art, are no longer seen as separate from the feedback processes of nature. Recovering from Copernican insult and Darwinian injury, anthropocentrism has been dealt yet another reeling blow by Gaia. This blow, however, should not send us into new depths of disillusion or existential despair. Quite the opposite: we should rejoice in the new truths of our essential belonging, our relative unimportance, and our complete dependence upon a biosphere which has always had a life entirely its own.

NOTES

1. James E. Lovelock, *Gaia: A New Look at Life on Earth* (Oxford and New York: Oxford University Press, 1982).

2. Lynn Margulis and James E. Lovelock, "Biological Modulation of the Earth's Atmosphere," *Icarus* 21 (1974): 471–89.

3. Ibid.

4. Andrew J. Watson, James E. Lovelock, and Lynn Margulis, "Methanogenesis, Fires, and the Regulation of Atmospheric Oxygen," *BioSystems* 10 (1978): 293–98.

5. J. Shukla and Yale Mintz, "Influence of the Land-Surface Evapotranspiration on the Earth's Climate, *Science* 215 (1982): 1498–1501.

6. Daniel B. Botkin and Edward A. Keller, *Environmental Studies: The Earth as a Living Planet* (Columbus, Ohio: Charles E. Merrill Pubs., 1982); G. Evelyn Hutchinson, *Biogeochemistry of Vertebrate Excretion* (New York: American Museum of Natural History, 1954).

7. W. Ford Doolittle, "Is Nature Really Motherly?" *CoEvolution Quarterly* 29 (1981): 58–63; Robert M. Garrels, A. Lerman, and Fred T. MacKenzie, "Controls of Atmospheric Oxygen: Past, Present, and Future," *American Scientist* 61 (1981): 306–15.

8. Lynn Margulis, *Early Life* (Boston: Science Books International,

1982); J. William Schopf, ed., *Precambrian Paleobiology Research Group Report* (Princeton, N.J.: Princeton University Press, 1983); Malcolm J. Walter, ed., *Stromatolites: Developments in Sedimentology* vol. 20 (Amsterdam, Oxford, and New York: Elsevier, 1976).

9. Stanley M. Awramik, J. William Schopf, and Malcolm J. Walter, "The Warrawoona Microfossils," *Precambrian Research* 20 (1983).

10. Michael J. Newman, "Evolution of the Solar 'Constant'," in *Limits to Life*, ed. C. Ponnamperuma and Lynn Margulis (Dordrecht, Holland: Reidel Pub. Co., 1980).

11. Ibid.

12. Conrad H. Waddington, concluding remarks in *Evolution and Consciousness*, ed. Erich Jantsch and Conrad H. Waddington (Reading, Mass.: Addison Wesley Pub. Co., 1976).

13. James E. Lovelock, "Gaia as Seen through the Atmosphere," in *The Fourth International Symposium on Biomineralization*, ed. Peter Westbroek and E. W. deJong (Dordrecht, Holland: Reidel Pub. Co., 1983).

14. Andrew J. Watson and James E. Lovelock, "Biological Homeostasis of the Global Environment: The Parable of 'Daisy World'," *Tellus* 35b (1983): 284–89; James E. Lovelock, "Daisy World: A Cybernetic Proof of the Gaia Hypothesis," *CoEvolution Quarterly* 31 (1983): pp. 66–72.

15. See notes 13 and 14.

16. Dorion Sagan and Lynn Margulis, "What Gaia Means to the Ecologist," *The Ecologist: Journal of the Post-Industrial Age* 15 (1983).

17. Incidentally, Lovelock is an inventor as well as a scientist. He devised the "electron capture device," a sensor for gas chromatographs that detects freon and other halogenated compounds in concentrations of far less than one part per million in the air. Indeed it was Lovelock's invention and observations that in large part sparked off ecological worries of ozone depletion, ultraviolet light-induced cancers, and general atmospheric catastrophe.

18. James E. Lovelock and Lynn Margulis, "Is Mars a Spaceship Too?" *Natural History Magazine* (1976): 86–90; Lovelock, *Gaia: A New Look at Life on Earth*.

19. Watson, Lovelock, and Margulis, "Methanogenesis, Fires, and the Regulation of Atmospheric Oxygen."

20. Doolittle, "Is Nature Really Motherly?"

21. Richard Dawkins, *The Extended Phenotype* (New York: W. H. Freeman Co., 1982), p. 17.

22. See note 14.

23. Lynn Margulis and Dorion Sagan, *The Expanding Microcosm* (New York: Summit Books, forthcoming).

24. Sharon Kaveski, Donna C. Mehos, and Lynn Margulis, "There

Are No One-Celled Animals or Plants," *The Science Teacher* (forth-coming).

25. Both are quoted in J. Donald Hughes, "Gaia: An Ancient View of our Planet," *The Ecologist: Journal of the Post-Industrial Age* 13 (1983): 54–60.

26. A. V. Lapo, *Traces of Bygone Biospheres*, trans. V. Purto (Moscow: Mir Pubs., 1982).

27. Lovelock, *Gaia: A New Look at Life on Earth*, p. 95.

28. Ibid.

Nature in Cross-Cultural Perspective

5

The Wild and the Cultivated
in Greek Religion

CARL RUCK

THE TWELVE DEITIES known collectively as the Olympians have come to symbolize for us some of the perfection for which ancient Greek culture is still admired today. We think of the wisdom of Athena, the musical grace of Apollo, and so on. They were said to have all been members of a single family that resided together in splendid houses on top of Olympus, the highest peak in the Greek lands. The head of the family was Zeus, imagined as a virile male at the age of full paternity, and indeed he was related to several of the others as their father and he bore the supreme epithet as father of both gods and human beings. These are the Greek gods that most people know from a reading of Homer.

A closer look at this decently patriarchal family, however, reveals a number of irregularities. Athena, for example, dressed as a male and was born full-grown without a mother out of her father's head, as though the mind, as Plato thought (Plato *Symposium* 206b ff.), were some kind of superior womb where males gestated something better than the biological infants that women give birth to. Hephaestus, in contrast, didn't have a father, but was solely the creation of his mother, as if the divine couple were vying with each other for procreative supremacy. And indeed, the husband and wife were notoriously ill-suited to each other, despite the equality of their bloodlines, for they were brother and sister. One can sense the uneasy nature of their marital bond in the only Olympian who was their joint offspring. He was Ares, the god of war. His paramour, Aphrodite, also showed a certain competitive-

79

ness between the sexes, for she was the goddess of love, a woman superior even to Zeus, and born actually two generations his senior, although her beguiling femininity masked the fact that originally she was just a phallus, supposedly castrated from her father.

It is, of course, understandable that beneath the calm of their Olympian existence there would be many tensions, for each of the twelve had lived originally in different circumstances and only recently had they come to their classical identities, just as the Greeks who worshipped them were a relatively new people, composed from different assimilated ethnic strains. Zeus himself had come with the tribal migrations that brought the Indo-Europeans in the second millennium B.C. from their northern Asiatic homeland into the Mediterranean Greek lands, where eventually they would dominate politically and culturally. They imposed their language, which we know as Greek, upon an earlier populace which was partly aboriginal and partly the result of earlier migrations from the East. Amongst these earlier inhabitants were the so-called Minoans, who had already achieved a high level of sophisticated culture on Crete and the Aegean islands. If Zeus, therefore, was not native to Greece, obviously he could not always have presided over Olympus, and although there was a story about his divine birth in a cave on Crete, that could only have been a second birth that identified him in Hellenic circumstances. It was strange, however, for him to have been born in a cave, for his name, which is Indo-European, associates him not with the darkness of the subterranean womb, but with the celestial realm of the shining day. The same etymological root gives the words in Latin for "day" (*dies*) and "god" (*deus*), and the Romans called him Jupiter, which is merely his name with the paternal epithet *pater*.

Unfortunately, this supreme father could not have chosen a less auspicious place to bring his people, for the earlier cultures worshipped a supreme mother. The Great Goddess, who was Earth, was not the snowbound inhospitable mountaintop, far removed from human concerns in the sunlit sky. Instead she was the plowland, in the midst of her people, or the soil to which the seed is entrusted in darkness, or the night itself, ruled by the lunar phases that match her womb's fertility and involved with the cavern in the earth, the tomb, sleep, and dreams. Whereas Zeus, like the other gods that he brought to Olympus, was immortal, a spirit

shunning contamination with human matter, she was a deity of repeated deaths and resurrections, one not adverse to human putrefaction, which was merely the transitional mode for life's renewal. And although Zeus liked to dominate his sibling wife, there was a time in these Greek lands when the Goddess ruled, and her consort was nothing but a creature of her own body.

Just as the Indo-Europeans assimilated words from these pre-Hellenic peoples for things that were alien to them in their homeland (for example, the word for "sea"), they also assimilated aspects of this chthonic religion, for it is the common pattern that diverse ethnic strains are reconciled in forging a national identity. Thus, alongside the Olympians in the classical age, there existed another class of deities, the chthonic ones, in whose subterranean realm the Goddess was still more important than her mate, the lord of death.

For the Olympians, the sacred place was a temple, an architectural replica of a sacred grove, a peripteral colonnade with a pitched roof. This design is not Mediterranean in origin but more appropriate for shedding the burden of snows in more northern climes. The temple was merely the house for the god's effigy, and worship took place before its opened door, in the free air beneath the shining sun. In contrast, the sanctuary of a chthonic deity was an enclosed space, a cave or its architectural replica. The worshippers, as in a church, entered the space to commune with the god, sometimes through incubation or a sacred meal. The Olympians were largely the guardians of Hellenic culture, the higher arts, the city, physical perfection, or the noble bloodlines of the dominant Indo-Europeans and the wealthy leaders of society. The Olympians originally had little sympathy for humankind and its mortal lot, and classical Greeks, when faced with the crises of their human condition, would turn to the chthonic ones to solve the problems of sickness, death, or infertility.

The two kinds of gods, however, were not completely separate. In the course of the assimilation, Indo-European deities had been equated with the Mediterranean ones, and thus the Olympians all had their darker *personae* from more primitive times, just as the chthonic ones might have a brighter side. A deity could not be worshipped in total exclusion of its past identities, for the dishonored *personae* would then be angered and rise up to undermine

the reconciliation that had been the foundation of Hellenic culture. Cultic rites, instead, renewed the reconciliation by according appropriate honor to all aspects of the deity, both the primitive and the civilized. Then the darker aspects would not pollute culture, withholding fertility and poisoning the progress of evolution. Instead, the present would be rooted securely in the past, nourished by the beneficent transmutation of what would otherwise be the forces of recidivism, pestilential putrefaction. In psychological terms, the pattern is analogous to the need to integrate the infantile libido into the balanced mature individual. Or in agrarian terms, which is the way the Greeks would have sensed it, rotting matter when correctly used is not poisonous but a source of fertility.

I should like to illustrate a few examples of this assimilation and integration with regard to several of the sacred plants that figured in Greek religion, specifically, the Eleusinian Mysteries, the rite of sacrifice, and the cults of Dionysus and Apollo. Amongst the earliest knowledge that people organized into a science must have been the attempt to categorize plants: those that were edible; those that were poisonous; and those that seemed to mediate between life and death, that is, the medicinal drugs and magical herbs which altered the state of the body, in particular the ones which opened a vision to a different world. These vision-inducing plants were often the genesis of religious experience in the form of shamanism. They seemed to have a divinity within them, and therefore they can appropriately be termed *entheogens*.[1]

The religious traditions of both the Indo-Europeans and the Mediterranean peoples involved this kind of entheogenic shamanism. This is clear in the case of the Earth Mother from the role played by the opium poppy, a plant that induces a deathlike sleep and a journey into dreams. For the Indo-Europeans, we have the tradition most clearly extant in the Indo-Iranian context, the branch of these people who, in a parallel migration to the one that entered the Greek lands, moved into what is now the Iranian plateau and the valley of the Indus. They carried with them religious traditions from their original homeland. These were originally formulaic and oral but were later recorded in written form in the canonic collection of Sanskrit hymns known as the Ṛg Veda. Amidst a complex pantheon appears the god Soma, who is a plant that

was pressed to extract an inebriating drink, a ritual that is still practiced today, although with various surrogates, for the identity of the original entheogen was long ago forgotten, probably because it was no longer easily obtainable after the migration. Even though it is not known, however, its properties and attributes are faithfully remembered in the ancient hymns. R. Gordon Wasson has noted that no mention is ever made of the plant's flowers, leaves, or roots, and he has proposed that the only plant which would lack these essential botanical elements would be a mushroom — in particular, the *Amanita muscaria* or fly-agaric, which fits the other descriptions of Soma and was used until just recently in Asiatic shamanism.[2] The theory has received substantial confirmation through the discovery that one of the earliest surrogates for Soma in India was actually a mushroom, one that was not in fact entheogenic, but symbolically associated with animate existence and (because of its rapid disintegration and corpselike odor) corporeal putrefaction, which through ritual is transmuted into fragrant spirit.[3] Wasson suspected that, if his theory was right, we should expect that the Indo-Europeans had brought their shamanic cult also to other of their ancient migratory destinations, and he proposed to me that we investigate the Greek Eleusinian Mysteries.

This was the most important religious rite of the classical world, lasting well into the Christian era from beginnings that go back to the period of assimilation between Mycenaean Indo-Europeans and the Minoan peoples. It was, in fact, the prime competitor of the proselytizing Christians, and Christianity itself may have been influenced by one of its early heretical sects. As a so-called mystery, it merely was the most famous of the other mysteries, which all involved some form of initiatory rites about which it was forbidden to speak. The Eleusinian initiation was a likely place to look for confirmation, for there is clear evidence that the experience involved a vision which was not theatrically staged but induced after the drinking of a special potion.

The ingredients for the potion are recorded in the Homeric hymn to Demeter, our earliest written evidence for the Mystery. They are given as water, mint, and barley. Carl Kerenyi, the great Hungarian classical mythologist, had supposed that the mint (*Mentha pulegium*) was the cause of the visionary experience,[4] but the herb is, in fact, not entheogenic. It is certainly not strong enough

to have warranted its profane use, despite the capital penalty for profanation of the Mystery, as happened in the great scandal that came to light toward the end of the fifth century. Here, a third collaborator, Dr. Albert Hofmann, the Swiss chemist who discovered the psychoactive properties of LSD, was able to tell us that ergot or rust, a common fungal parasite on grains and grasses, contained several poisonous alkaloids, as well as one that is closely related to LSD. The latter, moreover, is easily separable from the others since it is the only water-soluble component.[5] It remained to see whether ergot figured in Greek botanic lore and the Eleusinian traditions in a way that would have made it an appropriate entheogen for the Mystery, and hence an early fungal surrogate for Soma in Greece.

The primary symbol of the Eleusinian Mystery was the sprouted seed and the cultivation of barley, the art that was supposed to have been taught to a prince at Eleusis by the goddess Demeter (the same goddess that the Indo-Europeans called the Earth Mother in their language). This prince, Triptolemus, is said to have then traveled throughout the world, civilizing it by proselytizing converts to the cultivation of barley. This art of cultivation must be understood in ancient terms, for the Greeks believed that cultivated plants were evolved and hybridized forms of more primitive, inedible, or poisonous plants, and, in particular, that barley had its avatar in a common weedy grass, *aira (Lolium temulentum*, in botanic Latin, or "drunken" *lolium*), called "darnel," "cockle," or "tares" in English. If barley, moreover, were not correctly tended with the appropriate religious rituals, the barley would revert to its weedy predecessor. This weed is commonly infested with ergot, from which it earns its botanical epithet, for it contains no inebriants of its own. The way that the ergot would spread from the weed to the cultivated crop would have suggested the recidivist tendency that had to be appeased if barley were to maintain its hybridized form.

This opposition between cultivated foods and wild poisons is very much a part of the sacred Eleusinian myth, for the story that ended with the mission of Triptolemus began not in the plowlands, but at the frontier with the otherworld in a place where wild plants grow. There Persephone, who is the Mother Goddess with her pre-Hellenic name, was still a maiden, picking flowers. There she

chanced upon a special one, the *narkissos,* a word from a pre-Greek language, but one that in classical times was understood as implying narcotic attributes. Immediately the lord from the nether realm appeared to her and abducted her away as his concubine. This was an illicit abduction, not a marriage. At the end of the story, however, just as the supposedly narcotic wild flower was supplanted by the cultivated grain, Persephone became the wife of the former abductor, accepted as such by her mother and certified in her honorable role by the laws of civilized society. This opposition is reflected in the two plants which were the cited ingredients of the potion. The wild mint was supposed to have been metamorphosed from the nether lord's concubine as a sign that the mother could not countenance the illicit abduction. Mint, therefore, in contrast to the cultivated barley, signified the precivilized condition, and, in fact, all such fragrant herbs in Greek botanic lore connoted concubinage, as opposed to certain evil-smelling plants that signified the marital state.

Ergot mediated between this dichotomy of primitivism and culture. Mushrooms are prototypically a wild plant, for the spores by which they propagate themselves require a microscope to be seen. To the ancients, therefore, they appeared to be seedless growths, defying cultivation, but sprouting spontaneously instead, it was thought, wherever the thunderbolt inseminated the earth. Since they cannot be grown, they must be hunted like a wild animal. Ergot, however, appears to be a seed. The mycelium of ergot forms a hardened mass or sclerotia that deforms and completely replaces individual kernels in the stalk with what appears to be an enlarged kernel of the characteristic purple that gives this fungus its botanic name, *Claviceps purpurea.* Like all the higher fungi, this is only one form of its growth, and under the right conditions it sends up tiny fruiting bodies of the recognizable mushroom shape. When the purple kernel falls to the ground, like the barley itself, the uncultivatable appears to have been tamed. In either form, it is poisonous. It would still require the intervention of civilized arts, in the form of the secret science of its water-soluble preparation, to release the entheogen. The entheogen induces, not narcosis like the abductor's plant, but a heightened vision.

This opposition was further dramatized in that there were actually two levels to the Mystery, the Lesser Mystery and the Greater.

The former preceded the latter by half a year and occurred in February, the winter, which in Greece is the season for wild flowers. The ceremony was held at a sanctuary near the walls of Athens, dedicated to the symbolism of the Hunt. Exactly what was done there was kept secret, but we are told that it was a mimesis of Persephone's abduction, and it involved a metaphor that can be traced to India as an attribute of Soma and that still occurs today in Asiatic shamanism in descriptions of the entheogenic properties of *Amanita muscaria*.[6] The Lesser Mystery would seem, therefore, to have centered upon the sacred wild plant or its surrogate in Greece, which metaphorically, at least, was fungal. For the Greater Mystery, the initiates would walk the sacred road to the village of Eleusis at the end of summer, with the coming of the rains that marked the beginning of the planting season for grain. They journeyed in imitation of a trip to the other world, for that was the significance of Eleusis, founded amidst the fertile plain, beside a chasm that was an entrance to the nether realm. After further exhausting themselves after the long walk by dancing into the night, they entered the great hall of initiation, the architectural replica of a cave, carved into the Eleusinian acropolis. There they drank the potion and perhaps journeyed in the spirit, as is done by other peoples in such rites, across the threshold to the other world. Then, at the moment of the revelation, the hierophant would intone that Persephone had returned and had borne a son. He had many names, but he symbolized her triumph over the primitivism of her abduction, the transmutation of death into life and of the nether lord into a beneficent Hellenic manifestation in a greater cosmic plan. He had a secret name which was probably Triptolemus, the proselyter of grain's cultivation.

In returning to this world, the pre-Hellenic Persephone, who had gone to the chthonic realm as a maiden, was reunited with her mother, the one called by the Hellenic name of Demeter. Now, of course, Persephone herself was also a mother. The religion was called "the Mystery of the two goddesses," without specificity of name, for they had many names and the two roles were interchangeable. The two had come about through the schism of the primordial Great Goddess into maiden daughter and mother, and in their reunion at Eleusis the totality was restored in a transmuted and assimilated version: Demeter was an Olympian, whose

daughter belonged to the rival house of the husband in the chthonic realm.

There is a further aspect to this reintegration that mediates the dilemma of sexual superiority of male or female, for the primordial Goddess had once been hermaphroditic and self-sufficient. In order to create the world, however, she severed the phallus from her own body to be her mate. In its Eleusinian version, that male principle of the female became the chthonic son. The Goddess held a pomegranate as symbol of this transformed completeness, for it had grown originally, it was thought, out of the blood shed at her castration. Now the profusion of seeds embedded in its bloody juice proclaimed the fertility of the womb into which she took the chthonic seed in order to tame the world through the birth of her son. It also commemorated the capsule of narcotic poppy, which it resembles, the now supplanted entheogen, replaced by the Indo-European fungal surrogate.

This same assimilative process commemorating a deity's darker and civilized *personae* can be demonstrated with the god Dionysus. As a Hellenic god, he taught the art of viticulture in a proselytizing mission parallel to that of Triptolemus. There was a time in his mad youth, however, when he had not yet discovered the art of growing grapes. In those days, he was driven wild throughout Asia Minor by the Great Goddess, whose consort he originally was. In fact, he was no better than Persephone's abductor.[7] That primordial union had occurred at a place called Nysa. When the Indo-Europeans arrived, they recognized that he was one of the principal male deities of the Mediterranean lands. He was like their own god Zeus and they named him the Nysian Zeus, for that is what his name Dionysus apparently means. In a pre-Greek language he was called Bacchus. The Indo-Europeans assimilated him by making him into a son of Zeus, but one so involved with chthonic rites that he never made it to Olympian status, except as a visitor.

To beget him in the assimilated form, Zeus inseminated a Great Goddess named Semele, a princess at Thebes. He used the same manner that begets wild mushrooms in the earth: he struck and destroyed her with his thunderbolt. He then sewed the fetus in his thigh, where it gestated for a second birth, by which Zeus demonstrated his own equality to the Goddess. As in her act of self-

castration, he too severed the male creature from his body. Thus the possessing spirit of Indo-European shamanism became identified with the consort figure in the Mediterranean rites.

That consort at first was associated with various entheogens, amongst which we can document the narcotic poppy. In Asia Minor, however, where the art of viticulture developed alongside the cultivation of edible grains, a cult of the deity resident in wine apparently came into being and spread westward, with the cultivation of the vine, to the Mediterranean. The god became identified and assimilated with the other versions of the Goddess's consort. The word for the product of the grape's ferment, "wine" or *(w)oinos*, in Greek, should have originated along with viticulture itself in the non-Indo-European context. In that case, its cognates in all the ancient and modern Indo-European languages would have been assimilated from that pre-Greek source. On the other hand, the word could be Indo-European, in which case it must have referred to some intoxicant or entheogen other than wine, in usage in their homeland before the migrations. If the latter is true, the etymology of the word for wine can be connected to a metaphor and ideogram for a mushroom as a spoked circular rim, as of a wheel. The Indo-Europeans, in that case, would have applied their own term to the new entheogen, just as they too assimilated its deity to their own tradition of shamanism.

This is perhaps not so remarkable, for the Greeks thought of mushrooms as a fermentation of the earth and sensed that the wine-making process was similarly fungal, as in fact it is. It is dependent upon the growth of microscopic yeast, a mushroom of the lower order that does not produce fruiting bodies. They would have come upon this knowledge by analogy with the moldering growth that overspreads dead matter, and we should expect that anything so commonly associated with death and putrefaction would have been carefully noted for its religious relevance. The other world was, in fact, imagined as a moldy place, and "mushroom" was a metaphor for the tomb. Upon the body of the dead grape that is the harvest god, the wild mushroom could be once again tamed and cultivated. It produced an entheogen that is actually a fungal surrogate of Soma in the Greek lands, and one that is associated, in accordance with the same pattern, with higher civilization. The fermentation of wine, moreover, is analogous to a similar advance

in the preparation of a food associated with Demeter. This is the leavening of the bread, or, as the Greeks called it, fermented bread, a process that for them was more obviously a taming of the same fungal putrefaction. Their method corresponded to the modern sourdough, a mixture marked by a distinctly foul odor. Thus both Demeter and Dionysus, in their Hellenic manifestations, nourished the human race, the Greeks thought, the one with dry food and the other with liquid.

Here too, however, the more primitive predecessors of Dionysus could not be discarded or dishonored. As a cultured deity, he would ordinarily be celebrated at a drinking party or symposium. These affairs were essentially for men, often joined in a homoeroticism that excluded women. If women were included, they were likely to be professional entertainers and prostitutes who stood outside the citizen class and therefore posed no threat to a male-dominant society. The inebriation that the symposium was intended to induce was also in the service of strengthening civilized society, for customarily the drinkers would recite poetry that indoctrinated the younger members into the traditions and ethos of their culture. But there was another way that Dionysus could be celebrated. This was primarily for the women of the citizenry. For a time, they abandoned their subservient role and regressed to a more primitive age, leaving the city and all it stood for and going to the wild mountainside, where they were possessed by a madness, for which they were named *maenads* or "mad women." Something was drunk to induce this madness, but symbolically, at least, it was the botanic avatar of the cultivated god. It was not the ferment grown upon the grapes of the tended vine, but the primitive predecessor of the vine, the wild ivy, which was thought to be a poisonous plant whose diminutive clusters of grapelike berries deranged the mind and whose wintertime growth on upright stems was like a sinister mockery of its hybridized descendant.

The primitivism of these winter rites of maenadism was symbolized by the animal skins with which the women clothed their bodies and by the serpents which they handled, like the women in the Minoan period, to whom these rituals of shamanism go back. From the art of that age we have evidence of women, portrayed as insects or bees, as they experienced mystical possession amidst wild flowers. The prime symbol of the maenads' activity was the

thyrsos, a pre-Greek word that designated a hollow stalk stuffed with ivy leaves, as herb gatherers would do with the plants they found. The women were supposed to have hunted on the mountain and to have devoured their catch raw, whether animate or botanic, without the civilized art of cooking. The nature of their spiritual possession could be seen in the ithyphallic satyrs who sexually attacked them. These were goatlike men, and the goat was a representative of the god's primitive *persona*. Because of its grazing habits, the goat was actually an enemy of the civilized *persona* in the form of the cultivated vine. It was they upon whom was placed the blame for the murder that was the harvesting of the grape. In actual practice, the harvest was accomplished to the music of lament, and the grape treaders disguised themselves as satyrs to divert the guilt upon the appropriate agent. Then the god's blood, which was the juice of the trodden grape, flowed into subterranean urns similar to those used for burial. While he gestated there in the tomb, the winter months belonged to the forces which seemed to have triumphed in his death. This was the regressive time of his avatars, before he had himself discovered the vine, when he was tended in his infancy by his maenadic nurses and the goatlike satyrs at Nysa. These avatars, symbolized by the ivy, included both pre-Greek and Indo-European entheogens, for the hunter god was portrayed with a crown of narcotic poppies amidst his maenads in their night of revelry, and the *thyrsos* of their gathering ritual was a descriptive metaphor for a mushroom.

When the fermentation was completed, the tomb was opened and the spirit of the god was released, new born as an infant into the new age, just as the elder Dionysus in the second generation himself had a son called Bunch of Grapes. Together with the resurrection of the god in the form of the new wine, the other graves throughout the land yielded up their spirits, and the living cautiously were reunited for a time with their departed friends for a banquet. The god had shown the way to the joining of the living and the dead, and of the primitive and civilization. He was the prefiguration of our own human lot, and at a very young age children at this feast impersonated the baby god and were initiated into his gift of drunkenness.

Even the wine, however, could not exclude token commemorations of the cultured god's predecessors, for it was flavored with

herbs and spices, and, like modern retsina, had a taste of pine. The pine tree was sacred to the god, perhaps because its fermented sap was once associated with one of his earlier *personae*. These additives were not always inert, but apparently added to the inebriating properties of the wine. The Greeks did not know about alcohol as a chemical. They had no word for it, nor did they know how to separate or concentrate it through distillation, which was a process to be discovered much later by the medieval alchemists. The alcoholic content of their wines was solely a product of natural fermentation and could not have exceeded twelve to fourteen percent. Alcohol is produced as a by-product of the growth of the yeast on the sugars of the juice, and the process is completed either when the sugars are depleted or the concentration of the alcohol reaches the lethal limit for the yeast, which is pickled by it. Despite the fact that the Greek wines did not have an extraordinarily alcoholic content, they were customarily drunk diluted with water, usually three- or fourfold, and certain wines could not be drunk safely without being diluted as much as eight times. As little as four small cups of diluted wine, moreover, were sufficient, according to an ancient poet, to induce drunkenness, and the effects of different wines could be diametrically opposite. Wine drunk undiluted could cause death or permanent brain damage. Clearly, these wines contained other, more primitive manifestations of the god, and like the Eleusinian potion, the drink was a symbolic totality of the god's *personae*.

As a triumph of culture, the wine transmuted the wild hysteria of the winter maenads into higher inspiration. This inspiration is evident not only in the social indoctrination of the symposium, but in the special madness of the god's poets, who celebrated him at the great festivals of drama. Again, there is a masculine bias that the Indo-European tradition gave to this higher culture, for the poets were men and all the roles in their plays were impersonated by males. They donned the traditional masks and felt themselves possessed by the mythical figures who, through the god's grace, returned from the distant past to serve the paedeutic purpose of indoctrination into the city's heritage and ethos.[8]

The festival, like the various aspects of the god, was a symbolic totality. The comedies exalted the libidinous willfulness of the phallic god, whose hero was the common person, at odds with

established society. Through the power of fantasy he was able to overthrow it and remake it in his own baser image. In satyr plays, the dancers impersonated the primitive god's familiars and mocked the pretensions of higher culture. In tragedies, however, these wilder natures had to yield. Tragedy was, as the name implies, the goat song, the song sung for the sacrifice of the goat, a lament. He was a version of the god, but an enemy of his civilized evolution, an enemy who had to fall. Typically in tragedy, the hero discovers his unsuspected darker *persona* and finds that it is his role to play the victim whose honored sacrifice will appease the forces of primitivism and restore the world to its established balance.

This in general was the meaning of sacrifice for the Greeks. The victim was an animal which could be viewed symbolically as the god's primitive familiar: a goat for Dionysus, a pig for Demeter, and so on. The animal had to acquiesce in its own slaughter, and it was tricked into giving some sign that could be so interpreted. The sacrifice was an attempt to ritualize the human dependence upon the dead for sustenance, for it is dead matter that must nourish life, and if its spirit is not appeased, evolution will convert to regression. The sacrifice thus was a ritual meal. To the chthonic deities, often an animal that it was taboo to eat was offered, a horse or a dog. The ceremony was performed at night, and the carcass was left in a pit to rot. To the Olympians, however, the offering was made in the sunlight, and the butchered victim was cooked upon an altar. The culinary arts are another aspect of the progress from primitivism. The cooking was done in a manner that was supposed to recapitulate evolution, both in the progress from earlier to more civilized styles of cooking and in the imagined ontogeny of the beast itself, with its most fundamental organs cooked first.

Some portion of the animal, the least desirable, was burnt completely in the fire so that as fragrant smoke it would rise to the heavens, where the Olympians received it as their share in the nourishment. The burning transmuted matter into the aery substance appropriate to their pure immortal *personae*. Ordinarily, their traditional foods on Olympus, their ambrosia and nectar, were totally divorced from mortal matter; but through these rites of sacrifice they were tricked into eating the worst parts of themselves. This transubstantiation of their own atavistic *personae* reinforced

their civilized image as benefactors of those who offered the sacrifice. For this reason, in the Eleusinian myth, the great evolutionary plan of Zeus would have been frustrated if the chthonic realm would not nourish the humans who were to offer up these transmuted versions of the Olympian avatars. Human worship was essential in maintaining the civilization overseen by the deities of the Hellenic age.

As a final example of the assimilative process we have been noting in the Indo-European and Mediterranean traditions, let us look briefly at a special secret offering that was made to the god Apollo. Each year the Greek cities sent first fruits to the sanctuary of the god on the sacred island of Delos as part of the great celebration of him as the patron of higher culture. These first fruits were samplings of the grain crop, harvested before it had matured. The unripe sheaves were symbolic of the wild avatars that had to be appeased in order to free the hybridized crop from the regressive threat of its primitive avatars. The secret offering amongst these symbolic victims was supposed to have been sent from the land of the Hyperboreans, the original homeland of the god amongst his Indo-European peoples.

The Hyperboreans were, of course, a mythical people, but the precise route for the transfer of the offerings was carefully preserved, and we can trace them back to the forested slopes of the Altai Mountains, on the western edge of the central Asiatic massif.[9] The actual secret offering must have been some plant closely associated with the mythical traditions of the Hyperboreans and native to the forested mountain slopes of central Asia.

The Hyperborean homeland, however, was only one version of Apollo's origins, for he had another ancestral people in southern Asia Minor amongst the Lycians. Apollo, like the other Hellenic gods, was an assimilation of an Indo-European and a pre-Greek deity, both of them gods of thresholds and mantic prophecy. Amongst the Lycians, he would have been a consort figure in chthonic worship, for even into the classical period the Lycians reckoned relationship by matrilineal descent. In becoming a Hellenic deity, he too was reborn as a son of Zeus and then fought numerous battles against symbolic representatives of his earlier existences. One version of these atavistic *personae* was his own brother, Dionysus, in his primitive maenadic state. At Delphi the two ac-

tually shared the sanctuary, with Apollo withdrawing amongst his Hyperboreans for the winter months. At that time the worship shifted to Dionysus at the cave high up on the mountain where the original Lycian Apollo had once delivered chthonic oracles.

Both the Hyperboreans and the Lycians were associated with magical plants and shamanism. Amongst these sacred plants were the olive and the laurel, but these could only be surrogates for the original which, unlike them, was clearly entheogenic. As preserved in the mythical traditions, the original was fungal and bore some remarkable properties in common with *Amanita muscaria*, a mushroom that grows on the Altai slopes. It was apparently this that was the secret offering, the primordial botanic identity of the Indo-European god, sent as token commemoration and sacrificial victim to the classical deity who, beyond all others, expressed the spirit of Hellenism. The Greeks, unlike their later admirers, could not, even here, ignore the primitive *persona* that lurks in nature behind the sublime cultured mask of the god.

NOTES

1. Literally, "engendering a god within." *Entheogen* replaces *psychotropic, hallucinogenic, psychedelic,* and similar words and neologisms in current usage, all of which have unfortunate connotations of contemporary illicit drugs or of adverse and biased judgments about altered states of consciousness as imitative of psychoses. An entheogen is defined in a strict sense as "only those vision-producing drugs that can be shown to have figured in shamanic or religious rites; in a looser sense, the term could also be applied to other drugs, both natural and artificial, that induce alterations of consciousness similar to those documented for ritual ingestion of traditional entheogens." This term does away with the awkwardness of having to say, for example, that a shaman took a psychedelic drug. The word has begun to appear in scholarly usage. See Ruck, Bigwood, Staples, Ott, and Wasson, "Entheogens," *Journal of Psychedelic Drugs* 11 (1979): 145–46.

2. R. Gordon Wasson, *Soma: Divine Mushroom of Immortality* (New York: Harcourt Brace Jovanovich, 1968).

3. Stella Kramrisch, "The Mahāvīra Vessel and the Plant Pūtika," *Journal of the American Oriental Society* 95 (1975): 222–35.

4. Carl Kerenyi, *Eleusis: Archetypal Image of Mother and Daughter* (New York: Pantheon, 1967), translated from the German manuscript

revised by the author from publications in 1960 and 1962, appendix 1. Dr. Albert Hofmann, whose opinion Kerenyi cites as to the vision-inducing properties of *Mentha pulegium*, now claims that the mint is not entheo-genic.

5. R. Gordon Wasson, Albert Hofmann, and Carl A. P. Ruck, *The Road to Eleusis: Unveiling the Secret of the Mysteries* (New York: Harcourt Brace Jovanovich, 1978).

6. Carl A. P. Ruck, "Mushrooms and Philosophers," *Journal of Ethnopharmacology* 4 (1981): 179–205.

7. This presentation of the shamanic nature of Dionysian cult is summarized from Carl A. P. Ruck, "The Wild and the Cultivated: Wine in Euripides' *Bacchae*," *Journal of Ethnopharmacology* 5 (1982): 231–70.

8. See my discussion of the relevance of Dionysian cult to the meaning of Greek drama in Ruck, "The Wild and the Cultivated: Wine in Euripides' *Bacchae*," pp. 263ff.

9. This presentation of the Apolline rite is summarized from Carl A. P. Ruck, "The Offerings from the Hyperboreans," *Journal of Ethnopharmacology* (forthcoming).

6

Buddhist Views of Nature:
Variations on the Theme of
Mother-Father Harmony

ROBERT A. F. THURMAN

THE BUDDHIST SCRIPTURE, the *Teaching of Vimalakīrti,* opens on
a scene of great magnificence. The Buddha is presented in the
center of a vast host of monks, *bodhisattvas,* gods, humans, and
nonhuman mythical creatures of various sorts. He appears as the
mountainous force of nature, and his first act of teaching is to manifest a vision of ecological splendor to his audience.

> Dominating all the multitudes, just as Sumeru, the king
> of mountains, looms high over the oceans, the Lord Buddha
> shone, radiated, and glittered, as he sat upon his magnificent
> lion-throne.
>
> Thereupon, the Licchavi *bodhisattva* Ratnakara, with
> five hundred Licchavi youths, each holding a precious parasol
> made of seven different kinds of jewels, came forth from the
> city of Vaisali and presented himself at the grove of Amrapali.
> Each approached the Buddha, bowed at his feet, circumam-
> bulated him clockwise seven times, laid down his precious
> parasol in offering, and withdrew to one side.
>
> As soon as all these precious parasols had been laid down,
> suddenly, by the miraculous power of the Lord, they were
> transformed into a covering for this entire billion-world ga-
> lactic universe. The surface of the entire billion-world galaxy
> was reflected in the interior of the great precious canopy,

96

where the total content of this galaxy could be seen: limitless mansions of suns, moons, and stellar bodies; the realms
of the gods, dragons, elves, fairies, titans, *garuḍas*, *kiṃnaras*,
and *mahoragas*, as well as the realms of the four Maharajas;
the king of mountains, Sumeru; Mount Hīmādri, Mount Mu-
cilinda, Mount Mahāmucilinda, Mount Gandhamadana,
Mount Ratnaparvata, Mount Kalaparvata, Mount Cakra-
vāḍa, and the Mahācakravāḍa range; all the great oceans,
rivers, bays, torrents, streams, brooks, and springs; finally, all
the villages, suburbs, cities, capitals, provinces, and wilder-
nesses. All this could be clearly seen by everyone. And the
voices of all the Buddhas of the ten directions could be heard
proclaiming their teachings of the Dharma in all the worlds,
the sounds reverberating in the space beneath the great precious canopy.[1]

As symbolic matrix of the teaching of this Scripture, the Buddha artfully creates a temporary holographic planetarium to prepare the audience to face the facts he presents: the emptiness, in-
substantiality, or illusoriness of the ordinary, objective, culturally
given reality, the inconceivable interpenetrative relativity of all
things, and the overwhelming power of love and compassion manifesting liberative art.

The luminous contemplation of the realities of nature is the
very heart of the Buddhist experience. Too often the holy fact of
suffering,[2] the uncompromising starting point of the experiential
(*adhigama*) Dharma, is mistaken for the whole of the Buddhist
attitude. "Life is a horror, a great heap of misery," we hear the Buddha say, and we mistakenly think there is nothing more to do than
to accept a prescription for the cold, anaesthetic ether of a lifeless
nirvana, if indeed we were to follow such a heartless, nihilistic
teacher. In fact, even in the beginning he said only that the unexamined life is not worth living, or in his own terms, our "ego-
centered, selfish lives are not worth living," especially for human
beings, who can so easily experience the truth of selflessness.

One cannot meditate, in English, on the Buddhist views of
nature without first considering the complex usages of the English
words and then looking for those words in the Indian languages
which might be used in similar ways. The Oxford English Diction-

ary's[3] fourteen meanings trace the life of the word *nature* in an interesting way, moving from "essential properties of a thing" *(svabhāva, svalakṣaṇa)*, through "inherent power or force by which the physical and mental activities of man are sustained" *(karma)*, and "the creative . . . physical power . . . conceived of as operating in the material world and as the immediate cause of all its phenomena . . . sometimes personified as a female being" *(prakṛti, māyā)*, up to "the material world, or its collective objects and phenomena . . . the features and products of the earth itself, as contrasted with those of human civilization." No Sanskrit word fits this last, which could be opposed to *culture*, or *society*, the word *loka* always including the social realm with the natural. But this is the important usage of *nature* in our present context, which leaves us with some careful thinking to do. What indeed happened to the nature vs. spirit, *prakṛti* vs. *puruṣa*, female vs. male, dualism that started out so strongly in Indian culture in the Samkhya philosophy and remained a strand in many of the later systems of thought and belief? How did the mainstream of Indian civilization, with its vast empires, complex social organizations, developed sciences and technologies, and intricate philosophies, preserve overall a sense of the organic natural-social continuum? How did it keep to the margins the extreme dualisms manifested in other cultures as radical nature-rejecting spiritualism and equally radical naturalistic materialism?[4] And what role did Buddhist culture play in this respect?

At the time of the Buddha we see nature-affirmation and nature-rejection developing in strongly polarizing trends in the Vedic and Upaniṣadic/Śramanic movements, respectively. Buddha's own monastic teaching seems on the surface to go along with the nature rejection, condemning mother *prakṛti* as *saṁsāra*, the natural cycle of births, and recommending a pure spiritual realm of nirvana. But there is a very important difference between his escape from nature and that of the other Śramanas. For the Buddha the realm of escape is hollow and empty. There is no *puruṣa*, no *ātma*, no person or self to enjoy a blissful, supernatural release. When the essential male flees from the engaging female, he loses himself rather than finding any isolated final aloofness. In this hollow victory of the dualistic quest for final independence lie the seeds of the eventual Mahayanist explication of ultimate nonduality, of

the integration of emptiness and relativity, and of the ultimate as Father and Mother in union, not just as spiritual Father or as earthly Mother. This same reconciliation of opposites is clearly present even in the earliest monastic teachings.

The Buddha myth[5] itself contains powerful symbols of the balance of the nature-culture, body-mind, relative-absolute dichotomies. His mother is Mother Nature herself, Queen Māyā, the creative magic of life, while his father is Pure Grain, Suddhodhana, the sustenance of civilization, cultivated food. He is a king in a palace in a powerful city. The Buddha conception occurs without sexual involvement of the father, during Māyā's time of purification, yet he appears to enter her womb as a glorious white elephant, symbol of royal power and military might, the most powerful animal in nature tamed. She does not give birth in the palace, but feels an impulse to leave the city. The actual birth occurs in a garden, surrounded by a blooming nature, un-naturally rejoicing at the divine birth. In his first words he proclaims himself the supreme human, the highest product of evolution. His long evolutionary struggle toward perfection is eventually documented in the numerous *Jātaka* nature tales with which he delights and defies his hearers. In his second words, on the other hand, he declares that he will have no more births, that he is nature gone beyond itself. During his pre-Buddhahood career, nature recedes with the early death of his mother, and his whole struggle focuses on his father.

It is prophesied that he will be king of kings, the consummation of culture. He will also be Buddha, "Awakened" and "Blossomed," the culmination of natural evolution, subsuming human culture. The Buddha's father resists this latter strenuously,[6] so the prince enjoys love and marriage. Eventually, however, he finds it too unnatural, a mere artifice unsuccessful in forestalling death, decay, suffering, and ignorance. This he balances by entering the realm of death, going out into nature to examine the ascetic methods of transcendence. He masters the samadhic trances in nothingness and in the fourth state beyond consciousness and unconsciousness, and he then rejects them. Pure spirit, pure transcendence is no solution, and asceticism is but another extreme. He returns to a garden, under a tree. Nature returns, his mother in the forms of Sujata who nourishes him, and Mother Earth herself, who

testifies to his evolutionary sacrifices to tame Māra, who challenges his Buddhahood as the very echo of his father.

As a Buddha, he has the body of a king of kings, and reappropriates the royal wheel, now Wheel of Dharma, and the lion-throne, now a stage for his Teaching. He has a mind of pure Wisdom, perfectly attuned with nature, knowing the causes of creation and destruction. And his speech masters and re-creates all culture, turning it from a prison house to a realm of liberation. He founds a new kingdom, that of the Saṃgha, the Holy Community, avoiding both city and wilderness, planting his monasteries in between, in the suburbs, so his monks can remain attuned with nature while exerting an influence on culture. He admits women as well as men to his order, repudiating the association of the male with spirit, the female with materiality. He helps those seeking transcendence to find what they really seek through *samādhi*, and he helps those committed to the world by teaching an ethic of non-violence and love in *sila*. He upholds the wisdom *(prajñā)* of self-lessness as supreme for both, and introduces his audiences to its presence in themselves by every possible method: ethical, religious, and philosophical. Finally, while manifesting extravagant super-natural powers, he undergoes a natural death, showing the inevitability of causation in evolution. As a final subtlety, his Parinirvana is not attained as an ultimate transcendence, beyond the formless realms, but is mysteriously entered at the boundary between the form and formless realms, later the cosmological location of the Pure Lands.

This heroic myth of the conquest of life and death, of nature and super-nature, is rich with symbols of balance and integration at every point. It thus served as a legendary matrix of a broad middle way, an ideal of interpenetration of culture and nature, body and mind, absolute and relative. It could satisfy the monastic, the spiritualist determined for transcendence, by presenting the ideal of the Great Ascetic, who achieved the transcendent goal through a moderate form of asceticism. It could satisfy the citizens, aristocratic or bourgeois, materialists determined to build a better world, by presenting the ideal of the Enlightenment Hero *(bodhisattva)*, who achieved the immanent purification of the Buddha-land through love and compassion.[7] And it could delight the great artists of life, the Great Adepts, who were determined for experi-

ential, individual integration of all dichotomies, living out the Father-Mother-union of bliss-void-indivisible.[8]

Of course, this ideal of balance was by no means achieved all in one ahistorical flash. We can now discern the unfolding of this attitude in historical social process as well as in a philosophical individual dialectic. I will approach it as a four-stage progression of views of nature: as evil, as empty, as good, and as inconceivable.[9]

If we turn to the Individual Vehicle (*Hīnayāna*), monastic form of Buddhism, we cannot fail to recognize a strong rejection of nature. The Four Holy Facts (as I prefer to call the Four Noble Truths) were the Buddha's first turning of the Wheel of Dharma, performed for the five ascetics who were his first monastic disciples. "All this (the five psychophysical aggregates) is suffering." This suffering, which is a fact for a holy (*ārya*) person, must be recognized first of all. It is the essential first step of the path. In terms of our inquiry, this means that nature is a *saṃsāra*, an endless life cycle determined by evolutionary impulses (*karma-saṃskāra*), and afflicted by passional addictions to delusion, lust, and hate (*moha-kāmarāga-dveṣa-kleśa*). Every aspect of such a life cycle in the state of nature is miserable: birth, sickness, aging, death, parting from the agreeable, meeting with the disagreeable. Happiness is suffering because it is ephemeral. Suffering is obviously suffering. All creation is suffering because it is compounded, and must dissolve. Every conceivable evolutionary form of life is vividly depicted as suffering: the hot hells, the cold hells, the crushing hells, the cutting hells, the *preta* realms of inconceivable hunger and thirst, the animal realms of one eating another, the human realms of strife, frustration, and death, the titan realms of constant warfare, and even the heavens, wherein the long-lived happy gods experience more suffering in their final days than other beings do in lifetimes. Contemplation of these world-rejecting teachings generates an intense revulsion, a will singly devoted to transcendence at any cost, a radical renunciation wherein the desire for liberation is as powerful as the desire for immersion in water of a person whose hair and clothes are blazing on fire. There is no longer any interest in anything else. And such intense will is then focused on the eradication of the cause of this *saṃsāra* of suffering.

Now the cause of this hellish nature of life is ignorance, or misknowledge (*avidyā*). The original sin in the individual being's

character that causes the entire misery is the egocentric delusion of being a real self, an "I am." This apparently self-evident knowledge of self-existence was proclaimed to be in fact a misknowledge, since upon investigation the Buddha discovered no physical or spiritual thing, no phenomenon and no noumenon that could serve as an irreducible self-sufficient, real core of individual being. But, far from being frustrated, he found his awakening to the absence of an absolute, static self to be the supreme enlightenment, liberation from the delusive presumption of self-existence through the wisdom of selfless relativity. And in that insight he could clearly see how the natural state of any being caught in that delusion was intolerable. To be struggling to maintain one little self against an infinity of other beings and things and an eternity of relentless processes is an inherently frustrating experience. Honesty and integrity would demand that one carry on, if there turned out to be something real at the core of that experience. But if there turned out to be no such thing, honesty and integrity would demand that the egocentric complex be abandoned. And Buddha was able to find no such thing. He then found that that lack was the key to liberation. His whole teaching is a canon of therapies to help other beings accomplish the same turn-around of perception, idea, habit, even instinct.

Since the first step in any of those therapies is the acknowledgment that the world under that delusion is completely unsatisfactory, there are innumerable cautionary, even horrific, renunciation-generating teachings. These are so spectacularly effective that most outside observers of Buddhism regard it as one of the archetypical examples of world-rejecting asceticism. But it is clear to see that the holy fact of suffering is merely the first of four facts. It is not that difficult to win freedom from such a miserable state of nature. One can discern its cause, follow a path to terminate the causes and then the suffering, and then experience the termination of that suffering. Apparently millions of people did so.

Thus, even this most nature-rejecting form of Buddha's teaching rejected nature only as experienced by egocentric, deluded beings. In nature/culture terms, it cannot be said that only egocentrist culture was rejected, since the Buddhist view is that animals are much more sunk into egocentric instinctual cycles. Egocentric nature and culture both are rejected, and nonegocentric nature and culture are embraced, as the third holy fact, nirvana, and the fourth

holy fact, the eightfold path of authentic view, intention, speech, action, livelihood, effort, mindfulness, and meditation. Historically this primary teaching was emphasized and institutionalized in the wide-spreading monastic establishment, with its mobilization of the populace into support of the *bhikṣus* and *bhikṣunis*. The institution of monasticism was a crucial factor in opening a middle ground in the culture between excessive naturalistic materialism, with its attendant violence and exploitation, and excessive spiritualism, with its attendant extreme asceticism and neglect of society. Based on a hollow dualism, it was able to entice the more extreme dualists from their polar positions into moderation. Its ability to perform this function is proven by its historical success over the first five centuries after Buddha.[10] Symbolically, the ultimate reality is represented by the Patriarchal Buddha, the King of Dharma, the Founder of a higher culture *(adhisikṣa)* based on discovery of a higher nature beyond the state of nature and the natural state of society. As in the society of the times, and as in the Buddha myth, the Mother is there, but not in the foreground.

The second stage in the process and dialectic, as I have schematized it, is marked by the emergence of the Universal Vehicle *(Mahāyāna)*, approximately five centuries after Buddha. Although this is tied mythically to the exploits of Nāgārjuna (ca. 100 CE), it had been emerging from the implications of the third and fourth holy facts, from the Buddha myth with its expansion in the exploits of the *bodhisattva* in the *Jātakas,* from the cultural activities of the lay Buddhist community, and from doctrinal developments within the Mahasamghika sects. The foundation of this stage is the further explication of the insight of selflessness, applying it to natural phenomena/supernatural noumena *(dharma)*, as well as more subtly to persons *(pudgala)*. Thus nature was seen to be empty *(śunyā)* of any intrinsic core reality, character, essence, substance, or objectivity, just as persons had been discovered to be selfless. Here we find an interesting overlapping of the first English usage of *nature*, mentioned above as "essential character," and the main current usage for the nonhuman universe. And, ironically, this critical intuition of the absolute naturelessness of all nature was the key for bringing a relative living nature back into central prominence as relativity, universally relativistic nature *(pratītyasamutpāda)* (Latin *natura* and Sanskrit *utpāda* both mean "birth").

This insight is basic to the two later stages of the Universal

Vehicle view of nature. It is a view of nature that fails to find any such real, irreducible thing as nature. This intellectual nondiscovery of any real nature becomes experiential when sustained through concentrated critical contemplation, which systematically dissolves all apparent objective natures of phenomena or noumena. These include any apparent nature of undiscoverability and any apparent realm of objective voidness. The perception of intrinsic objectivities is, of course, so instinctive that it feels intuitive. The intellectual conviction that no relative object of perception can be intrinsically real must be strenuously cultivated, as persistently counterintuitive. Eventually, however, such contemplative cultivation pays off in an erosion of the instinct for egocentrist perception. This releases the noumenal intuition called the "tolerance of the unborn (unnatural)," (*anutpattikadharmakṣānti*) or "transcendent wisdom" (*prajñāpāramitā*), until that nonegocentrist perception of emptiness itself becomes intuitive, and the instinctual perceptual habit is transcended. Crucial here is that no dualistically absolute realm of emptiness is objectively absolute. Emptiness itself is not objectively discovered. Emptiness is empty of itself. The absolute itself is found to be just relativity. "Matter is emptiness and emptiness is matter. Emptiness is not found beyond matter. The very nature of matter itself *is* emptiness."[11] This nonduality of relative and absolute can also be expressed as their absolute unity sustaining relative duality. This is extremely hard to understand without losing the dynamic tension between the two poles and falling into absolutism or nihilism.[12] It can also be called a relativism centered between absolutism and nihilism.[13] The subjective way of expressing this is that wisdom (*prajña*) is the womb (*garbha*) of, and is indivisible from, compassion (*karuṇā*).[14] The absolute openness to naturelessness becomes the relative empathy toward animate and inanimate nature. The intellect becomes relativistically open to nature's transcending its grasp, and the will becomes absolutistically committed to reducing the amount of suffering it feels. This complete freeing of the great Mother Nature into absolute emptiness allows her to give forth her richness of abundant relativity, leaving the Father-will no ground but that of universal love (*maitrī*), the selfless will to universal happiness. In this stage of the Universal Vehicle view, the Father compassion is just there, unexplicated, nondual in the background. The Mother Śūnyatā is very prominent, as Prajnaparamita, the Mother of All Victors (*sarvajinamātā*).

Historically, there developed an institutional mediation between the monastic Samgha and the lay community in the expansion of the *bodhisattva* ethic. The monasteries themselves gradually evolved into universities. This movement took hold first on the fringes of the Aryan Gangetic heartland, in Gandhara, in the seacoast kingdoms of Andhra and Maharashtra, and at the jungle border in eastern Bihar and Bengal. These less Brahmanized cultures may have been less patriarchal, hence less rigidly dualistic, and therefore more open to the liberation of Mother Nature into her glory as Mother Wisdom.[15]

The third stage presupposes and includes the first, the rejection of egocentrist nature; and the second, the insight into natureless nature and the entrance into nondualism. It concerns itself with Father Compassion. It is sometimes called the "stage of the path of magnificent ethics," in contrast to the second "stage of the path of the profound view," but in our quest of views of nature the third stage has its own kind of view. It is a view of nature as wholly excellent, as a perfect vessel of positive evolution of beings from selfish suffering to selfless bliss. It is a view of the world as an infinite panorama of Buddha-lands. We have already glimpsed this view in the opening passage from the *Vimalakīrti*. It is rendered more explicit later in the same chapter, in a context where Śāriputra is confused about the Buddha's talk of the exquisite nature of a Buddha-land. The implication is that this world is Shakyamuni's Buddha-land, but he sees it as a horrible mess. The Buddha scolds Śāriputra for his faulty insight, and then:

> Thereupon the Lord (Buddha) touched the ground of this billion-world galactic universe with his big toe, and suddenly it was transformed into a huge mass of precious jewels, a magnificent array of many hundreds of thousands of precious gems, until it resembled the universe of the Tathāgata Ratnavyūha, called Anantaguṇaratnavyūha ("infinite array of jewels of excellence"). Everyone in the entire assembly was filled with wonder, each perceiving himself seated on a throne of jewelled lotuses.[16]

The Buddha goes on to tell Śāriputra that "this Buddha-land is always thus pure, but the Tathāgata makes it appear to be spoiled by many faults, in order to bring about the maturity of inferior living beings." Shortly thereafter he picks up his toe and the world

reverts to its ordinary appearance. And the rest of the *Vimalakīrti* can be understood as a vehicle of coming to terms with that statement, that confusion between the habitual perception of evil and the revelational view that good is overwhelmingly more powerful than evil and hence that nature is good, that the world is really a Buddha-land.[17] The treatise of Maitreyanatha, *Analysis of the Jewel Matrix*, systematizes this view in relation to the doctrine of the Buddha-nature (*tathāgatagarbha*), present in every being, saying that its "fruit has the supernatural qualities of purity, self, happiness, and permanence." Since the Four Seals of the Dharma used in the early, world-rejecting stage are that all of nature is impure, selfless, suffering, and impermanent, the third stage formulation is purposely provocative. That the new view is a further mediation is expressly stated in the commentary: "In brief, the fruit of these purifying causes (in the Buddha-nature) represents the remedy *both* to the four ways of straying from the Body of Truth (*Dharmakāya*) *and* to their four Individual Vehicle antidotes."[18] Thus, the Buddha-nature is pure, because its ultimate nature is pure and because it is free of evolutionary instincts. It is true self, because fabrications of self and selflessness have been pacified. It is happiness, because it terminates the mentally constructed five compulsive aggregates and their causes. And it is permanent, because it realizes the unity of *samsāra* and nirvana.

In sum, our first stage was preoccupied with the first two holy facts, suffering and origin. The second stage was preoccupied with the third holy fact, cessation or nirvana. This third stage is preoccupied with the fourth holy fact, the path, both to nirvana and beyond nirvana. It aims to encourage the *bodhisattva* to an obligatory ethic of transcendent virtue. It displays the splendor of the Father Love, once wedded to Mother Wisdom. And it is not just an obscure philosophical view. It underlies the great cheerfulness found in the arts, literature, and faces of the peoples of the Buddhicized civilizations, even in situations of hardship and deprivation. This is a glow from solid faith in the mysterious saving graces of the innumerable Buddhas and *bodhisattvas*. Historically, this view begins with Asaṇga in the fourth century and relates to the outreach activity of the Buddhist universities in permeating the growing Brahminical philosophical and religious movements, such as Vedānta and various *bhakti* cults.[19]

The fourth stage view of nature we could call either the magical or the artistic view. It emerges in the esoteric teachings of the Great Adepts. It is prefigured in the Universal Vehicle scriptures in certain key moments, such as the "apparition of the jewel stupa" in the *Lotus*,[20] the "Buddha-toe" episode in the *Vimalakīrti*,[21] and numerous revelatory incidents in the *Garland*, especially the Vairocana tower episode.[22] It is exoterically systematized in the Chinese schools, particularly in the Hua Yen school, with its doctrine of interpretation of phenomena (*shih-shih wu-ai*).[23]

The fourth stage view unpacks the final implications of nonduality on the nature of relative reality. The second stage view had opened the door of nonduality and had introduced relativity as equivalent to emptiness. The third stage view elaborated the magnificence of a world of nature shaped by infinite compassion. The fourth stage view combines these two, but imaginatively assumes responsibility for that shaping. It is the view of those who are at the state wherein confusion about the three previous views no longer allows the *bodhisattva* to wait for the big toe to come down. A future manifestation of a Buddha-land will no longer quench the flames of sufferings. This view focuses on emptiness and the illusoriness of relativity. It determines, out of compassion, to master that relativity to accelerate fulfillment. It views relativity as dependent (*prajñapti upādāya*), as structured by the creative imagination of cultures, whether of humans, gods, or Buddhas. One with such a view thus resolves to use the creative, benevolent imagination. One will never waver from awareness of the absolute emptiness of all creations, however, and the destructive, imprisoning, misknowledge-governed imagination.

In the technical psychology of the Tantras, the *bodhisattvas* in stages two and three must alternate between the vision of naturelessness and that of magnificence. They cannot perceive any object and its emptiness simultaneously until Buddhahood. *Bodhisattvas* on stage four, however, train to perceive both simultaneously. It is thus a view of nature as a malleable matière, the raw material of the supreme artistry, the artistry of liberated life. Again, the *Vimalakīrti* presents the seed of this fourth view in the chapter called "The Inconceivable Liberation." Before giving this teaching, Vimalakīrti magically produces thirty-four-hundred-thousand league-high lion-thrones, and seats all his guests upon

these Buddha-thrones, helping them adjust the size of their bodies to the appropriate dimension, through magical power or through faith, according to ability. Then, when they are receptive, he addresses them:

> Reverend Śāriputra! For the Tathāgatas and the *bodhisattvas*, there is a liberation called "Inconceivable." The *bodhisattva* who lives in the inconceivable liberation can put the king of mountains, Sumeru, which is so high, so great, so noble, and so vast, into a mustard seed. He can perform this feat without enlarging the mustard seed and without shrinking Mount Sumeru. And the deities of the assembly of the four Maharajas and of the Trayastriṃśa heaven do not even know where they are. Only those beings who are destined to be disciplined by miracles see and understand the putting of the king of mountains, Sumeru, into a mustard seed. That, reverend Śāriputra, is an entrance into the domain of the inconceivable liberation of the *bodhisattvas*.[24]

Vimalakīrti continues to mention further miraculous deeds, turning an eon into a moment, a moment into an eon, moving galaxies here and there, swallowing hurricanes and even supernovas, manifesting multiple incarnations, and so forth, a veritable riot of imagination of cosmic deeds benefiting living beings.

The Hua Yen school in China elaborates the "ten mysteries" to cope with the same vision of the *Garland* scripture;[25] every atom contains the entirety of universes, yet remains itself part of its own universe and is contained in every other atom. Even the view of evil is incorporated here, from the first stage view, and reenvisioned into the perfect whole. Mara is proclaimed by Vimalakīrti to be a *bodhisattva* in the inconceivable liberation, literally playing the devil to test the *bodhisattvas'* compassion and tolerance,[26] and Devadatta is praised by the Buddha in the Lotus, thanked for having been his original initiator on the path, and given personal revelation of future Buddhahood.[27] In the *Blue Cliff Record*, Hsueh Feng teaches his community: "Pick up the whole great earth in your fingers, and it's as big as a grain of rice. Throw it down before you: if like a lacquer bucket you don't understand, I'll beat the drum to call everyone to look."[28]

In the Vajrayana, there are innumerable space- and time-

distorting visualizations used to similar effect in the early stage, known as the creation stage. In the ultimate stage even these are transcended, and the contemplations are conducted on an extremely subtle level in a realm of subatomic dreamlike imagery. I cannot enter into these dimensions here.[29] It was only necessary to evoke this fourth view of nature to complete the catalogue of the Buddhist views.

Standing as ultimate over the first view of the evil of the egocentrist nature was the stern Father, ascetic Buddha. Over the second floats the gentle Mother Wisdom. In the third, the kind Mother allows the Father to shine forth in his splendor as Boundless light Amitābha, the eternal Shakyamuni, Amitāyus of the Boundless Life, and so forth. At least in the fourth, both Wisdom and Love, Voidness and Relativity, are nakedly revealed in the primal symbol, that of Father and Mother in intimate union, Vajra and Bell, compassion's great-bliss-illusion-body and wisdom's clear light brilliant voidness; indivisible, nondual, radiant with the rainbow-lights of universal love that effect the liberation of all beings.

The four views of my scheme are of course only for purposes of elucidation, as no one individual Buddhist's view would be a pure example of any of the types. However, modern schools of Buddhism, and views deeply ingrained in cultures that are no longer Buddhist nominally, may be understood as containing strands of the above four in various permutations. Second, the question of human nature is worth the briefest description. A human is considered a mutation of a lower animal or a degeneration of a higher one, such as one of the types of gods. Human life is considered a precious jewel obtained by an individual being after countless lives of evolutionary development. But the fitness of the being who wins humanity is not caused by aggressive competitiveness or egocentrism. It is caused by generosity, moral sensitivity, and patience. Love is the greatest strength in the Buddhist universe, and the human form culminates an evolutionary progression of love up from the more painful states of egocentrism in hells, *preta* realms, and animal realms. So, while ultimately there is no nature, and relatively all sentient beings contain instinctual potentialities for every evil as long as they are still imprisoned in the egocentrist delusion, the mere fact of embodiment in a human form of mind and body signifies a more powerful relative nature of goodness, love, and in-

telligence. A human thus is closest of all beings to Buddhahood, defined as the evolutionary perfection of body, speech, and mind. That is why Buddhist cultures consider human life so very precious that they enshrine nonviolence as the highest virtue. To waste human life out of greed or hate is compared to throwing a royal diamond into filth. It is such a rare and precious opportunity for everyone who has it that they should make the best of it; or at the very least, refrain from preventing others from doing so. This, one might say, is the bottom line of all the Buddhist views of nature.

Let me seal this essay with a quote from the great Mongolian Lama, Jangkya Rolway Dorje, who flourished in Peking and Wu T'ai Shan in the time of Ch'ien Lung in the eighteenth century.

> The mutual interdependence
> Of the Mother Emptiness,
> In whom nothing has real status,
> And Father Relativity,
> In whom everything appears —
> It is exactly this
> Which must be understood.
>
> Seeking my old Father,
> The just not finding
> Is the actual discovery
> Of my kind Mother Emptiness!
> Then, calm in my Mother's lap,
> I found my old Father!
> I a child of such kind parents
> Cried out to them for refuge! . . .
>
> Though things do, surely,
> Exist here somehow,
> Their real nature seems not to be
> A sort of horned incompatibility.
> Since this delicate intimacy
> Of Father-Mother-Communion
> Seems to be inseparably
> Gentle and delightful ease! [30]

NOTES

1. Robert A. F. Thurman, trans., *The Holy Teaching of Vimala-kīrti* (University Park, Pa.: Pennsylvania State University Press, 1976), p. 12.

2. *Arya-duhkhasatya.*

3. *Oxford English Dictionary,* compact ed., s.v. "nature."

4. These extremes were embodied in the Ajivaka and Lokayata schools of thought, respectively, neither of which ever became central in Indian culture.

5. See, for example, Edward Byles Cowell, trans., *Buddhacarita,* in *Buddhist-Mahāyāna Texts* (New York: Dover, 1969), or numerous other treatments of Buddha-life.

6. In an India supposedly devoid of the Oedipal complex, the father's deeds are presented in the myth as strikingly similar to the later deeds of Māra, the Devil, who also makes a strenuous effort to block the enlightenment.

7. *Buddha-ksetra-parisodhana,* ("purifying the Buddha-land") is a Mahāyāna way of expressing the attainment of enlightenment with reference to the world-transformative drive of great compassion that becomes the Buddha's Form Body.

8. The Great Adepts (Mahasiddha) were the champions of the Vajrayana school of the Mahāyāna, as well as the probable initiators of the Ch'an tradition in China. "Bliss-void-indivisible" was their way of expressing the nonduality of relative and absolute.

9. The following table may be useful to keep the view-typology in mind:

nature as:	holy facts emphasized:	metaphysically:	institutionally:
evil	first and second	dualistic	monastic individualist
empty, relative	third	nondualistic	messianic universalist
good	third and fourth	monistically nondualistic	messianic universalist
inconceivable	all four	dualistically nondualistic	individualistically messianic

10. The solid sociological study of Buddhist monasticism is just getting underway, with the work of S. J. Tambiah, *World Conqueror, World Renouncer* (Cambridge and New York: Cambridge University Press, 1976) setting a new standard.

11. Famous phrase found throughout the *Prajñāpāramitā Scriptures*.

12. Monism can result in either nihilism or absolutism, and also dualism.

13. Relativism is too easily confused with nihilism by absolutists or by those recently disillusioned with absolutism. It is the key problem of modern philosophy, in my opinion.

14. One thinks of Nāgārjuna's phrase, *śūnyatākaruṇāgarbham*.

15. This is speculative, having the virtue of allowing for *both* "Northern" and "Southern" origin theories of the Mahāyāna.

16. Thurman, *Holy Teaching of Vimalakīrti*, pp. 18–19.

17. There are numerous revelations in Mahāyāna scriptures of the enlightened vision of the universe as perfect, notably in *Lotus, Garland, Pure Land*, and *Great Final Nirvana* scriptures, as well as in the Vimalakīrti.

18. Maitreya and Asanga, *Uttaratantra*, trans. Holmes and Gyatso as *The Changeless Nature* (Scotland: Kagyu Samye, 1979).

19. Thus, from the fourth century, the Brahmins begin to write their great *sastras* in response to the Buddhist schools, the *Gita* comes to the fore as a nationalistic celebration of caste as well as a synthetic ground for *bhakti*, and *Avalokiteshvara*-like forms of Vishnu and Shiva are sculpted profusely.

20. Bunnō Kato, *Threefold Lotus Sutra* (New York: Weather Hill, 1975), pp. 195ff.

21. Thurman, *Holy Teaching of Vimalakīrti*, p. 18.

22. See D. T. Suzuki, *Outlines of Mahāyāna Buddhism* (New York: Schocken Books, 1963), pp. 173ff.

23. See Ch'eng-chi Chang, *Buddhist Teaching of Totality* (University Park, Pa.: Pennsylvania State University Press, 1971), pp. 153ff.

24. Thurman, *Holy Teaching of Vimalakīrti*, p. 52.

25. Chang, *Buddhist Teaching of Totality*, pp. 153ff.

26. Thurman, *Holy Teaching of Vimalakīrti*, pp. 54–55.

27. Kato, *Threefold Lotus Sutra*, pp. 207–14.

28. Thomas Cleary, *The Blue Cliff Record* (Boulder, Colo.: Shambhala, 1977), p. 31.

29. See my essay on "Unexcelled Yoga Tantra," in *Practice in Buddhism*, ed. S. Park (New York: SUNY Press, forthcoming).

30. Thurman, *Song of Mother Emptiness* (San Francisco: Vajra Bodhi Sea, 1977), p. 78.

7

The Continuity of Being:
Chinese Visions of Nature

TU WEI-MING

THE CHINESE BELIEF in the continuity of being, a basic motif in Chinese ontology, has far-reaching implications in Chinese philosophy, religion, epistemology, aesthetics, and ethics. F. W. Mote comments:

> The basic point which outsiders have found so hard to detect is that the Chinese, among all peoples ancient and recent, primitive and modern, are apparently unique in having no creation myth; that is, they have regarded the world and man as uncreated, as constituting the central features of a spontaneously self-generating cosmos having no creator, god, ultimate cause, or will external to itself.[1]

This strong assertion has understandably generated controversy among Sinologists. Mote has identified a distinctive feature of the Chinese mode of thought. In his words, "the genuine Chinese cosmogony is that of organismic process, meaning that all of the parts of the entire cosmos belong to one organic whole and that they all interact as participants in one spontaneously self-generating life process."[2]

However, despite Mote's insightfulness in singling out this particular dimension of Chinese cosmogony for focused investigation, his characterization of its uniqueness is problematic. For one thing, the apparent lack of a creation myth in Chinese cultural history is predicated on a more fundamental assumption about reality; namely, that all modalities of being are organically connected. An-

cient Chinese thinkers were intensely interested in the creation of the world. Some of them, notably the Taoists, even speculated on the creator (*tsao-wu chu*) and the process by which the universe came into being.[3] Presumably indigenous creation myths existed although the written records transmitted by even the most culturally sophisticated historians do not contain enough information to reconstruct them.[4] The real issue is not the presence or absence of creation myths, but the underlying assumption of the cosmos: whether it is continuous or discontinuous with its creator. Suppose the cosmos as we know it was created by a Big Bang; the ancient Chinese thinkers would have no problem with this theory. What they would not have accepted was a further claim that there was an external intelligence, beyond human comprehension, who willed that it be so. Of course the Chinese are not unique in this regard. Many peoples, ancient and recent, primitive and modern, would feel uncomfortable with the idea of a willful God who created the world out of nothing. It was not a creation myth as such but the Judeo-Christian version of it that is absent in Chinese mythology. But the Chinese, like numerous peoples throughout human history, subscribe to the continuity of being as self-evidently true.[5]

An obvious consequence of this basic belief is the all-embracing nature of the so-called spontaneously self-generating life process. Strictly speaking, it is not because the Chinese have no idea of God external to the created cosmos that they have no choice but to accept the cosmogony as an organismic process. Rather, it is precisely because they perceive the cosmos as the unfolding of continuous creativity that it cannot entertain "conceptions of creation *ex nihilo* by the hand of God, or through the will of God, and all other such mechanistic, teleological, and theistic cosmologies."[6] The Chinese commitment to the continuity of being, rather than the absence of a creation myth, prompts them to see nature as "the all-enfolding harmony of impersonal cosmic functions."[7]

The Chinese model of the world, "a decidedly psychophysical structure" in the Jungian sense,[8] is characterized by Joseph Needham as "an ordered harmony of wills without an ordainer."[9] What Needham describes as the organismic Chinese cosmos consists of dynamic energy fields rather than static matter-like entities. Indeed, the dichotomy of spirit and matter is not at all ap-

plicable to this psychophysical structure. The most basic stuff that makes the cosmos is neither solely spiritual nor material but both. It is a vital force. This vital force must not be conceived of either as disembodied spirit or as pure matter.[10] Wing-tsit Chan, in his influential *Source Book of Chinese Philosophy*, notes that the distinction between energy and matter is not made in Chinese philosophy. He further notes that H. H. Dubs's rendering of the indigenous term for this basic stuff, *ch'i*, as "matter-energy" is "essentially sound but awkward and lacks an adjective form."[11] Although Chan translates *ch'i* as "material force," he cautions that since *ch'i*, before the advent of Neo-Confucianism in the eleventh century, originally "denotes the psychophysiological power associated with blood and breath," it should be rendered as "vital force" or "vital power."[12]

The unusual difficulty in making *ch'i* intelligible in modern Western philosophy suggests that the underlying Chinese metaphysical assumption is significantly different from the Cartesian dichotomy between spirit and matter. However, it would be misleading to categorize the Chinese mode of thinking as a sort of pre-Cartesian naïveté lacking differentiation between mind and body and, by implication, between subject and object. Analytically Chinese thinkers have clearly distinguished spirit from matter. They fully recognize that spirit is not reducible to matter, that spirit has an independent ontological status, and that axiomatically spirit is of more enduring value than matter. There are of course notable exceptions. But these so-called materialist thinkers are not only rare but also too few and far between to constitute a noticeable tradition in Chinese philosophy. Recent attempts to reconstruct the genealogy of materialist thinkers in China have been painful and, in some cases, far-fetched.[13] Indeed, to characterize the two great Confucian thinkers, Chang Tsai (1020–1077) and Wang Fu-chih (1619–1692), as paradigmatic examples of Chinese materialism is predicated on the false assumption that *ch'i* is materialistic. Both of them did subscribe to what may be called philosophy of *ch'i* as a critique of speculative thought but, to them, *ch'i* was not simply matter but vital force endowed with all-pervasive spirituality.[14]

The continuous presence in Chinese philosophy of the idea of *ch'i* as a way of conceptualizing the basic structure and function of the cosmos, despite the availability of symbolic resources

to make an analytical distinction between spirit and matter, signifies a conscious refusal to abandon a mode of thought that synthesizes spirit and matter as an undifferentiated whole. The loss
of analytical clarity is compensated by the reward of imaginative
richness. The fruitful ambiguity of *ch'i* allows philosophers to explore realms of being which are inconceivable to people constricted
by a Cartesian dichotomy. To be sure, the theory of the different
modalities of *ch'i* cannot engender ideas such as the naked object,
raw data, or the value-free fact, and thus cannot create a world
out there, naked, raw, and value-free, for the disinterested scientist to study, analyze, manipulate, and control. *Ch'i*, in short, seems
inadequate to provide a philosophical background for the development of empirical science as understood in the positivistic sense.
What it does provide, however, is a metaphorical mode of knowing, an epistemological attempt to address the multidimensional
nature of reality by comparison, allusion, and suggestion.

Whether it is the metaphorical mode of knowing that directs
the Chinese to perceive the cosmos as an organismic process or it
is the ontological vision of the continuity of being that informs
Chinese epistemology is a highly intriguing question. Our main
concern here, however, is to understand how the idea of the undifferentiated *ch'i* serves as a basis for a unified cosmological theory. We want to know in what sense the least intelligent being, such
as a rock, and the highest manifestation of spirituality, such as
heaven, both consist of *ch'i*. The way the Chinese perceive reality
and the sense of reality which defines the Chinese way of seeing
the world are equally important in our inquiry, even though we
do not intend to specify any causal relationship between them.

The organismic process as a spontaneously self-generating life
process exhibits three basic motifs: continuity, wholeness, and dynamism.[15] All modalities of being, from a rock to heaven, are integral parts of a continuum which is often referred to as the "great
transformation" (*ta-hua*).[16] Since nothing is outside of this continuum, the chain of being is never broken. A linkage will always
be found between any given pair of things in the universe. We may
have to probe deeply to find some of the linkages, but they are there
to be discovered. These are not figments of our imagination but
solid foundations upon which the cosmos and our lived world
therein are constructed. *Ch'i*, the psychophysiological stuff, is ev-

erywhere. It suffuses even the "great void" (*t'ai-hsü*) which is the source of all beings in Chang Tsai's philosophy.[17] The continuous presence of *ch'i* in all modalities of being makes everything flow together as the unfolding of a single process. Nothing, not even an almighty creator, is external to this process.

This motif of wholeness is directly derived from the idea of continuity as all-encompassing. If the world were created by an intelligence higher than and external to the great transformation, it would, by definition, fall short of a manifestation of holism. Similarly, if the world were merely a partial or distorted manifestation of the Platonic Idea, it would never achieve the perfection of the original reality. On the contrary, if genuine creativity is not the creation of something out of nothing, but a continuous transformation of that which is already there, the world as it now exists is the authentic manifestation of the cosmic process in its all-embracing fullness. Indeed, if the Idea for its own completion entails that it realize itself through the organismic process, the world is in every sense the concrete embodiment of the Idea. Traditional Chinese thinkers, of course, did not philosophize in those terms. They used different conceptual apparatuses to convey their thought. To them, the appropriate metaphor for understanding the universe was biology rather than physics. At issue was not the eternal, static structure but the dynamic process of growth and transformation. To say that the cosmos is a continuum and that all of its components are internally connected is also to say that it is an organismic unity, holistically integrated at each level of complexity.

It is important to note that continuity and wholeness in Chinese cosmological thinking must be accompanied in the third motif, dynamism, lest the idea of organismic unity imply a closed system. While Chinese thinkers are critically aware of the inertia in human culture which may eventually lead to stagnation, they perceive the "course of heaven" (*t'ien-hsing*) as "vigorous" (*chien*) and instruct people to model themselves on the ceaseless vitality of the cosmic process.[18] What they envision in the spontaneously self-generating life process is not only inner connectedness and interdependence but also infinite potential for development. Many historians have remarked that the traditional Chinese notion of cyclic change, like the recurrence of the seasonal pattern, is incompatible with the modern Western idea of progress. To be sure, the

traditional Chinese conception of history lacks the idea of unilinear development, such as Marxian modes of production depicting a form of historical inevitability. It is misleading, however, to describe Chinese history as chronicling a number of related events happening in a regularly repeated order.[19] Chinese historiography is not a reflection of a cyclic world view. The Chinese world view is neither cyclic nor spiral. It is transformational. The specific curve around which it transforms at a given period of time is indeterminate, however, for numerous human and nonhuman factors are involved in shaping its form and direction.

The organismic life process, which Mote contends is the genuine Chinese cosmogony, is an open system. As there is no temporal beginning to specify, no closure is ever contemplated. The cosmos is forever expanding; the great transformation is unceasing. The idea of unilinear development, in this perspective, is one-sided because it fails to account for the whole range of possibility in which progress constitutes but one of several dominant configurations. By analogy, neither cyclic nor spiral movements can fully depict the varieties of cosmic transformation. Since it is open rather than closed and dynamic rather than static, no geometric design can do justice to its complex morphology.

Earlier, I followed Mote in characterizing the Chinese vision of nature as the "all-enfolding harmony of impersonal cosmic function" and remarked that this particular vision was prompted by the Chinese commitment to the continuity of being. Having discussed the three basic motifs of Chinese cosmology — wholeness, dynamism, and continuity — I can elaborate on Mote's characterization by discussing some of its implications. The idea of all-enfolding harmony involves two interrelated meanings. It means that nature is all-inclusive, the spontaneously self-generating life process which excludes nothing. The Taoist idea of tzu-jan ("self-so"),[20] which is used in modern Chinese to translate the English word *nature*, aptly captures this spirit. To say that *self-so* is all-inclusive is to posit a nondiscriminatory and nonjudgmental position, to allow all modalities of being to display themselves as they are. This is possible, however, only if competitiveness, domination, and aggression are thoroughly transformed. Thus, all-enfolding harmony also means that internal resonance underlies the order of things in the universe. Despite conflict and tension, which are

like waves of the ocean, the deep structure of nature is always tranquil. The great transformation of which nature is the concrete manifestation is the result of concord rather than discord and convergence rather than divergence.

This vision of nature may suggest an unbridled romantic assertion about peace and love, the opposite of what Charles Darwin realistically portrayed as the rules of nature. Chinese thinkers, however, did not take the all-enfolding harmony to be the original naïveté of the innocent. Nor did they take it to be an idealist utopia attainable in a distant future. They were acutely aware that the world we live in, far from being the "great unity" (ta-t'ung) recommended in the *Evolution of the Rites*,[21] is laden with disruptive forces including humanly caused calamities and natural catastrophes. They also knew well that history is littered with internecine warfare, oppression, injustice, and numerous other forms of cruelty. It was not naïve romanticism that prompted them to assert that harmony is a defining characteristic of the organismic process. They believed that it is an accurate description of what the cosmos really is and how it actually works.

One advantage of rendering *ch'i* as "vital force," bearing in mind its original association with blood and breath, is its emphasis on the life process. To Chinese thinkers, nature is vital force in display. It is continuous, holistic, and dynamic. Yet, in an attempt to understand the blood and breath of nature's vitality, Chinese thinkers discovered that its enduring pattern is union rather than disunion, integration rather than disintegration, and synthesis rather than separation. The eternal flow of nature is characterized by the concord and convergence of numerous streams of vital force. It is in this sense that the organismic process is considered harmonious.

Chang Tsai, in his celebrated metaphysical treatise, "Correcting Youthful Ignorance," defines the cosmos as the "Great Harmony":

The Great Harmony is called the Tao. It embraces the nature which underlies all counter processes of floating and sinking, rising and falling, and motion and rest. It is the origin of the process of fusion and intermingling, of overcoming and being overcome, and of expansion and contraction. At the com-

mencement, these processes are incipient, subtle, obscure, easy, and simple, but at the end they are extensive, great, strong and firm. It is *ch'ien* ("heaven") that begins with the knowledge of Change, and *k'un* ("earth") that models after simplicity. That which is dispersed, differentiated, and discernible in form becomes *ch'i*, and that which is pure, penetrating, and not discernible in form becomes spirit. Unless the whole universe is in the process of fusion and intermingling like fleeting forces moving in all directions, it may not be called "Great Harmony."[22]

In his vision, nature is the result of the fusion and intermingling of the vital forces that assume tangible forms. Mountains, rivers, rocks, trees, animals, and human beings are all modalities of energy-matter, symbolizing that the creative transformation of the Tao is forever present. Needham's idea of the Chinese cosmos as an ordered harmony of wills without an ordainer is, however, not entirely appropriate. Wills, no matter how broadly defined, do not feature prominently here. The idea that heaven and earth complete the transformation with no mind of their own clearly indicates that the harmonious state of the organismic process is not achieved by ordering divergent wills.[23] Harmony will be attained through spontaneity. In what sense is this what Mote calls "impersonal cosmic function"? Let us return to Chang Tsai's metaphysical treatise:

> *Ch'i* moves and flows in all directions and in all manners. Its two elements (yin and yang) unite and give rise to the concrete. Thus the multiplicity of things and human beings is produced. In their ceaseless successions the two elements of yin and yang constitute the great principles of the universe.[24]

This inner logic of *ch'i*, which is singularly responsible for the production of the myriad things, leads to a naturalistic description of the impersonal cosmic function. Wang Fu-chih, who developed Chang Tsai's metaphysics of *ch'i* with great persuasive power, continues with this line of thinking:

> The fact that the things of the world, whether rivers or mountains, plants or animals, those with or without intelligence, and those yielding blossoms or bearing fruits, provide bene-

ficial support for all things is the result of the natural influence of the moving power of *ch'i*. It fills the universe. And as it completely provides for the flourish and transformation of all things, it is all the more spatially unrestricted. As it is not spatially restricted, it operates in time and proceeds with time. From morning to evening, from spring to summer, and from the present tracing back to the past, there is no time at which it does not operate, and there is no time at which it does not produce. Consequently, as one sprout bursts forth it becomes a tree with a thousand big branches, and as an egg evolves, it progressively becomes a fish capable of swallowing a ship. . . .[25]

The underlying message, however, is not the impersonality of the cosmic function, even though the idea of the moving power of *ch'i* indicates that no anthropomorphic god, animal, or object is really behind the great transformation. The naturalness of the cosmic function, despite human wishes and desires, is impersonal but not inhuman. It is impartial to all modalities of being and not merely anthropocentric. We humans, therefore, do not find the impersonal cosmic function cold, alien, or distant, although we know that it is, by and large, indifferent to and disinterested in our private thoughts and whims. Actually, we are an integral part of this function; we are ourselves the result of this moving power of *ch'i*. Like mountains and rivers, we are legitimate beings in this great transformation. The opening lines in Chang Tsai's *Western Inscription* are not only his article of faith but also his ontological view of the human:

> Heaven is my father and earth is my mother, and even such a small being as I finds an intimate place in their midst. Therefore, that which fills the universe I regard as my body and that which directs the universe I regard as my nature. All people are my brothers and sisters, and all things are my companions.[26]

The sense of intimacy with which Chang Tsai, as a single person, relates himself to the universe as a whole reflects his profound awareness of moral ecology. Humanity is the respectful son or daughter of the cosmic process. This humanistic vision is distinc-

tively Confucian in character. It contrasts sharply with the Taoist idea of noninterference on the one hand and the Buddhist concept of detachment on the other. Yet the notion of humanity as forming one body with the universe has been so widely accepted by the Chinese, in popular as well as elite culture, that it can very well be characterized as a general Chinese world view.

Forming one body with the universe can literally mean that since all modalities of being are made of *ch'i*, human life is part of a continuous flow of the blood and breath that constitutes the cosmic process. Human beings are thus organically connected with rocks, trees, and animals. Understandably, the interplay and interchange between discrete species feature prominently in Chinese literature, notably popular novels. The monkey in the *Journey to the West* came into being by metamorphosis from an agate;[27] the hero in the *Dream of the Red Chamber* or the *Story of the Stone*, Pao-ÿu, is said to have been transformed from a piece of precious jade;[28] and the heroine of the *Romance of the White Snake* has not completely succeeded in transfiguring herself into a beautiful woman.[29] These are well-known stories. They have evoked strong sympathetic responses from Chinese audiences young and old for centuries, not merely as fantasies but as great human drama. It is not at all difficult for the Chinese to imagine that an agate or a piece of jade can have enough potential spirituality to transform itself into a human being. Part of the pathos of the White Snake lies in her inability to fight against the spell cast by a ruthless monk so that she can retain her human form and be united with her lover. The fascinating element in this romance is that she manages to acquire the power to transfigure herself into a woman through several hundred years of self-cultivation.

Presumably, from the cosmic vantage point, nothing is totally fixed. It need not be forever the identity it now assumes. In the perceptive eye of the Chinese painter Tao Chi (1641–1717), mountains flow like rivers. The proper way of looking at mountains, for him, is to see them as ocean waves frozen in time.[30] By the same token, rocks are not static objects but dynamic processes with their particular configuration of the energy-matter. It may not be far-fetched to suggest that, with this vision of nature, we can actually talk about the different degrees of spirituality of rocks. Agate is certainly more spiritual than an ordinary hard stone and per-

haps jade is more spiritual than agate. Jade is honored as the "finest essence of mountain and river" (*shan-ch'uan ching-ying*).[31] By analogy, we can also talk about degrees of spirituality in the entire chain of being. Rocks, trees, animals, humans, and gods represent different levels of spirituality based on the varying compositions of *ch'i*. However, despite the principle of differentiation, all modalities of being are organically connected. They are integral parts of a continuous process of cosmic transformation. It is in this metaphysical sense that "all things are my companions."

The uniqueness of being human cannot be explained in terms of a preconceived design by a creator. Human beings, like all other beings, are the results of the integration of the two basic vital forces of yin and yang. Chou Tun-i (1017–1073) says, "the interaction of these two *ch'i* engenders and transforms the myriad things. The myriad things produce and reproduce, resulting in an unending transformation."[32] In a strict sense, then, human beings are not the rulers of creation; if they intend to become guardians of the universe, they must earn this distinction through self-cultivation. There is no preordained reason for them to think otherwise. Nevertheless, the human being, in the Chinese sense of *jen* which is gender neutral, is unique. Chou Tun-i offers the following explanation:

> It is man alone who receives [the Five Agents] in their highest excellence, and therefore he is most intelligent. His physical form appears, and his spirit develops consciousness. The five moral principles of his nature (humanity, rightness, propriety, wisdom, and faithfulness) are aroused by, and react to, the external world and engage in activity; good and evil are distinguished; and human affairs take place.[33]

The theory of the Five Agents or the Five Phases (*wu-hsing*) need not concern us here. Since Chou makes it clear that "by the transformation of yang and its union with yin, the Five Agents of Water, Fire, Wood, Metal, and Earth arise" and that since "the Five Agents constitute a system of yin and yang,"[34] they can be conceived as specific forms of *ch'i*.

That humankind receives *ch'i* in its highest excellence is not only manifested in intelligence but also in sensitivity. The idea that humans are the most sentient beings in the universe features prominently in Chinese thought. A vivid description of human sensitiv-

ity is found in the "recorded sayings" (yü-lu) of Ch'eng Hao (1032–1085):

> A book on medicine describes paralysis of the four limbs as absence of humanity (pu-jen). This is an excellent description. The man of humanity regards heaven and earth and all things as one body. To him there is nothing that is not himself. Since he has recognized all things as himself, can there be any limit to his humanity? If things are not part of the self, naturally they have nothing to do with it. As in the case of paralysis of the four limbs, the vital force (ch'i) no longer penetrates them, and therefore they are no longer parts of the self.[35]

This idea of forming one body with the universe is predicated on the assumption that since all modalities of being are made of ch'i, all things cosmologically share the same consanguinity with us and are thus our companions. This vision enabled an original thinker of the Ming Dynasty, Wang Ken (1483–1540), to remark that if we came into being through transformation (hua-sheng), then heaven and earth are our father and mother to us; if we came into being through reproduction (hsing-sheng), then our father and mother are heaven and earth to us.[36] The image of the human that emerges here, far from being the lord of creation, is the filial son and daughter of the universe. Filial piety connotes a profound feeling, an all-pervasive care for the world around us.

This literal meaning of forming one body with the universe must be augmented by a metaphorical reading of the same text. It is true that the body clearly conveys the sense ch'i as the blood and breath of the vital force that underlies all beings. The uniqueness of being human, however, is not simply that we are made of the same psychophysiological stuff that rocks, trees, and animals are also made of. It is our consciousness of being human that enables and impels us to probe the transcendental anchorage of our nature. Surely, the motif of the continuity of being prevents us from positing a creator totally external to the cosmic organismic process, but what is the relationship between human nature and heaven which serves as the source of all things? Indeed, how are we to understand the ontological assertion in the first chapter of the Doctrine of the Mean that our nature is decreed by heaven?[37] Is the Mandate of Heaven a one-time operation or a continuous

presence? Wang Fu-chih's general response to these questions is suggestive:

> By nature is meant the principle of growth. As one daily grows, one daily achieves completion. Thus by the Mandate of Heaven is not meant that heaven gives the decree (*ming*, mandate) only at the moment of one's birth. . . . In the production of things by heaven, the process of transformation never ceases.[38]

In the metaphorical sense, then, forming one body with the universe requires continuous effort to grow and to refine oneself. We can embody the whole universe in our sensitivity because we have enlarged and deepened our feeling and care to the fullest extent. However, there is no guarantee at the symbolic nor the experiential level that the universe is automatically embodied in us. Unless we see to it that the Mandate of Heaven is fully realized in our nature, we may not live up to the expectation that "all things are complete in us."[39] Wang Fu-chih's refusal to follow a purely naturalistic line of thinking on this is evident in the following observation: "The profound person acts naturally as if nothing happens, but . . . he acts so as to make the best choices and remain firm in holding to the Mean."[40] To act naturally without letting things take their own course means, in Neo-Confucian terminology, to follow the "heavenly principle" (*t'ien-li*) without being overcome by "selfish desires" (*ssu-yü*).[41] Selfish desires are forms of self-centeredness that belittle the authentic human capacity to take part in the transformative process of heaven and earth. In commenting on the *Book of Change*, Ch'eng Hao observes:

> The most impressive aspect of things is their spirit of life. This is what is meant by origination being the chief quality of goodness. Man and heaven and earth are one thing. Why should man purposely belittle himself?[42]

Forming a trinity with heaven and earth, which is tantamount to forming one body with the myriad things, enjoins us from applying the subject-object dichotomy to nature. To see nature as an external object out there is to create an artificial barrier which obstructs our true vision and undermines our human capacity to experience nature from within. The internal resonance of the vital

forces is such that the mind, as the most refined and subtle *ch'i* of the human body, is constantly in sympathetic accord with the myriad things in nature. The function of "affect and response" (*kan-ying*) characterizes nature as a great harmony and so informs the mind.[43] The mind forms a union with nature by extending itself metonymically. Its aesthetic appreciation of nature is neither an appropriation of the object by the subject nor an imposition of the subject on the object, but the merging of the self into an expanded reality through transformation and participation. This creative process, in Jakobson's terminology, is "contiguous," because rupture between us and nature never occurs.[44]

Chuang Tzu recommends that we listen with our minds rather than with our ears; with *ch'i* rather than with our minds.[45] If listening with our minds involves consciousness unaffected by sensory perceptions, what does listening to *ch'i* entail? Could it mean that we are so much a part of the internal resonance of the vital forces themselves that we can listen to the sound of nature or, in Chuang Tzu's expression, the "music of heaven" (*t'ien-lai*)[46] as our inner voice? Or could it mean that the all-embracing *ch'i* enables the total transposition of humankind and nature? As a result, the aesthetic delight that one experiences is no longer the private sensation of the individual but the "harmonious blending of inner feelings and outer scenes"[47] as the traditional Chinese artist would have it. It seems that in either case we do not detach ourselves from nature and study it in a disinterested manner. What we do is to suspend not only our sensory perceptions but also our conceptual apparatus so that we can embody nature in our sensitivity and allow nature to embrace us in its affinity.

I must caution, however, that the aesthetic experience of mutuality and immediacy with nature is often the result of strenuous and continual effort at self-cultivation. Despite our superior intelligence, we do not have privileged access to the great harmony. As social and cultural beings, we can never get outside ourselves to study nature from neutral ground. The process of returning to nature involves unlearning and forgetting as well as remembering. The precondition for us to participate in the internal resonance of the vital forces in nature is our own inner transformation. Unless we can first harmonize our own feelings and thoughts, we are not prepared for nature, let alone for an "interflow with the spirit

of Heaven and Earth."[48] It is true that we are consanguineous with nature. But as humans, we must make ourselves worthy of such a relationship.

NOTES

1. Frederick W. Mote, *Intellectual Foundations of China* (New York: Alfred A. Knopf, 1971), pp. 17–18.

2. Ibid., p. 19.

3. For a thought-provoking discussion on this issue, see N. J. Girardot, *Myth and Meaning in Early Taoism* (Berkeley: University of California Press, 1983), pp. 275–310.

4. For a suggestive methodological essay, see William G. Boltz, "Kung Kung and the Flood: Reverse Euhemerism in the *Yao Tien*," *T'oung Pao* 67 (1981): 141–53. Professor Boltz's effort to reconstruct the Kung Kung myth indicates the possibility of an indigenous creation myth.

5. Tu Wei-ming, "Shih-t'an Chung-kuo che-hsüeh chung te san-ko chi-tiao" [A preliminary discussion on the three basic motifs in Chinese philosophy], *Chung-kuo che-hsüeh shih yen-chiu* [Studies on the history of Chinese philosophy] (Peking: Society for the Study of the History of Chinese Philosophy) 2 (March 1981): 19–21.

6. Mote, *Intellectual Foundations of China*, p. 20.

7. Ibid.

8. See Jung's Foreword to the *I Ching (Book of Changes)*, translated into English by Cary F. Baynes from the German translation of Richard Wilhelm, Bollingen Series, vol. 19 (Princeton, N.J.: Princeton University Press, 1967), p. xxiv.

9. Needham's full statement reads as follows: "It was an ordered harmony of wills without an ordainer; it was like the spontaneous yet ordered, in the sense of patterned, movements of dancers in a country dance of figures, none of whom are bound by law to do what they do, nor yet pushed by others coming behind, but cooperate in a voluntary harmony of wills." See Joseph Needham and Wang Ling, *Science and Civilization in China*, 2 vols. (Cambridge: Cambridge University Press, 1969), 2: 287.

10. Actually, the dichotomy of spirit and matter does not feature prominently in Chinese thought, see Tu, *Chung-kuo che-hsüeh shih yen-chiu*, pp. 21–22.

11. Wing-tsit Chan, trans. and comp., *A Source Book in Chinese Philosophy* (Princeton, N.J.: Princeton University Press, 1969), p. 784.

12. Ibid.

13. For a notable exception to this general interpretive situation in

the People's Republic of China, see Chang Tai-nien, *Chung-kuo che-hsüeh fa-wei* [Exploring some of the delicate issues in Chinese philosophy] (T'ai-yuan, Shansi: People's Publishing Co., 1981), pp. 11–38; 275–306.

14. For a general discussion on this vital issue from a medical viewpoint, see Manfred Porkert, *The Theoretical Foundations of Chinese Medicine: Systems of Correspondence* (Cambridge, Mass.: MIT Press, 1974).

15. Tu, "Shih-t'an Chung-kuo che-hsüeh," pp. 19–24.

16. A paradigmatic discussion on this is to be found in the *Commentaries on the Book of Changes.* See Wing-tsit Chan, *Source Book in Chinese Philosophy*, p. 264.

17. See Chang Tsai's "Correcting Youthful Ignorance" in Wing-tsit Chan, *Source Book in Chinese Philosophy*, p. 501.

18. For this reference in the *Chou I*, see *A Concordance to Yi Ching*, Harvard-Yenching Institute Sinological Index Series Supplement No. 10 (reprint; Taipei: Chinese Materials and Research Aids Service Center, Inc., 1966), 1/1.

19. The idea of the "dynastic cycle" may give one the impression that Chinese history is nondevelopmental. See Edwin O. Reischauer and John K. Fairbank, *East Asia: The Great Tradition* (Boston: Houghton Mifflin Co., 1960), pp. 114–18.

20. Chuang Tzu, chap. 7. See the Harvard Yenching Index on the *Chuang Tzu*, 20/7/11.

21. See William T. de Bary, Wing-tsit Chan, and Burton Watson, comps., *Sources of Chinese Tradition* (New York: Columbia University, 1960), pp. 191–92.

22. Wing-tsit Chan, *Source Book on Chinese Philosophy*, pp. 500–1.

23. Ibid., pp. 262–66. This idea underlies the philosophy of change.

24. Ibid., sec. 14, p. 505. In this translation, *ch'i* is rendered "material force." The words *yin* and *yang* in parentheses are added by me.

25. Ibid., pp. 698–99.

26. Ibid., p. 496.

27. Wu Ch'eng-en, *Hsi yu chi*, trans. Anthony C. Yü as *Journey to the West*, 4 vols. (Chicago: University of Chicago Press, 1977–), 1: 67–78.

28. Ts'ao Hsüeh-ch'in (Cao Xuequin), *Hung-lou meng* [Dream of the Red Chamber], trans. David Hawkes as *The Story of the Stone*, 5 vols. (Middlesex, England: Penguin Books, 1973–), 1: 47–49.

29. For two useful discussions on the story, see Fu Hsi-hua, *Pai-she-chuan chi* [An anthology of the White Snake story] (Shanghai: Shanghai Publishing Co., 1955) and P'an Chiang-tung, *Pai-she ku-shih yen-chiu* [A study of the White Snake story] (Taipei: Students' Publishers, 1981).

30. P. Ryckmans, "Les propos sur la peinture de Shi Tao traduction et commentaire," *Arts Asiatique* 14 (1966): 123–24.

31. Teng Shu-p'in, "Shang-ch'uan ching-ying — yü te i-shu" [The finest essence of mountain and river — the art of jade], in *Chung-kuo wen-hua hsin-lun* [New views on Chinese culture] (Taipei: Lien-ching, 1983), Section on Arts, pp. 253–304.

32. Wing-tsit Chan, *Source Book in Chinese Philosophy*, p. 463. This translation renders *ch'i* as "material force."

33. Ibid.

34. Ibid.

35. Ibid., p. 530.

36. Wang Ken, "Yü Nan-tu chu-yu" [Letter to friends of Nan-tu], in *Wang Hsin-chai hsien-sheng ch'üan-chi* [The complete works of Wang Ken] (1507 edition, Harvard-Yenching Library), 4.16b.

37. Wing-tsit Chan, *Source Book in Chinese Philosophy*, p. 98.

38. Ibid., p. 699.

39. *Mencius*, 7A4.

40. Wing-tsit Chan, *Source Book in Chinese Philosophy*, pp. 699–700.

41. For example, in Chu Hsi's discussion of moral cultivation, the Heavenly Principle is clearly contrasted with selfish desires. See Wing-tsit Chan, *Source Book in Chinese Philosophy*, pp. 605–6.

42. Ibid., p. 539.

43. For a suggestive essay on this, see R. G. H. Siu, *Ch'i: A Neo-Taoist Approach to Life* (Cambridge, Mass.: MIT Press, 1974).

44. Roman Jakobson, "Two Aspects of Language and Two Types of Aphasic Disturbances," in Roman Jakobson and Morris Halle, *Fundamentals of Language* ('sGravenhage: Mouton, 1956), pp. 55–82. I am grateful to Professor Yu-kung Kao for this reference.

45. *Chuang Tzu*, chap. 4. The precise quotation can be found in *Chuang Tzu ying-te* (Peking: Harvard-Yenching Institute, 1947), 9/4/27.

46. *Chuang Tzu*, chap. 2 and *Chuang Tzu ying-te*, 3/2/8.

47. For a systematic discussion of this, see Yu-kung Kao and Kang-i Sun Chang, "Chinese 'Lyric Criticism' in the Six Dynasties," American Council of Learned Societies Conference on Theories of the Arts in China (June 1979), to be included in *Theories of the Arts in China*, eds. Susan Bush and Christian Murck (Princeton, N.J.: Princeton University Press, forthcoming).

48. *Chuang Tzu*, chap. 33 and *Chuang Tzu ying-te*, 93/33/66.

PART III

Human Nature in the Natural World

8

The Alienation and Liberation
of Nature

JÜRGEN MOLTMANN

1. *Karl Marx and the alienation of nature*

Science and technology require a particular relationship of humanity to nature.[1] In natural science, nature is the object which the human subject wishes to discern methodically. In work and technology, nature is the stuff which the human subject can dispose of, appropriate, and shape. In natural science and technology, humans experience themselves as the ruling subjects of their world, not only the center and reference point of all things, but also the ontological foundation, the first and all-determining being.[2] Nature is made into an object through science and technology. It is real only as it is available to the human subject. Humans take nature seriously on the way to their seizure of power. They dominate it through work. And in this work it encounters them as the essence of the worked-upon objects.

There have been many philosophical attempts to overcome the splitting of the world into subjectivity and objectivity, into *res cogitans* and *res extensa*. One can also regard the subjectivizing of humanity and the objectivizing of nature as a historical relation, mutually conditioned. Then history becomes the true subject. It differentiates itself into the human subject and the natural object, but remains the unity behind this differentiation.

If a historical dialectic replaces an ontological dualism as the interpretive framework for the difference between subject and object, then one must ask about a future in which this difference is

transformed into a higher unity so that tensions and contradictions are overcome. The philosophies of history in German idealism were devoted to this problem. But the dialectical interpretation of the difference between subject and object only grasps the human relationship to nature, not nature itself. In the historical dialectic nature appears only as the object of human perception and action. It is respected insofar as it can be taken into the history of humanity through knowledge and work. Nature standing on its own cannot be understood in this way.

Karl Marx attempted to overcome idealistic subjectivism by proposing a dialectical materialism which would resolve the conflict between humanity and nature. In his early writings, communism overcomes the alienation of both humanity and nature, bringing both to their true being. Communism is thus a perfected naturalism.

> It is first here that his natural existence becomes his human existence and nature itself becomes human for him. Society, then, is the perfected mode of being of humans with nature, the true resurrection of nature, the completed naturalism of humanity, and the completed humanism of nature.[3]

When, through the abolition of private property and the overcoming of alienating work, humans become truly human, they will also discover the human essence of nature, for they will have then found the natural essence of humanity. Humans and nature will overcome their mutual alienation and become a living unity. In this living unity, Marx presents humans, following Goethe, as natural beings: "The real, corporeal human, standing on the solid, well-founded earth, breathing all of nature's power in and out. . . ." The logical element in this picture of breathing in and out is dialectical identity, which originates in Schelling's philosophy of nature.[4]

> This communism is a perfected naturalism equal to humanism, a perfected humanism equal to naturalism; it is the true resolution of the conflict between humans and nature, and other humans; the true resolution of the conflict between existence and being, between objectification and self-confirmation, between freedom and necessity, between individual and kind. It is the solution to the riddle of history, and knows itself as such.[5]

2. Ernst Bloch's nature subject

Ernst Bloch took up the idea of the naturalization of humanity in order to tie the dialectical materialism of Karl Marx even more closely to Schelling's nature philosophy.[6] Bloch starts from a correspondence between humanity and nature. Creative humanity corresponds to productive matter; hoping humanity to a material realm of the real-possible. Bloch sees the human subject in partnership with a corresponding nature subject. It is not until nature is recognized as standing on its own as subject that its own history, independent of humans, can be discerned. Then its own independent future can be respected. And only then can a community of humanity and nature come about in which both can be at home.

A nature subject is not a remystification of nature as the great Mother, but rather "the not yet manifest That-impulse (the most immanent material reagent) anywhere in the real."[7] There is within nature itself a seat of production. Nature is always *natura naturans* (Spinoza). In humanity nature reaches its "highest bloom," as Bloch poetically expressed it, but in so doing it remains subject and does not become the object of the human subject. From this follows the idea of "alliance technology," mediated through the respective subjectivity of humanity and nature. "In place of the technologist as mere cheater or exploiter, firmly stands the society-oriented, self-mediated subject, increasingly self-involved with the problem of the nature subject."[8] Alliance technology — or as we say today, soft technology — recognizes and accepts the complementary productivity of the nature subject. Humans want to produce and reveal their true being, but now nature also can manifest its own uniqueness.

Spinoza's idea of *natura naturans* presupposes, according to Bloch, a notion from the Cabala, of *natura abscondita*, a nature pressing for its own revelation. Thus "nature in its final manifestation" lies within the horizon of the future of those alliances mediated through humanity and nature: "The more straightforwardly . . . alliance technology, mediated with the complementary productivity of nature, becomes possible, the more surely the imaginative powers of a frozen nature will be released anew. . . . Up to now our technology has operated in nature like an army of occupation in enemy territory, knowing nothing of the interior — the matter of the thing is transcendent to it."[9] Bloch, in his time, was

able to formulate these ideas only with the help of romantic conceptions of nature, yet with their help he anticipated important ecological principles. The idea of the subjectivity of complex life-systems as well as the methods of communicative discernment follow up on his ideas.

Bloch's philosophy of nature was a far cry from today's orthodox Marxism. The condemnation of Bloch by Marxist scientists written in 1956 dismissed his ideas as "an anti-Marxist doctrine of world redemption"; the thesis concerning the appearance of a nature subject is an idealistic-mystical dogma; there is no other subject of nature besides the working human; Bloch's conception is not only unscientific, but downright hostile to science; his dogmas contradict socialist practice: "In reality, becoming-human and the entire history of humanity is a process whereby nature is utilized by humans in material production. . . . Even in socialism and communism there is no 'identity' in the sense of a wedding between humans and the nature subject within a common 'home.'"[10] The only subject of nature is humanity. Any higher development of nature's creative resources will take place through humanity, not independently. Freedom exists only for humans, not for nature.

Karl Marx himself had taken leave of the nature philosophy visions of his early writings by the time of *Das Kapital.* In *Das Kapital* there is no more talk of a "naturalization of humanity" or the "resurrection of nature." "The new society is to benefit humanity alone, and indeed unequivocally at the cost of external nature. It shall be ruled through gigantic technological means with the smallest expenditure of time and work and serve as the material substratum for all the conceivable requisites of all humanity."[11] Nature appears again only as "nature matter" and "work object," to be transformed by humanity into articles of use. Working humanity subjugates the performance of nature's powers. For the later Marx the conflict between humanity and nature remains. Despite all attempts at mediation, nature's necessity and human freedom remain in the end unresolved.

Marx's views in *Das Kapital,* however, had already been prepared for in his early writings. There he regarded nature as natural powers, and objects as products of the objective activity of humans. He never described the relation between humanity and nature as involving a common home, but always regarded it simply as a necessary exchange of matter. This concept of matter exchange be-

tween humanity and nature, taken from Moleschott, leaves no room for the greater hope of the future cherished by Bloch.

Marx acknowledged only one transformation of the self-alienation of humanity, achieved at nature's cost, the exploitation caused by a capitalism which would be overcome. But in communism as well, nature remains the submissive slave of humanity. Marx remained within the framework of the humanity-nature conceptions put forth by Bacon and Descartes, so that his dialectical materialism is substantively similar to modern idealism.

The reason for this is that Marx and orthodox Marxism only acknowledge a practical relationship to nature. This practice is work. From the perspective of work, humans can't perceive nature as anything but an object to be worked upon, as raw materials for their own purposes. The perspectives and aims of work, furthermore, have so shaped reason itself that humans are only able to discern that which they produce, as Kant had already established. The independence of nature vanishes before the objectivizing production orientation of humans.

Only insight into the ecological crisis of modern industrial societies can lead to a new point of view among Marxists. As Alfred Schmidt writes in a 1971 postscript to his book *Der Begriff der Natur in der Lehre von Marx*, which first appeared in 1962: "'Resurrection of nature', 'humanization of humanity'— today, these are no longer products of eschatological fantasy. Their achievement is the prerequisite for whether humanity enters into a more reasonable state of existence, indeed for whether it even survives."[12] This amounts to a subsequent justification of Ernst Bloch's position, as is noted with respect to his philosophy of nature in the same book: "It is all the same to what extent Bloch's ponderings go back to Renaissance philosophy, Jakob Böhme, or Schelling's romantic speculation on nature; they are, in their entirety, incompatible with a materialistic position."[13] Now either an ecological understanding of the world is incompatible with materialist positions or else materialism as it has thus far been presented is incompatible with that reasonable state in which humanity along with nature has a chance to survive.

3. The common home in nature

In their relation to the natural environment humans have at least two basic interests. One is the already presented interest of

work. Humans work upon nature in order to obtain food and to construct their own world. From the perspective of work, humans are always active, while nature is passive. They are the masters; it is their slave. But is there any other basic human need which ought to determine humanity's relation to nature? There is. Up to this point it has been theoretically overlooked and held back by the construction of industrialized big cities, causing damage to both humans and nature. It is the concern for a place to live. Not only must humans work upon nature, they must also be able to live in it. The concern for a place to live is different from the concerns of work. We can summarize the concern for a place to live under the concept of *home.* Home is not initially linked to any regressive origins dream, encompassing fatherland and mother tongue and childlike safety. Home exists only in freedom, not in slavery.

Home designates a network of relaxed social relations: I am at home where people know me, where I am acknowledged without fighting for recognition. In such relaxed social relations a balance arises which supports humans, relieving us of the burdens of struggle and care. The natural environment also contributes to such a network of peaceful social relations. Human society must be attuned to the natural environment. This demands a respect for the regenerative ability of nature, and an adaptation to its cycles. Nature on its own terms, however, is no home for humanity. Our natural constitution shows that we are an unprepared, environmentally unfit form of life. It is not until nature has been shaped into an environment that it becomes a home for us in which we can stay and live. Nature truly becomes a home only when we utilize it without destroying it. Exploitation only leads to estranged, homeless groups of people. Utilizing nature without destroying it preserves its continuing ability to exist as nature. The development of ecological garden projects and the upkeep of the landscape give evidence of the possibilities of human-natural symbiosis. They also show the senselessness of the rape of nature.

Up to now industrialization has been centralized and slanted toward major industries and industrial combines. By placing the primary burden upon the natural world, it caused irreparable damage to nature. Industrialized areas are becoming uninhabitable. Humanizing industrial society means balancing the interests of capital and work in production on the one hand and the interests

of a livable world on the other. Citizens' initiatives against further construction of environmentally burdensome industries make this point. By taking away livability these industries destroy the possibilities of human existence.

Humans have not only a right to work, but also what might be called a right to residence. Both of these interests must be balanced. This is not simply a demand relating to society and politics; it is also a demand for a reversal in the basic relationship between humanity and nature. The ecological mentality must transform the one-sided, pragmatic-utilitarian mentality toward the world. The rediscovery of nature out there remains, however, incomplete if it is not accompanied by the concurrent rediscovery of nature within, that nature which humans in their corporeality themselves are.

4. The animation of the body

Are there models and examples of this in other areas of life? In Europe the new ecological mentality has its intellectual roots in psychosomatic medicine.[14]

Even Descartes himself was unable to apply the strict subject-object dichotomy to human existence. He did not find the connection between *res cogitans* and *res extensa* within the human person. His assumption that it was the pineal gland which connected soul and body hardly did justice to his own conditions. The rise of modern medicine and its scientific methods still could not ignore the fact that the object of medical research and treatment is the human subject. In medicine, the person as treating subject stands over against the person as treated subject. The patient remains a person. Medically speaking, the rigorous differentiation between humans and nature cannot be carried out with respect to humans themselves.

People exist bodily as long as they live. They can stand apart from themselves and objectivize the corporeal existence, which they are, as the body, which they have. But they remain their bodies and their bodies remain themselves. Human beings never become completely objectivized and disposable. If they did, they would no longer be human. Even those who are sick always remain subjects, as sick people, no matter how much they become objects of therapeutic treatment.

Psychosomatic medicine began with the demystification of

scientific objectivism through the introduction of the subject-nature of the sick person into pathology. It recognized how extensively people are able to shape the course of their illness through their distinctively human influence.[15] By acknowledging human subjectivity medicine deals with illness through the ill people involved. A truly humane medicine cannot presuppose a subject-object relationship but must, rather, presuppose a subject-subject one. It must overcome the alienation of the body as it occurs in a merely body-oriented medicine. It must supplement concepts of having a body with concepts of being a body.[16] It must encompass the entirety of the human person.

The alienation of people from their bodies is the inner side of the ecological crisis in modern industrial society. Due to the influences of religion and education, humans were brought to the point where they were only able to identify themselves as subjects of knowledge and will. They could only objectivize and subjugate their bodily existence. They became lords and owners of themselves. They learned to rule over themselves, controlling all bodily feelings and needs. They became slaves and property to themselves. Self-rule and self-control were the moral maxims of industrial society.[17] Only by following these principles could people be ready at all times to offer themselves as workers and consumers. Purpose-oriented conduct in work, trade, and consumption is the presupposition of an industrial society. Time as lived experience is reduced by the clock to mechanical time. The result is the alienation of people from their corporeality. The body becomes an instrument of work and pleasure. One is only aware of it if it fails to perform its duty and becomes sick. It is unknown as a medium of the whole person's emotions. The receptivity and spontaneity of the whole person is lost, as people are increasingly made into the subjects and objects of themselves.

The discovery of the physical-mental wholeness of persons in medicine and the acceptance of bodily self-experience in the life of the individual and the community are moves toward overcoming the ecological crisis of people in relation to their own bodily nature. The provision of a home for human society in its natural surroundings demands a corresponding provision for the human soul in the bodily existence of the human person. Without a liberation of humanity's own bodily nature from subjugation by the

subject, there will be no liberation in the environment of a nature alienated through domination and exploitation. Being at home in nature and animating one's own bodily existence belong together.

5. *The naturalization of humanity*

Overcoming the alienation of nature caused by humanity is unthinkable without the naturalization of humanity itself. This is not a romantic return to nature, but rather a new human self-understanding and a new interpretation of the human world within the framework of nature.

If the modern metaphysic of subjectivity can be held responsible for the alienating objectification of nature, then the new self-interpretation of humanity must be grounded in a nonsubjectivistic metaphysic. If the centralized construction of modern industries has a destructive environmental effect, then the new interpretation of the human world must be grounded in a noncentralized metaphysic. The Cartesian subject metaphysic was just as much a centralized theory of the world as the Aristotelian substance metaphysic. Both can be positively transformed only through a metaphysic of the relativity of humanity and the world. This is the direction in which newer theories appear to be going, as they become involved in the ecological situation of the modern world.[18]

In Germany the discussion has turned toward a humanization of nature.[19] With the help of a theory of open systems and new theories of information it has become possible to see in the natural environment a measure of subjectivity at various levels. The growing indeterminacy of behavior in complex, open systems, their time structure, and their realm of possibility allowed them to take on a subjectivity of their own sort, a subjectivity which cannot be objectivized by the human subject. Thus a communicative form of discernment must take the place of one based on domination: discernment itself becomes a cognitive life-relationship. The object becomes the receiver and sender of information, reacting as a subject in its own way, and taken seriously as such. But even with this model for the overcoming of nature's alienation, humanity remains the great and central subject for nature.

The other possible direction for an ecological theory aims at the naturalization of humanity.[20] Here humanity does not stand against nature, but is itself a product of nature. Nature is the great

subject which brings forth ever new shapes and forms of life, including humanity. Humanity is therefore the object of productive nature. This applies to the rise and development of the human kind out of the animal-human field of transition, and also to the rise and development of the human world in modern industrial societies. Nature, as the essence of all material and life systems, developed in the evolution of human societies its most complex form, relatively speaking. In human societies nature found a relative concentration and a relative centralization. Nature is the ecosystem for human societies. This means, however, that in the human knowledge of nature, nature perceives itself; and that in the human objectivization of nature, nature objectivizes itself. The subject for the subject-object relationship of humanity to nature is, according to this model, nature itself. If this is acknowledged, then the human subject must acknowledge the subjectivity of nature and continually arrange its own world within the encompassing context of nature and its evolution.

Humanity is therefore not subject ruling over nature as object, but rather the product of nature. In theological terms we must not understand ourselves primarily as *imago Dei*, but rather as *imago mundi*. Then another conception of natural experience also arises: We don't make experience or bring something into experience. Experiences happen to us. We are impressed, take them seriously, and receive them. They condense themselves to our perception. From observations we then form conceptions, frameworks for observation within which we can order and identify the flow of events. There are several starting points for this turnaround in the modern, hostile-to-nature, subjectivistic form of human conception.

Max Scheler, in his influential work *Die Stellung des Menschen in Kosmos,* which strongly stressed the special place of humanity, still added the inquiry: "Isn't this as if there were some scale upon which a primeval form of being, in the building of the world, contorted itself to an even greater extent in order to become itself on ever higher levels and within ever new dimensions — in order, finally, to have and to grasp itelf as a whole in humanity?"[21]

The idea of "eccentric positionality," introduced by Helmut Plessner into the new philosophical anthropology, also points in this direction: Humans exist in themselves, but yet at the same time

stand over against themselves. They always experience themselves concurrently in the mode of being and in the mode of having. They merge into neither of the two orders: "Neither *are* they body alone nor *have* they body alone. Every claim of physical existence demands a balance between being and having, outside and inside."[22]

In the modern human world, nature-having has been extended ever wider through science and technology. Modern science has achieved its success in an area one could characterize as body-having. All the same, humans are nature, and the body which they objectivized as their property is, at the same time, themselves in their bodily existence. To localize the human world within the history of nature, and once again discover nature in body-being, is not a romantic escape from responsibility for the power humankind has won. It means, rather, that we can discover suppressed and displaced dimensions of life and use them to overcome the inhumanity and unnaturalness of the modern world.

The nature-being of humanity is the original given; nature-domination and nature-possession are secondary facts. They remain dependent upon the original given because they build upon it and live from it.

NOTES

1. See W. Schmidt-Kowarzik, "Die Dialektik von gesellschaftlicher Arbeit und Natur," *Wiener Jahrbuch für Philosophie* 10 (1977): 143–76; and E. Rudolph, "Entfremdung der Natur," in *Humanökologie und Frieden* (Stuttgart, 1971), pp. 319–41. In this critique I agree with some of the propositions; however, I am not sympathetic with the labor-oriented view of the relation to nature through an aesthetic similarity.

2. Martin Heidegger, "Die Zeit des Weltbildes," in *Holzwege* (Frankfurt, 1957), pp. 69ff.

3. Karl Marx, *Die Frühschriften* (Stuttgart, 1953), p. 237.

4. This has been proven in K. Bockmühl, *Leiblichkeit und Gesellschaft: Studien zur Religionskritik und Anthropologie im Frühwerk von Ludwig Feuerbach und Karl Marx* (Göttingen, 1961), pp. 234ff.

5. Marx, *Die Frühschriften*, p. 235.

6. Ernst Bloch, *Das Prinzip Hoffnung* (Frankfurt, 1959), chap. 37: "Wille und Natur, die technischen Utopien," pp. 729ff., especially 802ff.

7. Ibid., p. 786.

8. Ibid., p. 787.

9. Ibid., p. 807.

10. R. Schulz, "Blochs Philosophie der Hoffnung im Lichte des historischen Materialismus," in *Ernst Blochs Revision des Marxismus* (Berlin, 1957), p. 65.

11. Alfred Schmidt, *Der Begriff der Natur in der Lehre von Marx,* (Frankfurt, 1971), p. 159. See also Rudolph, "Entfremdung der Natur," pp. 334ff.

12. Schmidt, *Der Begriff der Natur,* p. 211.

13. Ibid., p. 163.

14. This shows the parallels and the connections between the founder of the environmental theories, Jacob von Uexküll, who wrote *Umwelt und Innenwelt der Tiere* (Berlin, 1921), and *Theoretische Biologie* (Berlin, 1928); and the founder of psychosomatic medicine, Viktor von Weizsäcker, who wrote *Der Gestaltkreis: Theorie der Einheit von Wahrnehmen und Bewegen* (Stuttgart, 1950). For the theological interpretation see Michael von Rad, *Anthropologie als Thema von psychosomatischer Medizin und Theologie* (Stuttgart, 1974).

15. For a discussion on the theses of Viktor von Weizsäcker and L. von Krehl see Jürgen Moltmann, "Die Menschlichkeit des Lebens und des Sterbens," in *Das Experiment Hoffnung* (Munich, 1974), pp. 177–94.

16. Erich Fromm, *Sein und Haben* (Frankfurt, 1972); and Balthasar Staehelin, *Haben und Sein* (Zurich, 1969).

17. Max Weber, "Die protestantische Ethik und der Geist des Kapitalismus," in *Gesammelte Aufsätze zur Religionssoziologie* (Tübingen, 1947), pp. 17–236.

18. F. Capra, *Wendezeit* (Munich, 1983).

19. E. von Weizsacker, ed., *Theorie der offenen Systeme* (Stuttgart, 1974).

20. Günther Altner, *Grammatik der Schöpfung* (Stuttgart, 1971).

21. Max Scheler, *Die Stellung des Menschen im Kosmos* (Munich, 1949), p. 44.

22. Helmut Plessner, *Die Stufen des Organischen und der Mensch* (Berlin, 1974), pp. 127ff.

9

They Think Not,
Neither Do They Care —
The Place of Matter in Reality

J. N. FINDLAY

THE AIM OF MY ESSAY is to determine the place of Matter in being.

Matter has generally been accorded a very low place, if any place at all. In Hellenic and Scholastic thought, Matter is a characterless, inert substrate, a mere something or other, which owes all its positive attributes to the imposition on it of organizing pattern or Form. Such Form exists in its purity apart from Matter, and either exists for, or in, an immaterial Mind or Intelligence. On the Aristotelian view, God or the unmoved, immaterial Mover of all things, holds in thought all the organizing principles which give pattern to Matter, but holds them in so intimate a fashion that in knowing them God is only knowing God. On the Platonic and Neoplatonic view there is similarly a demiurgic Master Intelligence, an Absolute Mind as such, in which all other intelligences participate in varying degrees, but which holds its vision eternally trained on all the formative patterns, which it also embraces intimately in itself, and which it or its minions impose on the emptiness of mere space, and on the confused movements that in some inscrutable manner are present in space. Matter, or the principle of the indeterminate and unorganized, here owes all its beautiful fillings and determinings to the divine Πέρας or Limit which is wholly immaterial, and which has already given rise to the beautiful hierarchy of numbers, which likewise represent an imposition of Form or Limit on what is indefinitely multiple. Plotinus, of course, made

145

Matter the principle of all evil, and compared it to a decorated corpse, to something only known in a very poor fashion, but emptying one's mind of all true knowledge.

These miserable views of materiality persisted through the Middle Ages, and if Christianity compelled the acceptance of a resurrected body, as a necessary element in a complete person, the latter was only to be resurrected in a very analogical manner. The same depreciation of Matter and body is of course characteristic of the idealism of the main modern philosophers: all but a few of them make material objects parasitic upon the minds and mental acts that perceive or conceive them. In Berkeley a material object is replaced by a systematically organized set of sensibly perceptible ideas. These have no existence apart from the minds to which they are sensibly present, except in so far as they are also present to other minds beside any given one. They are also present to the Supreme Mind, God, who has fitted up, and fitted together, all the sensible appearances which are appearances to or for anyone. Husserl's phenomenology of 1913, despite many strong disclaimers, is merely an updated version of Berkeley, in which material objects are systems of sensible *Abschattungen* or perspectives, which are infinitely fragmented in the human case, but which we can conceive as completely present to, and necessary for, the comprehensive understanding we might credit to a God.

In Kant, there is some mercy shown toward Matter in that he admits the obligatory thinkability of things-in-themselves which affect us who are ourselves merely other percipient things-in-themselves, for the benefit of whose sensibility the relationships among outer things-in-themselves have, in some inscrutable manner, been translated into the phenomenal relationships of space and time. Our own thoughts and feelings are attributed by us to a Transcendental Ego whose existence or character we cannot know or prove. In the same way phenomenal Matter is attributed by us to the timeless interaction of a set of dynamic centers endowed in some extraordinary manner with mutual attractions and repulsions. These, in some inscrutable fashion, generate the appearance of many moving bodies in space. In his *Opus Postumum* Kant becomes rather kind to Matter: he claims an *a priori* certainty regarding the existence of an Aether necessary for both movement in space and succession in time. There must presumably be

something in things-in-themselves which underlies this appearance of an Aether.

In Fichte, however, Kant's strange doctrine of an unconscious consciousness called the Productive Imagination, which primordially translates impacts from things-in-themselves into appearances in space and time, is transformed into an Imagination which freely *fabricates* the spatio-temporal universe. It helps itself to do so by mistaking its own first outgoing, and then afterward returning, energies for the impact on itself of a non-Ego quite alien to itself. We are only saved from living in a private world of our own fabrication by the fact that we are all one and the same Absolute Ego. This Ego can only successfully posit itself by also positing a world of mindless objects that stand over against itself. It also posits itself in a large number of distinct persons, each of whom posits all the others, and also endows them all with imaginary bodies. The dialogue among persons is genuine, but it is a dialogue among the many embodiments of the same self which has also posited the common world that they all inhabit.

If we now turn to Hegel, Matter is treated with a little more ceremony, principally because his Absolute is primarily an Idea and a shared Spirit, and not anything that is narrowly subjective as opposed to objective. The Absolute Idea in Hegel can only fully implement and actualize itself if it can also become alienated from itself, and can then overcome that alienation. It can be nothing but an eternal return to itself, and a seeing of itself in its Other. To see itself in its Other, it must, however, transform itself into that Other, and the Other of the Absolute Idea has all the properties of fragmentation and mutual externality of parts. The self-alienated Idea becomes Nature, with parts infinitely outside of each other in space, and infinitely before and after one another in time, and belying its own intrinsic unity in the most scandalous manner. And it must go through a long temporal dialectic of mechanics, physics, and organics in order to arrive at the self-aware, world-mastering inwardness of Spirit. In the end everything becomes a modality of Spirit, but only after long wanderings in a bodily wilderness. Hegel's accounts of these wanderings involve much that is realistic and materialistic; and he accepts the geological record, and believes that Life and Intelligence, though first in Idea, do not emerge first in time. There was a time when there was nothing on earth like

the conscious spiritual life that we now enjoy: Marx and Engels never realized how much of their dialectical materialism was already fully acknowledged by Hegel.

The dialectical spiritualism of Hegel thus had few who understood its granting of a dialectical place to Matter and materialism: the *Philosophy of Nature* was in the nineteenth century largely unread and thought to be wholly outmoded. After Hegel's death there was a great surge of thought back to Kant, and to Kant understood as a subjective constructivist, one who regarded knowing as a case of making or of Productive Imagination in the most literal sense of the word. Here there were no things-in-themselves whose unknowable relationships had in an unknowable manner to be translated, according to laws inherent to the mind, into a world of phenomena in time and space. The transcendental syntheses which generated phenomena might have arts hidden in the darker depths of the soul, but they did not fundamentally differ from the imaginative syntheses which take place in the full daylight of consciousness, when we interpolate or extrapolate what the senses show us. They were in fact the conscious acts by which the world was fabricated or constituted by the Transcendental Subject, whose self-consciousness was in fact inseparable from the syntheses in which it set a regular world before itself.

It was the same conscious subject which, by unifying material phenomena in a categorially regular manner, also achieved its own unity as a thinking subject. It was itself only a unity because it unified phenomena categorially. On this view things-in-themselves become a mere as-if. The appearances which seemed to stem from a Transcendental Object really stemmed from the Transcendental Subject and its unifying activities. The situation is not much altered if the appearances of material objects are attributed to a vaguely generic *Bewusstsein überhaupt*, which is itself, at best, an as-if construct, so that material objects and their properties become the constructs of a construct. And if God or the World-Spirit or the World-Will is invoked as the fabricator of the material world, we tie our constructions to a construct which is even more totally obscure. There is in fact nothing in human experience, apart from the creative imagination, which corresponds to the *Mens fabricans* of all these idealistic constructions. Creative imagination, in our experience, always arises out of a soil from

which creativity is wholly absent. If people could create and modify material objects by their pure acts of thinking and willing, as yogis and mediums are alleged to do, there would be some basis for these constructivist fantasies; but most of us have, alas, no such powers. Material objects impose themselves upon us whatever we may think or wish, and it is this character of compulsive imposition that is the most essential trait of what is material. If we could modify our bodies and the environing world as we sometimes do in our dreams, we should certainly have eliminated Matter, for it is arguably not its mere sensuousness which makes Matter Matter, but the compulsive character of the vision it forces upon us.

But constructivism is to be rejected not merely because it fails to do justice to our compulsive sense-experience, but also because it is at odds with all the higher values of the Spirit. For all the higher spiritual activities require the compulsive resistance of Matter. The construction of works of art and beauty requires the difficulties of arriving at *le mot juste* or *le ton juste* or *la forme juste:* one must struggle hard before one's *rêve flottant se scelle dans le bloc resistant.* In the same way, the major acts of the moral life, its great deeds of generosity, courage, and sacrifice require the mastery of many recalcitrances which have their roots in what is material. And the activities and enjoyments of love would be deprived of all value were their passion not needed to overcome many difficulties and obstructions having their source in what is material. The higher life of the Spirit requires the body, and the body that it requires must be not phantasmal but gross. It must be exposed to the possibility of many injuries, possibly even to such a supreme injury as crucifixion. We may also hazard the view that there is something wonderful and admirable about the resistant simplicity of material things. They are not infected with the hesitancies and twisted variations which infect the living and conscious and above all the self-conscious. They are simply and solidly what they are. They react in their characteristic manner or express their inbuilt messages whenever the circumstances warrant or compel this. Carbon, hydrogen, and oxygen join or separate in countless ways consistent with their sort when there are fitting confrontations between them. They do not dither or consider the effect of their interactions, nor wonder whether they will be doing quite the right thing.

It is the invariance of Matter which makes it admirable. It

is the invariance which makes the North Germans refer to a virtuous person as *ein solider Kerl*. That *solider Kerl* was exemplified by one who held the chair of philosophy at Königsberg, and by the timing of whose daily walk all the less solid citizens set their watches and adjusted their activities. And it is the utter reliability of material objects which led to many a religious metaphor. There is the Rock of Ages in which we hope to hide ourselves; or the Fire of the Zoroastrian dayspring; or the Johannine Light which lighteth every one that cometh into the world; or the Brahman which is subtly dissolved in all things like salt in water; or the *Tao* of Lao-Tze which is without shape or resistance yet like water penetrates everywhere. There is something in the essential honesty of material objects which makes us, by contrast, seem counterfeiters and practicers of *mauvais foi*. This honesty is fitly consecrated in the fixity of what is divine. Plainly there are other values in the cosmos beside those of Matter, but the merits of Matter are none the less essential to the health, beauty, and virtue of the cosmos.

There must be a material world of extended things that impinge on us through the senses, and to which we ourselves in our bodily capacity belong. The phenomenal character of this material world may not accurately represent what it is *an sich*, but the former is at least a genuine logical picture of the latter, having no items or differences which do not correspond one for one with items or differences in its material original. The world, qua phenomenon, represents, we may say, a translation of the world *an sich* into a language that we may call phenomenalese. God may, if you like, be ultimately responsible for the translation, though God does not carry it out in each instance. We may, however, rightfully balk at the Kantian notion that space and time belong only to the phenomenalese translation, and that the original is timeless and spaceless. It seems to me that mutual externality or *Aussersichsein*, as well as one-after-anotherness or *Nacheinandersichsein*, are of the essence of phenomenal Matter, and hence also of the nonphenomenal Matter that underlies them. It may not have all the sensuous characters of size and shape, nor the finely nuanced characters of temporal passage, but it must surely embody their logical pattern of multiplicity and dimensional difference if it is to be their adequate correlate and underlying source.

I turn with horror from any view of Matter that would make

it into a swarm of monads, or, worse still, of detached happenings with trailing prehensions and objective immoralities. The glory of material objects is that they simply *are*, and simply are what they are, and neither think about anything nor care about it. What we call mechanism, an inflexible regularity of lifestyle, is what distinguishes Matter, and without this as a background and foundation there would be no role for the Spirit and all its fine, impalpable, infinitely variable, purposive gifts and performances. I therefore stand alongside the outmoded, discredited Cartesian-Lockean theory of primary and secondary qualities: to cast it aside is gravely to impoverish the sum of things. But I am enough of a Hegelian overcomer and unifier to believe that Matter, the ever thoughtless other of Spirit, requires and implies the presence of Spirit. It has an ineluctable tendency to pass from unorganized mechanism to systematic teleology, on which, in the fullness of time, all the appurtenances of conscious thought and feeling will come to be built.

I cannot conceal my disillusioned disappointment that Matter seems to have gone so small a distance in the direction of organic and spiritual unification in most of the known universe. I cannot pretend that the total lifelessness of the moon, Mars, Venus, and other places visited by astronauts and robots is anything but embittering. Life and consciousness may be necessary outgrowths of Matter, but they should make their regular appearances in appropriate circumstances. There ought to be canals on Mars, and inhabitants who made them and maintain them. A universe with its spiritual population confined to the earth is worthy of Genesis and Archbishop Usher. It could give delight to no one but a fundamentalist. By contrast with this, I like the open horizons, the endless Pralayas and Manvantaras of Hindu cosmology, and the worlds beyond worlds and states beyond states of their wonderful mythology.

My belief in the essential relevance of Matter and Mind to one another means, further, that I believe, with the eighteenth-century German metaphysician Crusius, in the preformation of all our cognitive faculties to the general structure of Matter. Prior to all experience, we are prepared for the mutual outsideness of things in space, and the successiveness of their states in time, as well as for the limitation of variety involved in substantial permanence and

causal regularity. Being material-spiritual beings, belonging to a material-spiritual universe, we are primitively adjusted to the spectacles that will greet us, and with the right hermeneutic to interpret them. Though phenomena are not of our making, they fit ourselves and our conscious comprehension *a priori*, just as they also constitute the structure of Matter. Many of us have in fact got minds as mechanistic as the phenomena they understand and like best.

Do I, however, believe in an immaterial or spiritual as well as a material region of the world? I do in fact do so. I think, in fact, that what we call the material world is only the outer periphery of being, characterized above all by hard sensuous outline, by temporal vanishingness, and by mutual outsideness of part and part. But the periphery of being is not the whole of being, and in imagination, thought, and love, we move into regions where there is no sensuous definiteness, no hard externality of thing to thing, or thing to person, or person to person. We in fact move through a spectrum of states which tends toward a limit, a center where all things come together in unity, in a single concentrated vision, where they are as it were conflated together, *quasi conflato insieme*, to use Dante's paradisal phrase, and are seen in a creativity of which everything finite is only an excerpt.

The center of all things is plainly spiritual rather than material, since its *Ineinander*, its concentrated unity, is more like that of a mind than of a body. But on my view it can just as well be described in terms of material as of spiritual analogies: it is the Rock of Ages, the light that lighteth every one that cometh into the world, the living water of *Tao* which, though weak, flows everywhere. It has the solidity and wide extent of a Kingdom or of a House of many mansions, and it is approached by the *Dhyana* of infinite space as much as by the *Dhyana* of infinite consciousness, and can be compared to a wonderful Island-refuge as well as to a glorious Void. I myself, being Western, prefer the analogies of plenitude to those of emptiness, and the former analogies are those of Matter rather than those of Spirit. The *Upaniṣads* also tell us that, as in the act of love otherness between husband and wife vanishes, so in one's union with the Supreme Spirit one passes beyond the difference and opposition between subject and object. Life at the center, therefore, has a transparent *Haplosis* that has more anal-

ogy with the simplicity of material being than with the dualism
of conscious being.

My paper will have succeeded if it makes you realize that
there are merits to Matter as well as to conscious Spirit. God may
appear in the burning bush as much as in the still small voice.
And material objects are not incapable of dialectical penetration.
They declare what they are in the sort of dialogue that we call
experimental.

10

God and the Meaning of Life

CHARLES HARTSHORNE

IN A MUCH ADMIRED and brilliant book Robert Nozick has asked
whether the search for life's meaning can stop with the idea that
relation to God provides the meaning.[1] He explores various theories of God's functions and powers including the gnostic idea of
a God above the creator of our universe. Even with the "top God,"
he holds, and whatever the divine functions, we can always ask,
What is God's meaning? Can a God without meaning give our lives
meaning? It seems we can always step outside any totality and ask
for its meaning. So why not go back to the starting point, our own
human reality, and be content with its meaning for us?

First of all, we must consider the reasons that have led people
to look beyond our humanity for the meaning of that humanity.
Why is the value of human life not thought sufficiently statable
in merely humanistic terms? Nozick considers one reason that can
be given: the certainty of our dying. He is right so far; this is a basic reason that theists have had in mind. But, since God is virtually defined as immortal, this reason cannot be given for looking
beyond God for God's meaning. Had Nozick been playing entirely
fair, would he not have conceded this point? But does he? Immediately after introducing the subject of death Nozick distracts attention from the obvious point I have just referred to by asking,
"If our lives went on forever would that solve *our* problem of meaning?" I answer, It would not; but it remains true that God's immortality solves the problem of God's meaning *for God*, so far at
least as mortality is concerned. Moreover, though *human* immortality, in the sense of going on forever, would not provide meaning for *our* lives, this is because of other aspects of human existence

154

than its mere mortality. There are additional limitations, among them the fact that our memories of our own past are so faint that the value of yesterday's hearing of a symphony, for instance, can add only a little to today's experience. Thus, as Santayana said, each day "celebrates the obsequies of its predecessor." The problem of transience is deeper than death; it is forgetfulness. We do a million times more forgetting than remembering — and in giving this high ratio I do not exaggerate. God, conceived as not forgetting at all, would not have this second reason for looking beyond self and kind for meaning. Some would say that God neither remembers nor forgets but simply knows; I would not; but either way here is a second win for the theistic side of the argument.

The two points just made are compatible with Frankl (who is cited in the book) and with Heidegger, who argues that our temporal finitude is part of what makes our lives meaningful. An endlessly prolonged yet nondivine life has no conceivable good meaning, as all attempts to make paradise attractive tend to bring out. Only God could assimilate an infinitely prolonged experience to the integrity of a single individuality without unbearable monotony. Definite individuality other than divine means temporal finitude. Indeed, the term *finite* falls short of expressing our limitation. Even God, in one aspect, is finite; but we, unlike God, are fragmentary in space-time. Finitude as not divine is fragmentariness. Other finite things are outside of us spatially and before and after us temporally. This is as it should be.

We have not yet exhausted the reasons for looking beyond humanity for humanity's meaning. Being fragments of the spatial whole of things, we yet have interests in other members of that whole than ourselves. These others we only partly know or understand, and some of them will outlive us. We have responsibilities for many of them. We are bound to ask, What is the value of the whole of humanity? No human being will ever adequately appreciate such a comprehensive value. Insofar as value consists in something like happiness, there is, in merely human terms, no value of humanity as a whole. The sum of happiness in the world is not itself a human happiness. "Greatest happiness of the greatest number" must be valued in other terms. An economist I knew asked utilitarian economists, "Why do you want to maximize happiness? For the contemplation of the Lord?" I told him that my answer

was yes. But we agreed that his fellow economists probably did not have that in mind. Here then is a third reason for looking beyond the human for the meaning of the human. Although most theologians have missed the opportunity by making certain intellectual mistakes, a theist has an option that a nontheist lacks, that is, the possibility of giving a meaning to creaturely happiness as a whole in terms, not of a mere sum of happinesses, but of a single superhappiness, the divine. For God is usually conceived as loving the creatures, and to love is to rejoice in the welfare of others. But no human being can do this so as to possess in himself or herself the full value of another's experiences. If God has this capacity, the welfare of all the creatures does add up to a single good, good in the same generic sense as my welfare just now or yours just now, that is, a *good experience*, the joy of God appreciating the world now. Mere fragments of reality, fallible in all our powers, we look to the divine life as adequately, infallibly treasuring forevermore all that happens, all achieved values, and as thus being in itself the inclusive good by which all lesser goods are given their due.

We look beyond ourselves spatially. God does not, for there is nothing beyond God spatially. God is ubiquitous. We look beyond ourselves temporally, partly because of death, but more basically because our future can never, even while we live, do justice to our present or past. Does God look beyond God temporally? In a sense yes, in another sense no. I hold with Berdyaev that there is a kind of divine time. Hence God has a future. But this future too is divine and is God in subsequent experiencing. It is not beyond God, but only beyond God as so far actualized. The Creator too is in process of being created, not simply self-created or simply created by the creatures, but the two together. And in this philosophy every individual is both self-created and created by others. Divine creativity (or, using Nozick's word, *originativeness*) is the eminent, all-others-surpassing form of creativity. Yet there is a common category for Creator and creatures.

I agree with Nozick that one can in thought stand outside any whole and ask what its meaning is. However, God is not merely a whole in the sense in which Nozick's proposition is true. God-as-experiencing-us-now is such a whole; but the next moment there will be a partly new divine whole experiencing partly new creatures. Nevertheless one cannot step outside God; for there can be

no such outside. God constantly transcends God while retaining self-identity. This is the all-surpassing, self-surpassing Integrity. Roughly analogous to Nozick's concept of self-identity in persons, God is always the closest continuant of God as already actualized. In us the closeness is a highly relative matter. In deep sleep, where am I as a conscious being? Also, there is multiple personality. The personal identity of God is the all-surpassing genetic identity. But it is not strict (Leibnizian) identity, for nothing actual can be that, with one exception to be considered below.

The analysis of freedom in *Philosophical Explanations* is both profound and brilliant. It is refreshing to see, for once, a sharp focus on the concept of sufficient reason, which is precisely what distinguishes deterministic from indeterministic theories of causation. Most theories admit the idea of strictly necessary causal conditions, but determinists want to add also strictly sufficient conditions or reasons. Nozick sees that a really significant meaning for freedom means precisely that sufficient reason must be qualified. We had to have the ancestors we had, to be what we now are; but it does not follow by any rule of formal logic that they had to have us as descendants. Moreover, they did not "have" us, so far as the evidence goes. For them, we were only rather indefinite potentialities. But we have them — at least we can designate them individually. Memory, other traces of the past, and belief in the significance of history imply that the past is quite real and definite, whereas the future is a realm of possibilities and probabilities or partial necessities.

This is the asymmetry of time. Determinism unduly exalts symmetry, a common practice of philosophers. Nozick is, I think, only partly free from this. From present or near past conditions, both earlier and later events are by determinists supposed to be equally inferrible, given ideal knowledge of the conditions and laws. Causes and effects are not, for determinism, distinguishable by the logic of their relationships. Peirce emphasized this point. Determinism is a counterintuitive notion of becoming. Intuitively, time is deeply asymmetrical; the past is settled and definite while the future is what we and others are about to settle, to make more definite. No other view has a pragmatic meaning. Determinism is not a doctrine anyone lives by. So why worry about what is compatible with determinism?

Nozick is the first philosopher, other than Wolfson the incom-

parable historian of medieval philosophy, that I have found who refers to Philo Judaeus's doctrine of freedom, in God and human beings, as partly transcending causal necessity. Nozick does not go on, apparently, to note that in recent times something like this idea has been generalized by Peirce and others to cover not only God and human creatures but all creatures, so that it becomes what the medievals called a transcendental, applicable to all actualities, including God. It follows that the classical theological problem of evil is exposed as an artificial puzzle, quite avoidable by a theist. For, if all creatures are partly self-determined here and now, rather than determined by causal conditions, then even divine causation leaves something open for creaturely freedom to determine. From "it happened" to "God did it" or "God made it happen" is a non sequitur. The book of Job can be read in this fashion.

Nozick reads the book somewhat differently. He puts the usual stress on the mystery of God's purposes but rather neglects the mystery of God's power; what it means to say that God makes — or even permits — events. God's purpose is at least the welfare of the creatures, for instance, the animals' young being fed. But in a world chock-full, as it seems to be, of creaturely doings and decidings, what room is there to interject divine doings and decidings? We are free only if we are co-creators — or, adapting Nozick's language, co-originators — with God. This was William James's lucid idea. It implies that the standard notion of omnipotence is a pseudo-idea and that, in our decisions, we do not merely reiterate decisions God has made for us. We make the decisions, as ordinary language says we do. It is odd that linguistic analysts seem not to notice this incongruity in classical theism. Instead, they seem mostly to accept omnipotence at face value but wonder how a good or loving God could make so many unhappy, sad, or ugly things happen.

Philonian freedom, generalized for all creatures, is found in Peirce's doctrine of *tychism* and the spontaneity of feeling, also in a similar doctrine of Varisco in Italy, in Bergson's mature thought, in W. P. Montague, Whitehead, and Berdyaev. It is the radical solution of the problem of evil — rejecting omnipotence, not as too much divine power, but as the nonsensical idea of power to create the powerless. As Plato said, being is power. Every soul, or sentient being at least, has the power of self-motion, self-determination.

This brings us to two further problems. If all creatures, even atoms, have some freedom (and quantum physics seems to allow this), then either all creatures have some form, however primitive or otherwise, of mind or the psychical, so that in principle the field of comparative psychology is universal and covers all nature; or there are two kinds of freedom, that of mind and that of mere dead, insentient matter. I miss in Nozick any reference to the issues suggested by terms like materialism or dualism. Peirce pointed to the nonmaterialistic and nondualistic possibility when he said, "Mind . . . the sole self-intelligible thing . . . is . . . the foundation of existence," and when he called his ontology objective idealism. Whitehead's reformed subjectivism is similar, but more carefully spelled out. Bergson was basically of the same persuasion, as was Varisco. Idealism in that sense, not discussed in Nozick's book, has been a doctrine of a select minority ever since Leibniz first sharply stated a form of it.

The twentieth-century version of theistic metaphysics fits best into the history of ideas, and gains most coherence, if it rejects the concept of mere matter, irreducible to mind in its most generalized sense, and accepts a universal theory of mind as, even in its lowest forms, not wholly lacking in creativity or transcendence of causal necessity. This is the radical way to get rid of omnipotence. No creature is a mere absolutely controlled puppet. Einstein was brilliantly and exactly wrong: God does throw dice; God takes a chance on what free creatures will do.

Some of Nozick's intellectual experiments with the idea of God are so remote from what the best theists mean by the term that the experiments seem almost wasted motion. Consider his example of laboratory mice and the scientist who uses them for experiments. The mice are means to an end having nothing to do directly with their pleasures, pains, or welfare. Yet Nozick says that the scientist is as God to the mice. Here we have one form of what I call the tyrant conception of deity. There is nothing of this in Bergson, Peirce, or Whitehead. Plato and Aristotle were already above this idea. God persuades the creatures, said Plato. The divine excellence moves the world, said Aristotle, adapting Plato's doctrine of human love as the attempt to realize absolute beauty. In process theology, as in Berdyaev or Whitehead, God charms the world, has charisma for all creatures, who cannot but respond to the divine fascination even though in their responses there is an element of creative freedom, however slight. For Whitehead, God's power is to inspire worship. And why is God thus inspiring? This is no absolute mystery, and we have analogies for it. Why do children respond to wise and unselfish love in parents? Why did many men and women respond to the unselfish love of Jesus, or of Buddha?

We have a still more illuminating analogy. It is Plato's idea of the World Soul, whose divine body is the cosmos in its entirety. It seems to be true that if tissue cells surrounding one's nerves are even slightly damaged, one tends to feel pain. Two hypotheses emerge: one's suffering is either one's human feeling of some of one's cells subhuman feelings; or it is one's feelings of mere, though highly organized, bits of matter. I say that the former view is truer to the direct evidence. It seems that one sympathizes with some of one's bodily members, feeling their sufferings as also one's own. I see no rival theory that is comparably clear even in principle. If the hypothesis is correct, then human sensory experience is an intuitive love, not conscious of itself as such, for some of one's own cells; it is participation in their feelings. This transforms Plato's analogy into the Whiteheadian view of God as physically prehending, that is, feeling the feelings of the creatures. Every creature is to God as some members of my body are to me. We tend to feel the feelings of some of our cells, their pleasures and pains, and God in an unsurpassable way does this with all creatures. So if the creatures respond, it is to love, embracing them and countless others, that they respond.

This is the simplest answer I know of to the question, How does God influence the world? At the same time, it also answers the question, Is God influenced by the world? Of course God is, as we are influenced by our bodies, except that God's response to the creatures is unsurpassably adequate to each creature. God loves us perfectly as we cannot love ourselves or anyone else. We simply cannot resist the appeal of such love.

It may still be questioned, Does all this really give our lives meaning? Is it enough for us that our welfare is appreciated and immortalized in God, along with the welfare of all those we care about?

I answer that the becoming of human experience is either continuous or discontinuous. By discontinuous I mean quantized, coming to be in least temporal units; and by continuous I mean not quantized, so that in any time, however short, there can be a succession of experiences, rather than a single experience with no internal succession. Peirce says that the present of experience is infinitesimal, but William James and Whitehead say it is finite, coming in least drops or buds. Each of these drops is what Whitehead calls an actual entity. Such an entity does not change; it merely becomes or is created — in a sense it creates itself, using its predecessors as data. Memory and perception are the two forms of this using of predecessors as data to constitute successive units of experiencing. The name Whitehead gives such self-creation of experience out of previously created actualities is "prehension."

Creativity and prehension are two aspects of one idea. Whitehead derives freedom in its most general sense from experiencing as such. The given data formed by past actualities cannot dictate just how they will be synthesized into new actual experiences. "The many become one and are increased by one." This is among the most powerful of all short sayings in the history of philosophy. The emergent synthesis of data into a new unitary experience is the ultimate emergence, the ultimate freedom. Freedom of behavior is derivative from that. Just how we remember or perceive what has been happening is our present decision. The previous many cannot increase itself by one in a completely prespecified manner; for the unity of the new actuality is no mere mosaic or rearrangement. Becoming creates an actuality which was not there beforehand even as a definite singular possibility. Possibility, as Peirce said, is continuous. He never quite did justice to his own insight that continuity is the law of possibility — an idea which loses its point if continuity is the law of actuality also. Peirce's synechism tries to have it both ways in the theory of actual becoming.

One may put the argument in Leibnizian terms. Definite plurality, reasoned Leibniz, implies definite singularity, real units. Applied to time as well as space, this means that if there are definite pluralities of successive items then there must be single items. The final monad, conceived spatiotemporally, cannot be the changing individual, as Leibniz assumed. Not I and you but I-now and you-now, or I-then and you-then, are the final concrete subjects in our experiencing.

Let us now consider the question of motivation. The next tenth or twentieth of a second there will be a new I-now or you-now, a new subject bearing our name. Each momentary subject enjoys itself and its remembered-perceived world. But then this enjoyment becomes past and begins to be forgotten, so far as human beings are concerned. So what is the importance of its having occurred? Theists have the most direct, radical answer possible, if they want to use it. First, they can agree with nontheists that the importance of the moment includes what it contributes to future moments in one's own or other creatures' experiencing. However, the reception of this contribution grows fainter and fainter and more and more uncertain and problematic. It is also spread wider and wider in more and more individuals whose collective or total good is not actually enjoyed by any of them. Only if creaturely satisfactions are contributory to an inclusive, divine satisfaction can the idea of importance have definite meaning for human lives, taking the long-run future into account.

To have meaning is to have a realizable rational aim, reasonable in view of the future — by the future meaning all that may come after the ultimate present, which in human experience occupies not more than a tenth of a second. Optimizing one's contribution to the divine future can be the aim, if one is a theist who holds, as even Karl Barth does, that there is change in God. Uncertainty, possibilities of tragedy, being forgotten by posterity, our lives and works not used as we had hoped by offspring, pupils, friends, colleagues — all these remain; but one radical frustration is absolutely excluded: intrinsic values achieved in one's own experience, or in the experience of those we have helped, will never be nullified. All will be retained as imperishable treasures "where neither moth nor rust consumes and where thieves do not break in and steal" (Matt. 6:20). What we ultimately wanted to accomplish will have been accomplished definitively and once for all — to enrich the Everlasting Life with as harmonious human, or other creaturely, experiences as we manage to achieve in ourselves or enable others to achieve. This much we will have done and enjoyed doing.

An important part of the meaning of life on the human level, as compared to the meaning on subhuman levels, is that our satisfactions depend substantially on our being able to have some con-

scious grasp of our situation and its relations to the future generally. We would like to understand what we are accomplishing, and not merely instinctively manage to accomplish it. Not only can the new theism, properly formulated, give us a theory of what our lives contribute to reality, it also enables us to "explain," to use Nozick's word, some basic features of that reality.

One such feature is the interdependence of the entities composing the cosmos. Nozick argues against the idea which was insisted upon by the absolute idealists of the early part of the century, that of absolute interdependence or organic unity. As Nozick suggests, this is a false ideal of world understanding. It is the block universe, William James's *bête noire*, excluding all creative freedom and all genuine individual decision making. But I miss in Nozick a sharp focus on the problem of dependence and independence, that is, internal and external relations. There must be both: without dependence or internal relations no part of the world implies any other part and all inference from here to there or from now to then lacks intelligible basis; without independence or external relations there are no distinguishable world parts, everything is an aspect of the whole, and only ignorance makes it seem a distinguishable thing at all.

Hume was half right: the distinguishable must be separable. Half right, because separable is nonsymmetrical but distinguishable is symmetrical. I am distinguishable from my ancestors and they from me; but, while they existed without me, I do not exist without their having existed and having contributed to my being. Determinists will say that my ancestors having existed is matched by my having been destined to exist in due time. I say that this idea of destiny is sheer superstition, while my ancestors having existed is fact.

Apart from the asymmetry of time nothing is intelligible. Peirce's view that the past is the sum of accomplished facts, together with his saying "Time is . . . objective modality," and his view of the future as irreducibly a matter of not fully definite or particularized possibilities, implies a view of historical truth which logicians such as Quine, who eternalize all truth, will never understand. Futurity is the key to possibility, as pastness or prehendedness is to necessity.

Another welcome feature of Nozick's book is his long discus-

sion of whether it makes sense to ask, Why is there something rather than nothing? Is nothingness the natural state, any departure from which needs explaining, or is somethingness the natural state? Or is there no natural state? I find this last position a leaning over backward to give the benefit of a highly artificial tolerance to a baseless notion. The rejection of coercive argumentation goes here, if not too far, at least to the extreme limit of the useful. How can it make sense to speak of nothing as natural? Nothing has no nature. Nothingness as a state of things, or of truth or reality, is contradictory. Somethingness has a nature. Metaphysics is the attempt to analyze this nature.

We are told that one cannot assume *a priori* that either nothing or something is the natural state. If this means that we must have reasons for the assumption, then yes. But if it means that the reason must be empirical, then no. I think the question is *a priori*. The function of the word *nothing* is such that absolutizing it to mean "nothing at all of any kind, or worth noticing for any purpose" deprives it of meaning. And so the view that there might have been nothing is nonsense or contradiction. Imagine some thieves looking through several rooms for something worth stealing and then concluding, "There's nothing in this room." They do not mean nothing at all (no dust, no bacteria, no air). I agree with Bergson: when we really *mean* something by the word *nothing* we do mean *something*, and when we do not mean something, then we do not mean — period. *Nothing*, when language is not idling, always means something useless for the purpose in hand. Otherwise we would be claiming to experience or know, with nothing to experience or know. To know or experience nothing is simply not to experience or know.

I connect this issue with another, seemingly different one: Are there any merely negative truths, or does every truth have positive implications? "Nothing exists" would be merely negative, and for me this rules it out. The word *nothing* does not function as so used. It does no work.

The axiom that every truth has some positive implications has great power to rule out various forms of nonsense — for instance, the skeptical worry: assuming that you are constituted physically approximately as I am, with the human organs and cellular structures, including nervous system and brain, all in healthy condi-

tion, and with your appearance and behavior normal for an individual not in a coma, still perhaps you, unlike me, are a wholly insentient, mindless automaton. The fact of this insentience or mindlessness would be a merely negative truth, devoid of positive significance. I refuse to take it seriously for that reason alone.

Again, take the question of whether atoms are sentient, have something like feeling. They respond to what can be regarded as stimuli, they keep moving about, their state now is influenced by their just preceding state, and these are the most general behavioral indications of something like perception and memory. What could conceivably show that atoms do *not* feel? I can see only two qualities which logically exclude feeling: one is complete inactivity as a whole; the other is lack of unity. A chair, for example, is an ensemble of molecules not as a whole dynamically unified, by comparison with each one of these molecules. So the chair, by two criteria, is shown to be insentient. It is an inactive aggregate of entities themselves active and significantly unitary. I hold that it will always be open to attribute feeling to dynamic singulars. A tree is best viewed as an aggregate; but its cells are probably dynamic singulars and hence their sentience cannot be excluded.

Inactive and *unintegrated* are verbally negative, but here they have partly positive bearings. The real behaving units, the molecules or cells in the chair or tree, will be active in ways that would be different were they molecules in a cell or cells in a vertebrate animal. The weak unity but collective inactivity or stability of chair or tree have positive implications for the plural activities composing them and also for our use of chairs or trees. But mere insentience attributed to dynamic singulars is useless.

That philosophical arguments fall short of coerciveness is a position I too have taken, though with some difference, at least in emphasis, from Nozick's view. I think, for instance, that the argument against absolute organic unity is very strong indeed, and should produce some approach to consensus, so that determinism would become a minority position (as it perhaps is in physics now), whereas in the time of Kant almost no first-rate thinker dared to challenge it. Since Peirce in this country, and several German and French philosophers a bit earlier, argued forcefully against it, the reputation of determinism among scientists and philosophers has been sinking steadily. I also think that an argument can be coer-

cive enough for some philosophers, and that we do not all need to be as indecisive and open-minded as Nozick perhaps is. My strategy in this matter is to set out the options, if possible in an exhaustive and mutually exclusive array, and then ask, Which of these options, if any, is credible? If there are, say, four options which, on certain apparently safe assumptions, are exhaustive, and all but one are incredible to so-and-so, then for so-and-so, the argument may seem coercive.

I give one example here of a noncoercive argument for theism which for me is practically coercive. These are the options: (1) The world has no general order and is simply chaotic. (2) The world is orderly (not necessarily so strict in its order as to exclude freedom, but still sufficiently ordered for freedom to operate significantly); however, there is no supreme cosmic power or influence ordering things, setting limits to the chaotic aspects which freedom, if it exists, makes not wholly avoidable. (3) The world is orderly and is ordered by a cosmic power, but this power is not divine; it lacks the goodness or wisdom attributed to God. (4) The world is orderly and is ordered by a cosmic power that is divinely good and wise. For me the last option is credible; the others are not. This fourfold progression of options plus a judgment of credibility form one of six similarly structured arguments which make theism virtually coercive for me. The argument from life's meaning is another of the six.

One can give supplementary arguments in each of the six cases to show the incredibility of the nontheistic options, but these subarguments will be coercive only in the same partly subjective way as the main argument. So I do not claim to settle the question for everyone. But I also think it is not necessary to be quite so far from definitive results as Nozick's way of going at things seems to be.

Nozick's problems of whether there could be nothing at all, and of whether, given a certain past, there are or are not open possibilities for what happens next (that is, whether there is freedom), and of whether, given any part of the world, every other part is as it must be because of the organic unity of the whole; and even his problem of whether the meaning of life involves God; all these can be most clearly envisaged, I hold, only if one attacks the problem of *contingency*. The question is, Of all that exists, what, if

anything, might not have existed and what is the principle of the distinction between necessity and contingency?

I see two keys to finding the answer. Given a certain universal, say animality, then, from "There is an animal" it does not follow that "There is a fox"; whereas from the latter statement the former does follow. Every step from universal to more nearly particular involves contingency. Perhaps then from the most universal ideas, say, that of something, every definite step toward the more specific is a contingent step. It does not, however, follow that there might have been nothing more specific than merely something. In other words, it may be entirely contingent that particularization of mere being or somethingness should take the form it has taken, yet altogether necessary that it take some form or other. That the most general class could not be empty does not entail that its members must be the very ones there are. (Quine's purely extensional view of a class is not the most useful one in philosophy.) The idea of a necessarily nonempty class whose members are contingent is one key to the modality problem. The other is the asymmetry of time or becoming. Given the past, any particular future is contingent, but it is not, for all that, contingent that there will be some particular future or other. It is as though Something says irresistibly to reality, at every moment, "You must decide somehow; you may, within such and such limits, decide freely, provided, however, that not deciding, or deciding in favor of nothing, is ruled out." Becoming cannot end, but there is always more than one possible way in which it can continue.

My belief is that the foregoing allows for every sort of contingency which does any real work in thought that understands itself. Moreover, the two clues offered for contingency belong together. At every moment, while alive and awake, each of us particularizes some universals. We have aims, purposes, and these are always less particular than any actual bit of behavior. Life is a constant process of particularization. What becomes is always partly new particularity, enriching the definiteness of the total reality, and only vaguely anticipated (even in the divine mind). But always, necessarily, some particularization takes place.

In the foregoing I am conforming to the principle of contrast which forbids applying one pole of a universal polarity like universal-particular, or necessary-contingent, while rejecting all

applications of the other pole, as Spinoza's necessitarianism at least seems to do, or as the assertion that there might have been nothing clearly does, for it makes every aspect of reality contingent, apart from merely conditional necessity (for example, if you, then your ancestors).

That God is the necessary being, a dictum I accept, does not entail that God is necessary in all respects, or with exclusively necessary and no contingent qualities. Quite the contrary, there are grounds for holding that God excels all other beings both in the scope of the divine necessity and in that of the divine contingency. Whatever is necessary at all is a necessary possession of God, and whatever is a contingent reality at all is a contingent possession of God. I call this the principle of dual transcendence, which applies to other comparably abstract or ultimate contraries, such as infinite-finite, absolute-relative, subject-object, unlimited-limited, and a number of others.

Altogether I find metaphysical problems to have a clearer logic than Nozick seems to give them in his fascinating, tantalizing, and always interesting book.

To summarize, the meaning of life is love in a generalized sense. God, who loves us better than we can love ourselves or one another, is the inclusive object of love. The true self-love is included in love of God. We cannot begin to fully appreciate even our own past experiences. These past experiences are our most direct offerings to God, our contributions to the divine glory. I warmly agree with the emphasis on aesthetic ideas in *Philosophical Explanations*. Whitehead said that beauty, as he defined it, was the aim of God and, each in its own way, of every creature. Sufficient analysis will show, I think, that love and beauty, or harmony of experiencing, are two aspects of one ultimate idea, beyond which, in its two *a priori* forms — divine or all-surpassing, and nondivine or surpassable-by-others — we cannot go.

NOTES

1. Robert Nozick, *Philosophical Explanations* (Cambridge, Mass.: Harvard University Press, Belknap Press, 1981). See especially pp. 573, 576, 580, 585–94, 600–10.

11

Human Nature and the Human Hope

JOHN C. BENNETT

I HAVE BEEN ASKED to discuss the changes in Christian thought in which I have participated in regard to hope for human history. I was part of the movement known as the Social Gospel in its latest period. That provided an example of liberal progressivism. I was close to those who developed in the 1930s and 40s what came to be called Christian Realism. One of my early books had those words as a title. Reinhold Niebuhr was the major thinker and prophet of Christian Realism. He was a product of the Social Gospel and one of its greatest representatives, but he also became its most powerful critic, while remaining loyal to some of its objectives. I shall have some things to say about his thought.

Many of us have lived in a period in which it was common to share the highest expectations for humanity in this world. All of us now live in a period in which we are aware of the greatest empirical threats that have ever darkened the future of humanity in this world. As Henry Steele Commager wrote, "Our dreams of the future are mostly nightmares."[1] It may seem a wonder that those of us who have lived in both periods are as sane as we are and as free from panic.

It sometimes seems that those who have had only the experience of the second period, the awareness of the dark threats, are more troubled than those of us who have plunged from one kind of expectation to the other. Perhaps some of the earlier confidence has remained with us in a chastened form. I think that when we try to interpret the meaning of this change of expectation we need to be humble and avoid either pessimistic or fatalistic or cynical dogmatism. There are few occasions on which even wise people

are more mistaken than when they predict the future. I shall not engage in an adventure in futurology. Rather, I shall reflect on what light we may receive from Christian faith and theology in regard to our hopes and fears for the future.

First I shall remind us of what the earlier hopes of human progress were.

Great expectations for the future were a natural outgrowth of faith in the triumph of reason which reached a high point in Western thought when our nation was founded. The expectation of human perfectibility had a special form in this country where there was a common belief that humanity had a fresh start free from sins and conflicts and the institutionalized irrationalities of the old world. John Adams was not one of the more temperamentally optimistic of our founders, but he represented this hope when he said: "I always consider the settlement of America as the opening of a grand scheme and design of Providence for the illumination of the ignorant and the emancipation of the slavish part of mankind all over the world."[2]

In recent times a deposit of this early American optimism has been the idea that all problems can be solved if Americans try hard enough. I associate that with one of our greatest modern achievers, Franklin Roosevelt, and one gets a glimpse of it in a less buoyant form in his present successor. Roosevelt rallied a fearful and frustrated nation by declaring in his First Inaugural that there is nothing to fear but fear itself. It was not really true then and it is less true now. Yet those words provided a necessary lift for the nation at that time. Some words are needed to lift a discouraged nation, but those words now would not have enough credibility to have that effect.

In the period of the Social Gospel that I remember well, it was widely assumed that education, the extension of Western civilization, and the spread of Christianity to all continents would be the instruments of progress. We saw them at work and there was no limit to our hopes for a humane and peaceful world. The slogan "the evangelization of the world in this generation" was current and sent thousands of Christians to the mission field with hope of Christian success. The slogan meant not that the whole world would be converted but that it would hear the Gospel. But even that was a great hope for Christian change.

The Social Gospel had its greatest strength from about 1880 to 1930, and its ablest and wisest representative was Walter Rauschenbusch. I shall quote from his expectations in 1912, but before I do so I want to say that five years later he wrote a book which showed that he had a greater sense of the stubbornness of evil than most of his liberal contemporaries. In 1912 he wrote a book entitled *Christianizing the Social Order.* The title is characteristic of the period. Today we are likely to speak not of a Christian social order but of a more just or peaceful or humane social order. It is amazing that Rauschenbusch, who was generally much wiser than these words suggest, said: "The largest and hardest part of the work of Christianizing the social order has been done."[3]

He wrote a chapter on the Christianized sections of the social order. With qualifications he said that the following aspects of the social order were Christianized or on the way to being Christianized: the home, the church, the school system, and political life. Then he said that there was one area that was still unchristian and indeed unjust and inhumane, and that was the economic institutions, especially business. His views of economic life were so dark that this helped him to think of the other areas as being far along toward the light.

We can make sport of these ideas but they reflected the time. Today we see many of our most shocking problems in family life, in schools, and in government; and we never make such claims for the churches. One of the most discouraging realities is the difficulty in establishing governments that are effective without being tyrannical. But even more significant was the fact that, two years after those words were written, hell broke loose with World War I. In Europe the First World War was the shocking event that changed Christian expectations and stimulated profound changes in theology. In this country the war itself, for a short time, was seen to be the final crusade, the war to end war and the war to make the world safe for democracy. That expectation turned sour in a few years, for many in a few months.

But something broader was involved than the war itself. We were at the very beginning of a period in which we were able to see the fateful and even terrifying nature of global problems. Today the most serious threats are global, and that means that if things go too far wrong all humanity will suffer disaster. What puzzles

me most about the earlier period is the comfortable white people who were on top of the world, with their empires in Asia and Africa, with most of the peoples of the world under their control, and who seemed to have so little vision of what was ahead. It took years of revolutionary struggles and World War II to dissolve their empires, and then they could see the fate of most of humanity with fewer blinders.

It is generally admitted that the Social Gospel and its progressivism had no understanding of the depth and pervasiveness of racial injustice or of the poison of white racism in this country, much less on other continents. The Social Gospel people in this country were preoccupied with economic problems in the North where they lived. Racial issues were still outside their field of perception.

In the late twenties and early thirties in this country several dark realities entered into the hopeful American consciousness. Disillusionment concerning the results of the First World War had become complete. Disillusionment about the League of Nations and the schemes for collective security, the rise of Fascism and especially Hitlerism, and the growing realization of the enormities of Stalinism were shocks to our democratic hopes. The Great Depression disturbed us most directly. The havoc that it created for a large part of our population and the doubts that it stimulated about the American economic system many of us remember.

Also, among Christian thinkers in this country there was influence from European thought which rejected both liberal hopes and the liberal assumptions about human nature. The traditional belief of the Reformation in the depth and universality of sin challenged our complacencies about human virtue and social progress and began to undermine the conclusions of liberal theology. I put it that way because I believe that the critical methods of liberal theology were generally accepted by those who felt the influence of the revival of Reformation theology. In its most radical form represented by Karl Barth it never had a wide following in this country, but the radical questions were disturbing.

A convenient date for the beginning of a changed outlook in American Protestantism is 1932, the date of the publication of Reinhold Niebuhr's *Moral Man and Immoral Society*.[4] This was a powerful manifesto for what came to be called Christian Realism.

It is now dated, but it was a shocking event for most liberals, and Niebuhr was sometimes regarded as a betrayer of the liberal faith in human progress. Niebuhr came to see that we cannot expect natural large-scale groups, especially nations but also economic groups controlled by common interests, to be affected by moral ideals and moral persuasion in the same way in which this is possible among individual persons or selected groups at their best. Even the motives of individuals in their public commitments may be better than the commitments themselves.

That last point is illustrated by Niebuhr's statement that "patriotism transmutes individual unselfishness into national egoism."[5] The very loyalty and self-sacrificing character that are morally fulfilling for the individual are often used not only by nations but by any group that has a cause to advance to support unjust and socially destructive ends. That perception needs to be put with another: that nations and other large groups are able to develop moral rationalizations of their interests which deceive the individual. Niebuhr goes so far as to say that "perhaps the most significant moral characteristic of a nation is hypocrisy."[6] This does not mean that most citizens are conscious hypocrites. Rather they are in varying degrees self-deceived. Massively induced self-deception is the defense of narrow interests and destructive policies.

The background for all of these factors is the social distance that limits the imagination of all of us. It is very difficult for people to see the world as it appears to those who live far away, those who have different experiences or opposing interests. At this moment we in our country never seem to be able to imagine that the Soviet Union fears our intentions and our power as much as we fear its intentions and its power. Also at this moment comfortable Americans seem unable to perceive the degree of misery created by national policies for the poor, for the unemployed, and especially for the sick who are poor.

There is another factor that is especially important in the case of nations, and that is that so much is at stake. The very mention of national security seems to justify almost any policy or action. We live in a dangerous world that is only a few steps away from international anarchy. Nations do feel threats to their way of life, and building up defenses against these threats becomes for nations often the primary concern. It becomes the justification of the arms

race and of harsh nationalistic policies which we observe on all sides. Fear is behind much of this. It is often partly justified and it leads to a vicious circle of fear. When these special moral problems of nations are seen as compounding the sin of egoism and pride, over-defensiveness and hardness of heart, it is easy to see why there are so many obstacles to human progress.

Niebuhr never became a fatalist or a dogmatic pessimist or a cynic. With all of his emphasis on sin he also saw that divine grace was a counteracting factor. The grace of forgiveness could be morally creative and could enable people to overcome destructive results of pride and self-righteousness which he always regarded as the deepest source of both personal and social evil. He opposed the expectations of perfectionism and utopianism, and it was the promises of utopianism which seemed to him to be the justification of the most cruel means to gain power in order to be able to realize those promises. Much of Niebuhr's thought is expressed in these words: "The sad experiences of Christian history show how human pride and spiritual arrogance rise to new heights precisely at the point where the claims of sanctity are made without due qualification."[7] He often made the same point about ideological utopian claims that characterize political movements.

Niebuhr encouraged more modest hopes for justice rather than perfect love, proximate rather than absolute social goals. He emphasized indeterminate possibilities for humanity. He liked to talk about common grace, that is not dependent on Christian revelation, as a power in the world for justice and peace. Since he is generally identified with his discovery of the depth and pervasiveness of sin I want to get this other side of his thought into the record.

The activity of God in history

When we think about the activity of God in history three forms of it are most emphasized: creative activity, redemptive activity, and divine judgment upon our self-centered and pretentious ways. In relation to hope for history I do not think that the creative and redemptive activities of God can be separated. The former involves the persuasion of nations and other large groups. The deep redemptive inner change of persons and the drawing of the public conscience to the light of God's purpose are closely related. Signs of judgment have great persuasive power. These can be most

readily observed. There is a sentence by Whitehead which expresses much of what is involved: "The instability of evil is the moral order of the world."[8] I used to take great comfort from that. There is a positive warning and a promise to us all in the extent to which evils are so unstable that they become self-defeating. This is still true, and it is still a beneficent warning that pushes even the most wayward societies into new ways. But today I worry more than I did about the fact that evil, in defeating itself, also defeats so much good. Always it has been true that there are multitudes of innocent victims of the processes of judgment. Now it may be that all the good continuities of civilization will be brought to an end by nuclear war.

Before I deal with that most fateful enemy of hope, I shall give some examples of what we may regard as results of the creative and redemptive work of God. There are so many monstrous evils and so many frustrating experiences in the world today that these signs of hope only begin to provide light on our predicament. But I speak of them as illustrations of one side of the work of God, and they are very important in themselves. There has been interaction between the Church and the world in developing in very wide circles a more humane ethic, and in the Church a more humane theology. This tendency does mean that groups that have been excluded are now included as having fully human rights and claims. I give my students a list of eighteen examples of real changes in what churches have accepted as true, though in many cases this has come about by pressure of the world upon the churches.

I shall speak of five cases of change, theologically, ethically, and in matters of public policy. I am covering all of this ground briefly so that we may see these five cases together. They all lead to the humanization of both thought and conduct. These changes together illustrate the persuasive work of God on reason and conscience. They also reveal God's judgment.

The first is the movement away from the idea that intolerance is implied in religious faith and responsibility. This has been completely abandoned in principle both by Catholics and by most Protestants. Protestants in general stumbled on this change partly because there were so many varieties of them and they had to live with each other. The Roman Catholic Church for the first time renounced intolerance dogmatically and as a matter of faith at the

Second Vatican Council in its Declaration on Religious Freedom. Freedom for all, even those in religious error, was meant. I wonder if any declaration of a church council has so quickly had beneficent effects. Today the Roman Catholic Church is in many countries, especially in Latin America, the greatest defender of human rights for all, including religious liberty.

A second case is the movement in the churches away from anti-Judaism as an aspect of the Christian faith itself. Anti-Judaism is not the same as racist anti-Semitism, but it has often stimulated anti-Semitism with its most horrible results in our time. Liberal Protestants have moved away from this religious position, but there are conservative forms of Protestantism with a very mixed record. Some still teach that contemporary Jews share responsibility for the death of Christ and that because of this there is a curse on them which explains their special suffering. The fact that these ideas are still around was evident when the head of the Southern Baptist Convention blurted out that God does not hear the prayers of the Jews. This statement was repudiated by many other Southern Baptists and he himself was led to change his position. Here again the Roman Catholic Church, in the reports of Vatican II, decisively broke from the past and repudiated anti-Judaism. Anti-Semitism is on the moral defensive more than ever before, though it is far from dead and appears in many places in ugly forms. I think that we can say that the distinctively Christian stimulus for anti-Semitism has lost most of its support in the churches.

My third case is in terms of practice not far along. There is, however, an irreversible movement away from the patriarchalism that assumed male supremacy and the inferiority of women. Women are more articulate than ever and have more power to push. Laws are increasingly in their favor. The old ways are on the moral defensive as never before. Economic discriminations against women are still scandalous. Many churches have moved in principle but they do not give full professional opportunities for women. The institutional Catholic Church has not moved at all, but it is hearing from able, trained, articulate women. One fact is astonishing evidence that this movement is irreversible, the fact that in this country the majority of first-degree students in higher education are women. It may prove to be the deepest change of all when this more than half of the human race more fully achieves opportunity

to be itself and to make its insights and gifts available for historical change.

My fourth case is the movement away from the *acceptance* of racism as the inspiration of social habit and policy. I hardly dare say "the movement away from racism," though there is such a movement in many circles. But at least it is true that most of those who defended white racism are quiet about it. Legal victories for racial justice have been notable. Religious defenses of white supremacy which once were powerful are not known except in isolated corners. If expressed they would soon be repudiated. Also, the entering of the nonwhite majority of humanity into global debates and struggles for justice has shown up the folly of white domination of the world.

My fifth example is the growing commitment to economic justice in this century. We have hardly begun to face the claims of justice in the third world, but the ferment in many third-world countries is strong, and the United States makes itself ridiculous in seeing in this ferment a stimulus from Communist countries. In our own country great gains were made in terms of economic justice and protection of the poor in the 1930s and the years following. In many other democracies much greater gains have been made. Today there is in our country an attempt to reverse much that was accomplished, and now when the human consequences of these recent efforts become visible there is hope of being able to reverse the reverses. Justice for the poor and neglected remains a struggle, but its claims are clearer than in other centuries. The Catholic Church in many declarations has made the words "preferential option for the poor" the testing of its own agenda.

In all five of these examples we see a common humanizing trend, and we see that it has gained strength because of the converging of pressures from the victims, which is a sign of divine judgment; and the sensitizing of consciences, which is a sign of the divine persuasion, creative and redemptive. It is on this process that our hopes for history depend.

Nuclear war and human hope

Now I shall discuss the most difficult question of all: the effect of the possibility of nuclear war on human hope. Nothing that anyone says about this can be regarded as surely true of the future.

Also, nothing that anyone says in view of what we now know can give us great comfort. It may help to give us perspective to realize that, while World War II was terrible in its destructiveness and global in its effects, today the nations that suffered most and lost the war seem almost to have been the winners, so strong is their economic life. Also their political life is far healthier than it was before the war.

We are in a situation in which the two major powers are poised for each other's annihilation as nations. The effort to make the bomb originally was caused by the fear that Hitler might get a bomb first. Even Einstein pushed for this, near pacifist that he was. Then governments and experts became trapped in a technological momentum that was difficult to stop. The nuclear experts live in a world of their own, and both scientific curiosity and professional ambition drive them on to invent more and more monstrous weapons.

There developed another trap for nations, a vicious circle of obsessive hostility and fear. We should realize that from their standpoint the Russians are as afraid of us as we are of them and with good reason. In both of these traps national pride and national fear, illusions about the other nation, and an idolatrous trust in military power as guaranteeing security developed national psychologies that make very difficult fundamental criticism of national assumptions.

Some Christians have assurance that, since God is the creator and ruler of history, God will never allow human folly to bring the human experiment to an end. Others believe that God has not set such limits to human freedom, that we can bring judgment upon ourselves and that it may take the form of nuclear war. There are limits to human success, but there are no limits to human failure because of our freedom.

In 1946 I was a member of a commission of Protestant theologians that brought in a report about the Christian approach to the atomic age. The commission had twenty-two members, and many of the best-known Protestant theologians were involved. The report put its emphasis on preventing nuclear war, but it did suggest the possibility of the extinguishing of all earthly life and raised the question as to how this could be consistent with the mercy and justice of God. This was an entirely new question, and there was

no very helpful answer. There was no vote on the subject, but my own vivid memory is that few were able to deny human freedom to end history. It is difficult to imagine a possible intervention as either superpower unleashes its most powerful bombs against the other.

The report did emphasize the probability that a human remnant would survive. We can even think of libraries in Australia and New Zealand preserving many of the results of Western civilization. It is most likely that the earthly and atmospheric environment of the Northern Hemisphere would be most seriously damaged, but Jonathan Schell, after five years of interviewing experts, projects in his book *The Fate of the Earth* the possibility of human extinction.

Jerome Wiesner, the former president of Massachusetts Institute of Technology, in a review of that book, is cautious about Schell's projection of extinction, but he says of the book that Schell had for the first time analyzed systematically as a coherent whole the full range of the consequences of nuclear war. He says that Schell found "that these separate effects of a nuclear war reinforced each other to a degree not appreciated even by the experts; that the many different aspects of a nuclear war would interact on each other to such an extent that the total damage would be much worse than most of us had thought."[9]

There are those who say that humanity will not be able to occupy this planet forever. Cosmic changes will prevent that. So why, they ask, would the death of the planet as a home for humanity ten or twenty years from now raise such a great problem in principle?

All that I can say about that is that the years of the cumulative development of humanity and of its ability to exercise the gifts that have given greatness to its life have been so very few in relation to the immensity of the period of cosmic and biological preparation, and that for our human history to be cut short now would be a tragic failure beyond words to express. At this moment many people have thrown off shackles that denied them opportunity for full human expression and are becoming for the first time participants in world history. For history to end before so much of the flowering of humanity could begin makes the failure even more tragic. Also, granting that human freedom, human sin, and human

finiteness with its follies would have brought this about and not the initiatives of God, such an outcome of the whole human experiment would raise deeper questions about the problem of evil and the providence of God than have ever been raised before.

Several considerations should be in our minds when we think about the prevention of nuclear war.

I. The first is that the two superpowers have as a common interest the prevention of nuclear war. There is nothing that is more important to either of them. Today they put their trust in mutual deterrence based upon mutual hostility and mutual fear. Since this is their common interest may we not hope that before long they may find positive ways to cooperate to prevent nuclear war? There is a beginning of this in the negotiations for arms reductions, to put a stop to the arms race which now has no limits. It is difficult for many Americans to be confident that our government is willing to accept any plan that takes the special needs of the Russians into account. It is difficult to know its real intentions and how far its proposals are only a starting point. This is an area, obviously, in which American public opinion can make a difference, and the new awareness in this country of the meaning of nuclear war as shown in the extraordinary movement for a nuclear freeze is a sign of hope that this may happen. The deepest question is whether our government really wants enough nuclear weapons to prevent their use or whether it seeks enough nuclear weapons to fight a nuclear war and "prevail," a word used in the Pentagon.

It would also be useful for our government to take seriously the fact already mentioned, that the Soviet Union is as much afraid of us as we are of it. This is not strange in view of the sixty-five years of American hostility toward the Soviet Union. Also, we are the only nation that has ever used nuclear bombs on populations. It is significant that Robert McNamara says that the Soviet build-up of nuclear armaments in recent years is partly the result of its fear of a first strike by us. He even goes so far as to say that in view of what they see to be our intention, "I would [if I were in their shoes] do some things that were very similar to what they did. I am talking about the action they took to build up their force."[10]

II. We all belong to the common humanity loved by God, of which two things should be said: All people are created in God's image, and all people are sinful but redeemable. All people are in-

clined to pride and self-righteousness that create hardness of heart, and they are inclined to blinding self-concern. Yet they are capable of love and compassion as well. This mixed view of humanity is a realistic view which includes a hopeful view. This means that there are no absolute enemies. A particular regime may be an absolute enemy of humanity, but it is also an enemy of its own people. Americans should take seriously this mixed view of humanity when they look at themselves and when they look at the Soviet Union. George Kennan knows the Soviet Union and the Russian people as a scholar and as a diplomat who has lived many years in Russia, and most recently as ambassador to the Soviet government, by which he was expelled because of his criticisms of the Soviet Union. (Kennan is no admirer of the Soviet system.) Many of us have seen articles by him about the danger of nuclear war. Here is one of his statements:

> But there is something else, too, that will have to be altered, in my opinion, if we are to move things around and take a more constructive posture. . . . I find the view of the Soviet Union that prevails today in our governmental and journalistic establishments so extreme, so subjective, so far removed from what any sober scrutiny of external reality would reveal, that it is not only ineffective but dangerous as a guide to political action.
>
> And we shall not be able to turn these things around as they should be turned, on the plane of military and nuclear rivalry, until we learn to correct these childish distortions — until we consent to see there another great people, one of the world's greatest, in all its complexity and variety, embracing the good with the bad — a people whose life, whose views, whose habits, whose fears and aspirations, are the products, just as ours are the products, not of any inherent iniquity, but of the relentless discipline of history, tradition, and national experience.
>
> Above all, we must learn to see the behavior of the leadership of that people as partly a reflection of our own treatment of it. Because if we insist on demonizing these Soviet leaders — on viewing them as total and incorrigible enemies, consumed only with their fear or hatred of us and dedicated

to nothing other than our destruction — that, in the end, is the way we shall assuredly have them, if for no other reason than that our view of them allows for nothing else, either for us or for them.[11]

III. My last concern is the possible motive the Soviet Union might have to initiate a nuclear war against this country. Again I refer to an experienced public servant. Former Senator Fulbright said the following in testimony before the House Armed Services subcommittee:

> The essence of our problem with the Soviet Union is not their capability to do us harm with their nuclear weapons, about which we can do little, but their intention, about which we can do a great deal. If we insist on viewing the Soviets as total and incorrigible enemies, that is the way we shall have them, for that view allows for nothing else; and I believe down the road we will find catastrophe. We must recognize that our own policies have a direct and powerful influence upon the intentions of the Soviets and upon the ultimate outcome of our rivalry.

Consider what Soviet intentions may or may not be. If Soviet leaders are influenced by a residue of Marxism they would not want to destroy the achievements of capitalism but rather to inherit them for the sake of Communism. They must know that they could not establish Communism in a radioactive wasteland. On the other hand, if the Soviet Union is not controlled by revolutionary intentions but rather is a great power inclined to expand when it is not too risky to do so, and concerned about its own security, it would not be seeking the world domination which many of our leaders regard as its aim. More likely it would be concerned to hold on to what it now has and more likely it would want to have equality with the United States as a world power. This question about Soviet intentions is very little debated in this country. Usually the view that the Russians are seeking world domination is taken for granted. How tempting would domination of a destroyed world be? What would the world look like to the "victors" of a nuclear war? They would be surviving on the edge of hell, assuming that such survival were possible. They would face a world so destroyed

that they would suffer in their own souls, and they might be condemned by other survivors in a distant part of the world. Would this be a victory for any nation? Would this be a fate — victory or not — that the survivors could do anything but curse?

We in this country at present have a strange sense of helplessness. Our morale as the world's most powerful nation is low. Yet if we could come to ask some of the questions I have suggested, is it not possible that we could use our power to do more than stop the other superpower? If we could be free from our obsessive hostility and fear of the Soviet Union and Communism, there would be hope of a more beneficent relation with the Soviet Union than we now believe possible, and more hope of preventing nuclear war. The Soviet Union does need to change; but we can do more about ourselves. To rid ourselves of hostility and fear is to nourish our resources for hope.

NOTES

1. *Los Angeles Times,* 22 August 1982.

2. John Adams, quoted in Hannah Arendt, *Meaning of Revolution* (New York: Viking Press, 1965), p. 15. Today it seems strangely ironic that Adams used the word *slavish,* when slavery in its literal sense was a chief blot on this new providential experiment and its greatest handicap for the future.

3. Walter Rauschenbusch, *Christianizing the Social Order* (New York: Macmillan, 1912), p. 155.

4. Reinhold Niebuhr, *Moral Man and Immoral Society* (New York: Scribner's, 1932).

5. Ibid., p. 91.

6. Ibid., p. 95.

7. Reinhold Niebuhr, *The Nature and Destiny of Man,* 2 vols. (New York: Scribner's, 1935), 2: 122.

8. Alfred North Whitehead, *Religion in the Making* (New York: Macmillan, 1927), p. 95.

9. Jerome Wiesner, review of *The Fate of the Earth* by Jonathan Schell, *Manchester Guardian Weekly,* 9 May 1982.

10. Robert McNamara, quoted in Robert Scheer, *With Enough Shovels: Reagan, Bush, and Nuclear War* (New York: Random House, 1982), pp. 215–17.

11. *Christian Science Monitor,* 7 February 1981.

Author Index

Subject Index